- Where would you find the most information about Existentialism?

- What are the most informative books on computer usage today?

- What are the landmark texts on the evolution of human-kind?

- What outstanding poetry did the English Renaissance produce?

- What are the best books about the American Indians?

- What books are considered "classics" in the study of art?

- Which modern writers are worth reading?

Whatever your field of interest, *Good Reading* will tell you what book you are looking for and what books are awaiting your discovery.

"RECOMMENDED!"
—*Library Journal*

"A FINE SOURCE BOOK."
—*Los Angeles Heritage*

ARTHUR WALDHORN is Professor Emeritus of English at The City College of New York.

OLGA S. WEBER is the Managing Editor of Professional/ Reference Books at R.R. Bowker Company in New York City and the widow of J. Sherwood Weber, for many years the editor of *Good Reading*.

ARTHUR ZEIGER is a resident professor at The City College of New York.

GOOD READING

A GUIDE FOR SERIOUS READERS

22nd EDITION

EDITORS

Arthur Waldhorn
Olga S. Weber
Arthur Zeiger

A MENTOR BOOK

NEW AMERICAN LIBRARY

NEW YORK AND SCARBOROUGH, ONTARIO

MENTOR TRADEMARK REG. U.S. PAT. OFF. AND FOREIGN COUNTRIES

REGISTERED TRADEMARK—MARCA REGISTRADA

HECHO EN CHICAGO, U.S.A.

SIGNET, SIGNET CLASSIC, MENTOR, PLUME, MERIDIAN and NAL BOOKS are published *in the United States* by New American Library, 1633 Broadway, New York, New York 10019, *in Canada* by The New American Library of Canada Limited, 81 Mack Avenue, Scarborough, Ontario M1L 1M8

First Mentor Printing, July, 1986

1 2 3 4 5 6 7 8 9

PRINTED IN THE UNITED STATES OF AMERICA

Affectionately dedicated to the memory of
J. Sherwood Weber,
the distinguished editor of
Good Reading for many years

Contributors

Oswaldo Arana, *California State University at Fullerton*
William Ray Arney, *The Evergreen State College*
Saul N. Brody, *The City College of The City University of New York*
Irene Quenzler Brown, *University of Connecticut*
Joseph A. Byrnes, *New York University*
Ardavan Davaran, *College of Notre Dame*
Paul Friedman, *Pratt Institute*
Sally M. Gall, *EIDOS/The International Prosody Bulletin*
Daniel Gerzog, *Pratt Institute*
Bruce R. Grob, *Drew University*
George Hochfield, *State University of New York at Buffalo*
Marshall S. Hurwitz, *The City College of The City University of New York*
Glenderlyn Johnson, *The Schomburg Center for Research in Black Culture*
Suzanne J. Kessler, *State University of New York College at Purchase*
Connie L. Lobur, *State University of New York College at Purchase*
Gary B. Mills, *University of Alabama*
Naomi Ogawa Moy, *California State University Dominquez Hills at Carson*
Roger W. Oliver, *Brooklyn Academy of Music*
Thomas Prapas, *The College of Staten Island*
Philip Roddman, *Pratt Institute*
Asela Rodriguez de Laguna, *Rutgers, The State University of New Jersey*
Mark Schulman, *The City College of The City University of New York*
Joan Schulz, *State University of New York at Albany*
George Sessions, *Sierra College*
Paul Shepard, *Pitzer College*

Oscar Shaftel, *Pratt Institute*

Gordon Teskey, *Cornell University*

George N. Thompson, *New York University*

Arthur Waldhorn, *The City College of The City University of New York*

Kenneth G. Wallace, *Pratt Institute*

Elizabeth Weatherford, *Museum of the American Indian* and *School of Visual Arts*

Bernerd C. Weber, *University of Alabama*

Stanley Wecker, *The City College of The City University of New York*

Arthur Zeiger, *The City College of The City University of New York*

Contents

Contributors   vii
To the Reader   xi
100 Significant Books   xvii
Key to Publisher Symbols   xix

I HISTORICAL PERIODS

1. Greece *Marshall S. Hurwitz*   3
2. Rome *Marshall S. Hurwitz*   12
3. The Middle Ages *Saul N. Brody*   18
4. The Renaissance and Reformation *Gordon Teskey*   28
5. The 17th Century *Joseph A. Byrnes*   42
6. The 18th Century *Joseph A. Byrnes*   50

II REGIONAL AND MINORITY CULTURES

7. The Middle East *Ardavan Davaran*   63
8. East and Southeast Asia *Oscar Shaftel*   74
9. Africa *Glenderlyn Johnson*   88
10. Latin America *Oswaldo Arana*   96
11. American Minority Cultures   106
    Native American *Elizabeth Weatherford*   106
    Asian-Pacific *Naomi Ogawa Moy*   114
    Black *Glenderlyn Johnson*   120
    Chicano-Hispanic *Asela Rodriguez de Laguna*   127

III LITERARY TYPES

12. The Novel   135
    19th-Century Continental Novels *Arthur Waldhorn*   135
    20th-Century Continental Novels *Arthur Waldhorn
    and Arthur Zeiger*   142

19th-Century British Novels *Joan Schulz* 151
20th-Century British Novels *Arthur Zeiger* 159
19th-Century American Novels *Daniel Gerzog* 170
20th-Century American Novels *Arthur Waldhorn* 178
    1900–1945 178
    1945–Present 184

13. The Short Story *Arthur Zeiger* 193

14. Poetry *Sally M. Gall* 203

15. Drama *Roger W. Oliver* 216

16. Biography *Philip Roddman* 224

17. Essays, Letters, Criticism, Magazines
    George Hochfield 236

18. Language and Communications
    Mark Schulman 246

IV HUMANITIES AND SOCIAL SCIENCES

19. Fine Arts and Performing Arts
    Kenneth G. Wallace 259

20. Philosophy *Philip Roddman* 272

21. Religion *Bruce R. Grob* 287

22. History *Gary B. Mills and Bernerd C. Weber* 295

23. Politics *Connie L. Lobur* 307

24. Economics *Thomas Prapas* 314

25. Anthropology *Elizabeth Weatherford* 323

26. Sociology *William Ray Arney* 330

27. Psychology *Suzanne J. Kessler* 338

28. Women's Studies *Irene Quenzler Brown* 346

V SCIENCES

29. Physical Sciences and Mathematics
    Paul Friedman 363

30. Biological Sciences *Stanley Wecker* 373

VI SPECIAL SECTION

31. Reference Books *George N. Thompson* 389

INDEX 408

To the Reader

A Fragment of Publishing History

Welcome to the 22nd edition of *Good Reading*, the most comprehensive and the most useful yet. From its first appearance in 1932 as a pamphlet, through all its subsequent revisions and expansions, *Good Reading* has served as a guide to supplementary reading for students, and for others who wanted direction as they wandered among bookstores and library stacks. In 1947 it became a full-sized paperback, and three editions prior to the 22nd have been published in hardback as well, primarily, but not exclusively, for libraries.

The Range of *Good Reading*

Today, as an R.R. Bowker publication, *Good Reading* has developed into an extensive survey not only of literature but of the humanities, social sciences, and sciences as well. Every chapter and every booklist has been revised and updated or written anew, and there have been several additions—"Women's Studies," for example. Though earlier editions have included books by and about women, the entries were scattered and, as one critic acerbically noted, the reader had to scurry between index and text to discover the author whom she or he was searching for—hidden, perhaps, in "Sociology," or "20th-Century American Novels," or "Biography."

Cross-Referencing as an Energy-Saving Device

We've decreased, but not eliminated, the reader's need to rummage. Should Grace Paley be sought in "The Short Story" or in the "Women's Studies" chapter? One might argue cogently for either location. We've tried to settle the argument, or at least soothe the arguers, by cross-referencing whenever there seems to be a reasonable doubt (or even, on occasion, a less than reasonable doubt). Thus, Grace Paley, annotated, has been assigned to ''The Short Story'' and cross-referenced to ''Women's Studies.''

Not only will consistent cross-referencing help readers locate their authors more easily, it may enforce their awareness of the complex inter-relatedness of the several disciplines. Sociobiology, for example, straddles (or spans) sociology and biology. The philosophy of religion, psycholinguistics, poetic drama, and many more have dual tenancies.

Reading *Good Reading*

Most readers, it is likely, will initially turn to the chapter that chiefly interests them, perhaps ''Fine Arts and Performing Arts,'' perusing essay and booklist, occasionally asterisking an entry (if the book belongs to them) or noting it on a card or scrap of paper (if it doesn't). Other readers, with pencil similarly in hand, will prefer to browse as mood, temperament, or chance suggests. We applaud either choice, as long as it impels them to read the books asterisked or noted, and read in a purposive and systematic way—or, for that matter, in a casual and random way. ''Reading maketh a full man [or woman], . . .'' Bacon pointed out long ago, adding ''if he [or she] read little, he [or she] had need have more cunning, to seem to know that [which] he [or she] doth not.'' But since the reader is clutching *Good Reading* now, we hardly need to dwell on Bacon's notation.

Excuses and Explanations

''Of making many books there is no end,'' Ecclesiastes observed. We have rejoiced in that fact generally, regretted it occasionally. There are dozens—hundreds—of books that we wanted to include but omitted in order to keep *Good Reading* portable. The reader will question our omissions, often denounce us for them. And often we will be at a loss to defend ourselves. We have sometimes admitted only one book by an author when we should have liked to admit two or three or more. We have characteristically selected for inclusion the most representative work of an author, the most available, the most attractive, or the most useful (useful, that is, as a starting point for further reading in the author). We have balanced one claim against another, and we have surely lost balance at times.

Structure: Sections and Chapters

Good Reading has five sections, plus an addendum on Reference Books. The five deal successively with Historical Periods, Regional and Minority Cultures, Literary Types, Humanities and Social Sciences, and Sciences. The sections are divided into varying numbers of chapters, and some chapters are further subdivided. Thus, the chapter on American Minority Cultures comprises four essays and annotated booklists: Native American, Asian-Pacific, Black, and Chicano-Hispanic cultures. Each introductory essay runs from 500 to 2,000 words, and endeavors within its course to outline its subject historically or thematically. Each booklist embraces 40 to 200 titles and annotations; each annotation aims at determining the interest and worth of the books listed, to locate its thesis (if it has one), and to encapsulate its plot or suggest its content.

We've obviously imposed a rigorous order on neither essays nor booklists. Rather, within limits, we've countenanced variations from the norm in length, method, and style for the purpose of dodging a dull conformity. The reader who studies the essay and listings of the "Philosophy" chapter, for example, will be afforded a succinct history of philosophy from Plato to Derrida. The "Reference" section, too, bursts through the boundaries we set, and presents a wide survey of books to consult for history, biography, poetics, musical theory, and a plenitude of other matters—including a bibliography of bibliographies.

Booklist Form

The pattern of entries in the booklists should offer no serious difficulty to the reader. There are three main arrangements of data:

1a. A book with one author
   Entry:

   WOOLF, VIRGINIA 1882–1941. **To the Lighthouse** (1927). From shifting centers of consciousness, this beautifully textured symbolic novel shows rather than describes Mrs. Ramsay and her widening effect (even after she has died) on the lives that touch hers. *H & P—HarBraceJ.*

   Explanation:
   Author, last name first.
   Author's dates.

Title in boldface.

Date of publication in parentheses.

Annotation.

Edition:　H = hardcover

　　　　　P = paperback

Publisher:　Harcourt Brace Jovanovich, Inc. (For a full roster, see ''Key to Publisher Symbols,'' page xix.)

1b.　A book with two or more authors
　　　Entry:

　　　ROSEN, CHARLES b. 1927 and HENRI ZERNER b. 1939. **Romanticism and Realism: The Mythology of 19th Century Art** (1984). A new definition of avant-garde and traditional art and a distinction between high art and low. *H—Viking Pr.*

2a.　A book with one editor (Ed.) or translator (Tr.)
　　　Entry:

　　　FLAUBERT, GUSTAVE 1821-1880. **The Letters of Gustave Flaubert** (1954). Ed. and Tr. Francis Steegmuller. A fascinating portrayal of the agony of modern authorship. *H & P —Harvard U Pr. 2 vols.*

2b.　A book with two or more editors or translators
　　　Entry:

　　　The Modern Tradition: Backgrounds of Modern Literature (1965). Eds. Richard Ellmann and Charles Feidelson. The nature of modernism explored through topically organized statements by writers, philosophers, artists, scientists. *H—Oxford U Pr.*

3a.　An anthology
　　　Entry:

　　　Anthology of Japanese Literature (1955–56). Ed. Donald Keene. Not an exhaustive collection, but flavorful. *P—Doubleday.*

The Problem of Permanence

Where we could, we tried to list paperbacks that we hope will endure—at least until the 23rd edition of *Good Reading*. That it is a fragile hope, we are aware: of the unmaking of paperbound books there is no end. And even hardbacks now seem to fade *o.p.*(out of print) more rapidly. when the *o.p.*'s are distinctly better than the in-print survivors, we have given them reluctant room. They will surely be available in libraries, and many of them will likely be back in print before this decade ends. Check our listings with the latest *Paperbound Books in Print* and *Books in Print*, both yearly publications (*Bowker*).

The Purpose of Good Reading

These words of J. Sherwood Weber, the late editor of *Good Reading*, still represent our purpose: ". . . to lead an increasing number of people to savor the great or significant books, both those that strive to light the dark places in our understanding of our complex world and our equally complex selves, and those that aim simply to delight."

THE EDITORS

100 Significant Books

This list offers a representative selection of 100 books that many people have found rewarding to know; they are not necessarily the best or greatest works of imagination and thought. Originally compiled for the 1934 edition of *Good Reading*, the list has been revised several times, including for this edition. Revisions were made by the editors in consultation with many distinguished teachers, writers, and critics.

Ancient Times

AESCHYLUS, **The Oresteia**
AESOP, **Fables**
ARISTOPHANES, **Comedies**
ARISTOTLE, **Nicomachean Ethics**
THE BIBLE
CONFUCIUS, **The Analects**
EURIPIDES, **Dramas**
HOMER, **Iliad and Odyssey**
LAO-TZU, **The Way of Life**

LUCRETIUS, **The Nature of Things**
PLATO, **Republic** and **Symposium**
PLUTARCH, **Lives**
SOPHOCLES, **The Theban Plays**
THUCYDIDES, **The Peloponnesian Wars**
VERGIL, **Aeneid**

Middle Ages and Renaissance

The Arabian Nights
BACON, **Essays**
BOCCACCIO, **Decameron**
CERVANTES, **Don Quixote**
CHAUCER, **Canterbury Tales**
DANTE, **Divine Comedy**
MACHIAVELLI, **The Prince**
MALORY, **Le Morte Darthur**
MOHAMMED, **Koran**

MONTAIGNE, **Essays**
MORE, **Utopia**
OMAR KHAYYÁM, **The Rubáiyát**
RABELAIS, **Gargantua and Pantagruel**
SHAKESPEARE, **Complete Tragedies, Comedies, and Histories**

17th and 18th Centuries

BOSWELL, **Life of Samuel Johnson**

BUNYAN, **Pilgrim's Progress**
BURNS, **Poems**

DEFOE, **Robinson Crusoe**
DESCARTES, **Discourse on Method**
DONNE, **Poems**
FIELDING, **Tom Jones**
GIBBON, **The Decline and Fall of the Roman Empire**
HAMILTON et al., **Federalist Papers**
KANT, **Critique of Pure Reason**
LOCKE, **Essay Concerning Human Understanding**

MALTHUS, **Principles of Population**
MILTON, **Paradise Lost**
MOLIÉRE, **Comedies**
PAINE, **The Rights of Man**
ROUSSEAU, **The Social Contract**
SMITH, **The Wealth of Nations**
SPINOZA, **Ethics**
STERNE, **Tristram Shandy**
SWIFT, **Gulliver's Travels**
VOLTAIRE, **Candide**

19th Century

AUSTEN, **Pride and Prejudice**
BALZAC, **Eugénie Grandet**
BROWNING (ROBERT), **Poems**
BYRON, **Poems**
CHEKHOV, **Plays**
DARWIN, **The Origin of Species**
DICKENS, **David Copperfield**
DICKINSON, **Poems**
DOSTOEVSKI, **The Brothers Karamazov**
ELIOT, **Middlemarch**
EMERSON, **Essays**
FLAUBERT, **Madame Bovary**
GOETHE, **Faust**
HARDY, **Tess of the D'Urbervilles**
HAWTHORNE, **The Scarlet Letter**

HUGO, **Les Misérables**
IBSEN, **Dramas**
KEATS, **Poems**
MARX, **Capital**
MELVILLE, **Moby Dick**
NIETZSCHE, **Thus Spake Zarathustra**
POE, **Short Stories**
SHELLEY, **Poems**
STENDHAL, **The Red and the Black**
THACKERAY, **Vanity Fair**
THOREAU, **Walden**
TOLSTOI, **War and Peace**
TWAIN, **Huckleberry Finn**
WHITMAN, **Leaves of Grass**
WORDSWORTH, **Poems**

20th Century

DREISER, **An American Tragedy**
EINSTEIN, **The Meaning of Relativity**
ELIOT, **Poems and Plays**
ELLISON, **Invisible Man**
FAULKNER, **The Sound and the Fury**
FRAZER, **The Golden Bough**
FREUD, **Introduction to Psychoanalysis**

FROST, **Poems**
HEMINGWAY, **The Sun Also Rises**
JAMES, **The Ambassadors**
JOYCE, **Ulysses**
LAWRENCE, **Sons and Lovers**
MANN, **The Magic Mountain**
O'NEILL, **Plays**
PROUST, **Remembrance of Things Past**
SHAW, **Plays**
YEATS, **Poems**

Key to Publisher Symbols

The 39 *Good Reading* booklists use the following abbreviated publishers' names. These are the same symbols employed by both *Books in Print* and *Paperbound Books in Print*. The current price for any title can be secured from your bookstore or from the latest annual *Books in Print*, available in your bookstore or your public or college library. *Good Reading* no longer lists publishers' addresses—first, because experience indicates that many will change addresses during the lifetime of this revision, and second, because many publishers do not distribute their own books. Consult the latest annual *Books in Print* for the publisher's or distributor's address if you wish to order a book by mail.

The hardcover publisher for each title is listed, following the annotation, after *H—;* the paperbound publisher(s) after *P—.* Publishers cited only a few times are not listed below but are given in identifiable form.

A-W	Addison-Wesley Publishing Co., Inc.
Abington	Abington Press
Abrams	Harry N. Abrams, Inc.
Adlers Foreign Bks	Adler's Foreign Books, Inc.
Airmont	Airmont Publishing Co., Inc.
Aldine	Aldine Publishing Co., Inc.
Allyn	Allyn & Bacon, Inc.
Am Chemical	American Chemical Society
Atheneum	Atheneum Publishers
Augsburg	Augsburg Publishing House
Avon	Avon Books
Ballentine	Ballentine Books, Inc.
B&N NY	Barnes & Noble Books
Bantam	Bantam Books, Inc.
Barron	Barron's Educational Series, Inc.
Basic	Basic Books, Inc.
Beacon Pr	Beacon Press, Inc.

Berkley Pub	Berkley Publishing Corp.
Biblio Dist	Biblio Distribution Center
Bobbs	Bobbs-Merrill Co., Inc.
Cambridge U Pr	Cambridge University Press
Citadel Pr	Citadel Press
Columbia U Pr	Columbia University Press
Cornell U Pr	Cornell University Press
Crown	Crown Publishers, Inc.
Da Capo	Da Capo Press, Inc.
Dell	Dell Publishing Co., Inc.
Dodd	Dodd, Mead & Co.
Doubleday	Doubleday & Co., Inc.
Dover	Dover Publications, Inc.
Dutton	Dutton, E. P.
Eerdmans	Eerdmans, William B., Publishing Co.
Fawcett	Fawcett Book Group
Free Pr	Free Press
FS&G	Farrar, Straus & Giroux, Inc.
Greenwood	Greenwood Press
Grove	Grove Press
HarBraceJ	Harcourt Brace Jovanovich, Inc.
Har-Row	Harper & Row, Publishers, Inc.
Harvard U Pr	Harvard University Press
Heath	Heath, D.C., Co.
Hill & Wang	Hill & Wang, Inc.
HM	Houghton Mifflin Co.
HR&W	Holt, Rinehart & Winston, Inc.
Ind U Pr	Indiana University Press
Intl Pub Co	International Publishers Co.
Iowa St U Pr	Iowa State University Press
Irvington	Irvington Publishers
Johns Hopkins	Johns Hopkins University Press
Kelley	Kelley, Augustus M., Publishers
Knopf	Knopf, Alfred A., Inc.
Krieger	Krieger, Robert E., Publishing Co., Inc.
La State U Pr	Louisiana State University Press
Little	Little, Brown & Co.
Liveright	Liveright Publishing Corp.
Longman	Longman, Inc.
McGraw	McGraw-Hill Book Co.
McKay	McKay, David, Co., Inc.
Macmillan	Macmillan Publishing Co., Inc.
MIT Pr	MIT Press

Modern Lib	Modern Library, Inc.
Monthly Rev	Monthly Review Press
Morrow	Morrow, William, & Co., Inc.
NAL	New American Library
Natural Hist	Natural History Press
NE U Pr	Northeastern University Press
New Directions	New Directions Publishing Corp.
Norton	Norton, W. W., & Co., Inc.
NYU Pr	New York University Press
Odyssey Pr	Odyssey Press
Open Court	Open Court Publishing Co.
Oxford U Pr	Oxford University Press
Pa St U Pr	Pennsylvania State University Press
Pantheon	Pantheon Books
PB	Pocket Books, Inc.
Penguin	Penguin Books, Inc.
Peter Smith	Smith, Peter, Publishers, Inc.
P-H	Prentice-Hall, Inc.
Praeger	Praeger Publishers
Princeton U Pr	Princeton University Press
Random	Random House, Inc.
Regnery-Gateway	Regnery Gateway, Inc.
S&S	Simon & Schuster, Inc.
Schocken	Schocken Books, Inc.
Scribner	Scribner's, Charles, Sons
St Martin	Saint Martin's Press
Stanford U Pr	Stanford University Press
Stein & Day	Stein & Day
T Y Crowell	Crowell, Thomas Y., Co.
U of Ala Pr	University of Alabama Press
U of Cal Pr	University of California Press
U of Chicago Pr	University of Chicago Press
U of Mich Pr	University of Michigan Press
U of Minn Pr	University of Minnesota Press
U of Nebr Pr	University of Nebraska Press
U of Notre Dame Pr	University of Notre Dame Press
U of Pa Pr	University of Pennsylvania Press
U of Tex Pr	University of Texas Press
U of Wis Pr	University of Wisconsin Press
U Pr of KS	University Press of Kansas
U Pr of New Eng	University Press of New England
UH Pr	University of Hawaii Press
Ungar	Ungar, Frederick, Publishing Co., Inc.

Viking Pr	Viking-Penguin, Inc.
Westminster	Westminster Press
WH Freeman	Freeman, W. H., & Co.
Wiley	Wiley, John, & Sons, Inc.
WSP	Washington Square Press, Inc.
Yale U Pr	Yale University Press

PART I

Historical Periods

CHAPTER 1

Greece

MARSHALL S. HURWITZ

The debut of Western literature took place in Asia Minor about the year 800 B.C. Somewhere along the coastline of Turkey, the poet Homer, writing in a European language, produced the first great literary work of Western civilization—the *Iliad*, a full-length narrative poem, an epic without antecedent. Homer's writing did not, like Athena, "spring into light fully grown." A long tradition of oral literature already existed. Homer effected a transition to a more complex stage—written literature. Since the Trojan War in 1200 B.C., bards had sung of its episodes, characters, and themes. Homer focused on a single event—the confrontation between Agamemnon and Achilles—and with his sense of the concrete and his poetic genius, transformed an entertaining story into a significant human experience.

Lyric poetry, too, may derive from oral sources (folk songs), but in the 7th to 5th centuries B.C., it developed into more complex forms. Iambic poetry criticized and satirized customs and institutions. Elegiac poetry roused the emotions. The names of most of the poets are generally forgotten—or remembered faintly by scholars. But Sappho, whose lyrics tell of the joys and agonies of love, and Pindar, whose odes celebrate his devotion to the gods, to his native Thebes, and, especially, to triumph in athletic contests, still figure in world literature, both for their excellence and their influence.

Even as the Greeks transformed a primitive oral culture into a highly sophisticated written literature, they shaped as well a wholly new conception of the purpose of human life—a humanistic view, a rational yet idealistic approach to the practical problems of living and enjoying life. As assimilative, analytical, and creative people, the Greeks interpreted and adapted all they inherited. In almost every activity of the human mind—from architecture and medicine to government and philosophy, from poetry and drama to athletics—we remain indebted to the Greeks of the 5th and 4th centuries B.C.

Greek philosophy, for example, an outgrowth of efforts to understand the rational ordering of the physical universe, was developed in the 6th century by the pre-Socratics and expanded by the Sophists, itinerant scholars who accepted fees for discoursing to such students as were willing to pay. Socrates shifted the direction of philosophy from science—speculation about the order and nature of the universe—to ethics—the principles governing a good life—and to metaphysics—the quest for the reality underlying appearances. Plato's "Socratic dialogues" draw upon a wide range of earlier philosophic theories, harmonizing and arranging them to chart a logical course toward truth. Plato's Academy, "the world's first university," lured the best minds, among them Aristotle, perhaps the greatest systematizer of all time. Aristotle also opened an intellectual center that drew together scholars and researchers as well as students. Aristotle systematically evolved what may be the most influential concept in philosophy, perhaps in any discipline: that rational analysis, logical arrangement, and reduction to first principles enable us to perceive and to understand.

Particularly in the 5th century B.C., the city-state of Athens was the hub of Greek commercial, intellectual, and political life. Because it dominated the seas, Athens garnered large sums as tribute from the other city-states it protected. Income poured in as well from its merchant fleet, its silver mines, and its marble quarries. A huge slave labor force assured architects the economic freedom to design handsome buildings for sculptors and painters to decorate. The climate of free thought attracted intellectuals and artists from scattered points of the Mediterranean world. For Athenian citizens, a version of democratic government prevailed, though only a fifth of the population qualified as voters (women, slaves, and resident aliens were not enfranchised).

In time, as the historian Thucydides and others would point out, domestic and foreign stress would expose the weaknesses of the democracy: Resources were wasted, policies muddled, faction spread, demagoguery ruled. Eventually, Athens would fall victim to Sparta, then to Philip of Macedon, and finally to

Rome. Paradoxically, each new conquest resulted in a wider spread of Greek language, thought, and culture. Thus, Alexander Hellenized Egypt and the Near East, while Rome carried Greek culture to western Europe, North Africa, and the British Isles.

What the Greeks passed on to the future was a vision of fairness and honesty, a sense of proportion and moderation. Leavening government and formal thought, these qualities show forth in artistic and literary production as well. Greek sculpture, vases, and architecture (particularly the Parthenon, designed by Ictinius and adorned by Phidias) are models of simplicity, grace, and symmetry. Like epic and lyric poetry, Greek tragedy probably had its origin in oral tradition—a choral lyric (*dithyramb*) sung in honor of the god Dionysus. When Thespis, in the 6th century B.C., had an actor speak the parts of the characters in the poem, drama was born. Greek comedy served to amuse and to expose people, policies, and institutions to public ridicule. Only Aristophanes' comedies have come down to us, really, but they are quite as vibrant and alive today as they were twenty-four centuries ago. The three great tragic poets—Aeschylus, Sophocles, and Euripides—drew upon stories people knew from childhood; they projected life steadily and whole, portraying without rancor or sentimentality the sad but ennobling workings of human fate.

Look at collections of Greek art and architecture in museums or books; read Greek tragedies, epics, and lyrics; ponder the probings of Greek philosophers—and you will discern the glory that was Greece.

Greek Literature

Collections

Complete Greek Tragedies (1959). Eds. David Grene and Richmond Lattimore. Generally first-rate translations of the surviving dramas of Aeschylus, Sophocles, and Euripides; soundly edited and excellently introduced. *H—U of Chicago Pr 4 vols*. Selections from each dramatist: *P—U of Chicago Pr 3 vols*.

The Greek Anthology (1981). Ed. & tr. Peter Jay. A good short introduction to Greek literature. *P—Penguin*.

Greek Lyrics (1960). Tr. Richmond Lattimore. A good selection of early Greek poets in a fine modern poetic translation. *P—U of Chicago Pr*.

The Portable Greek Historians (1959). Ed. M. I. Finley. Generous selections from Herodotus, Thucydides, Xenophon, and others, with illuminating introduction and notes. *P—Viking Pr.*

The Portable Greek Reader (1948). Ed. W. H. Auden. The best one-volume collection, containing 720 pages of entire works and excerpts plus an acute introduction, bringing together the significant high spots of Greek literature and thought from Homer to Galen. *P—Penguin.*

Individual Authors

AESCHYLUS 525–456 B.C. **Tragedies.** In tense, taut, oblique verse, Aeschylus projects his stern moral view of the universe through myths fashioned into dramas. Best known is **The Oresteia,** the only surviving Greek trilogy, comprising **Agamemnon, Choephoroe,** and **Eumenides,** superb tragedies of bloodshed, revenge, and moral regeneration. The most readable translations are by Richmond Lattimore (*P—U of Chicago Pr*), Paul Roche (*o.p.*), and Robert Fagles (*H—Viking Pr; P—Penguin*). *Over 20 other eds. of indiv. or coll. plays.*

AESOP c. 6th cent. B.C. **Fables.** Delightful animal stories illustrating folk morality with pointed, sometimes cynical wit. *Over 20 eds.*

ARISTOPHANES c. 448–380 B.C. **Comedies.** Lyrical, topical burlesques, combining boisterous farce with poetic beauty: on Socrates, **The Clouds;** on war and women, Lysistrata; on utopian schemes, **The Birds.** *Over 20 eds. of indiv. or coll. plays.*

ARISTOTLE 384–322 B.C. **Nicomachean Ethics.** A profound pioneer analysis of the modes, methods, and values of human conduct. The most encyclopedic Greek thinker carefully interprets the good life as achievement of well-being or fullest virtue, the mean between too much and too little in social relations. See also "Philosophy," page 248. *H—Harvard U Pr, Oxford U Pr; P—Bobbs.*

——. **Politics.** See "Politics," page 275.

DEMOSTHENES 383–322 B.C. **Orations.** The best in rhetoric and oratory. *H—Gordon Pr, Harvard U Pr, Oxford U Pr.*

EURIPIDES c. 484–408 B.C. **Tragedies and Tragi-Comedies.** Realistic, human, highly theatrical dramas by the most modern of the great Greek playwrights, whose favorite targets were irrationality, war, and women's rights. His best-known plays include **Hippolytus, Medea, The Suppliants,** and **The Trojan Women.** *Over 30 eds. of indiv. and coll. plays.*

HERODOTUS c. 484–425 B.C. **History.** Lively narrative (with anthropological digressions) of the crucial struggle between democratic Greece and totalitarian Persia in the 5th century B.C. *Over 6 eds.*

HESIOD c. 770 B.C. **Theogony** and **Works and Days.** Myths of the gods, fables, proverbs, social protest, moral advice, prayers, and religious chants, by a probable contemporary of Homer. *H—Ayer Co, Harvard U Pr, Oxford U Pr, U of Mich Pr; P—Bobbs, Johns Hopkins.*

HOMER c. 800 B.C. **Iliad.** In moving verse, the epic develops the tragic consequences of Achilles' anger against Agamemnon over the distribution of war spoils. Through this slight incident in the Trojan War, Homer projects the total life view and standard of values of early Greeks as well as creates many memorable characters. The most faithful and readable verse translation is by Richmond Lattimore (*o.p.*); also very readable is that of Robert Fitzgerald (*H & P—Doubleday*). *Over 12 other versions.*

———. **Odyssey.** The exciting and varied experiences of Odysseus during his ten-year trip home from Troy demonstrate the ability to triumph over human, natural, and supernatural obstacles, and etch brilliantly the world of Odysseus. This "novel" provides a splendid introduction to Homeric myth and religion, social institutions, and cultural values. The recommended verse translations are by Robert Fitzgerald (*P—Doubleday*) and Richmond Lattimore (*P—Har-Row*). The prose version by E. V. Rieu reads much like a modern novel (*P—Penguin*). *Over 10 other versions.*

LUCIAN c. 125–210. **Dialogues of the Dead** and **Dialogues of the Gods.** Pungent and witty satires with philosophic implications. *H—Harvard U Pr 8 vols.* Selections: *P—Norton.*

PINDAR 522–443 B.C. **Odes.** Chief writer of choral or "Pindaric" odes celebrating Olympic triumphs and special events. Richmond Lattimore's translations are excellent: *P—U of Chicago Pr.*

PLATO c. 427–347 B.C. **The Republic.** While developing in detail a definition of justice and the characteristics of a utopian state, Plato expounds his theory of Eternal Ideas, his influential views on education, his paradoxical concept of the philosopher-king, and other fundamental aspects of his world view. The skillfully annotated abridged translation by F. M.

Cornford is recommended: *P—Oxford U Pr. Over 6 unabr. eds*.

————. **Dialogues.** See "Philosophy," page 282.

PLOTINUS. **The Enneads.** See "Philosophy," page 282.

PLUTARCH c. 46–120. **Lives.** Short biographies, paralleling the lives of famous Greeks with the careers of famous Romans. Remarkable character interpretations. *Over 6 eds*.

POLYBIUS 204–122 B.C. **Histories.** An outstanding interpretation of Rome's rise to power. *H—Greenwood 2 vols., Harvard U Pr 6 vols*.

SOPHOCLES 496–406 B.C. **Tragedies.** In the whole range of Greek tragedy, two of his "Theban plays"—**Oedipus Rex** for plot, **Antigone** for wide-ranging moral significance—are the most widely known. The best translations of the Theban trilogy are by Robert Fagles (*P—Penguin*) and Dudley Fitts and Robert Fitzgerald (*o.p.*). *Over 15 other eds. of indiv. or coll. plays*.

THUCYDIDES c. 470–400 B.C. **The Peloponnesian Wars.** An acutely analytical yet stirring account of the fateful struggle for power between Athens and Sparta. A classic work of history. *Over 6 eds*.

XENOPHON 431–355 B.C. **Anabasis.** Describes the military campaigns of Cyrus of Persia and the retreat of the Greek mercenaries across the Arabian deserts to the Black Sea. *P—U of Mich Pr, Penguin*.

Books about Greece

Ancient Greek Literature (1980). Ed. K. J. Dover. Essays by many different specialists in various genres of Greek literature. Useful bibliography. *H & P—Oxford U Pr*.

BOWRA, C. M. 1898–1971. **The Greek Experience** (1958). Brilliant popular analysis of Greek life, thought, and culture. *P—NAL*.

DODDS, E. R. 1893–1979. **The Greeks and the Irrational** (1951). Fascinating discussion of shame culture (in which conduct is governed by the opinion of others), magic, and other aspects that constituted the darker side of the Greeks. *P—U of Cal Pr*.

DURANT, WILL 1885–1981. **The Life of Greece** (1939). Comprehensive yet eminently readable survey of Greek civilization from remote times to the Roman conquest. *H—S&S*.

FARRINGTON, BENJAMIN 1891–1974. **Greek Science** (1939). Illuminating survey of the physical and economic forces and of the speculative minds that laid foundations for modern science. *o.p.*

FINLEY, M. I. b. 1912. **The World of Odysseus** (1954). The best popular introduction to the world and works of Homer. *H—Viking Pr; P—Penguin.*

———. **The Ancient Greeks** (1963). A sound, readable account of ancient Greek history and culture, rich in anecdote and illuminating in assessing Greek strengths and shortcomings. *P—Penguin.*

FRANKEL, HERMANN F. 1899(?)—1977. **Early Greek Poetry and Philosophy** (1962). A detailed discussion of the literature and thought of the Greeks before the Golden Age. *H—Irvington.*

GRANT, MICHAEL b. 1914. **Myths of the Greeks and Romans** (1962). Excellent presentation of the major myths via the most important sources. Applies different theories of myth, stressing the continuing influences of the tradition. *P—NAL.*

GRAVES, ROBERT 1895–1985. **Hercules, My Shipmate** (1945). Imaginative reconstruction of the savage, lusty, daring adventures of the Argonauts, who sought the Golden Fleece. *H—Greenwood; P—FS&G.*

———. **The Greek Myths** (1955). The complete story of the Greek gods and heroes assembled—with many fresh insights and occasional idiosyncrasies—into one continuous narrative by a poet and novelist of great learning and ability. *H—Doubleday; P—Penguin 2 vols.*

HADAS, MOSES 1900–1966. **History of Greek Literature** (1950). An intelligent and discriminating survey of the major writers of ancient Greece. *H—Columbia U Pr.*

———. **Hellenistic Culture** (1954). Some of the major trends and themes in Greek literature and civilization after Alexander the Great. *P—Norton.*

HAMILTON, EDITH 1867–1963. **The Greek Way** (1930). Entertaining and stimulating study of Greek writers and their influence in ancient as well as modern times. *H & P—Norton; P—Avon.*

HARRISON, JANE 1850–1928. **Prolegomena to the Study of Greek Religion** (1903). Fascinating scholarly account of deities, ceremonials, sacrifices, and other elements of primitive Greek religion. *H & P—Humanities; H—Ayer Co.*

HIGHET, GILBERT 1905–1978. **The Classical Tradition** (1949). With both scholarship and charm, analyzes the major influences of Greek and Roman literature and thought on contemporary Western culture. *H—Oxford U Pr.*

JAEGER, WERNER 1888–1961. **Paideia** (1939). Profound, difficult, but highly rewarding study of the development of Greek thought and ideals. *H—Oxford U Pr 3 vols; P—Oxford U Pr Vol. 1 only.*

KITTO, H. D. F. 1897–1982. **The Greeks** (1954). A witty, sometimes opinionated popular introduction, focusing on social conditions in ancient Greece. *P—Penguin.*

————. **Greek Tragedy** (3rd rev. ed. 1966). Informed, perceptive, unusually illuminating analysis of Greek tragedies and their backgrounds. *P—Methuen Inc.*

LESKY, ALBIN b. 1896. **History of Greek Literature** (1966). An excellent and detailed survey of all stages of Greek literature from Homer to early Christianity. Bibliographies. *H & P—T Y Crowell.*

————. **Greek Tragic Poetry** (1983). The best survey of scholarship on the remains of Greek tragedy. Detailed bibliographies. *H—Yale U Pr.*

MacKENDRICK, PAUL L. b. 1914. **The Greek Stones Speak** (rev. ed. 1962). A lively, well-illustrated survey of recent archeological work in Greek lands. *H & P—Norton.*

Oxford Classical Dictionary (2nd ed. 1970). Eds. N. G. Hammond and H. H. Scullard. Scholarly articles in alphabetical order on all phases of Greek and Roman civilization. Brief bibliographies. *H—Oxford U Pr.*

RENAULT, MARY (MARY CHALLANS) 1905–1983. **The King Must Die** (1958). Another clear, delicate evocation of ancient Greece, centering around the legendary Theseus. *H—Pantheon; P—Bantam.*

SNELL, BRUNO b. 1896. **Discovery of the Mind in Early Greek Philosophy and Literature** (1982). Stimulating essays on perception, the gradual awareness of self and other philosophical motifs in Greek literature. *P—Dover.*

STANFORD, W. B. 1910–1985. **The Ulysses Theme** (1968). Traces the myth of Odysseus in its many manifestations in Western literature from Homer to James Joyce. *P—U of Mich Pr.*

WARNER, REX b. 1905. **The Greek Philosophers** (1958). Useful as an introductory study of the major philosophers and their predecessors. *P—NAL*.

CHAPTER 2

Rome

MARSHALL S. HURWITZ

The word "Roman" conjures up a vision of blocks of masonry—strong, massive, durable—and with reason; for many of the roads, temples, bridges, aqueducts, amphitheaters that the Romans built still survive. But they made contributions to Western culture even more enduring. Their network of roads and their settlements helped give modern Europe its shape. Their language, Latin, was the main source of eight modern languages, including Italian, French, and Spanish. Their political system strongly influenced the founding fathers of America, among others. And their law is the core of one of the two major legal systems in Western civilization.

Such accomplishments of the Roman gift for social organization are important, but they leave a misleading impression. Efficiency implies hard practicality, perhaps even lack of feeling. Yet the Romans, like other Mediterranean peoples, were also emotional and excitable, as their literature abundantly reveals. Though the Romans did not match the intellectual and artistic originality of the Greeks, their literature often exhibits wit, emotional insight, and esthetic power. The uniqueness of Latin literature lies in the fusion of sophistication with the moral force and earnestness produced by a strong orientation toward public affairs and social issues.

A sampling will show the variety. The comedies of Plautus, written near the beginning of Latin literature, are full of lively humanity. His comic animation and chaotic plots stand in sharp contrast to Terence's quieter, more polished and sensitive comedies of manners.

In the literature of the first half of the 1st century B.C., the outstanding names are Cicero and Caesar in prose and Catullus and Lucretius in poetry. The orations and letters of Cicero reveal a humane politician and a consummate orator. The strong and brilliant personality of Caesar appears vividly in his accounts of the Gallic and civil wars. These two writers, political enemies, help us to know deeply a crucial period in world history when republic was yielding to empire. Catullus pictures in his lyrics the sophisticated society of poets, rakes, and beauties, using his art for the graceful expression of erotic feeling. Lucretius undertakes in *The Nature of Things* to crush superstition and ignorance with the materialistic thought of Epicureanism.

The following half century, the "Augustan Age," produced equally notable works. Vergil's *Aeneid*—the most significant single Latin book to read—portrays the cultural mission of Rome with grandeur and intelligence. Horace's lyrics—sometimes delicate, sometimes weighty, usually brilliant—and his pungent satires have been relished by many readers. Ovid's *Metamorphoses* fascinates with its remarkable narrative power. In a period memorable mainly for its poetry, Livy's epical history of Rome is a prose masterwork.

The reader will find much that seems contemporary in the social criticism of Roman decadence that permeates the best writing of the early centuries of the Christian era. The precursors of novelists, Petronius and Apuleius, wrote bawdy, satiric social romances. The materialism and immorality of Rome are the targets of Juvenal's satires. Also critical of the times are Tacitus' devastating historical analysis of the emperors and Seneca's Stoic writings. Stoicism was the source of much social liberalism, as is shown in a Senecan letter challenging slavery: "Just remember that he whom you call your slave was born from the same seed, enjoys the same sky, and equally breathes, lives, and dies."

The continuous movement from pagan to fully Christian times is reflected in the literature from the 4th century through the 6th. Jerome, whose favorite authors were Plautus and Cicero, was primarily responsible for the great Latin translation of the Bible known as the Vulgate. Augustine's *Confessions* records his conversion to Christianity from and through classical thought. Boethius clings firmly to the rationality of pagan philosophy as a support to the faith of Christianity. So new vitality arises from old.

Literature of the Roman Era

Collections

An Anthology of Roman Drama (1960). Ed. P. W. Harsh. Selected comedies of Plautus and Terence, tragedies of Seneca. *P—HR&W*.

Latin Poetry in Verse Translation (1957). Ed. L. R. Lind. An excellent anthology of poetry in Latin from the beginnings to the Renaissance. *P—HM*.

The Portable Roman Reader (1951). Ed. Basil Davenport. A competent survey of Roman literature and thought, generously representing the poets, playwrights, historians, satirists, and philosophers. *P—Penguin*.

Individual Authors

APULEIUS, LUCIUS c. 160. **The Golden Ass.** The only complete surviving Latin novel, about an adventurer who is changed into an ass and doomed to fantastic experiences until the goddess Isis allows him to resume human form. *H—Harvard U Pr; P—Ind U Pr*.

AUGUSTINE. **The City of God.** See "Philosophy," page 278.

———— **Confessions.** The odyssey of a powerful mind from materialism through Platonism to Christian belief, acutely analyzing "time" and "creation." *Over 6 eds*.

BOETHIUS 480–524. **The Consolation of Philosophy.** A moving dialogue concerning pagan philosophy and Christianity by "the last great pagan author." *P—Bobbs, Penguin*.

CAESAR, GAIUS JULIUS 100–44 B.C. **Commentaries.** The conqueror of Gaul and Britain and the victor in civil war gives propagandist reports of crucial campaigns and political struggles. *H—AMS Pr*.

CATULLUS, GAIUS VALERIUS 84–54 B.C. **Poems.** A hypersensitive young artist expresses intense emotion in lyrics ranging from personal feeling to contemporary life to the world of myth. *H—Godine, U of Cal Pr; P—U of Mich Pr*.

CICERO, MARCUS TULLIUS 106–43 B.C. **Selected Works.** Essays on philosophy and rhetoric, forceful orations, and revealing personal letters, written by a Roman active equally in politics and the arts. *Over 6 eds*.

HORACE (QUINTUS HORATIUS FLACCUS) 65–8 B.C. **Poems.** Polished lyrics, sophisticated satires, and poetic essays by one who belonged to the court circle but retained independence of mind. His name symbolizes urbanity and wit. *Over 20 eds.*

JUVENAL (DECIMUS JUNIUS JUVENALIS) c. 60–140. **Satires.** Bitter, realistic attacks on vices, abuses, and follies of imperial Rome, by an idealist driven to indignation. *Over 6 eds.*

LIVY (TITUS LIVIUS) 59 B.C.–A.D. 17. **Early History of Rome.** Picturesque account of the growth of the Roman state from the earliest times, emphasizing that the decline in moral values of the Roman world would cause its downfall. *P—Penguin.*

LUCRETIUS. **On the Nature of Things.** See "Philosophy," page 281.

MARCUS AURELIUS ANTONINUS. **Meditations.** See "Philosophy," page 281.

OVID (PUBLIUS OVIDIUS NASO) 43 B.C.–A.D. 17. **The Art of Love.** Playful, risqué verses on the devices of love; full of charm and humor. The Rolfe Humphries version is superior (*P—Ind U Pr*). Also: *H—Harvard U Pr.*

———. **Metamorphoses.** Tales of miraculous transformations by a versatile narrative poet. Its broad coverage of Greek and Roman myth has made it an important source book. Again, the Humphries translation is preferred (*H & P—Ind U Pr*). Others: *H—Harvard U Pr; P—NAL, Penguin.*

PETRONIUS, GAIUS d. 66. **The Satyricon.** Picaresque novel about the adventures of three rascals, incoporating· both social and literary criticism. This hilarious satire provides useful information about everyday life in Rome. The William Arrowsmith translation is recommended (*P—NAL*). Others: *H—Harvard U Pr; P—Penguin.*

PLAUTUS, TITUS MACCIUS c. 251–184 B.C. **Comedies.** Rollicking farces about tricky servants, braggart soldiers, identical twins, courtesans, et al. *H—Oxford U Pr.*

PLUTARCH. **Lives.** See "Greece," page 8.

SENECA, LUCIUS ANNAEUS c. 5 B.C.–A.D. 65. **Works.** Essays and letters applying stoic thought to perennial human problems and conditions of Roman life; Stoic melodramas showing the destruction of reason by passion. *H—Harvard U Pr, Oxford U Pr; P—Bobbs, Norton, Penguin.*

TACITUS, CORNELIUS c. 55–117. **Works.** History of the Roman Empire to A.D. 70 and of the Roman occupations in Britain and Gaul, written from a republican bias and exhibiting ironical insights as well as sustained literary qualities. *Over 10 eds.*

TERENCE (PUBLIUS TERENTIUS AFER) c. 195–159 B.C.

Comedies. Polished, refined comedies of manners stressing moderation. *Over 5 eds.*

VERGIL (PUBLIUS VERGILIUS MARO) 70–19 B.C. **Aeneid.** A great national epic glorifying the Latin temperament as well as the historical tradition and the universal cultural mission of Rome. The Robert Fitzgerald translation is preferred (*H & P—Random*). *Many other versions.*

————. **Eclogues.** Ten pastoral poems blend sensitive descriptions of nature with political commentary. *H & P—Cambridge U Pr, Ungar; H—Harvard U Pr, St Martin; P—Ind U Pr, Penguin.*

Books about Rome

BARROW, R. H. b. 1893. **The Romans** (1949). Clear sketch of their traits, history, achievements, and contributions to modern times. *P—Penguin.*

BULWER-LYTTON, EDWARD 1803–1873. **The Last Days of Pompeii** (1834). A colorful historical romance about the life that perished beneath the ashes of Vesuvius. *H—Biblio Dist.*

Cambridge History of Classical Literature: Latin Literature (1982). Eds. E. J. Kenney and W. V. Clausen. Up-to-date articles by leading specialists on the major authors and movements in Roman literature. Detailed bibliographies. *H & P—Cambridge U Pr.*

CARCOPINO, JEROME 1881–1970. **Daily Life in Ancient Rome** (1940). A description of many aspects of Roman life at the beginning of the empire. Based on original sources. *P—Yale U Pr.*

DUDLEY, DONALD R. 1910–1972. **The Civilization of Rome** (1960). An up-to-date, popular account of Rome from 753 B.C. to 476 in the Christian era, including history, politics, religion and art. *P—NAL.*

DUFF, J. W. b. 1866. **A Literary History of Rome: From the Origins to the Close of the Golden Age** (3rd ed. 1953) *o.p.*, and **A Literary History of Rome in the Silver Age: Tiberius to Hadrian** (3rd ed. 1964). The standard work on Roman literature. Balanced, perceptive accounts of each of the major and some of the minor writers. *H—Greenwood.*

DURANT, WILL 1885–1981. **Caesar and Christ** (1944). Well-informed, fluently written cultural history of Rome and Christianity from their beginnings to A.D. 325. *H—S&S.*

GIBBON, EDWARD 1737–1794. **The Decline and Fall of the Roman Empire** (1776–78). A monumental masterwork of great analytical power that has become a classic of history. *H—Biblio Dist 6 vols., Modern Lib 3 vols.; P—Dell.*

GRANT, MICHAEL b. 1914. **The World of Rome** (1961). Illustrated, readable interpretation of Roman history and culture and of their subsequent influence *o.p.*

GRAVES, ROBERT 1895–1985. **I, Claudius** (1934). Fictional autobiography of a strange emperor, which makes excellent use of historical sources. *H—Modern Lib; P—Random.*

HIGHET, GILBERT 1906–1978. **Poets in a Landscape** (1962). Biographical and literary assessments of Catullus, Vergil, Propertius, Horace, Tibulus, Ovid, and Juvenal by an incisive and witty critic. *H—Greenwood.*

OGILVIE, R. M. 1932–1981. **Roman Literature and Society** (1980). A good general introduction to Roman literature and its audience. *P—Penguin.*

PATER, WALTER H. 1839–1894. **Marius the Epicurean** (1885). Many-sided picture of Roman life and thought in the 2nd century A.D. as seen by a young patrician. *H—Garland Pub.*

Roman Civilization: Sourcebook (2 vols. 1966). Eds. Naphtali Lewis and Meyer Reinhold. A first-rate anthology of the primary sources illustrative of the political and social history of Rome with brief notes on the authors and context. *P—Har-Row.*

ROWELL, HENRY T. 1904–1974. **Rome in the Augustan Age** (1962). An expert analysis of the factors that made classical Rome a significant world capital. *P—U of Okla Pr.*

WILDER, THORNTON 1897–1975. **The Ides of March** (1948). The assassination of Julius Caesar vividly told through imaginary letters and documents. *o.p.*

WILKINSON, L. P. b. 1907. **Golden Latin Artistry** (1963). A significant contribution to the literary analysis of the authors of the 1st century A.D. *o.p.*

YOURCENAR, MARGUERITE b. 1903. **Memoirs of Hadrian** (1954). Brilliant novelistic re-creation of an intelligent emperor's reflections on the Roman world of his times. *H & P—FS&G; H—Modern Lib.*

CHAPTER 3

The Middle Ages

SAUL N. BRODY

In coming to read the literature of the Middle Ages, one thing to keep in mind is the prejudice contained in the very name "Middle Ages." With its implication that the era was merely an interlude between the classical and Renaissance periods, times when cultural life was *really* lived, the phrase betrays an unfortunate cultural myopia.

The richness of the medieval period is apparent to anyone who troubles to explore it. Its architectural monuments, such as the great cathedrals, embody not simply an extraordinary esthetic vision but also confirm the remarkable technical achievements of the period's mathematicians, architects, sculptors, masons, and glassmakers. Though not generally appreciated, even the work of medieval scientists should not be lightly dismissed. Among the scientific gifts we have received from the Middle Ages are such things as eyeglasses and mechanical clocks, the distillation of alcohol, the transmission from the Greeks of the basic ideas of theoretical explanation in science, and the application of mathematics to physical science.

In many ways, the Middle Ages were much like our own time, not least of all because of the sinister forces that gripped the era. Violence and war were commonplace then as now, poverty was everywhere, disease was a constant companion. Fourteenth-century England offers a ready illustration of these conditions. The year 1337 saw the beginning of the prolonged bloodbath known as the Hundred Years' War—a struggle between the English and the French that lasted well into the 15th century. The bubonic plague, also called the Black Death, struck first in 1348 and within two years carried off approximately one-third of England's population. In the decade of the sixties, the plague returned again three times, and on each occasion with catastrophic results. The decimation of the population naturally produced labor shortages, the labor shortages strained the relationship between the landed classes and the peasants, and the tension between the two classes ultimately helped bring about the Peasants' Rebellion of 1381. A distant mirror, perhaps, but the reflection in it is disconcertingly familiar.

Any sketch of medieval history will show how the period was marked by profound conflicts. These conflicts are the major themes of the period's literature, and their presence helps make that literature important to use as a place in which the human condition is accurately, if often grimly, described.

Medieval authors were driven by impulses we immediately recognize and by others that are less familiar. Modern writers usually do not write to obtain or to please patrons, but poetry written in praise of noble sponsors was commonplace then, for the ability to praise a nobleman inventively and persuasively could mean the difference between a warm bed and a night in the rain. Neither do modern writers, except perhaps the writers of textbooks, usually set out to conserve learning; the printing press has made obsolete the medieval need to copy and compile. But especially in the early Middle Ages, the business of transcribing and assembling anthologies of the work of venerated predecessors was a serious and ordinary undertaking. Also more prominent in the Middle Ages than now is the didactic strain in literature. The desire to convey religious doctrine, to teach moral behavior, was widely and deeply felt. The need to write in God's service—rarely encountered in our own skeptical age—was among the most common of medieval authorial impulses. It gave rise to hymns, religious lyrics, sermons, allegories, plays, and collections of saints' lives. Much of this literature was pedestrian, imitative, and repetitive, but among the many tedious examples stand some works that are treasures of world literature. Dante's *Divine Comedy*, for example, is an unparalleled masterpiece.

Closely tied to the religious motivation in medieval authors is the desire to set society on a proper path. If the individual needed to be directed to salvation, then society also needed to be saved from its sinful and destructive impulses. While in early medieval literature satire tended to be an exercise in imitation of classical models, by the late Middle Ages the satirical impulse was expressed in original and even passionate ways. Fourteenth-century England, for example, produced an extraordinary poem called *Piers Plowman*, an allegory that exposes the creativity of humans in undermining God's laws.

The urge to explore social problems is also seen in romances, stories that examine the values implicit in the courtly ethos, and especially the conflict between passionate, erotic love and the demand for loyalty to a God or society that opposed that love.' This issue is at the heart of many of the greatest medieval books about knights and their ladies, including the memorable Arthurian romances of Chrétien de Troyes, Thomas Malory's *Le Morte Darthur*, and (arguably the supreme instance) Gottfried von Strassburg's *Tristan*.

The epic, a second medieval genre populated by warriors, recounts and celebrates a nation's heroic past as it is embodied in a hero. An epic hero, such as Roland, Beowulf, or Siegfried, is the incarnation of the country's national identity. In Roland, for instance, we meet a proud and fierce warrior who defends his king, country, and God against the threats of their villainous heathen enemies. In Roland's virtues, and even in his flaws, is captured a greatness meant to define the sources of his country's strength. Giving definition to that strength was yet another urge that moved medieval writers.

If much medieval literature set out to improve human behavior, or to comment on its moral complexity, there was also some that had no redeeming social purpose. Writers, of course, have always delighted in showing us at our worst, and among medieval writers were many who shared that delight. Their impulse? Perhaps nothing more than to entertain. The worm's-eye view of life will always be expressed, and in the Middle Ages it was no different. The pleasure in lecherous lyrics and stories of adultery, trickery, and perversity was there, as we can see, for example, in the tales of Tyl Eulenspiegel and among Chaucer's brilliant *Canterbury Tales*.

Many readers, in their first encounters with medieval literature, are surprised by its sophistication. They come to it with the expectation that the earlier world, being a simpler one than ours, will also be more simple-minded. To their delight, they find it is not so much simple as different, and then to their greater delight, less different than at first appears. For instance, readers may find the medieval habit of mind that imbued human experience with rich symbolic import strange, a way of thinking that produced a richness in language and even narrative levels that are foreign to our modern empirical sensibility. Nevertheless, such obstacles to the appreciation of medieval literature are not so formidable as to place it out of our reach. Its power is there, and the modern reader need only open these books to discover it.

Medieval Literature

ANDREAS CAPELLANUS fl. 12th cent. **The Art of Courtly Love** (c. 1185). Tr. John J. Parry. Fascinating formulation of the theory and practice of courtly love by the chaplain of the Countess Marie of Champagne. *H & P—Ungar.*

Arabian Nights. See "The Middle East," page 67.

AUGUSTINE. **The City of God** and **Confessions.** See "Rome," page 14, and "Philosophy," page 278.

Beowulf (8th cent.). Anglo-Saxon epic about a legendary hero's struggles for humanity in a savage world. *Over 15 trans. and eds.*

BOCCACCIO. **The Decameron.** See "The Renaissance and Reformation," page 33.

BOETHIUS. **The Consolation of Philosophy.** See "Rome," page 14.

The Book of Beasts. Tr. T. H. White. An adaptation of a 12th century Latin bestiary—a collection of descriptions of animals real and imagined. *P—Dover.*

CHAUCER, GEOFFREY 1340?–1400. **Troilus and Criseyde** (c. 1385). A tragic love story, set in doomed Troy; one of the greatest English narrative poems. *10 trans. and eds.*

———. **The Canterbury Tales** (1387–1400). A wonderful panorama of English life, thought, and social types of the 14th century, drawn in character sketches and stories touched with wit, pathos, and common sense and shaped through superb literary art. *Nearly 40 trans., and eds., in whole and in part.*

CHRÉTIEN DE TROYES fl. late 12th cent. **Arthurian Romances** (c. 1170—c. 1181). Tr. W. W. Comfort. Verse tales of love and chivalry, marked by irony and wit. *H & P—Biblio Dist.*

DANTE ALIGHIERI 1265–1321. **The Divine Comedy** (1300–21). This brilliantly imagined epic journey through Hell, Purgatory, and Paradise, by one of the world's greatest poets, synthesizes medieval religion, politics, learning, and philosophy in a timeless story of faith and love. *Over 12 trans. and eds.*

ENGLISH DRAMA BEFORE SHAKESPEARE. Medieval miracle and mystery plays, interludes, and early 16th-century plays have been variously anthologized and titled by at least six different publishers. An excellent collection, including examples of Continental plays, is **Medieval Drama** (1975). Ed. David Bevington. *H—HM*.

ENGLISH LYRICS OF THE MEDIEVAL PERIOD. Several anthologies of Old English and Middle English lyric poetry exist. One good collection is **One Hundred Middle English Lyrics** (1964). Ed. Robert D. Stevick. *P—Bobbs*.

Fabliaux: Ribald Tales from the Old French (1965). Tr. Robert Hellman and Richard O'Gorman. Comic stories of lechery and sexual deceit. *H—Greenwood*.

FROISSART, JEAN 1333?–1400? **Chronicles of England, France, and Spain** (1373–90). The classic contemporary history of the first half of the Hundred Years' War. *H—AHS Pr 6 vols., Walter J. Johnson 2 vols.; P—Penguin*.

GEOFFREY OF MONMOUTH 1100?–1154. **History of the Kings of Britain** (c.1136). Idealized, usually imaginary history that underlies much of Arthurian romance. *P—Dutton, Penguin*.

GEOFFREY DE VILLEHARDOUIN 1160?–1212? and JEAN DE JOINVILLE 1224?–1317? **Memoirs** (also **Chronicles**) **of the Crusades** (c. 1207 and 1309). Vivid and fascinating first-hand accounts of the 4th and 7th crusades. *H—Greenwood; P—Penguin*.

German and Italian Lyrics of the Middle Ages (1973) *o.p.*, and **Lyrics of the Troubadours and Trouveres** (1973). Ed. & tr. Frederick Goldin. A superb bilingual anthology of lyrics extolling "the dignity, and even the spirituality, of passionate love," with detailed introductions. *H—Peter Smith*.

GOTTFRIED VON STRASSBURG fl. 1210. **Tristan** (c. 1210). Tr. A. T. Hatto. The story of Tristan and Isolde, in what is arguably the supreme example of an Arthurian romance. *P—Penguin*.

GUILLAUME DE LORRIS 1215?—1278? and JEAN DE MEUN d. 1305. **The Romance of the Rose** (c. 1236). One of the most popular and influential poems of the Middle Ages, this dream allegory is really two poems, one embracing courtly love, the other satirizing it. *H—AMS Pr 3 vols.; P—Dutton, U Pr of New Eng*.

KHAYYÁM. **The Rubáiyát.** See "The Middle East," page 69.

Koran. See "Religion," page 289.

LANGLAND, WILLIAM 1332?–1400? **Piers Plowman** (c. 1360–c. 1400). A powerful social protest in vigorous verse. *Over 10 eds. and trans.*

MALORY, SIR THOMAS 1430?–1471. **Le Morte Darthur** (1485). Sometimes lusty, sometimes idealized fiction of chivalric combat and courtly love, much of it written in prison. *Over 15 eds. and trans.*

MANDEVILLE, JOHN d. 1372. **Travels** (1371). An entertaining compound of geographic facts and legendary marvels. *P—Penguin.*

MARIE DE FRANCE fl. late 12th cent. **Medieval Fables** (1160–99). Tr. Jeanette Beer. Tales in verse, known as Breton *lais*, about love and adventure in Celtic settings. *H—Dodd.*

MARTORELL, JOANOT 1415?–1480? and **MARTI JOAN DE GALBA** d. 1490. **Tirant lo Blanc** (1490). Tr. David H. Rosenthal. A Catalan novel of chivalry, praised by Don Quixote's curate as "the best book of its kind in the world." *H—Schocken.*

Nibelungenlied (c. 1200). The German heroic epic surrounding Siegfried and the overthrow of the Burgundian kingdom by the Huns; the basis for Wagner's operatic cycle *Der Ring des Nibelungen. Over 5 trans.*

POLO, MARCO 1254?–1324? **Travels** (1300–24). Colorful autobiographical account of the adventures of a Venetian merchant who was for a time an official of the great Kublai Khan in China. *Over 8 trans.*

Sir Gawain and the Green Knight (c. 1375–c. 1400). The compromised attempt of an Arthurian knight to preserve his king's and his own reputation. *Over 15 eds. and trans.*

The Song of Roland (c.1090–c. 1105). The French heroic epic recounting Ganelon's betrayal of Charlemagne in order to revenge himself on his nephew Roland. *More than 12 eds. and trans.*

THOMAS À KEMPIS 1380–1471. **The Imitation of Christ** (c. 1471). A famous devotional work reflecting the ideas of the medieval Church. *Over 15 eds.*

THOMAS AQUINAS, SAINT 1225–1274. **Writings.** The greatest Catholic theologian and philosopher, on God, humanity, and human destiny. *Over 20 eds.* See also "Philosophy," page 283.

VILLON, FRANCOIS 1431–1463? **Poems.** Compelling, power-fully charged lyrics by a 15th-century Parisian poet-outlaw. *Over 6 eds.*

WOLFRAM VON ESCHENBACH c. 1170–c. 1220. **Parzival** (c. 1200–c. 1212). A version of the Grail legend by one of the greatest poets of the medieval period. *H—AMS Pr; P—Penguin, Random.*

Books about the Middle Ages

ADAMS, HENRY 1838–1918. **Mont-Saint-Michel and Chartres** (1904). Penetrating, sensitive analysis of the medieval spirit in architecture and literature. *H & P—Princeton U Pr; H—Gordon Pr.*

BARBER, RICHARD W. b. 1941. **The Knight and Chivalry** (2nd ed. 1975). A learned and witty treatment of knighthood from origin to decline and of its medieval social setting. *H—Rowman; P—Har-Row.*

BATTERBERRY, MICHAEL b. 1932. **Art of the Middle Ages** (1972). Lively, informative, lavishly illustrated account, from the catacombs to the 15th century. *o.p.*

BAUTIER, ROBERT-HENRI. **The Economic Development of Medieval Europe** (1972). A clear and vivid survey. *o.p.*

BLOCH, MARC 1886–1944. **Feudal Society** (1960). Creates in detail a vast panorama of the social system of the Middle Ages; one of the most important books on the subject. *P—U of Chicago Pr 2 vols.*

BOGIN, MEG b. 1950. **The Women Troubadours** (1980). This study and translation of some 20 women poets of medi-eval Provence, with an introduction on courtly love, is valu-able both in its own right and as a corrective to the male troubadours' views of women and love. *P—Norton.*

BULLOUGH, DONALD b. 1928. **The Age of Charlemagne** (1966). Portrays the social and religious history, the arts, and the learning of the Carolingian period, as well as the first and last European emperor. *o.p.*

COULTON, GEORGE G. 1858–1947. **Medieval Panorama** (1947). Richly detailed narrative of the English scene from the Norman Conquest to the Reformation. *P—Norton.*

CROMBIE, A. C. b. 1915. **Medieval and Early Modern Science**

(1959). An illuminating overview of medieval technology and scientific theories. 2 vols. *o.p.*

ECO. **The Name of the Rose.** See "20th-Century Continental Novels," page 129.

GIES, JOSEPH b. 1916 and FRANCES GIES b. 1915. **Life in a Medieval City** (1969). First-rate account of the life of the burghers of the Middle Ages. *P—Har-Row*.

————. **Life in a Medieval Castle** (1974). Chepstow Castle in Monmouthshire and the lives of its knights and villagers, with generous quotations and illustrations from contemporary sources. *P—Har-Row*.

HASKINS, CHARLES HOMER 1870–1937. **The Renaissance of the Twelfth Century** (1927). The 12th-century revival of learning: science, philosophy, jurisprudence, and the beginnings of universities, to cite but four examples. *P—Harvard U Pr*.

HEER, FRIEDRICH b. 1916. **The Medieval World** (1961). Learned, vigorous account and analysis of the people, institutions, and culture of the High Middle Ages. *P—NAL*.

HUGO, VICTOR 1802–1885. **The Hunchback of Notre Dame** (1831). The love of a hunchback for a dancer. A great historical novel set in 15th-century Paris. *Over 6 eds*.

HUIZINGA, JOHAN 1872–1945. **The Waning of the Middle Ages** (1924). Colorful and original interpretation of the psychology of the late Middle Ages in France and the Netherlands, based on contemporary literature, art, customs, and costume. *H—St. Martin*.

JACKSON, W. T. H. 1915–1983. **The Literature of the Middle Ages** (1960). A general account of the field, organized by literary types. *H—Columbia U Pr*.

KELLY, AMY b. 1878. **Eleanor of Aquitaine and the Four Kings** (1950). The life and times of one of the great women of the Middle Ages, wife of two kings and mother of two others. Biography and history that reads like a novel. *P—Harvard U Pr*.

MAURER, ARMAND b. 1915. **Medieval Philosophy** (1962). "The monumental structure of ideas and beliefs created in the course of one of the most inspired intellectual and spiritual quests of all ages." *o.p.*

MAYER, HANS E. **The Crusades** (1972). Causes, Crusades, consequences: a fine one-volume survey. *P—Oxford U Pr*.

OLDENBOURG, ZOÉ b. 1916. **Destiny of Fire** (1961). Compassionate and moving novel based on the 13th-century atrocity known to history as the Albigensian Crusade. *o.p.*

PERNOUD, REGINE b. 1909. **Joan of Arc** (1967). Contemporary documents—letters, chronicles, trial testimony—with connecting commentary bring the Maid of Orleans to life as a credible human being. *P—Stein & Day*.

POUILLON, FERNAND b. 1912. **The Stones of the Abbey** (1970). Recreating the building of a 12th-century French abbey, this finely wrought short novel captures the flavor of the Middle Ages and illuminates the problems involved in the creation of medieval monasteries and cathedrals. *o.p.*

POWER, EILEEN 1889–1940. **Medieval People** (1925). Fine scholarship and stylistic grace re-create six medieval lives in memorable fashion. *H & P—B&N*.

————. **Medieval Women** (1975). Ed. M. M. Poston. The editor's attractive personal approach is contained in the texts of lectures given at various places and times. *P—Cambridge U Pr*.

READE, CHARLES 1814–1884. **The Cloister and the Hearth** (1861). Vigorous, realistic novel about Erasmus' parents, set in Flanders, France, Germany, and Italy. *o.p.*

ROWLING, MARJORIE b. 1900. **Everyday Life in Medieval Times** (1968). A sound, sensitive, well-documented account of how all classes of people lived from the time of Charlemagne to the Renaissance. *o.p.*

SCOTT, SIR WALTER 1771–1832. **Ivanhoe** (1819). Famed romance of Old England, with Richard the Lion-Hearted, Robin Hood, tournaments, robber barons, and love. *Over 6 eds*.

TIERNEY, BRIAN b. 1922 and SIDNEY PAINTER 1902–1960. **Western Europe in the Middle Ages** (4th ed. 1983). Outstanding one-volume history of the civilization from 300 to 1475. *H—Knopf*.

TUCHMAN, BARBARA W. b. 1912. **A Distant Mirror: The Calamitous Fourteenth Century** (1978). An exceptionally lively history, focusing on France. *H—Knopf; P—Ballantine*.

UNDSET, SIGRID 1882–1949. **Kristin Lavransdatter** (1920–22). A trilogy about a woman's life in 14th-century Norway, notable for its historical verisimilitude; by the winner of the 1928 Nobel Prize for Literature. *H—Knopf; P—Bantam*.

VALENCY, MAURICE J. b. 1903. **In Praise of Love** (1958). A brilliant, original analysis of the poetic tradition of the troubadours in its historical, social, and psychological setting. *H & P—Schocken; H—Octagon*.

WADDELL, HELEN 1889–1965. **Peter Abelard** (1933). Deeply

moving novel about one of the most famous true love stories of all time and about the brilliant, passionate scholar whose love for Heloise brought tragedy. *o.p.*

WHITE, LYNN b. 1907. **Medieval Technology and Social Change** (1964). A remarkable and convincing effort to relate profound social developments to humble technological innovations such as the stirrup and the heavy plow. *P—Oxford U Pr.*

CHAPTER 4

The Renaissance and Reformation

GORDON TESKEY

The word "Renaissance" (Fr. "rebirth") is used to denote the synergic complex of changes that took place in all aspects of European culture in a period beginning about 1300 in Italy and drawing to a close in northern Europe toward the end of the 17th century. Although we regard it as a historical period distinct from the "Middle Ages" that preceded it and the "Enlightenment" that followed, it is important to note that the Renaissance brought about profound changes in the history of the West that affect us today.

It was called a "rebirth of antiquity" (*rinascimento dell' antichità*—the phrase is Vasari's) because the sudden and intense developments that took place in literature, painting, sculpture, architecture, and science were due in large measure to the inspiration of recently discovered classical models. As the term "rebirth" suggests, people of the Renaissance were attracted to a new conception of history as a cycle of loss and recovery in which one age may be separated from another by an intervening period that is different from, even alien to, both. The nine centuries that separated the world of Plato and Cicero from that of Erasmus and Petrarch were therefore described as "medieval" (*medius*, "middle"; *aevum*, "age"), and people of the Renaissance imagined themselves looking back across a wide gap of time to that distant and luminous ideal of "sacred antiquity" (*sancta vetustas*). Thus, when Brunelleschi, having studied the Pantheon, threw a gigantic dome without any supporting columns over the altar of the cathedral of Florence—a feat of engineering unattempted since Rome—it must have seemed as if the prophecy of Francis Petrarch, the first of the great Italian Renaissance humanists, was being dramatically fulfilled: "After the darkness has been dispelled," he declared, "our grandchildren will be able to walk back into the pure light of the past."

While Petrarch's confident assessment of what the new age would accomplish was to be amply justified—most of classical literature as we know it was recovered, the arts were dramatically transformed, and modern science in its practice (Galileo) and theory (Bacon) was born—the notion of a "renaissance," taken too literally, can distort our perspective. On the one hand the classics had not been lost quite so completely as was thought (there were at least two minor revivals, or "renascences," before the Renaissance itself), and on the other hand the notion of a "rebirth of antiquity" underestimates the scope and power of the changes that actually occurred, most notably in the development of empirical science. It was in the Renaissance that modern man, not remarkable for his veneration of the classics, was born.

Since the middle of the 19th century, when Burckhardt's influential study was published, scholars have questioned not only the date of the Renaissance but even its validity as a historical concept. The reasons for this are not hard to find: No consensus on a movement of cultural transformation involving so many independent national traditions, from Portugal to Germany, can be expected to hold up for long; and it is not likely that economists, historians, political theorists, geographers, classicists, art historians, literary scholars, musicologists, and historians of science and technology will readily agree that they are talking about the same thing. Although the term "Renaissance" is indispensable to university curricula, there is so little agreement about its precise meaning that many scholars avoid using it as being unprofessionally vague.

This is needlessly coy; for despite the enormous complexity of the problem, one thing is clear: a constellation of powerful changes came together from which modern Europe emerged. It is reasonable to think that the general world view of someone in England in 1700 would have more in common with ours, almost 300 years later, than with that of someone only a generation before. The changes might be summarized as follows: A new sense of human dignity and power appears, only to be contradicted by an equally new awareness of the body as a fragile machine; nature is conceived of in material rather than semiotic terms, so that it is no longer thought of as a reflection of God; and history is conceived of as an array of distinct, internally coherent periods any of which the observer might examine on its own without having to look *through* all the events in between. While biblical or classical figures represented in medieval art always look medieval (Homeric heroes jousting like 12th-century knights), a Roman or Greek scene in the hands of Renaissance painters like Mantegna or Raphael gives us the sense of looking through a window in time into a separate world.

This compartmentalized view of history made critical historiography and scientific antiquarianism possible, but its greatest significance lies in the implicit realization that people are not the same from one age to the next. Thus the foundation was laid in the Renaissance for a conception of human nature that is irreducibly temporal, an idea that was to be enunciated later, and in different ways, by Nietzsche, Darwin, and Marx. Such changes provoked a new and profound concern about what it means to be human, and scholars expressed that concern primarily within a tradition of liberal studies directed toward an ideal standard that was thought to have been contained in the classics. The search for "Man" (a collective term for both genders) had begun.

With the invention of printing in the 16th century, the newly discovered texts of classical antiquity could be widely and rapidly disseminated, thus bringing into being a class of learned churchmen, administrators, and teachers dedicated to the *studia humanitatis*, or "humane studies," and calling themselves "humanists." Preferring the more informal style of the dialogue or colloquium, in imitation of Plato and Cicero, the humanists were scornful of the technically impressive accomplishments of medieval theology. Instead of dealing in what they regarded as arid abstractions, they sought to make all learning applicable to practical affairs.

Writing for a much wider audience, the humanists therefore addressed questions of morals, statecraft, and history—and they did so in a colloquial style that would be easy and, it was hoped, delightful to read, a style that these dwellers in cities like Florence, Rotterdam, and London would have called *urbanitas*, or "civility." Because they regarded the ancients as a store of wisdom that was almost as venerable as Christian truth ("Saint Socrates, pray for us!" Erasmus exclaimed not entirely in jest), they gave weight to this colloquial style by frequent quotation from the classics—as one sees particularly in the essays of Montaigne. Humanism, then, is a movement committed to the ideal of a common, nonspecialist discourse that can be shared by all learned people, and it was for this reason that so many humanist works employed the framework of a "banquet," or *convivium*, of talk. To the humanists, however, an elegant style was not an end in itself; for they aimed at nothing less than the restitution of human nature, through reason and education, to its original perfection: "The end of learning," wrote Milton, "is to repair the ruins of our first parents by regaining to know God aright." No medieval author could have made that assertion with anything like Milton's confidence.

In its overriding concern with defining, in classical terms, an ideal of "Man," humanism was not so much an achievement in its own right as a coordinating principle in every area of Renaissance culture: "Man," in the popular expression of Protagoras, "is the measure of all things." Yet, as Hamlet's remarks on the dignity of man would suggest, this newly won confidence brought with it some disturbing contradictions. We can see something of what this means by juxtaposing two of the most influential works of the period that take Man as their subject: Pico della Mirandola's *Oration of the Dignity of Man*, in which we are said to have the freedom to degenerate into beasts or to expand our powers to rule the cosmos, and what is perhaps the most extraordinary scientific achievement of the age, Vesalius' detailed anatomy text, *On the Structure of the Human Body*. Taking these together, we can observe the formation in the Renaissance of a view of human nature that is profoundly contradictory: a boundless human will—what Marlowe called the "aspiring mind"—directs all its force *against* nature, as a thing to be conquered, while remaining tied to the limitations of a fragile, organic structure.

The hectic insecurity that such a contradiction imposes may help to explain why the Renaissance ideal of Man is almost always expressed in images of balance—from the titanic *contraposto*, the titanic counterpoise, of Michelangelo's *David* to the "perfect hero" who balances on the pinnacle at the climax of Milton's *Paradise Regained*. Renaissance Man aspires, and in us still aspires, to stand serenely omnipotent above the complex ecology of nature and to owe nothing to its laws of process and exchange. The moral ideal of balance and prudent restraint is therefore the mask of an insatiable will. The ability to manage this contradiction politically was called *virtù* by Machiavelli, an economy of prudent restraint and unrestrained violence. And the same contradiction, in Bacon, organizes the relation between method and goal in empirical science: The investigator humbly "buckles" his mind to nature's law, but only so that he may eventually win absolute control. We find this mask, and what it partly conceals, in the most seemingly innocuous places: "Virtue is in the middle way," reads an "embleme" from Spenser's *Shepherds' Calendar* that typifies the spirit of the time, "but happiness resides at the top": "*In medio virtus. In summo felicitas.*"

The *Reformation*, which took place during the Renaissance, was the movement of revolt from the Roman Catholic Church initiated by Luther and eventually established throughout northern Europe in the various Protestant sects. Among the principal tenets of Reformation theology are (a) that no rite, observance, or authority can be binding on any Christian if there is no clear mention of it in scripture ("*sola scriptura*"); and (b) that the Christian will be justified before God by his *faith*, not by his *works*. (*Works* in practice did not mean "good deeds" but observance of the rituals and obedience to the discipline of the Roman Catholic Church.) These principles still characterize all varieties of Protestantism today. The Protestant interest in the early fathers of the church and in the original languages of the Bible was consonant with much of the humanist movement. We find in it the same notion of returning to a source, removed at some distance in time, without having to account for anything that happened in the intervening period. Just as Cicero's Latin is the pure fountainhead muddied by later Scholastic writers, so the simple piety of the worshippers in the early church, and the simplicity of Jesus himself, are to be preferred to the worldly glory of the Roman Church. By the middle of the 16th century the latter had begun to react with a full-scale *Counter-Roman Reformation*.

Renaissance

ARIOSTO, LODOVICO 1474–1533. **Orlando Furioso** (1532). Great romance epic of the Italian Renaissance. Highly varied and inventive narrative that is comic, satirical, passionate, and grave by turns. The Renaissance translation of Sir John Harrington (1591) is superb: *H—Walter J. Johnson*. Of several modern translations, Barbara Reynolds' translation is a good one: *P—Penguin 2 vols*.

BACON, FRANCIS 1561–1626. **Advancement of Learning and New Atlantis** (1605). The theoretical and imaginative foundations of empirical science in the 17th century. Good introduction. *Several eds. of both works separately in print.*

————. **Essays** (1597, 1612, 1625). Shrewd, aphoristic studies of human life. *Over 6 eds.*

BOCCACCIO, GIOVANNI 1313–1375. **The Decameron** (c. 1350). One hundred tales of love, intrigue, and adventure by an early master of Renaissance narrative. *Over 10 eds.*

BROWNE, SIR THOMAS 1605–1682. **Selected Writings** (1968). Ed. Sir Geoffrey Keynes. Supreme English prose stylist of the 17th century. *P—U of Chicago Pr.*

BURTON, ROBERT 1577–1640. **The Anatomy of Melancholy** (1621–32). Bewildering, encyclopedic, and satirical medical treatise on the disease of "melancholy." Written in an "extemporal style," which the author compares to a running sore. *H—AMS Pr 3 vols., Walter J. Johnson; P—Random, Ungar.*

CASTIGLIONE, BALDASSARE 1478–1529. **The Courtier** (1528). The enormously influential expression of the Renaissance ideal of courtly manners, set in the ducal palace of Urbino. Renaissance translation by Thomas Hoby. *H & P—Biblio Dist; H—AMS Pr; P—Doubleday, Penguin, Ungar.*

CELLINI, BENVENUTO 1500–1571. **Autobiography** (1728). A portrait of the artist as rogue and assassin, set in the rich world of Florentine politics, manners, and morals. *H—St Martin; P—Penguin.*

CERVANTES SAAVEDRA, MIGUEL DE 1547–1616. **Don Quixote** (1605–15). Picaresque novel satirizing both the morals of the time and the fashion for extravagant novels of adventurous romance. *Over 10 eds.*

DA VINCI, LEONARDO 1452–1519. **The Notebooks.** Anatomical drawings, inventions, titanic engineering projects, studies of all aspects of the natural world, secret writing, and much more. A mysterious record of genius. *H—Peter Smith 2 vols.; P—Dover 2 vols., Oxford U Pr.*

DONNE, JOHN 1573–1631. **The Complete English Poems** (1983). Ed. A. J. Smith. The man whose cynical, passionate, and devout poems Samuel Johnson called "metaphysical." *P—Penguin.*

Elizabethan Critical Essays. Ed. Gregory Smith. A collection of writings on poetry and poetics by authors of the English Renaissance. Includes Sidney, Puttenham, and Nashe. *o.p.*

Elizabethan Narrative Verse (1967). Ed. Nigel Alexander. An anthology of narrative poems in English in the tradition of

Ovid, recounting various stories of metamorphosis. Typical of Renaissance poetic sensibility. *o.p.*

England's Eliza (1939). Ed. Elkin C. Wilson. Contemporary documents bearing witness to the idealization of Queen Elizabeth. *H—Octagon*.

English Drama: 1580–1642 (1933). Eds. C. F. Tucker Brooke and N. B. Paradise. Excellent anthology of major plays by contemporaries of Shakespeare, including Marlowe and Kyd. *H—Heath*.

ERASMUS, DESIDERIUS 1466–1536. **In Praise of Folly** (1512). Witty satire on human irrationality in general, and false learning in particular, by the most influential humanist of the northern Renaissance. *H & P—Yale U Pr; P—Princeton U Pr, U of Mich Pr*.

Famous Utopias of the Renaissance (1955). Ed. Frederic R. White. An anthology of utopian literature exemplifying the new tendency of the age to conceive of human problems as being capable of solution through rational social organization. Includes More's **Utopia** and Bacon's **New Atlantis.** *P—Hendricks House*.

HAKLUYT, RICHARD 1552–1616. **Voyages and Discoveries** (1982). Superb narratives of the English voyages of discovery to the New World. *P—Penguin*.

HERBERT, GEORGE 1593–1633. **The English Poems of George Herbert** (1974). Ed. C. A. Patrides. High Anglican devotional poems of extraordinary intensity and wit. Editor's introduction very useful for Renaissance theology. *H & P—Rowman*.

JONSON, BEN 1572(?)–1637. **Plays.** A skillful satirist, especially in his comedies **Volpone** and **The Alchemist.** Strongly influenced by the classics, unlike his friend Shakespeare. *Over 20 eds. of indiv. and coll. plays*.

————. **Poems** (1975). Ed. Ian Donaldson. Superb, English neoclassical poems concerned with the possibility of ideal social relations. See especially "To Penshurst" and "Inviting a Friend to Supper." *H & P—Oxford U Pr*.

LOPE DE VEGA CARPIO, FÉLIX 1562–1635. **Five Plays** (1961). A mere sampling of the enormous output of one of the greatest dramatists of the Renaissance. *o.p.*

MACHIAVELLI, NICCOLÒ 1469–1527. **The Prince** (1513). A brilliant, and notorious, analysis of the brutal realities of getting power and keeping it. Written by a man who lived in the midst of the chaotic politics of Renaissance Italy; "The Prince," he said, "must have the head to plan and the arm to strike." *Over 10 eds.*

MILTON, JOHN 1608–1674. **John Milton: Complete Poems and Major Prose** (1957). Ed. Merritt Hughes. Author of *Paradise Lost*, the greatest epic poem in English, Milton was a paragon of the Renaissance man: encyclopedic in his learning, yet also devoted to an active life of public service. *H—Odyssey Pr.*

MONTAIGNE, MICHEL DE 1533–1592. **Essays** (1580–88). A fascinating adventure of self-exploration by one of the great masters of French prose. A probing series of *essais*, or "attempts," to examine all aspects of life. *H—AMS Pr 3 vols.; P—Penguin.*

PETRARCH, FRANCIS 1304–1374. **Petrarch: Selected Sonnets, Odes and Letters** (1966). Ed. Thomas G. Bergin. A selection of the work of the first, and perhaps the greatest, of the Renaissance humanists and one of the greatest lyric poets of any period. *P—Harlan Davidson.*

The Portable Elizabethan and Jacobean Poets (1977). Eds. W. H. Auden and Norman Holmes Pearson. Wide-ranging collection of all the major and several of the minor poets. *P—Penguin.*

The Portable Renaissance Reader (rev. ed. 1958). Eds. James B. Ross and Mary M. McLaughlin. An excellent and very wide selection of texts from the period illustrating all aspects of Renaissance culture. Very helpful bibliography. *H—Viking Pr; P—Penguin.*

The Protestant Reformation (1968). Ed. Hans J. Hillerbrand. Documentary overview of the great movements and leaders of the Reformation. *P—Har-Row.*

RABELAIS, FRANCOIS 1494(?)–1553. **Gargantua and Pantagruel** (1533–34). Farcical, obscene, satirical, and prodigiously inventive masterpiece by one of the most learned and irreverent authors of the French Renaissance. *H—AMS Pr 3 vols., Biblio Dist; P—Harlan Davidson, Penguin.*

SHAKESPEARE, WILLIAM 1564–1616. **Poems and Plays.** Arguably the greatest poet of all time, who, in his fascination with all aspects of the human condition and his transcendent love of beauty, is typical also of his own time. His works are available in countless editions.

SIDNEY, PHILIP 1554–1586. **Prose Works.** Ed. Albert Feuillerat. Contains his great prose romance, **Arcadia**, which is ornately rhetorical in style and aristocratic in sentiment, and his famous **Apology for Poetry**. *o.p.* Several P and H eds. of both. Indiv. eds. of *Apology for Poetry: H—Walter J Johnson, R West; P—Bobbs. Arcadia: P—Penguin.*

————. **Poems.** Ed. W. A. Ringler. Contains the famous sequence of sonnets "Astrophel and Stella" ("Fool! Look in thy heart and write!") and the experiments in quantitative measure from the *Arcadia. H—Oxford U Pr.*

Source Readings in Music History: The Renaissance, Vol. 2 (1965). Ed. Oliver Strunk. An unusual anthology, especially enlightening to readers with some knowledge of music theory and terminology. *P—Norton.*

SPENSER, EDMUND 1552–1559. **Poems.** The greatest nondramatic English poet of the Elizabethan age. His **Faerie Queene** combines myth and complex moral theory in an immense, and marvelously imagined, allegorical romance. *Over 6 eds.*

VASARI, GIORGIO 1511–1574. **The Lives of the Artists** (1550). A student of Michelangelo and Andrea del Sarto, Vasari was the first historian of art to proclaim a "rebirth of antiquity" in Italian art and to record its development from Giotto through Masaccio to Michelangelo. An excellent abridged version: *P—Penguin. Over 6 eds.*

VESALIUS, ANDREAS 1514–1564. **The Illustrations from the Works of Andreas Vesalius** (1950). An extraordinary instance of collaboration between art and science, this great study of the human body revolutionized our conception of scientific research and of human nature itself. *H—Peter Smith; P—Dover.*

VESPASIANO DA BISTICCI, FIORENTINO 1421—1498. **Lives of Illustrious Men** (1839). Lively thumbnail biographies of the most gifted and important men of the author's time, largely from personal recollection. *o.p.*

Books about the Renaissance and Reformation

ADAMCZEWSKI, JAN and EDWARD J. PISZEK. **Nicolas Copernicus and His Epoch** (1974). Illustrated and informative account of the life and times of the man who invented the theory Galileo was later to prove. *o.p.*

ANTHONY, KATHARINE 1877–1965. **Queen Elizabeth** (1929). An animated biography that gives a strong sense of Elizabeth Tudor's life and times. *H—Arden Lib, Norwood Edns.*

BAKER, HERSCHEL b. 1914. **The Race of Time: Three Essays on Renaissance Historiography** (1967). An elegantly written and streamlined account. *o.p.*

BERENSON, BERNARD 1865–1959. **Italian Painters of the Renaissance** (1897). A superbly written, fundamental study of the Venetian and northern schools and of the Florentine and central Italian schools of painting. *P—Cornell U Pr.*

BLUME, FRIEDRICH 1893–1975. **Renaissance and Baroque Music** (1967). Comprehensive survey of the rich achievements of the period, especially recommended to readers with some knowledge of music theory and terminology. *P—Norton.*

BLUNT, ANTHONY 1907–1983. **Artistic Theory in Italy, 1450–1600** (1956). Excellent and readable study of the intellectual background to one of the greatest epochs in the history of Western art. *H & P—Oxford U Pr.*

————. **Art and Architecture in France: 1500–1700** (1977). A richly informative and engrossing study. *H—Viking Pr; P—Penguin.*

BURCKHARDT, JACOB 1818–1897. **The Civilization of the Renaissance in Italy** (1860). The great work of historical synthesis that remains the point of departure for all studies of the Renaissance. 2 vols. *H—Modern Lib, Peter Smith; P—Har-Row, Merrimack Pub Cir.*

BUSH, DOUGLAS 1896–1983. **The Renaissance and English Humanism** (rev. ed. 1956). A brief and readable study of the humanistic movement and its influences in England. *P—U of Toronto Pr.*

————. **Mythology and the Renaissance Tradition in English Poetry** (rev. ed. 1963). More far-reaching than its title suggests, this work is a landmark in our understanding of the literary culture of the English Renaissance. *o.p.*

————. **English Literature in the Earlier Seventeenth Century: 1600–1660** (3rd ed. 1966). The standard, comprehensive study. *H & P—Oxford U Pr.*

CHAMBERS, E. K. 1866–1954. **Shakespeare, a Survey** (1925). A stimulating collection of a great scholar's introductions to the plays. *o.p.*

CLARK, SIR KENNETH 1903–1983. **Civilization: A Personal View** (1970). Chapters on the Renaissance are an absorbing and beautifully illustrated introduction to the event as a comprehensive European phenomenon. *H & P—Har-Row.*

————. **Leonardo da Vinci** (1976). A fine study of the greatest genius of the age. *P—Penguin.*

————. **The Art of Humanism** (1983). Excellent for the intellectual context it gives to the art of the Renaissance. *H—Harper Row*.

CROMBIE, A. C. b. 1915. **Mediaeval and Early Modern Science, Vol. 2** (1959). The beginnings of the scientific revolution and the foundations of modern science and technology expertly summarized. *o.p.*

DURANT, WILL 1885–1981. **The Renaissance** (1953) and **The Reformation** (1957). Lively and encyclopedic popular histories. *H—S&S*.

FERGUSON, WALLACE K. b. 1902. **Europe in Transition, 1300–1520** (1964). Excellent introduction to the Renaissance, integrating social, political, economic, and cultural history. *o.p.*

FOUCAULT, MICHEL b. 1926. **The Order of Things: An Archaeology of the Human Sciences** (1973). An influential study of concepts of order, intelligibility, and knowledge in the 16th century and how these contribute to the emergence of the concept of "Man." *P—Random*.

GARIN, EUGENIO b. 1909. **Italian Humanism: Philosophy and Civic Life in the Renaissance** (2nd ed. 1976). Like the following entry, an elegant and readable study by a master. *H— Greenwood*.

————. **Astrology in the Renaissance** (1983). A fascinating account of science in transition. *H—Routledge & Kegan*.

GILMORE, MYRON P. b. 1910. **The World of Humanism 1453–1517** (1952). Still the best general overview of the rise of the "New Learning" throughout Europe. *H—Greenwood*.

GRANVILLE-BARKER, HARLEY 1887–1946. **Prefaces to Shakespeare** (1944–47). An outstanding producer-director's important analyses of plot, character, and language. *H & P—Princeton U Pr; P—David & Charles*.

GREENBLATT, STEPHEN b. 1943. **Renaissance Self-Fashioning from More to Shakespeare** (1980). An interesting study of new conceptions of human nature and their political consequences. *H & P—U of Chicago Pr*.

GURR, ANDREW b. 1936. **The Shakespearean Stage, 1574–1642** (2nd ed. 1981). A compact and fascinating study of the world of the theater in Shakespeare's London. *H & P—Cambridge U Pr*.

HALE, J. R. b. 1923. **Renaissance Exploration** (1972). A reliable and beguiling account. *P—Norton*.

HARRISON, GEORGE B. b. 1894. **Introducing Shakespeare**

(1939). Still the best brief introduction to Shakespeare. *H—Somerset Pub*.

————. **The Story of Elizabethan Drama** (1972). An entertaining and readable account. *H—Folcroft*.

HARTT, FREDERICK b. 1914. **History of Italian Renaissance Art** (1969). The best text and the first to offer an integrated discussion of the painting, sculpture, and architecture. *H—Abrams, P-H*.

HENINGER, S. K. b. 1922. **Touches of Sweet Harmony: Pythagorean Cosmology and Renaissance Poetics** (1974). A wide-ranging study of esoteric, Pythagorean philosophy and its influence on Renaissance poetics and poetry. *H—Huntington Lib*.

HILLERBRAND, HANS J. b. 1931. **Christendom Divided: The Protestant Reformation** (1971). Excellent study of the religious reform movements and their leaders in historical context. Other works by same author also of interest. *o.p.*

KRAILSHEIMER, A. J. b. 1921. **The Continental Renaissance 1500–1600** (1971). A comprehensive survey with bibliographies. Useful reference work. *H—Humanities*.

KRISTELLER, P. O. b. 1905. **Renaissance Thought and the Arts: Collected Essays** (1980). A wide-ranging, diverting, and profoundly learned collection of essays on the diffusion of humanism throughout Europe, the role of Neoplatonism in speculative philosophy, and the relation of the new learning to the development of the arts. *P—Princeton U Pr*.

LACEY, ROBERT b. 1944. **Sir Walter Raleigh** (1974). A fast-paced biography of the adventurer, courtier, and poet. Profusely illustrated. *P—Atheneum*.

LEWIS, CLIVE S. 1898–1963. **English Literature in the Sixteenth Century** (1954). The standard survey, richly entertaining. *H & P—Oxford U Pr*.

MEE, CHARLES L. b. 1938. **Lorenzo de' Medici and the Renaissance** (1969). Outstandingly illustrated introduction to the most glamorous of Renaissance princes and to Florence, the most glamorous of Renaissance cities. *H—Har-Row*.

A New Companion to Shakespeare Studies (1971). Eds. Kenneth Muir and S. Schoenbaum. An excellent collection of essays by eminent scholars on such subjects as Shakespeare's language, the playhouses, his intellectual and cultural milieu, and the history of criticism about him. *P—Cambridge U Pr*.

PANOFSKY, ERWIN 1892–1968. **Meaning in the Visual Arts** (1955). Contains important essays on such subjects as the theory of human proportions in Renaissance painting. A beautifully written and exciting book. *P—U of Chicago Pr.*

————. **Renaissance and Renascences in Western Art** (1972). A series of essays, including " 'The Renaissance': Self-Definition or Self-Deception?" constituting the best general introduction to the complex and controversial problem of defining and understanding the Renaissance. A landmark of scholarship and a pleasure to read. *P—Har-Row.*

————. **Studies in Iconology: Humanistic Themes in the Art of the Renaissance** (1972). *H—Peter Smith; P—Har-Row.*

PATRIDES, C. A. b. 1930. **Premises and Motifs in Renaissance Thought and Literature** (1982). An extremely learned and interesting study of various aspects of the Renaissance imagination. *H—Princeton U Pr.*

PILL, DAVID H. **The English Reformation** (1973). A good popular study. *o.p.*

PLUMB, J. H. b. 1911. **The Italian Renaissance** (1961). A stimulating and richly informative historical study. *P—Har-Row.*

QUINT, DAVID b. 1950. **Origin and Originality in Renaissance Literature** (1983). A comparative study of Renaissance poetry in several languages, examining the growth of new thought patterns as the period drew toward its close. *H—Yale U Pr.*

ROWSE, A. L. b. 1903. **The Elizabethan Renaissance: The Cultural Achievement** and **The Elizabethan Renaissance: The Life of Society** (1972). Together these form a good, comprehensive introduction to the world of Shakespeare, Marlowe, and Spenser. *H—Scribner.*

RUOFF, JAMES E. b. 1925. **Crowell's Handbook of Elizabethan and Stuart Literature** (1975). A good reference work on writers and literature of the English Renaissance. *o.p.*

SCHOENBAUM, S. b. 1927. **William Shakespeare: A Compact Documentary Life** (1977). A masterful synthesis, providing a full consideration of all the documents concerning Shakespeare in a lively narrative that is free of romantic conjecture. *H & P—Oxford U Pr.*

SCOTT, SIR WALTER 1771–1832. **Kenilworth** (1821). A historical novel about Elizabethan times. *H—Biblio Dist; P—Airmont.*

SEZNEC, JEAN b. 1905. **The Survival of the Pagan Gods** (1972). Tells the fascinating story of how the gods of the ancients survived through the Middle Ages and reemerged in the Renaissance as a system of signs and concepts to be exploited by poets and painters. *P—Princeton U Pr*.

Shakespeare's England (1917). An engaging collection of essays by various hands describing many aspects of social and cultural life in Shakespeare's time. 2 vols. *o.p*.

SPINGARN, JOEL E. 1875–1939. **A History of Literary Criticism in the Renaissance** (1976). Written at the turn of the century, this remains the most concise and readable introduction. *H—Greenwood, R. West*.

SYMONDS, JOHN ADDINGTON 1840–1893. **The Renaissance in Italy** (1875–86). Encyclopedic, monumental study, often richly entertaining. *H—Peter Smith 3 vols*.

TILLYARD, E. M. W. 1889–1962. **The Elizabethan World Picture** (1943). An excellent and readable summary of Elizabethan ideas about the structure of nature and the place of humanity within it. *P—Random*.

TUVE, ROSEMOND 1903–1964. **Elizabethan and Metaphysical Imagery** (1947). Learned and detailed study of imagery in one of the most important and conspicuous periods of transition in English poetry. *P—U of Chicago Pr*.

WILKINS, ERNEST H. 1880–1966. **Life of Petrarch** (1961). A biography of the humanist scholar and poet who, more than any other individual, initiated Renaissance literature and humanistic studies. *o.p*.

WILLEY. **The Seventeenth-Century Background.** See "The 17th Century," page 45.

WIND, EDGAR 1900–1971. **Pagan Mysteries in the Renaissance** (rev. ed. 1969). A fascinating study of esoteric symbolism and its importance in painting, poetry, and philosophy. *P—Norton*.

YATES, FRANCES 1899–1981. **Giordano Bruno and the Hermetic Tradition** (1964). In addition to examining the hermetic tradition as a whole, a lively account is given of one of the most powerful intellects of the Renaissance. Bruno was eventually burned by the Inquisition for his extraordinarily original, and peculiarly modern, scientific ideas. *P—U of Chicago Pr*.

CHAPTER 5

The 17th Century

JOSEPH A. BYRNES

The politically turbulent and intellectually active 17th century, the century of genius, as it has been called, served as both twilight of the Renaissance and dawn of the Age of Reason. In science, the century began with the new cosmology of Copernicus and Galileo; it ended with the Newtonian law of gravitation. It saw the experimental methods advocated by Bacon and Descartes, the founding of the English Royal Society and the French Academy of Sciences, and inventions and discoveries crucial for the future: the telescope and microscope, the calculus and logarithms, and Harvey's demonstration of the "Motion of the Heart and the Blood." In the arts, painting had distinguished practitioners: Rembrandt, Hals, Rubens, Van Dyck, Vermeer, Poussin, and Velasquez. In music, Monteverdi, Lulli, Corelli, and Purcell, England's greatest native-born composer, developed the baroque style, as polyphony yielded to harmony, madrigal to opera.

These impressive and peaceful accomplishments took place while Europe was torn by political, economic, and religious strife. During the Thirty Years' War (1618–1648), Catholics and Protestants piously and zealously and thoroughly devastated most of Germany. Victims of religious persecution fled; many, like the Huguenots and the Pilgrims, sought liberty of conscience in the wilderness of the New World. Spain's great empire was steadily weakening; the French monarchy, with brilliant administrators like Richelieu and Mazarin, established its supremacy domestically, although on an uncertain financial basis. The English, during and after their Civil War (1642–1649), modified their government—in part by killing one king, expelling another, and importing a third, and in part by applying the liberal political tenets advocated by men like Milton and Locke. Europe's merchant classes made weapons of their wealth in their vigorous drive toward power, nowhere with more success than in England. Energetic, practical, forward-looking, predominantly radical-Protestant, they were eventually to triumph over the conservative aristocrats.

Religion, long a source of bitter controversy, found itself harassed from a new quarter by doubts induced by the "new science." Problems of faith versus reason began increasingly to trouble speculative minds. Although the bulk of partisan sectarian writing is unreadable today, not all religion was acrimonious: among Englishmen, Fox and Bunyan achieved serene personal approaches to God; Donne and Herbert spoke poetically for Anglican moderation.

Philosophy, too, was especially concerned with religion and politics. Descartes began with a complete and radical skepticism; Hobbes postulated man's inhumanity to man, advocating absolutism as the safeguard of domestic tranquility. Locke's *Two Treatises of Government* later formed part of the intellectual heritage of America's founding fathers. Spinoza geometrically reexamined the fundamentals of ethics and religion; Pascal, moralist and mathematician, paradoxically exalted faith. In educational theory, the Moravian Comenius offered an idealistic proposal for universal free education.

During the 17th century, Spain's foremost contributions to European letters were created: Cervantes' comic knight and the dramas of Calderón and Lope de Vega. French drama likewise found its most sublime classical formulation in Corneille and Racine, and its supreme comic vision in Molière. English literature began the century with the glory of Shakespeare and the Jacobean dramatists, and with Donne and his fellow metaphysical poets, who compressed their world into intense, striking images. Unlike the metaphysicals, the greatest Puritan literary spokesman, Milton, was deeply committed to politics as well as to his attempts to "justify the ways of God to men." His rejection of royal absolutism and his fervent pleas in the *Areopagitica* for the free exchange of ideas unhampered by censorship are seminal propositions in the British and American view of democratic life.

In England, after years of Puritan repression, the Restoration of 1660 ushered in not only a king but also the social reaction reflected in its witty, rationalistic comedies about eager gentle-men in pursuit of equally eager ladies. Life in the England of Charles II was reported with humor and frank self-revelation by the prince of diarists, Pepys. The style of verse changed, and the varied stanzas and subtle lyrics of the metaphysicals, Herrick, and the Cavaliers were replaced by Dryden's pointed, balanced, rational, "heroic" couplets. English prose, the best of it nonpolemic, developed rapidly. What the English sentence lost throughout the century in Elizabethan exuberance (and length), it gained in power, precision, and suppleness. The magnificent phrasing of the King James Bible, the cadences of Sir Thomas Browne, the devotional simplicity of Bunyan, the rational power of Dryden's critical essays—all influenced the development of the language.

During the Renaissance, Western civilization reached the thresh-old of the modern world and in the 17th century entered fully into it, with its conflicts and confusions—some of which still plague us today. We have inherited from that age some of the scientific and philosophic principles we still live by, as well as the enduring literary record of its agonies, delights, and accomplishments.

17th-Century Literature

AUBREY, JOHN 1626–1697. **Brief Lives** (1813). Informal, revealing sketches, with often amusing details, of a host of persons. *H—B&N Imports, Darby Bks; P—Penguin.*

Authorized Version of the Bible (King James translation, 1611). "The noblest monument of English prose." See "Religion," page 257.

BACON. **Essays.** See "The Renaissance and Reformation," page 32.

BEAUMONT, FRANCIS 1584–1616 and JOHN FLETCHER 1579–1625. **Selected Plays.** Excellent theater, violent and exotic, elegant, poetic, witty. *Over 15 eds. of indiv. and coll. plays.*

BEHN, APHRA 1640–1689. **Selected Writings.** Clever, witty, occasionally sentimental, often indelicate, "the George Sand of the Restoration" was England's first professional woman author. *H—Greenwood; other sels. & eds.*

BROWNE, SIR THOMAS 1605–1682. **Religio Medici** (1643). The style—stately, cadenced, lucid, and personal—distinguishes the reasoned liberalism of Browne's Platonist doctor's faith. *P—Oxford U Pr*.

BUNYAN, JOHN 1628–1688. **Pilgrim's Progress** (1678). An allegory of the Christian's journey to self-fulfillment by a humble tinker and religious visionary; the most abiding scripture of English Puritanism, with a strong influence on later English prose style. *Over 20 eds*.

BURTON. **The Anatomy of Melancholy.** See "The Renaissance and Reformation," page 33.

CERVANTES. **Don Quixote.** See "The Renaissance and Reformation," page 30.

Colonial American Poetry (1968). Ed. Kenneth Silverman. No Miltons or Marvells here, but the high culture of the homeland did more than flicker in the new wilderness. *P—Hafner*.

CONGREVE, WILLIAM 1670–1729. **Comedies.** Satire on, and for, fashionable society; brilliantly cynical situations; dialogue of amazing finish and verve. *H—U of Chicago Pr; H & P—Cambridge U Pr*. There are also numerous collections and single volumes of Congreve and his fellow Restoration dramatists (Etherege, Wycherley, Otway, et al.).

CORNEILLE, PIERRE 1606–1684 and JEAN RACINE 1639–1699. **Plays.** These two playwrights created many of the masterpieces of France's neoclassical theater. Theirs is a world of formal tragedy, phrased in polished verse, following the classic unities in presenting irreconcilable conflicts of reason and passion. *Many eds. of indiv. and coll. plays*.

DESCARTES. **Discourse on Method.** See "Philosophy," page 248.

DONNE. **Poems.** See "The Renaissance and Reformation," page 30.

DRYDEN, JOHN 1631–1700. **Poems.** Poet laureate and pioneering drama critic, a titan of 17th-century English letters in drama, translation, criticism, and lyric and especially satiric poetry. *Over 5 eds*.

EVELYN, JOHN 1620–1706. **Diary** (1818). More sobersided than his younger contemporary, Pepys, Evelyn kept his historically invaluable diary during most of his long life. *H— Biblio Dist, R West, Oxford U Pr*.

FOX, GEORGE 1624–1691. **Journal** (1694). The Quaker leader's 34 years of "enlightening" the people. *H—Octagon*.

GRIMMELSHAUSEN, HANS JACOB CHRISTOFFEL VON 1625?–1676. **Simplicius Simplicissimus** (1669). A satiric fantasy, cast in a picaresque mold, of an innocent at large in the Thirty Years' War. *P—U of Nebr Pr, Ungar*.

HERRICK, ROBERT 1591–1674. **Poems** (1648). Piquant, poignant, graceful lyrics, encompassing both religious devotion and an Epicurean feeling for life and love. *o.p.*

HOBBES. **Leviathan.** See "Philosophy," page 279.

LAFAYETTE, MADAME DE 1634–1693. **The Princess of Clèves** (1678). Profoundly delicate fiction, notable for psychological realism, about a woman in a triangle. *H—French & Eur, Greenwood; P—Penguin.*

LA FONTAINE, JEAN DE 1621–1695. **Fables** (1668–94). Traditional beast fables from Aesop and other sources adapted to the not-too-nice world of Louis XIV. *H—Gannon; P—Dover, Penguin.*

LEIBNIZ, GOTTFRIED WILHELM VON 1646–1716. **Philosophical Writings.** The philosophy of rationalized optimism that was later to be Voltaire's target in *Candide. H & P—Rowman.*

LOCKE, JOHN 1632–1704. **Two Treatises of Civil Government** (1689). The source of much of the early political theory of America, especially Jefferson's. *Over 6 eds.*

————. **An Essay Concerning Human Understanding.** See "Philosophy," page 281.

LOPE DE VEGA CARPIO. See "The Renaissance and Reformation," page 34.

MARVELL, ANDREW 1621–1678. **Poems.** Puritan, politician, and poet, author of one of the greatest love poems in English ("To His Coy Mistress"). *H—AMS Pr, Folcroft, Oxford U Pr; P—Penguin, Routledge & Kegan.*

Metaphysical Lyrics and Poems of the Seventeenth Century (1921). Ed. H. J. C. Grierson. A classic anthology, with a helpful introduction to this knotty but fascinating verse. *H—Greenwood; P—Oxford U Pr.*

MILTON. See "The Renaissance and Reformation," page 35.

MOLIÈRE (JEAN BAPTISTE POQUELIN) 1622–1673. **Comedies.** Comic genius, expert theatricalism, and classic art united in satiric portrayals of society. Translations of Molière vary in quality; those by Richard Wilbur are superb. *P—HarBraceJ. Many other trans. and eds.*

Oxford Book of Seventeenth-Century Verse (1934). Eds. H. J. C. Grierson and G. Bullough. A standard collection representing more than 100 English poets. *H—Oxford U Pr.*

PASCAL, BLAISE 1623–1662. **Pensées (Thoughts)** (1670). Reflections of a sensitive mathematician on nature, humanity, and God. *Over 10 eds.*

PEPYS, SAMUEL 1633–1703. **Diary** (1825). Pepys reformed the Royal Navy, collected books, attended the theater, chased women, observed society and politics, and wrote it all down in a shorthand deciphered years later. A fascinating and frank picture of work and play in Charles II's London. *Over 10 eds., some abr.*

SÉVIGNÉ, MARIE, MARQUISE DE 1626–1696. **Letters.** Charming, witty, superbly styled, and natural letters that give a fine picture of the times of Louis XIV. *H—Folcroft 2 vols.; P—Penguin.*

SEWALL, SAMUEL 1652–1730. **The Diary of Samuel Sewall.** Almost all aspects of colonial life as reported by one of Massachusetts Bay's most observant men of affairs. *H—Ayer Co, Russell.*

SPINOZA. **The Ethics.** See "Philosophy," page 283.

WALTON, IZAAK 1593–1683. **The Compleat Angler** (1653). Generations of fishermen have delighted in this serene recommendation of the contemplative sport, with its interpolations on literature and life. *H & P—Oxford U Pr; P—Biblio Dist.*

Books about the 17th Century

BAZIN, GERMAIN b. 1907. **Baroque and Rococo Art** (1964). A brief but excellent and well-illustrated introduction to the visual arts of the age by the former curator of the Louvre Museum. *P—Oxford U Pr.*

CATHER, WILLA 1873–1947. **Shadows on the Rock** (1931). French pioneers on the Quebec frontier struggle to maintain the decorum of their homeland. *H—Knopf; P—Random.*

CHUTE, MARCHETTE b. 1909. **Two Gentle Men: The Lives of George Herbert and Robert Herrick** (1959). Caroline England gracefully evoked, with enlightening details, through the lives of two great lyric poets. *H—Dutton.*

DEFOE, DANIEL 1660–1731. **A Journal of the Plague Year** (1722). A vividly detailed, quasi-journalistic, re-creation of the nightmare world of the London pestilence of 1665. *H & P—Biblio Dist; H—AMS Pr; P—NAL, Penguin.*

DUMAS, ALEXANDRE 1802–1870. **The Three Musketeers** (1884). Swashbuckling adventure in the court of Louis XIII. *Over 6 eds.*

DURANT, WILL 1885–1981 and ARIEL DURANT 1898–1981.

The Age of Reason Begins (1961) and **The Age of Louis XIV** (1963). A panoramic view of Western civilization during the formative years of the modern world. Engagingly written with illuminating detail. *H—S&S*.

FRASER, ANTONIA b. 1932. **Royal Charles: Charles II and the Restoration** (1979). The king seen not only as the ''merry monarch'' of legend but also as a supremely astute politician who preserved order and his throne in troubled times. *H—Knopf; P—Dell*.

————. **The Weaker Vessel** (1984). In this ironically titled volume, wherever possible the actual words of women themselves have been quoted to portray women's lot at all social levels in 17th-century England. *H—Knopf*.

GRIERSON, H. J. C. 1886–1960. **Cross Currents in Seventeenth-Century English Literature** (1929). The age-old oppositions of world, flesh, and spirit, as manifested in a complex milieu. *H—Arden Lib*.

HALLER, WILLIAM 1885–1974. **The Rise of Puritanism** (1938). Even without Cromwell's New Model Army in the field, Puritanism became a force to be reckoned with. This standard study traces the movement from its humble beginnings. *P—U of Pa Pr*.

HAWTHORNE, NATHANIEL 1804–1864. **The Scarlet Letter** (1850). The classic American novel set in Puritan New England, highly dramatic and cannily symbolic, with masterly examination of the characters and their motives. *Over 30 eds*.

JOHNSON, SAMUEL 1709–1784. **The Lives of the English Poets** (1779–81). Cowley, Milton, and Dryden are among the English poets of the 17th century appraised with sturdy independence and common sense by the 18th century's greatest literary critic. *H—Adlers Foreign Bks 3 vols., Octagon 3 vols., Oxford U Pr; P—Biblio Dist (sels.), Oxford U Pr (sels.)*.

LEWIS, WARREN H. 1895–1973. **The Splendid Century** (1953). A wide-ranging view of the great and the lowly in French society during the reign of Louis XIV. *P—Morrow*.

MACAULAY, THOMAS B. 1800–1859. **The History of England** (1855). Scholarship joins dramatic imagination to present English history, with a Whig political bias. *H—AMS Pr 6 vols., Biblio Dist 4 vols.; P—Penguin (abr.)*

————. **Essays.** Lively criticism of Bacon, Milton, Bunyan, and the drama. Much good sense, despite a dogmatic style that may at first tend to alienate the modern reader. *H—Biblio Dist 2 vols*.

MANZONI. **The Betrothed.** See "The Novel: 19th-Century Continental Novels," page 139.

MILLON, HENRY A. b. 1927. **Baroque and Rococo Architecture** (1961). A concise and well-illustrated introduction to an era of impressive creations. *P—Braziller.*

ROSTAND, EDMOND 1868–1918. **Cyrano de Bergerac** (1897). A tour de force romantic drama about a real-life poet and playwright, lover and swordsman in Louis XIV's Paris. Various translations, none ideal. *H—Knopf, R. West; P—Bantam, NAL.*

SCOTT, SIR WALTER 1771–1832. **Old Mortality** (1816), **The Fortunes of Nigel** (1822), and **Woodstock** (1826) are among Scott's novels set in the 17th century. Of these, *Old Mortality*, a tale of Presbyterian revenge, resolution, and fortitude under royalist persecution, is the best. *P—Penguin.*

SILVERMAN, KENNETH b. 1936. **The Life and Times of Cotton Mather** (1984). Impressive warts-and-all portrayal of the great Puritan divine, "the first American celebrity," setting him firmly in the colonial New England milieu. *H—HarRow.*

STARKEY, MARION L. b. 1901. **The Devil in Massachusetts** (1949). A vivid, horrifying, and strictly factual narrative of the delusion that seized the good people of Salem and led to the infamous witch trials of 1692–93. *H—Peter Smith; P—Doubleday.*

TAWNEY, RICHARD H. 1880–1962. **Religion and the Rise of Capitalism** (1926). A now classic argument, relating the Protestant work ethic to the economic development of Western Europe. *H—Peter Smith.*

VAN LOON, HENDRIK W. 1882–1944. **The Life and Times of Rembrandt** (1943). An imaginative presentation of a great man and artist in a great time. *H—Liveright.*

WILLEY, BASIL 1897–1978. **The Seventeenth-Century Background** (1934). Primarily literary-philosophical and sometimes difficult, these essays examine English religion and poetry against contemporary climates of opinion. *H—Columbia U Pr.*

CHAPTER 6

The 18th Century

JOSEPH A. BYRNES

The philosophers of the Renaissance and 17th century bequeathed to their successors a more or less coherent intellectual system for viewing the world. Fundamentally rational, the 18th century perhaps found its characteristic expression in the Newtonian laws that were to dominate physics for nearly 200 years. The spirit of experimentation flourished and the tools of science were further refined. Things we take for granted—the beginnings of precise measurement, the exact composition of air and water, the relation of lightning to electricity, Lavoisier's chemical equations, Hutton's view that the earth has a geologic history, the Linnaean classification system in biology, the refutation of the accepted view that heat was a substance—all were discovered or established and, once established, led to subsequent discoveries, both scientific and technological. Interest in practical engineering was spreading, as manifested by the attention given to machines and industrial processes in the French *Encyclopedia*. Later in the century, the creation of canal systems and the invention of the steam engine, textile machinery, and hard-paved roads started Europe on the way to what we know as the Industrial Revolution, the rapid growth of which left a poet like Blake lamenting "Among these dark Satanic mills."

In philosophy, thinkers from Berkeley through Hume to Condorcet, whatever their premises, based their systems on reason, and Kant's insistence on the innate logicality of the mind is still the principle behind our computers and linguistic science. Not only among philosophers was reason honored; satirists and critics like Swift and Voltaire complained in its name, and rational religion (Deism) even seemed to threaten orthodox faith. Politically, the concept of the "rights of man" had been foreshadowed by the two English revolutions in the 17th century and by Locke's argument that people create government. However, it remained for America and France to carry through greater and more comprehensive revolutions. In economics, Adam Smith restored to the mainstream of European thought the Platonic doctrines of trade and the division of labor. A sobering warning on the relation of population increase to food supply was issued by Malthus long before technological and medical advances generated modern population pressures.

In spite of setbacks like the financial collapse of 1720 (the "South Sea Bubble"), European expansion continued. England and France were drawn by their conflicting economic interests onto battlefields as far-flung as Canada and India, where English victories led to the consolidation of the British Empire—that greatest of the 19th-century politicoeconomic powers, the collapse of which in our own time has left a vacuum still being painfully filled.

A reasonable and pragmatic age—one that could produce and admire Benjamin Franklin—did not approve of extremes of individualism or emotion, however it might at times allow itself to behave. There were dissidents, of course, the most prominent being Rousseau, whose influence helped spark not only the French Revolution but also the 19th-century Romantic movement and such earlier, tentative manifestations as the cultivation of "sensibility" in England and France and the "storm and stress" experienced by German youth in the 1770s.

The new literary form, born and developed in the century, was the novel, specializing in the realistic portrayal of individual men and women against recognizable backgrounds. Written mostly by and for the middle class, the novel appeared in a great variety of styles: realism (serious and comic, respectively) in Defoe and Fielding, psychological penetration and "sentiment" in Richardson, the philosophical tale in Voltaire, freewheeling extravaganza in Sterne, even the Gothic thriller in Walpole. The drama of the age is less striking than its fiction. An 18th-century tragedy could be acted today only as a curiosity; among the comedies, however—by Goldoni in Italy, Sheridan and Goldsmith in England, Marivaux and Beaumarchais in France—there are superb examples: witty, polished, brilliantly theatrical, and perceptively satiric.

Form dominated poetry and poetic diction when the century began. In England, the heroic couplet, as perfected by Pope, was unsurpassed for pithy epigram and witty satire. Later, when literary rebels like Burns and Blake wanted to express their often unconventional feelings, they sought less confined lyric forms. Ending the century, the Romantic Wordsworth declared for simplicity, urging poets to write in "a selection of language really used by men."

Among the other arts, painting, though much cultivated, fell short of earlier achievements. Perhaps the noblest and most enduring art of the century was its music: opera developed steadily; the form for the symphony was created. Bach, Handel, Haydn, and Mozart composed music that blends elegance, precision, and order with a touch of passion under firm control.

Old certainties, like the idea of an unchanging social and political order, crumbled during these years. By 1800, after two major revolutions, that concept was no longer tenable; even faith in reason had been shaken. Serious questions had arisen: how to cope with the irrational, with industrialization, with humanity's striving for equality—for all of which the 18th century produced no definitive answers. It is not too much to say that we are still seeking them.

18th-Century Literature

ADDISON, JOSEPH 1672–1719 and **SIR RICHARD STEELE 1672–1729. The Spectator** (1711–12). Polished and witty commentary on the fashions, foibles, and fops of Queen Anne's London. *H—Biblio Dist 4 vols.; P—HR&W (abr.).*

The Age of Enlightenment (1956). Ed. Isaiah Berlin. Generous selections from the major philosophers of the 18th century with helpful commentary by the editor. *H—Ayer Co; P—NAL.*

BEAUMARCHAIS, PIERRE CARON DE 1732–1799. The Barber of Seville (1775) and **The Marriage of Figaro** (acted 1784). Comedies satirizing class privilege, best known now in the operatic versions by, respectively, Rossini and Mozart. *P—Barron, Penguin.*

BERKELEY, GEORGE 1685–1753. A Treatise Concerning the Principles of Human Knowledge (1710). Platonic idealism reworked in the light of Newtonian science. *H & P—Hackett Pub; P—Bobbs, Open Court*. See also "Philosophy," page 278.

BLAKE, WILLIAM 1757–1827. **Poems.** As both artist and poet, Blake was simple and original, profound, lyrical, and challengingly symbolic in his best work. *Over 10 eds*.

BOSWELL, JAMES 1740–1795. **The Life of Samuel Johnson** (1791). The sturdy common sense and literary judgments of an impressive mind, recorded by a shrewd and devoted friend in one of the greatest biographies ever written. *Over 6 eds., some abr*.

BURKE, EDMUND 1729–1797. **Reflections on the Revolution in France** (1790). A conservative defense of gradual change, opposed to the violence Burke predicted for France. *P—Bobbs*.

BURNS, ROBERT 1759–1796. **Poems.** Songs and meditations, mostly in Scottish dialect, that speak for the common folk and have proved enduringly popular. *Over 10 eds*.

CASANOVA DE SEINGALT, GIACOMO 1725–1798. **Memoirs** (1826–38). Most of the adventures he reports were amorous, some doubtless exaggerated; the filler sketches very ably etch the times. *P—Da Capo*.

CHESTERFIELD, LORD 1694–1773. **Letters to His Son** (1774). Urbane advice on manners and morals for a worldly and aristocratic society. *H—R West 2 vols.; P—Biblio Dist*.

Constitution of the United States and **Declaration of Independence.** Basic American documents every citizen should know. Found in almost every history of the United States and in many encyclopedias and almanacs.

CRÈVECOEUR, ST. JOHN DE 1735–1813. **Letters from an American Farmer** (1782). These letters to an imaginary friend in Europe reflect both an idealistic and a realistic view of life in young America. *H—Peter Smith; P—Biblio Dist, Penguin*.

D'ALEMBERT, JEAN LE ROND 1717–1783. **Preliminary Discourse to the Encyclopedia of Diderot** (1751). Mathematician and philosopher, a representative mind of the Enlightenment, D'Alembert was co-editor at first of the *Encyclopedia*. *P—Bobbs*.

DEFOE, DANIEL 1660–1731. **Robinson Crusoe** (1719). The original and immortal desert island story. *Over 20 eds*.

————. **Moll Flanders** (1722). A realistic novel about one woman's life through many marriages and many crimes. *Over 6 eds*.

DIDEROT, DENIS 1713–1784. **Rameau's Nephew and Other Works** (1762). Satire and preachment by the chief editor of the great *Encyclopedia;* only Voltaire, among French authors of the age, was more versatile. *H—Irvington; P—Bobbs, Penguin.*

Federalist Papers. See "Politics," page 311.

FIELDING, HENRY 1707–1754. **Joseph Andrews** (1742). Adventures of a chaste footman and a sturdy parson, told in mockery of 18th-century sentimentalism. *Over 10 eds.*

———. **Tom Jones** (1749). The long, lusty, zestful, superbly plotted story of an engaging hero, from childhood to marriage, filled with lively characters and adventures. *Over 6 eds.*

The Fire of Liberty (1984). Comp. & ed. Esmond Wright. Firsthand accounts (from diaries, letters, and reports) by participants and bystanders in the American Revolution. *H—St Martin.*

FRANKLIN, BENJAMIN 1706–1790. **Autobiography** (1791, 1818, 1868). A great American, prototype of the pragmatic man, explains his rise to fame and fortune in aphoristic prose. *Over 10 eds.*

GAY, JOHN 1685–1732. **The Beggar's Opera** (1728). Rollicking burlesque of politics and society; thieves, highwaymen, harlots, and crooked jailers sing false sentiments to old ballad tunes. The source for the Brecht–Weill *Threepenny Opera. H & P—U of Nebr Pr; P—Barron, Harlan Davidson.*

GIBBON. **The Decline and Fall of the Roman Empire.** See "Rome," page 17.

GOETHE, JOHANN WOLFGANG VON 1749–1832. **The Sorrows of Young Werther** (1774). An early, very "romantic" novel in which the hero kills himself for unrequited love. *P—HR&W, Ungar.*

———. **Faust** (1808, 1832). Goethe worked for 60 years on this monumental two-part drama on the meaning of life. Randall Jarrell's translation of Part I is recommended (*o.p.*). *Many other trans. and eds.*

GOLDONI, CARLO 1707–1793. **Comedies.** Actable and natural comedies by one of the few good dramatists of the century. *H—Hyperion Conn, Greenwood; P—Penguin. Other eds. of single plays.*

GOLDSMITH, OLIVER 1728–1774. **The Vicar of Wakefield** (1766). A novel relating the amusing tribulations of a gentle and gullible clergyman and his family. *Over 10 eds.*

———. **She Stoops to Conquer** (1773). A comic masterpiece

and one of the most actable of all plays of the period. *P—Barron, Harlan Davidson, Norton, PB, WSP*.

HUME. **Enquiry Concerning Human Understanding.** See ''Philosophy,'' page 279.

JEFFERSON, THOMAS 1743–1826. **Autobiographical and Political Writings.** A multitalented founding father writes clearly and eloquently on many subjects still very much of concern to Americans. *Over 6 eds*.

JOHNSON, SAMUEL 1709–1784. **Samuel Johnson** (1984). Ed. Donald Greene. The most generous one-volume selection available of the works of the great literary dictator of his age. *H & P—Oxford U Pr*.

KANT. See ''Philosophy,'' page 280.

LACLOS, P. A. F. CHODERLOS DE 1741–1803. **Les Liaisons Dangereuses** (1782). A novel in letters describing the behavior and motives of heartless but intelligent debauchees among the French aristocracy. *H & P—French & Eur; H—AMS Pr; P—Routledge & Kegan*.

MALTHUS, THOMAS ROBERT 1766–1834. **Essay on the Principles of Population** (1798). Classic study of the relationship between population growth and the means of subsistence. *H & P—Norton; P—Biblio Dist, Penguin*.

MONTESQUIEU, CHARLES DE 1689–1755. **The Spirit of the Laws** (1748). Sometimes called the greatest French work of the century, it treats laws as the products of men and as codes that relate differently to different societies. *H & P—U of Cal Pr; P—Hafner*.

PAINE, THOMAS 1737–1809. **The Rights of Man** (1791). Paine's impassioned answer to Burke's criticism of the French Revolution. *H—Biblio Dist; P—Citadel Pr, NAL, Penguin*.

———. **The Age of Reason** (1794–95). A spirited defense of Deism, the religion of many 18th-century intellectuals. *P—Bobbs, Citadel Pr*.

POPE, ALEXANDER 1688–1744. **Poems.** Devastating social satire, political ridicule, philosophic optimism, some restrained emotion—all wrought into neat epigrammatic heroic couplets by the greatest master of the technique. *Over 6 eds*.

PRÉVOST, ANTOINE 1697–1763. **Manon Lescaut** (1731). The story of a young man fascinated, and ultimately ruined, by a courtesan—the source of the operas by Puccini and Massenet. *H—Hyperion Conn; P—Larousse*.

RICHARDSON, SAMUEL 1689–1761. **Pamela** (1740). In letters that reveal the ''sentiments'' of the age, a maidservant tells how she resisted her young master until he offered marriage. *H—AMS Pr; P—Biblio Dist 2 vols., HM, NAL, Norton, Penguin.*

ROUSSEAU, JEAN JACQUES 1712–1778. **Émile** (1762). A didactic novel, important for proposing the theory of progressive education (though not for women). *H & P—Basic, Biblio Dist; P—Barron (abr.).*

———. **The Social Contract** (1762). An argument credited with helping to bring about the French Revolution. *H—Darby Bks; P—Hafner, Penguin, Regnery-Gateway.*

———. **Confessions** (1781–88). These uninhibited self-revelations by a romantic egoist are endlessly fascinating, despite the weight of self-justification and complaining. *P—Penguin.*

SHERIDAN, RICHARD BRINSLEY 1751–1816. **The Rivals** (1775) and **The School for Scandal** (1777). Two famous and still standard comedies, noted for wit and good humor, intricate plots, and memorable caricatures (e.g., Mrs. Malaprop). *Over 6 eds.*

SMITH, ADAM 1723–1790. **The Wealth of Nations** (1776). The classic explanation of the economic advantages of free trade and of specialization of labor. *Over 10 eds.*

STERNE, LAURENCE 1713–1768. **Tristram Shandy** (1760–67). Comic domestic episodes in an almost bewildering assortment of styles—whimsical, digressive, extravagant. *Over 6 eds.*

SWIFT, JONATHAN 1667–1745. **Gulliver's Travels** (1726). Imaginary journeys that amuse children but are really first-rate, highly inventive, and unrelenting attacks on irrationality and inhumanity. *Over 30 eds. Recommended: P—HM, NAL, Norton, Penguin.*

VOLTAIRE (FRANCOIS MARIE AROUET) 1694–1778. **Candide** (1759). A short, funny, well-spiced adventure story and a masterly satire on optimism, war, religion, government, romantic love, wealth, and a host of perennial human follies by one of the greatest minds and the most versatile literary figure of the century. *P—Bantam, Biblio Dist, WSP.*

WALPOLE, HORACE 1717–1797. **Letters.** The activities of the civilized 18th century come to life in these charming letters to and about his friends. Selections: *H—Biblio Dist.*

———. **The Castle of Otranto** (1764). The first famous Gothic novel of horror and the supernatural. *H—Arden Lib; P—Dover, HR&W, Macmillan, Oxford U Pr.*

WOLLSTONECRAFT, MARY 1759–1797. **A Vindication of the Rights of Woman** (1792). The most prominent feminist of the age argued for educational and other forms of equality for men and women. *Over 6 eds.*

Books about the 18th Century

BATE, W. JACKSON b. 1918. **Samuel Johnson** (1977). A model of the modern biographer's art, proving Johnson every bit as admirable as the hero-worshiping Boswell thought. *H & P—HarBraceJ.*

BECKER, CARL LOTUS 1873–1945. **The Heavenly City of the Eighteenth-Century Philosophers** (1932). A lively, scholarly, provocative analysis of 18th-century thought. *P—Yale U Pr.*

BUTTERFIELD, SIR HERBERT 1900–1979. **The Origins of Modern Science** (rev. ed. 1965). A classic on the history of science, particularly good on 18th-century developments and their effects. *P—Free Pr.*

CARLYLE, THOMAS 1795–1881. **The French Revolution** (1837). A long and almost overdramatic account, more bedazzled with Napoleon than the facts warrant. In the *Works of Thomas Carlyle: H—AMS Pr.*

CASSIRER, ERNST 1874–1945. **The Philosophy of the Enlightenment** (English tr. 1951). A thoughtful, balanced, illuminating corrective to Becker's *Heavenly City. P—Princeton U Pr.*

COBBAN, ALFRED 1901–1968. **A History of Modern France** (1965). Volume 1 is regarded as the best short history of the period. *P—Penguin 3 vols.*

COOPER. See "The Novel: 19th-Century American Novels," page 155.

CUNLIFFE, MARCUS b. 1922. **George Washington: Man and Monument** (rev. ed. 1984). A successful effort to recreate Washington's life as it really was, rather than as legend and myth have presented it. *P—NAL.*

DARNTON, ROBERT b. 1939. **The Great Cat Massacre: And Other Episodes in French Cultural History** (1984). History, sociology, and psychology blend in enlightening pictures of some byways of the *ancien régime*. *H—Basic*.

DICKENS, CHARLES 1812–1870. **A Tale of Two Cities** (1859). A tale of self-sacrifice during the French Revolution, famous for Sydney Carton and Madame Defarge. *Over 15 eds*.

DURANT, WILL 1885–1981 and ARIEL DURANT 1898–1981. **The Age of Voltaire** (1965) and **Rousseau and Romanticism** (1967). Entertainingly written, well-illustrated presentations of the historical, social, and cultural developments of the century. *H—S&S*.

FLEXNER, JAMES T. b. 1908. **Washington: The Indispensable Man** (1974). A judicious study of the father of his country, balancing virtues and faults and stressing the cohesive effect of his presence. (For a fuller treatment, see the same author's four-volume biography *H—Little*.) *H—Little; P—NAL*.

GAY, PETER b. 1923. **The Enlightenment: An Interpretation** (2 vols., 1966, 1969). A study of the genesis, development, and effects of the movement throughout the century, ending with its involvement in the American Revolution. *P—Norton*.

LEFEBVRE, GEORGES 1874–1959. **The Coming of the French Revolution** (1939). A balanced, authoritative history. *P—Princeton U Pr*.

MILLER, PERRY 1905–1963. **The New England Mind** (1953). A classic study by the most distinguished historian of American thought. *P—Harvard U Pr*.

MORGAN, EDMUND S. b. 1916. **The Birth of the Republic, 1763–89** (rev. ed. 1977). Perhaps the best short treatment of an often-handled subject. *H & P—U of Chicago Pr*.

NOCK, ALBERT J. 1872–1945. **Jefferson** (1926); also issued as **Mr. Jefferson.** A short, penetrating biography, good on the character; economically naive. *P—C Hallberg*.

SCOTT, SIR WALTER 1771–1832. **Waverley** (1814). The Jacobite rebellion of 1745 is the setting for the first of the romantic "Waverley novels." *H & P—Biblio Dist; P—Penguin*.

STEVENSON. **The Master of Ballantrae.** See "The Novel: 19th-Century British Novels," page 141.

TOCQUEVILLE, ALEXIS DE 1805–1859. **The Old Regime and the French Revolution** (1855). Shrewd observations on the subject by a wise Frenchman. *H—Peter Smith*.

The World of George Washington (1984). Comp. Richard M. Ketchum. Essentially a book of illustrations (many in color) giving a full picture of life in colonial and early independent America. *H—Crown*.

PART II

Regional and Minority Cultures

PART II

Regional and Minority Cultures

CHAPTER 7

The Middle East

ARDAVAN DAVARAN

Perhaps longer and more consistently than any other region of the world the Middle East has maintained a basic and profound significance in the history of Western civilization. On the banks of its rivers Western man has searched for the Indo-European origins of his birth; on the floors of its valleys and the shores of its seas he has developed an awareness of the cycles of vegetation, drought, and rebirth; in the vast landscapes of its deserts he has sought responses for his spiritual aspirations; and in the heart of its lands and the depths of its waters he continues to delve for material sources of his energy and his sustenance.

To study the literature of such an area completely would be to look for the very first signs of man's attempts to communicate his feelings and thoughts, his fears and his curiosities, his preoccupations and his expectations. Realistically, the endeavor might begin with Zoroaster's *Avesta* (7th century B.C.) and the Old Testament (8th to 5th centuries B.C.), the earliest significant writings. But historical events prevented or interrupted the development of a Middle Eastern literature in Avestan or Hebrew for centuries. The chief cause: the appearance and spread of Islam. No phenomenon in the entire history of the Middle East has had an impact so enduring. Literary historians, in tracing the development of Arabic, Persian, and Turkish literatures, begin by referring to a pre-Islamic period that ends in the early years of the 7th century A.D. But though an oral tradition has been preserved by bards, singers, and story-tellers (a tradition that has left a clear impression on subsequent literature), little remains of Arabic or Turkish writings identifiable as pre-Islamic.

63

Why is there so little recorded literary work until long after the appearance of Islam? The Moslems, who spread their faith by force of arms, were intolerant of the literature of the people they conquered or converted. Indeed, most fine arts seemed to violate their religious beliefs, and literature was, at least, suspect. Not until hard-line Islamic thought moderated and Persian and Turkish rulers established their own powers did Arabic, Persian, and Turkish literatures flourish.

For Arabic literature, the 8th to the 13th centuries were the period of growth, a growth linked to the more tolerant and culturally sophisticated Abbasid Caliphate. Among the writers were historians (al-Yaqubi, Mohammad ibn Jarir Tabari), poets (Bashar ibn Burd, Abu Nuwas, Abu Al 'faraj al'Isfahani, and the triumphant poet of the classical age, Mutanabbi), and prose writers (Hariri of Basra and Ibn Khaldun, philosopher of history).

Persian literature emerged in the 10th century as dynasties rose in the Eastern provinces. The first literary epic was Ferdowsi's *Shāh-nāme*, completed in the 11th century. Omar Khayyám's *Rubáiyát*, Nizámí's *Xosro va Shirin*, the mystic poet Attâr's *Mantiq al-tâ'ir* (*Conference of the Birds*) and *Tazkerat al Aulia* (*Lives of the Moslem Saints*), Rūmī's *Masnavi*, and Sadi's epics *Golestan* (in prose) and *Bustan* (in verse) are among the greatest works. The culmination is in the noble achievement of Hafiz of Shiraz and in the establishment of the classical age that ends in the 15th century with the mystical writings of the poet Jami.

Turkish literature began later than Arabic or Persian and also in time achieved classical stature. In both form and content, a literary tension suffuses Ottoman poetry from the mid-13th century, much of it lively, witty, and satirical narrative read aloud for social entertainment. Such are Gülşehri's *Mantiku 't-tayr* (*Conference of the Birds*) and Ahmedia's *Iskendarnāme* (*Book of Alexander*). Prose too was popular for sessions of social reading, *Kirk Vizier* (*Forty Viziers*) being an especially beloved work. In the same vein, and technically more significant, was the native syllabic poetry practiced mainly by the dervish poets, outstanding among them Yunus Emre. At the same time, however, writers sought after high seriousness, as in the solemn poetry of Zāti and Khayli in the 16th century and in the noble *Qazals* of Nedim, the most famous of classical poets in the 18th century.

Periods of temporary literary decline followed the classical ages, particularly in Arab lands subjected to Ottoman conquest and in Persia during the political upheavals of the 18th century. In the 19th century, however, a series of events spurred new vitality in all three literatures. Napoleon's expedition to Egypt, England's ventures in India, and European (mainly French) spheres of influence in Turkey and Persia—all stimulated the translation of Western literature, especially Romantic works, and a host of extended versions and imitations as well. With the arrival in the Middle East of convenient modes of transportation, travel of students abroad to acquire Western education accelerated; the reading audience enlarged and, as a consequence, modern fiction with plots and characters similar to European models began to appear.

Pioneering efforts toward modernizing Arabic literature are associated with the religious rationalist Muhammad Abduh. The most influential cultural figure in Arabic thought, he reconciled Islamic and modern ideas and paved the way for modern Arabic literature. Among earlier writers, Jirji Zaidan, the Syrian Christian novelist and historian, stands out, along with Mutran, a Lebanese resident of Egypt who translated some of Shakespeare's plays into Arabic. In Persian literature, translations of a few textbooks from European originals and publication of the first Persian newspapers, not only within but also beyond the Persian-speaking lands, marked the first steps toward colloquial prose usable in writing stories and novels for a larger public. The travelogues of the Qajar king Naser-addin and the fictional work *Siāhatnāme-ye Ebrāhim-beg* (*Travelogues of Ebrāhim-beg*) were among the early models. At the turn of the century, the constitutional movement gave rise to an abundance of satirical and social writings in prose and poetry composed for a large Persian public. In Turkish literature periods of reform and modernization aroused the writers of poetry, fiction, and even drama: men like Tevfik Fikrat, Ahmed Nimhat, who was also a journalist, and Namik Kemal who wrote the first play performed, *Vetan* (*Fatherland*).

Twentieth-century events effected closer relations between the Middle East and the rest of the world. The backwash of World War I to some extent and of World War II to a larger degree spread into the Middle East. New nations came into being in the Arab-speaking lands; Persia shrank in size and political influence, becoming modern Iran; the Turkish language adopted the Latin alphabet, creating a literary gap between the Turkish literature of the past and literature produced by the new generation of Turks in the modern republic.

The opening of borders, the possibilities of travel, and modern economic and industrial expansion brought people of the world into more frequent contact with one another. Modern means of communication made the reporting of events in different corners of the world a common experience. Awareness of what was happening in different parts of the world helped diverse ethnic and linguistic segments of the modern Middle East realize increasingly their own identity and imparted a new energy to distinct national and ethnic literatures.

The establishment of the modern state of Israel has supplied an impetus to modern Israeli literature, which reflects centuries of Hebrew literature—a literature largely evolved in countries and lands far from the Middle East. Because of the harsh realities of political life, Hebrew writers had left the Middle East but had not ceased their literary activity. For centuries Hebrew literature developed in Spain and subsequently in other parts of Europe. Indeed, Judhah Halevi of Toledo brought postbiblical Hebrew to its highest pitch in the 11th century and Immanuel of Rome combined elements of the Hebrew tradition and of the Italian renaissance two centuries later. But in the 20th century, Israeli writers write of return to Israel and reflect upon life in the modern Middle East generally and in Israel particularly. Poets like Shlorsky and Dahlia Ravikovich and writers of fiction like S. J. Agnon, A. B. Yeshoshua, and M. Shamir in their various ways speak of the journey back and of life in the new land.

The literature of the Middle East undergoes a dramatic development in the 20th century through structural innovations, innovations powerfully influenced by the discovery of Western genres and formal variations. In Arabic literature, such formal changes were impelled by a neoclassical surge associated with Shawqi, the Egyptian court poet, then Zahabi and his energetic experiments in verse, and later Badr Shakir al-Sayyab and al-Bayati (all of Iraq). In Persian literature, Nima Yushij is the poet most responsible for freeing modern verse from symmetrical and repetitive patterns in rhyme and rhythm. The novels of Sadeq Hedayat, the acknowledged pioneer of modern fiction, are free of pretension or artificiality. Similarly, Nazim Hikmat is the first Turkish writer of free verse to succeed in synthesizing traditional and modern techniques.

Arabic, Persian, Turkish, Israeli, Pakistani, Urdu, Armenian, and other Middle Eastern literature have more in common today with Western literature than they have had in the past. But although these literatures come to the Western reader in familiar genres and forms, they render a view of life and a curve of sensibility refreshingly different and vigorously humanistic. In its finest moments, recent Middle Eastern writing reflects the rich and resourceful tradition from which it has evolved.

Arabic Literature

ABU AL-ALA AL-MA'ARRI 973–1057. "The Meditations of Ma'arri," in **Studies in Islamic Poetry** (1921). Tr. R. A. Nicholson. Poetry centering on moral, philosophical, and rather pessimistic speculation about humanity. *o.p.*

AL-MUTANABBI, ABU AL-TAYYIB AHMAD IBN AL-HUS-SAIN 915–965. **The Diwan of Abu Tayyib Ahmad ibn al-Hussain al-Mutanabbi** (1971). Tr. Arthur Wormhoudt. Considered the height of achievement in classical tradition, Mutanabbi's panegyric poetry attains remarkable subtlety of meaning and serenity of language. *o.p.*

An Anthology of Modern Arabic Poetry (1974). Eds. & trs. Mounah A. Khouri and Hamid Algar. A well-chosen body of modern Arabic poetry by the most significant figures in modern and contemporary Arab poetry from different nationalities of the Middle East. Bilingual texts and informative biographical notes. *P—U of Cal Pr*.

Arabian Nights (compiled from 8th–15th cent). A collection of tales full of intrigue, adventure, passion, and pleasure in the magic atmosphere of a fairy-tale Orient, rendered through centuries of oral tradition, finally put together in Egypt in 1450. *P—Ace Bks*.

Arabic Writing Today (1970). Ed. & tr. Mahmoud Manzalaoui. Contains a generous number (30) of short stories by Arab writers from various parts of the Middle East. *o.p.*

IBN KHALDUN 1332–1406. **The Muqaddimah: An Introduction to History** (1967). Tr. Franz Rosenthal. This "introduction" to a lesser known study of Arab history is renowned as an independent work in the philosophy of history. *o.p.*

JABRA, IBRAHIM JABRA b. 1919. **The Ship** (1982). Trs. Adnan Haydar and Roger Allen. Exciting new novel by a Palestinian writer and critic who lives in Iraq. Characters who meet on a ship cruising the sea recollect their past. *o.p.*

LICHTENSTADTER, ILSE b. 1907. **Introduction to Classical Arabic Literature** (1976). An insightful introductory study, including selections from representative works in English. *o.p.*

Modern Egyptian Drama: An Anthology (1974). Tr. Farouk Abdel Wahab. Includes works by four of the most significant figures in modern Arabic drama: Tawfig al-Hakim, Mikhail Roman, Rashad Rushdy, and Yusuf Idris. *H—Bibliotheca*.

TAHA HUSSEIN 1889–1973. **al-Ayyam.** In three parts: **An Egyptian Childhood** (1932), *P—Three Continents;* **The Stream of Days: A Student at the Azhar** (1948), *o.p;* **A Passage to France** (1976), *o.p.* This autobiographical work by one of Egypt's foremost men of letters gives a personal view of 20th-century life in Egypt.

Persian Literature

ATTAR, FARID ADDIN d. 119? **Muslim Saints and Mystics** (1966). Tr. A. J. Arberry. An anecdotal account of the lives of mystic saints; full of energy and wit. *H—Routledge & Kegan*.

BROWNE, EDWARD G. 1862–1926. **A Literary History of Persia,** 4 vols. (1928). Uneven but informative historical account of Persian literature from pre-Islamic times through the first quarter of the 20th century; lives and times are interspersed with textual extracts in Persian followed by translations. *H—Cambridge U Pr*.

FERDOWSI, ABULGHASEM 932–1021. **The Epic of the Kings** (1973). Tr. Reuben Levy. A serviceable though not wholly satisfactory translation of a rich epic, a chronicle of mythical and historical dynasties up to the time of the Arab invasion of Iran early in the 7th century, involving the life and trials of the mythical hero Rostam. *H—Routledge & Kegan*.

HAFIZ, KHAJA QAVAMADDIN 1329–1389. **Poems from the Divan** (1928). Tr. Gertrude Bell. Lyrical attempts at translating a few untranslatable masterpieces from a collection of some of the finest Persian poetry. *o.p.*

HEDAYAT, SADEGH 1903–1951. **The Blind Owl** (1958). Tr. D. P. Costello. The most important novel in Persian, considered the first complete achievement in that genre in Persian. Its surreal atmosphere, provocative assumptions, and simple yet poetic language have fascinated 20th-century intellectuals and critics. *P—Grove*.

KHAYYÁM, OMAR d. 1123? **The Rubáiyát** (1952). Tr. A. J. Arberry. Short quatrains of quantitative verse in the original, all in the same meter, on the vanity of worldly possessions and of living for the virtues of the moment. This translation is supplemented by the famous translations, or rather re-creations, of Fitzgerald. *H—R West; P—Airmont, Branden, Penguin*.

Modern Persian Short Stories (1980). Ed. Minoo Southgate. Readable translation of short stories by representative writers of fiction in modern Iran. *H & P—Three Continents*.

New Writing from the Middle East (1978). Eds. Leo Hamalian and John D. Yohannan. Translations of exemplary poetry, fiction, and drama from among the most significant contemporary writers of the Middle East (Arabic, Persian, Turkish, Israeli, and Armenian). *H—Ungar*.

RŪMĪ, MAWLANA JALĀL ALDĪN 1207–1273. **Masnavi** (1925). Tr. R. A. Nicholson. The most influential mystic classic in narrative verse, with anecdotes and maxims quoted and remembered more than any other in the literature of mysticism. *H—Kazi Pubns*.

SA'DI MOSLEH-ADDIN 1184–1291? **Golestān** (1965). Tr. Edward Rehatsek. Anecdotes (some autobiographical), quotations, and maxims serve to elucidate the author's insight and his commonsense approach to varied questions about life and survival. The original is in rhymed prose of the highest merit. *o.p.*

Turkish Literature

ADIVAR, HALIDE EDIB 1884–1964. **The Clown and His Daughter** (1935). Among the more successful early novels in Turkish dealing with social problems; the influence of the English novel form is apparent. *o.p.*

FUZULI, MEHMET 1494–1555. **Leyla and Mejnun** (1970).

Tr. Sofi Huri. Famed in Arabic, Persian, and English, this love story is superficially akin to that of Romeo and Juliet. *o.p.*

GUNTEKIN, RESAT NURI 1889–1956. **The Autobiography of a Turkish Girl** (1949). Tr. W. Deedes. An endearing picaresque novel, it recounts the life of a young schoolteacher. *o.p.*

KEMAL, YASHAR b. 1923. **Memed, My Hawk** (1961). Tr. Edouard Roditi. In a simple yet poetic prose enhancing an interesting plot, Kemal relates the harsh and tragic life of the Turkish peasant. *P—Pantheon.*

NESIN, AZIZ b. 1915. **Istanbul Boy** (2 parts 1977, 1979). Tr. Joseph Jacobson. An autobiography by the leading satirist in modern Turkey, whose stories lambast both bourgeoisie and bureaucracy. *P—U of Tex Pr.*

The Penguin Book of Turkish Verse (1978). Ed. Nermin Menemencioglu. A comprehensive anthology providing examples of Diwan, folk and popular, mystic, transitional, and modern Turkish poetry—from the 14th century to the present. *o.p.*

SHEYK-ZADA. **Forty Viziers** (1886). Tr. E. J. W. Gibb. One of the best-known collections of tales and romances, intended to be read in nightly sessions to an audience. *o.p.*

Tales Alive in Turkey (1966). Eds. Warren S. Walker and Ahmet S. Vysal. Collection of tales and riddles from the oral folk tradition of Turkey: supernatural, humorous, moralistic, anticlerical, anecdotal—displaying the shrewd insight of the peasant mind. *o.p.*

YUSUF-I MEDDAH fl. 14th cent. **Varga ve Gulsah** (1976). Tr. Grace Martin Smith. Romance intended to be read as entertainment, written originally in narrative verse. *o.p.*

Modern Israeli Literature

AGNON, SAMUEL JOSEPH 1888–1970. **In the Heart of the Seas** (1947). Tr. I. M. Lask. A story of a journey to the land of Israel. Drawings by Herzl Rowe. *P—Schocken.*

————. **Twenty-One Stories** (1970). Ed. Nahum Glatzer. Collection of short stories, some of them among the best known in modern Hebrew literature, by the 1966 Nobel Prize winner. *P—Schocken*.

ALTER, ROBERT b. 1935. **After the Tradition: Essays on Modern Jewish Writing** (1969). Discerning critical essays that place modern Israeli and Jewish writing in proper perspective. *o.p.*

Contemporary Israeli Literature: An Anthology (1977). Ed. Elliot Anderson. Ranges over poetry and prose. A useful afterword by Robert Alter. *o.p.*

Modern Hebrew Poetry (1966). Ed. & tr. Ruth Finer Mintz. An illuminating experience in modern Hebrew poetry, this collection provides bilingual texts as well as a helpful introduction and notes. *H—Greenwood; P—U of Cal Pr*.

Modern Israeli Drama: An Anthology (1983). Ed. Herbert S. Joseph. Representative works by modern playwrights, often combining analysis of contemporary social problems of Israeli society with comment on modern Western technique. *H—Fairleigh Dickinson*.

OZ, AMOS b. 1939. **My Michael** (1972). Tr. Nicolas deLang. A novel by one of the most influential modern writers in Israel, involving the lives of university students and younger intellectuals in Jerusalem against a background of current social problems. *o.p.*

Penguin Book of Hebrew Verse (1981). Ed. & tr. T. Carmi. Bilingual. Excellent prose translations that come remarkably close to capturing the original. *P—Penguin*.

SINGER. See "The Short Story," page 179.

YEHOSHUA, ABRAHAM b. 1936. **The Lover** (1978). Tr. Philip Simpson. Story of an upper-middle-class educated couple whose daughter falls in love with an Arab boy. *o.p.*

A Postscript on Armenian Literature

Geographically, Armenia exists today only as one of the Soviet Socialist Republics. But because substantial Armenian minorities are scattered throughout the Middle East and represent a significant culture, a brief, separate introduction as well as a reading list is appended.—*Eds*.

Armenian literature dates from the 5th century, soon after Armenia became the first nation to embrace Christianity, and the monasteries became centers of intellectual and cultural life. From that time until the late 19th century, Armenian literature was dominated by history and theology. The opposition of the Church and domination of foreign invaders suppressed freer expression. Still, some poems, tales, proverbs, an "epic," and occasional plays have survived. They are perhaps most available to the general reader in anthologies and particular collections, and we have therefore emphasized such listings.

Today, Armenian literature is enjoying a renaissance. In Yerevan, in Soviet Armenia, poets like Paruir Sevag, Gevorg Emin, and Sylvia Gaboudikian are highly regarded. Yet other Armenians have begun to regroup after the political events that disrupted their lives in Lebanon. Among these, one of the best is Antranik Zaroukian, a distinguished poet, novelist, and critic who now lives in Paris. Though writers in the diaspora have characteristically tended to assimilate, their work often has a distinctive Armenian reference.

Armenian Folk-Tales and Legends (1972). Tr. Charles Downing. Authentic and often enchanting selections from Armenian folklore and folk wisdom. *H—Oxford U Pr.*

Armenian Legends and Poems (1916). Ed. Zabelle Boyajian. A varied and useful anthology. *o.p.*

Daredevils of Sassoun: The Armenian National Epic (1874). Tr. Leon Surmelian. The "greatest achievement of the oral literature," this medieval epic was first published in 1874. The translation, though apparently not the most literal, is the most vivid among several versions: **David of Sassoun** (1964). Tr. Artin K. Shalian. *o.p.;* **David of Sassoun** (1961). Tr. Aram Tolegian. *o.p.*

MIRAK, ROBERT. **Torn Between Two Lands: Armenians in America, 1890 to World War I** (1984). How Armenian refugees readjusted to the problems of a new life in a new world. *H—Harvard U Pr.*

New Writing from the Middle East. See page 62.

One Hundred Armenian Tales and Their Folkloric Significance (1966). Ed. Susie Hoogasian-Villa. A ranging scholarly collection. *H & P—Wayne State U Pr.*

We of the Mountains: Armenian Short Stories (1972). Tr. Fainna Glagoleva (from the Russian). Nineteen Soviet-Armenian short stories, representing several generations and diverse trends. *H—Imported Pubns.*

Books about the Middle East

ANTONIUS, GEORGE b. 1891. **The Arab Awakening** (1939). A fundamental introduction to the Arab national movement in the 20th century. *H—Gordon Pr, Intl Bk Ctr*.

DIEHL, CHARLES 1859–1944. **Byzantium: Greatness and Decline** (1957). The classic study by the great French Byzantinist. Contains a fine bibliography. *P—Rutgers U Pr*.

FISHER, SYDNEY N. b. 1906. **The Middle East** (1959. 3rd rev. ed. 1978). The best introductory survey of Islam, the Ottoman Empire, and the modern Middle East. *H—Knopf*.

HITTI, PHILIP KHURI 1886–1978. **History of the Arabs from the Earliest Times to the Present** (10th ed. 1970). The standard text for the history of the Arab peoples down to the 16th century, but superficial on the last four centuries. *P—St Martin*.

Jewish Society Through the Ages (1972). Eds. H. H. Ben-Sasson and S. Ettinger. Contains many essays, most of high quality, on a wide range of important aspects of Jewish life from ancient to modern times. *o.p.*

Jews and Arabs (1975). Ed. S. D. Goitein. A scholarly presentation of the social and intellectual relations of Jews and Arabs through the ages, useful for lending perspective to contemporary views of Jews and Arabs. *P—Schocken*.

Mythologies of the Ancient World (1961). Ed. Samuel N. Kramer. Using new translations, ten scholars discuss the myths of individual Middle East cultures in essays the general reader can comprehend and enjoy. *P—Doubleday*.

Professor Davaran's comprehensive essay and extensive reading list have been edited and shortened to conform with the particular needs of *Good Reading*. A list of books about the Middle East, including a section on Armenian literature, has been added. For the latter we are indebted to Professor Leo Hamalian (The City College of New York).

CHAPTER 8

East and Southeast Asia

OSCAR SHAFTEL

Political and economic forces are radically changing the lives of
Asian men and women. A new, often a global, perspective is
progressively transforming traditional national attitudes. Japan,
whose history swings between emulation of advanced foreign
ways and a cool rejection, is today caught up in an expression of
national sensibility in international competition in fashion, industrial design, film, and literature. China, after three decades of
attempted revolutionary self-reliance, turns its face outward and
welcomes foreign trade, technology, consumer goods, and models of freer creative expression. India, emerging from the cultural
attraction of British political and literary forms, makes more
sophisticated use of the major native languages for national
concerns, while continuing a vigorous use of English adapted to
daily needs. In Southeast Asia, war and dictatorship have stifled
but not wholly stilled dissent from the power of the palace.

Asian writers are, of course, not isolated from the effects of so
much turmoil. Japan, with almost universal literacy, rising aspirations, and a precarious hold on prosperity (a piquant enlarge-
ment to national scale of the situation nine centuries ago in the
Heian court that brought forth the world's first great novel, *The
Tale of Genji*), is a tension-fraught scene for its artists. Nature
and seasonal change, traditional images for human feeling, are
obscured by urban settings and occupations. The salaried man
replaces the samurai. Traditional Kabuki and puppet plays are
still patronized as operatic spectacles, but are also recast and
presented as costume films for popular entertainment. Poets,
especially women poets, are breaking the old molds, borrowing

forms, themes, and imagery from Western verse and finding translators. Improved translations of the classics continue to appear. The fine collection of court poetry, the *Manyoshu*, compiled in 765, is available, and the early legends, the sources of Shinto belief in the *Kojiki* (712) and the *Nihon Shoki* (*Chronicles of Japan*, 720), can be found in various collections. Chinese characters, used at first for both meaning and sound, and still indispensable for specific traditional meanings, were supplemented in the 9th century by *kana*, syllabaries suited for Japanese sounds and for use by women, who lacked or hid knowledge of Chinese. The introspective estheticism of the Heian period (10th to 11th centuries) found expression in the tales of Lady Murasaki (*Genji*) and her fellow and rival attendant on the empress, Sei Shonagon, and in diaries, especially the latter's gossipy *Pillow Book*.

The effete court was shoved aside in the struggle between the Taira and Minamoto clans in the late 12th century. The *Heike Monagatari* is a chivalric celebration of the brutal conflict, and of the sad end of Yoshitsune, the victorious captain condemned by his jealous brother, Minamoto Yoritomo, the first shogun. The tales found new expression in drama, both courtly and popular. The Noh, a highly stylized poetic form restricted to court audiences, expressed Buddhist themes of sadness and reconciliation (*Atsumori* of Seami, c. 1400). Kabuki and Bunraku (a puppet medium) presented both traditional and topical incidents.

In 1937 the third Tokugama shogunate ejected all Europeans; until the Meiji Restoration in 1868, contact with the outside world was restricted. Such isolation meant, among other things, a diminished interest in military virtues and a growth in respect for other kinds of excellence. The mysteries and beauties of nature found expression in the haiku of Basho (1644–1694), the finest Zen poetic sensibility of the era. Like the samurai of an earlier age, the emerging merchant class had its own strong, if less violent, sense of obligation and loyalty. Thus commoners began to appear as central characters in the plays of Chikamatsu (1653–1725) and the earthy novels of Saikaku (1642–1693).

After the Restoration, Western technology, dress, food, and then literature and social ideas were tested as models. But revised Shinto doctrine urged ultranationalism and justified Nipponese "elder-brother" exploitation of neighbors. Defeated in war and freed of heavy military outlay, Japan emerged as a leader in industry and in literature. Writers and filmmakers questioned both traditional loyalties and the human costs of commercial success. Old themes of Confucian obligation, Buddhist sacrifice, and unearthly bewitchment were applied to modern discontents, as in Mishima's stories and modern Noh plays, while others, like the 1970 Nobel Laureate Kawabata and, more recently, Oë, explored neurotic monomanias. Tanizaki, a subtle stylist and analyst of change, in his later years turned to social realism in *The Makioka Sisters*. The trauma of Hiroshima left its open wound, probed most notably in Ibuse's *Black Rain*. Women writers are now being recognized and their work is being increasingly translated too. Poetry, freed from traditional forms, is also acquiring an international audience.

Historians of Chinese literature will observe a significant date: On December 31, 1984, a congress of writers called for artistic freedom, with the approval of government leaders. The new program, in line with the opening to Western cultural and commercial exchange, recalls the revolt against archaic Confucian doctrine and style after the overthrow of Ching in 1911. Colloquial language and realistic observation in place of stilted allusive prose and a turning to Western democratic practices to free China from Western exploitation characterized the new voices of the 1920s. Lu Xun and Ba Jin, old transliteration Pa Chin, chairman of the 1984 meeting, were a bridge to the revolutionary 1930s. The victorious People's Republic set universal literacy as a goal and gave artists the task of guiding and exhorting the released energies of workers and peasants, and especially of women, who "hold up half the sky." The great Proletarian Cultural Revolution of 1966–1975, professing to safeguard the masses from the mandarinism and elitism of cultural and political leaders, is now regarded by the many victims of its excesses as "ten lost years." Now the hope is for a truer era of 100 flowers blooming and ideas contending than Mao's short-lived promise in 1957.

The dominant Chinese classical form, since the *Book of Odes* collected in Confucian times, was poetry, the pastime and solace of scholar-administrators, such as Li Bai and Du Fu of Tang times. Ghost stories and folktales, at first the domain of the street storyteller, were borrowed and published shamefacedly by literati down on their luck. And once the popular drama took hold in the 13th century, the old stories (especially the two great hero books, *The Three Kingdoms* and *The Water Margin*) found new expression, and did so yet again when the complex form called Peking opera developed its themes and formal traditions. Four great fictional classics, weighted with satire and social comment, are *Journey to the West, Dream of the Red Chamber, Golden Lotus,* and *The Scholars.*

As China turns away from dogmatic rejection of the "evil past," literary and archeological studies have brought new respect for the national heritage, and the classics are accorded new editions and translations. The works of victims of the Cultural Revolution, such as Ba Jin, Ding Ling, and the late Lao She, are being republished. Satire against officials who do not serve the people is again approved, and personal emotions, including love and courtship, are not unrevolutionary. Women now write more freely about their extra share of work and the strains of the population policy. Drama includes vigorous social comment, with inspiration from Western plays.

India, constitutionally a secular state, is emerging from a cultural framework pervaded by religious vocabulary. The 80 percent Hindu population still live with their myths and epics, but as both industrial power and individual poverty increase, social activism is replacing the acceptance of Karma. Communal strife between religious groups and intercaste conflict are recognized as economic as well as sociological or theological problems. Still proclaimed as the basis of Hindu belief, the Vedic hymns were originally prayers and magic spells of nomadic tribes who migrated from the northwest after 2000 B.C. Later the four collections of hymns were wielded by a self-specialized priesthood, the Brahmin caste, as ritual formulas. The speculative *Upanishads,* after 700 B.C., directly contravened the priesthood by exalting individual and mystical religious experience. Hinduism developed out of the merging of cultures—those of the various native and the Aryan invaders. Religious and social doctrine was expressed in the sprawling *Mahabharata,* an oft-interrupted and embellished epic that tells of the struggle of the five sons of Pandu against their cousins, the Kauravas, for a kingdom. It combines exemplary tales, retold myths, and religious speculation. The central document of Hinduism, the *Bhagavad Gita* (*Song of the Lord Krishna*), is a late insertion (after 300 B.C.) in the epic; in it a local low-caste folk deity (Krishna) is elevated to divine supremacy as an avatar of Vishnu. A comforting transformation, it legitimizes various ways to liberation from rebirth, especially selfless duty and *bhakti,* a way of devotion open even to outcastes and women.

The other great Indian epic alive in daily consciousness is the *Ramayana.* King Rama the just, also an avatar of Vishnu, and his faithful wife, Sita, are paradigms of social virtue. In a deeper folk tradition the great good Shiva presents fuller psychic complexity in conflicting roles as ascetic, mystic, destroyer, and consort of such embodiments of the mother deity as Durga and Kali. The various streams of myth reappear in the Puranas, religious wonder tales, and in the courtly refinements of Kalidasa, the foremost Sanskrit playwright, and Bhartrihari, an elegant erotic poet. A supreme celebration of Krishna as god and lover is Jayadeva's *Gita Govinda*, about A.D. 1200. The non-Sanskritic languages of southern India had rich expression in their own legends and in their versions of the Aryan epics.

First the Moslem invasions, culminating in Moghul power in the 17th century, and then the British raj profoundly affected Indian life. English, spoken by two million, is still the most widely accepted language, and education and law still follow the British patterns. Indian themes are expressed in Western forms—novels, short stories, and problem plays—and sometimes translated into English, like the stories of Premchand and the poems of the Nobel Prize winner Tagore. Translations from one regional language to another are fostered by the government. Writers in English have a growing audience abroad.

General

BURTT, EDWIN A. b. 1892. **The Teachings of the Compassionate Buddha** (1955). A sound introductory essay and useful selection of scriptures and other sources of Theravada, Mahayana, Zen, and other doctrines. *P—NAL*.

FAIRBANK, JOHN K. b. 1907, EDWIN O. REISCHAUER b. 1910, and ALBERT M. CRAIG b. 1927. **East Asia: Tradition and Transformation** (2nd ed. 1978). A first-rate history, representing a reworking and condensation of several earlier books by the same authors; contains much necessary information, good illustrations, and useful maps. *H—HM*.

Introduction to Oriental Civilizations: Sources of Indian Tradition (1958). *H—Columbia U Pr 2 vols.;* **Sources of Japanese Tradition** (1958). *o.p;* and **Sources of Chinese Tradition** (1960). *P—Columbia U Pr 2 vols.* Eds. William De Bary et al. An indispensable collection. Philosophical, religious, and historical materials are presented in depth; literary materials are less emphasized.

LEE, SHERMAN E. b. 1918. **A History of Far Eastern Art**

(rev. ed. 1982). A leading curator keeps abreast of a rapidly developing field. Well illustrated. *H—Abrams*.

Masterpieces of the Orient (rev. ed. 1977). Ed. G. L. Anderson. Contains many examples from the standard classical literatures as well as modern material, including a revolutionary Chinese opera. *P—Norton*.

A Treasury of Asian Literature (1959). Ed. John D. Yohannan. A very useful yet inexpensive selection, including Gita Govinda, Shakuntala, Tao Te Ching, and an early Genji chapter. *P—NAL*.

Collections

China

Anthology of Chinese Literature: Vol. I—From Early Times to the Fourteenth Century (1965); Vol. II—**From the Fourteenth Century to the Present** (1972). An attractive selection of traditional materials. *P—Grove*.

Roses and Thorns: The Second Blooming of the Hundred Flowers in Chinese Fiction 1979–1980 (1984). Ed. Perry Link. Post-Mao writing that stresses personal rather than political motifs and stylistic experimentation rather than conventional realism. *H—U of Cal Pr*.

Six Yuan Plays (1972). Tr. Liu Jung-en. Representing themes and styles of the rapid-growth years of drama during the Mongol dynasty. *P—Penguin*.

Sources of Chinese Tradition. See *Introduction to Oriental Civilizations* under "General," page 78.

Stories from a Ming Collection (1968). Ed. Cyril Birch. Popular themes—young scholars in love, faithful wives, scheming concubines, just and unjust officials, witches, murderers—in realistic settings. *H—Greenwood; P—Grove*.

Sunflower Splendor: Three Thousand Years of Chinese Poetry (1975). Eds. Liu Wu-chi and Irving Yucheng Lo. The largest and most impressive collection now available. *P—Doubleday*.

Japan

Anthology of Japanese Literature (1955–56). Ed. Donald Keene. Not an exhaustive collection, but flavorful. *P—Grove*.

Four Major Plays of Chikamatsu (1961). Tr. Donald Keene.

Representative pieces by Japan's greatest classical playwright. *P—Columbia U Pr.*

From the Country of Eight Islands: An Anthology of Japanese Poetry (1981). Trs. Burton Watson and Hiroaki Sato. Ranging broadly, the translations catch both the classical tones and modern rhythms. *H—U of Wash Pr; P—Doubleday.*

Manyoshu (1965). Tr. Nippon Gakujutsu Shinkokai, advised by Ralph Hodgson. One thousand of the 4,500 popular and court poems of the great 7th- and 8th-century collection. Hitomaro, Akahito, Lady Otomo, and Yakamochi are well represented. *P—Columbia U Pr.*

One Hundred Poems from the Japanese (1955). Ed. & tr. Kenneth Rexroth. A delightful collection of early poems from Akihito, Hitomaro, and others, plus some later haiku. *H & P—New Directions.*

Stories by Contemporary Japanese Women Writers (1982). Eds. & trs. Noriko Mizuta Lippit and Kyoko Iriye Selden. Twelve stories written between 1938 and 1977, breaking through the polite silence expected of women. *H & P—M E Sharpe.*

Women Poets of Japan (1982). Eds. & trs. Kenneth Rexroth and Ikuko Atsumi. More than 1,000 years of poetic genius recorded in varied forms. *P—New Directions.*

The Smaller Nations

Anthology of Korean Literature: From Early Times to the Nineteenth Century (1981). Ed. Peter H. Lee. Legends, poems, tales of wonder and heroism, satire, with echoes from classical Chinese literature, but with a Korean difference. *P—UH Pr.*

Contemporary Indonesian Poetry: Poems in Bahasa Indonesian and English (1975). Ed. & tr. Harry Aveling. Reflecting the strains of change from colony to a nation of diverse islands and cultures seeking personal and national identity. *H & P—U of Queensland Pr.*

Flowers of Fire: Twentieth Century Korean Stories (1974). Ed. Peter H. Lee. Testimony of an ordeal: living through Japanese oppression, civil war, and partition. *o.p.*

From Surabaya to Armageddon: Indonesian Short Stories (1976). Ed. & tr. Harry Aveling. Fifteen pieces by six contemporary writers responding to a world in painful flux. *H & P—U of Queensland Pr.*

Philippine Short Stories: 1941–1955 (1981). Ed. L. Y. Yabes.

From Japanese occupation to Marcos's martial law, the writers of 154 stories use English to report on their new nation's most critical period. *H—UH Pr*.

A Thousand Years of Vietnamese Poetry (1983). Tr. Nguyen Ngoc Bich, with B. Raffel and W. S. Merwin. The refinement of an ancient culture that persevered through conflict in newly translated classics and recent statements of pain and pride. *o.p.*

TOTH, MARIAN DAVIES. **Tales from Thailand** (1983). The folklore, retold, retains its Buddhist tinge, but modernity and conflict elbow in. *H—C E Tuttle*.

China

CONFUCIUS c. 551–479 B.C. **The Analects** (1938). Arthur Waley's translation and careful editing of the work that provided the basis for the Confucian system. *P—Random*.

CREEL, H. G. b. 1905. **Confucius and the Chinese Way** (1949). A scholarly but readable account of how the original ideas of Confucius were modified as they became "official" and of how they affected Western thought and modern China. *o.p.*

————. **Chinese Thought from Confucius to Mao Tse-tung** (1953). A basic popular study of the intertwining strands of developing ideas. *P—U of Chicago Pr*.

DING LING b. 1904. **The Sun Shines over the Sanggan River** (1948). The dean of women writers, now rehabilitated, wrote critically of early land reform. *P—China Bks*.

FUNG YU-LAN b. 1895. **A Short History of Chinese Philosophy** (1966). An abridged edition of a standard work by a universally respected scholar. *P—Free Pr*.

HINTON, WILLIAM b. 1919. **Fanshen: A Documentary of Revolution in a Chinese Village** (1966). A new classic, describing how peasants faced their former landlords and themselves. *H—Monthly Rev; P—Random*.

————. **Shenfan** (1983). Author returns to Long Bow in 1971 and reports on villagers coping with changing policies and techniques. *H & P—Random*.

HOOKHAM, HILDA 1915–1972. **A Short History of China** (1972). Up-to-date survey, well illustrated; ends with a sympathetic treatment of the revolutionary regime. *o.p.*

KINGSTON. **The Woman Warrior.** See "American Minority Cultures: Asian-Pacific," page 117.

LAO SHE 1898–1966. **Cat Country** (1970). Satirical novel of finance in 1930s. *H—Ohio St U Pr*.
———. **Camel Hsiang-tsu** (1981). New translation of **Rickshaw Boy** (1945), with original conclusion and introduction by author's widow. *H & P—Ind U Pr*.

LAO TZU c. 604–531 B.C. **Way of Lao Tzu: Tao Te Ching** (1963). Good edition by Wing-tsit Chan of the ancient classic. *P—Bobbs*.
———. **The Way of the Ways** (1985). Tr. and with a commentary by Herrymon Maurer. A laconic, vigorous rendering and a successful attempt to explain Tao in relation to Western spiritual teaching. *H—Schocken*.

LIU WU-XI b. 1907. **An Introduction to Chinese Literature** (1966). A pleasant survey, including excerpts from major writers and works. *H & P—Ind U Pr*.

LO KUAN-CHUNG c. 1330—c. 1400. **Three Kingdoms: China's Epic Drama** (1976). Ed. & tr. Moss Roberts. Folk tradition and noble ideals in rousing tales of post-Han wars. *P—Pantheon*.

LU XUN (CHOU SHU-JEN) 1881–1936. **Selected Stories** (1972). Eighteen stories by "the chief commander of China's modern cultural revolution." *H—Cheng & Tsui; P— Norton*.

MAO DUN 1896—1981. **Midnight** (1933). A leading novelist's early treatment of corruption, foreign and Chinese, in prerevolutionary Shanghai. *H—China Bks*.

MAO TSE-TUNG 1893–1976. **Selected Readings** (1971). An official collection of representative writings and speeches. *H—China Bks*.

NEWNHAM, RICHARD AND LIN-TUNG TAN. About Chinese (1971). An effective and engaging analysis of how the Chinese language works. *P—Penguin*.

PA CHIN (LI FEI-KAN) b. 1904. **Family** (1931). Conflict between old China and new, in first part of trilogy **Turbulent Stream**; the second part, **Spring**, and the third, **Autumn**, written 1939–40, are not available in English. *P—Doubleday*.

SCHURMANN, FRANZ b. 1926 and **ORVILLE SCHELL** b. 1940. **The China Reader** (1967). The last two centuries are covered in three volumes of documents on imperial, republican, and Communist China. The introductions are enlightening. *P—Random*.

SHIH NAI-AN c. 1350 and **LUO KUAN-CHUNG. Outlaws of the Marsh (Shui Hu Chuan)** (1981). Brigand army nobly opposes injustice in late Sung period. *H—Ind U Pr*. Other versions are **Water Margin** (1968). Tr. J. H. Jackson. 2 vols. *H—Cheng & Tsui*; and **All Men Are Brothers** (1933). Tr. Pearl S. Buck. *H—T Y Crowell*.

SZE MAI-MAI. **The Way of Chinese Painting** (1959). A delightful explanation of how Taoist practice is applied; includes the mustard-seed treatise on painting. *o.p.*

Tao Te Ching. Many translations exist of the great poetic, quietist, mystical, yet practical classic.

TSAO HSUEH-CHIN 1717–1764 and KAO NGO. **A Dream of Red Mansions (Hung Lou Meng).** Trs. Haien-Yi Yang et al. The downfall of a noble family, the result of slow, unheeding self-absorption (1978–80. 3 vols.). More familiarly known as **Dream of the Red Chamber.** *H—China Bks, Greenwood; P—Doubleday.*

WALEY, ARTHUR 1889–1966. **Three Ways of Thought in Ancient China** (1939). A conversational and anecdotal presentation of Taoism (Chuang Tzu), Confucianism (Mencius), and legalism, with side references to other doctrines. *P—Stanford U Pr.*

————. **Monkey** (1958). A free version of one-third of Wu Cheng-en's **Journey to the West.** Full of fun. *P—Grove.*

WELCH, HOLMES b. 1921. **Taoism: The Parting of the Way** (1966). A sympathetic historical and philosophical treatment of the two ways of Tao, esoteric and popular. *P—Beacon Pr.*

WU CHING-TSU 1701-1754. **The Scholars.** A bitter satire on the intelligentsia, the mandarin administrators during the Ch'ing dynasty. *H—Cheng & Tsui, China Bks.*

India

ANAND, MULK RAJ b. 1905. **The Untouchable** (1974). A fictional comment on India's abiding evil by the dean of Indian editors and fiction writers in English. *P—Ind-US Inc.*

BASHAM, A. L. **The Wonder That Was India** (3rd ed. 1968). A rich and readable cultural history of pre-Moslem times; well illustrated. *H—Merrimack Pub Cir.*

Bhagavad Gita (ca. 3rd c. B.C.). The most popular and influential book in Hindu religious literature. Many translations. One by P. Lal is graceful and literary (1982). *H—Ind-US Inc.* Also well known is **The Song of God.** Trs. Prabhavananda and Isherwood. *P—NAL.*

CHAUDHURI, NIRAD b. 1897. **Autobiography of an Un-**

known Indian (1968). A cantankerous Anglophile looks at and through his compatriots. *o.p.*

————. **Hinduism** (1979). Celebrating its vitality and psychic appeal, opposing the vague pieties of its swamis. *H & P—Oxford U Pr.*

FISCHER, LOUIS 1896–1970. **The Essential Gandhi** (1983). A useful collection of the Mahatma's utterances, both spiritual and political. *P—Random.*

GANDHI, MOHANDAS K. 1869–1948. **Autobiography: The Story of My Experiments with Truth** (1957). Records the development of his spiritual ideas, especially *ahimsa* (the sacredness of all life), rather than the events of his life. *P—Dover.*

Great Sanskrit Plays in Modern Translation (1964). Tr. P. Lal. Six pieces well rendered. *H—New Directions.*

KALIDASA c. 390–470. **Theater of Memory: Three Plays of Kalidasa.** Ed. Barbara Stoler Miller and trs. Edwin Gerow, David Gitomer, and Miller. The master poet of classical Sanskrit wrote for the sophisticated Gupta court. The three works represented are **Shakuntala, Urvasi,** and **Malavika and Agnimitra.** *H & P—Columbia U Pr.*

LANNOY, RICHARD. **The Speaking Tree: A Study of Indian Culture and Society** (1971). Wide-ranging religious, sociological, and psychological study. *H & P—Oxford U Pr.*

Mahabharata (1980). Selections of the great national epic. *Over 15 eds.*

NAIPAUL, V. S. b. 1932. **India: A Wounded Civilization** (1977). An expatriate Indian visits his ancestral land and finds it sadly lacking. *H—Knopf; P—Random.*

NARAYAN, R. K. b. 1906. **The Bachelor of Arts** (1980). A leading novelist in English treats gently the indigent semi-intellectual. *P—U of Chicago Pr.*

O'FLAHERTY, WENDY D. b. 1940. **Hindu Myths** (1975). Brief but enlightening prefatory materials to translations from the Sanskrit introduce the complex and often brutal bases of popular religion as well as the "great tradition." *P—Penguin.*

————. **Siva: The Erotic Ascetic** (1981). Fine scholarship and fascinating material. *P—Oxford U Pr.*

PREMCHAND (DHANPAT RAI SRIVASTAVA) 1881–1936. **Godan: The Gift of a Cow** (1972). The best-known novel by the foremost Hindi storyteller. *P—Ind-US Inc.*

RUSHDIE, SALMAN b. 1947. **Midnight's Children** (1982). Counterpointed lives and history, set in India in the years following independence (1947). A fusion of comic and tragic, the novel is a superb example of "magic realism." *H—Knopf; P—Avon*.

SINGH, KHUSHWANT b. 1915. **Train to Pakistan** (1956). On the blood spilling at the partition of British India in 1947. *H—Greenwood; P—Grove*.

TAGORE, SIR RABINDRANATH 1861–1941. **A Tagore Reader** (1966). Ed. Amiya Chakravarty. Contains poetry and prose of India's best-known literary figure. *P—Beacon Pr*.

WISER, WILLIAM H. 1890–1961 and CHARLOTTE VIALL WISER. **Behind Mud Walls: 1930–1960** (rev. ed. 1972). A classic study of the "unchanging" Indian village beginning to look around and change. A sequel appeared: **The Village in 1970** (1972). *H & P—U of Cal Pr*.

Japan

ABÉ, KOBE b. 1924. **The Woman in the Dunes** (1960). Tr. E. Dale Saunders. Trapped in the grainy fluidity of a sand dune, a man comes to terms with his existential fate. Prizewinning novel and film. *P—Random*.

BASHO MATSUO 1644–1694. **The Narrow Road to the Deep North and Other Travel Sketches** (1974). The greatest haiku poet walked the byways, lived frugally, exchanged poems with admirers, and wrote memorable, simple prose. *P—Penguin*.

BOWER, FAUBION b. 1917. **Japanese Theatre** (1952). A good introduction to the various traditional forms—Noh, Kabuki, and Bunraku—and helpful comments on modern drama. Contains three Kabuki plays. *H—Greenwood; P—C E Tuttle*.

GIBNEY, FRANK b. 1924. **Miracle by Design: The Real Reasons Behind Japan's Economic Success** (1982). Critical of Japan's failure to accept international responsibilities, Gibney surveys the social and managerial origins of Japan's cooperative-competitive practices. *H—Times Bks*.

HALL, JOHN W. b. 1916. **Japan** (1971). Formal in tone, sound in scholarship, ranging from prehistory to modern times. *P—Dell*.

HALLIDAY, JON b. 1939. **A Political History of Japanese Capitalism** (1975). A Marxian analysis of the interplay of internal forces and foreign pressures that led to the Meiji upheaval and subsequent expansion. *P—Monthly Rev*.

HENDERSON, HAROLD G. 1889–1974. **An Introduction to Haiku** (1958). Informative, with renderings of classic poets from Basho to Shiki. *P—Doubleday*.

HOUSTON, JEANNE WAKATSUKI b. 1934 and JAMES D. HOUSTON b. 1933. **Farewell to Manzanar** (1973). A gripping description of a Nisei family in the pressures of adjustment to a World War II relocation camp and afterward. *P—Bantam*.

IBUSE, MASUJI b. 1898. **Black Rain** (1969, 1980). Devastatingly quiet novel on aftermath of Hiroshima. *P—Kodansha*.

IHARA, SAIKAKU 1642–1693. **Life of an Amorous Woman and Other Writings** (1969). Ed. & tr. Ivan Morris. The realistic 17th-century gossip and humorist. *P—New Directions*.

KAWABATA, YASUNARI 1899–1972. **Snow Country** (1969). A fair example of the teasing indirection of Japan's Nobel laureate. *P—Putnam Pub Group*.

KEENE, DONALD b. 1922. **Dawn to the West: Japanese Literature in the Modern Era** (1984). Vol. 1—**Fiction**; Vol. 2—**Poetry, Drama, Criticism.** A full and eloquent survey of Japanese writers and literary movements since the opening to the West in 1868. Indispensable. *H—HR&W 2 vols*.

MATSUBARA, HISAKO. **Cranes at Dusk** (1984). Tr. from German by Leila Vennewitz. An outstanding novelistic account of the impact upon Japanese women of postwar adjustment. *H—Doubleday*.

MISHIMA, YUKIO 1925–1970. **Death in Midsummer and Other Stories** (1966). A good sampling of the violent themes of the decadent who yearned for a pure absolute. *P—New Directions*.

————. **Five Modern Noh Plays** (1973). Retellings in modern settings of Noh classics. *P—C E Tuttle*.

MORRIS, IVAN 1925–1977. **The World of the Shining Prince** (1964). A fascinating description of court life in ancient Japan during the era of Prince Genji. *P—Penguin*.

MURASAKI, LADY 978–1031? **The Tale of Genji.** The world's first novel and still one of the greatest. The 1976 translation by Edward G. Seidensticker is superb. *P—Knopf*.

OË, KENZABURO b. 1935. **A Personal Matter** (1964). Tr. John Nathan. By rejecting the impulse to kill his deformed, brain-damaged child, the hero learns how to live between rebellion and responsibility. Powerful and often brutal. *P—Grove*.

The Pillow Book of Sei Shonagon (1971). Tr. Ivan Morris. The diary classic of Lady Murasaki's court rival. *P—Penguin*.

SANSOM, SIR GEORGE B. 1883–1965. **Japan** (rev. ed. 1952). Overall, the most balanced and penetrating study of the cultural history of Japan. *H & P—Stanford U Pr*.

Sources of Japanese Tradition. See *Introduction to Oriental Civilizations* under "General," page 78.

STATLER, OLIVER b. 1915. **Japanese Inn: A Reconstruction of the Past** (1982). The business of Japan flows past the inn on the Tokaido Road since the 16th century. *P—UH Pr*.

TANIKAWA, SHUNTARO. **Selected Poems** (1893). Tr. Harold Wright. A leader in the use of Western forms and images superimposed on Japanese sensibility. *o.p.*

TANIZAKI, JUNICHIRO 1886–1965. **The Makioka Sisters** (1957). A directly told depiction of the persistence of old ways of thought in modern Osaka. *H—Knopf; P—Putnam Pub Group*.

WARNER, LANGDON 1881–1955. **The Enduring Art of Japan** (1952). A loving tribute to old Japanese craft artistry. *P—Grove*.

The Smaller Nations

DEVKOTA, LAXMIPRASAD 1909–1959. **Nepali Visions, Nepali Dreams** (1980). Tr. David Rubin. Selected poetry. *H—Columbia U Pr*.

DU, NGUYEN. **Tale of Kieu** (1983). Tr. & annot. Huynh Sanh Thong (1983). Early 19th-century Vietnamese verse narrative. *H—Yale U Pr*.

KANG, YOUNGHILL 1903–1972. **The Grass Roof** (1975). Autobiographical: Japanese occupation of Korea and life in the United States. Bound with Mirok Li's novel, **The Yalu Flows**, in one volume. *P—Norton*.

KHOKHAI, KHAMMAAN. **The Teachers of Mad Dog Swamp** (1982). Best-known novel of a distinguished Thai writer. *H & P—U of Queensland Pr*.

PROCTOR, RAJA. **Waiting for Surabiel** (1981). A novel on the effects of modernization on village life in Sri Lanka. *H & P—U of Queensland Pr*.

RAWSON, PHILIP b. 1924. **The Art of Southeast Asia** (1967). A compact but detailed treatment of the art of Cambodia, Vietnam, Thailand, Laos, Burma, Java, and Bali, with numerous illustrations well keyed to the text. *P—Oxford U Pr*.

RIZAL Y ALONSO, JOSE 1861–1896. **The Subversive** (1891, 1968). Tr. of *Filibusterismo*. An anticolonial Philippine revolutionary political novel. *P—Norton*.

CHAPTER 9

Africa

GLENDERLYN JOHNSON

Africa, the cradle of civilization, is a complex mosaic of peoples, cultures, and traditions. More than 1,000 ethnic groups live on the continent. They share many cultural similarities, but there are as well numerous linguistic and social differences. Despite this diversity, a sense of historical unity is apparent in the rich body of written literature created by African authors.

The roots of written African literature can be traced to the continent's centuries-old oral tradition, which is still very much alive throughout Africa. For centuries, African storytellers (commonly known as griots throughout West Africa) have served as oral custodians of Africa's history, legends, folktales, and traditions. Their distinct narrative style is especially vivid in the African novel, by far the most widely used genre in modern African literature.

Written African literature on a large scale is a relatively recent development, and even more recent is its introduction to an international audience. Most African authors write in the linguae francae of the colonists—English, French, and, to a lesser extent, Portuguese. If one were to select a date that introduced modern Francophone African writing to an international audience, it would probably be 1922, when René Maran won the coveted Prix Goncourt for *Batouala*, the best novel written in French in that year. He was the first black writer to win this award.

Maran was born on the island of Martinique, but he lived in the Central African Republic for more than twenty years. *Batouala* is based on his experiences there as a military officer. It is a gripping tale of daily life in what is now the Central African

Empire. Viewed by the French establishment as a scathing attack on colonialism, *Batouala* was banned in all French African colonies. The ban, however, heightened the novel's political impact, and *Batouala* soon became a literary catalyst in Africa's pre-independence movement.

It was some time later that Anglophone African writers gained an international audience. The Nigerian author Amos Tutuola is considered by most critics to be the forerunner of modern African writers in English. His first book, *The Palm-Wine Drinkard* (1952), caused quite a controversy when it was originally published. How, readers asked, could this semi-educated Yoruba, writing in a type of pidgin English, perform such wonders with the folktales of Yoruba oral tradition? Tutuola's novel was simultaneously hailed and reviled, but it eventually took its place as one of the most popular African novels ever written. It is required reading in many African literature courses.

Following the independence movement that swept the continent in the late 1950s and 1960s, a popular motif used in the novel was the clash of African cultures with Western mores. Chinua Achebe, a leading figure in Africa's first generation of writers, and the continent's foremost novelist, vividly describes this clash in his classic novel, *Things Fall Apart* (1958). Through the liberal use of symbolism and African proverbs, Achebe draws his readers into the traditions of Ibo society and exposes them to the dilemmas faced by the villagers of Umofia when Christian missionaries arrive.

Another pioneer of modern African fiction was the late Guinean author Camara Laye, whose first novel, *L'enfant noir (The Dark Child)* (1953), focuses on traditional African life. In this poignant, autobiographical narrative, Laye evokes the rich customs and traditions of his childhood days in Guinea. Considered a masterpiece by many literary critics, *L'enfant noir* firmly established Laye as a major African novelist.

In the works of Africa's second generation of writers, there is a noticeable shift from the postcolonial nostalgia of their predecessors to more contemporary political themes, such as nationalism, urbanization, and the role of women in modern African societies.

The last topic is becoming increasingly popular, among female authors in particular. Their works have opened up new vistas in African literature. The late Mariama Bâ's highly acclaimed novel, *Une si longue lettre (So Long a Letter)* (1979), is a moving account of a Moslem woman's emotional survival following her husband's abrupt decision to take a second wife. Bâ shares with the Nigerian novelist Buchi Emecheta the courage to address issues affecting African women, issues that, until recently, were considered sacrosanct.

It is language, however, that has emerged as the central issue among contemporary African authors. The fundamental implications of language are raised by the two most frequently asked questions: Whom are we writing for, and who is reading our works? Increasingly, African authors are choosing to write in the vernacular, aware of the limited accessibility of their earlier works to African audiences.

Among the most committed to indigenous writing is Kenyan author Ngugi wa Thiong'o, one of the most politically significant authors in Africa today. His plays, written in his mother tongue Gikuyu, carry an explicit political message, and they have a strong appeal to the masses. The political impact of his work was the probable cause of his detention, in 1977, by the Kenyan government.

No introduction to African literature is complete without acknowledging the contributions of writers belonging to the *négritude* movement. This ideology emerged in the 1930s as a response to what severel French-speaking African and Caribbean writers perceived as a dissolution of their African heritage. Simply put, *négritude* is an affirmation of one's Africanness, an idea espoused by the leading apostles of the movement (Léon Damas, Aimé Césaire, and Léopold Sédar Senghor) and depicted so dramatically in their works. A detailed analysis of this controversial philosophy, which was heatedly debated by African writers, is given in Ezekiel Mphahlele's *African Image*.

What does the future hold for African literature? No doubt African writers will continue to follow the tradition of their griot forebears and preserve African history and culture. The novel is the dominant genre, and culture and politics are still overwhelmingly favored topics; however, there is a noticeable shift toward largely unexplored genres such as children's books, literary surveys, biographies, and drama. Increasingly, African literature reaches ever larger audiences, both in Africa and abroad, and is no longer judged from an exclusively Eurocentric perspective, as much of it was in the past.

African Literature

ABRAHAMS, PETER (South Africa) b. 1919. **Mine Boy** (1946). One of the first novels to portray, vividly and passionately, the dehumanizing system of apartheid. *P—Heinemann Ed.*

ACHEBE, CHINUA (Nigeria) b. 1930. **Things Fall Apart** (1958). Achebe's first novel, now a classic, is a simple but powerful story of the disintegration of Ibo village life once Christianity and Western culture are introduced. *P—Astor-Honor, Fawcett, Heinemann Ed.*

AIDOO, AMA ATA (Ghana) b. 1942. **No Sweetness Here** (1971). Ghanaian women's survival in traditional and urban settings is the central theme in this collection of short stories. *o.p.*

ARMAH, AYI KWEI (Ghana) b. 1939. **The Beautyful Ones Are Not Yet Born** (1969). Gripping tale of violence and corruption in a newly independent African nation. *P—Heinemann Ed.*

BÂ, MARIAMA (Senegal) 1929–1981. **So Long a Letter** (1981). Modupe Bode-Thomas's translation of *Une si longue lettre*. This "cry from the heart" is an intensely moving account of a widowed Moslem woman's grief, courage, and dignity in a transitional polygamous society. *P—Heinemann Ed.*

BETI, MONGO (Cameroon) b. 1932. **The Poor Christ of Bomba** (1971). Witty, satirical novel centers around a Catholic mission school for girls run by French priests in French colonial Africa. Its publication stirred the ire of the French church. *P—Heinemann Ed.*

EKWENSI, CYPRIAN (Nigeria) b. 1921. **People of the City** (1954). Africa's foremost urban novelist focuses on decadence in a West African city. *P—Heinemann Ed.*

EMECHETA, BUCHI (Nigeria) b. 1944. **The Bride Price** (1976). Tragedy befalls an Ibo family after they refuse to pay the traditional bride price. *H & P—Braziller.*

FAGUNWA, DANIEL OROWOLE (Nigeria) 1903–1963. **Forest of a Thousand Daemons** (1983). Tr. Wole Soyinka. Charming Yoruba folktale filled with ghosts and other supernatural spirits, by one of the most popular writers in Africa. *H—Random.*

GORDIMER, NADINE (South Africa) b. 1923. **Selected Stories** (1976). Short stories by a writer internationally acclaimed for her works showing the cruelty and injustice of apartheid. *H—Viking Pr; P—Penguin.*

HEAD, BESSIE (South Africa) b. 1937. **Maru** (1971). Intraracial prejudice between Bantu and Bushmen is skillfully attacked in this memorable love story set in Botswana. *P—Heinemann Ed.*

LAYE, CAMARA (Guinea) 1928–1980. **The Dark Child** (1954). The author's childhood in Guinea is tenderly narrated in this classic autobiographical novel. *P—FS&G.*

————. **The Radiance of the King** (1956). A thought-provoking, complex novel, considered by many literary critics as an ingenuous allegory about man's search for God. *o.p.*

MARAN, RENÉ (Martinique) 1887–1960. **Batouala** (1921). Controversial, prizewinning first novel depicting French colonialism. *o.p.*

NGUGI, JAMES (NGUGI WA THIONG'O) (Kenya) b. 1938. **A Grain of Wheat** (1968). This penetrating novel by East Africa's foremost writer probes Kenya's pre- and post-independence struggles. *P—Heinemann Ed.*

————. **Detained** (1981). Imprisoned by the Kenya government, the author kept a diary describing the degradation he experienced in prison. *P—Heinemann Ed.*

NIANE, DJIBRIL TAMSIR (Mali) b. c. 1920. **Sundiata** (1965). Beautiful tale about the ancient empire of Old Mali, told by a descendant of a long line of griots. *o.p.*

NWAPA, FLORA (Nigeria) b. 1931. **Efuru** (1966). A provocative first novel compassionately portraying the heroine's rejection of the traditional role of African women. *P—Heinemann Ed.*

OMOTSO, KOLE (Nigeria) b. 1943. **The Combat** (1972). One of the most popular of Africa's second generation of writers allegorizes the Nigerian civil war in his second novel involving two friends fighting over paternity rights. *P—Heinemann Ed.*

OYONO, FERDINAND (Cameroon) b. 1928. **Houseboy** (1966). Humorous, biting satire on French colonialism taken from the "diary" of a houseboy. *P—Heinemann Ed.*

PATON, ALAN (South Africa) b. 1903. **Cry, the Beloved Country** (1948). A noted critic of apartheid brings to life the race question in this intense, pulsating novel, which has become a classic. *H & P—Scribner.*

SEMBÈNE, OUSMANE (Senegal) b. 1923. **God's Bits of Wood** (1962). Internationally famous filmmaker and novelist, Sembène focuses his pen on the Dakar-Niger railroad strike of African workers in 1947–48. *o.p.*

SENGHOR, LÉOPOLD SÉDAR (Senegal) b. 1906. **Nocturnes** (1971). Senegal's first president is recognized by many literary critics as Africa's leading poet. A member of the Académie Française, many of his most sensitive poems are in this collection. *P—Heinemann Ed.*

SOYINKA, WOLE (Nigeria) b. 1934. **Kongi's Harvest** (1967). A musical comedy that takes aim at a post-independence African dictator. *P—Oxford U Pr.*

————. **Aké** (1983). A delightful autobiography of the author's Yoruba childhood in western Nigeria. A master craftsman, Soyinka is Africa's most versatile writer—dramatist, poet, novelist, and critic. *H & P—Random.*

TUTUOLA, AMOS (Nigeria) b. 1920. **The Palm-Wine Drinkard** (1952). Peopled with ghosts and other imaginary creatures, this titillating folktale, written in a type of pidgin English, centers on the adventures of a palm-wine drinker in search of his dead palm-wine tapster. *H—Greenwood; P—Grove.*

Books about Africa

AWOONOR, KOFI b. 1935. **The Breast of the Earth: A Survey of the History, Culture and Literature of Africa South of the Sahara** (1976). Ambitious, scholarly, thoroughly readable survey of Africa's literary traditions. *H & P—NOK Pubs.*

BEBEY, FRANCIS b. 1929. **African Music: A People's Art** (1975). Excellent introduction to traditional music and culture. The generous use of illustrations enhances the reader's understanding of the significance of music in African societies. *o.p.*

BROWN, LLOYD W. b. 1938. **Women Writers in Black Africa** (1981). First full-length study of African women writers. *H—Greenwood.*

CHINWEIZU b. 1943, et al. **Toward the Decolonization of African Literature, Vol. 1** (1983). A forceful attack on critics who judge African literature from a purely Eurocentric perspective. *H & P—Howard U Pr.*

Critical Perspectives on Lusophone Literature from Africa (1981). Compiled by Donald Burness. An excellent introduction to some of the leading Afro-Portuguese writers. *H & P—Three Continents.*

DAVIDSON, BASIL b. 1914. **Africa in History** (rev. ed. 1974).

Compact, clear, thematic presentation of African history from ancient times to the revolutionary movements of southern Africa. *P—Macmillan*.

DIOP, CHEIKH ANTA b. 1923. **The African Origin of Civilization** (1974). Historical, archeological, and anthropological data, with copious illustrations supporting the thesis that Egyptian civilization is of black origin. *H & P— Lawrence Hill*.

DU BOIS, WILLIAM E. 1868–1963. **The World and Africa: Inquiry into the Part Which Africa Has Played in World History** (rev. ed. 1965). A pioneer work by a noted scholar that projects Africa in clear, historical relation to the rest of the world. *H—Kraus Intl; P—Intl Pub Co*.

FANON, FRANTZ 1925–1961. **The Wretched of the Earth** (1965). Regarded as a "textbook" for colonized people during the 1960s, Fanon's work lays bare the dehumanizing nature of colonialism and offers solutions for the oppressed of the Third World. *P—Grove*.

FINNEGAN, RUTH b. 1933. **Oral Literature in Africa** (1970). Oral literature and its manifestations in prose, poetry, music, and other forms of African culture is richly highlighted, with cogent examples and a substantial bibliography. *P—Oxford U Pr*.

JAHN, JANHEINZ 1918–1973. **Muntu: An Outline of the New African Culture** (1961). Broad survey of African culture embracing art, religion, and philosophy. Jahn was a primary agent in the introduction of African culture to Europe and the United States. *P—Grove*.

JORDAN, ARCHIBALD CAMPBELL 1906–1968. **Towards an African Literature** (1973). Twelve scholarly essays analyzing Xhosa literature. *H—U of Cal Pr*.

KENYATTA, JOMO 1893–1978. **Facing Mount Kenya** (1938). A fascinating account of the social and political structure of the Gikuyu people written by the nation's first president, the grandson of a Gikuyu medicine man. *H—AMS Pr; P—Random*.

MANDELA, NELSON b. 1918. **No Easy Walk to Freedom** (1973). A piercing collection of the writing, speeches, and the trial testimony of this invincible South African freedom fighter, who is currently serving a life sentence at the infamous Robben Island prison. *H—Heinemann Ed*.

MBITI, JOHN S. b. 1931. **Introduction to African Religion** (1975). A clear and insightful introduction to religion in Africa by one of the continent's noted theologians. *P—Heinemann Ed*.

MOORE, GERALD b. 1924. **Twelve African Writers** (1980). Lucid, crisp examination of Africa's most important writers, along with detailed comparisons of their works. A good geographical cross-section is represented. *H—Ind U Pr.*

MPHAHLELE, EZEKIEL b. 1919. **The African Image** (rev. ed. 1974). A searching social and political analysis of the "African personality" by a major South African writer. *o.p.*

A New Reader's Guide to African Literature (rev. ed. 1983). Ed. Hans M. Zell. The most comprehensive bibliography available on African literature. Richly annotated with current information, includes essays, criticisms, biographical sketches, and photographs. *H & P—Africana Pub.*

NKRUMAH, KWAME 1909–1972. **Africa Must Unite** (rev. ed. 1970). Ghana's first president describes the steps the African nations must take before full freedom and national development can be achieved. *P—Intl Pub Co.*

————. **Ghana: The Autobiography of Kwame Nkrumah** (1971). The struggles and triumphs that culminated in Ghana's independence. *H & P—Intl Pub Co.*

RODNEY, WALTER 1942–1980. **How Europe Underdeveloped Africa** (rev. ed. 1982). Provocative Marxian analysis of African history. *H—Howard U Pr.*

SCHMIDT, NANCY J. b. 1936. **Children's Books on Africa and Their Authors** (1975). The most thorough bibliography available on this subject. It contains more than 800 entries, each with descriptive and critical annotations, and biographical information. A supplement was published in 1979. *H—Holmes & Meier.*

SNOWDEN, FRANK M., JR. b. 1911. **Blacks in Antiquity** (1970). Engrossing historical account, with ample illustrations, of the role of Ethiopians in the Greco-Roman world. *P—Harvard U Pr.*

WILLIAMS, CHANCELLOR b. 1905. **The Destruction of Black Civilization** (1974). Clear, informative, scholarly analysis of the worldwide social, cultural, and political contributions of Africa. Contradicts many "dark continent" myths. *P—Third World.*

CHAPTER 10

Latin America

OSWALDO ARANA

Latin American writing has gone through three distinct stages. During the colonial period, writers—like artists and architects—found their models in Spain and Portugal. During the revolutionary period, which extended over two centuries, the literature of France—first the France of the Encyclopedists, then of the Symbolists—was the vital influence. Only very recently has Latin American literature entered a renaissance. Compounded of North American techniques and developing from indigenous roots, it has the vitality of the plastic arts of the 1930s. This is especially true of the novel.

The Indians have always been a key (and problematic) figure in Latin American letters. During the various revolutionary cycles, they were first Rousseauesque "noble savages" and, afterward, faceless symbols of the oppressed. For the new generation of writers, however—especially in Mexico and to a lesser extent in Peru and Guatemala—they are complex protagonists of a deeply split but extraordinarily rich culture. Mexican writers, such as Juan Rulfo, Rosario Castellanos, and Carlos Fuentes, uncover in the Indian an ancient wisdom that the Toltecs and Maya possessed centuries before the conquistadores arrived on the scene. José Mariá Arguedas (Peru) and Miguel Ángel Asturias, Nobel Prize winner from Guatemala, concentrate on probing the soul of the Indian in the struggle between the myths and symbols of a great past and the imperatives of a rather meager present.

In their creative preoccupation with who they are and what they mean, contemporary Latin American writers have a fruitful literary tradition to explore and to which to return. The pre-

Columbian legends—preserved by priest-ethnologists of the caliber of Sahagún and Ximénez and (today) Angel Garibay, or by European-educated natives such as the Inca Garcilaso—have a stylistic and symbol-packed richness resembling that of the Upanishads and the Old Testament. Works such as *Chilam Balam* and *Popol Vuh*, compiled long after the people whose legends and history they preserve had vanished, range in style and theme from a Grimms' (and Freudian) fairy tale, through an Old Testament curse on the conquerors, to a Blakean myth of a New Jerusalem.

The colonial period produced some works of lasting importance. An Alarcón, a Sor Juana Inés de la Cruz—even a Lizardi, whose quasi-picaresque novel *The Itching Parrot* was the first written and published in the Western hemisphere—deserve more attention from students of international literature than they have been given.

During the revolutionary cycles, which can be divided into the 19th-century wars of independence and the continuing struggles against native dictators, much of the major writing was done by intellectuals turned soldiers—from Hidalgo to Martí. Their manifestos often took the form of poetry, novels, newspaper columns, and philosophic essays. To the latter phases of the revolutions we owe such vital works as those by Alegría (Peru), Arciniegas (Colombia), Azuela (Mexico), Da Cunha (Brazil), Gallegos (Venezuela), and Quiroga (Uruguay). Most such novels suffer, however, from being written too close to the scene—either as protest novels or as combat diaries compiled by the light of the campfire on the eve of battle. In this genre the semifictionalized accounts of the Villa campaigns by Martín Luiz Guzmán (Mexico) are notable. Though there is still no Latin American *War and Peace*, some of the writers have composed battle scenes as convincing as Stephen Crane's.

The novelists and journalists fought and wrote. The poets tended to retreat to the ivory towers that Mallarmé and other Symbolists inhabited with great style. The early poetry of Rubén Darío (Nicaragua), the leader of the *modernistas*, is a prime example of this group. In Mexico the retreat took the form of the complex and opaque death-and-God-centered poetry of Villaurrutia and Gorostiza. The Spanish Civil War added a social focus to the anguished and esoteric poetry of César Vallejo (Peru) and Octavio Paz (Mexico). And the whole spectrum of human feelings and concerns runs through the poetry of Gabriela Mistral and Pablo Neruda, both Nobel Prize winners from Chile.

Meanwhile, a special genre of Latin American writing, which echoes the bitter epigrams of *Chilam Balam* and borrows from such diverse sources as La Rochefoucauld and O. Henry, deserves attention. In the short story, prose poem, or short essay, such Latin Americans as Jorge Luis Borges and Julio Cortázar (Argentina) and Ramón López Velarde, Juan Rulfo, and Juan José Arreola (all of Mexico) have perfected forms as stylized as the Japanese haiku. Combining a European elegance of style with Indian impassivity, these pieces are a sharp commentary on human weakness and social conditions.

In recent years American and European publishers have enthusiastically translated the works of world-renowed Latin American authors, and now they are adding to their lists the names of newer and younger voices. Julio Cortázar (Argentina), Mario Vargas Llosa (Peru), Alejo Carpentier, Gabriel Cabrera Infante, José Lezama Lima (all of Cuba), Gabriel García Márquez (Colombia), José Donoso (Chile), Juan Carlos Onetti, Mario Benedetti (both of Uruguay), and Manuel Puig and Luisa Valenzuela (of Argentina) provide remarkable examples of diverse and innovative techniques. The audacity of form and theme and the dazzling language of their novels or short stories must be the joy and despair of the best translators. And the university presses in particular have been newly translating, or bringing back into print, Latin American classics, old and new. Many are available in paperback.

Travel books on Latin America and journalistic accounts of contemporary events are often good reading as well as good guides. Not to be missed are John Dos Passos on Brazil (*Brazil on the Move*), Edmund Wilson on Haiti (*Red, Black, Blond, and Olive*), Graham Greene and Kate Simon on Mexico (*Another Mexico* and *Mexico: Places and Pleasures*), Sacheverell Sitwell on Peru (*Golden Wall*), Selden Rodman on a number of countries, and Joan Didion on El Salvador today.

We shall probably have to wait a generation, as we did after the Mexican Revolution, before writers of the stature of Rulfo and Fuentes can assess the Cuban happenings in terms of fictional art. Luisa Valenzuela has already given us a glimpse of the terrors of Argentinian military violence in *Strange Things Happen Here*. Meanwhile, a book such as Azuela's *The Underdogs* etches a timeless picture of what revolution does to the revolutionaries.

Since Latin Americans blame North Americans for long neglect of their area and problems, we should do more to find out what they have to say about themselves. The quest for and the urge to assert national and cultural identity are a prime concern of Octavio Paz, Victor Alba, Samuel Ramos, Germán Arciniegos, Ezequiel Martínez Estrada, Gilberto Freyre, García Márquez, and others. Their works provide a keen insight into the multifaceted world of Mexicans, Cubans, Puerto Ricans, Chicanos, and other Latinos whose varied contributions are making a lasting mark on the culture of the United States.

Finally, scholarly research has produced a great number of studies on Latin America by experts in diverse fields in an effort to analyze the complex traditions inherited from the past and the sociopolitical and economic changes pointing to the future. Works by W. Rex Crawford, Edwin Lieuwen, Kalman H. Silvert, Carleton Beals, Hubert Herring, Walter La Fever, Judith Adler Hellman, and Thomas E. Skidmore and Peter H. Smith are worthy of our attention.

Latin American Literature

ALEGRÍA, CIRO (Peru) b. 1909. **The Golden Serpent** (1935). One of the great novels. Reminiscent at times of Mark Twain, it deals profoundly and compassionately with boat people who live on the Amazon and the Indian villagers who live beside it. *o.p.*

AMADO, JORGE (Brazil) b. 1912. **Gabriela, Clove, and Cinnamon** (1962). Rabelaisian novel about a pretty country woman's effect on a seaport town. *P—Avon.*

———. **Dona Flor and Her Two Husbands** (1969). A charming novel about the Bahian people of northeast Brazil who blend reality and magic in their search for happiness. *P—Avon.*

ANDRADE, CARLOS DRUMMOND DE (Brazil) b. 1902. **In the Middle of the Road** (1965). Poems in which irony, sadness, humor, and other traits of human life are vividly intertwined. *o.p.*

An Anthology of Mexican Poetry (1958). Ed. Octavio Paz. This bilingual edition has a vital introduction by Paz and first-rate translations by Samuel Beckett. *o.p.*

ASTURIAS, MIGUEL ÁNGEL (Guatemala) 1899–1974. **El Señor Presidente** (1964). A forceful portrayal of the brutalization of life under the rule of a man who is the personification of the evils found in all dictators. *P—Atheneum.*

AZUELA, MARIANO (Mexico) 1873–1952. **The Bosses** (1917) and **The Flies** (1918). Two pungent novelettes about the Mexican Revolution. Published under the title **Two Novels of Mexico.** *P—U of Cal Pr.*

————. **The Underdogs** (1927). A stark and incisive novel about the Mexican Revolution. Probing the symptoms of revolution and the aftereffects, Azuela shows that in the end those who are betrayed are the people themselves. *P—NAL.*

BENEDETTI, MARIO (Uruguay) b. 1920. **The Truce** (1969). An excellent novel, in diary form, about a man trying to find some meaning for his life amidst the strangling Uruguayan bureaucracy. *o.p.*

BORGES, JORGE (Argentina) b. 1899. **Ficciones** (1962). A master of poetic tour de force and literary legerdemain pursues the unknowable in essays, detective stories, prose poems, and literary parodies. *P—Grove.*

————. **Labyrinths** (1962). Another anthology of literary fireworks based on Borges's favorite symbol, showing this great stylist at his best. *H—Modern Lib; P—New Directions.*

————. **A Personal Anthology** (1967). In this collection, on which the author wants his reputation to rest, Borges mixes satire, myth, and parable in a way resembling Kafka, Mallarmé, and Swift. *P—Grove.*

CARPENTIER, ALEJO (Cuba) 1904–1980. **The Lost Steps** (rev. ed. 1967). The search for the origins of Spanish-American culture set in a novel dominated by the magic realism of a lost but still longed-for world. *P—Avon.*

CASTELLANOS, ROSARIO (Mexico) 1915–1974. **The Nine Guardians** (1959). A rich novel about contemporary descendants of the Mayans. *o.p.*

CORTÁZAR, JULIO (Argentina) 1914–1984. **Hopscotch** (1966). Irony, humor, and a whimsical structure are skillfully combined in a cosmopolitan novel that questions through its characters the authenticity of various aspects of life. *P—Avon.*

————. **A Change of Light and Other Stories** (1980). A fine selection of stories showing Cortázar's masterful handling of language, fantasy, and reality. *H—Knopf.*

CUNHA, EUCLIDES DA (Brazil) 1866–1909. **Rebellion in the Backlands** (1902). An epic narrative of Brazil's struggle from tropic jungle to modernity. *P—U of Chicago Pr.*

DARÍO, RUBÉN (Nicaragua) 1867–1916. **Selected Poems** (1965). A varied sampler of rich poetry by a great innovator and a leading *modernista. o.p.*

DONOSO, JOSÉ (Chile) b. 1924. **The Obscene Bird of Night** (1973). Decadence and disintegration in a feudal Chilean family, seen through the eyes and mind of characters who create a surrealistic world to disguise their own sordid reality. *P—Godine*.

FUENTES, CARLOS (Mexico) b. 1928. **The Death of Artemio Cruz** (1964). Through the eyes of a dying robber baron, we glimpse the tragedy of Mexico: the failure of the revolution. *P—FS&G*.

————. **A Change of Skin** (1968). Fuentes's most ambitious novel, an existentialist epic involving four different kinds of travelers in a tragedy with Aztec overtones. *o.p.*

————. **Terra Nostra** (1976). A sprawling novel that spans from Genesis to New Year's Eve, 2000. A fantastic journey through reality as perceived by Fuentes's imagination, using key events in Western history as points of departure. *H & P—FS&G*.

GALLEGOS, RÓMULO (Venezuela) 1884–1969. **Doña Barbara** (1942). A symbolic novel about a femme fatale, developing the conflict between barbarism and civilization. *H—Peter Smith*.

GARCÍA MÁRQUEZ, GABRIEL (Colombia) b. 1928. **One Hundred Years of Solitude** (1970). A masterpiece in the neobaroque style. A century-long history of a town and of a family, with subtle insights into the psychology of the people and the mores of Colombia. *H—Har-Row; P—Avon*.

————. **The Autumn of the Patriarch** (1976). A novel about a dictator who spends his life in the ruthless exercise of power, told in brilliant language and with a deep awareness of the dictator's intimate tribulations and loneliness. *H—Har-Row; P—Avon*.

————. **Chronicle of a Death Foretold** (1983). A short, masterful narrative about love and dishonor resulting in an expected ritual revenge, set in a Colombian village. *H—Knopf*.

GARCILASO DE LA VEGA (Peru) c. 1540–1616? **Royal Commentaries of the Incas and General History of Peru** (1609). Son of an Inca princess and a Spanish conquistador, Garcilaso compiled an authentic chronicle of the origin, growth, and destruction of the Inca Empire to correct the false picture given by the historians of his day. *H—U of Tex Pr 2 vols*.

GUZMÁN, MARTÍN LUIS (Mexico) 1890–1968. **The Eagle and the Serpent** (1930). A participant's fast-paced, deadpan novel about campaigning with Pancho Villa. *H—Peter Smith*.

LEZAMA LIMA, JOSÉ (Cuba) 1910–1976. **Paradiso** (1974). An intense, complicated novel with autobiographical overtones, written in a nontraditional manner, about some Cuban families at the turn of the century. *o.p.*

MACHADO DE ASSIS, JOAQUIM MARIA (Brazil) 1839–1908. **Epitaph of a Small Winner** (1880). Ironic psychological novel about a 19th-century Brazilian George Apley. *P—Avon*.

———. **Esau and Jacob** (1904). Aristocratic twin brothers vie in turn for love of mother, a woman, and political power. Witty, urbane political satire and "novel of the absurd." *H—U of Cal Pr*.

MISTRAL, GABRIELA (Chile) 1889–1957. **Selected Poems** (1957). Langston Hughes's translation of representative verse by Nobel Prize winner *o.p.*

Modern Brazilian Short Stories (1974). Ed. William L. Grossman. A remarkable selection of contemporary writers exploring the complexities of the human condition in Brazil. *H & P—U of Cal Pr*.

NERUDA, PABLO (Chile) 1904–1973. **Residence on Earth and Other Poems** (1973). An excellent bilingual edition of the *Residencias*, probably the most important work by this Nobel Prize winner. Poetry ranging from surrealistic verse of alienation to works deeply concerned with social and political justice. *H—Gordian*.

Neruda and Vallejo: Selected Poems (1971). Ed. Robert Bly. A well-selected, wide-ranging anthology of the best poems by Neruda and Vallejo. Goes from the earliest to the latest periods of both authors. *P—Beacon Pr*.

ONETTI, JUAN CARLOS (Uruguay) b. 1909. **A Brief Life** (1976). A captivating novel about a middle-aged man facing a life without meaning and bereft of options. *H—Viking Pr*.

PAZ, OCTAVIO (Mexico) b. 1914. **Early Poems 1935–1955** (rev. ed. 1973). Verse by Mexico's major poet, beautifully translated by Muriel Rukeyser. *H—Ind U Pr; P—New Directions*.

Popul Vuh: The Sacred Book of the Ancient Quiché Maya (date unknown). A marvelous myth put into English by Delia Goetz and Sylvanus G. Morley. *o.p.*

PUIG, MANUEL (Argentina) b. 1932. **Betrayed by Rita Hayworth** (1971). A novel dealing with alienation and boredom in an Argentinian provincial town where going to the movies becomes a way of life. *P—Random*.

QUIROGA, HORACIO (Uruguay) 1878–1937. **The Decapitated Chicken and Other Stories** (1976). Tales of love, madness, and death comparable to those by Poe, Kipling, and London. *H—U of Tex Pr*.

REYES, ALFONSO (Mexico) 1889–1959. **Mexico in a Nutshell and Other Essays** (1964). Scholar, humanist, classicist, and revolutionary, Reyes, who had a wide range and the respect of the young, is especially brilliant on native themes. *o.p.*

ROMERO, JOSÉ RUBÉN (Mexico) 1890–1952. **The Futile Life of Pito Perez** (1967). A picaresque classic—scathing, poetic, touching. Pito, a typical Mexican hero, is an honest rogue who battles the establishment and generally lands in jail. *o.p.*

RULFO, JUAN (Mexico) b. 1918. **The Burning Plain and Other Stories** (1967). Wryly compassionate vignettes of Mexican peasant life, informed by a religion that is part Catholic, part Aztec. *H & P—U of Tex Pr.*

The Spanish American Short Story: A Critical Anthology (1980). Ed. Seymour Menton. An excellent collection covering the last one and a half centuries, each preceded by an introduction on the author and followed by critical commentaries. *P—U of Cal Pr.*

VALENZUELA, LUISA (Argentina) b. 1938. **Strange Things Happen Here** (1979). A collection of stories and a short novel about the fears, terror, and violence underlying contemporary life in Argentina. *H—HarBraceJ.*

VALLEJO, CÉSAR (Peru) 1892–1938. **César Vallejo: The Complete Posthumous Poetry** (1978). Trs. Clayton Eshleman and José Rubia Barcia. Splendid bilingual edition, including poetry from 1923 through 1938. Excellent introduction by Eshleman, notes, and some facsimilies of Vallejo's worksheets. *P—U of Cal Pr.*

VARGAS LLOSA, MARIO (Peru) b. 1936. **The Time of the Hero** (1966). Action and suspense in a novel that inquires deeply into the nature of the Peruvian military caste as it perpetuates itself in a preparatory school for boys. *o.p.*

————. **Aunt Julia and the Scriptwriter** (1982). A hilarious novel where reality and illusion get mixed up in the life of an imaginative radio scriptwriter. *H—FS&G; P—Avon.*

————. **The War of the End of the World** (1984). Perhaps Vargas Llosa's most ambitious novel, based on a violent and historical uprising in the hinterlands of Brazil. *H—FS&G.*

YÁÑEZ, AGUSTÍN (Mexico) b. 1904. **Edge of the Storm** (1963). A probing study of the consciousness of a small Mexican town on the eve of the revolution, told in poetic and evocative language. *H&P—U of Tex Pr.*

Books about Latin America

ALBA, VÍCTOR b. 1916. **The Mexicans: The Making of a Nation** (1970). An incisive analysis of the culture, problems and possibilities by a keen observer. *o.p.*

ARCINIEGAS, GERMÁN b. 1900. **Latin America: A Cultural History** (1967). A brilliant analysis of the peoples of Latin America, the richness of their culture, and their struggle to achieve maturity. *o.p.*

DÍAZ DEL CASTILLO, BERNAL c. 1492–1581. **Discovery and Conquest of Mexico** (1632). Blunt, engaging chronicle by one of Cortes's conquistadores. *P—FS&G.*

DIDION, JOAN b. 1934. **Salvador** (1983). A compelling account of the outrages resulting from the policies of terror and death in El Salvador. *H—S&S; P—WSP.*

DOS PASSOS, JOHN 1896–1970. **Brazil on the Move** (1963). A major novelist with Portuguese roots approaches modern Brazil with the feeling for landscapes and political figures that distinguishes his novels. *H—Greenwood.*

FREYRE, GILBERTO b. 1900. **Masters and the Slaves** (1964). Using buildings to symbolize Brazil's history from colonial times to the present, from country to city life, Freyre pontificates with verve. *o.p.*

HELLMAN, JUDITH ADLER b. 1945. **Mexico in Crisis** (2nd ed. 1983). An outstanding analysis of the political and social factors—starting with the revolution—behind the emergence of today's Mexico. *H & P—Holmes & Meier.*

HERRING, HUBERT C. 1889–1967. **History of Latin America** (3rd ed. 1968). The standard work, tracing a kaleidoscopic interplay of varied cultures and forces upon an immense, rich continent. *H—Knopf.*

LA FEBER, WALTER b. 1933. **Inevitable Revolutions** (1983). An incisive evaluation of the problems in Central America and the role of the United States in that troubled area. Written by a respected U.S. diplomatic historian. *H & P—Norton.*

LEWIS, OSCAR 1914–1978. **The Children of Sánchez** (1961). Tape-recorded interviews with a typical Mexico City slum family edited to produce an anthropological documentary on the culture of poverty that reads like a novel. *o.p.*

MADARIAGA, SALVADOR DE 1886–1970. **Latin America Between the Eagle and the Bear** (1962). A scholar's viewpoint of the two major forces pulling at the continent. *H—Greenwood.*

PAZ, OCTAVIO b. 1914. **The Labyrinth of Solitude** (1962). A major modern poet analyzes the ambivalence of Mexicans— their sudden pendulum swings from sensuality to asceticism, from rhetoric to taciturnity, from social explosion to solitariness—in a sociological and literary classic of our time. *P—Grove*.

PRESCOTT, WILLIAM HICKLING 1796–1859. **Conquest of Mexico** (1843) and **Conquest of Peru** (1847). Colorful classics of historical writing. *H—Irvington, Modern Lib*.

RAMOS, SAMUEL 1897–1959. **Profile of Man and Culture in Mexico** (1963). This acute analysis of the Mexican character by an Adlerian psychologist has had an immense influence on Mexican writers from Paz to Fuentes. Ramos underlines the split between past and present to explain the inferiority complex of the *mestizo. H & P—U of Tex Pr*.

SILVERT, KALMAN H. 1921–1976. **Essays in Understanding Latin America** (1976). An incisive analysis of this region's perennial problems and the possibilities for a better future. *H & P—ISHI PA*.

SKIDMORE, THOMAS E. b. 1932 and PETER H. SMITH b. 1940. **Modern Latin America** (1984). An excellent survey of Latin American history with emphasis on the 1880–1982 period. *H & P—Oxford U Pr*.

TORRES-RÍOSECO, ARTURO 1897–1971. **The Epic of Latin American Literature** (1959). A crowded panorama, filled with insight; an excellent guide to reading in the field. *H—Peter Smith*.

VAILLANT, GEORGE 1901–1945. **The Aztecs of Mexico** (rev. ed. 1962). A classic revised. *P—Penguin*.

WAGLEY, CHARLES b. 1913. **An Introduction to Brazil** (rev. ed. 1971). Illustrated and updated, this book provides a first-rate interpretation of the culture and civilization of contemporary Brazil. *H & P—Columbia U Pr*.

CHAPTER 11

American Minority Cultures

Native American

ELIZABETH WEATHERFORD

The history of American Indian and Eskimo societies is a rich and complex one. Today, approximately 290 bands, tribes, nations, village communities, and corporations exist in the United States, each with its separate identity, history, and language. The largest of these, the Navajo Nation of Arizona and New Mexico, numbers more than 160,000 people. The smallest tribes, such as the Pequot of Connecticut, now number fewer than a hundred.

The many diverse environments of North America supported the development of a variety of traditional cultures. By a systematic study of the nine distinct geographic zones inhabited by native cultures, scholars have illuminated shared customs and regional patterns. These culture areas are Arctic, Subarctic, Plateau, Pacific Northwest Coast, California, Great Basin, Southwest, Great Plains, and Eastern Woodlands. Within each area are many tribes and nations, sharing some modes of existence with each other but often distinguished by their own language and history.

In the first 300 years following European contact, Native America experienced enormous changes and, frequently, devastating disruption. The survival of traditional culture and the preservation of a record of techniques, ways of subsistence, beliefs and rituals, and social patterns have inspired many writers to research, interview, and record in detail the culture histories of each tribe.

Since the turn of the century writers have concerned themselves with the traditions and social realities of contemporary Native American life. Religious practices and philosophies startlingly relevant to a time of ecological crisis in America continue to attract much writing. Issues such as the pursuit of land and water rights and the health and economic problems many native peoples face are being analyzed more fully. Informed writers voice a concern that most non-Indians fail to recognize that native peoples exist as their contemporaries—believing that "real" Indian and Eskimo cultures died in the 19th century.

In recent decades there have been marked contrasts in how contemporary Native Americans live. Since 1950 the native population has been steadily growing, now numbering 1.5 million people. Lively centers of native life are found throughout the United States (although more than 70 percent of Native Americans live west of the Mississippi River). The three states with the largest Indian populations are Oklahoma, where many diverse tribes were relocated after being removed from their own lands by 19th-century government policies; Arizona, where numerous tribes have remained for generations on their traditional lands; and California, where today the largest urban population of Indians is centered.

Despite the growth in numbers, native peoples are, according to all reports, among the poorest and least healthy of all Americans. The survival of both traditional and contemporary American Indian and Eskimo cultures remains threatened. Approximately half of the Native American population lives on reservations, which provide the basis for continuing the customs and beliefs of the community. Some reservation economies are strong, but many reservations, depleted by land sales and rentals necessitated for economic survival, can provide only a meager livelihood for their inhabitants. The survival of the very lands on which the community is founded is under threat. For those Indians and Eskimos living off reservations or community lands, difficulties range from finding employment to sustaining a sense of purpose away from their own communities.

Since the 1970s, Native American goals have been more clearly asserted and better understood by the whole country. It has been an era of increased native pride and of cultural and spiritual revival. Major lawsuits have been brought by some tribes for the return of lands and the recognition of their sovereignty and other treaty-guaranteed rights. Some have opted for financial compensation, such as the Penobscot and Passamaquoddy of Maine. Others, such as the Lakota Sioux of the Black Hills, have been awarded a settlement of lands illegally seized in the

19th century but remain undecided about whether to accept this tacit sale or to continue to press for the return of their lands. Land issues are not merely economic; for in their relationship to their lands Native Americans discover, and reflect, deeply held spiritual values.

For American Indians and Eskimos there exists a plurality of experiences. Despite an oppressive sense of marginality within American life, Native Americans derive from their resiliency and native values the strength to continue to discover ways to survive as Native Americans. The complexity of their cultures, the bitter aspects of their history and contact with colonialism, the deeply philosophical nature of their spiritual ways, their present concerns, and their lively contemporary cultures—all shine forth in an extensive and fascinating literature.

American Indian Myths and Legends (1984). Eds. Richard Erdoes and Alfonso Ortiz. A compendium of oral traditions and tales, sacred myths, and history from throughout North America by an outstanding fieldworker and a Native American anthropologist. *H—Pantheon.*

America's Fascinating Indian Heritage (1978). Reader's Digest Editors. A handsomely illustrated and well-researched volume on traditional customs and history of all areas of North America. *H—Random.*

BATTAILLE, GRETCHEN b. 1944 and KATHLEEN M. SANDS. **American Indian Women: Telling Their Lives** (1984). By focusing on several outstanding life stories, presents autobiography as an expressive literary form for Native American women. *H—U of Nebr Pr.*

BOAS, FRANZ 1858–1943. **Kwakiutl Ethnography** (1966). Ed. Helen Codere. Richly detailed ethnography of a Northwest people by the major early American anthropologist, describing all aspects of traditional life. *H & P—U of Chicago Pr.*

BROWN, DEE b. 1908. **Bury My Heart at Wounded Knee** (1970). Narrates the military and political history of white settlement in the American West, 1860–1890, from the viewpoints of many Indian tribes, such as the Apache, Navajo, Cheyenne, and Nez Percé. *H—HR&W; P—WSP.*

CATLIN, GEORGE 1796–1872. **Letters and Notes on the Manners, Customs, and Conditions of the North American Indians.** (1844, repr. 1973). Colorful firsthand account by a 19th-century painter of his experiences among peoples of the

Plains, particularly the Mandan, Arikara, and Sioux. *P—Dover 2 vols*.

Coyote Was Going There (1977). Ed. Jarold Ramsey. Well-selected collection of Indian myths, legends, and oratory from diverse tribes of Oregon, including many tales of the trickster Coyote. *P—U of Wash Pr*.

CRONON, WILLIAM b. 1954. **Changes in the Land** (1983). A historical analysis that reconstructs the plant, animal, and human ecologies of New England and the impact upon them of the arrival of the Europeans. *H & P—Hill & Wang*.

DEBO, ANGIE b. 1890. **And Still the Waters Run** (1972). The story of U.S. federal government actions that resulted in tribes of the Southeast—the Five Civilized Tribes—being forcibly removed to Oklahoma. *H—Princeton U Pr; P—U of Okla Pr*.

DELORIA, VINE, JR. b. 1933 and CLIFFORD LYTLE b. 1932. **The Nation Within** (1984). Indian self-rule and the history of U.S. federal government and tribal relations are discussed in a readable account, co-authored by an eminent Indian lawyer and spokesman. *H & P—Random*.

DENSMORE, FRANCES 1867–1957. **Chippewa Customs** (1929, repr. 1979). A record of all aspects of traditional Ojibwa (Chippewa) life, including history, life cycle, and material culture. *H—Scholarly, Johnson Repr; P—Minn Hist*.

DUTTON, BERTHA P. b. 1903. **American Indians of the Southwest** (1975, rev. 1983). Authoritative introduction to the Southwest Indian cultures—the Pueblo tribes, the Apaches and Navajos, the Utes, the Paiutes, and the rancheria peoples, including the Papago and Yaqui. *P—U of NM Pr*.

EWERS, JOHN C. b. 1909. **The Blackfeet: Raiders on the Northwestern Plains** (1958, repr. 1976). Informative account of the 19th-century history and culture of the three tribes that make up the Blackfeet Nation—Piegan, Blood, and Blackfeet. *H & P—U of Okla Pr*.

FEEST, CHRISTIAN F. b. 1945. **Native Arts of North America** (1980). Well-written and illustrated history of American Indian and Eskimo arts and their techniques and styles. *H & P—Oxford U Pr*.

Finding the Center; Narrative Poetry of the Zuñi Indians (1972). Tr. Dennis Tedlock. A fine collection of ten narrative poems from Zuñi, translated with an unusual sense of the oral tradition and its dynamics. *H & P—U of Nebr Pr*.

FITZHUGH, WILLIAM W. b. 1943 and SUSAN A. KAPLAN. **Inua: Spirit World of the Bering Sea Eskimo** (1982). Beautifully illustrated catalog with essays, concerned with traditional Eskimo culture in western Alaska. *H & P—Smithsonian*.

GUILLEMIN, JEANNE b. 1943. **Urban Renegades** (1975). The complex experiences of Indians in urban areas, reflected in a thoughtful study of the Micmac Indian community in Boston. *H—Columbia U Pr*.

Handbook of North American Indians (1981–   ). Ed. William C. Sturtevant. A landmark 20-volume encyclopedia, the *Handbook* covers history, languages, biography, as well as all culture areas of North America, with essays by leading scholars. *H—Smithsonian*.

HOEBEL, E. ADAMSON b. 1906. **The Cheyennes: Indians of the Great Plains** (2nd ed. 1978). A classic history of the 19th-century traditional Cheyenne culture by an anthropologist noted for his work on traditional law. *P—HR&W*.

HOLDER, PRESTON B. b. 1907. **The Hoe and the Horse on the Plains** (1970). Analyzes two modes of Plains Indian life—corn cultivation and hunting from horseback—and how they fared following European contact. *H & P—U of Nebr Pr*.

HUDSON, CHARLES b. 1932. **The Southeastern Indians** (1976). Comprehensive introduction to the tribes of the Southeast, past and present, including the Cherokees, Creeks, Seminoles, and Choctaws. *H & P—U of Tenn Pr*.

HUNGRY WOLF, BEVERLY. **The Ways of My Grandmothers** (1980). A collection of stories, myths, and traditions gathered from interviews with many women elders from the author's tribe. *P—Morrow*.

JOSEPHY, ALVIN M. b. 1915. **The Patriot Chiefs** (1961). Nine stimulating chapters on such leaders of Indian resistance to white culture as King Philip, Pontiac, Tecumseh, and Crazy Horse. *P—Penguin*.

———. **Now That the Buffalo's Gone** (1982). Native American history fascinatingly recounted, clarifying issues of current concern for Indian and Eskimo communities, such as self-rule and land and water rights. *H—Knopf; P—U of Okla Pr*.

KROEBER, THEODORA 1897–1979. **Ishi in Two Worlds** (1961). Heart-rending account of a man who was the last member of his tribe, the Yahi Indians of California. *H & P—U of Cal Pr*.

LAUBIN, REGINALD and GLADYS LAUBIN. **Indian Dances of North America** (1977). Describes dances and dance costumes from all regions, with particular attention to Plains dances and music. *H—U of Okla Pr*.

MOMADAY, N. SCOTT b. 1934. **House Made of Dawn** (1967). Eloquent novel by a Kiowa author and scholar concerned with the experiences of a Pueblo veteran returning to his community following World War II. *H & P—Har-Row*.

MOONEY, JAMES 1861–1921. **The Ghost Religion and the Sioux Outbreak of 1890** (1896, abr. 1965). Report by a careful observer of a politically controversial religious movement that swept through many Western tribes at the end of the 19th century. *P—U of Chicago Pr*.

Mountain Wolf Woman. See "Anthropology," page 328.

NABOKOV, PETER b. 1940. **Two Leggings: The Making of a Crow Warrior** (1967). Remarkable first-person account of the psychological, religious, and social life of a 19th-century Plains Indian man. *P—T Y Crowell, U of Nebr Pr*.

————. (ed.) **Native American Testimony** (1978). A chronicle of Indian and white relations told and interpreted by native peoples in a selection of perceptive and candid accounts. *H & P—Har-Row*.

Native American Women: A Contextual Bibliography (1983). Ed. Rayne Green. An annotated listing by a Native American scholar. Almost 700 entries, with a long introduction on writings by and about American Indian and Eskimo women. *H—Ind U Pr*.

NEIHARDT, JOHN G. 1881–1973. **Black Elk Speaks** (1932, repr. 1979). The life story of a Lakota Sioux spiritual man and a record of his visions and the values he believed in, told to the author in Sioux and translated by his son. *H—U of Nebr Pr; P—WSP*.

NELSON, RICHARD K. b. 1941. **Make Prayers to the Raven** (1983). The animals of the northern forest, as they are described by the Koyukon Indians of Alaska, illuminating their origins, lifeways, and spiritual meaning. *H—U of Chicago Pr*.

The Newberry Library Series (1978–   ). Ed. Francis Jennings. A 30-volume series of excellent bibliographic essays, each serving as a guide to reliable sources on specific tribes and periods of Indian history, prepared by the Newberry Library Center for the History of the American Indian. *P—Ind U Pr*.

ORTIZ, ALFONSO b. 1939. **The Tewa World** (1969). An ethnography by a prominent Indian anthropologist dealing with the cosmology—space, time, and being—of the Pueblo Indian tribes of the Rio Grande. *H & P—U of Chicago Pr*.

ORTIZ, SIMON J. b. 1941. **From Sand Creek** (1981). Poems by an outstanding American Indian poet that reflect both bit-

terness of Indian history and the author's belief in the enduring
human spirit. *P—Thunder's Mouth*.

OWEN, ROGER C. b. 1928, JAMES J. F. DEETZ, and AN-
THONY D. FISHER. **The North American Indians** (1967).
A major sourcebook that includes articles from a wide range of
scholarly perspectives, covering anthropological topics and
concerned with all culture areas of North America. *o.p.*

The Portable North American Indian Reader (1972). Ed.
Frederick W. Turner III. A compendium of traditional oral
literature, accounts by white observers in early contact with
Indian tribes, and contemporary writings by Native Americans. *H—Viking Pr; P—Penguin*.

POWERS, WILLIAM K. b. 1934. **Oglala Religion** (1977).
Focuses on the persistence in the face of change of Oglala
Sioux social and cultural identity and the continuity of their
religious values. *H & P—U of Nebr Pr*.

RADIN, PAUL 1883–1959. **The Trickster** (1956). The myth
cycle of the Trickster, ambiguous creator and destroyer, translated from the Winebago traditional version and annotated by a
leading anthropologist. *H—Greenwood; P—Schocken*.

REICHARD, GLADYS A. 1893–1955. **Navajo Religion: A
Study of Symbolism** (1950). A clear, scholarly presentation
of the complex religion of the Navajo nation and its ceremonials, myths, and symbols. *P—U of Ariz Pr*.

SCHERER, JOANNA COHAN b. 1942. **Indians** (1973). Photographs made between 1847 and 1929 from the collection of the
Smithsonian Institution, including portraits and scenes of everyday life and ritual. *o.p.*

SILKO, LESLIE M. b. 1948. **Storyteller** (1981). Account of
traditional tales told poetically, preserving their mythic manner, by a noted Pueblo poet and author. *H & P—Seaver Bks*.

SPICER, EDWARD H. b. 1906. **The American Indians** (1982).
Concise survey of the history and present circumstances of
more than 200 Indian tribes in the United States. *P—Harvard
U Pr*.

Sun Chief (1942). Ed. Leo W. Simmons. Life story of a Hopi
man, Don Talayesva, spanning the first part of the 20th
century. *P—Yale U Pr*.

**Teachings from the American Earth: Indian Religion and
Philosophy** (1975). Eds. Dennis Tedlock and Barbara Tedlock.
A collection of thoughtful articles about Native American
sacred practices and beliefs. *H & P—Liveright*.

UNDERHILL, RUTH M. 1884–1984. **The Navajos** (1956, rev.

1967). A detailed history of the Navajo and their cultural values from early to recent times. *P—U of Okla Pr*.

WELTFISH, GENE 1902–1980. **The Lost Universe: Pawnee Life and Culture** (1965, repr. 1977). Pawnee life about 1867 as learned from the tales of elders living in Oklahoma in the 1920s. *H & P—U of Nebr Pr*.

WILSON, EDMUND 1895–1972 and JOSEPH MITCHELL b. 1908. **Apologies to the Iroquois: With a Study of the Mohawks in High Street** (1959, repr. 1978). Acute observation of the Iroquois Nations of New York State and Canada and their life in the 20th century. *H—Octagon*.

Words in the Blood (1984). Ed. Jamake Highwater. A collection of outstanding contemporary Native American writers, from both North and South America. *P—NAL*.

Asian-Pacific

NAOMI OGAWA MOY

Although Asian Americans—Asian-Pacific would be the more precise designation—are often stereotyped as a "model" minority, how they attained this perceived middle-class status is not widely known. Moreover, the history of Asian-Pacific Americans and their contributions to the building of this nation have yet to be recognized as an integral part of United States history, and so most of us grow up knowing very little about them.

"Asian-Pacific American" refers to a mosaic of ethnic groups: Chinese, Japanese, and Koreans from East Asia; Burmese, Cambodians, Indonesians, Laotians, Malaysians, Thais, and Vietnamese from Southeast Asia; East Indians and Pakistanis from South Asia; and Aleuts, Filipinos, Guamanians, native Hawaiians, and Samoans from the Pacific Basin.

When the pioneering Chinese, who were attracted initially to the gold fields of California, began to enter the labor force, a nativist movement ensued and resulted in the federal Chinese Exclusion Act of 1882, the first of many such measures. As Jack Chen vividly records in *The Chinese of America*, the Chinese were vital to the development of the West as entrepreneurs and laborers constructing railroads, farming, pioneering the fishery industry, and operating factories and restaurants.

The anti-Chinese movement established the hostile climate that later Asian immigrants, especially the Japanese, would encounter. Roger Daniels, in *The Politics of Prejudice*, describes the xenophobic actions of the press, labor unions, politicians, and nativist organizations that resulted in the alien land laws, Gentlemen's Agreement, and finally the Immigration Act of

1924, which virtually cut off all Asian immigration until 1952. This 1924 law, however, opened the door to Filipinos whose status as U.S. nationals enabled them to fill the need for farm laborers, domestics, and cannery workers. Among those laborers was Carlos Bulosan, whose autobiography *America Is in the Heart* describes the plight of the Filipinos during the 1930s.

The bombing of Pearl Harbor ushered in for Asian-Pacific Americans one of the darkest periods in American history. It was followed by the uprooting of 110,000 Americans of Japanese ancestry from their West Coast homes and their subsequent incarceration behind the barbed wire fences of the U.S. Relocation Authority Relocation Centers. This noxious action, especially, has engendered a plethora of works ranging from apologist statements to revisionist interpretations, such as those of Roger Daniels and Michi Weglyn.

In the aftermath of World War II, a new era for the Asian-Pacific Americans commenced as emigrants from the continuing turmoil in Asia began to arrive. The Communist takeover of China sent former officials and Kuomintang supporters fleeing; U.S. servicemen stationed in Japan and Korea returned with Asian brides; and economic conditions prompted migration from the Pacific Islands. Later, the Immigration Act of 1965 generated a new wave of Asian immigrants from Hong Kong, Taiwan, Korea, and the Philippines. With the collapse in 1975 of the South Vietnamese government came an exodus of Vietnamese refugees, followed by refugees from the political upheavals in Laos and Cambodia. While older immigrant groups have finally established themselves in the mainstream, the new immigrants have only begun to face the struggle to overcome language difficulties, cultural shock, employment problems, and racial discrimination.

Most of the published works on Asian-Pacific Americans treat them more as objects rather than subjects and all too often from a political or sociological perspective. The inclusion of autobiographies and literary works is an attempt to bridge this gap; for without the human dimension, our understanding of Asian-Pacific Americans would be incomplete.

Aiiieeeee! An Anthology of Asian American Writers (1974). Eds. Frank Chin et al. A provocative collection of literary works by Asian American authors; valuable for its "insider's" view of Asian America. *H & P—Howard U Pr*.

BULOSAN, CARLOS 1914–1956. **America Is in the Heart: A**

Personal History (1973). Bulosan's autobiography is a personal statement but reflects the experiences of Filipino immigrants in the 1930s. *P—U of Wash Pr.*

CHEN, JACK b. 1908. **The Chinese of America** (1982). An overview from the early Chinese immigration to current-day perspectives; particularly notable for its stories of the Chinese as pioneers in the development of the West. *P—Har-Row.*

CHU, LOUIS H. b. 1915. **Eat a Bowl of Tea** (new ed. 1979). Authentic, sensitive depiction of Chinatown's bachelor society as it begins to transform into a community of young families. *P—U of Wash Pr.*

DANIELS, ROGER b. 1927. **The Politics of Prejudice: The Anti-Japanese Movement in California and the Struggle for Japanese Exclusion** (1962). A detailed examination of the anti-Japanese movement from its inception in the late 1800s to the passage of the Immigration Act of 1924; relies heavily on local newspapers and official documents. *H & P—U of Cal Pr; P—Atheneum.*

————. **Concentration Camps North America: Japanese in the United States and Canada During World War II** (rev. ed. 1981). A concise and authoritative account of the World War II incarceration of Japanese Americans, which has been revised to include a chapter on the Japanese Canadian experience. *H—Krieger.*

East Across the Pacific: Historical and Sociological Studies of Japanese Immigration and Assimilation (1972). Eds. Hilary Conroy and T. Scott Miyakawa. A compilation of historical and sociological essays that brings together research on Japanese immigration and settlement in the Hawaiian and Pacific Islands, the continental United States, and Canada. *o.p.*

GLICK, CLARENCE b. 1906. **Sojourners and Settlers: Chinese Migrants in Hawaii** (1980). Focuses on the Chinese migrants to Hawaii, whose experiences contrast with those on the mainland. *H—UH Pr.*

IRONS, PETER b. 1940. **Justice at War** (1983). A meticulously researched revisionist exposure of the legal subterfuge surrounding the court cases that challenged the U.S. federal government's right to incarcerate Americans of Japanese descent during World War II. *H—Oxford U Pr.*

Island: Poetry and History of Chinese Immigrants on Angel Island, 1910–1940 (1980). Eds. Judy Yung et al. Preserves the poems expressing the despair, anguish, and anger of the Chinese immigrants who wrote on the barrack walls of their ordeal at the Angel Island detention station. *P—SF Stud Ctr*.

KIKUMURA, AKEMI b. 1944. **Through Harsh Winters: The Life of a Japanese Immigrant Woman** (1981). A poignant blend of autobiography and biography—the latter a daughter's account of the spirit and values of an Issei (first-generation Japanese American) woman who struggled to support her family as migrant farm worker, cook, maid, and internee. *H & P—Chandler & Sharp*.

KIM, ILLSOO b. 1944. **New Urban Immigrants: The Korean Community in New York** (1981). This perceptive and comprehensive analysis of Korean immigrants in metropolitan New York is valuable for the study of Korean American immigration and adaptation in general. *H—Princeton U Pr*.

KINGSTON, MAXINE HONG b. 1940. **The Woman Warrior** (1976). With powerful, poetic imagery, a Chinese American woman tells of her youth as she grows up trying to reconcile the paradoxes posed by the dreams and legends of her Chinese heritage with the realities of life in America. *H—Knopf; P—Random*.

————. **China Men** (1980). This companion to *Woman Warrior* uses a similar combination of myth and recollection to enlarge the experience of becoming Chinese American from the mundane to saga proportions. *H & P—Random; H—Knopf; P—Ballantine*.

KITANO, HARRY H. L. b. 1926. **Japanese Americans: The Evolution of a Subculture** (2nd ed. 1976). First published in 1969, this was a pioneering revisionist study that examined the Japanese American family and community to explain their success during the postwar period. *o.p.*

The Korean Diaspora: Historical and Sociological Studies of Korean Immigration and Assimilation in America (1977). Ed. Hyung-Chan Kim. Especially valuable for the discussion of cultural assimilation and the small business enterprises of post-1965 immigrants. *o.p.*

LYMAN, STANFORD M. b. 1933. **Chinese Americans** (1974). A scholarly sociological study of Chinese Americans. *P—Random*.

McCUNN, RUTHANNE LUM. **Thousand Pieces of Gold: A Biographical Novel** (1981). An engrossing, fast-paced biography of a strong-willed Chinese woman, known as Poly Bemis, who cherished her freedom and lived the life of a pioneer in an Idaho mining town. *H & P—Design Ent SF; P—Dell*.

MELENDY, H. BRETT b. 1924. **Asians in America: Filipi-**

nos, Koreans, and East Indians (1977). Discussions of conditions in the homeland, immigration, and life in America make this a concise introduction to three groups often neglected in general works on Asian Americans. *P—Hippocrene Bks*.

MILLER, STUART CREIGHTON b. 1927. **The Unwelcome Immigrant: The American Image of the Chinese, 1785–1882** (1969). Challenges previous assumptions regarding the development of anti-Chinese sentiments in the United States by focusing on the nation rather than the West Coast. *H—U of Cal Pr*.

MORI, TOSHIO 1910–1980. **The Chauvinist and Other Stories** (1979). Mori's eclectic stories depict diverse scenes from Japanese American life, characterized by the enduring spirit of his people. *P—Asian Am Stud UCLA*.

NEE, VICTOR G. b. 1945 and BRETT DE BARY NEE b. 1943. **Longtime Californ': A Documentary Study of an American Chinatown** (1974). Use of interviews gives a very personal, human quality to this sociohistorical study of the development of San Francisco's Chinatown and its residents. *P—HM*.

OGAWA, DENNIS M. b. 1943. **Kodomo No Tame Ni—For the Sake of the Children: The Japanese American Experience in Hawaii** (1978). Through a mixture of primary materials, book excerpts, journal articles, and literature, Ogawa shows that a belief in the future has served as a driving force in the development of the Japanese American community in Hawaii. *H & P—UH Pr*.

OKADA, JOHN 1924–1971. **No-No Boy** (1980). Powerful portrayal of self-contempt arising from the conflict of being neither completely Japanese nor completely American. *P—U of Wash Pr*.

TEN BROEK, JACOBUS 1911–1968, EDWARD N. BARNHART, and FLOYD W. MATSON b. 1921. **Prejudice, War, and the Constitution** (1954). Comprehensively surveys the incarceration of Japanese Americans and provides a cogent analysis of the constitutional and civil rights issues. *P—U of Cal Pr*.

WEGLYN, MICHI b. 1926. **Years of Infamy: The Untold Story of America's Concentration Camps** (1976). Rehearses again the revisionist analysis of the Japanese-American wartime experience, but important for use of documents and facts previously downplayed or ignored. *P—Morrow*.

WILSON, ROBERT A. b. 1910 and BILL HOSOKAWA b. 1915. **East to America: A History of the Japanese in the United States** (1980). A lucid general history. *P— Morrow*.

Black

GLENDERLYN JOHNSON

Written literature by black Americans was first published during the latter half of the 18th century. Two literary pioneers, both slaves, were Jupiter Hammon and Phillis Wheatley. Hammon's poem, "An Evening Thought: Salvation by Christ with Penetential Cries" (1760), and Wheatley's *Poems on Various Subjects, Religious and Moral* (1773), paved the way for other black writers to contribute their creative talents to American letters.

Black writers, centered in their own cultural milieu, as most are, have produced many richly illuminating works concerning the black experience. Their books give readers insightful and at times powerfully realistic views of black life and culture. A viable way of approaching black literature is through some of its distinct literary periods.

Prior to the Harlem Renaissance of the 1920s (also known as the Negro Renaissance), the works of only a minuscule number of black writers were known to the general public. One who was nationally acclaimed was Frederick Douglass—ex-slave, orator, journalist, and zealous abolitionist. His autobiography, *The Narrative of the Life of Frederick Douglass*, was published in 1845. Slave narratives were a popular literary genre during the abolitionist period, and Douglass's was by far the finest. This era also witnessed the publication of the first novel by an Afro-American, *Clotel, or, The President's Daughter* (1853), by William Wells Brown.

By the turn of the century, a transitional period in Afro-American literature, a select number of black writers had emerged, representing various literary styles. Paul Laurence Dunbar introduced black dialect verse to the reading public and it immediately became his trademark, although he preferred writing in "standard" English. W. E. B. Du Bois appealed to the "black intelligentsia" with his brilliant essays extolling black consciousness and racial pride. The talented short story writer Charles W. Chesnutt drew heavily on black folklore. Chesnutt created characters free of the typical racial stereotypes that up until then had been popular among many well-known white writers, such as Joel Chandler Harris.

Following this transitional phase came the Harlem Renaissance, a period unequalled in the flowering of creative black talent. Harlem was the cultural mecca of black writers and artists. Here they created some of the most important works of black literature ever published.

Though not a Harlemite, Jean Toomer was one of the most gifted writers of the period. His novel *Cane*, a work rich in imagery and sensuality, is credited by many as being the literary catalyst that sparked the Renaissance. Using the ethos of blacks in a southern setting as the book's structural frame, Toomer created what many critics consider a literary masterpiece. His work influenced other Renaissance writers—Zora Neale Hurston, Countee Cullen, and Langston Hughes, to name but a few.

Langston Hughes is one of the world's most celebrated writers. Often referred to as the poet laureate of Harlem and the people's poet, his work covers a diverse range of literary forms, including children's books, humor, librettos, lyrics, drama, radio scripts, journalism, autobiography, and, above all, poetry. The deep concern he had for black life and culture is clearly reflected in his work. He enjoyed a fruitful literary career that stretched from the Harlem Renaissance into the black consciousness era of the 1960s, the most propitious periods for black writers.

It should, however, be stressed that during the interim several extremely important works were written by highly talented individuals, most notably Richard Wright. Wright, who set the standard for other writers of his generation—such as Ralph Ellison and James Baldwin—delivered a powerful indictment of racism in America. Two of Wright's so-called protest novels, *Native Son* and his largely autobiographical *Black Boy*, both written in the 1940s, rank among the best fiction by any American author, black or white. Ralph Ellison's celebrated literary reputation is based mainly on his only novel, *Invisible Man*, for which he won the 1952 National Book Award for Fiction. A contemporary classic, it is required reading in black literature courses across the country.

Of all the black writers of the past or present, James Baldwin is perhaps the best known. Since 1953, when his first novel *Go Tell It on the Mountain* was published, Baldwin has continued to create not only novels but plays and brilliant essays as well. Like Hughes, Baldwin's career also extended into the 1960s, a turning point in black literature.

The 1960s was the black consciousness decade, and a fervent interest in one's Africanness (which was actually rooted in the Harlem Renaissance) was strikingly evident. Writers celebrated their heritage and wrote about it with vigor and originality. Their works explicitly reflected the passions and contradictions that black people had experienced for more than 200 years in America. Moreover, these writers were deeply committed to the social and political struggle being waged against racism and poverty.

LeRoi Jones (Amiri Baraka), poet, essayist, critic, novelist, editor, and playwright, was the most creatively versatile of the writers of this period. Together with Larry Neal, Jones edited *Black Fire: An Anthology of Afro-American Writing*, which not only brings together the works of some of the most influential writers of the 1960s but also captures the spirit that existed among them. The writers of the black consciousness generation left an indelible impression on black literature. Enthusiasm for their work was stirred to such a height that it was difficult for publishers to keep up with the demand.

One can only speculate about what the critics of the future will have to say concerning current black writers, for it is premature to reach a historical judgment. However, given their present standing, Alice Walker, Ishmael Reed, Toni Morrison, and John Edgar Wideman, among others, will surely not go unnoticed. They have already received critical acclaim and top literary awards, and like the pioneers Hammon and Wheatley, their works have contributed to the rich and striking tradition of black literature.

BALDWIN, JAMES b. 1924. **Go Tell It on the Mountain** (1953). Scorching (largely autobiographical) portrait of a 14-year-old boy growing up in Harlem and his complex relationship with his stepfather. *H—Doubleday; P—Dell*.

BARAKA, IMAMU AMIRI. See "Poetry," page 210, and "Biography," page 227.

BROOKS, GWENDOLYN b. 1917. **The World of Gwendolyn**

Brooks (1957). A collection of five highly acclaimed works by the poet laureate of Illinois. Included is her Pulitzer Prize winner *Annie Allen*, poems about black life in Chicago. *o.p.*

BROWN, CLAUDE b. 1927. **Manchild in the Promised Land** (1965). An extraordinarily vivid autobiography about growing up in Harlem and succeeding, despite some very formidable odds. *H—Macmillan; P—NAL*.

CHESNUTT, CHARLES WADDELL 1858–1932. **The Marrow of Tradition** (1901). Set in the post-Reconstruction era, this ambitious work is one of the first novels by a black writer to explore the race question. *H & P—U of Mich Pr; H—AMS Pr, Ayer Co, Irvington*.

CLEAVER, ELDRIDGE b. 1935. **Soul on Ice** (1968). An extremely provocative collection of essays, by one of the most important black revolutionary leaders of the 1960s. *H—McGraw*.

CULLEN, COUNTEE 1903–1946. **Color** (1925). A tremendously popular author during the Harlem Renaissance, this is Cullen's first and perhaps best collection of verse. *H—Ayer Co*.

DOUGLASS, FREDERICK 1818–1895. **Narrative of the Life of Frederick Douglass, an American Slave** (1845). Vivid account of the author's life from his childhood to his escape from bondage. *H & P—Harvard U Pr; P—Doubleday, NAL, Penguin*.

————. **My Bondage and My Freedom** (1855). A revised and extended version of the narrative, recounting not only his life as a slave but also his notable career subsequently, particularly his abolitionist labors. *H—Ayer Co, Johnson Chi, Peter Smith; P—Dover*.

DU BOIS, WILLIAM EDWARD BURGHARDT 1868–1963. **The Souls of Black Folk** (1903). Fourteen eloquently written essays, by America's foremost black intellectual, that address various aspects of the black experience, including the "color line" and black folk songs. *H—Dodd, Kraus Intl; P—NAL*.

DUNBAR, PAUL LAURENCE 1872–1906. **Complete Poems** (1913). In the genre of black dialect verse, Dunbar has no peer. This collection contains both dialect poems and verse in conventional English. *P—Dodd*.

ELLISON, RALPH b. 1914. **Invisible Man** (1952). In this compelling story, symbolic of modern alienation, an anonymous black man undergoes a series of baffling adventures, first in the South and later in New York, during a fervent quest for personal identity and social visibility. Often referred to as

the most important novel ever written by a black American.
H—Modern Lib; P—Random.

GAINES, ERNEST J. b. 1933. **The Autobiography of Miss
Jane Pittman** (1971). An engrossing fictional autobiography
recounting "Miss Jane's" life from slavery to the civil rights
era. Gaines skillfully combines humor, wrath, and authenticity
in this memorable novel. *H—Doubleday; P—Bantam.*

HUGHES, LANGSTON 1902–1967. **Selected Poems of Langston
Hughes** (1959). The highly colloquial, deliberately simple and
moving poems Hughes chose for this collection reflect his
intense concern about the "Negro condition in America" and
underscore his superb creative talent. *H—Knopf; P—Random.*

HURSTON, ZORA NEALE 1903–1960. **Their Eyes Were
Watching God** (1937). A master raconteur skillfully uses black
folklore to create an intriguing novel about a black woman in
search of love and fair treatment. Hurston was the most widely
published black woman writer of her era. *H—Greenwood, U
of Ill Pr.*

KILLENS, JOHN O. b. 1916. **And Then We Heard the Thunder**
(1963). Contradictions faced by black men during World War
II as soldiers and Americans are explored in this noteworthy
novel. *P—Howard U Pr.*

McKAY, CLAUDE 1890–1948. **Harlem Shadows** (1922). Clear,
sculptured, poetry—a landmark in black literature. *o.p.*

MALCOLM X. See "Biography," page 231.

MORRISON, TONI b. 1931. **Song of Solomon** (1977). In **Sula**
(1973), a modern black woman in the Midwest strives with
little success for an inner life that transcends race and feminism. The later novel is more complex. Problems of sex and
violence, identity and caste, arise and remain unresolved. But
the women in the novel—extensions of Faulkner's Dilsey—
endure and, as literary creations, prevail. *P—NAL.*

REED, ISHMAEL b. 1938. **Mumbo Jumbo** (1973). The ever-
spreading "Jes Grew" epidemic of the 1920s (read "black
power") began as an infection of the Egyptian god Osiris.
Hinkle van Hampton, a villainous publisher, has survived for a
thousand years on a secret diet. These are but two of the
outrageous mysteries in this experimental collage, a funny but
often bitter satire of racial conflict. *P—Avon.*

TOOMER, JEAN 1894–1967. **Cane** (1923). This richly sensual
work was a major influence on Harlem Renaissance writers.
Combining realism and mysticism, Toomer explores the ethos
of black Southern culture. *P—Liveright.*

WALKER, ALICE b. 1944. **The Color Purple** (1982). Jolting, compelling novel written in an epistolary style about a black woman's journey to self-awareness. Winner of the 1983 American Book Award and the Pulitzer Prize. *H—HarBraceJ; P—WSP*.

WIDEMAN, JOHN EDGAR b. 1941. **Sent for You Yesterday** (1983). Spanning three generations, the novel vividly explores the themes of family and community, continuity and tradition in a decaying Pittsburgh neighborhood. Winner of the 1983 PEN/ Faulkner Award for best American fiction. *P—Avon*.

WRIGHT, RICHARD 1908–1960. **Native Son** (1940). Magnetic story of "Bigger Thomas," a rebellious young Chicago black man coping in a racist and capitalist environment. Undoubtedly one of the most highly acclaimed novels ever written by a black author. *H—Har-Row*.

Books about Black Literature

Black Fire: An Anthology of Afro-American Writing (1968). Eds. LeRoi Jones and Larry Neal. Most comprehensive anthology ever published on the writers of the black power/black consciousness generation. Includes the essays, poems, short stories, and plays of more than 70 writers. *o.p.*

Black Women Writers (1950–1980): A Critical Evaluation (1984). Ed. Mari Evans. Fifteen contemporary writers reflect on their work in this landmark publication. Critical essays by noted observers of black literature as well as bibliographical and current biographical data, are also included. *H & P—Doubleday*.

BONE, ROBERT b. 1924. **The Negro Novel in America** (1958). In this early historical survey of the "Negro novel," Bone diligently traces this genre from the 1890s through the 1950s. *o.p.*

DAVIS, ARTHUR P. b. 1904. **From the Dark Tower: Afro-American Writers, 1900–1960** (1974). Penetrating overview of 28 significant black writers and their works. *H & P—Howard U Pr*.

The Harlem Renaissance Remembered (1972). Ed. Arna Bontemps. Written in a clear, crisp style, this perceptive collection of essays provides an in-depth study of some of the major patterns, themes, and writers of the Harlem Renaissance. Bontemps was a major writer of the era. *P—Dodd*.

Books about Blacks

ANDERSON, JERVIS. **This Was Harlem: A Cultural Portrait, 1900–1950** (1982). Engaging social history highlighting the famous personalities and the legendary cultural and social institutions that made Harlem the capital of black America. *H & P—FS&G*.

BENNETT, LERONE, JR. b. 1928. **Before the Mayflower: A History of Black America** (1969). This well-researched black history classic is now in its fifth revised edition. Designed for nonspecialists, it is a clear and concise history of black Americans from their African past to the present. *H—Johnson Chi; P—Penguin*.

————. **The Shaping of Black America** (1974). Differs from *Before the Mayflower* in its developmental rather than chronological approach to black American history. Includes information on the "black founding fathers" and relations between blacks and Native Americans, among other subjects. Illustrations by Charles White (1918–1979), noted black artist. *H—Johnson Chi*.

HARDING, VINCENT b. 1931. **There Is a River: The Black Struggle for Freedom in America** (1981). Harding, a prominent black scholar, boldly redefines the black experience in American history, from the slave ships to the end of slavery. *H—HarBraceJ; P—Random*.

HUGHES, LANGSTON 1902–1967, MILTON MELTZER b. 1915, and C. ERIC LINCOLN b. 1924. **A Pictorial History of Black Americans** (1963). Now in its fifth edition, copiously illustrated with current data covering 300 years of black history, this book is an excellent introduction for the layperson. *H—Crown*.

KATZ, WILLIAM LOREN b. 1927. **The Black West** (rev. ed. 1973). A fascinating, well-documented account of the black frontier experience, including famous black cowboys and all-black towns. Designed to be used as a school text. *H—Doubleday*.

Chicano-Hispanic

ASELA RODRIGUEZ DE LAGUNA

Hispanic literature as a minority manifestation in the United States is not a recent phenomenon. Ongoing studies properly trace the historical roots of Chicano literature to the U.S. Southwest during the 16th and 17th centuries. This first stage is characterized particularly by works in Spanish closely linked to epic and history, religious and missionary topics, and a rich oral tradition.

The immediate foundation of this literature rests in the 19th century, however, when U.S. expansionism dislocated the socio-cultural and political cultures of the Spanish-speaking inhabitants of those areas incorporated into the Union. Mexican Americans had to shape their lives accordingly, and it is from the confrontation and coexistence of bilingual and bicultural experience that Chicano or Mexican American literature emerges. Hispanic people, who left their lands for political or economic reasons, settled in the East and Southwest particularly. Since the 19th century, Spanish, Cubans, and later Puerto Ricans maintained active Hispanic communities, continually renewed by waves of Spanish-speaking immigrants—a movement advanced by political turmoil: the Spanish-American War, the Mexican Revolution, World Wars I and II, the Spanish Civil War, the Castro revolution, diverse coup d'etats, oppressive Latin American dictatorships. The constant influx of immigrants enhanced the production of literary works and publication of Spanish newspapers in the United States.

In the 20th century, a different kind of Spanish-American literature emerges, different in content, essence, and form. New and more firmly anchored generations of Chicanos, Puerto Ricans, and other Hispanic Americans have largely shifted their center of interest from the political and social movements of their homeland to their present experiences as a large minority in a sometimes hostile United States. Their writings deal with such matters as identity, cultural affirmation, and discrimination. Though occasionally they prefer Spanish, or blend English and Spanish, or reproduce the language of the ghetto and barrio streets, for the most part they write in English.

The two most prominent groups have been the Chicanos (or Mexican Americans) and the New York Puerto Ricans (pejoratively referred to as Nuyoricans or Newricans), but one must be aware of recent contributions by Cuban Americans. The emergence of a national Hispanic minority resulted inevitably from the sociopolitical and economic changes of the 1960s, when Mexican Americans and Puerto Ricans joined with other minorities to struggle for social, economic, and educational justice, to redefine their cultural identity, and to oppose the existing misconceptions and ethnic stereotypes with which they had been stigmatized and which, in part at least, provided a motive for their rejection.

Despite group differences and diversity in literary style, Chicano and Hispanic writers share common themes. Their subject matter emphasizes protest, social criticism, and the search for selfhood and cultural pride, encompassing both the Hispanic and Indian heritages: ancient legends and contemporary myths from their ghetto environment, separateness and assimilation, love and self-hate, resignation and rebellion, pride and humiliation, hope and surrender, the pull of Spanish and the enticement of English. They are troubled by the claims of religion—Catholicism, Protestantism, and "superstition"; they are oppressed by the conditions of their lives—exploited, underpaid, unemployed. They are enraged by the false promise held out by the "American dream" —their world too often one of drugs, prostitution, and racial and cultural discrimination. Although most Hispanic writers are, understandably, social realists, yet others (Tomás Rivera, Alurista) have transcended or evaded the imperatives of the urban situation and incorporated fantastic or mythic elements into both their fiction and poetry.

Poetry has been the most prolific genre of Hispanic writing in the United States. Among the best known poets are the Puerto Ricans (Pedro Pietri, Miguel Algárin, Victor Hernandez Cruz, Felipe Luciano, Tato Laviera, Sandra Maria Esteves, Louis Reyes

Rivera) and the Chicanos (Alurista, S. Elizondo, Richard García, Rolanti Hinojosa, Tino Villanueva, and Gary Soto). Two leading Hispanic dramatists are the Puerto Rican Miguel Piñero and the Chicano Luis Valdez. Piri Thomas, Nicholasa Mohr, Edward Rivera, Rudolfo Anaya, Ron Arias, Sergio Elizondo, Tomás Rivera, and Ricardo Suárez have made important contributions in prose fiction. The works of Chicano, Puerto Rican, and Hispanic Americans reflect, in general, a conflict between two cultures, two languages and two peoples, and their literature valiantly attempts to resolve the conflict.

ACOSTA, OSCAR "ZETA." **The Revolt of the Cockroach People** (1973). Sequel to **The Autobiography of a Brown Buffalo** (1972). An autobiographical novel of a Chicano who, amid drugs and sex, searches to attain his cultural identity and becomes a leader of his people. *o.p.*

ANAYA, RUDOLFO A. b. 1937. **Bless Me, Ultima** (1972). Story of a young Chicano seeking to understand the mysteries of life through the help of a *curandera*, or medicine man, in New Mexico. *P—Tonatiuh-Quinto Sol Intl.*

————. **Heart of Aztlan** (1976). Award-winning novel about an adolescent who searches to know himself through the guidance of a blind fortune-teller. Presents a broad vision of the Chicano ghetto of Albuquerque. *P—Editorial Justa.*

Borinquen: An Anthology of Puerto Rican Literature (1974). Eds. Maria Teresa Babín and Stan Steiner. More than 100 selections from Puerto Rican poets, novelists, playwrights, and intellectuals from Puerto Rico and New York. *o.p.*

COLÓN, JESÚS. **A Puerto Rican in New York and Other Sketches** (1961). Portrays Puerto Ricans as hardworking people with a strong sociopolitical commitment to freedom and justice during the period between World Wars I and II. *H—Ayer Co; P—Intl Pub Co.*

A Decade of Hispanic Literature: An Anniversary Anthology (1982). Ed. Nicolás Kanellos. Contemporary works by representative Hispanic American writers. *P—Arte Público.*

ESTEVES, SANDRA MARIA. **Yerba Buena** (1980). Poems about the saga of Puerto Ricans and other Caribbeans in the United States—about freedom, social justice, love, desolation, misery, and hope. Blend of Spanish and English. *P—Greenfld Rev Pr.*

GARZA, ROBERTO J. b. 1934. **Contemporary Chicano Theater** (1975). Contains eight plays by important Chicano playwrights, among them *Dawn* by Alurista; *The Day of the Swallows* by Estela Portillo; *Los vendidos and Bernabe: A Drama of Modern Chicano Mythology* by Luis M. Valdez. *H & P—U of Notre Dame Pr.*

HINOJOSA, ROLANDO b. 1929. **Estampas del valle y otras obras** (1973). Bilingual. Short vignettes on Chicano affairs and characters in fictitious Klail City. *o.p.*

LAVIERA, TATO. **La Carreta Made a U-Turn** (2nd ed. 1980) and **Enclave** (1981). Poems blending several popular Puerto Rican musical traditions. *P—Arte Público.*

MARTÍNEZ, MAX. **The Adventures of the Chicano Kid and Other Stories** (1983). Satiric and humorous short stories on different aspects of Chicano life. *P—Arte Público.*

Memoirs of Bernardo Vega (1984). Ed. Cesar Andreu Iglesias. Chronicle of the life of Puerto Ricans in New York from the viewpoint of a cigarmaker who migrated to New York in 1916. *H & P—Monthly Rev.*

MOHR, NICHOLASA b. 1935. **Nilda** (1973). Life in Spanish Harlem from 1941 to 1945 from a girl's point of view. Winner of the 1974 Jane Addams Children's Book Award. *o.p.*

————. **El Bronx Remembered** (1975). Collection of short stories about life in the South Bronx during 1945–1956 filled with love, nostalgia, and humor. For grades 7 and up. *H—Har-Row.*

————. **In Nueva York** (1977). Eight short stories about different aspects of living and struggling in New York City. For grades 7 and up. *H—Dial Bks Young.*

————. **Felita** (1979). A family moving away from the South Bronx to a better neighborhood and suffering signs of discrimination. For grades K–6. *H—Dial Bks Young; P—Dell.*

Nuyorican Poets (1975). Eds. Miguel Algarín and Miguel Piñero. Anthology of Puerto Rican poets from New York. *H—Morrow.*

PIETRI, PEDRO b. 1943. **Puerto Rican Obituary** (1973). Poems on misery, pain, and self-degradation of Puerto Ricans in New York. *P—Monthly Rev.*

PIÑERO, MIGUEL b. 1946. **Short Eyes** (1975). Received the 1973–1974 New York Drama Critics Circle Award. Powerful representation of the cruelty and difficulties of survival in prison. *H & P—Hill & Wang.*

PORTILLO DE TRAMBLEY, ESTELA b. 1936. **Rain of Scorpions and Other Writings** (1975). Nine short stories and a short novel about Chicanos torn between assimilation and rejection of their own heritage. About women's liberation and other subjects such as love and description of traditional family. *P—Tonatiuh-Quinto Sol Intl.*

The Puerto Rican Poets (1972). Eds. Alfredo Matilla and Iván Silén. Anthology of Puerto Rican poets from the island and New York. *o.p.*

RECHY, JOHN b. 1934. **City of Night** (1962). Exploration of the struggles of a homosexual from El Paso. *H & P—Grove.*

RIVERA, EDWARD. **Family Installments** (1982). Poignant, funny, charming memories of growing up Hispanic in New York. *H—Morrow; P—Penguin.*

RIVERA, TOMÁS b. 1935. **. . . Y no se lo trago la tierra (and earth did not part)** (1971). Winner of the Quinto Sol Library Prize for 1969–1970. Stories and anecdotes portraying a wide spectrum of situations typical to Chicano farmworkers. *P—Editorial Justa.*

THOMAS, PIRI b. 1928. **Down These Mean Streets** (1967). Bestselling autobiographical account of the author's search for positive identity in a childhood, adolescence, and adulthood seared by drugs and racial discrimination. *H—Knopf; P—Random.*

———. **Savior Hold My Hand** (1972). About the author's experiences in prison and his salvation. *o.p.*

———. **Seven Long Times** (1974). Important criticism, based on experience, of the devastating conditions in penal institutions. *o.p.*

———. **Stories from El Barrio** (1978). Eight vivid stories about Puerto Ricans in New York City for young readers. *P—Avon.*

VILLANUEVA, TINO b. 1941. **Hay Otra Vez Poems** (1972). Focuses on the imposed suffering and forced migration shared by each generation of Chicanos. Humor and irony, in a blend of English and Spanish. *P—Edit Mensaje.*

VILLAREAL, JOSÉ A. **Pocho** (1959). About the sociocultural changes of a Mexican family during the 1920–1940 period. *P—Doubleday.*

Woman of Her Word: Hispanic Women Write (1983). Ed. Evangelina Vigil. Poems, fiction, and essays by well-known Latin writers. *H—Arte Público.*

outer subjects such as love and descriptions of traditional family. —Jennifer Crider 20, 1981.

The Puerto Rican Poets (1972). Eds. Alfredo Matilla and Iván Silén. Anthology of Puerto Rican poets from the island and New York. ...

RIVERA, MARINA. *City of Muter* 1981. Exploration of the identities of a homemaker from a Chicana... —B. F.—Crow.

RIVERA, EDWARD. *Family Installments* (1982). Poignant, many candid memories of growing up Hispanic in New York. —Lindale.

RIVERA, TOMÁS b. 1935 ... *Y no se lo tragó la tierra* (and earth did not part) (1971). Winner of the Quinto Sol Literary Prize for 1969–1971. Stories and sketches portraying a ... of stoicism typical in Chicano manual workers. —Editorial (staff).

THOMAS, PIRI (1928). *Down These Mean Streets* (1967). ... portrait of the author's struggle for identity as a childhood experience... and childhood ... —Kayhan.

—— *Savior Hold My Hand* (1972). About the author's experiences in prison and the narcotic...

—— *Seven Long Times* (1974). Humane sympathy based on the experiences of the dehumanizing conditions in penal institutions.

—— *Stories from El Barrio* (1978). Eight vivid stories about Puerto Ricans in New York City for young readers. —Kayhan.

VILLANUEVA, TINO b. 1941. *Hay Otra Voz Poems* (1972). ... of the impact of suffering on a writer... of English and Spanish. ... and may be enjoyed ...

VILLARREAL, JOSÉ A. *Pocho* (1959). ... the sociocultural changes of a Mexican family during the 1920-1940 period. —Lindale.

Woman in Her Prime ... (1952?). ... spanish. Vigor. Racism, fiction, and peace; he is well-known ... and works. —John Palten.

PART III

Literary Types

CHAPTER 12

The Novel

19th-Century Continental Novels

ARTHUR WALDHORN

More good novels were written in Continental Europe during the 19th century than in any other place or period. It seems doubtful that this was mere happenstance. The arts flourished in peace, and there were no great wars after Napoleon's defeat in 1815. A novelist feeds on his or her time, and Continental Europe in the 19th century served varied and nourishing fare. Ferment in art, science, and politics leavened the age and infused the novel with new ideas and new points of view. For those with intellectual appetite, it was a zestful time to live and to write.

France and Russia showed the greatest activity. Out of the turmoil of French politics a new middle class was arising. Increasingly, careers were open to talent instead of to aristocratic privilege. The greatest French novelists—Balzac, Zola, Stendhal, Flaubert—were bourgeois, and it was the rise of their class that they portrayed with varying degrees of disapproval. Where the French Romantics saw men and women as passionate individuals, nobler or baser than they consistently were, Balzac placed the individual in society, and in his novels the Romantic goals of an abstract liberty or an exalted love change to money and social ambition. His *Comédie Humaine* had the most comprehensive plan any novelist ever made, nothing less than to depict in a series of novels a whole nation, the France of his time, as it actually was. For Zola, actuality was scientific: "Study men like simple elements and note their reactions," he advised. His novels about the Rougon-Macquart families shocked France to the core, although they never quite achieved the scientific objectivity he aimed for (a strong moral disapproval shows through). In his three chief novels Stendhal wrote the same story three times, that of a young man making his way in the world: in *The Red and the Black*, a poor young man in the real France; in *Lucien Leuwen*, a rich young man; but in *The Charterhouse of Parma* (sometimes called the greatest French novel), a young aristocrat fails to gain happiness in an imaginary Italian principality. The actions, operatic and extravagant, are moved by a hard-boiled modern psychology.

With Flaubert's *Madame Bovary*, the novel changed. Although Flaubert was called a realist in his time, it can now be seen that he not only fused the realistic and the Romantic ideas but he moved the novelist out of the book. The characters seem to think and act by themselves. His intense care for structure and the fall of the individual sentence gave novelists everywhere a new sense of the seriousness of their art; thus he is the bridge to Joyce and through him to the 20th century.

In Russia the situation was different. The czars, frightened by the democratic ideas that had spread from revolutionary France, tried to shut them out by suppressing freedom of assembly and imposing a strict censorship. It is possible that most Russian novels, although politically "correct," were a defiant response to these pressures. Tolstoi was a rich nobleman, an army officer, and had none but the artist's obligation to be a novelist at all. Yet in *War and Peace*, *Anna Karenina*, and *Resurrection*, he tries to portray the permanent, essential Russia, regardless of the accidents of politics, and his vision is so profound that he gives us not merely Russians but very human beings. After a term in Siberia as a political offender, Dostoevski was tormented by the problems of Christian belief and the existence of evil. His lifelong aim was to write a huge work called *Life of a Great Sinner*, but he never did. However, his great novels, *The Brothers Karamazov*, *Crime and Punishment*, and *The Possessed*, may be fragments of this work. He owed much to Dickens, but he treats his characters with a psychological penetration that often foreshadows Freud and makes Dickens seem at times naive. Turgenev, like Tolstoi, was rich, but boldly and unsentimentally depicted serfs as human beings in his *Sportsman's Sketches*. In *Fathers and Sons* he examines with great clarity the impact of liberal ideas on two generations of Russians. Isolated though they were, these Russian novelists have a power and intensity that abolished national boundaries.

Other European countries had fewer great novelists, but fine novels were published nevertheless. Manzoni's *The Betrothed* and Verga's *The House by the Medlar Tree* were the best to come out of Italy. The charm of Alarcón's *The Three-Cornered Hat* and Pérez Galdós's *Doña Perfecta* makes one wish that Spain had been more prolific. Among German novels, *Wilhelm Meister*, although not Goethe's greatest work, is still a product of one of the most fertile minds of the age. Novels by Scandinavian, Polish, Hungarian, Belgian, Dutch, and Portuguese authors had merit but made little stir internationally.

In 1800 the novel had been a new thing, scarcely to be ranked with poetry or drama as serious literature. By 1900 the novel was clearly the most popular and most influential of all literary forms.

ALARCÓN, PEDRO ANTONIO DE (Spain) 1833–1891. **The Three-Cornered Hat** (1874). After *Don Quixote*, the most famous of Spanish tales. A clever, witty, and charming account of how a miller's wife fooled an amorous mayor. *o.p.*

BALZAC, HONORÉ DE (France) 1799–1850. **Eugénie Grandet** (1833). One of the greatest of *La Comédie Humaine*, Balzac's series of novels that record French life from the fall of Napoleon to 1848. Grandet, a provincial bourgeois miser, sacrifices his daughter's happiness upon the altar of greed. Powerful realism and sweeping imagination color the portrayal of emotional sterility. *Over 6 eds*.

————. **Old Goriot** (1834). Balzac's version of the King Lear theme, an agonizing, searing, and relentlessly objective tale of an old father's humiliation at the hands of his monstrous daughters. *Over 6 eds*.

————. **Cousin Bette** (1846). "A serious and terrible study of Parisian manners," Balzac called it. Many consider this brutal study of vice, jealousy, and vanity his finest work. Certainly the characterizations—the vindictive Bette, the debauched Hulot, and the dazzling "beast of prey" Valerie—number among his most unforgettable. *P—Penguin*.

CONSTANT, BENJAMIN (France) 1767–1830. **Adolphe** (1815). One of the earliest psychological novels, it draws upon Constant's long and dramatic relationship with Mme. de Staël. *H & P—French & Eur; P—Manchester, Penguin*.

DOSTOEVSKI, FEDOR (Russia) 1821–1881. **Notes from Underground** (1864). A terrifying analysis of psychic alienation and impotence. In many ways the protagonist is the archetypal antihero of 20th-century existential fiction. *P—Bantam, Dutton, NAL, Penguin, U Pr of Amer*.

————. **Crime and Punishment** (1866). A half-starved student with superman aspirations murders two women, then seeks a motive for his crime. On one level a superb detective story; on a deeper level a trenchant analysis of human impulses. *Over 10 eds.*

————. **The Brothers Karamazov** (1880). Dmitri Karamazov and his debauched father vie for the affections of the loose and lusty Grushenka. Smerdyakov, an illegitimate son and an epileptic, murders the father, but Dmitri is tried and convicted on circumstantial evidence. Beyond the intricate plot and compelling characterizations, the novel gains force from its profound investigation of good, evil, and faith. The climactic novel of Dostoevski's career. The Magarshack translation is recommended. *P—Penguin. Over 6 other eds.*

DUMAS, ALEXANDRE (France) 1802–1870. **The Count of Monte Cristo** (1844). An exciting story that dramatizes French history with melodramatic romance and adventure. *H—Dodd, Lightyear; P—Bantam, Regents Pub.*

FLAUBERT, GUSTAVE (France) 1821–1880. **Madame Bovary** (1857). Often called the first modern realistic novel, *Madame Bovary* reveals consummate precision in language, structure, and irony. Emma Bovary seeks vainly in a dull marriage the romance she has read and dreamed of. Disillusioned, she searches for adventure in illicit amours, but again encounters disappointment and monotony. At last, she destroys herself, a victim of her own failure to distinguish appearance from reality. The Steegmuller translation is recommended. *H & P—Modern Lib. Over 10 other eds.*

FRANCE, ANATOLE (France) 1844–1924. **The Crime of Sylvestre Bonard** (1881). Presented against a background of gentle humor, pathos, and urbanity. Bonnard is one of the most lovable characters of French literature. *o.p.*

————. **Penguin Island.** See "The Novel: 20th-Century Continental Novels," page 145.

GAUTIER, THÉOPHILE (France) 1811–1872. **Mademoiselle de Maupin** (1835). A romantic, sensual love story by the fine poet who first preached the gospel of "art for art's sake." *H & P—French & Eur; P—Penguin, R West.*

GOETHE (Germany). See "The 18th Century," page 54.

GOGOL, NIKOLAI (Russia) 1809–1852. **Dead Souls** (1842). Chichikov, the rascally hero, journeys across Russia purchasing the names of dead serfs for their tax value. Beneath the genial, comic surface run twin streams of satire against fraud and compassion for the underprivileged. *H—Norton; P—Airmont, NAL, Penguin.*

————. **The Overcoat** (1842). "We have all come out of Gogol's overcoat," Dostoevski observed, conscious in his jest of Gogol's sure-handed style, pungent social satire, and heartfelt warmth. All appear in this curiously realistic tale that steps over into the realm of fantasy. The Magarshack translation of *The Overcoat and Other Tales of Good and Evil* (which also contains *The Nose*) is recommended. *P—Norton.*

GONCHAROV, IVAN (Russia) 1812–1891. **Oblomov** (1859). Oblomov, a rich landowner, is the laziest man in the world. The account of his getting up in the morning is one of the funniest, most touching passages in fiction. *H—Bentley; P—NAL, Penguin.*

HUGO. **The Hunchback of Notre Dame.** See "The Middle Ages," page 25.

————. **Les Misérables** (1862). Jean Valjean, Javert, and Fantine, three of the most memorable characterizations of the great French romanticist, act out their drama of pathos and poverty in post-Napoleonic France. *Over 6 eds.*

HUYSMANS, JORIS KARL (France) 1848–1907. **Against Nature** (1884). A lavish portrait of a decadent searching for relief from the banality of bourgeois life. The exotic proclivities of the aristocratic Des Esseintes whetted many tastes, not least among them Oscar Wilde's; *The Picture of Dorian Gray* avowedly imitates portions of Huysmans's fascinating tale. *P—Penguin.*

LERMONTOV, MIKAIL (Russia) 1814–1841. **A Hero of Our Time** (1840). Pechorin, the Byronic hero, is adventurous, passionate, egotistic, cynical—the prose heir to Pushkin's poetic *Eugene Onegin* (1831). *P—Doubleday, Penguin.*

MANZONI, ALESSANDRO (Italy) 1785–1873. **The Betrothed** (1826). A splendid historical novel of 17th-century Italy, replete with robber barons, the plague, and eternal love. *P—Biblio Dist, Penguin.*

MAUPASSANT, GUY DE (France) 1850–1893. **Bel-Ami** (1885). A scoundrel makes his way by his good looks. *H & P—French & Eur.*

MÉRIMÉE, PROSPER (France) 1803–1870. **Carmen** (1845). Famous in story, opera, and film, this Gypsy girl enslaves and destroys her lover but makes the experience seem worthwhile. *H—R West; P—Barron, EMC, French & Eur, Larousse.*

NERVAL, GÉRARD DE (France) 1808–1855. **Sylvie** (1853).

An affecting, semiautobiographical narrative of adolescent love recollected in maturity. *H—AMS Pr.*

PÉREZ GALDÓS, BENITO (Spain) 1843–1920. **Doña Perfecta** (1876). The finest of Galdós's several portraits of Spanish life. The scene is provincial, the time before the Carlist war, the treatment at once romantic and realistic. *H—Arden Lib; P—Barron.*

STENDHAL (HENRI BEYLE) (France) 1783–1842. **The Red and the Black** (1830). Julien Sorel, one of the supreme opportunists and hypocrites of literature, turns profitably from "red" (the military life) to "black" (the clerical life) in this sharply drawn study of post-Napoleonic France. Brilliant characterizations, memorable episodes, and an overwhelming irony combine to make one of the great novels of the century. *Over 6 eds.*

————. **The Charterhouse of Parma** (1839). An intricately wrought but colorful and forceful novel of love and politics. *Over 6 eds.*

————. **Lucien Leuwen** (1894). One of the sharpest political novels ever written. Published in America as two novels: **The Green Huntsman** and **The Telegraph.** *H—French & Eur; P—New Directions.*

TOLSTOI, LEO (Russia) 1828–1910. **War and Peace** (1866). One of the supreme novels of all time. Historically, it chronicles on an epic scale Napoleon's invasion of Russia. But its grandeur and sweep derive chiefly from the pulsating force of characterization, the dynamic interplay of ideologies in conflict. Noble and base, wise and foolish, heroic and cowardly— every type finds a place in Tolstoi's all-embracing scheme. *Over 6 unabr. eds.*

————. **Anna Karenina** (1877). An engrossing story of adultery among the Russian nobility. Thomas Mann called it the greatest novel of society in the history of the world. *Over 10 eds.*

————. **The Kreutzer Sonata** (1889). An absorbing problem novel about an unconventional attitude toward marriage. *H—Ayer Co.*

TURGENEV, IVAN (Russia) 1818–1883. **Sportman's Sketches** (1852). A vigorous attack on Russian serfdom, defending the peasant as a man possessed of "a soul of his own." A subtle book despite its propagandistic intent. *P— Penguin.*

————. **Fathers and Sons** (1862). Although Bazarov, the hero, embodies the principles of political nihilism that led to the

October Revolution, he is also a spokesman for youthful rebellion against the authority of the older generation. *Over 10 eds*.

VERGA, GIOVANNI (Italy) 1840–1922. **The House by the Medlar Tree** (1890). A graphic and tragic account of the lives of Sicilian fishermen. *H & P—U of Cal Pr; H—Greenwood*.

ZOLA, ÉMILE (France) 1840–1902. **L'Assommoir** (1877). The terrors of poverty, alcoholism, and debauchery hound Zola's tortured souls into animalized nonexistence. Some rate this novel second only to *Germinal* in its enormous force. *P—French & Eur, Larousse, Penguin*.

————. **Nana** (1880). With stunning if sometimes excessive detail—a characteristic of his naturalistic method—Zola describes the bizarre life of a harlot during the Second Empire. *Over 6 eds*.

————. **Germinal** (1885). Relatively free of the confining limitations of the "scientific method" of naturalism, the novel rages through the agonies of an unsuccessful strike by impoverished French coal miners. Scenes of brutality and bestiality, courage and compassion follow hard upon one another in this relentless but overwhelmingly moving story. The translation of L. W. Tancock is recommended. *P—Penguin*.

20th-Century
Continental Novels

ARTHUR WALDHORN AND ARTHUR ZEIGER

Works of literature form a continuum, and the centuries mark off convenient but artificial fragments. By the middle of the 19th century, realism had been firmly established with Stendhal and Flaubert, and soon Zola developed naturalism, a deterministic and characteristically pessimistic variation (or aberration, as some critics insist). Symbolism, inevitable in any fictional construct, became linked to a new theory and attained a new density in Huysmans and the decadents. Dostoevski's novels, integrated by a searing psychological vision, anticipated the findings of psychoanalysts by a half century and sometimes (as in *Notes from Underground*) of the existentialists as well. Hardly a genre, mode, or technique (hallucinatory images, stream of consciousness, expressionistic distortion, surrealistic fantasy, subverted narrative) that courses through the 20th-century novel has not its spring in the century—really, centuries—preceding.

And yet the shape of the modern novel, its total configuration, must impress us as very different. The multiple shocks our time has suffered—monstrous wars, genocide, cataclysmic redistribution of lands and peoples—have shattered traditional values and overthrown venerated authorities. The writer, deeply responding to these dislocations, has been driven to an intensified and heightened isolation. Without a compelling perception of wholeness, or even worth, of the sort that Balzac or Tolstoi had inherited, he or she cannot project images of coherence and symmetry. Characteristically, then, writers see their world as a landscape of despair, fragmented, torn by force.

The consequences for the modern novel are momentous. The

novelistic perspectives of the 19th century have been violently wrenched. The writers of our time introduce nightmare variations upon familiar themes, anathematize traditional certainties, like Céline. Or they escape the burden of reality through a mystic descent, like Hesse. Or they precisely and dispassionately annotate the phenomena of consciousness, like Robbe-Grillet. Or they devise a humanistic but contingent morality as a surrogate for a once-confident faith, like Camus. Or they arrange a counterpoint of pain and fantasy in evoking the past to evade its impact, like Grass. Or they attempt to evade authoritarian suppression by retreating to other, imaginary worlds, like Bulgakov and Lem.

These are schematic comments, however; novels may not be subsumed by catalogs of characteristics. For each of the writers cited, it would not be impossible to adduce, without much qualification, a 19th-century analogue. Despite a variety of differences, for example, Grass surely has affinities to Gogol. And Silone and Malraux, no less than Mauriac and Undset, are actuated by traditional principles of morality—though the traditions are of course diverse. Moreover, the novelists generally acknowledged to be the most significant of our century elude generalization. Proust, whose complex interweaving of themes is esentially modern, nevertheless presents a fictional world as solid as that created by any of his 19th-century forebears—distorted certainly, but compelling belief. And Mann, whose vast mythic journeys to discover the sources of our pervasive spiritual illness are still avant garde, is yet allied to Goethe and Schiller among other great ancestors. In every novelistic development in the 20th century, the "new" has been conditioned by the "old," the beginning is implicit in every progression.

BECKETT, SAMUEL (Ireland, now France) b. 1906. **Murphy** (1938). A comedy of failure: No individual escape into the recesses of self is possible for Murphy because the big booming confusion of the macrocosm (his friends, disciples, and beloved) keeps breaking through. *H & P—Grove; P—French & Eur*.

———. **Three Novels: Molloy; Malone Dies; The Unnamable** (1951–53). A trilogy (1959) of sorts: its element, despair; its matter, the absurdity of human existence; its manner, wit, and farce. *P—Grove*.

BÖLL, HEINRICH (Germany) 1917–1985. **Billiards at Half Past Nine** (1959). How three generations of a family of architects lived before, during, and after two world wars—

between 1880 and 1958. Böll characterizes better than he plots, affords a many-faceted experience. *H—Peter Smith; P—Avon, McGraw*.

BROCH, HERMANN (Austria) 1886–1951. **The Sleepwalkers** (1932). A trilogy of modern dissolution; set in Germany, 1888 to 1918, this masterly novel surveys the disparate lives of three men (romantic, anarchist, and realist) to achieve a kind of synthesis. *H—Octagon*.

BULGAKOV, MIKHAIL (Russia) 1891–1940. **The Master and Margarita** (1967). An "ironic parable of power," a fantasy centering on the devil's doings in Moscow and an exuberant entertainment. *P—Grove*.

CALVINO, ITALO (Italy) 1923–1985. **If on a Winter's Night a Traveler** (1981). Bewildered but enchanted, the reader tags along through the partial plots of ten novels, each abandoned at the moment of highest suspense. A playfully serious fantasist, Calvino wittily teases the simplistic expectations of readers, parodies popular narrative styles, and cudgels the excesses of literary criticism. *H—HarBraceJ*.

CAMUS, ALBERT (France) 1913–1960. **The Stranger** (1946). A compelling story of the absurdity of life when man's aspirations and values have no cosmic status. *H—Knopf; P—Random*.

———. **The Plague** (1948). Bubonic plague in Oran forces choices of action: bewildered faith, passivity, flight, suicide, helping others. Symbolically, the story of the Nazi occupation and of people's responses to any sort of human plague. *H—Knopf; P—Random*.

ČAPEK, KAREL (Czechoslovakia) 1890–1938. **War with the Newts** (1937). The Newts take over: science fiction, excellent as humor, social commentary, and story. *H—AMS Pr*.

CÉLINE, LOUIS FERDINAND (DESTOUCHES) (France) 1894–1961. **Journey to the End of the Night** (1932). The colloquially and semiautobiographically reported adventures and misadventures of Bardamu, first in World War I, then in America and Africa, and at last as an embittered doctor. Though gusty and vigorous, the novel is heavy with loathing for humanity and a pervasive sense of life's emptiness. *H & P—New Directions*.

———. **Death on the Installment Plan** (1936). Boyhood and adolescence in all their agony, comedy, and tenderness, but with a large measure of paranoia added for bad measure. *P—New Directions*.

COLETTE, SIDONIE GABRIELLE (France) 1873–1954. **Gigi,**

Julie de Carneilhan, and Chance Acquaintances (1976). *H & P—FS&G*.

————. **Chéri and the Last of Chéri** (1976). These and other novellas like *Claudine at School* and *Claudine in Paris* are the best introduction to a writer whose stylistic elegance no less than her subtle, precise, often malicious perception of life is an unfailing delight. *H—FS&G; P—Ballantine*.

DÜRRENMATT, FRIEDRICH (Switzerland) b. 1921. **The Pledge** (1959). Thought-arousing *recit*, sparsely written, of a police force captain whose logic is defeated by reality. *o.p.*

ECO, UMBERTO (Italy) b. 1932. **The Name of the Rose** (1983). Murder and mystery in a medieval monastery!—the case solved gratifyingly and learnedly by an English schoolman with an assist from Aristotle. *P—Warner Bks*.

FRANCE, ANATOLE (France) 1844–1924. **Penguin Island** (1908). Deceits, tricks, pathetic follies of the rich, poor, haters, lovers, predators, idealists when, as penguins become humans, they repeatedly make and break "civilizations." *H—Am Repr-Rivercity Pr; P—Leetes Isl*.

FRISCH, MAX (Switzerland) b. 1911. **Man in the Holocene** (1980). Alpine floods isolate an old man in a Swiss valley. To pass time, he cuts passages from the Bible, guidebooks, and encyclopedias (reprinted, incidentally, in their diverse typefaces). In this strange and disconcerting parable, each clipping suggests not only the old man's fears but also those of humanity: loneliness, aging, dying, and, above all, the apocalyptic end of our age—the Holocene—whether by flood, avalanche, or atomic holocaust. *H & P—HarBraceJ*.

GENÉT, JEAN (France) b. 1910. **Our Lady of the Flowers** (1942). The first novel by the notorious thief and literary man, a flamboyant but powerful narrative—idyllic, brutal, comic, and absurd—of love and death among Parisian pimps and male whores. *P—Grove*.

GIDE, ANDRÉ (France) 1869–1951. **The Immoralist** (1902). A masterfully patterned short novel tracing the career of the Immoralist from conformity to hedonism, leaving him poignantly aware of the nature and implications of his sexuality. *H—Modern Lib; P—Random*.

————. **The Counterfeiters** (1927). Technically, a virtuoso performance: a novel within a novel; multiple points of view and diverse accents. Thematically, a study of how we "counterfeit" our actual identity, deceiving ourselves as well as others. *P—Random*.

GRASS, GÜNTER (Germany) b. 1927. **The Tin Drum** (1959), **Cat and Mouse** (1961), and **Dog Years** (1963) are Rabelaisian diagnoses and prescriptions for the sick conscience of modern Germany—and by extension of the modern world. Difficult black humor as full of dirt and drollery as *Gulliver's Travels*. The author is Germany's most acclaimed writer since Thomas Mann. First title: *H & P—Random*. Second title: *P—NAL*. Third title: *P—Fawcett*.

HAMSUN, KNUT (Norway) 1859–1952. **Growth of the Soil** (1920). An unsophisticated farmer, Isak resists the temptations and corruptions of society to achieve a kind of serenity on his Norwegian farm. *H—Knopf; P—Random*.

HANDKE, PETER (Germany) b. 1942. **The Goalie's Anxiety at the Penalty Kick** (1972) *o.p.*, and **Short Letter, Long Farewell** (1974). Two short novels by the most important new talent to emerge in Germany in the past dozen years. Distinct in subject—the one a thriller that is also a psychological and philosophical study, the other a *bildungsroman* that is also a fantasy and a "scale model of America." Both are complex, intense, intriguing. *H—FS&G*.

HAŠEK, JAROSLAV (Czechoslovakia) 1883–1923. **The Good Soldier Schweik** (1923). With peasant guile, Schweik outwits and outlives both ally and enemy. Devoid of honor or morality, he epitomizes—with grim good humor—the brutal emptiness of war. *P—NAL*.

HESSE, HERMANN (Germany) 1877–1962. **Steppenwolf** (1929). An introspective, psychoanalytically oriented novel that probes the dilemma of the intellectual divorced from society and terrified of isolation. Harry Haller, the autobiographical hero, confronts the "steppenwolf" (animal) of his inward self in one of the most remarkable scenes in modern fiction. *H & P—HR&W; P—Bantam*.

KAFKA, FRANZ (Czechoslovakia) 1883–1924. **The Castle** (1926). At the same time a parable and a nightmare, the novel records the futile attempt of a surveyor to communicate with the Castle (to attain grace?), suggesting the essential nature of the metaphysical problem but not of its solution. *H—Knopf; P—Modern Lib, Random, Schocken*.

————. **The Trial** (1937). In this our life, Joseph K. is up for trial. But for what? He is never really tried by the High Court. Yet, finally, he is taken to a quarry and stabbed in the heart. Is this a neurotic man's anxiety dream—or a revelation for Everyman? *H—Knopf; P—Random, Schocken*.

KAPEK. See Čapek, page 144.

KAZANTZAKIS, NIKOS (Greece) 1885–1957. **Zorba the Greek** (1952). Zorba is fuller of the joy of life than continents of today's "hollow men." He obeys the law of his own being, which, like that of his prototype Ulysses, is compounded of cunning, fellowship, and picaresque heroism. *P—S&S*.

KOESTLER, ARTHUR (Hungary, England) 1905–1983. **Darkness at Noon** (1941). Penetrating, memorable dramatization of the ideological and psychological forces in a Communist purge trial. *H—Macmillan; P—Bantam*.

KUNDERA, MILAN (Czechoslovakia, now France) b. 1929. **The Unbearable Lightness of Being** (1984). In his earlier, more loosely knit *The Book of Laughter and Forgetting* (1980), Kundera posed insouciantly unanswerable questions: Why not laugh or forget when life becomes intolerable? In his more recent novel, a fractured narrative, he tells of four Czechs whose lives are variously affected by their political and sexual behavior. Ironic, comedic, and paradoxical. *H—Har-Row*.

LEM, STANISLAW (Poland) b. 1921. **Return from the Stars** (1961). A futurist novel by a polymath who is also a superlative storyteller, "the Borges of science fiction." An astronaut returns to a world, dislocated from him because of a time warp, in which he struggles to emerge from isolation and incomprehension to a kind of tolerable peace. *P—Avon*.

LEVI, CARLO (Italy) 1902–1975. **Christ Stopped at Eboli** (1945). A moving autobiographical novel about a genteel, sophisticated northern Italian discovering the agony and humanity of southern villagers under Fascist dominion. *P—FS&G*.

MALRAUX, ANDRÉ (France) 1901–1976. **Man's Fate** (1933). Individuals—Communists and non-Communists—together yet solitary, brave yet absurd, commit themselves to danger and death in the attempt to control Shanghai during the Chinese civil war (1927). Not history but existentialist vision; not man's fate but Malraux's fate for man. Malraux's heroes set the pattern for "picaresque saints." *P—Modern Lib, Random*.

MANN, THOMAS (Germany) 1875–1955. **Buddenbrooks** (1901). The ineluctable decline from wealth and honor to mean-spirited poverty and extinction of a too-complacent mercantile family. Interesting for its delineation of social changes; of temperaments, motives, marriages, and measures among the Buddenbrooks and their connections. *H—Knopf; P—Random*.

———. **The Magic Mountain** (1924). One of the most profound and provocative novels of our time, picturing a mountaintop sanitarium as a symbol of humanity in a pathological universe. *H—Knopf; P—Random.*

————. **The Joseph Tetralogy** (1924–44). A vivid, highly suggestive recreation of ancient Egypt and the biblical saga of Joseph. *H—Knopf.*

MAURIAC, FRANCOIS (France) 1885–1970. **Thérèse** (1927). A guilt-ridden woman remains inwardly tormented despite acquittal of trying to poison her husband. As in most of Mauriac's taut, absorbing fiction, characters try vainly to comprehend what can be known only to God. *P—FS&G.*

MILOSZ, CZESLAW (Poland, now United States) b. 1911. **The Issa Valley** (1955, 1981). An early autobiographical novel by the Nobel Prize poet and essayist. Old-fashioned and idyllic, the novel tenderly evokes a growing boy's love for the grandparents who raise him and for the natural beauty of the gentle Lithuanian valley countryside. *H & P—FS&G.*

MORAVIA, ALBERTO (Italy) b. 1907. **Two Adolescents** (1950). Agostino and Luca suffer the torments of social, familial, and sexual pressure in these two sensitively perceived novellas of youth. *H—Greenwood; P—Berkley Pub.*

————. **The Time of Indifference** (1953). That "indifference" itself is a kind of action is realized as the shocked reader watches the Marengos—mother, daughter, and son—maneuvered into sexual and moral ruin by an amoral businessman. Neorealistic satire without a smile. *P—Berkley Pub.*

MUSIL, ROBERT (Austria) 1880–1942. **The Man Without Qualities** (3 vols. 1931–43). Unfinished but heroic novel; set in pre-World War I Austria, it investigates the collapse of an empire and the disintegration of an individual consciousness. Witty, learned, passionate, ironic, it is a great, complex, and difficult work. *o.p.*

PASTERNAK, BORIS (Russia) 1890–1960. **Dr. Zhivago** (1958). Yuri Zhivago, orphaned at ten, later an upper-class doctor, poet, husband, lover, philosopher, struggles successfully, despite upheavals and regimentation in his beloved Russia, to preserve his humanity and spiritual independence. *H—Pantheon, U of Mich Pr; P—Ballantine.*

PAVESE, CESARE (Italy) 1908–1950. **The Moon and the Bonfire** (1950). His last, most autobiographical, and most mature novel. About the narrator's tragic quest in a Piedmontese village for the truth about his past and possibilities for the future. *H—Greenwood.*

PROUST, MARCEL (France) 1871–1922. **Remembrance of**

Things Past (1913–28). In recovering his past through the dedicated exercise of memory, Proust lays bare in a series of seven novels—from *Swann's Way* (the best known) to *Time Regained*—a growing self, a changing age, a many-stranded philosophy. To read Proust, slowly, is to experience, in entertaining and enlightening fashion, his special world. *H—Random 3 vols.*

REMARQUE, ERICH MARIA (Germany) 1897–1970. **All Quiet on the Western Front** (1929). Perhaps the best-known World War I novel; blends images of war's bestiality with scenes of the battle-born brotherhood of men. *H—Little; P—Fawcett.*

ROBBE-GRILLET, ALAIN (France) b. 1922. **The Voyeur** (1958). An exceptionally readable example of the French "new novel." Enveloped by ambiguity and charged with suspense, it records, with sometimes painful detail and unvarying objectivity, the surface consciousness of a man who may be a traveling salesman of watches or a monstrous criminal. *P—Grove.*

ROMAINS, JULES (France) 1885–1972. **The Death of a Nobody** (1911). A poignant, haunting account of the impact an unimportant man's death has upon the lodgers in his boardinghouse. *H—Fertig.*

————. **Men of Good Will** (1932–47). A 27-volume *roman fleuve* embracing the feverish years 1908 to 1933, commingling real characters (Lenin, Poincaré, the Kaiser) and imaginary ones; admirable for its epic scope and memorable tableaux (e.g., the battle of Verdun). Often talky and naive but a valuable document of misguided optimism. *o.p.*

SARRAUTE, NATHALIE (France) b. 1902. **The Golden Fruits** (1964). A sparkling brief satire on the vanities of literary critics and on how solid-seeming fictions dissolve into "process" when examined by many or when reexamined by one. *H & P—Riverrun NY.*

SARTRE, JEAN-PAUL (France) 1905–1980. **Nausea** (1938). Antoine Roquentin, the antihero protagonist, records in his diary the dizzying elements of his existential vertigo: time, things, bourgeois bad faith, others, and himself. A disturbing but bracing portrait of Sartre's wasteland. *H—Bentley; P—New Directions.*

SCHMIDT, ARNO (Germany) 1914–1970. **The Egghead Republic** (1956). A relatively accessible short novel by an important (and underread) modernist, who has been compared not unjustly to Joyce and Beckett: a virtuoso performance, erotic, ingenious, funny. Set in the darkly divided America of A.D. 2008–2009. *H & P—M Boyars*.

SHOLOKHOV, MIKHAIL (Russia) 1905–1984. **The Silent Don** (1934–41). Includes two novels of epic scope—**And Quiet Flows the Don** and **The Don Flows Home to the Sea**—about Russian life from late czarist days through World War I and the Revolution. *P—Random*.

SILONE, IGNAZIO (Italy) 1900–1978. **Bread and Wine** (1936). The hero, Pietro Spina, an independent Communist, is primarily a humanitarian who risks all to rally the exploited away from Mussolini. A novel that has everything: great story, memorable characterizations, humor and pathos—major implications for church, society, and the individual. *P—NAL*.

ŠKVORECKÝ, JOSEF (Czechoslovakia, now Canada) b. 1924. **The Engineer of Human Souls** (1977, 1984). A harshly comic "entertainment" that shifts through cinematic dissolves between the dark absurdities of Communist Czechoslovakia and the bright ones of an émigré community in Toronto. Like the author, the hero teaches literature at a democratic campus whose students are free "not to read, not to suffer, not to desire, not to know, not to understand." *H—Knopf*.

SOLZHENITSYN, ALEXANDER (Russia, now United States) b. 1918. **Cancer Ward** (1958). Last of three novels based partly upon the author's experiences under Stalin. **One Day in the Life of Ivan Denisovitch** (1962), a short novel, describes the suffering and injustice in a Russian labor camp. **The First Circle** (1964, 1968) delineates the terrorizing of free-minded scientists, writers, and other intelligentsia. In the final work, Solzhenitsyn draws from his own bout with cancer to dramatize life in a prison hospital. The novels are more journalistic than literary, but all are undeniably powerful. First title: *H—Modern Lib; P—Bantam, Dell*. Second title: *P—Bantam, NAL*. Third title: *P—Bantam*.

WERFEL, FRANZ (Austria) 1890–1945. **The Forty Days of Musa Dagh** (1934). Saga of seven Armenian villages resisting the Turks in 1915. *H—Amereon Ltd; P—Carroll & Graf*.

ZAMYATIN, YEVGENY (Russia) 1884–1937. **We** (1924). Orwell acknowledged his debt to this satiric fantasy of a metronomic metropolis where dreaming is a disease and an individual is always "we," never "I." *P—Avon*.

19th-Century British Novels

JOAN SCHULZ

With thousands of new novels published each year in the United States alone, with many of them addressed to concerns central to our lives today, and with hundreds of them available in the corner drugstore, why should anyone read a 19th-century novel?

Why indeed? To begin with, the great novels of Victoria's England not only give us a powerful feeling for the social texture of the period but also convey the sense of self that prevailed at the time. Second, the best of the Victorian novelists grapple with the questions of how people do live and how they should live their lives. Moreover, since the sources of a modern perspective surface in a muted—even at times ringing—form throughout 19th-century fiction, we can find the roots of our own psychological and moral problems there.

For students of literature, the form of the Victorian novel offers an intermingling of the traditional novel and disruptions of that tradition, disruptions that have flowered into new forms in the 20th century. For all readers, the great Victorians tell good stories, which is important because a novel ought to satisfy that primitive urge to hear an engrossing tale.

Start reading anywhere. Start with Sir Walter Scott and what he called his "Big bow-wow stuff"—those marvelously broad and spacious canvases that nevertheless seem crowded with vivid characters and intriguing events with all the stir and bustle of life, or spend some time with his Scottish novels, which seem to achieve an added dimension from his strong historical sense. Scott's novels are exciting also because he had the storyteller's awareness of the great scene and how to use it. So did Meredith, and so did Jane Austen, working on what she called her "little pieces of ivory . . . two inches wide," on which she created witty, perceptive satires out of the material of everyday life in a world where a clumsily handled teacup and the response it brought might reveal more about the persons involved than would a major crisis in their lives.

Or dip into Trollope, who, like Austen, possessed of a gift for sharp observation of human behavior, could turn the unremarkable into delightful stories, stories characteristically colored with either pathos or good-natured irony and not infrequently directed at the Establishment. While Trollope is the great armchair raconteur, Hardy is a storyteller out of the primitive oral tradition, able to combine an ancient tradition with a modern outlook derived from Darwin and the assumptions of empiricism. Hardy has the power to draw elemental figures who strive for human dignity in spite of the relentlessness and inevitability of their suffering.

Or try one of the most inventive and exciting storytellers of them all, Charles Dickens, who creates a world so lively and peoples it with characters so eccentric, exaggerated, or extravagant that we don't care how clumsy and overloaded his plots are. Generally speaking, with the exception of Jane Austen, whose novels are technically sophisticated, 19th-century novelists, great storytellers though they were, had creaky plots. So for a well-plotted novel, turn to Wilkie Collins, whose *The Moonstone* and *The Woman in White* are still among the best mystery and detective fictions ever written.

For stories in which the sensational and melodramatic have real significance, one must go either to Hardy or to the Brontë sisters, who brought poetry and passion to their brilliant novels. *Jane Eyre* convinces us that the sensational can exist within the commonplace and reveals an ability to move through realism to the highest romance; *Wuthering Heights*, which G. K. Chesterton said "might have been written by an eagle," recounts a story of fierce and transcendent human passions in conflict with the ordinary social world.

The Brontës were among the few 19th-century English novelists who explored in depth the private self and private emotions. Mainly the Victorian novel concerned itself with the problems of the human being in her or his relation to society, and many leveled powerful criticisms at that society. Among them are some of the novels of Dickens, whose pictures of social evil and inequity are as moving as his solution is puerile. Never merely a social reformer, Dickens was as much dedicated to symbolic attacks on oppressive institutions as to real attacks on existing ones. And there is Thackeray, who, though no social reformer, levels a satiric gaze on his society and uncovers in a vast panorama the snobbishness and hypocrisy of bourgeois society. Thackeray's achievement lies in the enormous variety of circumstances, in the succession of brilliant scenes, in the sharply drawn and contrasted characters, and in the incisiveness of his picture of human beings as social creatures.

If we then turn to George Eliot, who, herself a rebel against conventions, changed the course of the English novel chiefly by deepening it morally and making it a more serious work of art, we are in a different but no less exciting world. Eliot's world is dominated by intense moral concerns and inhabited by a large, diverse collection of characters given perceptive psychological and social analysis by their creator.

What, in sum, keeps the 19th-century novel alive? Certainly the enormous inventiveness of the Victorians as spinners of intriguing stories and as creators of memorable characters is partly responsible, as are the great liveliness and diversity of them. These novels are often fast-moving, seldom plodding; they are Gladstone bags stuffed with interesting things for our inspection. There is sharp satire and keen criticism, pure comedy and pathos and tragedy. Some are distinguished by high intensity in a narrow scope, others by a leisurely pace and panoramic views of human beings in society: The range is broad, the moods various.

AUSTEN, JANE 1775–1817. **Sense and Sensibility** (1811). In deft strokes of brilliant and sometimes brutal irony, this antisentimental but sympathetic domestic comedy traces the fortunes of two very dissimilar sisters—one a figure of subtle intelligence and good sense, the other a victim of romantic sentimentality. *Over 10 eds*.

————. **Pride and Prejudice** (1813). A sparkling comedy of manners, intense in vision, perfect in form; the hero's haughty pride of class is opposed by the heroine's understandable prejudice. *Over 20 eds*.

————. **Mansfield Park** (1814). To some, the protagonist, Fanny Price, is priggish and insipid; to others, she is touching and astute. For both, there is great delight in the marvelous portraits of the pompous, the vapid, and the selfish as seen through Fanny's perceptive gaze. *Over 6 eds*.

————. **Emma** (1816). An almost faultlessly structured novel in which a subtle irony is directed at the engaging and intelligent but too certain heroine for her misguided meddling in the love affairs of others and for her failures in self-knowledge. *Over 10 eds.*

BRONTË, CHARLOTTE 1816–1855. **Jane Eyre** (1847). A piercing and radical social analysis of what it meant to be female, poor, intelligent, and sexually passionate in mid-Victorian England. Early celebrated as a love story between Jane and the "Byronic" Rochester, it is, more significantly, a virtually unprecedented novel of a woman's quest for selfhood. *Over 20 eds.*

————. **Villette** (1853). More relentless than *Jane Eyre* in its account of a young woman, who, appearing colorless and uncommunicative to others, without beauty or family, and therefore without "prospects," nevertheless powerfully engages reader interest. Unwilling to be either "influence" or nurturer and strengthened by determination and clarity of vision, Lucy Snowe strives for her two most precious objectives—freedom and renewal. *H—Oxford U Pr; P—Biblio Dist, Penguin.*

BRONTË, EMILY 1818–1848. **Wuthering Heights** (1847). The action of this extraordinarily intense novel, conceived at the highest imaginative level, centers around the fiercely passionate relationship between Catherine and Heathcliff, figures of elemental force and towering strength. *Over 20 eds.*

BUTLER, SAMUEL 1835–1902. **Erewhon** (1872). A still-elevant and incisive satire upon sham in education, religion, social custom, and ethics. *H—Biblio Dist; P—Airmont, Penguin.*

————. **The Way of All Flesh** (1903). At once Victorian and modern, this semi-autobiographical novel is one of the earliest studies of a young man's alienation and search for identity. The novel is also savage in its attack on the hypocrisy and horror of the Victorian family and of Victorian Christianity. *Over 6 eds.*

CARROLL, LEWIS (CHARLES L. DODGSON) 1832–1898. **Alice in Wonderland** (1865). Ostensibly a children's story, this wildly fantastic and uproarious tale of Alice's adventures may be read as a terrifying journey into the subconscious mind. *Over 30 eds.*

COLLINS, WILKIE 1824–1889. **The Moonstone** (1868). The first full-scale detective story—an involved, action-filled mystery concerning the theft of a precious jewel. *Over 6 eds.*

CONRAD. See "The Novel: 20th-Century British Novels," page 163.

DICKENS, CHARLES 1812–1870. **Oliver Twist** (1838). The violence and terror of the 19th-century London underworld among the outcasts of society are powerfully depicted in a story of crime and punishment. *Over 10 eds.*

————. **David Copperfield** (1850). Dickens's favorite, perhaps because it reflects his own youth, this novel, in which reside some of the most fascinating characters Dickens ever invented, is essentially a long retrospective look into David's memory. *Over 10 eds.*

————. **Bleak House** (1853). On one level, an artfully contrived detective story employing melodramatic effects; on another level, Dickens's most mature criticism of the whole social fabric of Victorian society, in which the failure of caring and responsibility takes its enormous toll in human lives and well-being. *Over 6 eds.*

————. **Hard Times** (1854). Dickens's most straightforwardly serious response to contemporary civilization, this short novel shows the world of rational hardheadedness and calculated self-interest in all its absurdity and in all its potential for destructiveness. *Over 6 eds.*

————. **A Tale of Two Cities.** See "The 18th-Century," page 58.

————. **Great Expectations** (1861). Employing all the appurtenances of melodrama, Dickens manages to create a profoundly moving novel of symbolic import based on the rise, fall, and rise again of a humbly born young male orphan. *Over 10 eds.*

EDGEWORTH, MARIA 1767–1849. **Castle Rackrent** (1800). Told with verve and vivacity, this short novel shows the decline and fall of an aristocratic Irish family through three generations of riotous and unreformed living habits. *H—Biblio Dist, Garland Pub; P—Norton, Oxford U Pr.*

ELIOT, GEORGE (MARY ANN EVANS) 1819–1880. **Adam Bede** (1859). The charm of the English countryside pervades this simple story of four young people: the uncorruptible workman, Adam Bede; the rich, pleasure-seeking squire; the romantic young woman desired by both; and the Methodist preacher, Dinah Morris, whose healing influence is felt by all. *Over 6 eds.*

————. **The Mill on the Floss** (1860). Among the first to trace a young woman's development, Eliot creates a heroine, Maggie Tulliver, with aspirations beyond her station and gender. Thwarted, she ultimately expiates her "sins" through massive renunciation—of lover, friend, family, home—and dies trying to save the brother whose love and respect she could not achieve. *Over 6 eds*.

————. **Middlemarch** (1872). A comprehensive and penetrating analysis of early Victorian provincial life, employing a multiple plot integrated by the character of Dorothea Brooke, whose splendid aspirations are initially defeated by her failure in self-knowledge and by her ignorance of the limits set by her society on female behavior and ideal achievement. *Over 6 eds*.

GASKELL, ELIZABETH 1810–1865. **Mary Barton** (1848). One of the best of the 19th century's "protest novels," which extensively and realistically explore social problems, this novel examines in compelling detail the miserable living conditions of the poor and the hostile relations between masters and workers and recounts the life of a poor young woman caught in the dilemmas of being female in 19th-century England. *H & P—Biblio Dist; P—Norton, Penguin*.

GISSING, GEORGE 1857–1903. **The Odd Women** (1893). The "odd women" are those who, by choice or necessity, do not conform in their lives or temperaments to the Victorian conception of the role of women. In a moving and probing story of trouble and hardship, some of these women run risks, and a few remain true to their perceptions of themselves and of their claim to equality. *H—AMS Pr, R West; P—NAL, Norton*.

HARDY, THOMAS 1840–1928. **Far from the Madding Crowd** (1874). Hardy depicts a society of rural people who must compromise their ideals and consume much of their vital energy before attaining some degree of contentment. *Over 6 eds*.

————. **The Return of the Native** (1878). A story of joy, sorrow, and defeat set against the somber background of Egdon Heath in which characters attempt to create their lives. *Over 10 eds*.

————. **The Mayor of Casterbridge** (1886). A drunken man sells his wife and child to a stranger: Such is the extraordinary opening scene in this nearly classical tragedy, which tells the story of a man of heroic ambition who achieves great success and then is thwarted and finally destroyed by the extremes and immoderation of his own character. *Over 10 eds*.

————. **Tess of the d'Urbervilles** (1891). The poignant tragedy of a young girl who grows into womanhood dogged by unhappiness and misfortune—beginning with seduction and ending with murder. Though she is only remotely responsible for her anguished life, she achieves heroic quality by reaching out to claim responsibility for that life. *Over 10 eds*.

————. **Jude the Obscure** (1896). A shocking and powerful drama of a man and woman whose quests for intellectual fulfillment and emotional freedom are frustrated at every turn by past values, contemporary society, and their own limitations. *Over 6 eds.*

JAMES. See "The Novel: 19th-Century American Novels," page 175.

KINGSLEY, CHARLES 1819–1875. **Westward Ho!** (1855). Bitterly anti-Jesuit, but an exciting historical romance of the time when Queen Elizabeth knighted sea captains for piracy against the Spaniards. *P—Airmont.*

MEREDITH, GEORGE 1829–1909. **The Ordeal of Richard Feverel** (1859). The moving story of a young man "scientifically" educated by his misogynistic and dogmatic father and the disastrous effects of that education, on both young love and wholeness of being. *P—Dover.*

————. **The Egoist** (1879). High comedy in the prolix and convoluted Meredith manner. The story of a man whose solipsistic sense of self-importance is finally shattered by the women whom his aggressive selfishness has exploited, with consequences that arouse our delight and then, unexpectedly, some pity. *H—Oxford U Pr; H & P—Norton; P—Penguin.*

MOORE, GEORGE 1852–1933. **Esther Waters** (1894). This novel, which introduced French naturalism into England, is a sympathetic portrayal of lower-class life in the story of a servant whose brief enjoyment of life is overshadowed by overwhelming misfortune. *H—Liveright; H & P—Biblio Dist; P—Oxford U Pr.*

READE. **The Cloister and the Hearth.** See "The Middle Ages," page 26.

SCOTT, SIR WALTER 1771–1832. For his enduringly popular historical novels dealing with the Middle Ages, the Renaissance, and the 17th century, see pages 26, 40, and 49.

SHELLEY, MARY WOLLSTONECRAFT 1797–1851. **Frankenstein** (1818). Among the most famous of the Gothic romances and a precursor of science fiction, this highly charged drama of terror is also a horror-ridden birth myth. A scientist learns the secret of breathing life into the gigantic human figure he has fashioned and then suffers the horrific consequences of abandoning and betraying it. *Over 10 eds.*

STEVENSON, ROBERT LOUIS 1850–1894. **Dr. Jekyll and Mr. Hyde** (1886). Pre-Freudian prototypical novel of the divided self. An absorbing story in which fantasy and romantic adventure are used to explore the irrational forces of evil to be found in the depths of even the most rational and humane scientist. *Over 10 eds*.

————. **The Master of Ballantrae** (1889). Stevenson's best—a novel of character with a fast-moving and complicated plot of the successes and failures of two aristocratic Scottish brothers whose bitter hatred for each other reaches a ghastly climax in the wilderness of America. *H & P—Biblio Dist; P—Airmont, Oxford U Pr*.

THACKERAY, WILLIAM MAKEPEACE 1811–1863. **Vanity Fair** (1847–48). A sometimes merry, nearly always biting satire, complete with large and lively comic scenes, and two nonheroines—one an extremely clever, engaging, but hardheaded plotter, the other a virtuous, sweet, but conventional and pallid young woman. Their alternating, interrelated fortunes are the basis for a searching judgment on society. *Over 6 eds*.

TROLLOPE, ANTHONY 1815–1882. **The Warden** (1855). A delightfully muddleheaded and generous old clergyman and those under his care are made miserable by a well-intentioned young reformer who raises a delicate ethical question. *o.p.*

————. **Barchester Towers** (1857). A leisurely paced and gently satiric story about the petty gossip and sometimes involved intrigues of a small mid-19th-century English cathedral town is made especially attractive by the memorable characters created by Trollope. *o.p.*

WILDE, OSCAR 1854–1900. **The Picture of Dorian Gray** (1891). The protagonist, who, narcissus-like, falls in love with his own portrait, is granted his demonic wish to remain young while the picture ages. He pursues a hedonistic life that ends in horror. *Over 10 eds*.

20th-Century British Novels

ARTHUR ZEIGER

In the decade preceding World War I some very impressive British novels were written: John Galsworthy's *The Man of Property* (1906), the first volume of *The Forsyte Saga;* Arnold Bennett's *The Old Wives' Tale* (1908): and H. G. Wells's *Tono-Bungay* (1909). Produced by perceptive novelists who respected truth and their craft, these are serious and substantial works.

Yet the younger novelists found them unsatisfying. Galsworthy had conceived his Philistine saga ironically, but in execution the iron melted. The author became the novelist member of the Forsyte family, esteeming them, and their solid possessions, almost as much as they did. Sentiment blurred his vision, and the Forsytes seem never wholly in focus.

Bennett built compacter, perhaps more durable, structures. In his best, most deeply felt novel, he placed two sisters against a drab industrial background—Bursley, one of the "five towns" of Staffordshire. He pictured their unlovely, joyless lives in immense and accurate detail, so that one knows all *about* them but never quite *knows* them, never feels their life as they felt it. Like other naturalistic novels, *The Old Wives' Tale* impresses by its massed data, not by the immediacy with which it enables us to know the characters it describes.

H. G. Wells had formidable novelistic equipment: curiosity, intelligence, social conscience, fertility of invention, and an incapacity for dullness. Yet, proudly regarding himself as a journalist and deprecating the artist's role, he willfully sacrificed

159

form to social reform. His people seem frequently to illustrate a thesis rather than to live even a fictitious life.

Admitting the virtues of Wells, Bennett, Galsworthy, and their industrious school, Virginia Woolf, the most articulate advocate of the opposition, denounced their resolute externality, their documentary materialistic bias, their refusal to immerse in the stream of consciousness. *To the Lighthouse* (1927) illuminates her strictures. The author enters the consciousness of her characters, reproduces sensitively the quality and content of their feeling, and herself intrudes only obliquely. From the subtle, lambent prose, one deduces not only the characters and their relationships but also the environment itself. An admirable stylistic achievement, *To the Lighthouse* becomes at times impalpable and rarefied as the shadow of a flame. One admires, but longs for plot and incident, for more solidity, more substance.

Viriginia Woolf did not, of course, inaugurate the subjective novel: she acknowledges two great ancestors, Henry James and James Joyce. James's involute sentences, which at first block the reader's progress and obscure the dramatic structure of his fiction by their dislocated clauses, fragmented phrases, displaced adverbs, piled up punctuation, and wrenched rhythms, seem ultimately right; for they capture the delicate, fleeting, apparently ineluctable nuance of feeling. Joyce's mythic ordering of the flux of contemporary experience, his dedication to the word, his comic vision, and above all his power of rendering the inward life of his characters makes *Ulysses* a triumph of the introvertive method.

Because of the compelling examples of Joyce, James, and (to a lesser extent) Virginia Woolf, many novelists since have progressively shunned external reality, preferring instead to record—intensively, almost raptly—the feelings and thoughts it induces. The unhappy fact, however, is that the reality itself often attenuates or disintegrates. As practiced by most contemporary English writers, the novel has lost force and breadth (and readability) and gained technique. Writers in our time generally have turned their backs on the elements that vitalize technique.

But charting the development of the 20th century thus broadly, one inevitably distorts. A number of writers refuse to submit to facile classification. Two with whom Virginia Woolf is associated in the revolt against the realistic and naturalistic novel, E. M. Forster and D. H. Lawrence, escape the perils incident to both the extrovertive and introvertive novel. Each novelist has a central, governing theme. Forster, beautifully, lucidly, penetrates the moral situation of our time, the difficulties we have "connecting" with one another, establishing truly human attitudes. Lawrence, in passionate, thrusting prose, probes the vital relationship between men and women, their failures to achieve fulfillment, the deepest longings of their subterranean beings.

Other names arise to undermine generalization concerning the progressive inwardness of the novel during this century. Aldous Huxley, Evelyn Waugh, and George Orwell attained notable success in satire, a genre that, requiring a definite credo, finds the climate of our divided age inhospitable. Nevertheless, Huxley, Waugh, and Orwell, men firmly grounded in belief (the first in Vedanta, the second in Roman Catholicism, the last in socialism), withstood the forces impelling to unbelief.

Finally, traditional novelists—novelists who have never abjured plot, chronology, climax, never renounced the world outside us from which presumably our impressions derive—have flourished. Somerset Maugham, an astute craftsman, has produced clever and extremely readable novels, though hardly anyone would claim that they were searching or powerful creations, enlarging our apprehension or increasing our sensibility. Christopher Isherwood has not realized the promise of his Berlin novels—penetrating, moving, prophetic evocations of pre-Hitler Germany—but *The Last of Mr. Norris* and *Goodbye to Berlin* stand, perhaps, as the best "social" fiction in this century. Graham Greene freights his well-made novels of suspense with theological insight—unlikely matter, but far from capsizing, it imparts gravity and dimension to them. Joyce Cary, nearly alone among the contemporaries, has dedicated his splendid novelistic abilities—a marvelous creative vigor, a warm and sympathetic insight into human imperfections, a flexible and resilient style—to celebrating the enduring, vaulting spirit.

Though C. P. Snow and Lawrence Durrell received most attention, the 1950s were dominated by the Angry Young Men—writers like Kingsley Amis, John Wain, J. P. Donleavy, Alan Sillitoe, and John Braine. "Angry" certainly seems an inappropriate designation for most of them: Far more they were disaffected, disassociated, or "disaffiliated." No member of the group (whether he voluntarily enlisted or was dragooned by the critics) has yet published a great novel. And, in spite of their various excellences, the novels they have so far produced bear too marked a resemblance to one another.

While a literary critic with even minor qualifications as a prophet might have a decade earlier foreseen the remarkable increase of such phenomena as the long novel and the novel sequence, only one gifted with extraordinary clairvoyance could have divined the main course of English literature since 1960. The Angry Young Men have made their peace with things as they are; Amis and Braine, indeed, have migrated far to the right and now assault the currently estranged generation as vigorously (if not perhaps as cogently) as once they assaulted the old Establishment. Iris Murdoch, who seemed to have tenuous affinities with them, has seceded wholly: Her novels in the "crystalline" mode, informed by myth and structured by symbol, strain to reveal the pattern of our existence—but without much anger. Doris Lessing, after her sustained and dedicated concentration on the social, political, and sexual realities of our discordant age, has digressed to Sufism, a variety of mysticism that hardly seems to gear with her essential talent. Though competent and even admirable crafted works have appeared—those of Trevor, Drabble, and Pym, for example—the years between 1960 and the present have not been notable for new directions or brave new achievements in the English novel. The years they embrace have been, rather, a period of novelistic stasis, of consolidation. The stillness may be deceptive; it may signal, as recurrently in the novel's history, the gathering of force, the onset of a stirring age, a time when novels will once again show forth the shape and meaning of our lives through characters who inhabit the real world and are bound to it.

AMIS, KINGSLEY b. 1922. **Lucky Jim** (1954). A funny, at times cruel, story of a young, inept instructor on probation at an English college, his difficulties and fortunes in love. *P—Penguin.*

————. **One Fat Englishman** (1964). A destructive, immensely clever portrait of a "U-type" Englishman, whom some will loathe and others relish; it is also a sly critique of America and American ways. *o.p.*

ATWOOD, MARGARET b. 1939 (Canada). **Surfacing** (1973). The heroine "surfaces" literally and metaphorically: through a watery "rite of passage," she rises from a deadening apathy to a new inspiration, a new acceptance of herself. *P—Warner Bks.*

BECKETT. **Molloy.** See "The Novel: 20th-Century Continental Novels," page 143.

BEERBOHM, MAX 1872–1956. **Zuleika Dobson** (1911). Undergraduate Oxford is disrupted by the maddening beauty of

Zuleika in this deft comic fantasy. *H—Dodd; P—Penguin*.

BENNETT, ARNOLD 1867–1931. **The Old Wives' Tale** (1908). Slowly, almost imperceptibly, the grimy Midlands town presses life from Sophia and Constance Baines. *H—Ayer Co; P—Biblio Dist, Penguin*.

BOWEN, ELIZABETH 1899–1973. **The Death of the Heart** (1938). A deeply moving tragedy of adolescence, brought about by adult cruelty and insensitivity. *H—Knopf, Modern Lib; H & P—Random*.

BRAINE, JOHN b. 1922. **Room at the Top** (1957). A brilliant chronicle of the fortunes—and ultimate misfortune—of a young man who knows all prices but no values. *P—Methuen*.

BURGESS, ANTHONY b. 1917. **A Clockwork Orange** (1962). Remarkable for its linguistic virtuosity, this dystopian novel relentlessly presses its alternatives: a world in which men and women possess free will and are cruel, inhuman, bad; or one in which they have been deprived of free will and are powerless to do evil, and are gentle, tame, "good." *P—Norton*.

————**Earthly Powers** (1980). The candid, sometimes outrageous memoirs of an octogenarian "eminent novelist and world-famous homosexual," centering (with some sprawl) on his relations with a priest, ultimately pope and candidate for sainthood. Beguiling, dextrously plotted, replete with incident and incidental erudition. *P—Avon*.

CARY, JOYCE 1888–1957. **The Horse's Mouth** (1944). Last and best of a trilogy including **Herself Surprised** (1941) and **To Be a Pilgrim** (1942). Exuberant history of Gulley Jimson, visionary painter and outrageous person, told by himself. (In the other volumes, Sarah, his beloved, and Wilcher, his lawyer rival, tell their complementary stories.) *H—Har-Row*.

COMPTON-BURNETT, IVY 1892–1969. **Bullivant and the Lambs** (1948). A comedy of manners, couched in antinaturalistic epigrammatic dialogue, involving a stingy father, his sinister children, and Bullivant, the butler, who never loses control. *H—AMS Pr*.

CONRAD, JOSEPH 1857–1924. **The Nigger of the Narcissus** (1897). Extraordinary dilineation of a common man of the sea. *H—Doubleday; over 6 eds*.

————. **Lord Jim** (1900). The hero suffers dishonor through cowardice; he atones; endures heroic defeat, and gains redemption. *Over 10 eds*.

————. **Heart of Darkness** (1902). A short novel revealing the heart's darkness, deeper than Africa's. *Over 6 eds*.

————. **Nostromo** (1904). An intricately structured political novel, recounting in full detail the genesis and course of a South American revolution and pointing up the corrupting power of silver. *H—Beil, Modern Lib; H & P—Biblio Dist; P—NAL*.

DAVIES, ROBERTSON b. 1913 (Canada). **The Deptford Trilogy,** consisting of **The Manticore** (1971), **Fifth Business** (1975), and **World of Wonders** (1976), traces the various and peccant careers of a master illusionist, an ecclesiastical historian, and their extraordinary inamorata—traces them with wit, energy, and learning worn lightly. *P—Penguin*.

————. **Rebel Angels** (1982). Set in a Canadian university and centering on a beautiful young Gypsy woman who possesses a genius for language. An unremitting delight. *H—Viking Pr; P—Penguin*.

DOUGLAS, NORMAN 1868–1952. **South Wind** (1917). Amusing, cynical symposium on conventional morality. The setting is a Mediterranean island whose shifting winds effect shifts in moral values among its visitors. *H—Scholarly; P—Dover*.

DRABBLE, MARGARET b. 1939. **The Garrick Year** (1964). An intelligent, perceptive, and honest novel, an excellent starting point for the pursuit of the author. The heroine, attractive and aware, hugs her independence. An unsatisfactory love affair brings not disaster but a new insight, a steadier balance. *o.p.*

DURRELL, LAWRENCE b. 1912. **Justine** (1957), **Balthazar** (1968), **Mountolive** (1959), and **Clea** (1960). A stunning baroque "Quartet" of novels about Alexandria—the shimmering, monstrous, beautiful, unreal city—and the "truth" about some exotic people who live there told from shifting perspectives. *P—Dutton, WSP*.

FORD, FORD MADOX (FORD MADOX HUEFFER) 1873–1939. **The Good Soldier** (1915). A subtle, beautifully duplicitous account, told by an "obtuse narrator" (or are the readers obtuse?) of four people who moved together with an intimacy that seemed "like a minuet"—until the music shattered. *H—Octagon; P—Random*.

————. **Parade's End** (1924–28). A tetralogy comprising The Tietjens Saga, in which "the last Tory" emerges from manifold tribulations (World War I merely one of them) into the modern world—where he has no place. *P—Random*.

FORSTER, E. M. 1879–1970. **The Longest Journey** (1907). A sensitive young man regularly accepts illusion for reality, an error that leads to a destroying marriage and ultimate destruction. *P—Random*.

————. **A Passage to India** (1924). Focusing on a dramatic situation, this philosophical novel explores the tensions between the English and the Indians—and, symbolically, other, more basic tensions as well. *H & P—HarBraceJ*.

FOWLES, JOHN b. 1926. **The Magus** (1966) and **The French Lieutenant's Woman** (1969). Completely captivating narratives with strong story lines and deliberately ambiguous shadings. *H—Little; P—Dell, NAL*.

GALSWORTHY, JOHN 1867–1933. **The Forsyte Saga** (1906–21). A series of 12 novels affectionately centering on a large, wealthy, middle-class family from 1886 to 1920, and tracing the effect on them of property and the possessive instinct. *H & P—Scribner*.

GOLDING, WILLIAM b. 1911. **Lord of the Flies** (1954). "Boys will be boys"—which, Golding implies in this brilliant, merciless allegory, means they will be, quite literally, savage. *H—Putnam Pub Group*.

GREEN, HENRY (HENRY VINCENT YORKE) 1905–1973. **Loving** (1945). A comic-pathetic realistic novel set against a romantic Irish background; the story concerns the love of Edith, a housemaid, for Raunce, a butler. *P—Penguin*.

GREENE, GRAHAM b. 1904. **Brighton Rock** (1938). One of Greene's "entertainments," involving pursuit, gang warfare, and murder—encompassed by terror and informed with theological doctrine. *H—Viking Pr; P—Penguin*.

————. **The Heart of the Matter** (1948). A "theological thriller," but equally a tale of frustrated goodness and thwarted love. *H—Viking Pr; P—Penguin*.

HUGHES, RICHARD 1900–1976. **A High Wind in Jamaica** (also titled **The Innocent Voyage**) (1929). A revealing study of the separate world of childhood; children, captured by pirates, undergo a violent voyage into experience. *P—Har-Row*.

HUXLEY, ALDOUS 1894–1963. **Point Counter Point** (1928). Through "parallel contrapuntal plots," Huxley atomizes the upper-class world in pursuit of "pleasure"—sensuality, debauchery, parisitism, and purposelessness. *P—Har-Row*.

————. **Brave New World** (1932). Satire on the mechanized, dehumanized world of the future; the time is 632 A.F. (After Ford). *H & P—Har-Row*.

ISHERWOOD, CHRISTOPHER b. 1904. **The Berlin Stories** (1946). Two short novels that hauntingly evoke Berlin in the five years before Hitler—its degeneration, futility, ominous brutality. Source of the musical and film *Cabaret*. *H—Bentley; P—New Directions*.

JOYCE, JAMES 1882–1941 (Ireland). **Portrait of the Artist as a Young Man** (1916). A semi-autobiographical "novel of initiation": The young artist strives to gain his freedom—from religion, country, family—to practice his art untrammeled. *H—Viking Pr; P—Penguin*.

————. **Ulysses** (1922). Ostensibly the record of a single day filtered through the consciousness of Leopold Bloom and Stephen Dedalus; but more than that, a great comic-epic poem, a paradigm of modern man's search for values. *H & P—Random; H—Modern Lib*.

KIPLING, RUDYARD 1865–1936. **Kim** (1901). A vivid picture of India and its people is given in this exciting tale of secret-service activity. *P—Airmont, Bantam, Dell*.

LAWRENCE, D. H. 1885–1930. **Sons and Lovers** (1913). A semiautobiographical novel, powerfully dramatizing the sexually inhibiting force of excessive mother-love. *Over 6 eds*.

————. **The Rainbow** (1915) and **Women in Love** (1921). An analysis (sometimes concrete, sometimes mystical) of the nature of sexuality, divisive and unifying—and ultimately insufficient. *H—Modern Lib; P—Penguin*.

————. **Lady Chatterley's Lover** (1928). Long censored because of the author's unreticent description of the processes of passionate love, the novel seems old-fashioned today in spite of the plain language but is still valid as a study in contrasts—industrialism versus "nature," the decadent upper class versus the vigorous lower. *P—Bantam, Grove, NAL*.

LESSING, DORIS b. 1919. **Children of Violence** (1965–69). Five novels tracing the movement through several hells—social, political, and emotional—of Martha Quest, beginning in "Zambesia" before World War II and ending in an apocalyptic fate. Occasionally tedious, ultimately rewarding. *P—NAL*.

LOWRY, MALCOLM 1909–1957 (Canada). **Under the Volcano** (1947). A powerful phantasmagoric novel, "a vision of hell," centering on the last day in the life of a British consul in Mexico, whose compulsive drinking has led to his total alienation. *H—Har-Row; P—NAL*.

MAUGHAM, W. SOMERSET 1874–1965. **Of Human Bondage** (1915). An engrossing "educational novel," based on the author's life: The hero comes to the realization of his individual identity through suffering, defeat, and tragic love. *H—Ayer Co, Doubleday, Folcroft; P—Penguin*.

MURDOCH, IRIS b. 1919. **The Flight from the Enchanter** (1956). Fascinating simply as story, this symbolic "fantasia" centers on a group of Londoners drawn into the orbit of the powerful, shadowy enchanter, Mischa Fox, and on how each suffers change or extinction. *o.p.*

NAIPAUL, V. S. b. 1932 (Trinidad, now England). **A House for Mr. Biswas** (1961). A long, densely populated, richly comic novel—but with an underlying sadness—about Mohun Biswas's determination to give shape (by owning his own home) to an apparently shapeless existence in colonial Trinidad. *H—Knopf; P—Penguin*.

———. **Guerrillas** (1975). Loosely based on the actual murder of an Englishwoman in Trinidad, Naipaul's novel is set vaguely in the Caribbean. The internal landscape is, though never slavishly, Conradian: dark, turbulent, profoundly revealing of psychic torment and despair. *H—Knopf; P—Random*.

O'NOLAN, BRIAN ("FLANN O'BRIEN," "MYLES NA GO-PALEEN") 1911–1966 (Ireland). **At Swim-Two-Birds** (1939). An antinovel, embracing parodies of Irish literary traditions, encapsulated narratives; bawdy, extravagant, high-spirited, a bit mad, and often very funny. *P—NAL*.

ORWELL, GEORGE 1903–1950. **Animal Farm** (1945). Brilliant satirical allegory on dictatorship, especially on its penchant for devouring its own. *H—HarBraceJ; P—NAL*.

———. **1984** (1949). A nightmare projection of a future police state ruled by "Big Brother," where "War Is Peace" and all values are transvalued. *H—HarBraceJ; P—NAL*.

POWELL, ANTHONY b. 1905. **A Dance to the Music of Time** (1951–73). An 11-volume sequence (which Powell regards as a single novel) chronicling urbanely and wittily the adventures of Nicholas Jenkins and his odd friends, most very upper class, from before the wars to the recent past. The first installment, *A Question of Upbringing* (1951), is perhaps the best place to begin. *H—Little*.

PRIESTLEY, J. B. 1894–1984. **The Good Companions** (1929). Long, diverting, picaresque tale involving a troupe of wandering English players. *P—U of Chicago Pr*.

PYM, BARBARA 1914–1980. **Quartet in Autumn** (1977). A low-pressured, scrupulously detailed account of four people in their sixties, living alone, and of the contrivances they employ to evade despair. Unlike her social comedies (e.g., *Excellent*

Women, 1978), which are dimly reminiscent of Jane Austen's. *H—Dutton; P—Har-Row*.

RHYS, JEAN 1894–1979. **Quartet** (1928), **Good Morning, Midnight** (1939), and **Wide Sargasso Sea** (1966). Lately emerged, extraordinarily popular novels—but one may be enough for most readers. Each novel chronicles the downward spiral (always downward) of a woman deceived, humiliated, rejected. *P—Har-Row, Norton*.

SCOTT, PAUL MARK 1920–1978. **The Raj Quartet** (1976), comprising **The Jewel in the Crown** (1966), **The Day of the Scorpion** (1968), **The Towers of Silence** (1972), and **A Division of the Spoils** (1975). The four novels spread before us the immense panorama of India during the tumultuous years (1942–1946) leading to independence. Despite complex interweaving of many diverse characters and stories, the action rarely flags or loses focus. *H—Morrow; P—Avon*.

SILLITOE, ALAN b. 1928. **Saturday Night and Sunday Morning** (1958). The career of a young worker, trapped by the system and angry with it, described authentically from a proletarian (even a lumpenproletarian) point of view. *H—Knopf; P—NAL*.

SNOW, C. P. 1905–1980. **Strangers and Brothers** (1940–70). An 11-volume sequence that forms the fictional biography of Lewis Eliot, an English lawyer, in his wanderings in the "corridors of power." An absorbing entry into the sequence is *The Masters* (1951), a realistic and poignant account of the election of a new master to a Cambridge college. *H— Scribner*.

SPARK, MURIEL b. 1918. **Memento Mori** (1959). A group of oldsters, their prepossessions and prejudices merely ossified by time, take brief positions in this funny and sad dance of death. *P—Putnam Pub Group*.

THOMAS, D. M. b. 1935. **The White Hotel** (1981). The story of "Anna G," whose fantasies no less than her actual experiences define an epoch, from her analysis by and correspondence with Freud to her immolation at Babi Yar. Poetic, searing, technically adroit. *H—Viking Pr; P—PB*.

TOLKIEN, J. R. R. 1892–1973. **The Lord of the Rings** (1954–56). This trilogy, enormously popular with undergraduates (and others), consists of **The Fellowship of the Ring, The Two Towers,** and **The Return of the King.** The three novels describe the perilous exploits of two extraordinary hobbits, Frodo and Sam, their valiant efforts to destroy a ring and with it the power of the Dark Lord: at once an allegory, a heroic romance, a moral mythology, a fairy story, a repository of elflore, a fascinating language game, and, above all, an engrossing adventure story. *H—HM; P—Ballantine*.

TREVOR, WILLIAM b. 1928 (Ireland). **Other People's Worlds** (1980). An expertly crafted novel, painful at times but redeemed by its compassion and clearheadedness. A middle-aged woman is entrapped in love by a young man without stability or conscience. *H—Viking Pr*.

WAUGH, EVELYN 1903–1966. **A Handful of Dust** (1934). A satire of the contemporary wasteland: the career of Tony Last, the man of goodwill, ends up in tragic-absurd fashion, as captive reader to a Dickens-loving lunatic. *H & P—Little*.

————. **Brideshead Revisited** (1945). A muted satirist in this novel written from a Catholic stance, Waugh presents dissipation, boredom, and insurmountable hopelessness as the only alternative to faith and works. *H & P—Little*.

WELLS, H. G. 1866–1946. **Tono-Bungay** (1908). Vigorous history of the rise and fall of the promoters of a patent-medicine fraud, with perceptive sidelights on the evils commercialism breeds. *H & P—U of Nebr Pr*.

WHITE, PATRICK b. 1912 (Australia). **Voss** (1957). A dramatic multidimensional novel, set in 19th-century Australia but shedding a wide radiance. The most memorable work of an Australian Nobel Prize winner. *H—Viking Pr; P—Penguin*.

WILSON, ANGUS b. 1913. **Anglo-Saxon Attitudes** (1956). A witty and corrosive satire, centering on the ranging reactions of a scholar who discovers a fraud—a heathen idol buried in the tomb of a Saxon bishop. *o.p.*

WOOLF, VIRGINIA 1882–1941. **To the Lighthouse** (1927). From shifting centers of consciousness, this beautifully textured symbolic novel shows rather than describes Mrs. Ramsey and her widening effect (even after she has died) on the lives that touch hers. *H—U of Toronto Pr; P—HarBraceJ*.

19th-Century American Novels

DANIEL GERZOG

Cultural independence is harder to win than political independence. It took the American novel almost three quarters of a century after 1776 to finish its own struggle for liberty. Not until the middle of the 19th century can it be said to be completely free of English apron strings. In the meantime, scores of fictional early American heroines relived the moral anguish of Richardson's Pamela, and Yankee Robinson Crusoes survived among savages. Charles Brockden Brown transported Godwin's Gothic settings to the outskirts of Philadelphia, and H. H. Brackenridge fashioned a Pennsylvania Don Quixote and an Irish Sancho Panza, set them on the western frontier, and acknowledged the debt his satire owed to Fielding and Swift. Some of these early attempts have their moments, but none is an enduring work of art.

The first important American novelist, James Fenimore Cooper, consciously imitated Sir Walter Scott. Because America lacked knights in full panoply and the romance of the Highlands, he exploited the closest parallels—the frontier, with its noble savages and dauntless pioneers, and the Revolution, with its larger-than-life heroes on both land and sea. Like Scott, Cooper created some unforgettable scenes and characters, but his adventure stories are best read in adolescence. Mature readers have found, however, that the Cooper novels concerned with American social problems—*The Pioneers* and *The Prairie* (the best of the Leatherstocking series); the "Rent-War" trilogy, especially *Satanstoe;* and *Homeward Bound* and *Home as Found*—yield rewarding if highly opinionated insights into the growing pains of the turbulent, formative years of the United States.

While the American novel can be said to have started slowly and imitatively, it came of age in that creative efflorescence of the early 1850s that has come to be known as the first American renaissance. In successive years, two of the greatest novels in any nation's literature were published—Hawthorne's *The Scarlet Letter* and Melville's *Moby Dick*.

Not only had America discovered a subject matter in its own past and present, but it had found a form in which to present it. Although both novels are, in the broadest sense, romances (neither Hawthorne's Salem nor Melville's *Pequod* is a world that ever was), both men created out of the materials of romance rich fabrics of highly complex symbolism, woven through with dark threads of enigmatic moral and metaphysical inquiry. In Melville's words, they "dove deep" and surfaced with treasures that lie unseen by those who swim in the shallows of human awareness. Because Hawthorne and Melville raised troublesome questions in an essentially optimistic age, neither was fully appreciated in his time. But in our bleaker age they are rightly considered two of the giants of American—and world—letters. The depth of psychological insight and the profundity of theme in these novels will sustain the reader through several readings and many hours of reflection.

Hawthorne went on to write other provocative romances, but he never again achieved the economy of expression and tightness of form that elevate *The Scarlet Letter* and the best of his short stories to the highest level of literary accomplishment.

Moby Dick marks the high point of Melville's output. Of the five novels he produced in the five years before its publication, four are fictionalized accounts of his adventures at sea. One, *Mardi*, does attempt the philosophic scope of his masterpiece, but fails to achieve its dramatic and poetic power. After *Moby Dick*, Melville's somber vision produced two more novels, but neither strikes the happy balance between exciting realism and significant speculation that we experience following Ahab in search of the white whale. Late in life, in the short novel *Billy Budd*, Melville again used shipboard life as a microcosm to illuminate man's metaphysical dilemma. Read with sensitivity to its author's sharp satiric bent and powerful irony, it reaffirms the dark genius of the mind that spawned America's greatest novel.

The strength that the romance had achieved with Hawthorne and Melville dissipated over the next two or three decades. The serious literary figures from 1830 to 1870—perhaps still reflecting the Puritan skepticism of "storytelling"—wrote poetry or essays. The novelists ground out precursors of today's sentimental soap operas. *Little Women* illustrates the type, although its merits disqualify it as "typical." From this genre, too, came *Uncle Tom's Cabin,* important for its pervasive effect on the antislavery movement. We might pause to consider *Elsie Venner* by Dr. Oliver Wendell Holmes, whose medical interest in the nature of the mind and in the moral and social problems raised by psychological determinism has new significance in our post-Freudian times. But not until the novel received vital transfusions from two regenerative springs did it regain its lost power.

The United States emerged as a nation from the Civil War, and with the awareness of wider vistas came the desire to create real pictures of the sprawling country. The best of the "local color" writing appeared in short stories, but at least one of the novels arising from the movement, G. W. Cable's *The Grandissimes,* etches sharp portraits not only of individuals but of the impact of slavery and miscegenation on the culture of antebellum New Orleans. The movement helped encourage Mark Twain to write the novels whose wit, humor, and sharp social and political satire dominate the last quarter of the century. In his greatest novel, *Huckleberry Finn,* we travel down the mainstream of the nation on a raft—seeing not only the Mississippi but the world through the eyes and mind of a wise-innocent boy through whose vision Mark Twain forces us to question our basic assumptions about society. Twain chose satire as his weapon to attack the far from idyllic America of the 1870s and 1880s. Although he can hardly be called gentle or subtle, until late in his life he always made his readers laugh at what angered him.

The second powerful influence brought with it the seeds of a much harsher form of social criticism. William Dean Howells, who had spent the war years in Italy, brought home the gospel of literary realism. Howells was primarily concerned that the novel reflect a true image of the situations it portrayed. He wrote as he preached, observing carefully, but rarely penetrating the surface of what he saw. Perhaps more important than his novels was his pervasive influence as editor and literary critic. He praised, justly, De Forest's *Miss Ravenel's Conversion* for its realistic scenes; encouraged writers as different as Henry James and Mark Twain; and fought to gain public acceptance for younger writers like Garland, Crane, Norris, and the first important black American novelist, Charles W. Chesnutt.

This new realism took vastly divergent paths. Henry James used it as a magnifying glass to explore human consciousness in depth in novels that are subtle, carefully wrought studies of the motivations and interactions of real people. But for the younger group, the new realism was a harsh white spotlight to be cast, in the manner of Zola, into the dark corners of the contemporary scene. Stephen Crane wrote *Maggie* in 1893 and *The Red Badge of Courage* in 1895. Norris was soon to follow with *McTeague* and Dreiser with *Sister Carrie* in 1900.

The troublesome social and economic conditions that had prompted Twain's satire and Bellamy's utopian prescription in *Looking Backward* gave rise to a full-fledged literature of protest that carried the American novel into its position of dominance as a literary form in the 20th century.

Recent scholarship, fueled by the women's movement, has revived interest in the neglected fiction of women writers in the last decade of the century. Sarah Orne Jewett, whose *The Country of the Pointed Firs* is a prime example of New England regionalism, had an important influence on Willa Cather. Mary E. Wilkins Freeman in the Northeast and Kate Chopin in the South explored themes that revealed the oppression that trapped their sex in late Victorian America. And Charlotte Perkins Gilman published the early stories that presaged her provocative later career, most notably her brilliant "The Yellow Wallpaper."

ALCOTT, LOUISA MAY 1832–1888. **Little Women** (1868). A sentimental story of domestic life in New England. The characters exude a certain charm but live life as we would like it to be rather than as it is. *Over 20 eds*.

BELLAMY, EDWARD 1850–1898. **Looking Backward** (1888). One of the most popular utopian romances in English: a vision of the United States in the year 2000, showing how economic planning and nationalization of industry can create prosperity of both body and spirit. *Over 6 eds*.

CABLE, GEORGE WASHINGTON 1844–1925. **The Grandissimes** (1880). Episodic but rich, sensitive treatment of the New Orleans of the year of the Louisiana Purchase, by a man who loved the South while repudiating its values. *o.p*.

CHOPIN, KATE 1851–1904. **The Awakening** (1899). A pioneering novel about a woman whose independence and repudiation of convention shocked the author's contemporaries. It holds up surprisingly well. *Over 6 eds*.

COOPER, JAMES FENIMORE 1789–1851. **The Pioneers** (1823). The earliest and least idealized of the Leatherstocking tales. Cooper's pioneer hero, Natty Bumppo, past middle age, struggles against the encroachments of civilization on the New York State frontier in 1793. *H & P—State U NY Pr; H—Lightyear; P—Airmont, NAL.*

————. **The Prairie** (1827). The most lasting of the Leatherstocking series—tied together by the force of the Great Plains themselves. Natty Bumppo lives out his last days reflecting on and waiting for death among a cast of characters that ranges the social gamut from naked Indian to born-to-the-blood aristocrat. *H & P—State U NY Pr; H—Lightyear; P—Airmont, NAL.*

————. **Satanstoe** (1845). The first novel in a trilogy that presents the author's brief for the necessity of a landed aristocracy. In this story of the youthful adventures of Cornelius Littlepage, colonial life on three social levels is vividly portrayed. *o.p.*

CRANE, STEPHEN 1871–1900. **Maggie: A Girl of the Streets** (1893). A short, impressionistic novel about a young New York streetwalker. Social protest etched in the acid of bitter irony. *H & P—Norton; H—Schol Facsimiles; P—Airmont, Fawcett.*

————. **The Red Badge of Courage** (1895). This Civil War story divests that overromanticized war—or any war—of much of its false glory. So vivid that its readers cannot believe that Crane had never known war firsthand, yet subtly symbolic and far-reaching in its implications. *Over 20 eds.*

DE FOREST, JOHN WILLIAM 1826–1906. **Miss Ravenel's Conversion from Secession to Loyalty** (1867). A surprisingly realistic novel of manners, delineating characters neither good nor bad and projecting a well-balanced view of the Civil War. *H—Somerset Pub.*

FREDERIC, HAROLD 1856–1898. **The Damnation of Theron Ware** (1896). The story of a Methodist minister whose superficial faith, based on self-satisfaction, crumbles as he begins to see more deeply. By implication, the story symbolizes America's loss of innocence. *H—Somerset Pub; P—Harvard U Pr, HR&W.*

HAWTHORNE, NATHANIEL 1804–1864. **The Scarlet Letter.** See "The 17th Century," page 48.

————. **The House of the Seven Gables** (1851). A novel about sinister hereditary influences within an old New England family, sunnier than Hawthorne's other works despite its grim subject. *Over 15 eds.*

————. **The Marble Faun** (1869). The Fall of Adam reset

amidst the ruins and art treasures of Rome. *H—Ohio St U Pr; P—Airmont, NAL*.

HOLMES, OLIVER WENDELL 1809–1894. **Elsie Venner** (1861). A young woman's struggle with a hereditary moral flaw raises important questions of moral and social responsibility in a novel that would be greater if it had a less creaky structure. *H—Ayer Co*.

HOWELLS, WILLIAM DEAN 1837–1920. **A Modern Instance** (1882). A realistic study of average people, a young newspaperman and his wife, and of their marital difficulties. *H—Ind U Pr; P—HM, Penguin*.

————. **The Rise of Silas Lapham** (1885). A self-made man chooses not to recoup his losses at the expense of others and thus "rises" morally if not socially and financially. Made less trite than the plot line would suggest by Howells's careful attention to realistic detail and characterization. *Over 10 eds*.

————. **A Hazard of New Fortunes** (1890). Howells's best novel, written when his moral outrage at the injustices of industrial conflict had driven him toward a Tolstoian socialism. A personal experience with socioeconomic injustice awakens the novel's protagonist to his total involvement with his fellow man. *H—Folcroft; P—NAL*.

JAMES, HENRY 1843–1916. **The American** (1877). Wealthy, capable, candid Christopher Newman goes to Paris to "live" and to get a wife who would be "the best article on the market." An early novel, direct in style, and a good introduction to James. *Over 6 eds*.

————. **The Portrait of a Lady** (1881). Isabel Archer, the counterpart of Christopher Newman, hopes to find in Europe the best of life and men. Another incisive contrast of American and European types and codes. *Over 10 eds*.

————. **The Turn of the Screw** (1898). A fascinating psychological ghost story. *Over 10 eds*.

————. **The Wings of the Dove** (1902). Kate Croy and Merton Densher weave a subtle scheme to enmesh the American heiress Milly Theale who surprisingly reveals them to themselves in a complicated psychological novel with a background of stately London residences, shabby lodging houses, and twisting Venetian canals. *H & P—Norton; H—Kelley; P—NAL, Penguin*.

————. **The Ambassadors** (1903). James's richest novel, contrasting the European and American traditions. Slowly, slowly, in a novel of great psychological suspense, the American

Lambert Strether falls under the spell of the liberal European way of life and sheds his new-world provincialism. *Over 6 eds*.

————. **The Golden Bowl** (1905). In this story set in Victorian London, a beautiful but flawed golden bowl symbolizes the marriage of the Italian prince Amerigo and the wealthy American girl Maggie Verver, who eventually surmounts all difficulties in another working out of James's "international theme." *H—Kelley; P—Biblio Dist, Oxford U Pr, Penguin*.

JEWETT, SARAH ORNE 1849–1909. **The Country of the Pointed Firs** (1896). A series of sketches with a common narrator and setting that captures with loving sensibility the atmosphere and people of seacoast Maine. *H—Arden Lib, Peter Smith; P—Doubleday, Norton*.

MELVILLE, HERMAN 1819–1891. **Typee** (1846). A fictionalized account of Melville's stay in the Marquesas Islands. Chiefly descriptive of the islanders' simple and lovely way of life and critical of Western ways. *H & P—Northwestern U Pr; H—Literary Classics; P—Airmont, NAL, Penguin*.

————. **Omoo** (1847). Well-developed episodes and 20 characters sharply realized as Melville recounts in fictional form his Tahiti adventures. *H & P—Northwestern U Pr; H—Hendricks House*.

————. **Moby Dick** (1851). A rich, complex, highly symbolic narrative that explores the deepest reaches of our moral and metaphysical dilemma at the same time that it tells a gripping, realistic sea story. A paean to the human spirit that nevertheless faces up to its darker, less comforting side. Perhaps Melville raises more questions than he answers, but this is as it should be in the highest order of literary art. Soaring poetic prose, dramatic conflict, unforgettable characterizations—in a book to be read and reread. *Over 20 eds*.

————. **Billy Budd** (c. 1891, pub. 1924). Goaded beyond endurance, Adam-like Billy strikes down his satanic persecutor and is executed in a scene suggesting the Crucifixion in this ironic quasi-allegory of human and divine justice. *Over 10 eds*.

NORRIS, FRANK 1870–1902. **McTeague** (1899). A realistic study of the disintegration of character, ending in murder. *Over 6 eds*.

————. **The Octopus** (1901). The story of battles between California wheat growers and the intruding railroad "octopus" is the beginning volume of a naturalistic trilogy Norris never completed. *H—Lightyear; P—Airmont, NAL*.

STOWE, HARRIET BEECHER 1811–1896. **Uncle Tom's Cabin** (1852). Powerful antislavery propaganda. The prose is dated, but the characters are surprisingly vivid, especially when contrasted with stereotypes from later stage versions. *Over 10 eds.*

TWAIN, MARK (SAMUEL LANGHORNE CLEMENS) 1835–1910. **The Adventures of Tom Sawyer** (1876). This book for young and old pictures the life of boys in little, lazy Hannibal, Missouri, contrasting their superficial cussedness with their inner decency. *Over 15 eds.*

————. **Adventures of Huckleberry Finn** (1885). Mark Twain's imagination elevates this tale of a boy seeking freedom on a raft he shares with a runaway slave into a true comic epic of American life. Huck, who sees the world with a marvelous combination of wisdom and innocence, tells his own story in a direct, colloquial idiom that is a perfect vehicle for Twain's social satire. *Over 25 eds.*

————. **A Connecticut Yankee in King Arthur's Court** (1889). A modern American finds himself among the Knights of the Round Table and discovers that Yankee ingenuity is more than a match for medieval magic and superstition. *Over 10 eds.*

————. **Pudd'nhead Wilson** (1894). A nonconformist too wise for his backwoods community, Wilson solves several mysteries. Partly a triumph of bitter humor, partly a daring treatment of miscegenation. *P—Airmont, Bantam, NAL, Penguin.*

20th-Century
American Novels

ARTHUR WALDHORN

1900–1945

During the first five years of the new century, Henry James published a trio of novels (*The Wings of the Dove, The Ambassadors,* and *The Golden Bowl*) exquisite in psychological and moral perception (see "The Novel: 19th-Century American Novels"). James's refined achievement left sparse opportunity for immediate literary descendants. American fiction had urgent need for new voices, harsher and coarser perhaps, but more consonant with the rough energy of American life.

Theodore Dreiser was the first of these voices to be heard. For more than twenty years after he published *Sister Carrie* in 1900, Dreiser sounded his gloomy message that natural and social forces shape and direct human affairs, or, characteristically, misshape and misdirect them. What he lacked in stylistic grace and precision he made up in epic abundance of detail and craggy sincerity. However plodding and awkward his lengthy accounts of the sordid, his acute reportorial vision and his profound compassion for humanity affected generations of realistic and naturalistic American writers—from Jack London to Erskine Caldwell and Richard Wright.

A more able craftsman than Dreiser, Sherwood Anderson recorded the impact of inward as well as environmental forces, zeroing in on his characters' bewildered groping as they struggled with the vast emptiness of life in the corn belt.

Others focused their critical vision on regional centers. Upton Sinclair explored the slums of Chicago's South Side, while

Henry Roth concentrated on Jewish life in New York City's Lower East Side; Sinclair Lewis fixed narrowly on tribal manners among midwestern small-town ritualists; and Thomas Wolfe rhapsodized about his childhood in Asheville, North Carolina. Edith Wharton perceived the excesses of elegant urbanites, and Ellen Glasgow satirized the foibles of her fellow Virginians.

Some novelists stumbled beyond the geographic limits of their material into cosmic regions. Thus, Willa Cather's portraits were informed by a profound sense of human experience in her portrait of the Nebraska prairies and of those who live and work on them. And no American novelist of this century has more wholly captured a region at once particular and universal than has William Faulkner. His mythic Yoknapatawpha County, Mississippi, scene of most of his novels and stories, is populated by Indians, black servants, laborers, and farm workers, decadent southern aristocrats, and shrewd, amoral carpetbaggers. But Faulkner's people and themes are not merely southern; instead, they are universal and timeless—all humanity and its sense of unexpiated guilt, its struggle with nature, and its agonized effort to reconcile values past and present.

During the great years of the 1920s, when much of America's best fiction was being written, two of the most famous public literary figures—Ernest Hemingway and F. Scott Fitzgerald—wrote their finest work too, each memorializing the impact of the "lost generation," that Jazz Age outcropping of shattered idealism and morality that exploded lives into myriad paths, most of them dead ends.

By the end of the 1930s—whose sordid record of economic depression and social unrest was most effectively recorded by John Dos Passos, John Steinbeck, and James Farrell—America was again ready for new voices. But they would not be heard until the din of war had receded.

ANDERSON, SHERWOOD 1876–1941. **Winesburg, Ohio** (1919). In the vein of Edwin Arlington Robinson's Tilbury Town of New England and of Edgar Lee Masters's Midwestern Spoon River, this unified medley of tales—Anderson's finest work—is the prose equivalent of those poems, a gallery portrait of the frustrated men and women of a small town at the end of the 19th century. *P—Penguin*.

CALDWELL, ERSKINE b. 1903. **God's Little Acre** (1933). The Georgia mountaineer Ty Ty Walden and his daughters, Rosamund and Darling Jill, are the hilariously grotesque central characters of this notable American folk comedy. *P—NAL*.

CATHER, WILLA 1873–1947. **My Antonia** (1918). The red grass and white snows of the Nebraska prairies provide the scenery of this compelling story of a 19th-century immigrant and her American friends. *P—HM*.

————. **The Professor's House** (1925). There are two houses in Professor St. Peter's life and two worlds representing different values in this impressive scrutiny of American civilization in terms of a family's experiences. *P—Random*.

DOS PASSOS, JOHN 1896–1970. **U.S.A.** (1937). A powerful trilogy, including **The 42nd Parallel** (1930), **1919** (1932), and **The Big Money** (1936), of disillusion with the American dream. Dos Passos's "four-eyed vision"—an amalgam of diverse narrative techniques—adds dramatic force to his tale of ordinary and famous Americans during the first three decades of the 20th century. *H—HM*.

DREISER, THEODORE 1871–1945. **Sister Carrie** (1900). Carrie Meeber drifts upward—from poverty in Chicago to fame on the New York stage in the 1890s. The decline of her lover, Hurstwood, establishes a moving counterpoint. The only authoritative text appeared in 1981. Earlier editions were censored by Dreiser's publisher. *Over 10 eds*.

————. **The Financier** (1912). The best of his "Trilogy of Desire" based on the career of the Chicago robber baron Charles Yerkes. The famous scene of a lobster devouring a squid sets the tone for Frank Cowperwood's rise to power in finance and sex. The succeeding volumes, **The Titan** (1914) and **The Stoic** (published posthumously, 1947), suffer from excessive documenting and flaccid philosophizing. *P—NAL*.

————. **An American Tragedy** (1925). Drawn from an actual murder case, the story of Clyde Griffith's hollow dreams and nightmare reality is overly long but still gripping. Is Clyde's fall a tragedy of his failure of will or of the American way of success? *H—Bentley; P—NAL*.

FARRELL, JAMES T. 1904–1979. **Studs Lonigan** (1935). The overwrought but powerful Lonigan trilogy, including **Young Lonigan** (1932), **The Young Manhood of Studs Lonigan** (1934), and **Judgment Day** (1935), tells the story of the middle-class Irish on Chicago's South Side, particularly of the degenerating effects of school, church, and family upon the weak, bragging Studs in the years between World War I and the depression. *H—Vanguard; P—Avon*.

FAULKNER, WILLIAM 1897–1962. **The Sound and the Fury**

(1929). A superb evocation of the decay and degeneration of a southern family. Technically complex, its devices—stream of consciousness, multiple points of view, dislocated time sequence, and symbolism—nevertheless reward an attentive reader with a memorable image of human fate. *H—Random new corrected ed. 1984; P—Random*.

————. **As I Lay Dying** (1930). The Bundren family takes the ripening corpse of Addie, wife and mother, on a gruesomely comic journey that is interrupted by such elemental matters as fire and flood. *H & P—Random*.

————. **Light in August** (1932). A profound and violent tale of isolation and endurance. Of the people Faulkner studies here, Joe Christmas is the most affecting in his complex and fatal quest for a reason for living. *H & P—Random*.

————. **Absalom, Absalom!** (1936). The Civil War, miscegenation, and murder run through this macabre and complex chronicle of a decadent southern family. *H & P—Random*.

FITZGERALD, F. SCOTT 1896–1940. **The Great Gatsby** (1925). A major scrutiny of American values through the experience of a near-mythic hero and his grand though ill-fated masquerade during the Jazz Age. *H & P—Scribner*.

————. **Tender Is the Night** (1934). The slow, poignant dissolution of a gifted psychiatrist who gives too easily and too much to those who need him—and, ironically, whom he needs almost as much. *H & P—Scribner*.

————. **The Last Tycoon** (1941). Unfinished at Fitzgerald's death, this engrossing legend of Hollywood affords a compelling portrait of Monroe Stahr, a driving, artistic producer—the "last tycoon." *H & P—Scribner*.

GLASGOW, ELLEN 1874–1945. **Barren Ground** (1925). A poor young Virginian with aristocratic connections, Dorinda Oakley is betrayed by a weak-natured young doctor in this tale of madness and murder written elegantly but powerfully. *H—Peter Smith; P—Hill & Wang*.

HEMINGWAY, ERNEST 1899–1961. **The Sun Also Rises** (1926). In this masterwork, the hero, Jake, blasted in the war, lives in Paris among Left Bank expatriates who make sidetrips to Spain for the bullfighting and search for values through the alcoholic fog of the "lost generation." *H & P—Scribner*.

————. **A Farewell to Arms** (1929). Told in terse and rhythmic understatement, with nicely calculated repetitions, this starcrossed romance of an American ambulance driver and an

English nurse in the Italy of 1917 is one of the finest war novels of our time. *H & P—Scribner*.

————. **For Whom the Bell Tolls** (1940). Hemingway's most ambitious but not his most successful novel. Sprawling and occasionally sentimental, this panoramic story of the Spanish Civil War boasts, nevertheless, tremendous emotive power gained through magnificent scenes and unforgettable portraits of Spanish guerrillas. *H & P—Scribner*.

LEWIS, SINCLAIR 1885–1951. **Main Street** (1920). A doctor's wife and minor-league Madame Bovary, Carol Kennicott is severely defeated in her ill-considered attempts to bring culture to the midwestern town of Gopher Prairie. *H—HarBraceJ; P—NAL*.

————. **Babbitt** (1922). A clownish businessman in the mythical city of Zenith, George F. Babbitt (the prototype of the hustler and the conformist) tries to break the grip of tribal customs—and fails grotesquely. *H—HarBraceJ; P—NAL*.

LONDON, JACK 1876–1916. **The Call of the Wild** (1903). London's most popular story, about Buck, a dog who regresses to wolf after his master dies during the Klondike gold rush. *Over 10 eds*.

MARQUAND, J. P. 1893–1960. **The Late George Apley** (1937). Ostensibly a biographical tribute by a friend, this neat satire of a proper Bostonian holds the dignified but not unlovable Apley and his tribal rituals up to a bright comic light. *H—Little; P—WSP*.

MILLER, HENRY 1891–1980. **Tropic of Cancer** (1931). Miller's exuberant, influential, and controversial novel records, in simple but ecstatic prose, the adventures of an American vagabond merrily sponging on his Left Bank friends. *H—Modern Lib; P—Grove*.

O'HARA, JOHN 1905–1970. **Appointment in Samarra** (1934). The first and best of his novels, compact where later works are loosely jointed, this is the saga of a country club set in a Pennsylvania town during the bootleg era. *P—Random*.

ROTH, HENRY b. 1906. **Call It Sleep** (1934). Neglected for 30 years, since acclaimed as a masterpiece, this is a moving but never sentimental story about two years in a Jewish boy's childhood. Set in the slums of Brownsville and New York's Lower East Side between 1911 and 1913, the novel projects searing images of urban life. Its language (often Joycean) and portraits are superb, especially those of a radiant mother and a terrifying father. *H—Cooper Sq; P—Avon*.

SINCLAIR, UPTON 1878–1968. **The Jungle** (1906). An impressive piece of dramatized journalism that paints a grim picture of the Chicago stockyards of the period. *Over 6 eds.*

STEIN, GERTRUDE 1874–1946. **Three Lives** (1909). A trio of novellas about three women—two, German immigrants, the third, a black—who suffer painful and, at last, futile lives. Each tale experiments stylistically, but "Melanctha" (about a black woman's affair with a doctor) dares most. *P—Random.*

STEINBECK, JOHN 1902–1968. **In Dubious Battle** (1936). This dramatic story of a fruit pickers' strike in California remains Steinbeck's most impressive achievement. *P—Penguin.*

————. **The Grapes of Wrath** (1939). Steinbeck's most famous novel, it describes the plight of dispossessed Oklahoma dust bowl tenant farmers during the depression. The writing is vivid and compassionate but, too often, melodramatic. *H—Viking Pr; P—Penguin.*

WEST, NATHANAEL 1906–1940. **Miss Lonelyhearts** (1933). An unhappy newspaperman assigned to write the lovelorn column at first scorns the stricken people who write in but gradually becomes tangled in their destinies. *P—New Directions.*

————. **The Day of the Locust** (1939). A surrealistically grotesque comedy about Hollywood. Distorted, hopeless, but powerful dreams of beauty and romance translate into bizarre reality; enacted by an extraordinary array of psychically bankrupt characters. *P—NAL.*

WHARTON, EDITH 1862–1937. **The House of Mirth** (1905). Wharton's masterpiece is a compelling novel of manners in which the glamorous, well-connected but poverty-ridden Lily Bart desperately goes toward her doom. *H & P—NYU Pr; H—Scribner; P—Bantam, Berkley Pub, NAL.*

————. **Ethan Frome** (1911). Grim and icy New England dominates this tragedy of a farmer in love with the cousin of his wife who, after a catastrophe to the lovers, triumphs bitterly over them. *H & P—Scribner.*

WILDER, THORNTON 1897–1975. **The Bridge of San Luis Rey** (1927). The earliest of Wilder's three Pulitzer Prize novels and his most enduringly popular. Five travelers plunge to death when a bridge collapses in 18th-century Peru. A witness reconstructs their life histories to probe the justice of their fate. *H—Har-Row; P—Avon.*

WOLFE, THOMAS 1900–1938. **Look Homeward, Angel** (1929). Wolfe's best novel tells in occasionally forceful but too often rhetorical prose the story of the turbulent Eugene Gant's first

19 years in his native southern town and at his state univeristy. *P—Scribner*.

WRIGHT. **Native Son.** See "American Minority Cultures: Black," page 125.

1945—Present

At no time in our literary history has American fiction seemed more profoundly anxious than since World War II. The horrors of corporate, technologized war—in Europe and the Pacific, Korea, Vietnam, and Latin America—diminished radically the potential of the individual, the "imperial self," by debasing human dignity. Hero gave way to antihero; lyricism to parody; reason to madness. Norman Mailer, James Jones, and Joseph Heller, the best novelists of World War II, mirror the cancellations and negations of aspiration and decency. The novelists of the Vietnam experience, Michael Herr, Tim O'Brien, and Robert Stone, are no less embittered. With grim humor they prophesy the manner and message of a new age: a malignant survival of cruelty and injustice, an absurd, irrational persistence of destructive impulse.

Starting in the 1950s, many novelists stepped outside the mindless mainstream of history to contemplate their own images in a kind of desperate endeavor to salvage self. Bernard Malamud, Saul Bellow, Philip Roth, and many others puzzled over the complexities of being an American Jew. Ralph Ellison, James Baldwin, and Ishmael Reed were among many who examined sensitively and, often, angrily the exasperating alienation of the black in northern as well as southern America. The troubled consciousness of the southerner found powerful expression among the literary descendants of William Faulkner: Robert Penn Warren, William Styron, Carson McCullers, Flannery O'Connor. And some writers, particularly J. D. Salinger, sought in adolescence and childhood some shred of innocence to shore against the ruins. Vladimir Nabokov's *Lolita* effectively ended that scant hope.

By the 1950s paranoia passed, for many, as normal. The asylum, hallucination, junk artifacts, V-2 rockets, fire bombings, cannibalism—these are salient images in the fiction of Ken Kesey, William Burroughs, Donald Barthelme, Thomas Pynchon, Kurt Vonnegut, and John Hawkes, leaders of the vanguard of new fiction. Their vision coincides with that of John Barth, who reminds us, ironically and despairingly, in the title of one of his novels that we are *Lost in the Funhouse*. It is too late to *do* anything, the philosopher-novelist William Gass insists; the artist can only show us what reality is and write so compellingly that we must at least confront that reality, perhaps for the first and only time in our lives.

The fiction of the mid-1970s and 1980s has failed so far to fulfill the literary promise of the preceding decade. Frustration with reality and a search for alternate modes persist as themes. One of the most popular subjects has been women's quest for more than marginal selfhood. Yet even among the best of the women novelists—such as Lisa Alther, Marilyn French, Toni Morrison, Joyce Carol Oates, Marge Piercy, Anne Tyler, and Alice Walker—there lacks, as in most recent American fiction, the excitement of freshness or discovery. With occasional exceptions—Walter Abish, Russell Hoban, and William Kennedy—authors have failed to equal the innovative skill of Pynchon, Hawkes, Gaddis, Barth, or Barthelme. This is not to prophesy the end of the novel. Despite the omnipresence of violence and loss, novelists will stay at their craft and, one hopes, will again craft with virtuosity. A few, perhaps, will offer comfort of one sort or another. It is unlikely that the best will do more than bring us to a recognition of fatality.

ABISH, WALTER b. 1931. **How German Is It** (1980). The hero, a novelist whose father died in the plot against Hitler's life, tries to understand why his fellow Germans choose to erase the memory of their terrible heritage. Montage, quick cuts, and nonsequential narrative—all lend a cinematic quality to this cold-blooded vision of contemporary Germany. *H & P—New Directions*.

AUCHINCLOSS, LOUIS b. 1917. **The Rector of Justin** (1964). The famous head of a famous preparatory school, having reached his eighties, is viewed at various times in his career by various people who knew him and who make a composite picture of his many-faceted personality. *P—HM*.

BALDWIN. **Go Tell It on the Mountain.** See "American Minority Cultures: Black," page 122.

BARTH, JOHN b. 1930. **End of the Road** (1958). A classic case of contemporary psychic paralysis, Jacob Horner fails to escape his corner, despite innovative, often funny, but at last destructive efforts. *H—Doubleday; P—Bantam*.

————. **The Sot-Weed Factor** (1960). A freewheeling picaresque novel, a Rabelaisian satire of human pretensions, a bawdy prose extension of Ebenezer Cooke's 18th-century lampoon. *The Sot-Weed Factor,* or a "moral allegory cloaked in the material of a colonial history" (as the author affirms), is certainly an astonishing fusion of witty tour de force and comic epic. *P—Bantam.*

BARTHELME, DONALD b. 1933. **Snow White** (1967). An unsweetened parody in which Snow White finds no prince but settles grumpily for her dwarfs, with whom she shares occasionally bed and bath. *P—Atheneum.*

————. **The Dead Father** (1975). To his familiar techniques of collage, irony, and parody, Barthelme adds an Oedipal plot as a son accompanies his father's mammoth corpse ("dead only in a sense") to a burial site. Often comic, sometimes outrageous, the novel is also a painful gloss on modern culture and familial patterns. *H—FS&G.*

BELLOW, SAUL b. 1915. **The Adventures of Augie March** (1953). A plump novel about the wandering of a passive *picaro* from Chicago. War, sex, and shipwreck play roles in his maturation. *H—Viking Pr; P—Avon.*

————. **Seize the Day** (1956). A powerful short novel whose antihero, Tommy Wilhelm, struggles to survive and to understand despite his pitiable ineffectuality. *H—Viking Pr; P—Avon, Penguin.*

————. **Herzog** (1964). Both highly individualized and deeply representative, Moses Herzog is an extravagantly and sadly comic portrait of the modern intellectual caught in a series of emotional traps. *H—Viking Pr; P—Avon, Penguin.*

————. **Mr. Sammler's Planet** (1969). Though a septuagenarian, Mr. Sammler resembles most of Bellow's heroes in his compassion for his fellows and his commitment to the fullness of life. *H—Viking Pr; P—Penguin.*

BURROUGHS, WILLIAM b. 1914. **Naked Lunch** (1959). A panoramic excursion through the moral underground, this surrealistic and hallucinatory novel is a ferocious (and linguistically scatological) depiction of the horrors of unbridled appetite. *P—Grove.*

CAPOTE, TRUMAN 1924–1984. **Other Voices, Other Rooms** (1948). Capote's first and best novel about the grim rite of passage of a sensitive southern boy trapped in a decadent Gothic household. *H—Random; P—NAL.*

CHEEVER, JOHN 1912–1982. **The Wapshot Chronicle** (1958)

and **The Wapshot Scandal** (1964). An episodic, subtly farcical but haunted account of the failure of the solidly middle-class Wapshot family of St. Botolphs, Massachusetts—and particularly the brothers Moses and Coverly—to cope with the intricacies of contemporary mores and morality. *P—Ballantine*.

COOVER, ROBERT C. b. 1932. **The Universal Baseball Association, Inc., J. Henry Waugh, Prop.** (1968). A compelling allegorical fantasy about Waugh, a middle-aged accountant who peoples an entire baseball league with imaginary teams and players, complete with biographies and statistics—all dependent upon the dice Waugh throws to determine fate. *P—NAL*.

DOCTOROW, E. L. b. 1931. **The Book of Daniel** (1971). Doctorow's most popular novels are *Ragtime* (1975)—about America from the turn of the century to the first World War—and *Loon Lake* (1980)—about union struggles during the depression. Both are entertaining but lack the force and passion of this earlier, more intensely realized novel based on the Rosenberg case and narrated eloquently by one of the executed couple's children. *H—Modern Lib; P—Bantam*.

DONLEAVY, J. P. b. 1926. **The Ginger Man** (1955). Although for some years a resident of Ireland, Donleavy may still be counted as an American writer, notably for this vigorously funny picaresque story of a young American's adventures and misadventures in Dublin and London. *H & P—Astor-Honor; P—Dell*.

ELLISON. **Invisible Man.** See "American Minority Cultures: Black," page 123.

GADDIS, WILLIAM b. 1922. **Recognitions** (1955). Twenty years after its publication, this first novel of more than 900 pages at last won deserved acclaim (just as Gaddis's second novel, the equally long *JR*, made its appearance). At surface, a story about forging paintings, beneath is "recognition" that inauthenticity clutters and infects every aspect of our lives and ourselves. *P—Avon*.

GASS, WILLIAM b. 1924. **Omensetter's Luck** (1966). Novelist and philosopher Gass exercises a virtuoso control of language as he mounts a strange and imaginative conflict between good and evil in a rural midwestern setting. *P—NAL*.

HAWKES, JOHN b. 1925. **The Lime Twig** (1961). A novel of Gothic atmosphere and force about the English underworld, the theft of a racehorse, and the violent death of a man under the hooves of horses during a race. *P—New Directions*.

———. **Second Skin** (1964). Hawkes's finest work, a densely textured complex of images and episodes that records the central character's passage from nightmare and death to dream and life. *P—New Directions*.

HELLER, JOSEPH b. 1923. **Catch-22** (1961). The total madness and horror of war captured through a farrago of comic absurdities at an American bomber base in World War II. *H—S&S; P—Dell*.

HOBAN, RUSSELL b. 1925. **Riddley Walker** (1981). A chilling tale of life in Inland (England) 2000 years after the ultimate bomb. The narrator is a 12-year-old man come of age, like Huck Finn, to survive the devastation of atomic doomsday and stumble toward regeneration. The fabricated language—a unique re-creation of the remnants of English—is a triumph of imagination. *P—WSP*.

JONES, JAMES 1921–1977. **The Thin Red Line** (1962). Less melodramatic and sentimental than *From Here to Eternity* (1951) with its portrait of barracks life in Hawaii just before Pearl Harbor, but truer to the dully ferocious reality of combat. Here the mission is to recapture a group of hills on Guadalcanal. *H—Scribner*.

KENNEDY, WILLIAM b. 1928. **Legs** (1975), **Billy Phelan's Greatest Game** (1978), and **Ironweed** (1983). An unpromising trio, the heroes of Kennedy's remarkable "Albany cycle" manage to assume vibrant shape. A gangster, a hustler, and an ex-ballplayer—each is a curiously engaging version of the American dream, a social derelict endowed with the instinct to do more than merely survive—rather to prove that men must be warriors, not victims. *H—Viking Pr; P—Penguin*.

KESEY, KEN b. 1935. **One Flew over the Cuckoo's Nest** (1962). Set in a mental hospital, this story dramatizes the conflict between a stubborn patient and the bullying figure known as Big Nurse, a conflict full of dramatic tension and sometimes painful comedy. *H—Viking Pr; P—NAL, Penguin*.

KOSINSKI, JERZY b. 1933. **The Painted Bird** (1965). An accidentally abandoned child, terrified into loss of speech, drifts silently from place to place during World War II, spectator and victim alike to vicious abuses, each a kind of metaphor for what humanity has become. Not a line of dialogue appears in this stunning first novel that Kosinski has never bettered. *H—Modern Lib; P—Bantam*.

McCULLERS, CARSON 1917–1967. **The Heart Is a Lonely Hunter** (1940). A bizarre group in a southern town—a man who owns a lunch counter, a woman with musical ambitions, an alcoholic radical, and a black doctor—confide their troubles to a deaf mute in this beautifully fashioned story. *H—HM; P—Bantam*.

MAILER, NORMAN b. 1923. **The Naked and the Dead** (1948). A collective picture of a reconnaissance squad in action against the Japanese on an island in the Pacific; this is one of the finest and grimmest of American war novels. *H & P—HR&W*.

————. **Why Are We in Vietnam?** (1967). A psychopathic young narrator details the grotesqueries of an Arctic hunting expedition with his father and assorted Texans. Idylls give way to mayhem and madness as the barbarism of modern technology degrades and destroys what is good in nature. *P—HR&W*.

————. **Ancient Evenings** (1983). A long, variously engrossing and enervating tale of Egypt in 1100 B.C. The *ka,* or soul, of a 21-year-old is tutored by the thrice-reincarnated spirit of his grandfather. Mailer's vast and dark imagination is abundantly present, but it fails to glue together multiple strands of sex and death, self-propagation, telepathy, and existential desperation. *H—Little; P—Warner Bks*.

MALAMUD, BERNARD b. 1914. **The Assistant** (1957). An affecting novel in which a wayward young Italian "assistant" learns some special meanings of suffering from a profoundly human Jewish grocer. *H—FS&G: P—Avon*.

MORRIS, WRIGHT b. 1910. **The Works of Love** (1952). A touching, sympathetic portrait of Will Brady, a decent but weak midwesterner who offers love too freely and suffers inevitable frustration. *P—U of Nebr Pr*.

MORRISON. **Song of Solomon.** See "American Minority Cultures: Black," page 124.

NABOKOV, VLADIMIR 1899–1977. **Lolita** (1955). Not Nabokov's best book but his most popular; a hilarious but also rather chilling account of a nubile, predatory "nymphet" and her hapless middle-aged lover. *H—Putnam Pub Group; P—Berkley Pub*.

————. **Pale Fire** (1962). An extraordinary comic tour de force about appearance and reality. Nabokov teases, traps, and enchants readers in his labyrinth of passages and deadfalls leading to understanding the fatal implications of a seemingly harmless task—editing and commenting upon the four cantos of a poem called "Pale Fire." *P—Berkeley Pub, Putnam Pub Group*.

OATES, JOYCE CAROL b. 1938. **Them** (1969). A big and

rather old-fashioned naturalistic family chronicle about three decades in the lives of the Wendells of Detroit, a shabby, not-too-bright clan struggling to rise above their stifling emptiness. *H—Vanguard; P—Fawcett.*

O'BRIEN, TIM b. 1946. **Going after Cacciato** (1978). A deserter, Private Cacciato ("the hunted" in Italian) leads his army pursuers a mad and merry chase away from the nightmare of Vietnam to the beguiling delights of Paris. An ingeniously structured novel whose comedy and fantasy underscore the terrible reality of destruction. *P—Dell.*

O'CONNOR, FLANNERY 1925–1964. **The Violent Bear It Away** (1960). In *Wise Blood* (1952), her first novel, a young backwoods Tennessean loses his faith, determines to destroy all who hold false belief, and ends in murder and self-immolation. The later novel, equally rich in comic and macabre effects but more complex and ambitious in exploring disbelief, tells of a young man's terrifying initiation as a religious prophet. *P—FS&G, NAL.*

PERCY, WALKER b. 1916. **The Moviegoer** (1961). Percy's first and best novel, a National Book Award winner about a New Orleans broker who rejects the banalities of traditional society but can substitute only movies as functional reality. *H—Knopf; P—Avon.*

PURDY, JAMES b. 1923. **Malcolm** (1959). The Gothic adventures of a complicatedly simple young man who, before he dies unexpectedly, meets a bizarre group of people, including a midget, a black undertaker, a wealthy woman who calls her home "The Chateau," and a torch singer whom he marries. *P—Penguin.*

PYNCHON, THOMAS b. 1937. **V.** (1963). A landmark of black humor. *V.* is a lively picaresque novel set in America, Africa, Italy, and elsewhere, and tells an absurd story about two men, one of them on a classical "quest." A mysterious female, whose initial gives the book its title, overshadows the narrative. *P—Bantam.*

———. **Gravity's Rainbow** (1973). This time the quarry is V-2, a rocket rather than a spy. Physics (especially principles of entropy and indeterminacy), cybernetics, and a dollop of paranoia are metaphors of modern chaos in this long, funny, and often exasperating novel. *P—Bantam, Penguin.*

REED. **Mumbo Jumbo.** See "American Minority Cultures: Black," page 124.

ROTH, PHILIP b. 1933. **Portnoy's Complaint** (1969). The

ultimate fictional case history of the suffering that Jewish mothers inflict upon their sons. Pitiless comedy and inspired mimicry with a broad base of sadness and bitterness. *H—Modern Lib, Random.*

————. **My Life as a Man** (1974). An ingenious triple play in which a writer offers two of his short stories, then appends a lengthy autobiographical account of the miseries (not unlike Portnoy's; substitute wife for mother) that inspired the fiction. *o.p.*

SALINGER, J. D. b. 1919. **The Catcher in the Rye** (1951). In his own brand of flavorful but sometimes monotonous slang, a prep-school adolescent named Holden Caulfield relates his attempts to evade adulthood in this mischievous and slyly comic novel. *H—Little; P—Bantam.*

STONE, ROBERT b. 1937. **Hall of Mirrors** (1967). Morality reflected as oppression, nationalism as racism, and patriotism as conspiracy—these are the distortions that mirror the madness and agony of contemporary American life in this brutal, apocalyptic novel centered in New Orleans. *P—HM.*

————. **Dog Soldiers** (1974). Here and in **A Flag for Sunrise** (1981), Stone explores the dehumanizing impact of Vietnam. Experiences of war are remembered rather than observed. But they shadow the later lives of the characters—with heroin the image of moral decay in *Dog Soldiers*, political irresponsibility and immorality (in Central America) in the latter novel. *H & P—HM; P—Ballantine.*

STYRON, WILLIAM b. 1925. **Sophie's Choice** (1979). A brave novel about a hopeless love between a beautiful Pole, a non-Jewish survivor of Auschwitz, and a charming but mad New York Jew. Melodramatic and southern Gothic, the novel nevertheless reaches toward profundity in tormented analyses of human weakness. *H—Random; P—Bantam.*

TYLER, ANNE b. 1941. **Dinner at the Homesick Restaurant** (1982). In her ninth novel about somewhat fey characters resident in a deeply southern Baltimore, Tyler wittily but compassionately separates the tangled strands of a mildly warped family. *H—Knopf; P—Berkley Pub.*

UPDIKE, JOHN b. 1932. **Rabbit, Run** (1950), **Rabbit Redux** (1971), and **Rabbit Is Rich** (1981). Updike's finest work, a persuasive effort to comprehend the disparate forces of our time. The first novel scans the inward, private problems of the 1950s; its successors confront the explosive artifacts of middle America in the 1970s and 1980s. *H—Knopf; P—Fawcett.*

VONNEGUT, KURT b. 1922. **Slaughterhouse Five** (1969). The firebombing of Dresden warps Billy Pilgrim's consciousness of time, space, and reality, compelling him to seek refuge and perspective elsewhere—on Vonnegut's now familiar planet, Tralfamadore. Possibly the best of his imaginative if occasionally sentimental satires. *P—Dell.*

WALKER. **The Color Purple.** See "American Minority Cultures: Black," page 125.

WARREN, ROBERT PENN b. 1905. **All the King's Men** (1946). The best novel of a first-rate American poet, critic, and scholar tells the story of a corn-pone dictator, markedly like Huey Long. *H—HarBraceJ, Random.*

WIESEL, ELIE b. 1928. **Night** (1960). A Rumanian Jew by birth, survivor of Auschwitz and Buchenwald, Wiesel is now an American citizen. His first novel is one of the most searing accounts of the Holocaust—as experienced by a 15-year-old boy. *o.p.*

————. **A Beggar in Jerusalem** (1970). Although set during the Six-Day War, the agonies and aspirations of the characters are timeless. *o.p.*

CHAPTER 13

The Short Story

ARTHUR ZEIGER

From the first nameless storytellers, masters of oral narrative who enlarged on occurrences, interpreted rituals, and transmitted traditions, through the earliest papyri, centuries later, upon which tales were inscribed in hieroglyphics, through the great ages of literature, the short story had a long and not inglorious history before the 19th century distinguished it as a specific genre.

Though Washington Irving, Edgar Allan Poe, and Nathaniel Hawthorne have variously been called "Father of the Short Story," they are at best its stepfathers. Poe, however, did define most explicitly, and stringently, the requirements of the form: It must aim at a single effect and every line must conduce to that end. Consequently, to ensure its totality of effect, its "unity," it must require "from a half-hour to one or two hours for its perusal" —neither more nor less.

Poe succeeded admirably by following his prescription. But other writers refused to be confined. Romantic fantasy (Tieck and Hoffmann in Germany), realistic analysis (Mérimée and Balzac in France), local color verism (Bret Harte and Mark Twain in America), and psychological "depth diving" (Gogol and Dostoevski in Russia) demanded forms and techniques different from Poe's.

Yet a kind of design became increasingly apparent in the 19th-century story. Length became standardized within generous limits—from 500 to 15,000 words (shorter, it became a "short-short story"; longer, a "short novel"). Plot, a casual chain of episodes, dominated: the story had a beginning, a middle, and an end; a knot was tied, more or less complexly, and gradually untied—with enough doubt about the possibility of untying to generate suspense. Character tended to be subordinated to plot (though occasionally, as in Melville's tales, plot evolved from character). And a kind of unity, at least of feeling, was generally sought and in the best stories attained.

But as the century progressed, the "well-made story" suffered a series of assaults. Even Maupassant, exemplar of the taut story with a surprise ending, sometimes broke the restraints to write poignant, evocative, nearly plotless stories (e.g., "Little Soldier"). Henry James, while tracing the formal pattern of the story, transcended it—because of his dedication to the "organic principle," his belief that a work of fiction is "a living thing, all one and continuous" (e.g., "The Beast in the Jungle"). Turgenev, especially, centered on quite ordinary characters, and as they revealed themselves, casually, almost incidentally, they compose the story (e.g., "The Country Doctor"). The most important practitioner of the modern short story, however, is surely Chekhov. He perceived the essential falsity of the story grounded in plot, wedded to unitary effect, proceeding to climax, all precisely calculated like the shelves of a cabinet. He insisted on a "middle action," with little or nothing before or after: A coachman, oppressed by troubles, tries to tell them to his passengers and fellows; rebuffed by both, he goes to the stable and confides to his horse ("A Coachman"). The readers are forced into active collaboration: They flesh out the story through memory, sympathy, insight, and they feel its truth with the immediacy of a toothache. The story makes Poe's effects seem trumpery.

With significant exceptions (Faulkner, for example), the great forgers of modern short fiction have continued in the direction toward which Chekhov pointed: Joyce, Mansfield, Anderson, Lawrence, Hemingway are each unique, yet in some sense descended from Chekhov. Nevertheless, the well-made story still prevails, of course, and it ought to. It delights, or thrills, or sends shivers through us. The world of story would be much poorer without Saki, or Conan Doyle, or Shirley Jackson. Literature is large; it can include multitudes.

And it needs to. For in the last two decades other forms of story have proliferated. Some attempt to show the disconnection of things (Barthelme); others their occult connection (Borges). Some point to the hollowness at the center of our lives (Gass); others—fewer, certainly—to at least a fragile hope (Bellow). Some are grounded in hallucination (Cortázar); others in the enduring folk past (Singer). Some reject all religious sanction

(Camus); others accept it as a first principle (Flannery O'Connor). But if the diversity seems uncountable, it is a matter for rejoicing. The multitudinousness, the plentitude, of the story implies its continuing force and vigor. The more ways for fiction the better, if not the merrier.

Books listed in earlier chapters that contain short narratives not generally considered to be short stories include Aesop's *Fables* ("Greece"), Ovid's *Metamorphoses* ("Rome"), Chaucer's *The Canterbury Tales* ("The Middle Ages"), Boccaccio's *Decameron* and Cervantes' *Don Quixote* ("The Renaissance and Reformation"), Addison and Steele's *The Spectator* ("The 18th Century"), and *Arabian Nights* and the *Bible* ("The Middle East"). Collections of short stories by writers of the regions are listed in "The Middle East," "East and Southeast Asia," "Africa," and "Latin America"; those of U.S. minority cultures under "American Minority Cultures."

Anthologies

There are countless good paperback and hardback anthologies of short stories available, including an abundance devoted to those of a single country—*Modern Turkish Short Stories, Great Russian Short Stories, French Short Stories and Tales,* and the like. Because they tend to remain in print only briefly, it seems more useful to list only "serially published" volumes—those that have continued to appear for a number of years, generally once a year.

Best American Short Stories (1915–). *H—HM.*
New Directions in Prose and Poetry (1936–). Includes short stories, often "experimental." *P—New Directions.*
Prize Stories: The O. Henry Awards (1915–) *H & P— Doubleday.*
The Pushcart Prize: Best of the Small Presses (1976–). Includes short stories from the "little magazines." *H— Pushcart Pr.*

Individual Authors

ALEICHEM, SHOLOM (SHALOM RABINOWITZ) 1859–1916.
Stories and Satires. The "Jewish Mark Twain," Aleichem

writes with understanding, compassion, and love about the Yiddish-speaking Jews of Eastern Europe. *Over 6 colls.*

ANDERSON. **Winesburg, Ohio.** See "The Novel: 20th-Century American Novels," page 160.

BABEL, ISAAC 1894–1938. **Collected Stories** (1955). Stories of civil war and of Russian life before and after the Revolution by a Russian master believed to have died in a concentration camp. *P—NAL.*

BARTH, JOHN b. 1933. **Lost in the Funhouse** (1968). Witty, technically adroit, occasionally overingenious but immensely enjoyable nevertheless. *o.p.*

BARTHELME, DONALD b. 1933. **Sixty Stories** (1981). Brilliant, often surreal fragments by a satirist who is also an extraordinary stylist: perfect sentences, words that "twitter, bong, flash and glow signals of exquisite distress." *P—Dutton.*

BEATTIE, ANN b. 1947. **The Burning House** (1982). Sharply perceived portraits of men and women whose feelings are murky. Superior specimens of the *"New Yorker* school" of fiction. *H—Random; P—Ballantine.*

BIERCE, AMBROSE 1842–1914. **In the Midst of Life** (1898). Sardonic sketches of soldiers and civilians in the terrifying world of the American Civil War and after. *P—Citadel Pr.*

BORGES. **Ficciones** and **Labyrinths.** See "Latin America," page 90.

BRADBURY, RAY b. 1920. **The Golden Apples of the Sun** (1953). One of several first-rate collections of tales of fantasy and science fiction by a master of the genre. *H—Greenwood; P—Bantam.*

CALDWELL, ERSKINE b. 1903. **Complete Stories** (1953). Tales of ribald humor, social protest, and tragedy. *o.p.*

CAPOTE, TRUMAN 1924–1984. **The Grass Harp and A Tree of Night and Other Stories** (1950). Nebulous, haunting stories. *P—NAL.*

CHEEVER, JOHN 1912–1982. **Stories** (1978). Wry commentaries on individual and societal manners in the contemporary American metropolis, suburbia, and exurbia. *H—Knopf; P—Ballantine, Random.*

CHEKHOV, ANTON 1860–1904. **Short Stories.** Carefully wrought, skeptical commentaries on Russian life and character. Chekhov's indirect, implicational narrative technique has profoundly influenced 20th-century fiction. *Over 6 colls.*

COLETTE (SIDONIE GABRIELLE COLETTE) 1873–1954. **Stories** (1983). Reminiscences of childhood by one of the most celebrated French writers of this century. *H & P—FS&G*.

CONRAD, JOSEPH 1857–1924. **Stories.** The master of the sea story is equally the master of the psychological tale. Incisive probings into the dark places of the human psyche. *Over 15 colls*.

COOVER, ROBERT b. 1932. **Pricksongs and Descants** (1969). Biblical episodes, myths, and fairy tales transmuted by psychological realism into startling and intriguing modern stories. *P—NAL*.

CORTÁZAR. **A Change of Light and Other Stories.** See "Latin America," page 91.

CRANE, STEPHEN. 1871–1900. **Stories.** Narratives by a pioneer of realism in America. *Over 10 colls*.

DE LA MARE, WALTER 1873–1956. **Stories.** Fascinated by the "twilight side of life," de la Mare created stories and tales of an unforgettable world of fantasy, dreams, and the supernatural. *Over 6 colls*.

DINESEN, ISAK (BARONESSE KAREN BLIXEN) 1885–1962. **Seven Gothic Tales** (1934), **Winter's Tales** (1942), and **Last Tales** (1957). Jewellike, richly embroidered tales of a romantic past peopled by cavaliers, maidens, and ghosts. *P—Random*.

FARRELL, JAMES T. 1904–1979. **Stories.** Stories of 20th-century urban America by the author of *Studs Lonigan*. *H—Vanguard*.

FAULKNER, WILLIAM 1897–1962. **Collected Stories** (1977). Richly varied short fiction ranging in time from the early settling of Mississippi to post-World War II days, by a master of form, subtlety, symbolism, and psychological insight. *P—Random*.

FITZGERALD, F. SCOTT 1896–1940. **Stories** (1951). Gay and tragic stories by the spokesman for the Jazz Age. *P—Scribner*.

FORSTER, E. M. 1879–1970. **The Celestial Omnibus** (1911). Graceful, witty, delightful exercises in fantasy. *P—Random*.

GASS, WILLIAM b. 1924. **In the Heart of the Heart of the Country** (1968). Diverse and remarkable "experimental" stories—ranging from a dispassionate recording of correlatives of pain to the earthy interior monologue of a "latter-day Molly Bloom." *H—Har-Row*.

GOGOL, NICOLAI V. 1809–1852. **The Overcoat and Other Tales of Good and Evil** (1957). Seven stories, all enormously important in the development of modern fiction: grotesque, moralities, acute psychological revelations, biting satires. *P—Norton*.

GORDIMER. **Selected Stories.** See "Africa," page 83.

HAWTHORNE, NATHANIEL 1804–1864. **Stories and Tales.** Deeply symbolic and carefully wrought studies of sin and retribution and romantic tales of colonial New England, by a master who helped establish the form as a serious literary type. *Over 15 colls.*

HEMINGWAY, ERNEST 1899–1961. **Short Stories.** Various collections of the short fiction by one of the most significant, influential, and controversial writers of our time. *H & P—Scribner.*

HENRY, O. (WILLIAM SYDNEY PORTER) 1862–1910. **Short Stories.** Ingenious, swiftly paced, skillfully plotted trick- or surprise-ending stories by a most widely read and imitated practitioner. *Over 6 colls.*

IRVING, WASHINGTON 1783–1859. **Sketch Book** (1820). Warmly colored, romanticized sketches, tales, and essays, such as "Rip Van Winkle" and "Legend of Sleepy Hollow." *P—NAL.*

JACKSON, SHIRLEY 1919–1965. **The Lottery** (1949). Terrifying and macabre vignettes of the tensions underlying contemporary life. *P—FS&G.*

JAMES, HENRY 1843–1916. **Short Stories. (The Complete Tales,** 12 vols., 1961–1964, *o.p.*) Intricate analyses of conflicting personalities and their psychological and emotional reactions by a consummate craftsman. *Over 12 colls.*

JOYCE, JAMES 1882–1941. **Dubliners** (1914). Joyce sought his material in the lives of insignificant people in "dear, dirty Dublin." Rich in insight, subtly symbolic, essentially simple in structure, *Dubliners* is a towering landmark in the evolution of the short story. *Over 6 eds.*

KAFKA, FRANZ 1883–1924. **Complete Stories** (1983). Striking commentaries on the absurdity of human existence, the dislocation of actor and scene. *H—Schocken.*

KIPLING, RUDYARD 1865–1936. **Stories.** One of the last of the great Romantics ranges from the hill towns of India to the jungles of Mowgli, Kaa, and Rikki-Tikki-Tavi. *Over 12 colls.*

LARDNER, RING 1885–1933. **Best Short Stories.** Satirical tales—sometimes humorous, often bitter—debunking hypocrisy in American life. *H & P—Scribner.*

LAWRENCE, D. H. 1885–1930. **Complete Short Stories** (1961). Lawrence's "religion of the blood" animates these vigorous and provocative stories of confrontations between man and woman, child and adult. *P—Penguin 3 vols.*

THE LIBRARY OF AMERICA SERIES. A series still in progress that publishes comprehensive selections in authoritative texts of the most important American writers. The volumes that have appeared so far, anthologizing Melville, Hawthorne, Irving, Poe, Stowe, Crane, Twain, and London, include short stories. *H—Viking Pr*.

LONDON, JACK 1876–1919. **Stories.** Narratives of violence, action, and atmosphere, set from the Far North to the South Seas. *Over 12 colls*.

MALAMUD, BERNARD b. 1914. **Stories** (1983). Ironic, highly individualistic stories of American Jews at home and abroad, tempered by nostalgia for the Jewish past. *H—FS&G*.

MANN, THOMAS 1875–1955. **Stories of Three Decades** (1936). Masterly, lengthy short stories on themes ranging from the adolescent to the artist. *H—Knopf*.

MANSFIELD, KATHERINE 1888–1923. **Stories.** Penetrating character studies in the Chekhov manner, and impressionistic portraits of situations. *H—Knopf; P—Random*.

MAUGHAM, W. SOMERSET 1874–1965. **Collected Short Stories.** Dramatic accounts by a popular raconteur, often dealing with odd people in faraway places. *P—Penguin 4 vols*.

MAUPASSANT, GUY DE 1850–1893. **Stories.** Realistic impressions of French life, deftly constructed and brilliantly ironic. *Over 6 colls*.

MELVILLE, HERMAN 1819–1891. **Stories.** Deep-diving, searching, masterly tales. *Over 6 colls*.

Modern Brazilian Short Stories. Ed. William L. Grossman. See "Latin America," page 102.

O'CONNOR, FLANNERY 1925–1964. **A Good Man Is Hard to Find** (1955) and **Everything That Rises Must Converge** (1965). Artistry, social awareness, the grotesque, and the need for faith characterize these stories of the contemporary South. First title: *P—HarBraceJ*. Second title: *H & P—FS&G*.

O'CONNOR, FRANK 1903–1966. **Stories** (1981). Humor, insight, and satire mark these representative stories by a leading Irish writer. *H—Knopf*.

O'FAOLAIN, SEAN b. 1900. **Short Stories** (1961). Effective narratives about contemporary Ireland. *P—Little*.

O'HARA, JOHN 1905–1970. **Short Stories.** Social satire of individual and societal absurdities. *H—Modern Lib*.

OLSEN, TILLIE b. 1913. **Tell Me a Riddle** (1960). Stories that seem simple, generally about poor and troubled people; probing, often hurting, characterized by honesty and compassion. *H—Peter Smith; P—Dell.*

OZICK, CYNTHIA b. 1928. **Levitation** (1982). Jewish life and legend form the matrix of these superlatively written, intensely imagined tales. Even when flawed, as occasionally they are, they compel our interest and admiration. *H & P—Knopf; P—Dutton.*

PALEY, GRACE b. 1922. **The Little Disturbances of Man** (1959), **Enormous Changes at the Last Minute** (1974), and **Later the Same Day** (1985). Structured about an episode or a string of episodes, these are nearly plotless stories. They stay in memory, however, because the characters are "imagined into life," and because the truth of the episodes, of the lean colloquial speech, and most of all of the feeling come through forcefully. First title: *P—NAL.* Second title: *H & P—FS&G.* Third title: *H—FS&G.*

POE, EDGAR ALLAN 1809–1849. **Tales.** Memorable stories of atmosphere, horror, and ratiocination by a founder and master of short fiction. *Over 20 colls.*

PORTER, KATHERINE ANNE 1894–1980. **Stories** (1965). Beautifully wrought and subtle narratives of varied moods, themes, and settings. *P—HarBraceJ.*

PRITCHETT, V. S. b. 1900. **Stories** (1982). Mostly about the double lives of middle-class Britishers tormented by changing social forces. *H & P—Random.*

PURDY, JAMES b. 1923. **Color of Darkness** (1957) and **Children Is All** (1962). Misfits trapped in a purgatory of the unloved, the unwanted, and the alienated, by an outstanding "black humorist." First title: *o.p.* Second title: *H—Greenwood.*

QUIROGA. **The Decapitated Chicken.** See "Latin America," page 102.

ROTH, PHILIP b. 1933. **Goodbye, Columbus, and Five Short Stories** (1959). Roth writes with irony and understanding about the American Jew in a variety of settings ranging from army training camp to big city. *H—Modern Lib; P—Bantam.*

RULFO. **The Burning Plain.** See "Latin America," page 93.

SAKI (H. H. MUNRO) 1870–1916. **The Best of Saki** (1961). Sophisticated treatment of affectations of English society; short-short stories of fantasy and surprise with an undercurrent of serious commentary. *P—Penguin.*

SALINGER, J. D. b. 1919 **Nine Stories** (1953). Perceptive depiction of problems of children and childlike adults, narrated with warmth, understanding, and sympathy. *H—Little; P—Bantam.*

SAROYAN, WILLIAM 1908–1981. **My Name Is Aram** (1940). Fresh and exuberant stories of a young Armenian in Fresno, California. *H—HarBraceJ; P—Dell*.

SCHULZ, BRUNO 1892–1942. **The Street of Crocodiles** (1977). A loosely connected sequence of stories, fascinating and sometimes eerie, revolving about the image of the father, whose reality continually shifts and dissolves into hallucination. *P—Penguin*.

SINGER, ISAAC BASHEVIS b. 1904. **Stories** (1982). Marvelous stories, rooted deep in folk memory, intensely real even when the theme is supernatural. *H—FS&G*.

Spanish American Short Story. Ed. Seymour Menton. See "Latin America," page 103.

STAFFORD, JEAN 1915–1979. **Collected Stories** (1955). Disturbing depictions of neuroses in contemporary American life enlivened by occasional humorous stories of "bad" characters in Colorado. *H—FS&G; P—Dutton*.

STEINBECK, JOHN 1902–1968. **The Long Valley** (1938). Powerful short fiction about the American West. *o.p.*

THOMAS, DYLAN 1914–1953. **Adventures in the Skin Trade** (1955). Includes individualistic short stories and sketches, employing melodrama, fantasy, humor, and surrealism. *P—New Directions*.

THURBER, JAMES 1894–1961. **The Thurber Carnival** (1945). Selections from an American humorist, one of the best of our time, whose warmth and insight are tempered by a gratifying malice. *H & P—Har-Row; H—Modern Lib*.

TURGENEV, IVAN 1818–1883. **Sketches from a Hunter's Album** (1852). Enormously influential and absorbing stories in which plot evolves from character, naturally and convincingly. *P—Penguin*.

TWAIN, MARK (SAMUEL L. CLEMENS) 1835–1910. **Stories.** Collections of the shorter works of America's greatest humorist. *Over 6 eds*.

UPDIKE, JOHN b. 1932. **Pigeon Feathers and Other Stories** (1962). *H—Knopf; P—Fawcett;* **The Music School** (1966) *H—Knopf; P—Random;* **Museums and Women** (1972) *H—Knopf; P—Random;* and **Problems and Other Stories** (1979) *H—Knopf; P—Fawcett*. The often engaging stories of a prolific writer, but a master of his craft, intelligent and finely perceptive.

VALENZUELA. **Strange Things Happen Here.** See "Latin America," page 103.

VERGA, GIOVANNI 1840–1922. **She-Wolf and Other Stories** (1958, rev. ed. 1973). Highly skillful reconstructions of Sicilian life in the 1860s. *P—U of Cal Pr*.

WELTY, EUDORA b. 1909. **Stories** (1982). Sensitive, beautifully wrought tales about contemporary Mississippi. *H & P—HarBraceJ*.

WODEHOUSE, P. G. 1881–1976. **Most of P. G. Wodehouse** (1969). A generous sampling of the hilarious effects achieved by intricate plotting and soufflé dialogue. Psmith, Jeeves, Bertie Wooster, and Mr. Mulliner are perhaps stock characters but surely enduring ones. *P—S&S*.

WOLFE, THOMAS 1900–1938. **The Hills Beyond** (1941). Semiautobiographical stories reminiscent of his loose novels but more carefully and economically written. *P—NAL*.

WRIGHT, RICHARD 1908–1960. **Uncle Tom's Children** (1938) and **Eight Men** (1961). Relentlessly honest, moving accounts of the black experience in a hostile white world. First title: *P—Har-Row*. Second title: *o.p.*

CHAPTER 14

Poetry

SALLY M. GALL

Poetry is an art form whose medium is language, language heightened in such a way that it makes perceptible to the imagination the whole range of human experience and feeling: the bitter and squalid and hateful along with the joyous, the witty, the wise.

Of all the arts (visual, performing, literary), poetry can establish the most intimately satisfying relationship with its audience. Unlike paint or marble or clay, the poet's medium—language—is an old friend; we have all worked with it since we spoke our first words. Moreover, the individual reader is also the performer: No highly talented dancer, actor, singer, or musician is needed to bring the work to full realization. The rhythms and other auditory effects of a poem, more potently pleasing than those of any other literary form, are also peculiarly ours: It is our physical act of speech that brings them into being.

Finally, because it exists in language rather than in a tangible material substance, in a sense each poem is ours alone: It exists for our inner eye, ear, and being. This places a certain responsibility on each of us. Watching a film or listening to music, we can to some extent sit back passively and let the cinematic effects or tones impinge on our eyes or ears. Not so with a poem; unless we put our imaginations to work, images of thought and feeling and awareness simply won't form in our minds. Take W. B. Yeats's six-line lyric "Memory":

> *One had a lovely face,*
> *And two or three had charm,*

> *But charm and face were in vain*
> *Because the mountain grass*
> *Cannot but keep the form*
> *Where the mountain hare has lain.*

Good poems don't stand still; they change and develop, their compressed and patterned language presenting a succession of centers of emotionally and sensuously charged awareness. These dynamic shifts can be found even in so short a span as the Yeats poem. Compare the qualitatively different realms presented by the first three lines of "Memory" and the last three. The first lines suggest a slightly world-weary man counting off attractive women who have failed to hold his ardor—"one" had a lovely this, "two or three" had that. Then the poem leaps, startlingly, to a wild natural scene: a mountain and the long grass still flattened by the body of the animal that has slept there, but which has now—in accordance with its free spirit and like the poet's one true love—gone elsewhere. Her departure, then, is as painfully present in his memory as if she had only just left, her hold on him so extraordinarily strong that no other woman can overcome it. His continuing love for her is embodied not only by the sensuously concrete image of the grass, which retains the hare's shape as the poet's memory retains hers, but by the great gulf between the ordinariness of the casually reminiscent opening scene and the extraordinariness of the closing one.

"Memory" makes the specific quality of the poet's sense of loss tangible to our aroused imagination in a way that no simple statement, no matter how heartfelt and generally moving—"I really miss that woman," say—can do. This is poetry's prime glory: its ability to convey the exact quality of other human beings' experience of life, no matter how distant their times and cultures. Further, we see in the greatest poems a blending of sound and sense that brings language itself to a pitch of elegant precision impossible in any other literary form.

Guides and Anthologies

It should be remembered that the best prose "guides" are frequently provided by the poets themselves: Prefaces, introductions, critical essays, letters, and diaries can all be highly illuminating for an individual poet's practice.

ATTRIDGE, DEREK b. 1945. **The Rhythms of English Poetry** (1982). Outstanding discussion of metrics, especially accentual-syllabic meter; offers a highly useful method of scansion. *H & P—Longman.*

BROGAN, TERRY V. F. b. 1951. **English Versification, 1570–1980: A Reference Guide with Global Appendix** (1981). Indispensable, well-annotated bibliography of books and articles treating the technical aspects of poetry from Anglo-Saxon times to the present. *H—Johns Hopkins.*

BROOKS, CLEANTH b. 1906 and ROBERT PENN WARREN b. 1905. **Understanding Poetry** (4th ed. 1976). Set the standard for introductory texts based on the tenets of New Criticism and still valuable. *P—HR&W.*

Chief Modern Poets of Britain and America (5th ed. 1970). Eds. Gerald DeWitt Sanders et al. Well-chosen, extensive selections from Hardy and Dickinson to the present; paperback is in handy two-volume format. *H & P—Macmillan.*

Contemporary American Poetry (4th ed. 1985). Ed. A. Poulin, Jr. Generous selections from some 40 poets born in the 20th century. *P—HM.*

DEUTSCH, BABETTE 1895–1982. **Poetry Handbook: A Dictionary of Terms** (4th ed. 1982). Concise and sensible. *H—Har-Row; P—B&N, T Y Crowell.*

The Home Book of Verse: American and English 1580–1920 (6th ed.1926). Ed. Burton Egbert Stevenson. Revealing compilation of poems considered suitable for family viewing before modernism took hold (editions date back to 1912). *o.p.*

LANGER, SUSANNE K. 1895–1985. **Feeling and Form** (1953). Brilliant discussion by one of our leading philosophers of the relationship between poetry and the other arts and between art and human feeling. *P—Scribner.*

The Modern Tradition: Backgrounds of Modern Literature (1965). Eds. Richard Ellmann and Charles Feidelson. The nature of modernism explored through topically organized statements ("Symbolism," "Realism," "Cultural History," etc.) by writers, philosophers, artists, scientists. *H—Oxford U Pr.*

The New Oxford Book of English Verse, 1250–1950 (1972). Ed. Helen Gardner. A standard selection. *H—Oxford U Pr.*

The Norton Anthology of Modern Poetry (1973). Eds. Richard Ellmann and Robert O'Clair. Good, annotated selections, complemented by biographical and bibliographical information. *H & P—Norton.*

The Norton Anthology of Poetry (3rd ed. 1983). Eds. Alexander W. Allison et al. The handiest available anthology of British and American poetry from their origins. *P—Norton*.

Oxford Book of American Verse (1950). Ed. F. O. Matthiessen. A classic selection by a noted critic. *H—Oxford U Pr*. (See also *The New Oxford Book of American Verse*, ed. Richard Ellmann.)

PEARCE, ROY HARVEY b. 1919. **The Continuity of American Poetry** (1961). Argues incisively for the centrality of Whitman and the continuing desire of American poets to ''find a place for poetry in the life of modern man.'' *P—Princeton U Pr*.

PERKINS, DAVID b. 1928. **A History of Modern Poetry: From the 1890s to the High Modernist Mode** (1976). First of two volumes and excellent as far as it goes (the 1920s). *H & P—Harvard U Pr*.

The Poetry of Black America: Anthology of the 20th Century (1973). Ed. Arnold Adoff. Excellent, comprehensive anthology through the 1960s. *H—Har-Row*.

The Princeton Encyclopedia of Poetry and Poetics (enlarged ed. 1974). Eds. Alex Preminger et al. The most comprehensive and authoritative reference work in the field; covers poetry in foreign languages as well. *H & P—Princeton U Pr*. (See also the forthcoming *Princeton Handbook of Poetic Terms*.)

ROSENTHAL, M. L. b. 1917 and SALLY M. GALL b. 1941. **The Modern Poetic Sequence: The Genius of Modern Poetry** (1983). Comprehensive critical treatment of the work of major modern and contemporary English and American poets in terms of this crucial genre. *H & P—Oxford U Pr*. (See also Rosenthal's earlier books *The Modern Poets* and *The New Poets*.)

SHAPIRO, KARL b. 1913. **Prose Keys to Modern Poetry** (1962). Illuminating essays, mainly by modern poets (including foreign), of significance for their work and modernism in general. *o.p.*

Viking (Penguin) Book of Folk Ballads of the English-Speaking World (1982). Ed. Albert B. Friedman. Excellent introduction to this most important tradition of stories in song. *H—Viking Pr; P—Penguin*.

WAGGONER, HYATT H. b. 1913. **American Poets from the Puritans to the Present** (1984, 1st printing 1968). Generally useful; emphasizes the centrality of Emerson to the American poetic tradition. *H & P—La State U Pr*.

WAGNER, JEAN P. b. 1919. **Black Poets of the United States:**

From Paul Laurence Dunbar to Langston Hughes (1963; English translation by Kenneth Douglas 1973). Excellent first volume (two are planned) by a white French observer. *H & P—U of Ill Pr*.

Poets to 1800

The chapters in "Historical Periods" and "Regional and Minority Cultures" contain entries for major world poets from Homer to Chaucer, Shakespeare, and Milton, and from Basho to Blake and Goethe. None of these is relisted or cross-referenced in this chapter.

British and American Poets from 1800 to the Early 20th Century

The works of most of the poets listed below have appeared in numerous anthologies and collected and selected editions. Full bibliographical information is given only for editions of special interest. American poets have "(A)" after their dates.

ARNOLD, MATTHEW 1822–1888. **Poetical Works.** Most philosophical of the leading Victorian poets, with a strong social and moral critical bent. *H—Oxford U Pr*.

BROWNING, ELIZABETH BARRETT 1806–1861. **Poetical Works** (1974). Immensely popular lyric poet, best known for her *Sonnets from the Portuguese* and *Aurora Leigh*. *H—HM*.

BROWNING, ROBERT 1812–1889. **Poetical Works.** Victorian forerunner of modernism; see especially the innovative use of speech rhythms and rapid tonal shifts of his dramatic monologues. *H—HM*.

BYRON, LORD (GEORGE GORDON NOEL) 1788–1824. **Complete Poetical Works.** The most swashbucklingly racy and satirical of the Romantic poets. *H & P—Oxford U Pr*.

COLERIDGE, SAMUEL TAYLOR 1772–1834. **Complete Poetical Works.** Founder, with Wordsworth, of the English Romantic tradition; his poetry emphasizes the psychological terrors and mysteries that drive the human spirit. *H—Oxford U Pr*.

DICKINSON, EMILY 1830–1886 (A). **Complete Poems** (1960). Ed. Thomas H. Johnson. Greatest woman poet in the English language, whose fascicles stand with Whitman's sequences at the beginning of American modernism. *H & P—Little.* See also Johnson's three-volume variorum edition (*Harvard U Pr* 1955) and, for the fascicles, R. W. Franklin's **The Manuscript Books of Emily Dickinson** (*Harvard U Pr* 1981).

EMERSON, RALPH WALDO 1803–1882. (A). **Poems.** Leading American philosopher-poet; transcendentalist and radical social thinker. *Over 6 eds.*

HARDY, THOMAS 1840–1928. **Complete Poems** (1978). Prolific elegiac and narrative poet, whose poems powerfully reflect ordinary English life. *H & P—Macmillan; H—Oxford U Pr.* See also **The Dynasts** (1978). *o.p.*

HOPKINS, GERARD MANLEY 1844–1889. **Poems** (4th ed. 1967). Eds. W. H. Gardner and N. H. MacKenzie. Intensely religious and experimental poet; inventor of "sprung rhythm." *H & P—Oxford U Pr.* See also **Poems and Prose** (1953). Ed. W. H. Gardner. *P—Penguin.*

HOUSMAN, ALFRED EDWARD 1859–1936. **Collected Poems** (new ed. 1971). Best known for his much-loved *A Shropshire Lad,* in spirit close to the restrained pathos of *The Greek Anthology. P—HR&W.*

KEATS, JOHN 1795–1821. **Poems** (1978). Ed. Jack Stillinger. Quintessential younger Romantic poet, whose richly tragic odes became models for the modern lyric-contemplative poem. *H—Harvard U Pr.*

LONGFELLOW, HENRY WADSWORTH 1807–1882 (A). **Poetical Works.** America's most popular poet; a virtuoso transmitter of foreign influences into the mainstream of American poetry. *H—HM, Oxford U Pr.*

MELVILLE, HERMAN 1819–1891 (A). **Poems.** Least appreciated American poet of power and genuine psychological complexity of his time; an outstanding poet of the Civil War. *H—Folcroft, Hendricks House; P—HR&W, New Coll U Pr.*

POE, EDGAR ALLAN 1809–1849 (A). **Poems.** Closest in spirit to English Romanticism; a compelling though uneven poet. *Over 10 eds.*

ROSSETTI, CHRISTINA 1830–1894. **Poetical Works.** A poet of delicate sensibility writing in deceptively simple forms. (Her brother Dante Gabriel's poetry is also of interest.) *H—Ridgeway Bks.*

SHELLEY, PERCY BYSSHE 1792–1822. **Complete Poetical**

Works. Romantic poet of spiritual exaltation in the neoplatonic tradition. *H—Oxford U Pr*.

SWINBURNE, ALGERNON CHARLES 1837–1909. **Poems.** His poetry is a prime example of the triumph of sound and sensual resonance over all other poetic values. *Over 6 eds*.

TENNYSON, LORD (ALFRED) 1809–1892. **Poetical Works.** With Browning, one of the outstanding Victorian poets; especially notable, as in *Maud*, for his lyrical virtuosity and intense psychological expressiveness. *H—HM*.

WHITMAN, WALT 1819–1892 (A). **Leaves of Grass.** Metrically and thematically the single most revolutionary figure in modern poetry. (See in particular *Song of Myself*.) *Leaves of Grass* (1891–92) constitutes his complete poetry. An excellent edition, including the 1855 text of *Leaves of Grass*, is **Complete Poetry and Collected Prose** (1982). *H—Library of America*. See also the variorum edition, eds. Sculley Bradley et al. (*NYU Pr* 1982). *Over 20 eds*.

WHITTIER, JOHN GREENLEAF 1807–1892 (A). **Poetical Works.** With Longfellow, one of the most popular American poets of the 19th century; democratically humane and affectionately realistic. *H—HM*.

WILDE, OSCAR 1854–1900. **Poems.** Romantic lyrics, highly polished, occasionally—as in "The Ballad of Reading Gaol" —poignant. *H & P—Biblio Dist; H—AMS Pr; P—Lawrence Hill, Penguin*.

WORDSWORTH, WILLIAM 1770–1850. **Poetical Works.** First of the English Romantics; introspective inventor (in *The Prelude*) of the personal epic; proponent of natural idiomatic phrasing in verse. For a comparison of texts of his most famous poem, see **The Prelude: A Parallel Text** (1972). *Ч & P—Oxford U Pr; P—Penguin*.

Modern and Contemporary American and British Poets

Complete bibliographical information is given only for collected editions or, where one does not exist, for a key selected volume. Although these may not be available in paperback, numerous other editions of individual and selected volumes frequently are. British poets have "(B)" after their dates.

AUDEN, W. H. 1907–1973 (B). **Selected Poems** (1979). Ed. Edward Mendelson. England's technically most versatile modern poet; deeply influenced by Marxist, Freudian, and Christian thought. *P—Random.*

BARAKA, IMAMU AMIRI (LEROI JONES) b. 1934. **Selected Poetry** (1979). Outstanding contemporary black revolutionary poet. *H & P—Morrow.*

BISHOP, ELIZABETH 1911–1979. **The Complete Poems 1927–1979** (1983). Leading woman poet in the generation after Marianne Moore. *H & P—FS&G.*

CRANE, HART 1899–1932. **The Complete Poems and Selected Letters and Prose** (1946). Lyric poet; at his best matches Rimbaud's passionately active symbolist poetry. *H—Liveright; P—Doubleday.*

CUMMINGS, E. E. 1894–1962. **Complete Poems 1913–1962** (1972). Bohemian-pacifist poet; specialist in high-spirited, sometimes visually oriented verbal acrobatics. *H & P—HarBraceJ.*

ELIOT, T. S. 1888–1965. **Collected Poems 1909–1962** (1963). With Pound and Yeats a founder of poetic modernism, of which *The Waste Land* is the example par excellence. *H—HarBraceJ.*

FROST, ROBERT 1874–1963. **The Poetry of Robert Frost** (1969). Ed. Edward Connery Lathem. Foremost 20th-century poet of pastoral realism. *H & P—HR&W.*

GINSBERG, ALLEN b. 1926. **Collected Poems: 1947–1980** (1984). Leading "Beat"; a poet of wild imagination, buffoonery, and revolutionary rhetoric, as in *Howl* and *Kaddish*. *H—Har-Row.*

HUGHES, LANGSTON 1902–1967. **Selected Poems** (1959). First black American poet to gain wide popularity; his highly colloquial, deliberately simple and moving poems show the influence of jazz and blues. *H—Knopf; P—Random.*

HUGHES, TED b. 1930 (B). **New Selected Poems** (1982). Cultivator of a totemic, almost sadistic, savagery, as in *Crow*, unusual in contemporary British poetry. *H & P—Har-Row.*

LAWRENCE, D. H. 1885–1930 (B). **Complete Poems** (1977). Poet-novelist of a mystically and sexually oriented primitivism, whose poetry is perhaps more important for its compelling antitechnological vision than for its artistry. *P—Penguin.*

LOWELL, ROBERT 1917–1977. **Selected Poems** (1976). Leading "confessional" poet whose art is based on often humiliating private experience felt to be representative of a whole society in crisis. See also **Day by Day** (1977) and the complete text of **Life Studies** (1959). *P—FS&G*.

MacNEICE, LOUIS 1907–1964 (B). **Collected Poems** (1966). Anglo-Irish poet of great wit, social sympathy, and elegiac pain. *H & P—Faber & Faber*.

MOORE, MARIANNE 1887–1972. **Complete Poems** (1967). Coolest stylist among the famous modernists and virtuoso of syllabic verse. *H—Viking Pr; P—Penguin*.

MUIR, EDWIN 1887–1959 (B). **Collected Poems** (2nd ed. 1965). Scottish poet profoundly affected by Freud, Kafka, and European socialist thought. *H—Oxford U Pr; P—Faber & Faber*.

OLSON, CHARLES 1910–1970. **The Maximus Poems** (1983). Leading poet of the Pound- and Williams-influenced ''projectivist'' movement, which emphasized ''open form.'' *H—U of Cal Pr*.

OWEN, WILFRED 1893–1918 (B). **Collected Poems** (1964). Most powerful poet to record the shock of World War I trench warfare. *P—New Directions*.

PLATH, SYLVIA 1932–1963. **Collected Poems** (1981). Most precocious and accomplished of the younger generation of ''confessional,'' suicidal poets. *H & P—Har-Row*.

POUND, EZRA 1885–1972. **The Cantos** (1972–   ). The prime mover and shaker of poetic modernism whose *Cantos* represents its most ambitious effort; controversially associated with Italian Fascism. *H—New Directions*. See also **Collected Early Poems** (1982) and **Personae** (n.d.). Both from *New Directions*.

RANSOM, JOHN CROWE 1888–1974. **Selected Poems** (3rd rev. ed. 1978). Leading southern agrarian poet; master of the bitterly nostalgic elegy. *P—Ecco Pr*.

RICH, ADRIENNE b. 1929. **The Fact of a Doorframe: Poems Selected and New, 1950–1984** (1984). Feminist poet whose piercingly lyrical art is, especially in her later poems, often mixed with tendentious rhetoric. *H & P—Norton*.

ROBINSON, EDWIN ARLINGTON 1869–1935. **Collected Poems** (1966). Fine poet, though sometimes overly discursive, of subtle yet intense nostalgia for a vanishing America. *o.p.*

ROETHKE, THEODORE 1908–1963. **Collected Poems** (1982). Mystical, sometimes manic, poet, at his best in his ''greenhouse poems.'' *H—U of Wash Pr; P—Doubleday*.

SANDBURG, CARL 1878–1967. **Complete Poems** (1970). Midwest populist poet; exuberant celebrator of the common life who was also capable of delicately impressionistic sketches. *H—HarBraceJ*.

SEXTON, ANNE 1928–1974. **Complete Poems** (1982). The most forthrightly self-exposing of the suicidal "confessional" poets of Plath's generation. *H & P—HM*.

STEVENS, WALLACE 1879–1955. **Collected Poems** (1982). The great dandy of poetic modernism and its esthete extraordinaire—except when drowning himself in philosophical abstractions. *P—Random*.

THOMAS, DYLAN 1914–1953 (B). **Poems** (1971). Welsh poet similar to Hart Crane in his preoccupation with sex and death expressed through powerfully juxtaposed metaphors. *H & P— New Directions*.

THOMAS, EDWARD 1878–1917 (B). **Collected Poems** (1974). Darkly pastoral poet, killed in World War I, whose work has strong affinities to that of his friend Robert Frost. *H & P—Norton; P—Faber & Faber*.

WILLIAMS, WILLIAM CARLOS 1883–1963. **Selected Poems** (1969). Most consciously American of the great moderns, whose *Paterson* is an epic effort to uncover a "common language" of shared history and experience. See **Collected Earlier Poems, 1906–1939; Collected Later Poems, 1940– 1950; Pictures from Brueghel and Other Poems, 1950–1962;** and **Paterson** (1963). All from *New Directions*.

YEATS, WILLIAM BUTLER 1865–1939. (B). **Poems** (1983). Irish poet whose powerful genius and depth of vision made him the foremost poet in English of the modern age. *H—Macmillan*. See also the variorum edition (1957).

Poetry has flourished in the 20th century, and a short list such as this one is distressingly incomplete. Various anthologies should be consulted for additional poets and their works sought out. The following should be of particular interest:

Conrad Aiken, John Ashbery, Margaret Atwood, John Berryman, Paul Blackburn, Robert Bly, Gwendolyn Brooks, Basil Bunting, Robert Creeley, Countee Cullen, Robert Duncan, William Empson, Kenneth Fearing, Robert Graves, Ramon Guthrie, H. D. (Hilda Doolittle), Seamus Heaney, Geoffrey Hill, Randall Jarrell, David Jones, Galway Kinnell, Philip Larkin, Denise Levertov, Hugh MacDiarmid, Archibald MacLeish, Edgar Lee Masters, Edna St. Vincent Millay, Laura Riding, Louis Simpson, Allen Tate, Mona Van Duyn, Derek Walcott, Robert Penn Warren, and Richard Wilbur.

Note on recordings: Readings by many modern and contemporary poets are widely available on such labels as Caedmon and Spoken Arts. Two specialized catalogs are those of the Library of Congress Recorded Sound Section (Washington, D.C. 20540) and the Poets' Audio Center of The Watershed Foundation (Box 50145, Washington, D.C. 20004).

Continental Poets since 1800

Thanks to poets' skillful manipulation of sound values, poetry is the most difficult of the verbal arts to translate successfully. Thus, whenever possible, the poems of the writers listed here should be read in their original language, even if one is not completely fluent. This is not as difficult as it seems, in that numerous dual-language anthologies and editions of individual poets exist and should be attempted. One need only be able to pronounce the language reasonably correctly and to recognize the most ordinary words and constructions. Exact prose translations are best for such editions and can be a considerable boost to morale, because one finds that all sorts of words one doesn't officially "know" are quite easily recognizable.

While capturing the sound of poetry in another language can be a very great joy indeed, in cases where this is not possible one should realize not only that fine translations exist for most of the following poets but that they continue to be made. The anthologies recommended below reflect the truism that each generation deserves a new translation to keep up with the changes in English idiom.

(*Note:* The poets cited in parentheses are of lesser stature but still important.)

France

19th–20th centuries: Charles Baudelaire, Jules Laforgue, Stephane Malarmé, Arthur Rimbaud, Paul Valéry, Paul Verlaine. (Guillaume Apollinaire, Louis Aragon, André Breton, Tristan Corbière, Robert Desnos, Paul Eluard, Théophile Gautier, Saint-John Perse.)

An Anthology of French Poets from Nerval to Valéry (1958). Ed. Angel Flores. *o.p.*

Contemporary French Poets (1965). Eds. Alexander Aspel and Daniel Justice. *o.p.*

Penguin Book of French Verse (1975). Eds. B. Woledge, Geoffrey Brereton et al. *P—Penguin*.
Random House Book of Twentieth-Century French Poetry (1982). Ed. Paul Auster. *H—Random*.

Germany

19th–20th centuries: Johann Wolfgang von Goethe, Heinrich Heine, Friedrich Hölderlin, Else Lasker-Schüler. (Hans Arp, Gottfried Benn, Paul Celan, Nelly Sachs, Georg Trask.)
An Anthology of German Poetry from Hölderlin to Rilke in English Translation (1960). Ed. Angel Flores. *H—Peter Smith*.
Contemporary German Poetry (1976). Ed. & tr. Ewald Osers. *P—Oleander Pr*.
Penguin Book of German Verse (1980). Ed. & tr. Leonard Forster. *o.p.*

Greece

20th century: Constantin Cavafy, George Seferis. (Odysseus Elytis, Nikos Kazantzakis, Angelos Sikelianos.)
Modern Greek Poetry (1973). Ed. & tr. Kimon Friar. *o.p.*
Penguin Book of Greek Verse (1971). Ed. & tr. Constantine A. Trypanis. *o.p.*
Voices of Modern Greece: Cavafy, Sikelianos, Seferis, Elytis, and Gatsos (1981). Eds. Edmund Keeley and Phillip Sherrard. *H & P—Princeton U Pr*.

Italy

19th–20th centuries: Giacomo Leopardi, Filippo Marinetti, Eugenio Montale, Salvatore Quasimodo, Giuseppe Ungaretti.
Italian Poetry, 1960–1980 (1982). Eds. Adriano Spatola and Paul Vangelisti. *H & P—Invisible-Red Hill*.
Italian Poetry: A Selection from St. Francis of Assisi to Salvatore Quasimodo (1970). Ed. & tr. Luciano Rebay. *o.p.*
Twentieth-Century Italian Poetry: A Bilingual Translation (1975). Ed. & tr. Levi Robert Lind. *o.p.*

Spain

20th century: Federico García Lorca, Antonio Machado.
Anthology of Spanish Poetry: From the Beginnings to the Present Day (1979). Ed. John A. Crow. *H & P—La State U Pr*.

Modern Spanish Poems (1965). Ed. Calvin Cannon. *H—Macmillan*.

Penguin Book of Spanish Verse (1966). Ed & tr. John M. Cohen. *o.p.*

USSR (and Russia)

19th–20th centuries: Anna Akhnatova, Alexsandr Blok, Sergei Esenin, Mikhail Lermontov, Osip Mandelstam, Vladimir Mayakovsky, Boris Pasternak, Alexsandr Pushkin.

The New Russian Poets, 1953–1968 (1981). Ed & tr. George Reavey. *P—M Boyars, October.*

Russian Poetry: The Modern Period (1978). Eds. John Glad and Daniel Weissbort. *H & P—U of Iowa Pr.*

Selections from Russian Poetry and Prose (1966). Ed. & tr. Vladimir Rus. *o.p.*

CHAPTER 15

Drama

ROGER W. OLIVER

Although a play is certainly more complete in its written form than a composer's score or an architect's blueprint, like them it represents a starting point rather than a final destination. For it is only when the full resources of the theater—acting, directing, design, and the like—breathe life into the playwright's words and ideas that they achieve their full impact. Drama uses the theater's dimensions of space and time to show us (and not just tell about) images of ourselves.

As literature rather than theater, drama requires a rigorous effort on the reader's part. A good (not to say great) play will certainly reward the reader with characters, actions, themes, images and language of resonance and power. But the reader must exercise imagination to provide what the theatrical production would normally supply. This is especially true in large-scale works, where the dialogue between characters in a scene can form only a small section of a complex visual and aural tapestry.

Perhaps the key element missing in reading rather than seeing and hearing a play is its social aspect. In communicating to a group audience, the playwright must find those bonds that link people together and transcend personal differences. In exchange the playwright can establish certain tacit agreements or conventions with the audience (e.g., soliloquies, asides, disguises, extreme compression or expansion of time) that enrich the theatrical experience. Furthermore, the full impact of both comedy and tragedy is deepened by the knowledge that our response is shared by others.

Thus, from its origins in the huge open-air amphitheaters of

the ancient Greeks, drama has dealt with the complex relationships between the individual and society. As the theater buildings themselves have evolved into the proscenium (or picture
frame) structures of the past 300 years, drama has concerned
itself with the representation of more intimate personal relationships. Yet even here the social ramifications of these relationships cannot be ignored. The history of the theater is a rich and
multifaceted one, and the experience of play reading is certainly
complemented by a book like Oscar Brockett's *History of the
Theatre* or Peter Arnott's *Theatre in Its Time: An Introduction*.

In describing Cleopatra in Shakespeare's *Antony and Cleopatra*,
one of the characters speaks of "her infinite variety." Drama
and theater can also be characterized this way. From intimate
chamber dramas to full-scale epics, from historical dramas en-
capsulating the fates of nations to clinical case studies, from the
comic to the tragic, the romantic to the realistic, the melodramatic to the naturalistic, the dramatic form has afforded its
creators a wide choice of subject matter and varied means of
expression. Many of these plays are available in reasonably
priced paperbacks (either in anthologies or individual editions)
that allow the full range of the medium to be sampled.

Even though the theater is not exclusively a literary domain, it
has traditionally attracted great writers. Earlier chapters of the
book refer to some of the golden ages of drama: ancient Greece
with its trio of tragic geniuses, Aeschylus, Sophocles, and Euripides, and the comic master Aristophanes; Elizabethan and Jacobean
England with Shakespeare and his contemporaries; the 17th-
century France of Corneille, Racine, and Molière; Restoration
and 18th-century England, with Congreve, Sheridan, and
Goldsmith.

The 19th-century phenomena of naturalism and realism had a
far-reaching influence on the drama. Writers like Ibsen, Strindberg,
Chekhov, and, later, Shaw and O'Neill brought to the stage a
social awareness and attention to everyday detail that had been
missing in Romantic plays and melodramas. Realism and naturalism also generated countermovements like the expressionism
of Strindberg, O'Neill, and various German writers, the theatricalism of Pirandello, and the epic theater of Brecht.

More recently, the twin strands of realism and antirealistic
experimentation have both continued to flourish, often intertwining, as in the plays of such writers as Miller, Williams, Albee,
Shepard, and Pinter. The drama's ability to create significant
metaphors for contemporary life is evidenced by these writers, as

well as by such playwrights as Beckett, Ionesco, Genêt, Fugard, and others. Even though the mass media of cinema and television reach much larger audiences, the theater, by reinterpreting great dramatic works from the past and engendering new plays to continue their tradition, remains an important forum for bringing communities together to share ideas and emotional experiences.

Anthologies

Best American Plays (1952–1983). Ed. John Gassner. Eight volumes (the final one co-edited with Clive Barnes) that together suggest the broad spectrum of the drama this country has produced. *H—Crown*.

Character and Conflict (2nd ed. 1969). Ed. Alvin B. Kernan. An excellent introduction to drama, containing 11 plays from various periods with elaborate commentaries. *P—HarBraceJ*.

The Classic Theatre (1958–63). Ed. Eric Bentley. Good collections from major national theaters—Italian, German, Spanish, and French *o.p.*

Drama on Stage (1961, 2nd ed. 1978). Ed. Randolph Goodman. A first-rate introduction to the serious study of plays, containing sample dramas from major periods as well as many essays about theaters, dramatic productions, and acting. *P—HR&W*.

Eight Great Comedies (1957). From Aristophanes to Shaw. *P—NAL*.

Eight Great Tragedies (1957). From Aeschylus to O'Neill. *P—NAL*.

Four Russian Plays (1972). Four major pre-Chekhovian works, translated by Joshua Cooper. *P—Penguin*.

Grove Press Modern Drama (1975). Ed. John Lahr. Six plays by Baraka, Brecht, Feiffer, Genêt, Ionesco, and Mrozek epitomize the most nontraditional trends in world theater today. *o.p.*

Jacobean Drama: An Anthology (1968). Ed. Richard C. Harrier. A representative collection of early 17th-century plays. *P—Norton*.

Masters of Modern Drama (1962). Eds. Haskell M. Block and Robert G. Shedd. An impressively edited, monumentally proportioned anthology, containing 45 plays by 35 modern world dramatists from Ibsen and Strindberg through Beckett and Duerrenmatt. *H—Random*.

The Modern Theatre (1955–60). Ed. Eric Bentley. Stimulating collections containing 30 otherwise hard to find modern European and American plays. *H—Peter Smith*.

Modern Theatre (1964). Ed. Robert Corrigan. An extensive selection of plays from the late 19th century to the present, with brief theoretical essays by their authors. *H—Macmillan*.

The Play: A Critical Anthology (1951). Ed. Eric Bentley. One play each by Sophocles. Molière, Ibsen, Strindberg, Rostand, Wilde, and Miller and two by Shakespeare, plus unusually illuminating critical analyses, constitute an excellent introduction to the study of drama. *o.p.*

A Treasury of the Theater (1968). Ed. John Gassner. Two volumes of plays that provide a full picture of modern drama. Vol. I: From Ibsen to Sartre. Vol. II: From Wilde to Ionesco. *H—S&S*.

Twenty-three Plays: An Introductory Anthology (1978). Eds. Otto Reinert and Peter Arnott. Plays from the Greeks to the present with useful introductory essays. *P—Little*.

Classics of the Drama

For plays by, and books about, the classical Greek dramatists (Aeschylus, Sophocles, Euripides, Aristophanes), see "Greece," pages 3 to 10. Elizabethan and Jacobean drama, including Shakespeare, is covered in "The Renaissance and Reformation," pages 26 to 38. For classical French drama (Corneille, Molière, Racine), see "The 17th Century," pages 39 to 45. Distinctive plays from all the greater and lesser dramatic periods are contained in many of the critical and standard anthologies previously cited.

Modern Drama

Many plays by modern and contemporary playwrights are inexpensively available in anthologies such as those listed previously. Chiefly collections of a single dramatist's work are included in the list following. An up-to-date listing of single plays in paperbound editions can be found in the latest *Paperbound Books in Print*, either in the author section under the author's name or in the subject section after "Drama."

ALBEE, EDWARD b. 1928. **Who's Afraid of Virginia Woolf?**
(1962). Remains a most powerful exploration of modern marriage and love and hatred coexisting in the same relationship.
P—Antheneum, NAL. See also **The Plays.** *P—Atheneum 4
vols.*

ANDERSON, MAXWELL 1888–1959. **Four Verse Plays** (1959).
Contains the best tragedies (including *Winterset*) of a modern
playwright who tried with varying success to blend poetry and
social commentary with his own tragic vision. *P—HarBraceJ.*

ANOUILH, JEAN b. 1910. **Five Plays** (1959). Distinctive and
diverse plays by a French master of theatricalism. *o.p.*

BOND, EDWARD b. 1934. **Bingo and The Sea: Two Plays**
(1975). Two acerbic social dramas mixing historical settings
and contemporary insights. *H—Hill & Wang.*

BRECHT, BERTOLT 1898–1956. **Collected Plays** (1971–73).
In dramas like *Mother Courage, Galileo*, and *The Caucasian
Chalk Circle*, this German master forces his audience to con-
sider images of war and economic exploitation. *P—Random.*

CHEKHOV, ANTON 1860–1904. **Plays.** Superb, realistic, subtle analyses of timeless human nature, with Russian variations.
Over 6 colls.

ELIOT, T. S. 1888–1965. **Complete Poems and Plays, 1909–
1950.** (1952). One of the most important modern poets in
English to date. *H—HarBraceJ.*

FUGARD, ATHOL b. 1932. **A Lesson from Aloes** (1981) and
Master Harold and the Boys (1984). A South African dramatist's eloquent condemnations of the evils of apartheid. First
title: *H—Random.* Second title: *P—Penguin.*

GENÊT, JEAN b. 1910. **The Blacks** (1960) and **The Balcony**
(1958). Striking theatrical images of social and sexual perversity. *P—Grove.*

GIRAUDOUX, JEAN 1882–1944. **Four Plays** (1958). Four
theatricalist dramas, including *The Madwoman of Chaillot*, in
Maurice Valency's excellent translations and adaptations from
the French. *o.p.*

HELLMAN, LILLIAN 1905–1984. **Collected Plays** (1972).
Hard-edged analyses of American life, often set in the
South, e.g., *The Little Foxes* and *Another Part of the Forest.*
o.p.

IBSEN, HENRICK 1828–1906. **Plays.** Naturalistic, symbolic,
poetic plays that have shaped significantly both the form and
the content of drama ever since his time. *Over 20 colls.*

IONESCO, EUGÈNE b. 1912. **Four Plays** (1958). Antirealistic, symbolic plays by a leading exponent of the experimental European theater since World War II. *P—Grove*.

LORCA, FEDERICO GARCÍA 1899–1936. **Three Tragedies** (1956). Powerful poetic tragedies by the leading author of 20th-century Spain. *P—New Directions*.

MILLER, ARTHUR b. 1915. **Collected Plays** (1957). Tragedies and social parables that prompt some critics to rank Miller as a major contemporary dramatist. *H—Viking Pr*.

O'CASEY, SEAN 1884–1964. **Three Plays** (1957). Three of the best plays, including *The Plough and the Stars*, by the most powerful modern Irish playwright. *P—St Martin*.

O'NEILL, EUGENE 1888–1953. **Long Day's Journey into Night** (1950) and **The Iceman Cometh** (1957). Two overwhelming tragic dramas by the father of serious American drama. First title: *H & P—Yale U Pr*. Second title: *P—Random*.

PINTER, HAROLD b. 1930. **The Homecoming** (1966), **Old Times** (1972), and **No Man's Land** (1975). Chilling yet comic dramas of manipulation and memory. *P—Grove*.

PIRANDELLO, LUIGI 1867–1936. **Naked Masks** (1952). In five enigmatic, provocative plays, an experimental Italian playwright probes the confusing nature of reality. *P—Dutton*.

SHAW, GEORGE BERNARD 1856–1950. **Plays.** Witty, talky dramas dedicated to the proposition that reason should rule over 20th-century men and women. *Over 6 colls*.

SHEPARD, SAM b. 1943. **Seven Plays.** Mythic images of contemporary America, rooted in, but not limited to, realism. *o.p.*

STOPPARD, TOM b. 1937. **Rosencrantz and Guildenstern Are Dead** (1967) and **Jumpers** (1974). Philosophical comedies featuring linguistic pyrotechnics, by an heir to the mantle of Wilde and Shaw. First title: *P—Grove*. Second title: *H & P—Grove*.

STRINDBERG, AUGUST 1849–1912. **Plays.** Moving dramas by a mordant Scandinavian playwright, important for his psychological probing and symbolist technique. *Over 12 colls*.

WILDER, THORNTON 1897–1975. **Three Plays** (1957). Includes *The Skin of Our Teeth* and *Our Town;* experimental, lucid, much-revived plays by a modern who retained his faith in humanity and God. *H—Har-Row*.

WILLIAMS, TENNESSEE 1914–1983. **Theatre of Tennessee Williams** (1972–81). Strange poetic tragedies about warped, frustrated lives by a leading American dramatist. *H—New Directions 7 vols*.

History and Criticism

ARNOTT, PETER b. 1931. **The Theater in Its Time: An Introduction** (1981). Theater history with a social dimension. *H—Little*.

ARTAUD, ANTONIN 1896–1948. **The Theatre and Its Double** (1958). Essays on the "theater of cruelty" that have greatly influenced the contemporary theater. *P—Grove*.

BENTLEY, ERIC b. 1916. **The Playwright as Thinker** (1955). Perceptive, informed analyses of the thought in drama of Cocteau, Ibsen, Pirandello, Sartre, Shaw, Strindberg—most useful after the reader knows the plays well. *P—HarBraceJ*.

BRECHT, BERTOLT 1898–1956. **Brecht on Theatre** (1964). Ed. John Willet. Theater writings by a proponent of alienation and the epic theater. *P—Hill & Wang*.

BROCKETT, OSCAR G. b. 1923. **History of the Theater** (4th ed. 1981). For both readability and scholarship, the best one-volume history of the theater from ancient Egypt down to "happenings." Rich in material, objective on controversial matters, with well-chosen but poorly reproduced illustrations. *H—Allyn*.

BROOK, PETER b. 1925. **The Empty Space** (1968). One of the most brilliant and controversial directors in the theater today explains his views on theatrical aesthetics. *P—Atheneum*.

BRUSTEIN, ROBERT b. 1927. **The Theatre of Revolt: An Approach to Modern Drama** (1964). Stimulating critical analyses of the major playwrights of modern drama. *P—Little*.

CARLSON, MARVIN b. 1935. **Theories of the Theater** (1984). A complete study of theatrical theory from Aristotle to the present. *H—Cornell U Pr*.

ESSLIN, MARTIN b. 1918. **Reflections** (1969). A series of essays in casual language offering sensible, perceptive, and thorough analyses of the whole theater situation today, viewing the newer trends (e.g., epic, absurdist) as fusing into the traditional mainstream. *o.p.*

LAHR, JOHN b. 1941. **Up Against the Fourth Wall** (1970). Stimulating essays on the radical theater of the 1960s (playwrights such as Pinter and Kopit, groups such as Living Theater and La Mama), viewing drama as a reflection of our social and cultural upheavals. *o.p.*

The Theory of the Modern Stage (1968). Ed. Eric Bentley. A ranging introduction to theater today through essays by representative directors, critics, and scholars. *P—Penguin.*

WILLIAMS, RAYMOND b. 1921. **Modern Tragedy** (1966). One of England's leading literary critics presents provocative analyses of the tragic form in our lives. *P—Stanford U Pr.*

Drama on Records and Videotape

Listening to recorded plays or seeing them on videotape is a compromise measure—sometimes better than reading them but less satisfying than seeing them performed live. Now, in addition to the extensive library of recorded plays that range from the Greek classics to the present, there are videotaped versions of filmed plays and staged performances, Schwann's catalog is a good source for recordings, and a videotape catalog can help suggest plays available in this medium.

CHAPTER 16

Biography

PHILIP RODDMAN

Is it possible to learn the truth about any individual, living or dead? And would the discovery of the truth explain the intricate, the accidental, the elusive life led from day to day by the subject of this truth? When reconstructing a life, all biographers must assume an affirmative answer to these two great questions. Whereas novelists and playwrights aim to *create* life in order to intensify the mystery of personality, biographers aim to *re-create* life in order to clarify the mystery. For the purpose of biography is to introduce, as history does, a sense of continuity into human affairs, as well as to excite our wonder and satisfy our doubts by making life a function of truth, as religion does. Biography is therefore a branch of history and frequently an ally of religious philosophy. In fact, for a culture such as ours, bred in the Judeo-Christian tradition, it has been the universal art form, as exemplified by the lives of the patriarchs and heroes of the Old Testament and by that of Jesus in the New. So it may well be that the enormous popularity of biography in our time—more than 2,000 are published annually in English alone—expresses the wish for a general, perhaps a religious, thaw in the icy reaches of Technopolis—biography being a reassuring documentary art form that infuses the meshes of history with the magic of personality.

There are, of course, many kinds of biography to fit the many kinds of truth. The thoughtful reader, seeking both pleasure and instruction, should examine the half-dozen masterpieces in the two mainstreams of biographical writing: the stream of being—what a person is—and the stream of action—what a person does.

The first stream flows from Plutarch's *Lives of the Noble Grecians and Romans*, the second from Suetonius's *Lives of the Twelve Caesars*. Plutarch, influenced by the idea of destiny in Greek tragedy, portrays human nature as changeless and the conflict between will and fate in terms of a morality play. Suetonius, influenced by Lucretius and the "atomists," conceives of the individual as a bundle of sensations, as an ever-changing I, a "coral reef of diverse personalities," as a vehicle for a fund of restless energies that add up to a "happening" rather than a play.

Plutarch's concept of "the ruling passion" and the unitary sense of things has been reinforced in modern history by Calvin's dogma of predestination, by Freud's theory of the ineluctable unconscious, and by Lenin's insistence on the inexorability of class determinism. Suetonius's emphasis on our mixed nature and the pervasiveness of chance has received support from the British empirical thinkers, from John Locke, David Hume, John Stuart Mill, and Charles Darwin, as well as from the libertarian ideas in the Declaration of Independence and from Einstein's theory of relativity.

The Plutarchian tradition of "the ruling passion" conferring symmetrical order upon the ages of man—youth, middle age, old age—appears in Dr. Johnson's *Lives of the Poets*, though not in his theories regarding experience. In Boswell's *The Life of Samuel Johnson*, the supreme biography in English, "the ruling passion" motif does not appear at all. Consider an example from each. After observing of Dean Swift that "he was always careful of his money," Johnson continues: "At last his avarice grew too powerful for his kindness; he would refuse a bottle to a guest, and in Ireland no man visits where he cannot drink." He then concludes that Swift's loneliness and desolation brought on his madness. The root cause, seemingly, of Swift's great misfortunes was in large part his "love of a shilling." Johnson's point of view is clear-cut and imposed with much force and wit. His biographer, James Boswell, on the other hand, follows the realistic tradition of Suetonius, where the character steadily characterizes himself—in and by his very voice, his style, and his habits. Here is Boswell's rendering of a dinner table conversation: "Mr. Arthur Lee mentioned some Scotch who had taken possession of a barren part of America, and wondered why they should choose it. Johnson: Why, Sir, all barrenness is comparative. The Scotch would never know it to be barren." Boswell tells us that Johnson kept dried orange peel in his pockets and that he had a dread of solitude. All manner of detail shapes and reshapes the Johnsonian presence. Boswell vividly re-creates the man who converted his outrageous prejudices into counters for fun and games and transmuted the ugly matter of physical pain and early sorrow into the bright essences of reason.

Of 20th-century biographies, among the most important in the first category are Ernest Jones's *The Life and Work of Sigmund Freud* and Edgar Johnson's *Charles Dickens: His Tragedy and Triumph*, while Lytton Strachey's *Queen Victoria* and Amy Kelly's *Eleanor of Aquitaine and the Four Kings* are examples of the second.

Ever since St. Augustine's *Confessions*, men and women have yearned to tell their own side of the story in the unequal struggle with existence, impelled as much by the need to obtain absolution as by the desire for self-justification in a cold and hostile universe. Autobiography, therefore, is as much a branch of psychology as of history. Its interest for us resides in the personal answer, both conscious and unconscious, which it gives to those four simple and all-encompassing questions that psychology is forever asking: Why do we laugh? Why do we cry? Why do we forget? Why do we lie? The responses to these questions in autobiographies of men and women of genius have universal value because they carry a charge of consciousness surpassed only by the greatest novelists. In projecting the self as hero, an autobiographer sets out to serve the secret fantasies of the heart, but ends by serving knowledge and truth. In the process of vindicating the massive illusions and ambitions of the inner life, he or she uncovers the way they are put together. Cellini's *Autobiography*, Rousseau's *Confessions*, Boswell's *London Journal*, Gibbon's *Autobiography*, De Quincey's *Confessions of an English Opium-Eater*, Mill's *Autobiography*, Gide's *Journals*, Planck's *Scientific Autobiography*, Einstein's *Out of My Later Years*, Van Gogh's *Dear Theo*, Stravinsky's *Themes and Episodes*, Frank Lloyd Wright's *Autobiography*, Stein's *The Autobiography of Alice B. Toklas*, Churchill's *Memoirs of the Second World War*, Sartre's *The Words*, and most recently, Russell's *Autobiography*—all attest to the variety, the wisdom, the psychological reality of this form of revelation.

The first eleven chapters of this book, dealing with "Historical Periods" and "Regional and Minority Cultures," list a few autobiographies and many biographies—both those written during the historical period or in the cultural area and those written mainly in recent decades about important political leaders and monarchs, writers, scientists, social reformers, and artists. These numerous biographies are not relisted or cross-referenced in this "Biography" chapter. The reader is advised to consult the "Books About" sections of Chapters 1 through 11 for additional recommendations and data about other biographies rewarding to read.

ACKERMAN, JAMES S. b. 1919. **Palladio** (1966). Perhaps the most imitated architect in history is presented in his social and cultural environment. *P—Penguin*.

ADAMS, HENRY 1838–1918. **The Education of Henry Adams** (1905). The scion of one of the "first families" of New England in quest of the meaning of life. *H & P—HM; H—Berg*.

ALLEN, GAY WILSON b. 1903. **The Solitary Singer** (1955). America's master poet, Walt Whitman, in a well-documented work that lays bare his life in his art. *o.p.*

————. **Waldo Emerson** (1981). The definitive biography of the "Sage of Concord"—America's sage as well: Emerson's life and thought luminously set forth. *H—Viking Pr*.

ARMITAGE, ANGUS 1902–1976. **The World of Copernicus** (1947). The life of the Renaissance cleric-astronomer who changed our view about the structure of the universe. *P— Beekman Pubs*.

AUDUBON, JOHN JAMES 1785–1851. **The Eighteen Twenty-Six Journal of John James Audubon** (1967). The personal record of the artist-ornithologist whose contribution to American culture is of unparalleled splendor. *H—U of Okla Pr*.

BAKER, CARLOS b. 1909. **Ernest Hemingway: A Life Story** (1969). The standard biography, massively documented and well written but lacking a coherent analytic overview. *H—Scribner; P—Avon*.

BARAKA, IMAMU AMIRI b. 1934. **The Autobiography of LeRoi Jones** (1984). The turbulent life of an American poet and playwright vividly drawn. *H—Freundlich*.

BEAUVOIR, SIMONE DE b. 1909. **All Said and Done** (1974). Views on feminism, religious belief, change, and chance as they form in the life experiences of the existentialist novelist and critic. *o.p.*

BELL, QUENTIN b. 1910. **Virginia Woolf** (1972). A major English novelist caught to the life in a frank biography by her nephew. *P—HarBraceJ*.

BERLIN, ISAIAH b. 1909. **Karl Marx** (4th ed. 1978). The mover and shaker of the modern world depicted by a celebrated English scholar. *H & P—Oxford U Pr*.

BERLIOZ, HECTOR 1803–1869. **Memoirs of Hector Berlioz** (1969). The great composer self-revealed as a passionate intellect. *P—Dover, Norton*.

BLAKE, ROBERT b. 1916. **Disraeli** (1966). The gifted and mysterious man—Queen Victoria's favorite prime minister—comes to life. *o.p.*

BLOTNER, JOSEPH LEO b. 1923. **Faulkner** (1974). A detailed life of the Nobel Prize novelist whose vision of southern anguish since the Civil War has enriched world literature. A condensed, updated, one-volume edition appeared in 1984 (also *Random*). *H—Random 2 vols*.

BOWEN, CATHERINE DRINKER 1897–1973. **Yankee from Olympus** (1944). The fascinating life of a magnificent man, Justice Oliver Wendell Holmes. *o.p.*

CHESTERTON, GILBERT KEITH 1874–1936. **Saint Thomas Aquinas** (1933). The authoritative theologian of Roman Catholicism refreshingly presented by a "prince of paradox" among biographers. *P—Doubleday*.

CURIE, EVE b. 1904. **Madame Curie** (1937). A daughter's tribute to the genius of her mother, a great scientist. *o.p.*

DAICHES, DAVID b. 1912. **Moses** (1975). The Hebrew lawgiver and prophet delineated by a many-sided Scottish scholar. *o.p.*

DANA, RICHARD HENRY 1815–1882. **Two Years Before the Mast** (1840). A young Harvard dropout adventuring aboard a windjammer more than a century ago. *Over 5 eds*.

DARWIN, CHARLES 1809–1882. **The Voyage of the Beagle** (1840). Perhaps the most significant voyage since that of Columbus, leading to the formulation of the theory of evolution and to a new concept of history. *H & P—Biblio Dist; H—Natural Hist*.

DELACROIX, EUGÈNE 1798–1863. **Journals** (repr. 1969). A towering artist of immense energy, interested in politics and literature and sex, setting himself down in a daily journal from the age of 23 to the year of his death. *H—Garland Pub; P—Cornell U Pr*.

DE QUINCEY, THOMAS 1785–1859. **Confessions of an English Opium-Eater** (1822). An account of drug addiction in brilliant prose. *H—Biblio Dist; P—Penguin*.

DU BOIS, WILLIAM EDWARD BURGHARDT 1868–1963. **Autobiography** (1968). The champion of complete civil and political equality for black Americans in a self-portrayal that reveals great nobility of character and mind. *H & P—Intl Pub Co*.

EDEL, LEON b. 1907. **Henry James** (1953–72). A five-volume definitive biography of the subtlest master of the American novel. *P—Avon.*

ELLMANN, RICHARD b. 1918. **James Joyce** (1959). An engrossing and immensely learned biography of a literary genius. *P—Oxford U Pr.*

ESSLIN, MARTIN b. 1918. **Antonin Artaud** (1977). A study of the lucid madman whose theories have revolutionized the modern theater. *P—Penguin.*

FRANK, ANNE 1929–1945. **Diary of a Young Girl** (1952). The unforgettable journal of an adolescent girl who with her family hid in an Amsterdam house before capture and death in a Nazi extermination camp. *H—Doubleday; P—WSP.*

FRANK, JOSEPH b. 1918. **Dostoevsky: The Seeds of Revolt, 1821–1849** (1976) and **Dostoevsky: The Years of Ordeal, 1850–1859** (1983). The first two volumes (thus far) of an engrossing biography, admirable in its insight. *H—Princeton U Pr.*

FRANK, PHILIPP 1884–1966. **Einstein** (1947). Einstein's successor in the professorship of theoretical physics at the University of Prague writes a magisterial account of a scientific genius. *o.p.*

FREEMAN, DOUGLAS SOUTHALL 1886–1952. **R. E. Lee** (1935). The hero of the Confederacy and his lieutenants delineated in a monumental work of historical scholarship. *H—Scribner 4 vols.*

GOLDSTONE, RICHARD HENRY b. 1917. **Thornton Wilder** (1975). A synthesis of the life and achievements of a widely read playwright, novelist, scholar, and critic. *o.p.*

GRAHAM, SHIRLEY 1907–1977 and GEORGE D. LIPSCOMB. **Dr. George Washington Carver** (1944). An engaging account of a black American scientist of international renown, whose work as an agricultural chemist has so extensively improved the culture of crops. *o.p.*

GUTMAN, ROBERT W. b. 1925. **Richard Wagner** (1968). The genius of the music-drama and "endless melody" brilliantly portrayed. *o.p.*

HAMMARSKJÖLD, DAG 1905–1961. **Markings** (1964). The spiritual struggle of a man who headed the United Nations like a modern Pericles. *H—Knopf; P—Ballantine.*

HESSION, CHARLES H. b. 1911. **John Maynard Keynes** (1984). A thorough study of the man who revolutionized capitalism and the way we live. *H—Macmillan.*

HIGHAM, CHARLES b. 1931. **The Adventures of Conan Doyle** (1976). The life of a great and just man, who in the Holmes-Watson team created one of the absolute successes in world literature. *H—Norton*.

HILDESHEIMER, WOLFGANG b. 1916. **Mozart** (1977). A wise and affectionate evocation of the genius who created an ideal world of matchless music. *H—FS&G; P—Random*.

HODGES, ANDREW b. 1949. **Alan Turing: The Enigma** (1983). The dramatic story of the man who built the first electronic brain and invented the "Turing test," which posed and answered the question: At what point, if ever, may we consider a computer truly "intelligent?" *H & P—S&S*.

HOMER, WILLIAM INNES b. 1929. **Alfred Stieglitz and the American Avant-Garde** (1977). About the photographer and painter who counseled and sustained native genius in the arts long before America's awakening to the existence of the school of Paris. *H & P—NYGS*.

HOWARD, JANE b. 1935. **Margaret Mead** (1984). A full-bodied account of the American anthropologist whose contributions to the emancipation of our minds have been of prime importance in education. *H—S&S*.

HUNT, JOHN DIXON b. 1935. **The Wider Sea: A Life of John Ruskin** (1982). The brilliant art critic and social reformer, the writer who inspired Tolstoy, Proust, Gandhi, portrayed in the full splendor of mind and in the suffering of disease. *H—Viking Pr*.

ISHERWOOD, CHRISTOPHER b. 1904. **Christopher and His Kind** (1976). Remarkably objective autobiography of the novelist who caught a vision of murderous inhumanity in the Berlin of the 1930s. *H—FS&G; P—Avon*.

JOHN XXIII, POPE 1881–1963. **Journal of a Soul** (1963). The record of a noble spirit in a troubled world, reminiscent of Thomas à Kempis's *The Imitation of Christ*. *o.p.*

JOHNSON, EDGAR b. 1901. **Charles Dickens** (1952). An outstanding work about the tragedy and triumph of one of the best and most beloved of English novelists. *H—Viking Pr*.

JONES, ERNEST 1879–1958. **The Life and Work of Sigmund Freud** (1953–57). A classic biography of the man who re-shaped the consciousness of the modern world. *H—Basic 3 vols.; P—Basic abr*.

KAPLAN, JUSTIN b. 1925. **Mr. Clemens and Mark Twain** (1966). The man, the writer, and the performer acutely studied, his comic genius perceptively analyzed. *H & P—S&S*.

KARL, FREDERICK ROBERT b. 1927. **Joseph Conrad: The Three Lives** (1979). The great novelist exhaustively presented as a boy in Poland, a merchant seaman in England, and a world-famous figure in literature. *H & P—FS&G*.

KELLER, HELEN 1880–1968. **The Story of My Life** (1903). A document of first importance about the miraculous achievements of a human being who in early childhood had lost the power to hear and see. *H—Doubleday; P—Airmont, Macmillan*.

KING, CORETTA SCOTT b. 1927. **My Life with Martin Luther King, Jr.** (1970). The poignant story of the assassinated human rights activist by his wife, a remarkable leader in her own right. *o.p.*

KLEE, PAUL 1879–1940. **The Diaries of Paul Klee** (1964). The painter who believed that art is *process* illuminates his own work and that of abstract impressionism. *P—U of Cal Pr*.

LÉLY, GILBERT. **Marquis de Sade** (1962). Novelist, diabolist, sadist, the Marquis, the ultimate monster in modern psychology, portrayed as neighbor and "our bedfellow." *P—Grove*.

LEVY, JULIEN 1906–1981. **Memoir of an Art Gallery** (1977). A rich record of the years 1931–1948 that recalls the struggle of the avant-garde to reach the American public at a time when the business aspect of art meant not money but lightness of heart, unorthodoxy of mind, and "plenty of pleasure." *o.p.*

LYONS, F. S. L. 1923–1983. **Charles Stewart Parnell** (1977). The fascination of a career, both political and romantic, that captured the imagination of geniuses like Yeats and Joyce as well as that of the average person. *o.p.*

MADARIAGA, SALVADOR DE 1886–1978. **Christopher Columbus** (1967). A well-conceived life of the explorer. *H—Greenwood*.

MALCOLM X 1925–1965. **The Autobiography of Malcolm X** (1964). A devastating depiction of life in the jungle of cities by a man of fine intelligence who rose, against heavy odds, above the bondage of his surroundings. *P—Ballantine*.

MARCHAND, LESLIE b. 1900. **Byron** (1957). A definitive biography of a great 19th-century poet, individualist, and activist. *o.p.*

MAUROIS, ANDRÉ 1885–1967. **Lelia: The Life of George Sand** (1953). The most famous woman in French letters, celebrated for 80 novels, a dozen liaisons, and numerous social reforms, drawn with a steel pen. *P—Penguin*.

———. **Prometheus: The Life of Balzac** (1966). The definitive biography of a titan of the novel and rated by French critics as Maurois's masterpiece. *P—Carroll & Graf*.

MEHTA, VED b. 1934. **Mahatma Gandhi and His Apostles** (1976). A vivid rendering of Gandhi's habits and daily conduct against the background of his beliefs, precepts, and enormous influence. *P—Penguin*.

MERTON, THOMAS 1915–1968. **The Seven Storey Mountain** (1948). Challenging account of a poet's conversion to Roman Catholicism and his discovery of a vocation in a Trappist monastery in Kentucky. *H—Octagon; P—HarBraceJ*.

MILL, JOHN STUART 1806–1873. **Autobiography** (1873). The education of a prodigy by a father whose psychological theories stressed environmental factors rather than heredity. *P—Columbia U Pr, HM*.

MILLER, EDWIN H. b. 1918. **Melville** (1975). A psychobiography whose primary evidence is Melville's fiction and poetry. *o.p.*

MIZENER, ARTHUR b. 1907. **The Far Side of Paradise** (1951). Fascinating account of F. Scott Fitzgerald, who in his novels caught the sense of life prevailing between the two world wars. *P—HM*.

MOORE, RUTH E. b. 1908 **Niels Bohr** (1966). A dramatic and thoughtful portrayal of the physicist and the milieu that helped place America first in the Atomic Age. *o.p.*

MORGAN, CHARLES H. 1902–1984. **The Life of Michelangelo** (1960). The pithiest one-volume account of the greatest sculptor between Phidias and Rodin and the most sumptuous of muralists. *o.p.*

MURRAY, K. M. ELISABETH b. 1909. **Caught in the Web of Words** (1977). The founding editor of the great *Oxford English Dictionary*, to whom we all owe "an unpayable debt," memorialized in a biography of drama and power. *H—Oxford U Pr, Yale U Pr*.

NABOKOV, VLADIMIR 1899–1977. **Speak, Memory** (1966). A masterly evocation of the aristocratic life in pre-Communist Russia by the author of *Lolita*. *H—Putnam Pub Group*.

NEWMAN, JOHN HENRY 1801–1890. **Apologia pro Vita Sua** (1864). One of the stellar stylists in English examines his life and his conversion to Roman Catholicism. *H—Oxford U Pr; P—HM, Norton*.

PAINTER, GEORGE D. b. 1914. **Marcel Proust** (1959–65). One of the great novelists of the 20th century delineated so vividly and precisely as to emerge as a Proustian creation. *P—Random 2 vols*.

PAWEL, ERNST b. 1920. **The Nightmare of Reason: A Life**

of Franz Kafka (1984). A comprehensive biography of the writer described by W. H. Auden as the Dante of the 20th century. *H—FS&G*.

PENROSE, ROLAND 1900–1984. **Picasso: His Life and Work** (1981). A striking portrait of the most celebrated artist, and best known name, of our entire century. *H & P—U of Cal Pr*.

PERNOUD, RÉGINE b. 1909. **Joan of Arc** (1969). A remarkable document illuminating an incredible life. *P—Stein & Day*.

PÉTREMENT, SIMONE b. 1907. **Simone Weil** (1976). A passionate thinker of the 20th century; mystic, rationalist, martyr, in a sympathetic biography. *H—Pantheon*.

RIIS, JACOB 1849–1914. **The Making of an American** (1901). A classic in the literature of immigration to the United States by a Dane who became a successful journalist and social reformer. *H—Century Book-bindery*.

RODINSON, MAXIME b. 1915. **Muhammad** (1971). The prophet and lawgiver of Islam in a biography that emphasizes his religious genius and political acumen. *P—Pantheon*.

SAMUELS, ERNEST b. 1903. **Bernard Berenson: The Making of a Connoisseur** (1979). A success story whose subject is the foremost specialist in the attribution of origin to the works of art of the Italian Renaissance *H & P—Harvard U Pr*.

SANTAYANA, GEORGE 1863–1952. **Persons and Places** (1944–53). The memories, reflections, and assessments of one of the wisest and most frequently quoted philosophers of our time. *o.p.*

SCHOENBAUM, S. b. 1927. **William Shakespeare: A Documentary Life** (1975). The best essential life to date. *H & P—Oxford U Pr*.

SCHWEITZER, ALBERT 1875–1965. **Out of My Life and Thought** (1933). The story of an amazing man—teacher, theologian, musician, humanitarian, doctor-missionary to Africa. *o.p.*

SHEAFFER, LOUIS b. 1912. **O'Neill: Son and Playwright** (1968) and **O'Neill: Son and Artist** (1973). A double biography of America's Nobel prize-winning playwright, perhaps the most autobiographical of all our artists. *H & P—Little*.

SOLOMON, MAYNARD b. 1930. **Beethoven** (1977). A masterly presentation of the isolated mystical intuitive man who, having created a promethean universe of sound, reverted to the impassive wisdom of Plutarch: "Plutarch has shown me the path of resignation." *H & P—Assoc-Mus*.

STEEGMULLER, FRANCIS b. 1906. **Cocteau** (1970). An account of the man, his work, and his banquet years that does justice to the kaleidoscopic artist: poet, novelist, playwright, filmmaker. *o.p.*

STEFFENS, LINCOLN 1866–1936. **Autobiography** (1931). One of the trail-blazing books about graft and corruption in American city politics during the early 1900s. *P—HarBraceJ 2 vols.*

STEIN, GERTRUDE 1874–1946. **The Autobiography of Alice B. Toklas** (1933). The classic re-creation of the life of geniuses living and working in the great epoch of early 20th-century Paris. *H—Modern Lib, Peter Smith; P—Random.*

STRACHEY, LYTTON 1880–1932. **Queen Victoria** (1921). A master biographer draws a vivid picture of the queen-empress in the enthusiasm of youth, the loneliness of middle age, and the eccentricities of old age. *H & P—HarBraceJ.*

SWANBERG, W. A. b. 1907. **Norman Thomas: The Last Idealist** (1976). The American voice of socialism and six times his party's candidate for president clearly portrayed as the product of the Protestant tradition of service and the Emersonian philosophy of optimism. *o.p.*

THOMPSON, LAWRENCE 1906–1973. **Robert Frost** (1966–77). America's "poet laureate" shown objectively, with all his strengths and weaknesses. *o.p.*

THOREAU, HENRY DAVID 1817–1862. **Walden** (1854). The essential American loner seeking communion with nature, self-revealed in classic prose. *Over 15 eds.*

TROTSKY, LEON 1879–1940. **Lenin: Notes for a Biography** (1925). A firsthand report of the international revolutionary figure by a messianic visionary who was his closest partner in the overturning of the czarist regime. *o.p.*

TROYAT, HENRI b. 1911. **Tolstoy** (1967). A knowing and loving biography of the master novelist, the influential prophet, and the elusive doom-haunted man. *H—Octagon; P—Crown.*

VAN GOGH, VINCENT 1853–1890. **Dear Theo** (1937). Perceptive letters to his brother by one of the tenderest and most anguished of artists. *P—NAL.*

WARD, AILEEN b. 1919. **John Keats** (1963). An award-winning biography of the immortal poet whose life has become an allegory of the suffering and transfiguration of early and ill-fated genius. *H—Octagon.*

WASHINGTON, BOOKER T. 1856–1915. **Up from Slavery** (1901). The epic story of a resurrection, from bondage to freedom, by the influential black educator. *H—Corner Hse, Doubleday; P—Airmont*.

WECHSBERG, JOSEPH 1907–1983. **Verdi** (1974). A life of the endearing composer whose music and whose humanism project what is most beautiful in Mediterranean civilization. *o.p.*

WILSON, EDMUND 1895–1972. **The Twenties** (1976). Fascinating journal by the dean of American literary critics about the high decade of love and poetry and aspiration in Greenwich Village and seacoasts of Bohemia. *H—FS&G*.

WRIGHT, FRANK LLOYD 1869–1959. **Autobiography** (1943). A wise, impressive, and provocative book covering the long career of a creative mind in architecture. *H—Horizon*.

WRIGHT, RICHARD 1908–1960. **Black Boy** (1945). Grim autobiography of an American who yearned for the intellectual and physical freedom denied him in a country ruled by whites. *H & P—Har-Row*.

YEATS, WILLIAM BUTLER 1865–1939. **Autobiography** (1936). The beautifully composed memoirs of the celebrated poet, Nobel Prize winner, founder of the Abbey Theatre, and Irish patriot. *P—Macmillan*.

CHAPTER 17

Essays, Letters, Criticism, Magazines

GEORGE HOCHFIELD

Essays are relatively short discursive writings in prose. They have commonly been distinguished as formal or informal, that is, tending either to rigorous argument and exposition or to loose, idiosyncratic, personal reflection. Until fairly recent times informality has been the dominant tradition, and even nowadays writers whose chief aim is to persuade by logical demonstration—Karl Popper is an excellent example—often allow themselves a certain freedom and intimacy of expression. It seems impossible, and even unnatural, for the essayist to seek perfect detachment from his subject. The essay, thus, despite recent developments, is a markedly individualized form in which the personality and voice of the writer are much more directly present than in other literary genres.

Essays did not exist in ancient literature. They are an invention of the Renaissance with its fresh appreciation for the rich possibilities of human character and experience. Montaigne in his *Essais* (1580) was the first to use the name—it carried the implication of ''trials'' or ''tests'' or ''forays''—and he was the model of a familiar, almost improvisatory, stylist. ''These are my humours and opinions,'' he wrote; ''I give them as representing what I myself believe. . . . I aim here at only disclosing myself, who may peradventure be a different self tomorrow. . . .'' Not long after, in 1597, Sir Francis Bacon published his *Essays or Counsels Civil and Moral*. They are less familiar, more rationally ordered and aphoristic, but equally reliant on the knowledge gained from firsthand observation of life. These two classic writers stand as the great progenitors of the literary essay.

Like other genres, the essay has evolved by adaptation to the times. The 18th century saw the emergence of a new type of informal writing: polished and urbane commentary on social manners and literary taste. The *Spectator* papers (1711–1714) are the most famous examples of this type of essay. In them the labors of art were disguised by a conversational style that suggested the intimacy of exchange among like-minded gentlemen. Samuel Johnson in *The Rambler* (1750–1752) and *The Idler* (1758–1760) introduced a note of moral severity and the hint of complex psychological depths.

In the 19th century new printing technology and large publishing concerns made the periodical press a true mass medium, and the essay flourished. Although Charles Lamb's *Essays of Elia* (1823) are remembered as classics of the familiar style, in general in this century essays became a serious matter: vehicles of social criticism, ideological contention, and literary and philosophical debate. Major writers like Carlyle, Ruskin, Arnold, George Eliot, and J. S. Mill participated in the intellectual wars of their age by means of essays in the monthly or quarterly journals. In America, one of the signs of growing literary independence was the establishment of successful magazines like *The North American Review* (1815), *Harper's* (1850), and *Atlantic* (1857). All the important figures of American literature, from Irving to Emerson to William and Henry James, saw their work appear in these or other journals. Emerson especially made the essay his own particular form, creating an original, sometimes intoxicating, mixture of poetry and philosophy.

In modern times the essay is the most widely diffused of literary forms, and its character has continued to change in accord with the development of society. The modern essay may, in a general way, be regarded as an instrument of democratic education. Though often polemical, its principal modes are explanatory and analytic, and its chief function is the dissemination of knowledge to generally educated readers. A good contemporary magazine is likely to carry several essays in various fields written by experts or specialized journalists: one on some question of foreign or domestic relations, let us say; another on science or technology; another on literature, or history, or popular culture, or business management, etc. By such means the reader is kept abreast of his world, and the extravagant variety of modern thought is circulated in the bloodstream of society.

Letters are normally private communications; that may be the reason for their peculiar fascination. A touch of voyeurism is no doubt involved. Still, the secrets of private life are not in themselves very interesting. The best letters are those in which the writer tells a story different from, though often complementary to, the stories he tells in public. Flaubert's letters about the composition of *Madame Bovary* are a wonderful example of such a story. In other letters we often find the stuff of personal experience before it is transmuted into works of art, the excited exchange of ideas, the drama of self-justification, the cool and witty appraisal of friends and enemies. All of these themes may be found in the marvelously expressive letters of such figures as Tolstoy, D. H. Lawrence, Virginia Woolf, Ernest Hemingway, and Scott Fitzgerald.

Criticism is the analysis, interpretation, and evaluation of works of art. It arises from the irresistible questions first asked, or adumbrated, by Plato and Aristotle: What is the purpose of art? What relation does it have to the world of common experience? What are its methods and materials? What are its effects on its audience? Every attempt to comment intelligently on books, or paintings, or musical compositions must wrestle (explicitly or not) with one or more of these important questions in some form. The reason for their importance is that art is the most fundamental, as well as the most complex, expression of human consciousness. It is the primary means by which mankind reveals itself to itself. Criticism is thus the ongoing, never-definitive effort to elucidate the human meanings contained in works of art and to make them available for new opportunities of thought.

ADDISON and STEELE. **The Spectator.** See ''The 18th Century,'' page 52.

ARNOLD, MATTHEW 1822–1888. **Essays in Criticism** (2 ser. 1865–88) and **Culture and Anarchy** (1869). An important body of work in their time, Arnold's essays are still prominent in contemporary debates over literature and culture. *Over 15 eds*.

AUDEN, W. H. 1907–1973. **The Dyer's Hand** (1962). Provocative reflections on a variety of literary subjects. *P—Random*.

AUERBACH, ERICH 1892–1957. **Mimesis** (1946). A classic work on realism in Western literature from Homer to Virginia Woolf. *H & P—Princeton U Pr*.

BACON. **Essays.** See ''The Renaissance and Reformation,'' page 32.

BERRY, WENDELL b. 1934. **Recollected Essays, 1965–1980** (1981). The work of a prolific and admirable writer whose world is the country known to farmers and naturalists. *H & P—N Point Pr.*

BLOOM, HAROLD b. 1930. **The Anxiety of Influence** (1973). A reinterpretation of literary influence in Freudian terms. *P—Oxford U Pr.*

CAMUS, ALBERT 1913–1960. **The Myth of Sisyphus and Other Essays** (1955). Earnest and thoughtful writings often dealing with the same themes that appear in his fiction. *P—Random.*

CHEKHOV, ANTON 1860–1904. **Letters of Anton Chekhov** (1973). Ed. A. Yarmolinsky. The most humane and ingratiating of Russian writers in letters touching on literature, the stage, and Russian life. *H—Viking Pr.*

CHESTERFIELD. **Letters to His Son.** See "The 18th Century," page 53.

CICERO, MARCUS TULLIUS 106–43 B.C. **Cicero's Letters to Atticus** (1965–68). Ed. & tr. D. R. Shackleton-Bailey. A unique and invaluable body of correspondence by a man deeply involved in the political struggles of his age. *P—Penguin.*

CRANE, HART 1899–1932. **The Letters of Hart Crane** (1952). Ed. Brom Weber. A record of the vagrant, poetry-obsessed life of one of the key figures of American modernism. *o.p.*

CULLER, JONATHAN b. 1944. **On Deconstruction: Theory and Criticism after Structuralism** (1982). Inspired by the French philosopher Jacques Derrida, Culler explains those strategies of deconstruction that subvert our conventional understanding of a literary text. *H & P—Cornell U Pr.*

ELIOT, T. S. 1888–1965. **Selected Essays** (1932). A book that contributed enormously to the profound change of literary attitudes in England and America in the years between World Wars I and II. *H—HarBraceJ.*

EMERSON, RALPH WALDO 1803–1882. **Essays** (1st ser. 1841, 2nd ser. 1844). The most original and important essays written by an American. *Over 20 eds.*

FITZGERALD, F. SCOTT 1896–1940. **The Letters of F. Scott Fitzgerald** (1963). Ed. Andrew Turnbull. An intimate, often funny, sometimes painful view of the author of *The Great Gatsby.* *H—Scribner.*

FLAUBERT, GUSTAVE 1821–1880. **The Letters of Gustave Flaubert** (1954). Ed. and tr. Francis Steegmuller. A fascinating portrayal of the agony of modern authorship. *H & P—Harvard U Pr 2 vols*.

FORSTER, E. M. 1879–1970. **Aspects of the Novel** (1927). An interesting attempt by an important novelist to gather together his thoughts about the art of novel writing. *P—HarBraceJ*.

———. **Two Cheers for Democracy** (1951). A delightful collection of personal opinions about literature, politics, friendship, and travel. *P—HarBraceJ*.

FRYE, NORTHROP b. 1912. **Anatomy of Criticism** (1957). A seminal work of modern criticism based on the analysis of "archetypes." *H & P—Princeton U Pr*.

GASS, WILLIAM H. b. 1924. **Fiction and the Figures of Life** (1971). Witty and intricate essays by a philosopher-novelist on the theme of art's divergence from life. *P—Godine*.

GOULD. **Ever Since Darwin.** See "Biological Sciences," page 378.

HAZLITT, WILLIAM 1778–1830. **Selected Writings** (1970). Ed. Ronald Blythe. Among the most readable examples of the personal essay in English literature—copious, opinionated, fiercely independent. *P—Penguin*.

HEMINGWAY, ERNEST 1896–1961. **Selected Letters, 1917–1961.** Ed. Carlos Baker. All the contradictory elements of an extraordinarily complex personality are revealed in these "often libelous, always indiscreet, often obscene" letters. *o.p.*

HOWE, IRVING b. 1920. **Celebrations and Attacks** (1978). A rich collection of essays on literature and society by a lucid, undogmatic, but committed writer. *H—Horizon; P—HarBraceJ*.

JAMES, HENRY 1843–1916. **The Art of the Novel** (1934). Ed. R. P. Blackmur. A collection of the subtle and highly suggestive prefaces written by James late in his life for the New York edition of his works. *P—NE U Pr*.

JAMES, WILLIAM 1842–1910. **The Will to Believe** (1956). First published in 1897 and called by James "essays in popular philosophy," the pieces contained in this volume are characteristically trenchant expressions of his thought. *H—Harvard U Pr; P—Dover*.

JOYCE, JAMES 1882–1941. **Letters of James Joyce** (1966). One of the towering figures of modern literature reveals a good deal about his states of mind and intentions during the composition of his books. *H—Viking Pr 3 vols*.

KAZIN, ALFRED b. 1915. **Contemporaries from the Nineteenth Century to the Present** (rev. ed. 1981). Thoughtful, well-written essays on 19th- and 20th-century American authors. *P—Horizon*.

KEATS, JOHN 1795–1821. **Letters of John Keats** (1959, 1970). The combination of precocious brilliance and painful mortality makes the reading of these letters an intensely moving experience. *H—Harvard U Pr 2 vols.; P—Oxfored U Pr*.

LAMB, CHARLES 1775–1834. **Essays of Elia** (1823, 1833). Perhaps the most famous of English personal essays, they are full of grace, invention, and tender feeling. *Over 6 eds*.

LAWRENCE, D. H. 1888–1930. **Studies in Classical American Literature** (1923). One of the most original and influential statements ever made concerning the literature produced by Americans. *P—Penguin*.

————. **Phoenix** (1936). A big collection of miscellaneous essays and reviews; all of Lawrence's varied passions and interests find expression here. *H—Viking Pr; P—Penguin*.

————. **Letters of D. H. Lawrence** (1979–84). Eds. J. T. Boulton and Andrew Robertson. One of the most forceful and original personalities in modern English literature in impassioned expression of his literary and social convictions. *H—Cambridge U Pr 3 vols.; P—Penguin, sels*.

LENTRICCHIA, FRANK b. 1940. **After the New Criticism** (1980). A lucid analysis of critical trends in the United States from about 1950 on. *H & P—U of Chicago Pr*.

MacDONALD, DWIGHT 1906–1982. **Against the American Grain** (1962). Intelligent and readable essays on the "effects of mass culture." *P—Da Capo*.

MANN, THOMAS 1875–1955. **Essays of Three Decades** (1947). Deeply thoughtful, occasionally ponderous, examinations of major literary figures, chiefly German. *o.p.*

MONTAIGNE. **Essays.** See "The Renaissance and Reformation," page 35.

ORWELL, GEORGE 1903–1950. **Collected Essays, Journalism, and Letters** (1968). Wide-ranging commentary on politics and culture in the 1930s and 1940s by the author of *1984*. *H & P—HarBraceJ 4 vols*.

POPPER, KARL b. 1902. **Conjectures and Refutations** (1963, 5th ed. 1974). A collection of essays on the methods and purposes of science by a pungent writer with a sharp mind. *P—Har-Row*.

POUND, EZRA 1885–1972. **The Literary Essays of Ezra Pound** (1954). Ed. T. S. Eliot. An opinionated, urgent writer, determined to transform the literary tastes and standards of his generation. *P—New Directions*.

RUSSELL, BERTRAND 1872–1970. **Unpopular Essays** (1969). One collection out of many by an outspoken, independent writer who was also one of the century's most popular philosophers. *P—S&S*.

SONTAG, SUSAN b. 1933. **Against Interpretation and Other Essays** (1966). A first collection by a brilliant essayist who writes on many aspects of modern artistic activity, from film and photography to tragedy and happenings. *H—Octagon*.

STEVENS, WALLACE 1879–1955. **The Necessary Angel** (1951). Illuminating essays on "poetry and the imagination" by one of the greatest of modern poets. *P—Random*.

STEVENSON, ROBERT LOUIS 1850–1894. **Virginibus Puerisque** (1881). Attractive informal essays by a writer now somewhat neglected. *o.p.*

THOMAS. **The Lives of a Cell: Notes of a Biology Watcher.** See "Biological Sciences," page 341.

TOLSTOY, LEO 1828–1910. **Tolstoy's Letters** (1978). Ed. & tr. R. F. Christian. Virtually an autobiography of Tolstoy, one of humanity's great seekers and passionate dogmatists. *o.p.*

TRILLING, LIONEL 1905–1975. **The Liberal Imagination** (1979). The leading representative of the Arnoldian tradition of cultivated, humane intelligence in modern American criticism. *H—HarBraceJ*.

WALPOLE. **Letters.** See "The 18th Century," page 56.

WILDE, OSCAR 1854–1900. **Selected Letters of Oscar Wilde** (1962). Ed. Rupert Hart-Davis. Letters of a clever and serious writer who thought of letter writing as an art. *P—Oxford U Pr*.

WILSON, EDMUND 1895–1972. **Axel's Castle** (1931). The first important book by a prolific critic and reviewer of modern literature; it helped introduce some of the great modernists to American readers. *P—Norton*.

————. **The Shock of Recognition** (1943, 1955). A splendid collection of essays, reviews, and letters by writers (chiefly American) about American writers. *H—Octagon*.

WOOLF, VIRGINIA 1882–1941. **The Common Reader: First Series** (1955). One of several collections of Woolf's sensitive critical prose. *P—HarBraceJ*.

————. **The Letters of Virginia Woolf** (1975–   ). Ed. Nigel Nicolson. Witty, shrewd, poignant letters by this century's most important English woman writer. *H & P—HarBraceJ 6 vols*.

Magazines

Magazines are regular publications, usually issued weekly, monthly, or quarterly, aimed at satisfying the intellectual or commercial interests of an astonishing variety of audiences, from video game players and classical music listeners to supermarket owners and health fanatics. As this range suggests, contemporary publishers have found that financial viability often requires specialization. Nevertheless, a certain number of ''general-interest'' periodicals still survive (sometimes tenuously), offering their readers thoughtful commentary and information on subjects traditionally regarded as appropriate for educated persons: world affairs, social and intellectual developments, and the arts.

Prototypes of the general-interest magazine, and still among the best, are the long-established monthlies *Atlantic* and *Harper's*. Both carry regular features on politics, some fiction and poetry, book reviews, and an array of timely articles. Several weekly and biweekly magazines do similar things, though their emphasis is political: *The Nation*, *The New Republic*, and *National Review* might be mentioned. Certain quarterlies like the *Yale Review* and *The American Scholar* are also intended for general readers; their tone is likely to be somewhat more sober and professional than the others.

Quarterlies in general represent the expert and professional wisdom of their fields. In a journal like *The American Historical Review*, to choose an example, one may find debate over fundamental questions and methodology, or over the interpretation of significant events like the Civil War or the New Deal, as well as highly detailed studies of particular bodies of historical material. These matters are all important to the life of the mind, even if their discussion is sometimes vitiated by intellectual fads and professional jargon. The function of the quarterlies at their best is to set standards and provide models for precision of thought and knowledge.

Listed below are some of the best magazines now available in the United States. The list is necessarily partial; and interested readers will easily find many more worthy of their attention.

The American Scholar (Quarterly—Washington, D.C.) An excellent review, slightly conservative, published by the Phi Beta Kappa Society, directed to the intelligent reader and covering a wide range of subjects.

The Atlantic Monthly (Monthly—Boston). Perhaps the best of the general-interest magazines, containing fiction, poetry, and reviews, as well as essays in many fields.

Bulletin of the Atomic Scientists (10/yr.—Chicago). Directed to the educated reader, offering informed, well-written articles on science and its role in world affairs.

Commentary (Monthly—New York). A highly literate magazine primarily interested in social and political affairs, with some special interest in Jewish matters. The leading journal of neoconservatism.

Commonweal (Biweekly—New York). A forum for fresh and serious thought about all matters pertaining to Catholicism, especially in the United States.

Daedalus (Quarterly—Cambridge, Mass.). Published by the American Academy of Arts and Sciences, a scholarly journal usually devoting entire issues to a single subject.

Dissent (Quarterly—New York). A thoughtful outlet for "democratic—socialist" criticism of American politics.

Economist (Weekly—London). Well-written, authoritative articles, organized in the newsmagazine style, on politics, economics, and world affairs.

Forbes (Biweekly—New York). Professional, informative magazine, aimed primarily at managers, business executives, and entrepreneurs.

Foreign Affairs (5/yr.—New York). The most authoritative American journal of matters relating to world politics.

Hudson Review (Quarterly—New York). An outstanding literary magazine, publishing fiction, poetry, and critical essays by some of the best contemporary writers.

Ms. (Monthly—New York). The leading popular journal of modern feminism.

The Nation (Weekly—New York). A well-written forum for liberal opinion on politics and the arts.

National Review (Biweekly—New York). The best-known outlet for the conservative position in American politics.

Natural History (Monthly—New York). Published by the American Museum of Natural History, it offers well-illustrated articles for the general reader on geographic, environmental, and ecological matters.

The New Republic (Weekly—Washington, D.C.). Important magazine of liberal opinion, with regular features on films and books.

New York Review of Books (Biweekly—New York). The best-written periodical for book reviews in the United States, frequently publishing long review essays or occasional pieces on politics or literature by writers of international stature.

The New Yorker (Weekly—New York). Including fiction, "profiles," cartoons, travel essays, features on jazz, sports, films, and books, this magazine—despite its monotony of style—remains one of the most readable in the country.

Newsweek (Weekly—New York). A summary of the week's news organized according to subjects, e.g., education, medicine, national and world politics, sports, etc.

Poetry (Monthly—Chicago). The most securely established and consistently valuable magazine specializing in poetry and criticism of poetry.

Salmagundi (Quarterly—Saratoga Springs, N.Y.). Lively intellectual journal concerned chiefly with social theory and modern literature.

Science (Monthly—Washington, D.C.). Published by the American Association for the Advancement of Science, a freshly written source of news about developments in the sciences.

Scientific American (Monthly—New York). A handsomely illustrated journal containing well-written articles that interpret scientific and technological research for general readers.

Time (Weekly—New York). The originator of the newsmagazine format, this is one of the world's most widely read periodicals.

Yale Review (Quarterly—New Haven, Conn.). A solid, thoughtful journal with articles on politics, literature, intellectual history, etc.

CHAPTER 18

Language and Communications

MARK SCHULMAN

Interaction among people depends on their competency in using language to communicate: We might say that social reality may be a function of the way we structure our worlds with words and gestures and images. In this chapter we consider the pertinent books on a variety of linguistic and communication themes. As disciplines, these share a common basis in their analysis of human cultures through the processes of encoding and decoding messages.

To examine the available material in this area, it makes sense to separate the reading lists into two distinct groups. Overlap is inevitable and, to pursue any aspects that appeal to you, freely select from either section. By following an eclectic but directed approach, you will be able to sample the stimulating atmosphere of disciplines in a period of rapid development and change. And you will experience the wide-ranging clash of ideas, a clash that suggests the still-to-be-defined nature of the fields themselves.

Languages

Definitions of language vary: Lock several linguists in a room and ask them to emerge only when they agree on a definition and you may never see the group again. Even more fierce is the debate about the nature and origin of languages and their relationship to the cultures within which they exist.

The purpose in developing the list that follows, then, is not to take a side in the debate but rather to offer a wide selection of readings through which the reader can trace the history and dimensions of the controversies. Perhaps a good place to begin is with some of the classics dealing with diverse perspectives on language: Sapir on the linguistic background; Pei on language history; Farb on sociolinguistics; Hayakawa on semantics. For an overview of linguistics, the essays in Anderson and Stageberg provide a convenient starting point. Other selections focus on more specific aspects of language: Hall on nonverbal communicaton; Dillard on black speech patterns; Frank and Anshen on gender differences and sexist usages; Williams on relationships between meaning and cultural change. A third group to sample includes controversial theorists who have transformed our thinking (or may yet do so) on the subject. Primary in this group would be Chomsky's explanations of his notions about grammar and the structures of human thought. Also included are Ong's tracing the development from oral to literate culture and Campbell's intriguing construct of a "grammatical man."

The most difficult readings in this section are those that explain recent developments in language theory. Many dull and inaccessible works have been omitted: The diligent reader will find references to those dense studies in the bibliographies of the less arduous volumes listed. The path through contemporary theory in this realm involves a step-by-step journey through divergent modern and postmodern terrains. The signposts read structuralism and semiotics; poststructuralism and deconstruction; reader-response theory and psychoanalytic criticism; phenomenology and hermeneutics. And these are just a few of the many possible directions to wander, often at the risk of losing one's way.

While it is beyond the scope of this brief essay to probe these complex topics, the common theme with which they are concerned is the relationship of *author, book and reader* (or, more precisely, *maker, text, and audience*), and how meaning is constructed out of that dynamic triangle. Using cultural forms other than books—films, advertisements, everyday language, for example—much recent study reaches toward a scheme of analysis of the *discourses* that bind people to, or allow them to transcend, their cultures. A good starting place to avoid dead ends along the way is Eagleton's excellent summary of many of these intellectual traditions. Thereafter, Hawkes's brief but solid work is appropriate. Other readings will take you deeper into the approaches: semiotics or the science of signs (Eco); structuralism and its myriad forms, a development out of anthropological thought (Kurzweil and Sturrock).

BARTHES, ROLAND 1915–1980. **Writing Degree Zero** (1953). Early work of the author, with the specific questions of language raised directly and in a style that is relatively easy to understand. *H & P—Hill & Wang.*

BERLITZ, CHARLES b. 1914. **Native Tongues** (1982). A compendium of tidbits on the subject of the world's languages. Not a scholarly work, but fun to read and still useful beyond cramming for trivia competitions. *H & P—Putnam Pub Group.*

CAMPBELL, JEREMY b. 1931. **Grammatical Man: Information, Entropy, Language, and Life** (1982). A whirlwind tour through a large number of topics that provide an overview of the concept of information and its relationship to human biology, psychology, and society. Artfully avoids oversimplification while remaining accessible. *H & P—S&S*

CHASE, STUART b. 1888 and MARIAN T. CHASE. **The Power of Words** (1954). A popular and highly simplified account of many topics in semantics and communication. Part II considers applications of concepts in semantics. *H—HarBraceJ.*

CHERRY, COLIN 1914–1979. **On Human Communication: A Review, a Survey and a Criticism** (3rd ed. 1978). One of the antecedent texts in communications. Because of conscientious updating, it is still relevant on questions of language as a communication process. *P—MIT Pr.*

CHOMSKY, NOAM b. 1928. **Reflections on Language** (1975). The "inventor" (or perhaps discoverer) of transformational grammar discusses the nature of the human mind in a series of essays. *o.p.*

DILLARD, J. L. b. 1924. **Black English: Its History and Usage in the United States** (1972). Though there have been other books on this subject in the last decade, this is still one of the strongest and most convincing arguments. It details the structure and proves the validity of black nonstandard English as an important dialect. *H & P—Random.*

EAGLETON, TERRY b. 1943. **Literary Theory: An Introduction** (1983). Clear, witty, polemical introduction to the most important strains of literary theory. The author makes clear his own socialist-feminist bias and still provides fair summaries of the contending philosophical positions. *H & P—U of Minn Pr.*

ECO, UMBERTO b. 1932. **The Role of the Reader: Explorations in the Semiotics of Texts** (1979). Deals with both the concepts and the applications of semiotics to cultural forms. Though advanced in its ideas, it is probably the best Eco to study, particularly his ideas on open and closed narrative structures. *H & P—Ind U Pr.*

FARB, PETER 1929–1980. **Word Play: What Happens When People Talk** (1973). The nontechnical explication of the tenets of sociolinguistics, or, says Farb, "the remarkable ability of human beings to play upon one another with their speech." *H—Knopf; P—Bantam.*

FRANK, FRANCINE and FRANK ANSHEN. **Language and the Sexes** (1984). Highly readable introductory summary of the latest research into gender and sexual differences in language usage. *H & P—State U NY Pr.*

HALL, EDWARD T. b. 1914. **The Silent Language** (1973). The interrelatedness of patterns in culture and language and the differences in these patterns among various ethnic groups. Original, and free from anthropological jargon. *H—Greenwood; P—Doubleday.*

HAWKES, TERENCE b. 1932. **Structuralism and Semiotics** (1977). Probably the best brief introduction to the subject; of course, the brevity contributes to an incompleteness in handling the range and complexity of the subject. But for clarity and avoidance of obtuse jargon, Hawkes excels. *H & P—U of Cal Pr.*

HAYAKAWA, S. I. b. 1906. **Language in Thought and Action** (4th ed. 1978). Fascinating semantic study of human interaction through communication, stressing the need for cooperation. *P—HarBraceJ.*

Introductory Readings on Language (4th ed. 1975). Eds. Wallace L. Anderson and Norman C. Stageberg. Selected readings in nontechnical language in such areas as the nature of language, word meanings and changes, logic, metaphor, semantics, dialects, structural grammar, and usage. *P—HR&W.*

LEITCH, VINCENT B. b. 1944. **Deconstructive Criticism: An Advanced Introduction and Survey** (1982). Summarizes well the work of Derrida, de Man, Barthes, and Foucault. Difficult reading though more accessible than the authors discussed, and worth the effort to gain some familiarity with deconstruction. *H & P—Columbia U Pr.*

MUELLER, CLAUS b. 1941. **The Politics of Communication: A Study in the Political Sociology of Language, Socializa-**

tion, and Legitimation (1973). In some ways this is a difficult book, but it merits careful reading for its well-documented analysis of the relationship among speech codes, information control, and political systems. *H—Oxford U Pr*.

NEWMAN, EDWIN b. 1919. **Strictly Speaking: Will America Be the Death of English?** (1975). Though not one of the most recent, still one of the best of the American-English-Is-Destroying-*Real*-English school. It is, in fact, erudite and witty. *P—Warner Bks*.

NORRIS, CHRISTOPHER b. 1917. **Deconstruction: Theory and Practice** (1982). A readable survey that details the work of the leading theorists and practitioners of the field. With annotated bibliography. *H & P—Methuen*.

ONG, WALTER b. 1912. **Orality and Literacy: The Technologizing of the Word** (1982). Ong elaborates the transformations that occurred in the movement from oral to written (literate) culture. His thesis is intellectually challenging and controversial; this book is the clearest introduction to his ideas and their relationship to other philosophical trends. *H & P—Methuen*.

PEI, MARIO 1901–1978. **The Story of Language** (rev. ed. 1984). An updated version, with some new material added to Pei's original work; a standard, clear history of languages, which, however, does not really reflect the recent thinking in the field. *P—NAL*.

Reader-Response Criticism: From Formalism to Post-Structuralism (1981). Ed. Jane P. Tompkins. Thirteen essays arranged chronologically so that the reader can follow the development of ideas. Outlines the emergence of the argument that a text cannot be defined solely through authorial intentions. *P—Johns Hopkins*.

SAFIRE, WILLIAM b. 1929. **I Stand Corrected: More on Language** (1984). The latest collection of alphabetized reflections by the *New York Times* columnist. Opinionated and sometimes idiosyncratic, but always fun to read. *H—Times Bks*.

SAPIR, EDWARD 1884–1930. **Language: An Introduction to the Study of Speech** (1955). A basic and classic treatment of one of the most characteristic of human behaviors—its sounds, grammatical processes and concepts, kinds of structures, and changes in the course of history. *P—HarBraceJ*.

SCHOLES, ROBERT E. b. 1929. **Semiotics and Interpretation** (1982) and **Structuralism in Literature** (1974). These two works are generally regarded as among the clearest, most concise yet not oversimplified, and readable introductions to structuralism and semiotics. Along with Hawkes, a good place for beginners to start. *H & P—Yale U Pr.*

Structuralism and Since: From Levi-Strauss to Derrida (1979). Ed. John Sturrock. A collection of essays concerning the work of Levi-Strauss, Barthes, Foucault, Lacan, and Derrida. After Hawkes and Scholes, this is perhaps the book to read next. *H & P—Oxford U Pr.*

Textual Strategies: Perspectives in Post-Structuralist Criticism (1979). Ed. Josue Harari. Fifteen essays plus a solid introduction by the editor on both French and American trends. Puts poststructural work into a theoretical and historical context; includes a very good annotated bibliography. *H & P—Cornell U Pr.*

WILLIAMS, RAYMOND b. 1921. **Keywords: A Vocabulary of Culture and Society** (1976). An intellectually stimulating discussion of meaning in relation to cultural change, traced through the development of semantic definitions of 155 keywords in English. *P—Oxford U Pr.*

Communications

Many teachers and scholars working in communications suffer at times from professional anxieties, if not from an outright identity crisis. The reason is that communications is an emerging discipline and borrows freely from established disciplines: anthropology, linguistics, psychology, and sociology in the social sciences; literature, speech, theater, and foreign languages in the humanities; biology, engineering, technology, and mathematics in the sciences. Communications draws freely from them all, as well as from less traditional domains like journalism, film, broadcasting, and computer studies.

Because of the spirited interdisciplinary debate, defining communications poses some difficulty. A useful distinction might be made between "communication" and "communications." "Communication" refers to the primary process of social interaction through the sending and receiving of messages; in this realm the connection to language studies is clear. "Communications" encompasses the secondary techniques (or means) of that primary process, those dependent upon technological intervention and operation. Thus, while every society communicates (in the past, it has been argued that communication is the foundation of culture), some societies have more sophisticated (but not necessarily more efficient, accurate, or humane) communications than others. The distinction, unfortunately, remains imprecise, and the two words usually become interchangeable.

The book list ignores the distinction, and attempts to suggest readings in both communication-oriented theoretical material (McLuhan and Williams) and communications-directed descriptive readings (Barnouw and Didsbury). Beyond these, several books consider the dialectic between communications and society (Bagdikian and Gurevitch); two are seminal sources for dozens of others on the theory of mass communication (DeFleur and Ball-Rokeach and McQuail); and two others represent new directions in media study (Dorfman and Mattelart and Mander). Were the list unrestricted in length, it would contain a more inclusive survey of the burgeoning publications about topics in mass communications or aspects of a scientific medium. But we offer only a small sampling: on television (Friendly and Gitlin), on the press (Liebling), on advertising and public opinion (Schiller), on the construction of news (Tuchman), on film (Monaco), on international communication (Tunstall), on children's television (Kaye), and on the alternative media (Armstrong).

Although the multitude of attitudes and approaches often confuses and occasionally confounds, it also creates a sense of dynamism and growth. Indeed, communications may well be *the* vocation for the rest of this century—for its economic and political clout, its recognition as a powerful social force, and its explosive boom as an area of study in secondary and higher education.

To plunge deeper into this turbulent subject—rolling with new ideas and their contentious proponents—search selectively through the bibliographies in most of the books cited. And watch for new publications, any one of which has the potential to press its mark on the future.

ARMSTRONG, DAVID b. 1945. **A Trumpet to Arms: Alternative Media in America** (1984). A comprehensive survey of the history of media outside the mainstream, demonstrating that there has always been a tradition of oppositional communications in this country. Particularly good treatment of the 1960s and 1970s. *P—South End Pr.*

BAGDIKIAN, BEN b. 1920. **The Media Monopoly** (1983).

Carefully documented analysis of the extent of corporate domination of the establishment media in the United States. Useful for understanding the current situation in mass communications. *H & P—Beacon Pr.*

BARNOUW, ERIK b. 1908. **Tube of Plenty: The Evolution of American Television** (rev. ed. 1982). The standard history of broadcasting in the United States. There is good reason that it has been in use for many years: It is unmatched for completeness, accuracy, and clarity. *H & P—Oxford U Pr.*

Communications and the Future (1983). Ed. Howard F. Didsbury, Jr. A wide-ranging collection of predictions and speculations on many aspects of the future and communication issues, including technology, access, and policy. *P—World Future.*

Contact: Human Communication and Its History (1981). Ed. Raymond Williams. A superb anthology. Covers what it promises in a series of excellent essays, though, as with most anthologies, some unevenness surfaces. *H—Thames Hudson.*

Culture, Society and the Media (1982). Eds. Michael Gurevitch et al. Though the authors and the examples are British, this collection is nevertheless essential to understand the latest thinking in communication studies. These readings were originally part of the curriculum at Open University—some are difficult, but all are worthwhile. *P—Methuen.*

DEFLEUR, MELVIN L. b. 1923 and SANDRA J. BALL-ROKEACH. **Theories of Mass Communication** (4th ed. 1981). This classic study is still valuable in its latest update as a survey of traditional communications theory. *H & P—Longman.*

DORFMAN, ARIEL b. 1942 and ARMAND MATTELART b. 1936. **How to Read Donald Duck: Imperialist Ideology in the Disney Comic** (2nd ed. 1984). Tr. David Kunzle. Fascinating and provocative, this treatment of the cultural penetration of the Third World focuses on comic books as the vehicles of imperialist values. The authors, now in exile, focus on their experiences in their native Chile during the early 1970s. *P—Intl General.*

FRIENDLY, ALFRED W. b. 1915. **Due to Circumstances Beyond Our Control** (1967). Insightful and entertaining anecdotal personal account of the author's years as president of CBS News. *P—Random.*

GITLIN, TODD b. 1943. **Inside Prime Time** (1983). What happens when a sociology professor formed by the politics of the New Left undertakes a massive research program to find out how networks program prime time? The answer makes for fascinating reading. *H—Pantheon*.

KAYE, EVELYN b. 1937. **ACT Guide to Children's Television: How to Treat TV with TLC** (rev. ed. 1979). Like its previous version, this volume provides a conceptual framework, based on the ideas of the media reform group Action for Children's Television, as well as practical advice for parents on this issue. *P—Beacon Pr*.

LIEBLING, A. J. 1904–1963. **The Press** (1981). A collection of the reporter-of-reporters' reflections on his craft, the trade, and the state of the world. One of the first forays, and still one of the best, in media criticism. *P—Pantheon*.

McLUHAN, MARSHALL 1911–1980. **Understanding Media: The Extensions of Man** (1964). Part sense and part nonsense, this is perhaps McLuhan's most important work on the media. Difficult reading because of the bizarre style, but worth the effort to understand why his influence persists. *P—McGraw, NAL*.

McQUAIL, DENIS. **Mass Communication Theory: An Introduction** (1983). Fine account of the development of theory with heavy emphasis on sociological aspects. *H & P—Sage*.

MANDER, JERRY b. 1936. **Four Arguments for the Elimination of Television** (1978). What the title says is what you get: four lucid, elegantly presented, well-designed reasons why the only solution to the TV dilemma is the abolition of the medium. A controversial approach but one that continues to be read and to influence opinion. *P—Morrow*.

MONACO, JAMES b. 1942. **How to Read a Film: The Art, Technology, Language, History, and Theory of Film and Media** (rev. ed. 1981). Despite the pretentious title, the book produces what it promises and does so creditably. *H & P—Oxford U Pr*.

SCHILLER, HERBERT I. b. 1919. **The Mind Managers** (1973). Though some of the author's arguments have been refuted, this work retains force as it describes the mechanics of manipulation through advertising and public opinion. *H & P—Beacon Pr*.

SMITH, ANTHONY b. 1938. **Goodbye, Gutenberg: The Newspaper Revolution of the 1980s.** (1980). Well-documented and fascinating analysis of the future of the daily newspaper in the light of vast technological changes in the production process. *P—Oxford U Pr*.

TUCHMAN, GAYE b. 1943. **Making News: A Study in the**

Construction of Reality (1978). Based on participant-observation with newspapers, a TV station, and in the women's movement, Tuchman delineates the method by which the construction of news defines reality. Among recent books on this subject, one of the best. *H & P—Free Pr.*

TUNSTALL, JEREMY b. 1934. **The Media Are American** (1977). Incisive, cogent, disturbing study of the effects of the spread of Americanized media throughout the global communications system. *H & P—Columbia U Pr.*

PART IV

Humanities
and Social Sciences

CHAPTER 19

Fine Arts and Performing Arts

KENNETH G. WALLACE

Art begins in necessity and culminates in gratification. When Stone Age folk fashioned their primitive tools, it is unlikely that they considered themselves artists. While they attempted generation after generation to make their hammers, scrapers, and stabbers even better and neater, more efficient and more shapely, it is doubtful that they conceptualized the relationship between form and function. But as form and function somehow fused and merged, control over human existence increased.

It is, of course, a truism—or should be—that humanity's needs are esthetic and spiritual as well as practical and material. If Stone Age people painted scenes from their daily lives on the walls of caves, they did so because they felt compelled to leave some evidence of having been on earth. If the result of this need was something we choose to call "beautiful" (an extremely dangerous if not meaningless word), then an esthetic need had been satisfied. As civilization moved through time, the needs remained pretty much the same; only the expressions changed.

These changes in the modes and methods of artistic expressions are responsible for the false notion, unfortunately widespread, that art is something special, fancy, precious, existing for the very few, and remote from life. While art is not life, in its finest form it is an honest evocation of life. The fact that any expression in words, paint, stone, or sound generally reflects a historical period or style should not block one's understanding about the nature of art, nor should it cause art to seem remote and removed from life. On the contrary, art can change existence at its very basis and involve people in the change.

Another false notion about the nature of art, resulting largely from Western civilization's espousal of Platonic idealism, is that it must possess utilitarian value, must offer some profit in the form of beauty, truth, goodness. A work of art offers none of these vague qualities inherently; at best—and surely this should be enough—it projects a vision of the joy, the fear, the despair, and the mystery of human experience. The "truth" that art offers lies in its very existence. When we avert our eyes or close our ears, the finest work of art has no meaning.

People with a sensitive awareness of humanity have not chosen to turn away from a painting, a building, a symphony; for experiencing art is similar to experiencing people. We reveal this when we speak of going "to hear Beethoven" or "to see a Picasso." As a rule before one can care deeply for a person, one must know that person very well. So with art. Before one can really grasp what attracts in particular art forms one must take the time to acquire an informed understanding. For one takes from a work of art—as from life in general—only in proportion to what one brings to it. Any person can take delight in or respond to Bach or Mozart, Renoir or Moore, without knowing a thing about them or their lives or their times. But if one knows something about the personalities involved, something about classicism or romanticism or impressionism, something about the various periods of expression in the work of Picasso, something about tone, volume, space, dynamics, rhythm—then one is prepared to hear in the music or see in the paintings or buildings significances and subtleties that the uninformed never recognize or recognize only dimly. By cultivating sensitive, sympathetic, and imaginative understanding of what any artist is attempting, one develops the capacity to come to terms more fully with the work of art, to probe more deeply, to enjoy more fully—in short, to become a part of the artist's vision.

The books listed here are a means—but only one of many—whereby the eyes and ears may be more widely and wisely opened, so that any person may be among those who relish fully the finest achievements of the greatest painters, sculptors, architects, composers, photographers, and dancers of all time. Through books about art and artists one can develop a capacity to understand and share some aspects of the human condition that any great artist offers.

Many specialized histories of art, architecture, and music deal with the arts of early historical periods or major cultural areas, and some biographies of leading artists from these periods or areas are listed in the "Books About" sections of Chapters 1 through 11. Additionally, the "Biography" chapter lists numerous biographies or autobiographies of painters, sculptors, architects, composers, and other artists. None of these many books about art and artists is relisted or cross-referenced in this chapter.

Basic Principles and General Histories

ARNASON, H. H. b. 1901. **History of Modern Art** (rev. ed. 1976). Exhaustive study of modern art from the late 19th century to the provocative movements of the 1970s. *H—Abrams, P-H*.

The Creative Process (1952). Ed. Brewster Ghiselin. Symposium by writers, painters, sculptors, and musicians about dealing with the process of creation. *P—NAL*.

EICHENBERG, FRITZ b. 1901. **The Art of the Print** (1976). A master printmaker himself, Eichenberg writes for the lay reader and artist alike a brilliant history of printmaking and explains lucidly its various techniques. *H—Abrams*.

FRY, ROGER E. 1866–1934. **Vision and Design** (1920). A famous art critic and former curator of the Metropolitan Museum of New York discusses the relation between perception and esthetic form. *P—Oxford U Pr*.

JANSON, HORST W. 1913–1982. **History of Art** (rev. ed. 1977). A splendid survey of the major visual arts from the beginning of history to the present. Magnificent illustrations include 80 color plates, many with gold. *H—Abrams*.

KRAMER, HILTON b. 1928. **The Age of Avant-Garde** (1973). Stimulating, perceptive essays on artists and movements of the last few decades, tracing the rise of the avant-garde as a historical phenomenon. *H—FS&G*.

MALRAUX, ANDRÉ 1901–1976. **The Voices of Silence** (1953). A monumental and unique history of art, profusely illustrated and based on the concept that "the museum without walls is by definition a place of the mind." *H & P—Princeton U Pr*.

Minimal Art (1968). Ed. Gregory Battcock. An impartial collection of valuable essays concerning the minimal art movement by critics and artists. *P—Dutton*.

The New Art (rev. ed. 1973). Ed. Gregory Battcock. A first-rate anthology of criticism by contemporary art critics, covering painting, sculpture, design, dance, and film. *P—Dutton*.

TAYLOR, JOSHUA C. 1917–1981. **Learning to Look: A Handbook of the Visual Arts** (1966). Clear, concrete explanations of what to look for in viewing art, particularly useful for the relatively uninitiated. *H & P—U of Chicago Pr.*

Painting and Sculpture

To enjoy fully great works of art, reading about them is less valuable than looking at them, studying them, getting to know them—as originals in museums, as good prints on the walls, as reproductions in the rich variety of excellent art books, hardcover and paperbound. Three series are outstanding:

Landmarks of the World's Art. Abbreviated but useful introductions to various periods in the history of world art. The series ranges from the ancient to the modern world and includes both Eastern and Western cultures. *o.p.*

Pelican History of Art. An unusually well-written and handsomely illustrated series of books on art and architecture of various countries, areas, and periods. *H—Penguin.*

Skira Art Books. Volumes with informed but dullish texts and magnificent color plates. Of special interest is the Art-History-Ideas series: 14 volumes giving the art-history-total cultural backgrounds of both the Eastern and Western worlds. *o.p.*

Also extremely valuable are four series of smaller, less ambitious, less expensive, but amazingly well-printed books.

BARNES AND NOBLE ART SERIES. *o.p.*
COMPASS HISTORY OF ART SERIES. *o.p.*
PRAEGER WORLD OF ART PAPERBACKS. *P—Praeger.*
UNESCO ART SERIES. *o.p.*

Art since 1945. A series of modest critical essays on the world art scene since 1945. Internationally known scholars write on the major European countries and the United States, often showing, for a change, how America influences Europe. *o.p.*

BARR, ALFRED H., JR. 1902–1981. **What Is Modern Painting?** (rev. ed. 1958). A clear introductory analysis of the methods and techniques of modern painting as well as an excellent explanation of how to look at modern art. *P—NYGS.*

BERENSON, BERNARD 1865–1959. **Aesthetics and History in the Visual Arts** (1948). A master critic analyzes the reasons for changing styles in the arts. *H—Somerset Pub.*

BOAS, FRANZ 1858–1942. **Primitive Art** (1927). The classic study of the subject by a great anthropologist. *H—Peter Smith; P—Dover.*

BOUSQUET, JACQUES b. 1923. **Mannerism: The Painting and Style of the Late Renaissance** (1964). Close to being the definitive study of one of the most controversial periods in art history, arguing convincingly for mannerism as a valid style. *o.p.*

BOWIE, HENRY. **On the Laws of Japanese Painting** (1952). Clear, fascinating explanation. *H—Peter Smith; P—Dover.*

CHASTEL, ANDRÉ b. 1912. **The Age of Humanism** (1963). Exhaustive study of one of the most productive periods in the arts—Europe from 1480 to 1530; profusely illustrated. *o.p.*

CLARK, KENNETH M. 1903–1983. **The Nude** (1956, 1959). Witty, learned, graceful analysis of the nude in art through the ages as an expression of imaginative idealized experience. *H & P—Princeton U Pr.*

————. **Civilisation** (1970). Remarkable, lucid exploration of history and culture through the creative works of Western man. *H & P—Har-Row.*

————. **The Romantic Rebellion** (1974). Clearly, but with considerable caution, dicusses the Romantic quality of 13 important artists from the middle of the 18th century to the middle of the 19th century. *H—Har-Row.*

————. **Landscape into Art** (rev. ed.1976). Authoritative analysis of four possible ways artists have tried to clarify the complexities of natural appearances. *H & P—Har-Row.*

FALLICO, ARTURO B. b. 1909. **Art and Existentialism** (1962). A significant attempt to reconcile art with the philosophy that interprets life as an encounter with nothingness. *o.p.*

The Flowering of the Middle Ages (1960). Ed. Dame Joan Evans. Magnificently illustrated study of the art and culture of the Middle Ages, containing readable essays by scholars of such caliber as Christopher Brooke, George Zarnecki, and John Harvey. *o.p.*

HUGHES, ROBERT b. 1938. **The Shock of the New** (1981). A significant study of the rise and fall of modern art. Attempts to answer the question: What was modernism? *H & P—Knopf.*

LARKIN, OLIVER W. 1896–1970. **Art and Life in America** (rev. ed. 1960). Solid, readable study of the relationship of the visual-plastic arts to the growth of American civilization. *o.p.*

LIPPARD, LUCY R. b. 1937. **Pop Art** (1966). Lucid, informative survey and appraisal of a controversial art style. *P—Oxford U Pr.*

LULLIES, REINHARD b. 1907 and MAX HIRMER. **Greek Sculpture** (rev. ed. 1957). Superior photographs are illuminated by Lullies' authoritative criticism of the successive trends. *o.p.*

MASTAI, MARIE-LOUISE. **Illusion in Art: A History of Pictorial Illusionism** (1975). Fascinating and comprehensive study of *trompe l'oeil* as practiced by nearly all famous artists in almost every generation since antiquity. *H—Abaris Bks.*

NADEAU, MAURICE B. b. 1911. **The History of Surrealism** (1965). The definitive study of this 20th-century art movement by a distinguished French critic. *o.p.*

NEWTON, ERIC 1893–1965. **The Romantic Rebellion** (1965). Valid, convincing, yet intensely personal view of Romanticism and the Romantic temperament which Newton sees as epitomized in "mystery, abnormality, conflict." *o.p.*

RHEIMS, MAURICE b. 1910. **Nineteenth Century Sculpture** (1977). A fresh appraisal of the 19th-century works by sculptors from 28 countries. *H—Abrams.*

RICHTER, HANS 1888–1976. **Dada: Art and Anti-Art** (1965). An excellent history of a highly controversial movement in 20th-century art by a man who was part of it. Contains many primary sources: documents, manifestos, etc. *P—Oxford U Pr.*

ROSEN, CHARLES b. 1927 and HENRI ZERNER b. 1939. **Romanticism and Realism: The Mythology of Nineteenth Century Art** (1984). A new definition of avant-garde and traditional art and of the distinction between high art and low. *H—Viking Pr.*

RUSSELL, JOHN b. 1919. **The Meanings of Modern Art** (1981). A study based on the author's thesis that the history of art is the "history of everything." Deals with all of the major movements in the arts from 1860 to the present. *H & P—Har-Row.*

SCHAPIRO, MEYER b. 1904. **Romanesque Art** (1977). A great art historian's collected innovative essays on Romanesque sculpture and medieval esthetic ideas. *H—Braziller.*

———. **Modern Art: 19th and 20th Century Selected Papers** (1978). Significant analysis of the introduction of modern art in America as well as the social meaning of abstract form. *H—Braziller.*

SCHORSKE. **Fin-de-Siècle Vienna: Politics and Culture.** See "History," page 301.

WILLETT, JOHN b. 1917. **Art and Politics in the Weimar Period** (1979). A meticulous and comprehensive study of one of the most creative and significant periods of the 20th century. Profusely illustrated. *P—Pantheon*.

Architecture and Design

Encyclopedia of Modern Architecture (1964). Ed. Wolfgang Pehnt. An invaluable aid to students, architects, critics, civil engineers, and lay readers for browsing or reference, involving the contributions of 31 authorities from 16 countries. *o.p.*

GIEDION, SIGFRIED 1893–1968. **Space, Time and Architecture** (1967). A fundamental text illuminating our times as well as the interrelation of materials, techniques, and human needs in terms of architectural design and city planning. *H—Harvard U Pr*.

GREENOUGH, HORATIO 1805–1852. **Form and Function** (1947). Remarks on art, design, and architecture by a prophet of modern architecture. *P—U of Cal Pr*.

GROPIUS, WALTER 1883–1969. **Apollo in the Democracy** (1968). Collection of profound essays and addresses by the founder of the famous Bauhaus School examining the cultural obligation of the architect. *o.p.*

LE CORBUSIER (CHARLES-ÉDOUARD JEANERET-GRIS) 1887–1965. **The Modular** and **Modular 2** (1954, 1958). Two volumes of provocative, intensely personal arguments for an ideal system of proportions based on the human body and the golden mean. *H & P—Harvard U Pr*.

MAKERS OF CONTEMPORARY ARCHITECTURE. A series of well-illustrated studies of influential modern architects, including Fuller, Johnson, Kahn, Saarinen, Tange. *H—Braziller*.

MASTERS OF WORLD ARCHITECTURE. A series of compact analyses of the works of outstanding modern architects and designers, with illustrations and biographies. Included are Aalto, Gaudi, Gropius, Le Corbusier, van der Rohe, Nervi, Neutra, Sullivan, and Wright. *H & P—Braziller*.

MUMFORD, LEWIS b. 1895. **The Culture of Cities** (1928). The past, present, and hoped-for future of urban civilization—a panoramic survey rich with factual data and challenging positions. *H—Greenwood; P—HarBraceJ*.

————. **Sticks and Stones** (rev. ed. 1955). Critical analysis of

American architecture from the 18th to the 20th century, stressing integration of structure with site. *P—Dover*.

NEVINS, DEBORAH b. 1947 and ROBERT A. M. STERN b. 1939. **The Architect's Eye** (1979). American architectural drawings from 1799 to 1978. Each drawing is accompanied by an essay on the architect and the drawing. *P—Pantheon*.

PEVSNER, NIKOLAUS 1902–1983. **An Outline of European Architecture** (rev. ed. 1960). A first-rate introduction, sound, readable, incisive. *o.p.*

————. **Pioneers of Design** (rev. ed. 1961). A standard work on designers from William Morris to Walter Gropius showing how these men moved from Victorianism to modernism. *P—Penguin*.

Who Designs America? (1966). Ed. Laurence B. Holland. Stimulating collection of critical essays by leading design critics showing the effects of both good and bad design in America. *o.p.*

WRIGHT, FRANK LLOYD 1869–1959. **The Future of Architecture** (1953). A collection of prophetic lectures concerning the author's own works as well as the future of architecture. *H—Horizon; P—NAL*.

————. **Writings and Buildings** (1960). Chronological summary of the master architect's major periods, with photography, drawings, floor plans, illustrative writings. *H—Horizon*.

Music

AUSTIN, WILLIAM W. b. 1920. **Music in the 20th Century** (1966). A panorama of musical composition designed not only as a history but also as a means of arousing the reader's interest in musical forms from Debussy to Stravinsky. *H—Norton*.

BARZUN, JACQUES b. 1907. **Berlioz and His Century** (1956). Splendid evocation of a man, his time, and his work. *P—U of Chicago Pr*.

BERNSTEIN, LEONARD b. 1918. **The Unanswered Question** (1976). Brilliant lectures by America's conductor-composer concerning the future of music, discussing music from primal sources to the most complex compositions. Boxed with three recordings. *H & P—Harvard U Pr*.

BLUME, FRIEDRICH 1893–1975. **Renaissance and Baroque**

Music (1967). A comprehensive survey by a distinguished musicologist, filled with fresh insights. *P—Norton*.

CHASE, GILBERT b. 1906. **America's Music from the Pilgrims to the Present** (rev. 2nd ed. 1966). Exhaustive study of American music from the Pilgrims to the age of electronics. *H—Greenwood*.

COPLAND, AARON b. 1900. **What to Listen for in Music** (rev. ed. 1957). A distinguished composer explains lucidly the interrelation of rhythm, melody, harmony, and tone color in musical patterns. *H—McGraw; P—NAL*.

EWEN, DAVID b. 1907. **Encyclopedia of Opera** (1963). A valuable comprehensive reference that answers almost any question about opera the reader may pose. *o.p.*

GRIFFITHS, PAUL b. 1947. **Modern Music: The Avant Garde since 1945** (1981). A somewhat technical analysis of musical change as heard in electronic sound synthesis in such musicians as Cage, Stockhausen, and Boulez. *H—Biblio Dist; P—Braziller*.

GROUT, DONALD JAY b. 1902. **A History of Western Music** (3rd ed. 1980). A shortened version of the author's lengthy history of music from the ancients to the modern masters of atonalism and dodecaphony. *H & P—Norton*.

A History of Song (1961). Ed. Denis W. Stevens. Covers all the noteworthy song composers in 15 Western countries from the Middle Ages to the present. *H—Greenwood*.

HODIER, ANDRE. **The Worlds of Jazz** (1972). An analysis of the various kinds of jazz, intended primarily for the lay person, emphasizing in depth the sociology of jazz. *o.p.*

LANG, PAUL HENRY b. 1901. **Music in Western Civilization** (1940). The definitive one-volume history—scholarly, detailed, yet very readable. *H—Norton*.

McKINNEY, HOWARD D. b. 1889 and W. R. ANDERSON. **Music in History** (1940). Relates music to the other fine arts and to the cultural climate in which it was written. *o.p.*

New Grove Composer Biography Series: Bach Family, Christopher Wolff et al.; **Beethoven,** Joseph Kerman and Alan Tyson; **Handel,** Winton Dean and Anthony Hicks; **Haydn,** Jens P. Larsen and Georg Feder; **High Renaissance Masters,** Gustave Reese et al.; **Italian Baroque Masters,** Denis Arnold et al.; **Masters of Italian Opera,** Andrew Porter et al.; **Modern Masters: Bartok, Stravinsky, Hindemith,** Laszlo Somfai et al.; **Mozart,** Stanley Sadie; **Schubert,** Maurice J. E. Brown and Eric Sams; **Second Viennese School,** Paul Griffiths et al.; **Wagner,** John Deathridge and Carol Dahlhaus. *H & P— Norton.*

SANDBURG, CARL 1878–1967. **The American Songbag** (1927). Gives unexcelled background for 280 songs, ballads, and ditties as well as the music for them. *P—HarBraceJ.*

SCHONBERG, HAROLD C. b. 1916. **The Great Pianists** (1963). Noted critic writes engagingly and knowledgeably about pianism and pianists for the music lover as well as for the specialist. *o.p.*

WINTERNITZ, EMANUEL 1898–1983. **Musical Instruments and Their Symbolism in Western Art** (1963). Excellent, informative discussion of the history of musical instruments, their creators, and aspects of the interconnection between the instruments and music of any given age. Exceedingly beautiful photographs by Lilly Stunzi. *H & P—Yale U Pr.*

Women in Music: An Anthology of Source Readings from the Middle Ages to the Present (1982). Ed. Carol Neuls Bates. Vividly presents accounts of women musicians and composers and their role in music. *o.p.*

The Dance

BALANCHINE, GEORGE 1904–1984. **Balanchine's Complete Stories of the Great Ballets** (rev. ed. 1977). The celebrated choreographer's stories of more than 100 ballets still performed; a guide to watching ballet, history of ballet, and discussion of the study of ballet—all directed to the balletgoer. *H— Doubleday.*

CROCE, ARLENE b. 1934. **Going to the Dance** (1982). A collection of penetrating essays of dance criticism ranging from individual dancers to the New York City Ballet to the international scene. *H & P—Knopf.*

FONTEYN, DAME MARGOT b. 1919. **Margot Fonteyn: Autobiography** (1976). The life of one of the world's great dancers, told with honesty and humility. *H—Knopf.*

HASKELL, ARNOLD 1903–1981. **The Wonderful World of Dance** (1960). Intended for children, this is also a good introduction to the dance for adults. It shows how people in various cultures reveal in their dances their way of living and thinking. *o.p.*

HUMPHREY, DORIS 1895–1958. **The Art of Making Dances**

(rev. ed. 1962). Illustrated guide to an appreciation of American modern dance as an art form, by a great dancer and choreographer. *P—Grove*.

LEATHERMAN, LEROY 1922–1984. **Martha Graham** (1966). Beautifully illustrated and fascinating biography of one of America's greatest dance innovators. *o.p.*

REYNOLDS, NANCY. **Repertory in Review: 40 Years of the New York City Ballet** (1977). A unique comprehensive history of a great ballet company, combining photographs, performance programs, interviews, and author's commentary. *o.p.*

SACHS, CURT 1881–1958. **World History of the Dance** (1937). A scholarly history of the dance in different cultures. *P—Norton*.

SIEGEL, MARCIA B. b. 1932. **Watching the Dance Go By** (1977). Clear-sighted essays on 80 performances from Balanchine to Meredith Monk. *o.p.*

———. **The Shapes of Change** (1979). Analyzes what is specifically American about dance in America as it has developed over the last 50 years. *o.p.*

SORELL, WALTER b. 1905. **Dance in Its Time** (1981). Explores the history of dance in its artistic, social, and political involvement from the 14th century to the present. *H—Doubleday*.

STODELLE, ERNESTINE. **Deep Song: The Dance Story of Martha Graham** (1984). Herself a former dancer, the author presents one more convincing argument for the greatness of one of the world's most controversial dancers and choreographers. *H—Macmillan*.

Photography and Film

CARTIER-BRESSON, HENRI b. 1908. **The World of Cartier-Bresson** (1968). An excellent collection of the work of a brilliant humanist photographer who strives for precise reporting of fact. *o.p.*

DENITTO, DENNIS b. 1929 and WILLIAM HERMAN b. 1926. **Film and the Critical Eye** (1975). Detailed and illuminating analyses—sometimes frame by frame—of 14 classical narrative films from Chaplin to Truffaut. *o.p.*

EISENSTEIN, SERGEI 1898–1948. **Film Form** (1969). Famous Soviet director's brilliant explanation of the esthetics of filmmaking. *P—HarBraceJ*.

————. **The Film Sense** (1969). Twelve essays demonstrating key points of the author's film theory, including diagrams and halftones. *P—HarBraceJ*.

Focal Encyclopedia of Photography (rev. ed. 1969). An informative reference work, presenting 2,400 articles by many experts. *H—Focal Pr*.

GOSLING, NIGEL 1909–1982. **Nadar** (1977). Contains 359 unusually fine photographs of leading artistic figures of the 19th century by the pioneer photographer Nadar, whose real name was Felix Tournachon (1820–1910). *o.p.*

GREEN, JONATHAN b. 1939. **American Photography: A Critical History 1945 to the Present** (1984). A substantial account of the history of photographers and the institutions and publications that have presented these photographers. *H—Abrams*.

HUSS, ROY G. b. 1927 and NORMAN SILVERSTEIN 1922–1974. **The Film Experience** (1968). An enlightening analysis of the principles and techniques of filmmaking from all periods and all countries. *P—Dell*.

JEFFREY, IAN. **Photography: A Concise History** (1981). Investigates the work of major photographers and carefully examines the current interest in photography as an art form. *H & P—Oxford U Pr*.

KAEL, PAULINE b. 1919. **When the Lights Go Down** (1980). Another collection of candid, perceptive, and often exasperating reviews of major films by the author of **I Lost It at the Movies** (1965, *P—Little*), **KissKissBangBang** (1968), *P—Little*), and **Going Steady** (1970, *o.p.*). *o.p.*

Master Photographers (1983). Ed. Pat Booth. Master photographers present their photographs and explain their art and technique. *H & P—Crown*.

SCHARF, AARON b. 1922. **Pioneers of Photography** (1976). Compelling story of the early years of photography, using excerpts from the diaries and letters of the photographers as well as 175 of their photographs. *o.p.*

SONTAG, SUSAN b. 1933. **On Photography** (1977). Brief but brilliant meditative essays by a leading philosophical critic about the form and function of photography. *H—FS&G; P—Dell*.

STEICHEN, EDWARD 1879–1973. **Family of Man** (1956). Reproduces the famous exhibition (503 photographs from 68 countries) created by Steichen for the New York Museum of Modern Art. *H—S&S; P—NAL*.

TRUFFAUT, FRANÇOIS 1932–1984. **Hitchcock** (rev. ed. 1984). The French New Wave director and master of humaneness and compassion interviews the British-born master of suspense and tension. The result: a harvest of insights into Hitchcock's technical expertise and genius. *H & P—S&S.*

CHAPTER 20

Philosophy

PHILIP RODDMAN

Philosophy is essentially a skill like medicine and an invention like music. The philosopher by means of language investigates the known, explores the unknown, and infers the unknowable. This art, as in doctoring and composing, entails many methods or procedures. The methods of philosophy are as various as the imaginations that entertain it. Of those imaginations, the mathematical, the commonsensical, the literary, and the religious are the most prominent in the philosophical thought of our time.

Contemporary thinkers tend to speak of philosophy as an activity rather than as a repository of wisdom. Accomplishments, in the sense of therapies for "mental cramp" and hints for penetrating existence, now count for more than doctrines about humanity's place in nature or supernature. Of the two most influential philosophies of the 20th century, one confines itself to the critique or analysis of language, while the other inquires into the predicament of the individual in the chaos of being. The analytic philosophers, whose appeal is either to mathematics or to common sense as manifested in ordinary speech, disclose the meaning and unmeaning of verbal constructions expressing beliefs and ideas. Examining articulations among and within codes of communication, they are much like physicians or surgeons diagnosing and prescribing for states of illness and delusion. The moral philosophers, whose appeal is to conditions of suffering and privation, to forces in a state of crisis, produce a poetry of feeling meant to educate the heart or suggest a new horizon to the mind. These philosophers are akin to musicians who inflect the pang of a painful emotion into its ideal import.

The linguistic philosophers use symbolic logic and everyday discourse, as far as these resources can go, to ascertain the meaning of facts, propositions, material objects, and the meaning of meaning. They call upon the authority of the senses and of the general rules of language to draw the line between sense and nonsense. The grammar of language, its structure and arrangement, in the opinion of the "logisticians," is a basic world view. Hence their metaphysics or system of first principles is the form and syntax of language itself, words used as signs or tools and as images or parables. They insist, quite literally, that in the beginning was the word.

The existentialists or moral philosophers dramatize a state of affairs in which acts, decisions, and resolutions create worlds of value. Their gospel reads that in the beginning was the deed. Although theirs is a cosmology that presupposes a totality devoid of purpose and design, they present a highly flattering, if overstrenuous, vision of the individual as his or her own invention: own keeper, own judge, and own priest.

For the logisticians, philosophy is "a battle against the bewitchment of our intelligence." For the existentialists, philosophy is a training in courage "for an attack on one's convictions."

It is precisely for leading the youth of Athens to lose faith in their convictions by exposing the inconsistencies and nonsense in their beliefs that Socrates, the patron saint of philosophy, was put to death. Socrates was both an analytic and a moral philosopher, a physician of the mind and a composer of new visions. His ontology (analytic metaphyics) and his cosmology (speculative metaphysics) are of a piece. Love for him is the cosmological process, the dynamo, that drives us to the ontological reality of truth, goodness, and beauty. Philosophy, a dialogue between sense and reason, culminates in a feast of intelligence and love. Compounded of the words *philos* ("love") and *sophia* ("wisdom"), philosophy, in the Socratic definition, is the passion for self-knowledge. To make our ideas and beliefs clear to ourselves and to others is to bring the truth out of hiding, to distinguish what we are and what we do from what we think we are and what we think we do. The key sentence in Socrates' life, still the most powerful declaration of moral principle in Western culture, occurs in Plato's *Apology:* "The unexamined life is not worth living."

But is self-knowledge possible? In fact, is reliable knowledge of any kind attainable? Doctrines of knowledge and truth, classified as "epistemology," have mustered much ingenuity in order to answer these still unanswered questions. Is true knowledge, as Plato says, a recollection, from prenatal existence, of an eternal Idea or Principle? Or is it, as Lenin says, a transition from nonknowledge to knowledge? In sum, is it a gift or a conquest?

If a gift, then it is the gift of self-recovery. Here the fundamental unit in morals is the individual giving birth to an authentic self. True knowledge harmonizes in us impulses and passions the way music organizes random sounds into intelligible forms. In the Socratic-Platonic theory, virtue and knowledge, morality and waking consciousness are one. It is not our experience of the world but our commitment to what is permanently best that can define the meaning of justice, courage, loyalty. The moral individual is like a fugitive dancer intuiting the timeless pattern of a dance.

Knowledge as conquest is knowledge for service, not for self-possession. The collectivity, of which the individual is a module, is the unit in morals. Marxism-Leninism holds that the class struggle in history shifts the accent of moral judgments according to the needs of the working class. Moral beliefs need constant revision, since moral values depend on modes of production and the alterable body of social life. The individual is a pawn aspiring to a command of the game, never to command the game.

Job in the Old Testament and Prometheus in Greek myth personify, in large measure, the two ethical systems under discussion. Job is in quest of himself; Prometheus, in quest of social justice. Job, in an access of cosmic piety, acknowledges the power that made him and must unmake him in the end as living proof of the moral government of the world. For Job the right is the good. Prometheus accuses the king of the gods of a vile conspiracy against humanity, of disloyalty to what makes for the good. For Prometheus, only the good can be right. Job bows before the divine secret that has brought about the kinship of all creation. Prometheus steals the secret of fire from the tyrant god in order to liberate humanity from the darkness of bondage. Job's recognition of the limits of his understanding frees him from illusion and inspires in him a boundless sympathy for all that lives and breathes. Prometheus's rebellion redeems humankind from alienation and endows it with consciousness of its own destiny. In both moral systems reason or understanding is the key to happiness. But in the Socratic-biblical system, understanding brings about a change of heart, while in the Promethean-

Marxist system, understanding brings about a change of situation. The life of reason may lead, as in Spinoza, to "the intellectual love of God"; or it may, in the reforming zeal of modern revolutionaries, govern passion by passion.

When the existentialists declare that "man creates his own values," they are close to the Marxist principle of value. So to a degree are those linguistic philosophers who reduce moral principles to the commitments we choose to make in life—games whose policy rules change with circumstances. Neither school subscribes to the historical determinism of Marxist ideology. Those linguistic philosophers who are also structuralists, however, imply that language is command, and its complex rules introduce a large element of determinism.

If we grant that language is command, we may well ask whose language is more likely to be obeyed: the classic language of the oppressor or the street language of the oppressed? Is it possible that languages collide, fight, and destroy one another as men and women and nations do? Moreover, experience and science everywhere remind us that there is a force in things that no set of invented forms can ever contain. Is there between the will-to-live and the will-to-dominate a web of indeterminate circumstance that neither a philosophy of freedom nor a philosophy of determinism can ever hope to encompass or circumvent?

The most recent philosophy of language, "deconstruction," asserts that far from mirroring a central reality and its underlying logic, language is as susceptible to endless interpretation as the signs and portents in our dreams. Disengaged from questions that call for definitive answers, rejecting allegiance to pure integral forms that imply "logocentrism," and bred on the free play of signs in modernist painting, the deconstructionist deprives the age-old problems in philosophy of privileged meaning, meanings that suggest a mental or spiritual order. Exploring texts, ocular art for a possible direction in the maze of traces (e.g., extruding visual and multilingual puns from the flux of written language), searching for a possible method in the madness of words, the deconstructionist is an artful Oedipus who does not answer but interrogates the sign-swarming sphinx. In "deconstructionism" the conscious life, the foreground of language, takes on the texture and infinite ambiguity of that hinterland of life which is the unconscious.

The ancient questions of whence? why? whither?—in metaphysics, in epistemology, in ethics—are like the Flying Duchman, doomed to sail the seas of thought forever, without hope of putting into some miraculously permanent haven. Yet the youngest branch of philosophy, esthetics, embracing families of felt quality (the Beautiful, the Ugly, the Tragic, the Comic, the Heroic, the Vulgar, the Noble, the Sublime, the Useful, the Useless, the Boring), has gained an independent haven in the fine arts.

The immense need for the assimilation of experience that has developed in industrial societies is creating a host of metaphysical, epistemological, and ethical issues that find their most attractive formulation in esthetic terms. Very likely, too, the mutations of religious categories have multiplied the perspectives of esthetics, for the same fundamental question resides in esthetics as in religion: What, without any ulterior reason, is objectively most admirable and infinitely cherishable?

Because works of art and criticism materialize esthetic feelings and perceptions more successfully, certainly more visibly, than other forms of human activity, the philosophy of art and the philosophy of criticism have proved as various and as polemical as the study of theology in the heyday of Scholasticism. Definitions of art are as multifarious as the ideologies and the imaginations of the definers. But about the role of the work of art there seems to be general agreement. It is this: A painting, a poem, a sculpture, a piece of music, when successful, serves as an organ of life. For a philosopher like Aristotle a work of art completes nature and thereby offers us a second life. For an artist like Tolstoy art expresses the morality of the brotherhood of man and hence is the essential condition of human life. For a critic like Walter Pater art lights the flame of perception and thus restores the powers of life.

In the esthetics of the 20th century, the major concern is the relation of function to form, of process to structure. In existentialist esthetics, form follows function, as essence follows existence, or as actuality precedes meaning or purpose. In structuralist esthetics function follows form, the way operations of a language follow its grammar, or as the movements of the body depend on the articulation of bone and muscle. To an existentialist the air of anxiety and dread informing a work by the sculptor Alberto Giacometti or by the painter Francis Bacon is the expression of a being choosing freedom, an existence choosing its essence, even, or especially, in a trap or cage. To a structuralist the same work is a transformation of several motifs in the history and in the medium of painting. Its meaning is its esthetic organization of, say, the composition of the age and the sensibility of technique of the artist—external and internal codes or forms deeply interfused. Here the meaning of a symbol is its power to translate into other symbols, as if we said that Socrates the philosopher is in one aspect the foe of tradition, in another the prototype of the Christian martyr. In existentialism, on the other hand, the symbol is a light beam that locates causes and consequences, as if we said that Socrates leading the life of the barefoot idler of Athens concretized philosophy. It is, however, possible to assert that the echo of Socrates' thought has grown so much more resonant than the actuality of the man in ancient Athens that essence has not only overtaken but completely swallowed existence. What, then, shall be our position in respect to knowledge that is given in nature and in social intercourse and knowledge formed by art and imagination?

At the outset we compared the discipline of philosophy to that of medicine and music—to a science and an art. We now add that philosophy, in a systematic manner, carries on the task suggested by those two world symbols earlier described: Job and Prometheus. Like Job, philosophy inquires into the nature and limits of knowledge. Like Prometheus, it indicates the possibilities of experience. Activities such as these, at least according to Aristotle, create the one permanent field of happiness.

Classics in Philosophy

The following descriptions, read in chronological order, from Plato through Wittgenstein, will give the reader a thumbnail history of philosophy.

ARISTOTLE 384–322 B.C. **Basic Works.** "The master of those who know" (Dante's phrase), Aristotle emphasizes "rationalism": the reliance on human capacities for intelligent behavior. The major works are **Nicomachean Ethics** ("the middle way" of common sense not as a compromise but as hitting the bull's eye in thought and action); **Physics and Metaphysics** (nature as the dynamic realm of matter and form set in eternal motion by the eternal unmoved first mover); and **Poetics** (art considered, like nature, a dynamic principle of creativity). *Over 6 eds. of each title.*

AUGUSTINE, SAINT 354–430. **The City of God.** Biblical fervor and Platonic ontology combine to create the philosophy of "illuminism." God (effluence of bright essence) enters history, preparing that mystical city where the individuality of the soul can efface the slave stamp of the body, as light obliterates darkness. The heavenly city is constituted of the union of souls in the love of the Divine Being. *H—Biblio Dist 2 vols., Cath U Pr 3 vols., Harvard U Pr 7 vols., Modern Lib; P— Doubleday, Penguin (abr.).*

BERKELEY, GEORGE 1685–1753. **Three Dialogues Between Hylas and Philonous** (1713). Berkeley repudiates the existence of a material world. His "empirical" or "subjective idealism," which identifies sense perception wholly with a mental reality, puts the source of all our knowledge in the divine language of our sensations. What Spirit, the eternal perceiver, creates has its passing moment of existence in the human mind and its eternal moment in the mind of God. *H & P— Hackett Pub.; P—Bobbs, Open Court.*

DESCARTES, RENÉ 1596–1650. **Discourse on Method** (1637). Assuming a mind-body dualism, Descartes makes thinking the essence of the individual, and mathematical dynamism the essence of matter. *Cartesianism* (philosophical dualism, or even tri-alism, with God as the connective) divorces science from theology and frees the individual consciousness from forms fixed by tradition, custom, and community. *Over 6 eds.*

DEWEY, JOHN 1859–1952. **Experience and Nature** (1925) and **Art as Experience** (1935). Effecting the union of theory and practice, as in Greek thought, but breaking with the dogma of a changeless superstatic truth, Dewey's "pragmatism" defines experience as a web of collective transactions. His "instrumentalism" looks to the scientific method and the democratic process as instruments for converting desire into intelligence. Since for Dewey meanings dwell neither in things nor in individual minds but in shared experience, he points the way toward activities whose fulfillment is esthetic and open-ended. First title: *H & P—Open Court; H—Peter Smith; P—Dover.* Second title: *o.p.*

HEGEL, GEORG W. F. 1770–1831. **The Phenomenology of Mind** (1807) and **The Philosophy of History** (1837). Hegel's "objective idealism" deduces the existence of the world from the idea of God. God is the self-realizing Spirit whose method is a dialectic of tensions and assimilations, packed with the whole realm of nature, humanity, and history, progressing to ever higher syntheses. Esthetically, Spirit is a composer and his dialectic a development of themes and counterthemes in ever richer complexities. Morally, Spirit is a fighter and his dialectic a machinery of conflict for achieving the coherence of one organic whole. First title: *H—Humanities*. Second title: *H—Peter Smith*.

HEIDEGGER, MARTIN 1889–1976. **Being and Time** (1927) and **Existence and Being** (1949). The key existentialist of the 20th century, Heidegger circles his main question, What does Being mean?, with reflection upon reflection: how it feels to choose a life that is primordial, inner-directed, anguished in a death-encasing skin, ontological, authentic, *existential*. What it means to be open to all possibilities, never another's other, subverting all conformities of the social self, unique in asking what Being is. Why, composed as one is of time and language, it is essential to engage in a "dialogue of sciences" (his phrase) that is the pure poetry of Being, poetry not heard but felt, not known but divined. First title: *H—Har-Row*. Second title: *P—Regnery-Gateway*.

HOBBES, THOMAS 1588–1679. **Leviathan** (1651). Breaking with all past philosophies of perfectionism and rationalism, and following the new science of Galileo and Bacon, Hobbes posits "materialism" (matter and motion as the basis of all perceptions) as the sole form of philosophy. His materialism views everything, including human beings, in terms of physical force, or matter in motion. It is the ferocious wolfishness of humanity in a state of nature that drives people to worship power and to accept, for reasons of survival, sovereign power in the state and in religion. *Over 6 eds*.

HUME, DAVID 1711–1776. **Enquiry Concerning Human Understanding** (1748). With a thoroughgoing "skepticism," the doctrine that the truth of all knowledge is in doubt, Hume undermines the entire traditional structure of philosophical and commonsensical thought and belief: the self, substance, identity, the existence of the external world, causal necessity. He uses as his means an empirical criterion, holding that every impression is a distinct, isolated, independent, particular unit of experience. *Over 6 eds*.

HUSSERL, EDMUND 1859–1938. **Ideas** (1913) and **Phenomenology and the Crisis of Philosophy** (1935). Husserl contends that "phenomenology," his philosophy of experience, will resolve the crisis in culture caused by science and naturalism. "Phenomenology" treats of experiences immediately present to us which produce truth and value as an inner possession. Husserl defines consciousness as a projection upon phenomena, intentional, interpretive, directed upon real and imagined objects and events the way a light beam delineates shapes and forms. By "bracketing off the fact-world" (his phrase)—holding in abeyance all material associations of things—Husserl thinks that we can pass from the cold fact of our existence to the meaning of our existence, to that inward sense of life as the free imagination of the artist intuits it. Husserl's emphasis on the subjective pole of consciousness has inspired the existentialists to make personal emotions the criterion of truth; his method of experiencing eternal essences in the environing "life-world" has lent Neo-Thomists a conception of ideal values to oppose to Marxian doctrine of material class values. First title: *H—Humanities; P—Macmillan.* Second title: *P—Har-Row.*

JAMES, WILLIAM 1842–1910. Pragmatism (1907) and **The Meaning of Truth** (1909). For James "the stuff" out of which everything is composed, including all connections and connectives, is experience, a cosmic continuum. In his particular kind of pragmatism, "radical empiricism," consciousness and truth are functions and instruments of experience. James opts for personal experience as knowledge itself. He thus restores a living warmth to the varieties of imagination and belief. First title: *H & P—Harvard U Pr, Hackett Pub; P—NAL, WSP.* Second title: *H—Harvard U Pr.*

KANT, IMMANUEL 1724–1804. The Critique of Pure Reason (1781), **The Critique of Practical Reason** (1788), and **The Critique of Judgment** (1790). "Transcendentalism" for Kant means the critique or analysis of all knowledge as arising from the structure of the human mind organizing experience. Kant discovers two selves in every human being: the phenomenal or empirical self that conforms to ordered sense-impressions, and the noumenal self that hints at eternal values. The phenomenal self, in tune with mechanical or causal necessity, makes scientific knowledge possible. The noumenal self, in tune with intimations of God, freedom, and immortality, leads to ethical and esthetic judgments of universal import. First title: *H & P—Biblio Dist; P—Doubleday, St Martin.* Second title: *P—Bobbs.* Third title: *P—Hafner, Oxford U Pr.*

LOCKE, JOHN 1632–1704. **An Essay Concerning Human Understanding** (1690). In revolt against Descartes's concept of innate ideas and their self-evident character of clarity and distinctiveness, Locke considers sensory experience the sole source of knowledge. This philosophy of "empiricism" induces Locke to describe the human mind as one long autobiography of unnumbered experiences anad to conceive nature, under the influence of Newton, as a free mechanism subject to indefinite change. *Over 6 eds.*

LUCRETIUS c. 94–55 B.C. **On the Nature of Things.** This classic work, based on the Epicurean philosophy of "atomism" (primary reality as a fertile dust—material and mechanical) and "naturalism" (nature as its own standard), announces that all creation arises from destruction. Everything tends toward death, and "death is the mother of beauty." *H & P—Norton; H—Harvard U Pr.*

MARCUS AURELIUS ANTONINUS 121–180. **Meditations.** In the most famous work of "Stoicism," a philosophy that weds "pantheism" (the order of nature defined as divinity) to "fatalism" (acceptance of the inevitable as recognition of the divinity that shapes our ends), the author balances a scientific logic (the stoic world-reason) against his personal life and vocation as emperor and general. *H & P—Hackett Pub; H—Harvard U Pr; P—Penguin.*

MARX, KARL 1818–1883. **Economic and Philosophical Manuscripts** (1844). From Hegel, Marx derives the belief that reason is central to history, but in terms of class conflict, not in Hegelian terms of nations and epochs playing subsidiary parts in the ultimate mission of Absolute Spirit. For Marx the idea of progress is not divine but human, going deeper than any code of ethics. He sees morals and religions as political passions, passions reflecting the way society makes its living and distributes its wealth. Divining the dénouement of future history as a prophet of old divined the Day of Judgment, Marx's "dialectical and historical materialism" holds that truth is the reality of power demonstrated in practice. *P—Intl Pub Co.*

NIETZSCHE, FRIEDRICH 1844–1900. **The Will to Power** (1906). Anarchist in morals, absolutist in politics, foe of social reform or progress, poet of the "eternal return" (the periodic reembodiment of certain patterns in world history), Nietzsche resurrects the Greek tragic hero, who, having outgrown his gods and rejected all limits, is to be the superman of the future. Converting Darwin's theory of natural selection and the struggle for life into the will-to-power, power to reverse all values at will, Nietzsche proclaims the terrible beauty of the imperial self, the philosophy of "romantic egotism." *H— Gordon Pr 2 vols.; P—Random.*

PLATO, c. 427–347 B. C. **Dialogues.** All philosophy is a footnote to Plato (Whitehead). Maintaining that all reality is mental, as do all idealists, Plato posits two principles: (1) the eternal Mind is changeless: (2) all motion arises from the love inspired by the Eternal Mind. Among the major dialogues are **The Phaedo** (the ontology or nature of Ideas), **The Timaeus** (the cosmogony), **The Meno** and **The Theaetetus** (the epistomology), **The Republic** (the structure of justice, of science, and of the soul), and **The Symposium** (love as the ladder to truth). *H—Random 2 vols.; P—WSP. Over 3 eds. of each title.*

PLOTINUS 204–275. **The Enneads.** Defining God as the Beloved whose emanations we are and whose center we forever seek, Plotinus creates a logic of feeling known as "Neoplatonism" that, for later centuries, becomes the ruling principle of such various institutions as Byzantine art, monastic discipline, feudalism, and the system of courtly love. *o.p.*

RUSSELL, BERTRAND 1872–1970. **An Inquiry into Meaning and Truth** (1940). A master logician (*Principia Mathematica*, 1913, with Alfred North Whitehead) and epistemologist (*Our Knowledge of the External World*, 1914), Russell wishes to assimilate philosophy to science. A leader in the movement known as logical analysis, Russell writes that its chief merits are "the introduction of scientific truthfulness into philosophy" and the invention of "a powerful method by which [philosophy] can be rendered fruitful." He is a mighty moralist in the tradition of Spinoza and John Stuart Mill. *H—Humanities.*

SCHOPENHAUER, ARTHUR 1788–1860. **The World as Will and Representation** (1819). Schopenhauer introduces his concept of evolution into the philosophy of "voluntarism" (will or desire as the primary factor in life) to prove his pessimistic doctrine that the Will-to-Live is savage, cruel, not to trust. This blind Will pursues its manifestations from the mineral to the vegetable to the animal to the human kingdom, the kingdom of extreme cruelty and madness. Only the Buddhist saint, who denies the Will-to-Live, achieves ultimate freedom. Only in a select few human beings, and only in rare moments, is the power of reflection, of imaginative projection, sufficient to eclipse the Will during the dispassionate contemplation of high art, that fine flower of the world as representation of "will-less, painless knowledge." *H—Peter Smith 2 vols.; P—Dover 2 vols.*

SPINOZA, BARUCH 1634–1677. **The Ethics** (1677). Spinoza assumes the eternal rightness, and therefore goodness, of God or Universal Nature. Of this Universal Nature, infinite in attributes, we know but thought and matter and their infinitude of instances. Descartes says: When I think, I am. Spinoza says: When I think, Nature thinks in me. Spinoza transforms pantheism, the belief that God is everything and everything is God, into "panentheism," the belief that God or Nature embraces everything. Spinoza's scientific attitude requires identifying necessity with freedom. For him, the understanding of the articulate structure of nature, what he calls "the intellectual love of God," offers the power and wisdom to elude the pitfalls of wishful thinking, illusion, and delusion. *H & P—Hackett Pub; P—Citadel Pr.*

THOMAS AQUINAS, SAINT 1225–1274. **Summa Theologica.** To close the gap between Creature and Creator and to fashion an undivided universe into a continuous hierarchy of intelligence, "Thomism" reconciles Aristotelian rationalism with divine revelation, reason with faith, in the synthesis of Christian humanism. Dante's *Divine Comedy* is a Thomist poem of the levels of reality, from the innermost recesses of the heart to the farthest reaches of the stream of destiny. *H & P—Chr Classics 5 vols.*

WITTGENSTEIN, LUDWIG 1889–1951. **Tractatus Logico-Philosopicus** (1921) and **Philosophical Investigations** (1953). Wittgenstein adopts ordinary language as the best instrument for toppling "the house of cards"—traditional metaphysics. Repudiating his earlier theory that propositions and concepts "picture" the world, Wittgenstein concludes that analysis of the ever-changing life of words is the arduous path to truth. Just as we may not apply rules of poker to umpiring a baseball game, we may not employ the same "language-game" (his phrase) in such different activities or "life forms" as religion, science and ethics, because each has its own language-game. The work of the philosopher is to calibrate the exactitude of any provisional system of words governing an inner or outer reality. First title: *H & P—Humanities; P—Routledge & Kegan.* Second title: *o.p.*

Modern and Contemporary Thought

AUSTIN, J. L. 1911–1960. **Philosophical Papers** (1961, 3rd ed. 1979). The significance of nuances in ordinary language by an Oxford professor noted for his theory of "speech acts." *H & P—Oxford U Pr*.

AYER A. J. b. 1910. **Language, Truth, and Logic** (1936). Important work in the exposition of logical empiricism. *H—Peter Smith; P—Dover*.

BERGSON, HENRI 1859–1941. **The Two Sources of Morality and Religion** (1935). The interplay of instinct and intelligence brilliantly presented in a seminal work. *H—Greenwood; P—U of Notre Dame Pr*.

BUBER, MARTIN 1878–1965. **Between Man and Man** (1947). A religious existentialist relating the "I-Thou" principle to communication, society, education, and modern philosophies. *o.p.*

CASSIRER, ERNST 1874–1945. **The Philosophy of Symbolic Forms** (1923). Detailed analyses of the significance of symbolic forms in the intellectual activities of our culture. *H & P— Yale U Pr 3 vols*.

CHOMSKY, NOAM b. 1928. **Rules and Representations** (1980). An expansion upon the "innateness hypothesis" of a universal grammar underlying the syntax of all human languages. *H & P—Columbia U Pr*.

DERRIDA, JACQUES b. 1930. **Of Grammatology** (1976) and **Margins of Philosophy** (1982). The subversion of the philosophy of language based on logic in an attempt to undermine the metaphysical foundations of Plato, Kant, Hegel, et al. *P—Johns Hopkins*.

FRANK, PHILIPP 1884–1966. **Modern Science and Its Philosophy** (1941). Einstein's successor at the University of Prague relating 20th-century physics to the logic of science, metaphysics, and education. *H—Ayer Co*.

KIERKEGAARD, SØREN 1813–1855. **Either/Or** (1843) and **The Sickness unto Death** (1849). Musical-erotic problems, "original sin," the importance of pure choice, the existing self as against Hegel's objective thinker dramatically examined by an exponent of Christian existentialism. First title: *P— Princeton U Pr 2 vols*. Second title: *H & P—Princeton U Pr*.

MERLEAU-PONTY, MAURICE 1907–1961. **Phenomenology of Perception** (1962). Phenomenology and pragmatism conjoined in the concept of a Nature which perception presents to us—a Nature which is not that of the sciences. *P—Humanities*.

MILL, JOHN STUART 1806–1873. **On Liberty** (1859) and **Utilitarianism** (1863). The great inductive logician and philosopher of science in a brilliant defense of individual freedom and the ethics of the greatest good for the greatest number. *Over 5 eds. each.*

MOORE, G. E. 1873–1958. **Some Main Problems of Philosophy** (1953). One of the fathers of analytical philosophy in essays relating problems in logic and metaphysics to common sense. *H—Humanities*.

OGDEN, C. K. 1889–1957 and I. A. RICHARDS 1893– 1979. **The Meaning of Meaning** (1938). The famous study of the influence of language upon thought and of the science of symbolism. *P—HarBraceJ*.

PEIRCE, CHARLES S. 1839–1914. **Philosophical Writings** (1940, 1955). Popular and technical essays on logic, evolution and the cosmos presenting key ideas in American thought. *H—AMS Pr; P—Dover*.

QUINE, W. V. O. b. 1908. **Word and Object** (1960). The definitive examination of the notion of meaning and the linguistic mechanisms of object reference in the philosophy of a noted logician. *P—MIT Pr*.

SANTAYANA, GEORGE 1863–1952. **The Life of Reason** (1906). Next to James's *Principles of Psychology*, Santayana's work is the most distinguished masterpiece in American philosophy. *P—Dover 3 vols*.

SARTRE, JEAN-PAUL 1905–1980. **Being and Nothingness** (1943). Atheistic existentialism presented by a philosopher who is also a novelist and playwright. *P—Philos Lib, WSP*.

SUZUKI, D. T. 1870–1966. **Zen Buddhism** (1956). The search for the entirely and vividly concrete. *P—Doubleday*.

WHITEHEAD, ALFRED NORTH 1861–1947. **Modes of Thought** (1938). The relations of value to language and physics to life explained by a philosopher whose work in mathematics and logic is of first importance. *P—Free Pr*.

Histories and Anthologies

Age of Analysis (1955). Ed. Morton White. Well-selected pages from key works of the 20th century with lucid commentaries. *P—NAL*.

The Chinese Mind (1967). Ed. C. A. Moore. Essays on essentials of Chinese philosophy and culture. *P—UH Pr.*

DURANT, WILL 1885–1981. **The Story of Philosophy** (rev. ed. 1983). Popular, readable, and selective account of Western thinkers. *P—S&S, WSP.*

Existentialism from Dostoevsky to Sartre (1956). Ed. Walter Kaufmann. An anthology for the layperson of selections from literary and religious imaginations in philosophy. *H—Peter Smith; P—NAL.*

FLOWER, ELIZABETH b. 1914 and MURRAY G. MURPHY. **A History of Philosophy in America** (1977). A comprehensive study of the origins and interrelations of American philosophical thought from Puritanism to conceptualistic pragmatism. *H— Hackett Pub 2 vols.*

JONES, W. T. b. 1910. **A History of Western Philosophy** (1952). The classical, the medieval, and the modern minds simply and forcefully presented. *P—HarBraceJ 5 vols.*

Logical Positivism (1959). Ed. A. J. Ayer. Authoritative expositions of doctrines associated with logical positivism. *H—Greenwood.*

MARÍAS AGUILERA, JULÍAN b. 1914. **History of Philosophy** (22nd ed. 1966). A Spanish scholar's philosophical treatment of the history of philosophy from the pre-Socratics to Heidegger and Ortega. *P—Dover.*

Readings in Philosophy (3rd ed. 1972). Ed. J. H. Randall, Jr. Excerpts from Plato through Descartes and Mill to Whitehead, grouped to emphasize philosophical perspectives. *P—B&N.*

RUSSELL, BERTRAND 1872–1970. **History of Western Philosophy** (1945). Lucid, candid, wise analysis of philosophical systems and of their connections with political and social circumstances. *P—S&S.*

Sourcebook in Indian Philosophy (1957). Eds. S. Radhakrishnan and C. A. Moore. Selections from the Vedic and Epi periods as well as from the heterodox and orthodox and contemporary systems with enlightening introductions. *H & P—Princeton U Pr.*

STUMPF, SAMUEL E. b. 1918. **Socrates to Sartre** (1966, 3rd ed. 1982). For beginners in philosophy an up-to-date introduction to the great issues of thought. *H—McGraw.*

WINDELBAND, WILHELM 1848–1915. **A History of Philosophy** (1901). A classic in its field by an idealist philosopher of some distinction. *H—Greenwood.*

CHAPTER 21

Religion

BRUCE R. GROB

Insatiably curious, people compulsively raise questions about the beginnings of things, about the origin and meaning of life. Everywhere we find that humanity is religious, "incurably religious," as one philosopher described it. On an individual level, religion is an intensely experienced and personal quest for a "way." It is an area of human experience where one comes upon mystery as a summons to pilgrimage. For the individual, religion is a vital search for that which might warrant one's "ultimate concern." Religious concern is ultimate in that it demands total surrender and promises total fulfillment. Detached objectivity is no longer possible. To be ultimately concerned is to be utterly committed.

Tolstoy believed that true religion was first of all the search for religion. The sacred texts, the literature and theology of the major religions, provide a vehicle for that search, affording one the opportunity to journey, to visit (literally, "to go see") the varied religious expressions of humankind. Common experience suggests that we sacrifice a great deal if we confine ourselves to the familiar. We grow and learn when we expose and acquaint ourselves with the experiences and ideas of other people.

In addition to the literature that pertains to the individual quest for meaning, a great body of work relates to the communal journey, the established institutions of religion—with their creeds, official rituals, and the weight of other traditions. The impact of world events constantly challenges these institutions to reassess and redefine their place and purpose in history. The interpretive literature of theology and ethics grows and changes in response to the continuing crises and revelations of history. New technologies, psychological insights, and political and social realities confront and question traditional moral codes. Eastern religions have become more and more important in the West, stimulating a vigorous spiritual renaissance. We have been catapulted from town and country onto a world stage. We all have our own perspectives, but they can no longer be cast in the hard molds of oblivion to the rest.

The vast literature of religion is not just a matter of facts in the historical sense; it is also a matter of meanings. An account may speak endlessly of gods and rites and beliefs, but unless it leads us to see how these things help people to confront and understand such problems as isolation, tragedy, and death, and to struggle with the questions of purpose and existence, that account may be impeccably accurate, but religion has only been partially touched. What the literature of religion takes fact and meaning to be is finally its ultimate agenda and its ultimate service.

Sacred Texts

BUDDHISM (564–483 B.C.). Anthologies of Buddhist scriptures vary widely. See E. A. Burtt (ed.), **The Teachings of the Compassionate Buddha** (1955). An anthology of the basic texts of Buddhism, with introduction and notes by Burtt. *P—NAL.* See also Allie M. Frazier (ed.), **Buddhism** (1969). Vol. 3 of **Readings in Eastern Religious Thought.** A well-balanced anthology that contains both introductory essays by leading interpreters and readings from scriptures. *P—Westminster.*

CHRISTIANITY AND JUDAISM. The scriptures of Judaism and Christianity in the Old Testament, the New Testament, and the Apochrypha now appear in more than 50 English translations ranging from the early **King James Version**, first published in 1611, to modern translations, which include **The New English Bible** (1961, rev. ed. 1970), *H & P—Oxford U Pr*; a Catholic translation, **The Jerusalem Bible** (1966), *H—Doubleday;* and the **American Revised Standard Version** or **RSV**, *H— Nelson; P—World Pub.*

————. Numerous biblical guides and commentaries are available to aid the reader. The most notable commentary is **The**

Interpreter's Bible (12 vols. 1952–57), *H—Abingdon*, and its companion, **The Interpreter's Dictionary of the Bible** (5 vols. 1962), *H—Abingdon*, which provide references to personalities, places, and topics of the scriptures.

————. The Dead Sea Scrolls, discovered in 1947, contain large portions of the Old Testament in Hebrew, which is of immense significance since these scrolls are a thousand years older than any other manuscript of the Hebrew Bible. Also in the scrolls are commentaries on the Bible and writings distinctive to the Qumran settlement and monastery, a community that flourished until about A.D. 69. Theodore Gaster's **The Dead Sea Scriptures** (2nd ed. 1976). *P—Doubleday*, is a translation of the scrolls with introductions and notes.

CONFUCIANISM (551–479 B.C.) Tr. Arthur Waley, **The Analects** (1966), *P—Random*; also, in **Three Ways of Thought in Ancient China** (1939), *P—Stanford U Pr*, Waley weaves together his own narrative and extracts from the Taoist Chuang Tzu, Mencius, and a "realist" philosopher, Han Fei Tzu.

HINDUISM. **Bhagavad Gita** (5th-3rd cent. B.C.). Notable translations are those by Mascaro, **The Bhagavad Gita** (1962), *P—Penguin*; Franklin Edgerton, **The Bhagavad Gita** (1944), *P—Harvard U Pr;* Radhakrishnan, **The Bhagavadgita** (1949), *P—Har-Row*; and Prabhavananda and Isherwood, **Bhagavad-Gita: Song of God** (3rd ed. 1972), *H—Vedanta Pr*.

————. **Upanishads.** Because English translations differ significantly, it is important and informative to compare them. Good translators of the Upanishads include those by Mascaro, **The Upanishads** (1965), *P—Penguin;* Radhakrishnan, **The Principal Upanishads** (1978), *H—Humanities;* and *Prabhavananda and Manchester*, **The Upanishads: Breath of the Eternal** (1945), *P—NAL*.

HUMANISM. A religion without revelation; its source is man; its values and ideas are human centered. There are, therefore, no humanist "scriptures." Corliss Lamont's **The Philosophy of Humanism** (6th ed. 1982) is a good review of the background and principles of humanism by one of its best-known spokesmen. *H & P—Ungar*.

ISLAM. Among the outstanding modern translations of the Koran in English are Pickthall, **The Holy Koran: Text and Explanatory Translation** (1983). *H—Kazi Pubns;* Dawood, **The Koran** (rev. ed. 1974), *P—Penguin;* and Arberry, **The Koran Interpreted** (1964), *P—Macmillan*, the preface to which is a very interesting discussion and comparison of the important English translations of the Koran.

LAO-TZU (604–531 B.C.) Difficulties in translating the Tao Te Ching make it evident that a comparison of the translations is necessary and revealing. Among the best are Wing-tsit Chan, **The Way of Lao Tzu** (1963), *P—Bobbs;* Waley, **The Way and Its Power** (1958), *P—Grove;* and Lin Yutang, **The Wisdom of Lao Tzu** (1948), *H—Modern Lib.* **Sacred Books of China** (1981), translated by J. Legge, remains one of the classic English translations of Taoist texts. *H—Krishna Pr. 6 vols.*

African Traditional Religions

African Systems of Thought (1965). Eds. M. Fortes and G. Dieterleu. Includes 21 essays covering such topics as indigenous systems of religious belief, ancestor worship, and Christianity and Islam in Africa. *o.p.*

MBITI, JOHN S. b. 1931. **African Religions and Philosophy** (1970). A thorough study of the nature and attributes of God, the problem of evil, anthropomorphism, the creation of man, worship, ethics, death, and other topics. *P— Doubleday.*

Comparative Religions

Disputation and Dialogue (1975), Ed. F. E. Talmage. This anthology brings together a variety of Jewish and Christian documents from antiquity to the present day. Each selection is preceded by a historical note that explains its background. *P—ADL, Ktav.*

NEILL, STEPHEN CHARLES b. 1900. **Christian Faith and Other Faiths** (2nd ed. 1970). Intended for the Christian's understanding of and dialogue with other religions. *P—Inter-Varsity.*

SMITH, HUSTON b. 1919. **Religions of Man** (1965). An inclusive portrait of man's religions, including their origin, nature, and form. *P—Har-Row.*

The Ways of Religion (1975). Ed. Roger Eastman. An anthology in comparative religion that combines pertinent and interesting primary sources and expository materials for each of the major religions. *P—Har-Row*.

Ethics

BIRCH, BRUCE C. b. 1941 and LARRY D. RASMUSSEN. **The Bible and Ethics in the Christian Life** (1976). A small book that contains a general survey of specific thinkers as well as an overall look at the issues. *P—Augsburg*.

CURRAN, CHARLES E. b. 1934. **Transition and Tradition in Moral Theology** (1980). Contains essays about recent changes in Roman Catholic moral theology. Curran not only reports developments, but he also interprets them. *H & P—U of Notre Dame Pr*.

FORELL, GEORGE W. b. 1919. **Christian Social Teachings** (1971). A reader in Christian social ethics from the Bible to the present. *P—Augsberg*.

Religion and Morality (1973). Eds. Gene Outka and John P. Reeder. This collection of essays constitutes a wide-ranging debate between philosophers, students of the ethics of Judaism and Christianity, and anthropologists on the relation of religion to morality. *o.p.*

General Histories

AHLSTROM, SIDNEY E. b. 1919. **The Religious History of the American People** (1972). The major study of the moral and spiritual development of the American people. *H & P—Yale U Pr*.

A Documentary of Religion in America (Vol. 1—1982, Vol. 2—1984). Ed. Edwin S. Gaustad. An anthology that accurately reflects the pluralistic nature of religious forms in the American experience. Gaustad provides learned and well-written introductions. *P—Eerdmans*.

The Pelican History of the Church, 6 vols. (1960–70). Ed. Henry Chadwick. An accessible and thorough compendium of the evolution and development of the institutional church. *o.p.*

SACHAR, A. L. b. 1899. **A History of the Jews** (rev. ed. 1968). The revised and enlarged 5th edition of Sachar's *History* outlines, in a lucid fashion, the salient events, ideas, and influences that have shaped the destiny of Jews and their role on the world scene. Sachar is concerned with the economic, political, and diplomatic factors, as well as with the purely social and religious, and stresses the diversified interaction between Jewish and non-Jewish life. *H & P— Knopf.*

Liberation Theologies

BROWN, ROBERT McAFEE b. 1920. **Theology in a New Key: Responding to Liberation Themes** (1978). Looks at issues for ethics raised by new liberation theologies. *P— Westminster.*

CONE, JAMES H. b. 1938. **A Black Theology of Liberation** (1970). Analyzes the role of Christianity and the theology of liberation in contemporary black American society. *P—Har-Row.*

McFADDEN, THOMAS M. b. 1935. **Liberation, Revolution and Freedom: Theological Perspectives** (1975). A helpful interpretation and analysis of the movement from political theology to ethics. *P—U Pr of Amer.*

RUETHER, ROSEMARY b. 1936. **Sexism and God Talk: Toward a Feminist Theology** (1983). *H—Beacon Pr.* See RUSSELL, below.

RUSSELL, LETTY M. b. 1929. **The Future of Partnership** (1979). Both Ruether and Russell relate feminist perspectives to human liberation themes in a wide context. *P—Westminster.*

New Religions

CASTANEDA, CARLOS b. 1931. **The Teachings of Don Juan** (1968), **A Separate Reality** (1971), **Journey to Ixtlan** (1972), and **Tales of Power** (1974). All portray the religious mysticism and world of the Yaqui Indian Don Juan, a ''sorcerer, medicine man, curer,'' and spiritual guide. *P—PB.*

NEEDLEMAN, JACOB b. 1934. **The New Religions** (1977). The best survey of transplanted Oriental mysticism in America (Zen, Subud, Meher Baba, Transcendental Meditation, etc.) that is available. *P—Crossroad NY.*

Religion for a New Generation (2nd ed. 1977). Eds. Jacob

Needleman et al. Fifty-seven reading selections on topics ranging from the "Spiritual Revolution" to "The Struggle with
Death." *P—Macmillan*.

Religious and Theological Currents

BENZ, ERNST b. 1907. **The Eastern Orthodox Church** (1963).
Still one of the best treatments of Eastern Orthodoxy—its
church, traditions, thought, and dogma. *o.p.*

BLAU, JOSEPH b. 1909. **Modern Varieties of Judaism** (1966).
A well-documented study of the most significant movements
within Judaism today, including Zionism. *H & P—Columbia
U Pr*. See also Neusner, Jacob. **Judaism in America: Adventure in Modernity** (1972). *o.p.*

FOWLER, JAMES W. b. 1940. **Stages of Faith** (1981). The
psychology of human development and the quest for meaning.
Fowler offers a clear, readable account of the stages he identifies in the development of a person's faith through the whole
span of life. *H—Har-Row*.

GUILLAUME, ALFRED 1888–1965. **Islam** (2nd rev. ed. 1956).
Muhammad, the Koran, the evolution of Islam, the various
schools of thought, and the place of Islam in the world. *P—
Penguin*.

HOPKINS, THOMAS J. b. 1930. **Hindu Religious Tradition**
(1971). A clear chronological and historical presentation of
Hindu values and traditions. *o.p.*

HUMPHREYS, CHRISTMAS 1901–1983. **Buddhism** (rev. 1958).
An exposition of the various schools of Buddhism, including
Zen. *o.p.*

JAMES, WILLIAM 1842–1910. **Varieties of Religious Experience**
(1902). Still the classic study of spirituality and spiritual experiences as psychological phenomena. *H—Modern Lib; P—Macmillan, NAL, Penguin*.

KÜNG, HANS b. 1928. **On Being a Christian** (1976). A major
Catholic theologian writes on "what Christianity and what
being a Christian really means." It is a relevant and opportune
introduction. *H & P—Doubleday; P—PB*. See also Küng's
Structures of the Church (1982). A major study of the
structures of the Catholic Church and its basic arguments
about ecclesiastical office, pope and council, teaching office,
and infallibility. *P—Crossroad NY*.

LEWIS, C. S. 1898–1963. **Mere Christianity** (1964). Lewis argues brilliantly (and wittily) for a conservative interpretation of Christianity. *H & P—Macmillan.* See also his **Screwtape Letters** (1982). *H & P—Macmillan; H— Fortress; P—Double-day, Revell;* and **Miracles** (1978) *P— Macmillan.*

SCHOLEM, GERSHOM 1897–1982. **Major Trends in Jewish Mysticism** (3rd ed. 1961). The purpose of Scholem's book is to outline the principal features of Jewish mysticism in the form of an analysis of some of its most important phases. He stresses the interpretation of mystical thought rather than the historical links between the various systems. *P—Schocken.*

UNDERHILL, EVELYN 1875–1941. **Mysticism** (1911). The classic study of mysticism drawing material from St. Teresa of Avila, Meister Eckhart, St. John of the Cross, William Blake, and others. *P—Dutton, NAL.*

Writings of the Great Theologians

Great Jewish Thinkers of the Twentieth Century (1963). Ed. Simon Noveck. A discussion of Jewish religious, intellectual, and social currents. *o.p.*

Great Voices of the Reformation (1952). Ed. Harry Emerson Fosdick. Major writings of Protestant reformers from Wycliffe to Wesley. Contains biographies and commentary. *o.p.*

A Handbook of Christian Theologians (1980). Eds. Martin E. Marty and Dean G. Peerman. A solid anthology of major theological voices. *P—Abingdon.*

Twelve Makers of Modern Protestant Thought (rev. 1971). Ed. George L. Hunt. Barth, Buber, H. R. and Reinhold Niebuhr, and Tillich are among those represented. *o.p.*

The Wisdom of Catholicism (1949). Ed. Anton C. Pegis. Important collection of writings from the Church fathers, mystics, Catholic philosophers, etc. *o.p.*

CHAPTER 22

History

GARY B. MILLS and BERNERD C. WEBER

Carl Becker defined history as "a knowledge of things said and done." But history at its best does more than present a miscellaneous collection of the varied experiences of the human race. It may show, although sometimes imperfectly, the whole spectrum of behavior and belief and illustrate the range and depth of human experience.

A knowledge of history can serve as a valuable corrective to the common habits of vague generalization or of too narrow particularism. Historical knowledge explains how things have come to be what they are and so may help to make the world more intelligible. The more one delves into the past, the deeper and broader will be one's comprehension of the present and insight into the future. The value of the knowledge of the past to the understanding of society today has been recognized by all the major historians from Thucydides on. Sir Charles Firth clearly supports these observations: "History is not easy to define; but to me it seems the record of the life of societies of man, of the changes which those societies have gone through, of the ideas which have determined the actions of those societies, and of the material conditions which have helped or hindered their development."

By its very nature, history is vibrant with life and inevitably concerns each of us. The 19th-century British historian Edward A. Freeman defined history as "past politics," but this definition is no longer considered adequate. Modern historians, in writing about the past, have increasingly turned attention to what James Harvey Robinson termed "the new history"—in other words, to economic, social, and cultural behavior of all people, as well as to political, military, and constitutional events. Geographically, too, the whole base of history has broadened. No longer are Western historians concerned just with Europe or the Americas: Africa, Asia, and the island world of the Pacific are vital parts of the total drama of human experience and endeavor. Thus, all that has been thought and done on this earth falls within the province of history.

One of the pleasures of history grows out of its relationship with literature. Since the time of Herodotus of Halicarnassus, written history has been a major form of literary expression, and many major historians of the past have been distinguished writers. Not only have historians created literature by writing history but, in varying degrees, a knowledge of the history they write is necessary for an understanding and appreciation of the poetry, drama, fiction, architecture, art, and music of any country or period.

History thus represents the sum of the total past of the world. If it is read and studied to any purpose, it is neither "a confused heap of facts" (Lord Chesterfield) nor a record "always tedious" (Anatole France); rather it makes an intelligent and often fascinating relationship between cause and effect that contains wisdom for all ages.

Many important historical books are listed in more than a dozen other chapters of *Good Reading*. For dates and other reference data, extremely useful volumes include *Annals of European Civilization, 1501–1900* (1949) by Alfred Mayer; *Encyclopedia of American History* (6th ed. 1982), edited by Richard B. Morris and Jeffrey B. Morris; *An Encyclopedia of World History* (5th ed. 1972), edited by William L. Langer; *Historical Atlas* (9th ed. 1964, *o.p.*) by William R. Sheperd; and *The Timetables of History: A Horizontal Linkage of People and Events* (rev. ed. 1982) by Bernard Grun. Available in paperback is *Historical Atlas of the World* (1965), edited by R. R. Palmer (*P—Rand*). See also the subdivision History in the "Reference Books" chapter.

General

Several hundred specialized histories—that is, histories limited to various historical periods and geographic areas—are contained in the book lists of Chapters 1 through 11. Histories that span the ages and often continents but examine only an aspect of culture (e.g., art, music, philosophy) are listed in the chapters on "Fine Arts and Performing Arts," "Philosophy," "Religion," "Economics," and "Anthropology." Additionally, many biographies of men and women important in history are listed in "Women's Studies" and "Biography." Because of the profusion of history titles listed elsewhere, none is cross-referenced in this chapter.

Becoming Visible: Women in European History (1977). Eds. Renate Bridenthal and Claudia Koonz. An excellent collection of essays by various scholars stressing the role of women throughout European history. *P—HM.*

BRINTON, CRANE 1898–1968. **Ideas and Men** (2nd ed. 1963). A well-written and sound analysis of the major concepts in Western thought that have helped shape the course of Western civilization. *H—P.H.*

—— et al. **History of Civilization** (5th ed. 1976). A readable, thorough, well-illustrated survey. *P—P.H.*

CHURCHILL, SIR WINSTON 1874–1965. **History of the English-Speaking Peoples** (1956–58). The great English statesman presents in his inimitable style the history of England, the United States, and the British Commonwealth as a unified story. *H—Dodd 4 vols.; P—Bantam 4 vols.*

CLYDE, PAUL H. b. 1896 and BURTON F. BEERS b. 1927. **The Far East** (6th ed. 1976). A well-organized and clearly written account that stresses the impact of the West upon East Asia. *H—P.H.*

DEAN, VERA MICHELES 1903–1972. **The Nature of the Non-Western World** (1957). A useful introduction emphasizing the West's influence upon older, traditional cultures. *o.p.*

FAIRBANK, JOHN K. b. 1907. **The United States and China** (4th enlarged ed. 1983). An excellent general introductory study of the history of American-Chinese relationships. *H & P— Harvard U Pr.*

HALECKI, OSKAR 1891–1972. **A History of Poland** (1976). A readable overview by a Polish-born scholar. *P—McKay, Regnery-Gateway.*

KNAPTON, ERNEST JOHN b. 1902 **France: An Interpretive History** (1971). A well-written, clearly organized narrative. *o.p.*

McNEILL, WILLIAM H. b. 1917. **The Rise of the West: A History of the Human Community** (1963). A fascinating and provocative work, monumental in scope, that attempts to integrate the entire history of human societies into one continuous and cohesive story. *P—U of Chicago Pr.*

————. **Plagues and Peoples** (1975). A lively analysis of the role of disease in history. *o.p.*

MAHAN, ALFRED T. 1840–1914. **The Influence of Sea Power upon History, 1660–1783** (1890). A work that has become a classic. *P—Hill & Wang.*

PINSON, KOPPEL S. 1901–1961. **Modern Germany** (2nd ed. 1966). A clear, readable history. *H—Macmillan.*

RANDALL, JOHN HERMAN, JR. 1899–1980. **The Making of the Modern Mind** (rev. ed. 1976). A learned and stimulating explanation of the forces from the Middle Ages onward that have contributed to modern ways of thinking and acting. *H & P—Columbia U Pr.*

TOYNBEE, ARNOLD J. 1889–1975. **A Study of History** (1934–61). A masterly monumental inquiry into the causes of the rise and decline of civilizations. *H—Oxford U Pr 12 vols.*

TREVELYAN, GEORGE M. 1876–1962. **History of England** (3rd ed. 1945). A classic work written by an outstanding English historian. Presupposes some previous knowledge of English history. *o.p.*

Ancient and Medieval

For many additional titles see Chapters 1 through 3.

CHILDE, V. GORDON 1892–1957. **The Prehistory of European Society** (1958). A useful exposition by a distinguished archeologist. *o.p.*

HAY, DENYS b. 1915. **Europe in the Fourteenth and Fifteenth Centuries** (1966). A well-organized survey of the last two centuries of the medieval period. *P—Longman.*

PARKES, HENRY B. 1904–1972. **Gods and Men** (1959). A good narrative history of the origins of Western culture, with a critical analysis of the important shaping of ideas and ideals. *o.p.*

PETERS, EDWARD MURRAY b. 1936. **Europe: The World of the Middle Ages** (1977). An excellent recent study, with extensive bibliographies for further reading. *o.p.*

PLUMB, JOHN HAROLD b. 1911. **The Italian Renaissance** (1965). A concise guide. *P—Har-Row*.

SHEVILL, FERDINAND 1868–1954. **The Medici** (1950). Traces with vivid detail the development of the city-state of Florence down to the 16th century. *H—Arden Lib*.

Women in Medieval Society (1976). Ed. Susan M. Stuard. A superb representative collection of essays on the role of women in the Middle Ages. *H & P—U of Pa Pr*.

Modern (1500–1900) Other than American

ALBRECHT-CARRIÉ, RENÉ 1904–1978. **A Diplomatic History of Europe since the Congress of Vienna** (rev. ed. 1973). A superior one-volume treatment, with useful maps and bibliography. *P—Har-Row*.

ALLEN, HARRY CRANBROOK b. 1917. **Conflict and Concord** (1960). Traces Anglo-American relations from 1783 to 1952 from the British point of view. *o.p*.

ASHLEY, MAURICE PERCY b. 1907. **The Golden Century** (1969). A well-written account of the 17th century, skillfully blending political and cultural forces to interpret the significance of a remarkable age. *o.p*.

BAINTON, RONALD H. 1894–1984. **The Age of the Reformation** (1956). A clear, concise summary, with excerpts from the primary materials of the period. *P—Krieger*.

The Berkshire Studies in European History. A first-rate series of popularizations by distinguished specialists. These short, clearly written studies include such outstanding works as *The Renaissance* by Wallace K. Ferguson (*o.p.*) and *The Age of Metternich* by Arthur J. May (*o.p.*).

BRAUDEL, FERNAND b. 1902. **Civilization and Capitalism, 15th-18th Century.** Vol. 1. **The Structure of Everyday Life** (1981); Vol. 2. **The Wheels of Commerce** (1983); Vol. 3. **The Perspective of the World** (1984). A prodigious work, examining almost every aspect of "material life" during three centuries. An important and influential study—founded on economics, yet extraordinarily readable. *H—Har-Row*.

————. **The Mediterranean and the Mediterranean World in the Age of Philip Second** (1976). A splendid, panoramic history, focusing on the Mediterranean world in the latter half of the 16th century, but ranging through an earlier part and illuminating our present world. *H & P—Har-Row 2 vols*.

BRINTON, CRANE 1898–1968. **The Anatomy of Revolution** (1950). This provocative book provides a comparative study of the English, American, French, and Russian revolutions. *H—Peter Smith; P—Random.*

CLOUGH, SHEPARD BANCROFT b. 1901. **European Economic History** (3rd ed. 1975). A clear perspective on the economic development of Western civilization. *H—McGraw.*

DANGERFIELD, GEORGE b. 1904. **The Damnable Question** (1976). An intriguing exploration of political, social, and cultural relations between Ireland and England from 1800 to 1922, remarkable for its grace, style, and inclusiveness. *H—Peter Smith.*

DAVIDOFF, LEONORE. **The Best Circles** (1973). One of the best analyses of the role of women in Victorian society. *o.p.*

ELLIOTT, JOHN HUXTABLE b. 1930. **The Old World and the New, 1492–1650** (1970). A concise and useful introduction to a vast subject. *H & P—Cambridge U Pr.*

GAY, PETER b. 1923. **The Enlightenment** (1966–69). A masterly and provocative study of the critical philosophical movement of the 18th century. *P—Norton 2 vols.*

GRIMM, HAROLD J. 1901–1984. **The Reformation Era, 1500–1650** (2nd ed. 1973). A clear and careful treatment of a complex era in modern history. *H—Macmillan.*

HERR, RICHARD b. 1922. **Spain** (1971). A competent history from the beginnings but with emphasis on the last two centuries. *o.p.*

The Norton History of Modern Europe. An admirable series: thorough and well-balanced volumes with extensive bibliographies. Individual titles include: **The Foundations of Early Modern Europe, 1460–1559** by Eugene F. Rice, Jr.; **The Age of Religious Wars, 1559–1689** by Richard S. Dunn; **Kings and Philosophers, 1689–1789** by Leonard Krieger; and **The Age of Revolution and Reaction, 1789–1850** by Charles Breunig. *P—Norton.*

PALMER, ROBERT ROSWELL b. 1909. **Twelve Who Ruled** (1941). A fascinating collective biography of the members of the Committee of Public Safety in France. *H & P—Princeton U Pr.*

————. **The World of the French Revolution** (1972). Illuminating: lucid explanations of the interrelationships among the various revolutionary movements of the 18th century. *P—Har-Row.*

PARRY, JOHN HORACE 1914–1982. **Trade and Dominion**

(1972). A well-drawn portrait of European overseas empires in the 18th century. *o.p.*

PLUMB, JOHN HAROLD b. 1911. **In the Light of History** (1972). A series of delightful essays, most of which deal with aspects of the 18th century. *o.p.*

RIASANOVSKY, NICHOLAS V. b. 1923. **A History of Russia** (4th ed. 1984). An informed, up-to-date history, emphasizing the periods since 1500. *H & P—Oxford U Pr.*

Rise of Modern Europe. Various specialists have written reliable and readable interpretations of various periods with detailed bibliographies for those who wish to read further. Representative titles include **Europe and the French Imperium** by Geoffrey Bruun (*H—Greenwood*); **The World of Humanism** by Myron P. Gilmore (*H—Greenwood*); **A Generation of Materialism, 1871–1900** by Carlton J. H. Hayes (*H— Greenwood*); and **The Triumph of Science and Reason** by Frank L. Nussbaum (*o.p.*)

SCHORSKE, CARL E. b. 1915. **Fin-de-Siècle Vienna: Politics and Culture** (1980). Essays in the culture and intellectual history of Vienna during the last decades of the 19th and the early decades of the 20th century (with some spillover). Broad in its perspective, acute and particular in its analyses. *H—Knopf; P—Random.*

SIMPSON, LESLEY BYRD b. 1891. **Many Mexicos** (4th ed. 1966). One of the best one-volume surveys of Mexican history from the beginnings. *H & P—U of Cal Pr.*

TAYLOR, ALAN JOHN PERCIVALE b. 1906. **The Habsburg Monarchy, 1800–1918** (rev. 1976). A sound and substantial work on a difficult subject. *H—AMS Pr; P—U of Chicago Pr.*

WEDGWOOD, CICELY VERONICA b. 1910. **The King's Peace** (1969) and **The King's War** (1958). Modern reappraisals of the background of the English Civil War and of the war itself written in a flowing narrative style. *o.p.*

YOUNG, GEORGE M. 1882–1959. **Victorian England** (2nd ed. 1964). A detailed, accurate, appealing portrait of an age. *P—Oxford U Pr.*

Contemporary (since 1900) Other than American

CHURCHILL, SIR WINSTON 1874–1965. **The Second World War** (1948–53). A six-volume personal narrative of the vital and dramatic war years—forceful and colorful. *H—HM.*

CRAIG, GORDON b. 1913 and ALEXANDER L. GEORGE b. 1920. **Force and Statecraft: Diplomatic Problems of Our Time** (1983). Combines a historical approach with methodology of political science to interpret international affairs. *H & P— Oxford U Pr*.

EISENHOWER, DWIGHT D. 1890–1969. **Crusade in Europe** (1948). The commander's report to the public on his assignment: clear, concise, judicious, still interesting. *H & P—Da Capo*.

FAY, SIDNEY BRADSHAW 1876–1967. **Origins of the World War** (rev. ed. 1938). An expert marshaling of the background of World War I, going back as far as 1871. *o.p.*

Fifty Major Documents of the Twentieth Century (1955). Ed Louis L. Snyder. An invaluable collection, including the Austro-Hungarian ultimatum to Serbia in 1914, the Munich agreement of 1939, the legislation enfranchising women in Britain and the United States in 1918–1919, the Nuremberg laws on race, Churchill's "Blood, Toil, Tears, and Sweat" address, the secret Yalta agreement, and the text of the Truman Doctrine. *P—Krieger*.

RAUCH, BASIL b. 1908. **Roosevelt from Munich to Pearl Harbor** (1950). An analysis of the development of the Roosevelt foreign policy before America's entry into World War II, challenging the views of extremists of both right and left. *H—Da Capo*.

ROBERTSON, PRISCILLA b. 1910. **An Experience of Women: Pattern and Change in Nineteenth-Century Europe** (1982). A clear discussion of the diversity among women and an analysis of various conditions that have affected their lives. *H & P—Temple U Pr*.

SHIRER, WILLIAM b. 1904. **The Challenge of Scandinavia** (1955). A history of the Scandinavian countries (Denmark, Finland, Norway, Sweden) since 1930, emphasizing the high level of social and economic well being they have achieved. *H—Greenwood*.

———. **The Rise and Fall of the Third Reich** (1960). The monumental and highly absorbing story of the rise and fall of Hitler based on personal observation and on the examination of voluminous documents. *P—Fawcett, S&S*.

The Times Survey of Foreign Ministries of the World (1982). Ed. Zara Steiner. This authoritative survey of how governments organize international relations covers 18 countries in Europe and 6 elsewhere, including the United States. *H—Meckler Pub*.

WOLFE, BERTRAM DAVID 1896–1977. **Three Who Made A Revolution** (rev. ed. 1984). Intriguing biographies of the men, and the forces shaping them, that brought on the Russian Revolution: Lenin, Trotsky, and Stalin. *H & P—Stein & Day*.

The United States

AMERICAN PRESIDENCY SERIES. The University Press of Kansas is publishing an exciting new series of interpretive works on the administrations of each president of the United States with each volume written by a leading scholar of the period. *H—U Pr of KS*.

BAILEY, HUGH C. b. 1929. **Liberalism in the New South** (1969). A careful study of the work and influence of southern social reformers and of the Progressive movement from 1877 to the end of the Wilson administration. *H—U of Miami Pr*.

BAILEY, THOMAS ANDREW 1902–1983. **A Diplomatic History of the American People** (10th ed. 1980). A sound popular work though not sufficiently critical for many contemporary tastes. *H—P-H*.

BOORSTIN, DANIEL J. b. 1914. **The Americans: The Democratic Experience** (1973). An excellent example of the "new history," emphasizing the changes, some revolutionary, that occurred in homes, farms, factories, and cities throughout the expanding nation. *P—Random*.

BURNER, DAVID b. 1937, ELIZABETH FOX-GENOVESE b. 1941, EUGENE GENOVESE b. 1930. and FORREST McDONALD b. 1927. **An American Portrait** (1982). An interesting examination of American history enhanced by vigorous commentaries from opposing conservative and Marxist viewpoints. *H—Revisionary 2 vols*.

Chronicles of America. More than 50 small volumes, each by a distinguished scholar and each covering a limited aspect of American history with accuracy and readability. *H—US Pubs*.

CRAVEN, AVERY ODELLE 1886–1980. **The Coming of the Civil War** (2nd ed. 1957). A readable, scholarly, objective study, developing the thesis that the democratic process "failed in the critical period that culminated in the Civil War." *P—U of Chicago Pr*.

CURTI, MERLE b. 1897. **The Growth of American Thought** (3rd ed. 1981). A sound and stimulating history of American social, intellectual, and scientific thought. *P—Transaction Bks*.

DEDERER, JOHN MORGAN b. 1951. **Making Bricks Without Straw: Nathaniel Greene's Southern Campaigns and Mao Tse-tung's Mobile War** (1983). A fresh and provocative comparison of American strategy in the War for Independence with modern revolutionary strategy. Also contains an excellent up-to-date bibliography. *P—Sunflower U Pr*.

DONALD, DAVID b. 1920. **Charles Sumner and the Coming of the Civil War** (1960). A careful, dispassionate anatomy of one of America's most complex and controversial leaders in the sectional conflict that culminated in the Civil War. *P—U of Chicago Pr*.

FILLER, LOUIS b. 1912. **The Muckrakers** (rev. ed. 1975). A vivid and cogent group portrait of the muckraking journalists who exposed the evils of the trusts and searched for an improved democracy during the first decades of this century. *H & P—Pa St U Pr*.

FLEXNER, ELEANOR b. 1908. **Century of Struggle** (rev. ed. 1975). More than a story of the women's rights movement in the United States and the enfranchisement of 26 million people, this volume traces the economic and social history of women in America through 1920. *H & P—Harvard U Pr*.

FOGEL, ROBERT W. b. 1926 and STANLEY L. ENGERMAN b. 1936. **Time on the Cross: The Economics of American Negro Slavery** (1974). An excellent example of the computer age methodology called "Cliometrics," this work has sparked debate and spurred further research on American black slavery. Among its startling and highly controversial findings is one arguing that slavery was both efficient and profitable, and that slaves were generally well treated and led lives materially superior to those of America's urban workers. *P—Little 2 vols*.

FRANKLIN, JOHN HOPE b. 1915. **From Slavery to Freedom: A History of Negro Americans** (5th ed. 1980). A scholarly and readable conspectus of Afro-American history from the African origins of America's black population through the modern struggle for civil rights. *P—Knopf*.

GRANTHAM, DEWEY W. b. 1921. **The Democratic South** (1963). A solid analysis of the forces that have molded the contemporary South. *P—Norton*.

HACKER, LOUIS MORTON b. 1899. **The Triumph of American Capitalism** (1940). American history to 1900, focusing on the economic and political forces that shaped the American version of capitalism. *o.p.*

HENRY, ROBERT S. 1889–1970. **The Story of the Confederacy** (rev. ed. 1957). A distinguished history: still a good place to begin one's study of the Civil War. *H—Peter Smith*.

HISTORY OF AMERICAN LIFE SERIES. Gen. eds. Arthur M. Schlesinger, Jr., and D. R. Fox. This series contains balanced, informed studies of limited periods in the economic, social, and cultural past of the United States. Representative titles include **The Revolutionary Generation, 1763–1790** by Evarts B. Greene; **The Irrepressible Conflict, 1850–1865** by Arthur C. Cole; **The Emergence of Modern America, 1865–1878** by Allan Nevins; and **The Age of the Great Depression, 1929–1941** by Dixon Wecter. *H—Macmillan*.

HOFSTADTER, RICHARD 1916–1970. **Anti-Intellectualism in American Life** (1963). A stimulating but often depressing study of the reaction of Americans to the intellectual currents of their history. Such works as this provide an antidote to the rosier versions of American history. *o.p.*

JENSEN, MERRILL 1905–1980. **The New Nation** (1981). A careful analysis of the United States during the formative years of the Confederation, 1781 to 1789. *H & P—NE U Pr*.

KARNOW, STANLEY b. 1925. **Vietnam: A History** (1983). A very popular account of the Vietnam War, the basis for the PBS program "Vietnam, A Television History." *P—Penguin*.

McDONALD, FORREST b. 1927. **Novus Ordo Seclorum: The Intellectual Origins of the Constitution** (1985). The most recent of several excellent works on the constitution by the leading authority in the field. *H—U Pr of KS*.

McWHINEY, GRADY b. 1928 and PERRY D. JAMIESON b. 1947. **Attack and Die: Civil War Military Tactics and the Southern Heritage** (1982). Certainly one of the best studies of Civil War tactics, greatly enhanced by a new cultural interpretation—the "Celtic thesis." *H & P—U of Ala Pr*.

MILLS, GARY B. b. 1944. **The Forgotten People: Cane River's Creoles of Color** (1977). A fascinating story of the rise of a slave family to the status of wealthy, slave-and-landowning free people of color, economically on the level of their aristocratic white Louisiana neighbors. *H & P—La State U Pr*.

NEW AMERICAN NATION SERIES. Eds. Henry Steele Commager and Richard B. Morris. This series attempts to synthesize the new and traditional history in studies covering the background and development of the American Nation from the age of discovery and exploration to the modern era. Some of the best volumes include **The Coming of the Revolution, 1763–1775** by Lawrence Henry Gipson; **The Era of Theodore Roosevelt, 1900–1912** by George E. Mowry; and **Woodrow Wilson and the Progressive Era, 1910–1917** by Arthur S. Link. *H & P—Har-Row*.

PANCAKE, JOHN S. b. 1920. **1777: The Year of the Hangman** (1977). Accurate, dramatic, and readable: the course of the American Revolution from Lexington and Concord in 1775 to the surrender of Burgoyne and the attempts to pen up the British in Philadelphia in 1777. *H—U of Ala Pr*.

PERKINS, DEXTER 1889–1984. **History of the Monroe Doctrine** (rev. ed. 1963). Definitive on the policy that has done so much to mold inter-American relations. *o.p.*

THE RIVERS OF AMERICA SERIES. ed. Carl Carmer. This series of more than 50 volumes on rivers—from the Allegheny to the Yazoo—gives the history of folklore of the area through which the title river flows. The best of these constitute superb historical writing. *H—HR&W*.

SPECTOR, RONALD b. 1943. **Eagle Against the Sun: The American War with Japan** (1984). The most recent outline of events leading up to the outbreak of war with Japan in 1941 and the ensuing four years of war in the Pacific, presented in a highly readable style. As a synthesis of the latest scholarship on the period, this volume covers all of the major controversies involving diplomatic machinations before the war: Pearl Harbor, General Douglas MacArthur, and the atomic bomb. *H—Free Pr*.

WEBB, WALTER PRESCOTT 1888–1963. **The Great Plains** (1957). An original, scholarly interpretation of the Great Plains by a distinguished authority, showing the importance of the horse, the six-shooter, the barbed-wire fence, and the windmill in the successful settlement of a large semiarid region. *P—U of Nebr. Pr*.

WILLIAMS, T. HARRY 1909–1979. **Lincoln and the Radicals** (1941). A dramatic and authoritative account of the efforts of radicals to dominate the Lincoln administration. *P—U of Wis Pr*.

WISH, HARVEY 1909–1968. **Contemporary America: The National Scene since 1900** (4th ed. 1966). A substantial history of the United States in the 20th century: first-rate. *o.p.*

CHAPTER 23

Politics

CONNIE L. LOBUR

As a form of human activity, politics consists of the theories and practices that define the collective goals of a society and determine the institutions of government that will be used to implement these goals. Whether or not one chooses to participate in politics actively, it is virtually impossible for modern industrialized societies to escape the effects of political decisions or the opinions and passions generated by political acts or ideologies. The variety of politics ranges from the negotiations of international treaties to the selection of street corners where traffic signs will be posted. Moreover, the guile and calculation so often associated with the politically powerful have been the source of almost limitless interest for laypeople, political savants, and literati alike.

Typically, the study of politics is divided into field areas. Each subfield consists of concentrated scholarship aimed at particular kinds of political inquiry and at the relevant institutions of government that have been constituted for the purpose of policy development and the resolution of social ills.

The most fundamental questions are philosophical and are the essence of political discourse. Classical political theorists like Plato and Aristotle or their modern counterparts like Marx and Rawls have addressed certain elemental questions: What is justice? Who should rule? For what end should governments be constituted? Is it possible to reconcile the desires of the few with the needs of the many? What is the proper relationship between politics and religion? These and other questions of politics are considered in the selected readings in the first section of the book list.

The development of and reliance on the written law as opposed to more traditional discretionary modes of resolving social
conflict are among the most significant critical achievements
characteristic of modern civilized societies. For those who are
interested in the forms of law, that is, constitutions and statutes,
as well as the more pragmatic aspects of the law such as enforce-
ment, the selection of judges, the judicial process, and the role
of law in the large environment, the selections under the heading
"The Legal Order" should provide valuable information and
insights.

If the reader wishes to grasp the processes and functions of the
institutions of government and extragovernment political forces,
the section entitled "Practical Politics and Government" sets
forth suggested reading. The books listed in this section are
representative of the scholarship being done in contemporary
political science.

The final section, "International Relations," includes books
that offer comparative studies of governments and ideologies as
well as more specific examinations of the foreign policies of
individual nations. The selections cited emphasize the global
ramifications of national policy decisions.

Theory

ARENDT, HANNAH 1906–1975. **On Revolution** (1963). A
provocative study of the modern concept of revolution, focusing on the diverse models of contemporary revolution, especially the American and French revolutions of the 18th century.
P—Penguin.

ARISTOTLE 384–322 B.C. **Politics** (1958). Ed. Ernest Barker.
Aristotle's view of politics emphasizes moderation and focuses
on the concept of distributive justice. It is a direct response to
the more elitist view of politics developed by Plato. *Over 6
eds*.

HARTZ, LOUIS. **The Liberal Tradition in America** (1955).
An exhaustive study of the liberal underpinnings of contemporary American political thought and attitudes. *P—HarBraceJ*.

HOBBES. **Leviathan.** See "Philosophy," page 279.

JACOBSON, NORMAN. **Pride and Solace: The Functions
and Limits of Political Theory** (1978). A comparative study
of Hobbes, Rousseau, and Machiavelli that sets the stage for

critical analysis of contemporary thinkers such as Nietzsche, Camus, and Arendt. *H—U of Cal Pr*.

LICHTHEIM, GEORGE 1912–1973. **Marxism: An Historical and Critical Study** (1965). A clearly written and well-researched study of Marxist thought and the criticisms directed against Marxism. *P—Columbia U Pr*.

LUKACS, GEORG 1885–1971. **Marxism and Human Liberation** (1973). A collection of the author's essays, suggesting the variety of his philosophical, esthetic, and political thought. Especially pertinent for the reader interested in the relationship between the arts and politics. *o.p.*

MACHIAVELLI. See "The Renaissance and Reformation," page 34.

MARX. **Economic and Philosophical Manuscripts.** See "Philosophy," page 281.

OKIN, SUSAN MOLLER b. 1946. **Women in Western Political Thought** (1979). An excellent survey of Western political theory pointing up the omission of women in theoretical discourse or, alternatively, the negative attitudes toward women embodied in the work of most political theorists. *H & P—Princeton U Pr*.

PLATO. **The Republic.** See "Greece," page 7.

RAWLS, JOHN b. 1921. **A Theory of Justice** (1971). A modern version of the utilitarian vision of Mill and Bentham, with an emphasis on the state's provision of a minimum standard of welfare. *H & P—Harvard U Pr*.

ROUSSEAU. **The Social Contract.** See "The 18th Century," page 56.

SCHAAR, JOHN b. 1928. **Legitimacy in the Modern State** (1981). A collection of essays that have quality and the ailing condition of the American democracy as their themes. *o.p.*

WOLIN, SHELDON. **Politics and Vision: Continuity and Innovation in Western Political Thought** (1960). A rich and provocative study of Western political theory that highlights the shift in focus from the community to the alienated individual. *H—Little*.

WOODCOCK, GEORGE b. 1912. **Anarchism: A History of Libertarian Ideas and Movements** (1962). An often fascinating presentation of the main intellectual and sentimental arguments, and sometimes of the lives and fortunes, of advocates of anarchism, which denies the legitimacy of any government. The study of anarchism makes a good beginning for the consideration of the basic question in politics: Why do we have government? *o.p.*

The Legal Order

ABRAHAM, HENRY J. b. 1921. **The Judiciary: The Supreme Court in the Government Processes** (6th ed. 1983). An exceptionally clear analysis of the place occupied by the federal judiciary and especially the Supreme Court within the processes of government. *P—Allyn*.

American Court Systems: Readings in Judicial Process and Behavior (1978). Eds. Sheldon Goldman and Austin Sarat. A useful collection of essays covering the spectrum of judicial process and behavioral analyses. *H & P—WH Freeman*.

BERMAN, HAROLD J. b. 1918 and WILLIAM R. GREINER. **The Nature and Functions of Law** (1980). A valuable introductory text for the student who wishes to learn about the origins of Anglo-American civil and criminal law. *o.p.*

GUNTHER, GERALD b. 1927. **Constitutional Law** (11th ed. 1985). A sophisticated survey which provides historical and political analyses as an accompaniment to case law materials. *H—Foundation Pr*.

KANOWITZ, LEO. **Women and the Law** (1967). An early and still illuminating text, discussing sex discrimination and tracing the development of antidiscrimination law in the United States as it affects women. *o.p.*

PRITCHETT, C. HERMAN b. 1907. **Constitutional Civil Liberties** (1984). A comprehensive and intelligent examination of the development of civil liberties through judicial decision making. *P—P-H*.

SMITH, DAVID G. b. 1926. **The Convention and the Constitution: The Political Ideas of the Founding Fathers** (1965). A compact analysis of the political ideologies affecting the shape of the American Constitution. *o.p.*

SPAETH, HAROLD J. b. 1930. Supreme Court Policy-Making: Explanation and Prediction (1979). A concise account of the political role of the allegedly "nonpolitical" branch of government. *P—WH Freeman*.

Practical Politics and Government in General

BURNHAM, WALTER DEAN b. 1930. **The Current Crisis in American Politics** (1982). A collection of the author's essays that examine the breakdown of the two-party system, the decline in voter participation, and the changing role of government in the American political culture. *P—Oxford U Pr*.

DOLBEARE, KENNETH M. b. 1930 and MURRAY J. EDELMAN b. 1919. **American Politics: Policies, Power and Change** (4th ed. 1981). One of the best introductions to American politics. Stimulating and challenging discussions about the form and function of American politics. *P—Heath*.

GREEN, PHILIP b. 1932. **The Pursuit of Inequality** (1981). An interesting look at the influence of science and social science on the kinds of political and legal opportunities and protections available to the less powerful segments of American society. *H & P—Pantheon*.

HAMILTON, ALEXANDER 1757–1804, JOHN JAY 1745–1829, and JAMES MADISON 1751–1836. **The Federalist Papers** (1787–88). A must for any student of American politics! For a firm hold on the foundations of American political thinking, *The Federalist Papers* provide the necessary starting point. *Over 4 eds*.

LOWI, THEODORE J. b. 1931. **The End of Liberalism: The Second Republic of the United States** (1969). A modern classic in the area of scholarship that addresses the incapacity of large government to govern. Lowi's recommendation for a solution to this dilemma is the creation of a juridical democracy, fashioned after the codified systems of Europe. *P—Norton*.

McCONNELL, GRANT b. 1915. **Private Power and American Democracy** (1967). A clearly written discussion of the predominance of private, elite interests in the formation of public policy. *P—Random*.

MILIBAND, RALPH. **The State in Capitalist Society** (1978). A historical survey of the parallel development of the centralized nation-state and the rise of capitalist economies in Western society. *P—Basic*.

POLSBY, NELSON b. 1934 and AARON WILDAVSKY b. 1930. **Presidential Elections** (6th ed. 1984). A clear and systematic survey of the process of being elected to the presidency and the formal and informal institutions that play a part in the process. *H—Scribner*.

SORAUF, FRANK b. 1928. **Political Parties in the American System** (1983). A thorough historical study of the political parties in America in conjunction with a provocative theoretical analysis of the parties as dependent and independent variables in the political environment. *o.p.*

TRUMAN, DAVID b. 1913. **The Governmental Process** (1951).

A seminal work in the field of American political processes. *H—Greenwood*.

International Relations

BARNET and MÜLLER. **Global Reach.** See "Economics," page 282.

CHOMSKY, NOAM b. 1928. **Towards a New Cold War** (1982). A collection of essays tracing the evolution of American foreign policy up to the current period. The essays are intellectually stimulating and are incisively critical. *H & P—Pantheon*.

FALK, RICHARD b. 1930. **The Endangered Planet** (1972). A clearly written argument that asserts global conditions such as terrorism, population growth, and exhaustion of natural resources necessitate the development of global politics and government. *o.p.*

HALBERSTAM, DAVID b. 1934. **The Best and the Brightest** (1972). An excellent introduction to America's involvement in Vietnam and the pitfalls of American foreign policy that were revealed by our participation in that war.   *H—Random; P—Fawcett, Penguin*.

LINDBLOM, CHARLES E. b. 1917. **Politics and Markets: The World's Political-Economic Systems** (1977). Lindblom's is a comparative analysis of capitalist and socialist market systems as a means of evaluating market mechanisms and authority structures. His conclusions are both significant and stimulating. *H & P—Basic*.

MERKL, PETER H. b. 1932. **Comparative Politics** (1967). An advanced text that emphasizes political culture, socialization, groups, parties, and institutional structures as factors of comparison in developing nations. *o.p.*

MORGANTHAU, HANS 1904–1980. **Politics among Nations** (5th ed. 1974). An important work in the area of international studies. Although much of the factual data is outdated, the book is a valuable contribution to the interpretation of global politics. *o.p.*

PUTNAM, ROBERT D. b. 1941. **Comparative Study of Political Elites** (1976). Putnam argues that elites rule governments and presents evidence of his theory as well as examines the consequences of elitism. *P—P-H*.

SCHELL, ORVILLE b. 1940. **In the People's Republic** (1977). A probing study of life in Chinese society, written by an American with extensive knowledge of Chinese culture and politics. *P—Random.*

SCHUMPETER. **Capitalism, Socialism and Democracy.** See "Economics," page 321.

CHAPTER 24

Economics

THOMAS PRAPAS

Economics is what economists do, Jacob Viner remarked a number of years ago. Just what they do, however, is no longer certain. Economics is an industry, the noted economist Cairncross recently observed, and went on to downgrade the product, question the wisdom of the producers, and lament the shortcomings of the means of production.

Not very long ago, economists stepped out of their academies to offer their services to a variety of patrons. From their think tanks, research institutes, and consulting firms, they were ready to make predictions about the growth of the gross national product, the level of interest rates, movements in exchange rates, changes in technology, and, if prodded, forecasts about the future of the human race. They moved into corporate and government offices to control the quantity of money, balance the federal budget, formulate corporate strategies, and organize the workplace. Their efforts earned them money, political influence, and social standing. Yet, today, some speak wistfully of the passing of the golden age of economics, while others still await its coming.

The difficulties are created by the very success that economists have enjoyed. As long as they explored the micro world of markets and prices, glamor and prestige eluded them. But post-World War II memories of the Great Depression provided an opportunity that Keynesian insights allowed them to exploit. Working with the premise that government can, and should, manage the level of spending to stabilize the economy, they devised policies that worked so well in early 1960s that there was talk of fine-tuning the economy so as to put an end to business cycles.

But their euphoria was short-lived. They were no longer in an ivory, or even a gold, tower, from which they could escape the harsh new realities of inflation and high unemployment, currency crises, and oil shortages. Their triumph proved fragile and temporary. Keynesian fought Keynesian, but the real attack came from conservatives who had not given up the faith. They had patiently amassed evidence and arguments with which to attack the "New Economics" when the moment was opportune. First monetarist, then supply-sider, challenged the liberal vision and confidently offered alternative visions, without government as the savior. But this was no mere struggle over the superiority of technical models. At stake was the very soul of the socioeconomic order. Issues as old as the study of economics lay beneath the surface: politics versus markets, individual versus collective choice, the pursuit of self-interest versus the conscious search for social purpose, efficiency versus equity.

Today the headlines belong to deficits, interest rates, the dollar, and defense spending, and the public is understandably distressed by the cacophony of voices with which economists speak. But there is less public awareness, and even less understanding, of the conflicts that represent deep divisions over social ends and fundamental human values: Is capitalism an irrational socioeconomic system that wastes human and other resources? Are democratic values being eroded by corporate power and growing concentration of wealth? Is freedom being threatened by the expanding economic role of the state? Are materialistic, hedonistic values consistent with the survival of the human race? Does the best hope for alleviating poverty and ameliorating sexual and racial discrimination lie with governments or markets?

This debate is taking place everywhere. Leaders in both China and the United States are challenging accepted economic wisdom and trying to revitalize the marketplace. A socialist government in France backs away from economic planning, while a conservative government in England attacks the welfare state. An economically distressed Soviet Union finds it almost impossible to dislodge the vested economic interests of a massive government bureaucracy in order to achieve desperately needed reforms. In many Western countries, leaders wonder how the Japanese do it, and turn their attention to the formulation of industrial policies to meet growing foreign competition.

The world is linked economically as never before, and the

strains are apparent. The energy crisis has temporarily passed, and the limits to growth are no longer urgently debated. The major concern now is the sluggish growth that characterizes much of the world's economy, leading the Third World to growing misery and debt and the advanced industrial nations to protectionist policies that heighten tensions and the prospects of an international economic disaster. Meanwhile, floating exchange rates favored by so many economists have not brought about stability, in part because the movement of funds around the world has reached levels never before imagined. The multinational corporation complicates the situation further. Some economists refer to the corporate force as the new imperialism; others view it as the most potent force for international economic growth yet devised. The noise becomes shriller when economists debate the responsibility of the West for the poverty and increasing debt of the Third World.

In the face of these growing complexities and uncertainties, what are economists doing? They are honing new tools, especially sophisticated mathematical models and elaborate statistical analyses that are made possible by the ability of computers to handle mountains of information. The results are not earthshaking, but the practitioners are convinced that their slow, carefully designed advances are moving economics to the status of "science." Certainly economics can now quantify what it could previously only describe with words. Many persons, including prominent economists, fail to be impressed. The models are too abstract, they protest, and trivial conclusions are drawn from narrow and implausible premises. Still the future is probably with the mathematicians, whose work is often inaccessible to other economists, let alone to the public at large.

But even these mathematicians, who so loudly proclaim their scientific objectivity, find it necessary to defend the values and techniques that separate them from their fellow economists. This debate over basic political, economic, and scientific values is available to the general reader, and provides essential knowledge for those who wish to understand what it is that economists do. There are many voices: old and new, calm and strident, detached and humane. All of them stimulate thought about matters as diverse as the shortcomings of economics as a practical science or the ability of the discipline to make intelligible the nature of economic reality and human purpose.

BARAN, PAUL 1910–1964 and PAUL M. SWEEZY b. 1910. **Monopoly Capital** (1966). A Marxist view of modern capitalism, stimulating and very readable. Political and corporate leaders are seen as contributing to an "irrational" system that wastes human and other resources. *P—Monthly Rev.*

BARNET, RICHARD J. b. 1929 and RONALD E. MÜLLER b. 1939. **Global Reach** (1975). More scholarly works on the multinational corporation are available, but few possess the clarity and vitality of this work: honest, documented, disturbing. *P—S&S.*

BAUER, P. T. b. 1915. **Equality, the Third World and Economic Delusion** (1982). In sharp contrast to Myrdal (see page 320), this conservative British economist argues that the search for egalitarianism in the Third World is delusion and that only a realistic agenda for economic change can avoid disaster. *P—Harvard U Pr.*

BERLE, ADOLF A. 1895–1971 and GARDINER C. MEANS b. 1896. **The Modern Corporation and Private Property** (1933). A pioneering work documenting the growing concentration of industrial wealth and the increasing separation of ownership from control in large corporations. *H—W S Hein.*

BOWLES, SAMUEL, DAVID M. GORDON b. 1944, and THOMAS E. WEISSKOPF. **Beyond the Waste Land: A Democratic Alternative to Economic Decline** (1983). A lucid and succinct defense of the proposition that neo-Marxist thought is better able to explain the crisis of American capitalism than conventional economic theory. *H & P—Doubleday.*

BROWN, LESTER R. b. 1934. **Building a Sustainable Society** (1981). A hardheaded, reformist account of the energy, environmental, and food crises confronting a rapidly expanding humankind. *H & P—Norton.*

CHANDLER, ALFRED D. JR. b. 1918. **The Visible Hand: The Managerial Revolution in American Business** (1977). An informed and fascinating study of the sources of change in the structure of American industry: explains why some industries are dominated by giant firms while others are not. *H & P—Harvard U Pr.*

ECKSTEIN, ALEXANDER 1915–1976. **China's Economic Revolution** (1977). Although written before the major changes in the Chinese economy, this work presents a wealth of information and probing analyses about the history and structure of this intriguing economy. *H & P—Cambridge U Pr.*

Economic Report of the President (Annual, issued each January). The writing is not scintillating, but the information contained within is worth the effort required to penetrate it. In addition to current data on the state of the nation's economy, the report outlines the basic assumptions and economic philosophy of the current administration. *H & P—US Government Printing Office*.

EICHNER, ALFRED S. b. 1937. **A Guide to Post-Keynesian Economics** (1978). Written for the beginner, this series of articles provides a comprehensive, and generally comprehensible, outline of the post-Keynesian argument that traditional theory pays insufficient attention to decision making under conditions of uncertainty. *H & P—Pantheon, M E Sharpe*.

FEDERAL RESERVE BANK OF ATLANTA. **Supply-Side Economics in the 1980's** (1982). A lively exchange between supporters and opponents of supply-side economics. *H—Greenwood*.

FRIEDMAN, MILTON b. 1912 and ROSE FRIEDMAN. **Free to Choose** (1980). In an elegant tribute to the efficiency and fairness of the market, the Nobel laureate and his wife argue that individual freedom and democracy can only survive under capitalism. *H—HarBraceJ; P—Avon*.

GALBRAITH, JOHN KENNETH b. 1908. **Economics and the Public Purpose** (1973). A graceful and witty attack on mainstream economics. The author condemns the failure of economists to consider power and planning in modern corporations and challenges them with a call for a new socialism. *H—HM; P—NAL*.

GOLDMAN, MARSHALL I. b. 1930. **USSR in Crisis** (1983). A short, informative survey of the origins, failings, and need for reform of the Soviet economic system and of the role played by the Stalinist model of economic development. *P—Norton*.

HAYEK, FRIEDRICH A. b. 1899. **The Road to Serfdom** (1944). A vigorous attack on national economic planning. Argues that collectivism leads to totalitarianism, and that only individualism and the market are compatible with freedom. *H & P—U of Chicago Pr*.

HEILBRONER, ROBERT L. b. 1919. **The Making of Economic Society** (7th ed. 1985). An economic history written with style and substance. Technology, society, the state, and ideology are expertly woven into this tale of the shaping of modern capitalism. *P—P-H*.

————. **The Worldly Philosophers** (5th ed. 1980). Lively,

highly readable accounts of the great economic thinkers and their doctrines. *P—S&S*.

——— and LESTER THUROW b. 1938. **Five Economic Challenges** (1981). Literate and engaging analyses of problems of inflation, recession, government budgets, the dollar, and energy—and thought-provoking solutions. *H—P-H*.

HELLER, WALTER W. b. 1915. **The Economy: Old Myths and New Realities** (1976). A highly readable account of the follies of economists. But Heller argues that, despite some embarrassing errors—resulting from a rapidly changing and increasingly complex reality—economics and economists do a great many things "right." *o.p.*

HERMAN, EDWARD S. **Corporate Control, Corporate Power** (1982). Of great value to the general reader who wishes to better understand the role of the corporation in American life. The managerial revolution is subjected to a thorough, often controversial treatment. *H & P—Cambridge U Pr*.

JOHNSON, CHALMERS b. 1931. **MITI and the Japanese Miracle** (1982). An important contribution to our understanding of the sources of strength of the Japanese economy. Examines how the competitive strategies of major Japanese corporations were complemented by appropriate government policies to achieve a performance that is the envy of all other nations. *H & P—Stanford U Pr*.

KEYNES, JOHN MAYNARD 1883–1946. **The General Theory of Employment, Interest, and Money** (1936). Hard to read, but simply cannot be ignored: a major turning point in the development of economic thought. Spurred by his concern for mass unemployment, Keynes launched an attack on classical theory that has produced more research and debate than the work of any other economist in the 20th century. *P—HarBraceJ*.

LEKACHMAN, ROBERT b. 1920. **Economists at Bay: Why the Experts Will Never Solve Your Problems** (1976). Entertaining, informative, and irreverent, a slashing indictment of the intellectual narrowness and disarray of the economics profession. *H & P—McGraw*.

LENIN, V. I. 1870–1924. **Imperialism: The Highest Stage of Capitalism** (1917). A classic examinaton of the stage of capitalism dominated by monopolies and finance capital and characterized by imperialism: polemical, provocative, and profoundly important. *P—Intl Pub Co*.

MAGAZINER, IRA C. and ROBERT REICH b. 1946. **Minding America's Business** (1982). Interesting case studies support the proposition that the United States needs an industrial policy to prevent further decline in its ability to compete with other nations. *P—HarBraceJ, Random.*

MALTHUS. **Essay on the Principles of Population.** See "The 18th Century," page 55.

MANDEL, ERNEST b. 1923. **The Formation of the Economic Thought of Karl Marx** (1971). A very useful introduction by a leading French Marxist to the early economic thought of Karl Marx. *P—Monthly Rev.*

MARSHALL, ALFRED 1842–1924. **Principles of Economics** (1890). Familiar economic concepts made accessible by the author's interest in everyday economic problems and by his insistence that the values underlying economic analysis be made explicit. *P—Porcupine Pr.*

MARX, KARL 1818–1883. **Capital,** Vol. 1 (1867). The most important critique of capitalist society ever written—but enormously difficult. Marx's categories, grounded in classical political economy and German philosophy, often prove elusive for the general reader. A reading of the work by Mandel may be a more realistic way to approach Marx. *H—Biblio Dist, Intl Pub Co.; P—Random.*

MILL, JOHN STUART 1806–1873. **Principles of Political Economy** (1848). Those who make the effort to penetrate this occasionally difficult book will be treated to enlightened talk of "higher" human purposes that are often ill-served by mere production and accumulation of wealth, and to surprising defenses of socialism and communism. *H—Kelley.*

MYRDAL, GUNNAR b. 1898. **Against the Stream: Critical Essays in Economics** (1972). A useful introduction to the writing of a humane man of letters, a Nobel laureate in economics, and a gifted social scientist. His profound commitment to egalitarianism and to the struggle against world poverty is amply demonstrated in these pages. *o.p.*

NOVAK, MICHAEL b. 1933. **The Spirit of Democratic Capitalism** (1982). A formidable defense of democratic capitalism that stands in sharp contrast to the position of Bowles et al. The moral and spiritual powers of capitalism are emphasized, not merely economic superiority. *H—S&S.*

OKUN, ARTHUR M. 1928–1980. **Equality and Efficiency: The Big Tradeoff** (1975). A succinct and lively defense of the position that a society's commitment to democratic values sometimes requires opting for an equality that compromises the efficiency of the market. *H & P—Brookings.*

O'TOOLE, JAMES et al. **Work in America** (1973). Produced for the Department of Health, Education, and Welfare by a special task force, this readable work provides useful information about unemployment and the deteriorating work environment in America. *P—MIT Pr*.

RAYBACK, JOSEPH G. b. 1914. **A History of American Labor** (1966). A short, well-written history of labor in the United States. Traces the development of the labor movement, its relationship to government, and its impact on the economy. *P—Free Pr*.

ROBINSON, JOAN 1903–1983. **Economic Philosophy** (1962). Taking as her point of departure the argument that an economic system cannot be described without moral judgments creeping in, this noted Cambridge economist exposes the "values" implicit in the "scientific writing" of classical, neoclassical, and Keynesian economists. *o.p*.

ROLFE, SIDNEY E. 1921–1976 and JAMES L. BURTLE b. 1919. **The Great Wheel: The World Monetary System** (1973). Invaluable to the general reader who is trying to understand the present instabilities of the international monetary system and how they came about. The authors put their faith in floating exchange rates, but allow the skeptical reader to examine alternative schemes for organizing the world's money. *P—MacGraw*.

ROTHSCHILD, EMMA. **Paradise Lost: The Decline of the Auto-Industrial Age** (1974). In a literate, forceful style, the author attacks the industry's failures and the excuses advanced by industry spokesmen for the apparent demise of the U.S. automobile industry in the 1970s. *o.p*.

SAMUELSON, PAUL A. b. 1915. **Economics: An Introductory Analysis** (12th ed. 1985). The leading elementary textbook since its first edition in 1948. *H—McGraw*.

SCHUMACHER, E. F. 1911–1977. **Small Is Beautiful: Economics As If People Mattered** (1973). An appealing call for economics on a small scale so as to allow for communal living and the full development of human potential. *H & P—Har-Row*.

SCHUMPETER, JOSEPH 1883–1950. **Capitalism, Socialism and Democracy** (3rd ed. 1950). An intriguing thesis: that the very success of capitalism creates changes that undermine the effectiveness of a key figure, the entrepreneur. The author fears the end of capitalism and the rise of an unwelcome socialism. *H—Peter Smith; P—Har-Row*.

SILK, LEONARD b. 1918. **The Economists** (1976). A thoroughly entertaining, superbly written introduction to the ideas of five contemporary economists. The diversity of viewpoints provides a powerful statement of a profession in conflict. *P—Avon.*

SMITH. **The Wealth of Nations.** See "The 18th Century," page 56.

SOWELL, THOMAS b. 1930. **Race and Economics** (1975). An unconventional and controversial perspective on the economic experience of blacks in the United States: Not discrimination but low social productivity has retarded the economic progress of blacks in the United States. *P—Longman.*

TABB, WILLIAM K. **The Political Economy of the Black Ghetto** (1971). Contrasts sharply with Sowell's analysis: Racism pervades every institution in America; the poverty of blacks derives from the colonial relationship between the ghetto and the larger society. *H & P—Norton.*

TAWNEY, RICHARD H. 1880–1962. **The Acquisitive Society** (1920). A classic work that challenges the assumption that the right to property is absolute. Defends, instead, the radical proposal that property should be given proprietary rights only when it discharges public functions. *P—HarBraceJ.*

THUROW, LESTER b. 1938. **Dangerous Currents: The State of Economics** (1983). A refreshing, well-written analysis of some key themes in contemporary economics. Makes imaginative suggestions to move economics and economists out of their present morass. *H & P—Random.*

VEBLEN, THORSTEIN 1859–1929. **The Theory of the Leisure Class** (1899). A radical, satiric, and penetrating critique of mainstream economics and of American consumers who define their lives not by what they invent and produce but by the quantity and quality of their consumption. *H—Kelley; P—NAL, Penguin.*

WEISSKOPF, WALTER b. 1904. **Alienation and Economics** (1971). An incisive critique of contemporary economic thought, the analysis focuses on the values neglected by economists and by industrial society: nonmaterial, intellectual, and spiritual. *o.p.*

Women and the American Economy (1976). Ed. Juanita Kreps. A leading authority on the economic status of women leads a diverse group of experts over a wide range of current issues. Stimulating and controversial. *o.p.*

CHAPTER 25

Anthropology

ELIZABETH WEATHERFORD

Anthropology is the comparative study of human beings and their societies. Although we are one biologically unique species, we exhibit a dramatic diversity of physical and behavioral characteristics. The study of humankind, therefore, demands a whole interrelated collection of specialized sciences, some historical, some documentary, some biological, and some sociological.

Anthropology consists of four specializations. *Archeology* tries to reconstruct the history of ancient societies by examining their material remains. *Linguistics* studies the growth and structure of one of humanity's most distinctive behaviors—language. *Physical anthropology* examines human evolution and studies the question of what behaviors are innate. *Cultural anthropology* focuses on the organization of all human societies and on the beliefs and practices of those who comprise them.

Cultural anthropology is of the most interest to the general reader because through the study of unfamiliar cultures one often comes to a better understanding of one's own. It teaches that what may seem unusual practices or beliefs are in fact alternative ways by which different peoples have tried to answer universal questions and solve real problems: how to ensure good harvests, to relate to unseen forces, to cure illness, to establish relationships with neighboring peoples, and the like.

Anthropological studies of many different societies have contributed countless examples for analysis and comparison, enabling the development of theories about how and why a society takes its form. Anthropology observes that such apparently diverse practices within a culture as its mythology, the organization of the family, and its pattern of government are profoundly interrelated, reflecting common patterns of structure. Some anthropologists have looked for these structures in human thought and symbolic systems. Others have focused on the correlation between the structure of social organization and the types of environments used by societies for their survival.

Typically, an anthropologist's research is conducted through participation in and observation of a particular culture's activities, ideas, and social relations over a one- to two-year period. The anthropologist often returns to that society to continue analyzing and recording life patterns. From this fieldwork the participant-observer writes an ethnography, that is, a detailed description of the culture, its characteristics, folkways, beliefs, and the like. Some anthropologists work in the field with a research group or with a documentary filmmaker.

Most early studies were of small-contained societies—bands, tribes, and chiefdoms—often unknown to nonspecialists. Many of these groups lacked writing and had simple, efficient technologies. These traditional cultures often became of interest as European and American culture expanded into their domains and drastically altered their world.

In recent years anthropologists have examined larger and more complex societies as well, partly because of their interest in how traditional cultures are affected by contact with new technology and other aspects of the industrialized world. The fate of tribal peoples whose domains have come under the jurisdiction of national governments, the changes wrought by the movement of peasant farmers to cities, and the possibilities for healing people by employing the best of both traditional knowledge and modern medicine are a few of the topics currently being studied. Other issues of contemporary interest include the examination of aggression as innate or learned behavior and the cross-cultural analysis of men's and women's roles and power.

Anthropology has two related concerns. One part of the discipline records descriptions of hundreds of traditional societies and subcultures within more complex societies. The other uses these data to generalize about the very nature of being human. Both scientific and humanistic, anthroplogy offers the reader a rich opportunity to learn about the breadth of human history.

Afro-American Anthropology (1970). Eds. Norman E. Whitten, Jr., and John F. Szwed. Twenty-two articles concerned with New World African cultures, including analyses of music and socioeconomic adaptations. *H—Free Pr*.

Anthropology and Art (1971). Ed. Charlotte M. Otten. Readings in cross-cultural esthetics and the relationship between art and culture. Part of the extensive Texas Press Sourcebooks in Anthropology series. *P—U of Tex Pr*.

BATESON, MARY CATHERINE. **With a Daughter's Eye** (1984). A memoir by the daughter of two great American anthropologists, Gregory Bateson and Margaret Mead. *H—Morrow*.

BOAS, FRANZ 1858–1942. **Race, Language and Culture** (1940). Essays by the pioneer American anthropologist arguing for a clearer understanding of the role of culture in shaping behavior. *P—U of Chicago Pr*.

BODLEY, JOHN H. **Victims of Progress** (2nd ed. 1982). Examines the fundamental differences between small-scale and industrial societies and the cultural and ecological results of contacts between them. *P—Mayfield Pub*.

BOWEN, ELENORE SMITH (LAURA BOHANNAN). **Return to Laughter** (1964). The difficulties of fieldwork are evoked in a humorous novel based on the author's experiences studying the Tiv of Nigeria. *P—Doubleday. Natural Hist*.

BRACE, C. LORING b. 1930 and ASHLEY MONTAGU b. 1905. **Man's Evolution** (1965). Clear presentation of the human fossil record and human evolution in the light of contemporary theory. *o.p*.

A Crack in the Mirror (1981). Ed. Jay Ruby. Twelve fine essays concerned with self-awareness and the process of observation and documentation in anthropology. *H—U of Pa Pr*.

DEETZ, JAMES b. 1930. **Invitation to Archeology** (1967). Brief introduction to the principles, methods, and problems of the present-day archeologist. *P—Nataural Hist*.

DIAMOND, STANLEY b. 1922. **In Search of the Primitive** (1972). Thoughtful essays critical of the ethos of Western culture, stressing the complexity of contact between anthropology and the traditional peoples being studied. *P—Transaction Bks*.

EAMES, EDWIN b. 1930 and JUDITH GRANICH GOODE. **Anthropology of the City** (1977). Introduces urban anthropology by examining current research and ideas of what anthropology may add to the study of cities. *P—H-H*.

Ethnic and Tourist Arts (1977). Ed. Nelson H. H. Graburn. Twenty essays concerned with continuing traditions and new forms in the arts of small-scale societies in all regions of the world. *H & P—U of Cal Pr*.

EVANS-PRITCHARD, EDWARD E. 1902–1983. **Witchcraft, Oracles, and Magic among the Azande** (1937). An absorbing study dealing with the philosophical and scientific beliefs of the Zande of Central Africa by a noted British anthropologist. *o.p.*

FAGAN, BRIAN M. b. 1936. **Clash of Cultures** (1984). A chronicle of contacts made by Europeans with traditional societies between the 15th and late 19th centuries. *H & P—WH Freeman*.

FARB, PETER. **Word Play: What Happens When People Talk.** See "Language and Communications," page 249.

———— and GEORGE ARMELAGOS. **Consuming Passions: The Anthropology of Eating** (1980). The fascinating connection between eating habits and human behavior explored with numerous examples. *H—HM; P—WSP*.

FRIEDLANDER, JUDITH b. 1944. **Being Indian in Hueyapan** (1975). Well-written account of an Indian village in central Mexico stressing the discrepancy between the actual life of the villagers and the national image of that life. *P—St Martin*.

Frontiers of Anthropology (1974). Ed. Ashley Montagu. Absorbing documentary history of anthropology based on writings of firsthand observers such as Christopher Columbus, Charles Darwin, and 20th-century anthropologists. *o.p.*

GERTZ, CLIFFORD b. 1926. **The Interpretation of Cultures** (1973). Analyzes society as a system of symbols shared by its individual members, drawing examples from fieldwork in Indonesia, especially Java and Bali. *P—Basic*.

GRIAULE, MARCEL 1898–1956. **Conversations with Ogotemmeli** (1975). Offers a unique firsthand account of the myth, religion, and philosophy of the Dogon of Mali as recounted by an elderly wise man. *P—Oxford U Pr*.

HALL, EDWARD T. b. 1914. **The Hidden Dimension** (1966). Examines the implications of the cross-cultural differences in the use of personal and business space. *P—Doubleday*.

Hallucinogens and Shamanism (1973). Ed. Michael Harner. Essays on the shamanistic practices of many cultures. *H & P—Oxford U Pr*.

HARRIS, MARVIN b. 1927. **The Rise of Anthropological Theory** (1968). A major history and critical analysis of anthropological theories of culture. *H—Har-Row*.

————. **Cows, Pigs, Wars, and Witches** (1974). Unusual human practices explained in lively essays centering on the material aspects of survival. *P—Random*.

HEIDER, KARL b. 1935. **Ethnographic Film** (1976). A history of ethnographic film, examining the development of methodology from the work of Robert Flaherty to the present. *P—U of Tex Pr*.

LANGNESS, L. L. b. 1929. and GELYA F. FRANK. **Lives: An Anthropological Approach to Biography** (1981). A bibliography and overview of the ways individual life-histories are recorded and used in anthropology. *P—Chandler & Sharp*.

Learning Non-Aggression (1978). Ed. Ashley Montagu. Eight essays about traditional societies, contradicting the popular theory of innate human aggression. *H & P—Oxford U Pr*.

LEE, RICHARD B. b. 1937. **The Kung San: Men, Women and Work in a Foraging Society** (1979). Excellent ethnographic account of traditional Kung life in the Kalahari Desert by a leader of the Harvard/Kung Bushman Study Project. *H & P—Cambridge U Pr*.

LÉVI-STRAUSS, CLAUDE b. 1908. **Tristes Tropiques** (1955). An astute account by a distinguished French anthropologist of his fieldwork experiences in Brazil and of the development of his structuralist thought. *H—Adlers Foreign Bks; P—Atheneum, WSP*.

LEWIS, I. M. b. 1930. **Ecstatic Religions** (1971). A study of cults of possession and ecstasy in Africa, the Arctic, Asia, and South America and their relationship to social marginality. *o.p*.

MALINOWSKI, BRONISLAW 1884–1942. **Argonauts of the Western Pacific** (1961). Classic monograph on the Trobriand Islanders, discussing among other things their system of ritualized exchange. By one of the founders of field observations. *P—Waveland Pr*.

MAUSS, MARCEL 1872–1950. **The Gift** (1925). The first systematic study of how the exchange of goods and gifts is a transaction basic to all social relationships and at the heart of traditional societies. *P—Norton*.

MEAD, MARGARET 1901–1978. **Sex and Temperament in Three Primitive Societies** (1935). An essay on the cultural definition of sex roles, drawing examples from a survey of three societies in New Guinea. *H—Peter Smith; P—Morrow*.

MEYERHOFF, BARBARA G. **Peyote Hunt: The Sacred Journey of the Huichol Indians** (1974). Based on participant observation and interviews with a Huichol spiritual leader, this work expertly presents a complex symbolic system. One of a series of works on symbol, myth, and ritual. *P—Cornell U Pr.*

MONTAGU, ASHLEY b. 1905. **Man's Most Dangerous Myth: The Fallacy of Race** (1974). A significant essay that clarifies misunderstandings about biological race and traces the development of an oppressive racial concept in Western society. *o.p.*

Mountain Wolf Woman (1961). Ed. Nancy O. Lurie. The autobiography of a Winnebago woman told and annotated by an anthropologist adopted as her kinswoman. *P—U of Mich Pr.*

The Pleasures of Anthropology (1983). Ed. Morris Freilich. Twenty-seven key essays on the many aspects of culture, from language to magic and from gender to war. *P—NAL.*

RABINOW, PAUL b. 1944. **Reflections on Fieldwork in Morocco** (1977). A report of the anthropologist's encounter with the culture of a Moroccan village and its effects upon him. *H & P—U of Cal Pr.*

RADIN. **The Trickster.** See "American Minority Cultures: Native American," page 112.

RAPPAPORT, ROY A. b. 1926. **Pigs for the Ancestors** (2nd ed. 1984). Theory and fieldwork method are discussed in this study of the function of religion in the human ecology of a New Guinea people. *H & P—Yale U Pr.*

Reinventing Anthropology (1973). Ed. Dell Hymes. Essays analyzing the impact of anthropological research on the people being studied and on the researchers. *P—Random.*

ROSMAN, ABRAHAM b. 1930 and PAULA G. RUBEL b. 1933. **The Tapestry of Culture** (2nd ed. 1985). A clear and concise introduction to the basic concepts of cultural anthropology. *P—Random.*

SAHLINS, MARSHALL b. 1930. **Stone Age Economics** (1972). Provocative essays that clarify the distinct nature of small-scale societies and their material life. *H & P—Aldine.*

Symbolic Anthropology (1977). Eds. Janet L. Dolgin, David S. Kemnitzer, and David M. Schneider. A fascinating selection of articles about symbols and meanings in many cultures as they reflect on art, myth, ideology, and ritual. *H & P—Columbia U Pr.*

Toward an Anthropology of Women (1975). Ed. Rayna Rapp Reiter. Essays examining women's roles in societies, the function of work in their lives and social status, and the situation of women's power in traditional cultures. *H & P—Monthly Rev.*

TURNBULL, COLIN b. 1924. **The Forest People** (1961). An intimate and engaging account of the Mbuti Pygmies of the Ituri Forest of northeastern Zaire. *P—S&S*.

VAN GENNEP, ARNOLD 1873–1957. **The Rites of Passage** (1909). The first work to note that in most cultures regular and significant rituals mark the transitional stages in life—birth, puberty, marriage, and death. *P—U of Chicago Pr*.

WOLF, ERIC b. 1923. **Europe and the People Without History** (1982). An exploration of the development of the modern world's social systems using historical and anthropological research. *H & P—U of Cal Pr*.

Women and Colonization: Anthropological Perspectives (1980). Eds. Mona Etienne and Eleanor Leacock. Fascinating case studies of women's economic and social roles in 12 societies and the changes that followed European colonization. *H & P—Bergin & Garvey, Praeger*.

WORTH, SOL 1922–1977 and JOHN ADAIR b. 1913. **Through Navajo Eyes** (1973). Engrossing investigation of cross-cultural communication, explored in a project in which Navajo Indians made their own films. *H & P—Ind U Pr*.

CHAPTER 26

Sociology

WILLIAM RAY ARNEY

Sociologists observe, describe, and explain organized human behavior. Their object of study is the social world that emerges from human interaction. All basic social institutions—religious, political, educational, familial, economic—are of interest to the sociologist. How do institutions arise? How are they related to one another? How do they influence individual behavior? How and why does the social world change? These are questions that organize sociological inquiry. Beyond these common interests, however, there are significant differences within the field.

Sociologists differ on even the simplest of issues, such as how one ought to observe human behavior. Some argue that face-to-face interaction—becoming a participant-observer in a group—is the only appropriate method for conducting sociological studies. Others are interested in macro-social behavior and try to develop factual accounts of the actions of large groups of people. Still others carry out their "observations" via questionnaires, telephone interviews, and other standard ways of collecting data on social behavior.

Schemes for description and explanation are equally diverse. The critical reader should be aware that theoretical differences in the discipline often indicate underlying political differences among proponents of various perspectives. For example, "functionalism," a dominant theoretical perspective in American sociology, tries to assess the ways in which various social institutions contribute to the smooth, orderly operation of society. A problem, from the perspective of this theory, is present if order is disrupted, if something is "dysfunctional." Functionalism rests

330

on a commitment to political stability. On the contrary, Marxism and the various conflict-oriented schools of thought that Marxism has spun off suggest that a fundamental restructuring of society is a necessary prerequisite to the solution of enduring social problems such as inequality, racism, and the oppression of women. Marxism thinks stability is a problem.

A recent president of the American Sociological Association has called on the profession to put its intellectual house in order so that sociologists may demonstrate what should not need demonstration—that sociology is a valuable discipline. Many other sociologists argue that the discipline demonstrates its values through its critical orientation toward existing social institutions.

There is considerable room in sociology for intradisciplinary dissent and debate concerning the ways in which social behavior is to be studied and the ends to which that study is to be directed. Edward Wilson's *Sociobiology* and other books that have followed in its wake have renewed debate about the biological bases of behavior. Feminist writers such as Daly, Ehrenreich, Firestone, de Beauvoir, and Friedan bring fresh perspectives to the discipline. European sociology, represented here by the works of Foucault, Habermas, Ariès and Lemert's reader, provides a counterbalance to the heavily quantitative approach of many American sociologists. Books such as those by Braverman, Bowles and Gintis, Piven and Cloward, and Freire question the entire conceptual framework from which we have tried to understand such common social institutions as education, public relief, and the division of labor in society. Becker and Chomsky challenge the assumptions and practices on which a century of sociology has rested.

Read sociology remembering that there is no agreement on disciplinary content or method. The profession is an intellectual battleground. Much of sociology is polemical, but an author usually wages war with an opponent whose identity you will learn only by reading diverse works in the field.

ALINSKY, SAUL D. 1909–1972. **Rules for Radicals** (1971). A proposal and practical primer for the radical organization of the middle classes. Projected outcome: a humanistic revolution. *P—Random*.

ARIÈS, PHILIPPE 1914–1984. **Centuries of Childhood: A Social History of Family Life** (1962). A sensitive study of the emergence of the notion of childhood. *P—Random*.

BEAUVOIR. **The Second Sex.** See "Women's Studies," page 352.

BECKER, ERNEST 1925–1974. **The Structure of Evil: An Essay on the Unification of the Sciences of Man** (1968). The analytical split between fact and value—so crucial to scientific endeavor—has permitted development of a social science of domination and control. A provocative and challenging thesis. *P—Free Pr.*

BERGER, PETER L. b. 1929 and THOMAS LUCKMANN b. 1927. **The Social Construction of Reality: A Treatise in the Sociology of Knowledge** (1966). Basic work outlining the way people construct their social world—institutions, authority, roles, etc.—and how that world is transmitted from generation to generation. *H—Irvington; P—Doubleday.*

BOWLES, SAMUEL and HERBERT GINTIS b. 1940. **Schooling in Capitalist America: Educational Reform and the Contradictions of Economic Life** (1976). Encyclopedic, scholarly analysis of extant data on the history, structure, and function of education in society. *P—Basic.*

BRAVERMAN, HARRY 1920–1976. **Labor and Monopoly Capital: The Degradation of Work in the Twentieth Century** (1975). An intelligent analysis of the transformation of work under modern monopoly capitalism. An insightful critique of the technological determinism of earlier literature on occupations. *H & P—Monthly Rev.*

CASTEL, FRANÇOISE and ROBERT CASTEL. **The Psychiatric Society** (1982). The first book to offer a thoughtful critique of the proliferation of therapies and the development of a "therapeutic state." *H—Columbia U Pr.*

CHOMSKY, NOAM b. 1928. **Reflections on Language** (1975). Thoughts on the nature of the human mind by a noted linguist. Challenges some of the basic assumptions of social science. *o.p.*

DALY, MARY b. 1928. **Gyn/Ecology: The Metaethics of Radical Feminism** (1978) The chart of the "rough journey" to the other side of patriarchy. Idiosyncratic, explosive, brilliant. *P—Beacon Pr.*

DURKHEIM, EMILE 1858–1917. **Suicide** (trans. 1951). The classic study of the correlates of suicide, still a model for a contemporary empirical research. *P—Free Pr.*

————. **The Elementary Forms of the Religious Life** (trans. 1961). A seminal contribution to the study of religion, the great symbolic stabilizer of society. *P—Free Pr.*

EHRENREICH, BARBARA b. 1941 and DEIRDRE ENGLISH b. 1948. **For Her Own Good: 150 Years of Experts' Advice**

to Women (1978). Raises the question of how a woman can achieve an identity of her own in the face of so much "good advice" on how to live a life. *P—Doubleday*.

ERIKSON, KAI T. b. 1931. **Everything in Its Path: Destruction of Community in the Buffalo Creek Flood** (1976). Erikson uses his sociological eyes and his human sensitivity to reveal the social ramifications of having one's community wiped out by a natural disaster. *P—S&S*.

FIRESTONE, SHULAMITH b. 1945. **The Dialectic of Sex: The Case for Feminist Revolution** (1970). A major statement of radical feminist theory. Firestone sees the biological relationship of women to men as the root of many social evils such as racism and gross economic inequality. Contains proposals for fundamental social reform. *o.p.*

FOUCAULT, MICHEL 1926–1984. **Discipline and Punish: The Birth of the Prison** (1979). A book, Foucault says, "that must serve as a historical background to various studies of the power of normalization and the formation of knowledge in modern society." The most important work on power since Marx's economic and philosophical manuscripts. *P—Random*.

————. **Herculine Barbin: Being the Recently Discovered Memoirs of a Nineteenth-Century French Hermaphrodite** (1980). The beautiful, poignant memoirs of a person born with both male and female genitalia. She was raised a woman, but later was administratively changed into a man when the birth certificate was "corrected." Herculine wrote the memoirs just before committing suicide. Foucault's introduction discusses the way one's "true sex" became a problem in the 19th century. *H & P—Pantheon*.

FREIRE, PAULO b. 1921. **Pedagogy of the Oppressed** (1971). An indictment of present pedagogical methods with recommendations for changes. The author has used his techniques to raise political consciousness among peasant laborers in South America. *P—Continuum*.

FRIEDAN, BETTY b. 1921. **The Feminine Mystique** (2nd ed. 1974). A 1963 bestseller that changed lives. A prime mover of feminism, Friedan drew attention to the post-World War II malaise of women: pushed by a consumer- and advertising-oriented society into the prescribed utopia of marriage/ motherhood/ suburban house-tending, guilt-ridden if they sought identity or expression except through husbands, children, and homes. *H—Norton; P—Dell*.

GEERTZ. **The Interpretation of Cultures.** See "Anthropology," page 291.

GOFFMAN, ERVING 1922–1982. **The Presentation of Self in Everyday Life** (1958). Everyday social behavior viewed as drama, with people as the actors and their social space as the state. *H—Overlook Pr; P—Doubleday.*

GOULDNER, ALVIN W. 1920–1980. **The Coming Crisis of Western Sociology** (1970). Contends that the functionalism of Parsons (see page 336) cannot deal with change and that Marxism can. A crisis will arise when sociologists must use a theoretical perspective that stands in opposition to the class interests of those who control the agencies that support academics. *P—Basic.*

HABERMAS, JÜRGEN b. 1929. **Toward a Rational Society: Student Protest, Science, and Politics** (trans. 1971). Theoretically integrated essays, expressing a radical view of diverse topics. *P—Beacon Pr.*

HARPER, DOUGLAS b. 1938. **Good Company** (1982). The beautiful—to eye and ear—firsthand account of life with hobos. *H & P—U of Chicago Pr.*

HARRINGTON, MICHAEL b. 1928. **The Other America** (1964). An early, important statement on poverty in America and a politically influential book. *P—Penguin.*

HOMANS, GEORGE C. b. 1910. **Social Behavior: Its Elementary Forms** (rev. ed. 1974). The structure and function of small groups. A basic treatment of social exchange. *o.p.*

ILLICH, IVAN b. 1926. **Gender** (1982). A controversial work that says we no longer live in a "gendered" world, a world in which men and women live in incommensurable realms. Illich argues that "male" and "female" are, in the modern era, just deviations from a universal, homogenizing variable called "sex." *H—Pantheon.*

INKELES, ALEX b. 1920. **What Is Sociology?** (1964). Straightforward exposition of the nature of the discipline and the profession. *P—P-H.*

JONES, JAMES H. b. 1943. **Bad Blood: The Tuskegee Syphilis Experiment** (1981). The well-told story of the 1932–72 "experiment" in which treatment for syphilis was withheld from 400 black men. Jones does not offer a simple explanation for this event in American science; he just lets the disquieting implications of the story sink in. *H & P—Free Pr.*

KUHN, THOMAS b. 1922. **The Structure of Scientific Revolutions** (2nd ed. 1970). Important discussion of changes in scientific theory, method, and fact. *H & P—U of Chicago Pr*.

LAZARSFELD, PAUL F. 1901–1976. **Qualitative Analysis: Historical and Critical Essays** (1971). A collection of papers by a grand master of sociological method. Also contains three essays on Lazarsfeld's work. *o.p.*

LEMERT, CHARLES C. b. 1937. **French Sociology: Rupture and Renewal since 1968** (1981). A selection of readings by leading French sociologists with a helpful, well-written introduction to French sociological thought by Lemert. *H & P—Columbia U Pr*.

MALCOLM, JANET. **Psychoanalysis: The Impossible Profession** (1981). Based on extensive interviews with "Aaron Green," a practicing, orthodox Freudian psychoanalyst, this book is the best introduction to the theory of analysis and the quirky social world of analysis. *H—Knopf; P—Random*.

MARCUSE, HERBERT 1898–1979. **Eros and Civilization: A Philosophical Inquiry into Freud** (1966). In this time when potshots at Freud are fashionable, this careful, optimistic reading of psychoanalysis and critique of the neo-Freudians remains refreshing and challenging. *P—Beacon Pr*.

MEAD, GEORGE HERBERT 1863–1931. **Mind, Self, and Society from the Standpoint of a Social Behaviorist** (1934). A person is a product of society. Mead discusses socialization and the way rationality and creativity emerge through social interaction. *H & P—U of Chicago Pr*.

MEADOWS, DONNELLA H. et al. **The Limits to Growth: A Report for the Club of Rome's Project on the Predicament of Mankind** (2nd ed. 1974). A readable report on computer simulations of the interaction of world population, natural resources, and economy. This book aroused considerable controversy in many academic disciplines. *H & P—Universe*.

MERTON, ROBERT K. b. 1910. **Social Theory and Social Structure** (enlarged ed. 1968). Classical essays on social structure. Contains arguments for the development of "middle range" theories—those that are concerned with social phenomena on less than a sweeping scale. *H—Free Pr*.

MILGRAM, STANLEY b. 1933. **Obedience to Authority: An Experimental View** (1974). Compelling report on the controversial research program showing that people obey authority even when their obedience will inflict pain and suffering on others. *H & P—Har-Row*.

MILLETT. **Sexual Politics.** See "Women's Studies," page 316.

MILLS, C. WRIGHT 1916–1962. **The Power Elite** (1956). Argues that the United States is controlled by a small, interlocking group of people from the military, politics, and business. *H & P—Oxford U Pr*.

————. **The Sociological Imagination** (1959). An important early critique of American sociology. Excellent essays by an original, radical thinker. *H & P—Oxford U Pr*.

PARSONS, TALCOTT 1902–1979. **The System of Modern Societies** (1971). Parson's work has shaped much of American sociology. Here, in a readable book, he develops a theory of social evolution and attempts to account for modern European and American history under his scheme. *o.p.*

PIVEN, FRANCES FOX b. 1932 and RICHARD A. CLOWARD b. 1926. **Regulating the Poor: The Functions of Public Relief** (1971). Views public relief as a device used by the haves to control the have-nots in times of potential political instability. *P—Random*.

RIESMAN, DAVID b. 1909 et al. **The Lonely Crowd** (1950). The changing social character of the American people from "inner directed" to "other directed." *P—Yale U Pr*.

ROSENBERG, STANLEY D. b. 1944 and BERNARD J. BERGEN b. 1930. **The Cold Fire: Alienation and the Myth of Culture** (1976). A sensitive study of alienation that comes to the provocative conclusion, "Alienation dwells upon those moments of silence each man knows in his own life, and tells us that such moments are rife with possibility." *H—U Pr of New Eng*.

SKOCPOL, THEDA R. b. 1947. **States and Social Revolution: A Comparative Study of France, Russia, and China** (1979). A scholarly, readable examination of the three revolutions that form the backdrop to modern politics. *P—Cambridge U Pr*.

STARR, PAUL b. 1949. **The Social Transformation of American Medicine: The Rise of a Sovereign Profession and the Making of a Vast Industry** (1982). A useful overview of the maneuverings that put modern scientific medicine in place and a good discussion of the ongoing takeover of medicine by the corporate sector. *H & P—Basic*.

WALLACE, WALTER L. b. 1927. **Sociological Theory: An Introduction** (1969). A splendid overview of contemporary sociological theory. Explains and gives examples of 11 "isms" that inform the discipline. *H—Aldine*.

WEBER, MAX 1864–1920. **The Protestant Ethic and the Spirit of Capitalism** (1930). One of the great sociological insights: the linkage of Protestant ideology to the emergence of industrial society. *H—Peter Smith; P—Scribner*.

WILSON, EDWARD O. b. 1929. **Sociobiology: The New Synthesis** (1975). Extraordinarily controversial book suggesting that attention be directed to the biological bases of social behavior. Denounced by some as a rationalization of stereotypes and the status quo and an attempt to resurrect racist and sexist biological determinism; hailed by others as a serious "fundamental intellectual challenge" to contemporary sociology. *H & P—Harvard U Pr*.

CHAPTER 27

Psychology

SUZANNE J. KESSLER

Psychology is defined as the science of human behavior and experience. Although many disciplines contribute to an understanding of why individual people do what they do—for example, literature and philosophy—psychology is distinguished from them in its commitment to scientific method. Controlled conditions of observation, objective assessment, and repeatability of the findings by any other researcher—these are criteria of scientific method. The experimental model has been applied with varied success to the understanding of child development, social behavior, personality styles, cognitive abilities, perceptual processes, learning strategies, motivation, and psychopathologies. Psychology interfaces with biology in research seeking to determine the precise relationship between thinking and what is going on in the brain—the presumed seat of the "mind."

By developing theories and testing them, both in the laboratory and in the real world, academic psychology has been able to make major contributions toward resolving complex problems. Thus, behavioral techniques have been developed for eliminating phobias; educational curricula have been adjusted to the stages of a child's level of understanding; and equipment has been designed to help people with special perceptual abilities or limitations.

Not only has psychology contributed to everyday life, but it has been responsive to it as well. One case in point is the subdiscipline of psychology of women. It grew out of an awareness in the early 1970s that not only were women not represented broadly enough in society but that psychology itself had focused primarily on male experience as representative of human experience.

Most lay people, when they think about psychology, do not focus on the academic aspect of psychology—theory building and testing—but rather on its clinical application. For them a psychologist is someone who practices some form of psychotherapy, which is indeed an important aspect of psychology today, with a long and intricate history. Though many psychotherapists adopt an eclectic approach, more generally they prefer one of three major perspectives: the psychoanalytic, the behavioral, or the humanistic. Each differs from the others in many ways, for example: the stress placed on unconscious motivation, the role of the therapist in structuring sessions and offering interpretations, the importance attributed to childhood experiences, the duration and intensity of treatment.

In trying to become familiar with the literature of psychology, readers may have difficulty selecting among the abundant offerings. An almost limitless supply of popular books on psychological topics is at hand, but many propose misleadingly simple answers to exceedingly complex questions. Such titles, we hope, do not appear here. The books below have been grouped into four categories to help readers become familiar with a broad range of psychological topics. The first group includes those books that will give readers an understanding of the history of psychology and its different schools of thought. Each author takes a position on the controversial question: What should psychology concern itself with—consciousness or only observable behavior? In the second category are books representing the major subdivisions of psychology. Although these are not the only useful and accessible texts, each is especially well written and provides a comprehensive overview of the most recent research findings. Section three lists books dealing with personality theory and the practice of psychotherapy, and reflects a wide range of legitimate approaches. The final category includes specialized psychological topics, each book written by a well-respected researcher or theorist. All of these books represent the difficult but exciting efforts of psychologists to discover who it is that we "really" are.

History of Psychology

JAMES, WILLIAM 1842–1910. **Principles of Psychology.** 2 vols. (1890). A brilliant classic by one of America's most important early psychologists and philosophers. *H & P—Harvard U Pr, Peter Smith; P—Dover*.

KOHLER, WOLFGANG 1887–1967. **Gestalt Psychology** (rev. ed. 1970). A clear exposition of the basic concepts of gestaltism, a theory that challenged early behaviorism, arguing that behavior is a response to a *whole* situation rather than to its *separate* elements. *P—Liveright, NAL*.

PAVLOV, IVAN P. 1849–1936. **Conditioned Reflexes: An Investigation of the Physiological Activity of the Cerebral Cortex** (1927) Ed. G. V. Anrep. Pavlov, a Nobel Prize-winning physiologist, contributed one of psychology's most important concepts when he discovered the conditioned response and developed a theory of learning based on it. *H—Peter Smith; P—Dover*.

PIAGET, JEAN 1896–1980. **The Moral Judgment of the Child** (1932). This sometimes difficult book presents a most prolific author's influential ideas about child development. *H & P—Free Pr*.

SKINNER, B. F. b. 1904. **Science and Human Behavior** (1965). Proposes a view of the person as ruled by the principles of conditioning through the reinforcement of reward and punishment. *P—Free Pr*.

WATSON, JOHN B. 1878–1958. **Behaviorism** (rev. ed. 1970). A precursor of Skinnerian behaviorism that argues for studying only observable behavior in animals and humans. *P—Norton*.

WATSON, ROBERT I. 1909–1980. **The Great Psychologists from Aristotle to Freud** (4th ed. 1978). Overviews the development of psychology through the works of the major historical figures from America and Europe; a good companion book to the classics above. *P—Har-Row*.

Overviews

ANASTASI, ANNE b. 1908. **Psychological Testing** (5th ed. 1982). The definitive work on the assessment of individual differences. A classic that is continually updated. *H—Macmillan*.

ARONSON, ELLIOT b. 1932. **The Social Animal** (4th ed. 1984). The most entertaining introduction to social theory and experiments, written by a foremost social psychologist. *H & P—WH Freeman; P—Viking Pr*.

BOOTZIN, RICHARD R. and JOAN ACOCELLA. **Abnormal**

Psychology: Current Perspectives (4th ed. 1984). Presents diverse theoretical perspectives and comprehensive descriptions of psychopathological categories. *H—Random*.

BOWER, GORDON H. b. 1932 and ERNEST R. HILGARD b. 1904. **Theories of Learning** (5th ed. 1981). A continually updated review of the major theories of learning. *H—P-H*.

CARLSON, NEIL R. **Physiology of Behavior** (2nd ed. 1981). Excellent review of what we know about physiological psychology and ways of researching the field. *H—Allyn*.

GARDNER, HOWARD b. 1943. **Developmental Psychology: An Introduction** (2nd ed. 1982). Weaves theory and research into an accurate account of all that is known about developmental processes—and without oversimplifying the issues. *H—Little*.

GLEITMAN, HENRY b. 1925. **Psychology** (1981). An inquiry into all the major subdivisions of psychology and the interconnections among them. *H—Norton*.

GLUCKSBERG, SAM and JOSEPH H. DANKS. **Experimental Psycholinguistics: An Introduction** (1975). Clearly summarizes classic studies in the psychology of language; touches on both culture-specific factors and language universals. *H—L Erlbaum Assocs*.

HALL, CALVIN S. b. 1909 and GARDNER LINDZEY. **Theories of Personality** (3rd ed. 1978). A detailed, classic reference work reviewing the entire range of personality theories. *H—Wiley*.

MATLIN, MARGARET. **Perception** (1983). Unlike some introductory books on perception, this one reviews research and theory relating to all the senses—seeing, hearing, touching, smelling, and tasting and provides excellent examples from everyday life. *H—Allyn*.

MISCHEL, WALTER b. 1930. **Introduction to Personality** (3rd ed. 1981). Covers not only the author's influential social-learning theory of personality but all other major theories; heavy emphasis on laboratory evidence for and against the various theories. *H—HR&W*.

NEISSER, ULRIC b. 1928. **Cognition and Reality: Principles and Implications of Cognitive Psychology** (1976). Selected topics in cognitive psychology by one of the leading cognitive psychologists, outlining his theory of how people construct a view of the world. Although not a comprehensive discussion, it is still the best introduction to this important subdiscipline in psychology. *P—WH Freeman*.

WILLIAMS, JUANITA H. b. 1922. **Psychology of Women** (2nd ed. 1982). An excellent text that thoroughly and engagingly reviews the most recent research in one of the newest areas of psychology. *P—Norton.*

Personality Theory and Psychotherapy

FRANKL, VIKTOR E. b. 1905. **Man's Search for Meaning** (1980). A proponent of existential psychotherapy discusses his theory in light of his experiences in a concentration camp. *P—PB.*

FREUD, SIGMUND 1859–1939. **A General Selection from the Works** (1957). Ed. John Rickman. Groups Freud's writings under convenient headings and moves from the earliest to the latest materials. *H—Liveright; P—Doubleday.*

————. **Introductory Lectures on Psychoanalysis: A General Introduction to Psychoanalysis** (1977). Accessible writings of the great master on topics for which he is best known, such as sexuality, neuroses, dream interpretation. *H & P—Liveright.*

HORNEY, KAREN 1855–1952. **Feminine Psychology** (1973). Ed. Harold Kelman. Female development from the point of view of a pioneering woman psychoanalyst who added a cultural dimension to Freudian theory. *P—Norton.*

JUNG, CARL G. 1875–1961. **The Portable Jung** (1976). Ed. Joseph Campbell. Selections of his better known works, deviating in a fascinating way from traditional Freudian psychoanalytic theory. *P—Penguin.*

KOVEL, JOEL b. 1936. **A Complete Guide to Therapy: From Psychotherapy to Behavior Modification** (1975). Describes the pros and cons of the many diverse therapies available. *P—Pantheon.*

LAING, R. D. b. 1927. **The Divided Self** (1965, 1969). An unconventional vision of sanity and madness based on the author's theory of personal alienation. *H—Pantheon; P—Penguin.*

ROGERS, CARL b. 1902. **On Becoming a Person** (1961). A moving and compassionate view of personal growth and development by the originator of client-centered therapy, a psychotherapy within the humanistic tradition. *H—HM.*

SELIGMAN, MARTIN E. b. 1941. **Helplessness: On Depression, Development, and Death** (1974). A discussion of the author's theory of the relationship between lack of control and depression, a theory that has stimulated a great deal of research. *P—WH Freeman*.

SHAPIRO, DAVID b. 1923. **Neurotic Styles** (1965). Elucidates from a psychoanalytic viewpoint the dynamics of four personality types: hysterical, impulsive, obsessive-compulsive, and paranoid. *H & P—Basic*.

SULLIVAN, HARRY S. 1892–1949. **The Psychiatric Interview** (1970). An analysis of the psychiatric interview as a special case of all interpersonal situations. Useful both for conceptualizing the psychiatric process and for the practical work of counseling or interviewing. *P—Norton*.

Special Topics

BEM, DARYL J. **Beliefs, Attitudes, and Human Affairs** (1970). Describes his theory of self-perception as well as summarizes the way social psychologists conceive the relationship of attitudes, beliefs, and behavior. *P—Brooks-Cole*.

CHODOROW, NANCY b. 1944. **The Reproduction of Mothering: Psychoanalysis and the Sociology of Gender** (1978). A difficult but stimulating and creative revision of psychoanalytic theory. Argues that traditional child-rearing arrangements create what are presumed to be universal personality differences between men and women. *H & P—U of Cal Pr*.

ELKIND, DAVID b. 1931. **Children and Adolescents: Interpretive Essays on Jean Piaget** (3rd ed. 1981). Lucid summaries of the main themes of the 20th century's most influential developmentalist. Piaget's own writings are not always accessible to the beginning reader of psychology. *H & P—Oxford U Pr*.

ERIKSON, ERIK H. b. 1902. **Childhood and Society** (1964). Major work on the social significance of childhood. *P—Norton*.

EYSENCK, H. J. b. 1916. **Intelligence Controversy: H. J. Eysenck vs. Leon Kamin** (1981). A debate between opponents on the effects of heredity and environment on intelligence. *H—Wiley*.

FESTINGER, LEON b. 1919 et al. **When Prophecy Fails: A Social and Psychological Study of a Modern Group that Predicted the Destruction of the World** (1964). A fascinating study of the relationship between attitudes and behavior, generalizing from one cult's experiences to everyday life. *P—Har-Row*.

FREEDMAN, JONATHAN. **Crowding and Behavior** (1975). Award-winning analysis of theory and research on the effects of crowding on human behavior and experience. *P—WH Freeman*.

GELMAN, ROCHEL b. 1942 and C. R. GALLISTEL. **The Child's Understanding of Number** (1978). Elegantly written description of studies showing how 2-, 3-, and 4-year-olds begin to use numbers. This short book is a model of sound empirical investigation in psychology. *H—Harvard U Pr*.

GIBSON, JAMES J. 1904–1979. **The Senses Considered as Perceptual Systems** (rev. ed. 1983). A controversial introduction to perceptual psychology from the ecological perspective. *H—Greenwood; P—Waveland Pr*.

GUTHRIE, ROBERT V. b. 1930. **Even the Rat Was White: A Historical View of Psychology** (1976). Reviews early research approaches to racial differences and the effects of psychology on the education of blacks. *P—Har-Row*.

KAGAN, JEROME b. 1929. **The Nature of the Child** (1984). Provocative examination of commonly held assumptions about child development, particularly the effects of early experience on later personality and behavior. *H—Basic*.

KESSLER, SUZANNE J. b. 1946 and WENDY McKENNA b. 1945. **Gender: An Ethnomethodological Approach** (1978). A radical perspective treating all aspects of gender as a social construction and giving an overview of more traditional approaches to understanding gender. *H—Wiley; P—U of Chicago Pr*.

LATANÉ, BIBB b. 1937 and JOHN M. DARLEY b. 1938. **The Unresponsive Bystander: Why Doesn't He Help?** (1970). A prizewinning account of the authors' series of studies on bystander intervention and factors that influence the likelihood of help being offered. *H—P-H*.

LIFTON, ROBERT J. b. 1926. **Death in Life: Survivors of Hiroshima** (1982). A psychohistory of one of the most traumatic events of modern time, seen through the eyes of the victims and analyzed by an astute and empathetic researcher. *H & P—Basic*.

MACCOBY, ELEANOR E. **Social Development: Psychological Growth and the Parent-Child Relationship** (1980). Discusses the influences of parents, peers, teachers, and television on social and personality development from infancy to adolescence. *P—Har-BraceJ*.

MILGRAM. **Obedience to Authority.** See "Sociology," page 299.

ORNSTEIN, ROBERT E. b. 1942. **The Psychology of Consciousness** (2nd ed. 1977). Highly readable introduction to a broad range of topics relating to human consciousness. *P—HarBraceJ, Penguin.*

SPRINGER, SALLY P. b. 1947 and GEORGE DEUTSCH. **Left Brain, Right Brain** (1981). Comprehensive study of how the two cerebral hemispheres function. *P—WH Freeman.*

CHAPTER 28

Women's Studies

IRENE QUENZLER BROWN

The relationship between reading and women is not a simple one, whether women are readers of women's or men's writings. Of course for most of human history women have read the works of men. Women as authors, writing not only for women but about women, is a relatively modern phenomenon, especially recognized by the formation of a new academic field known as Women's Studies. As the works listed at the end of this essay suggest, most of the new scholarship has been conducted by women. Women's voices are finally singing in that chorus of human culture confined to the rarefied atmosphere of the academy. This essay invites the reader to consider the significance of those voices, not only for the academy but for society at large.

This is the first edition of *Good Reading* to include a section drawn from Women's Studies. To familiarize the newcomer with certain fundamentals in Women's Studies, the reader is asked to glance quickly at the list of recommended books. Arranged alphabetically by author or editor, this short selection invites the reader to create an individual list. Such an exercise recognizes, as does Women's Studies generally, the importance of the reader's or the student's point of view. Such a cursory reading also shows how rapidly scholarship in Women's Studies is expanding. Many titles have only appeared in the last three years. Topics such as housework, motherhood, comparable worth, and lesbianism are also new subjects of scholarly inquiry, too complex to introduce quickly without oversimplifying.

To understand more fully why Women's Studies should command your interest, let us begin with a historical example of women readers. Then we will proceed to discuss what other features characterize Women's Studies today. We will consider the significance of an earlier good reading book that was published for women of Great Britain in 1714, one that remained popular into the 1770s; and we know that in the 1730s and 1740s, Jonathan Edwards, the theologian of the Great Awakening, lent his copy to parishioners living on the Massachusetts frontier. A French translation also existed.

At first sight *The Ladies Library* appears to be a classic, male-defined, elitist good-conduct book. A closer examination, however, reveals that its anonymous editor read very selectively. If a woman edited the work, we can appreciate how the female reader of the main—primarily male, androcentric—culture, prepared the way for the female writer of woman's experience.

That *The Ladies Library* was published with an eye on female readership is quite evident. Was the editor a woman, however? The title page of the three-volume work indeed declares it was "written by a lady." Yet scholars have doubted this, while expressing surprise about the feminist tone of the editorial work. Some suggest that the publisher, Richard Steele, simply lied about a woman editor in an effort to boost sales. That a publisher might feel compelled to invent a female editor to promote a work intended primarily for women is in itself significant.

Indeed it is prudent to accept Steele's assertion, since it provides the most economical and least anachronistic explanation. The third volume of this work promoting female moral force or agency was actually dedicated to his own wife. She was a woman whose reason and piety he admired, as we know from his correspondence. As to the origin of the manuscript, he explained that it was "first intended by the Compiler for a Guide to her own Conduct, and if thought worth publishing to be of the same Service to others of her sex."

Dissatisfied with any single conduct book, and conscious of the dignity of her sex and its capacity for reason and critical thought, this unknown "lady" fashioned her own good reader, initially for her own private edification. The most logical explanation of editorship points to a learned *and* pious lady of the late 17th century. Such a virtuous woman would be most reluctant to be publicly identified. Yet she would readily share her learning with other women. Hiding her identity also liberated her to defend her sex in a way that was not yet common and explains the book's feminist perspective. By judiciously selecting from among the various male authors, predominantly Anglican clergymen, she expressed her own outlook. Finally, it is significant that she included parts of a treatise also first published anonymously in 1694, *The Serious Proposal to the Ladies,* by England's early feminist, Mary Astell, another learned and most pious woman.

In her proposal Astell recommended the founding of a women's academy where some might spend a lifetime and others come only for an education before returning to the world and most likely to marriage. The academy would also be a place of reentry—for widows. Astell's plan only materialized very much later. Except for the remarkable medieval convents, women as a group were to remain excluded from formal higher education until the middle of the 19th century. Thereafter, only a small minority gained entrance to academe, and even that success proved a mixed blessing.

The pursuit of scholarly learning about women was easily overwhelmed even in women's colleges and still more so in coeducational institutions. Higher education in the 19th and 20th centuries introduced students to a male-oriented curriculum. Sanctioned by ancient classical humanistic culture, modernized through the transformation of the Renaissance and the Enlightenment, the basic curriculum spoke less to an inclusive humankind than to a particular mankind, mostly a male minority blessed with sufficient wealth and leisure to sustain that culture.

Yet there were also alternatives to that formal higher learning, open to the majority of people, including women. Growing literacy and cheaper production of books created a new form of popular culture that was also significantly tied to the ancient curriculum and to Judeo-Christian traditions. Yet there were differences between this more popular and the more formal high culture, because these readers were different. For women there were also two places where some could act collectively in a new way. Young women of some means could acquire a preparatory education. In America they even relied on a new version of our earlier text. Now called *The Ladies Pocket Library,* this work included many female writers from England and France. Second, female identity and solidarity were also promoted by older women's religious and social reform organizations, which served as incubators for organized feminist activities of the mid-19th century.

Nonetheless, significant advances were made in women's education and learning during that century—and here Elizabeth Cady Stanton's commissioning of *The Woman's Bible* comes to mind—and Women's Studies as such remained part of nonformal or preparatory education. It was not introduced in the newly reorganized research universities or in the colleges. The university model even inspired the curriculum of women's colleges in post-Civil War America.

On the other hand, while those college women did not formally pursue Women's Studies, they did gain a sense of common purpose, as well as excellent academic skills, that allowed them to compete with educated men. Both the solidarity and the pursuit of academic excellence were also influential in sustaining the first wave of feminism that lasted until suffrage was achieved in 1920.

Similarly, the resurgence of feminism in the 1960s was significantly connected with "overqualified" women from elite women's colleges. Betty Friedan and Adrienne Rich are examples of remarkably different feminists, both influential activists and intellectuals, who also helped shape the new interdisciplinary academic study of Women's Studies. The dialectic of higher education also affected Women's Studies in another way. At public institutions Women's Studies first gained an institutional footing, as did their more service-oriented sister programs: women's centers.

From the present vantage point, the progress of the last fifteen years is indeed remarkable and irreversible. Women's Studies has entered the academy. In the United States alone, more than 500 programs now exist. Forty research centers have been formed, with a council that coordinates research activities and helps set priorities. As the reading list suggests, there are also numerous scholarly journals devoted to disseminating a rich variety of feminist research. National and regional conferences annually bring thousands of researchers, students, and activists together. Connections with scholars abroad are also growing, which is especially significant if Women's Studies is to reflect more accurately the concerns of the Third World.

Today more than half of the world's population is female. As Women's Studies succeeds in building scholarly networks across nations and cultures, its effort to be inclusive will be challenged even more than it has been already. Let me conclude this introduction to Women's Studies, and how it exists in a state of becoming, by outlining very briefly five general characteristics that underlie this basic commitment to the value of inclusion.

First, there is the feminist perspective from which the inquiry begins, thereby excluding an androcentric perspective. Second, the study relies on gender as a fundamental category of social analysis as important as class, ethnicity, religious affiliation, or race. Third, cognizant of the fact that women's experience is profoundly fluid, Women's Studies scholars are also beginning to view social change involving women not so much as a dialectical but as a "polylectical" process. Women find and have found themselves living frequently with contradictions. There is, for instance, a tension between woman in her role as woman, worker, sexual being, family member, political activist. In these roles she occupies different social spaces. She may be needed as a worker; and while her role as mother is especially praised, it is also seen as being incompatible with work outside the home. If she is a known lesbian, her mothering is regarded as deviant. Fourth, there is a profound sense that women's lives have been marked by oppression; but women have also exercised power in their own behalf. Finally, Women's Studies tries to remain alert to differences among women, including those of privilege, or degrees of oppression. That sensitivity succeeds best where the community of scholars is also close to a diverse community of women.

Let us look more closely at some of these fundamentals and how they interrelate. The open admission that a feminist premise underlies all Women's Studies research becomes a legitimate check against traditional but mostly unacknowledged androcentric research in which women's capacity to act was often ignored, denied outright, or distorted into deviance. Just as class, birth order, race, and ethnic background are significant factors in behavior, so is gender. Unless we consciously look for the construction of female gender identity, however, we will not see women as active participants in society. Too many social forces and expectations—the need for modesty on the "lady's" part, for example—hide woman's actions from view. And one must accept that certain trends have contradictory consequences. Thus the increasing distinction between private and public life, drawn more and more since the Renaissance, succeeded in hiding women from view. For women of some means, however, the new cultivation of privacy also could gain them, "a room of their own." Nor can one attribute too great a force to these spheres or spaces for action. Women played multiple roles. Over her lifetime a woman moved not only from her family of birth to that of marriage; she might also enter a different class, or as a sexual object might be intimately connected with a man from a different class or culture.

Once woman's invisibility is removed, her true experience can be examined. It is far from a "traditional" or conformist life. It may well be that the very insistent ideology of woman's sphere and woman's place, so powerfully proclaimed in that great 19th century of change, became such a refrain because it contradicted reality. Women's Studies research seeks to assess these phenomena of mobility in Western society, a society on the move on so many frontiers—social and geographic, even psychological and spiritual—as the modern identity came into being. Women's capacity for transformation, prompted by the very real perception of living in a situation of conflicting norms, may have prepared women especially for modern existential predicaments.

Both a Hegelian and a Marxist dialectic are too simple for describing woman's continual lack of resolution in the face of an existence that is always shifting. This state of permanent impermanence, very much an existential condition, and not so wholly attributable to pre-Oedipal mother-daughter experiences, may explain why women seem to have such diffuse ego boundaries. Women have had to be ready to shift their egos at little notice. They have learned to be in a state of preparedness to act as the reserve labor pool on many fronts and in many wars, including those going on in the very privacy of their cottages, mansions, or tenements. And many have prepared themselves—not simply been conditioned—to love their father and raise their sons significantly in his image. Here the new research on the reproduction of mothering is most promising.

There is another dimension of signal importance in Women's Studies. Perhaps we should call it the fifth dimension, recalling the 1960s musical group that sought to inspire a generation with its idealism. In the case of Women's Studies there is also a visionary idealism that hopes to keep alive a commitment to pluralism, resisting restraints in the form of ideology, including that of feminism itself. Dialogue between feminists is of fundamental importance lest the sensitivity to difference and contradiction be blunted. Women, especially, have learned to live in a state of impermanence, where consciousness is never entirely consistent or fully authenticated for long but challenged again in the next encounter. As long as this existential condition prevails for women, one can expect that the majority of scholars in Women's Studies will be women. When this fact no longer seems shocking and somehow illegitimate, the pendulum will begin to shift. One can hope that the readership of Women's Studies will extend increasingly to both sexes (the fact that *Good Reading* has invited this essay is a hopeful sign). A shift may also be in the making as the academy begins another revision of the ancient classical curriculum. There are signs that it is replacing the version founded on the reforms of the 19th-century university—a time of supreme Western imperialism and cultural confidence, if not arrogance. A new curriculum may be in the making, one that includes not only women but also other groups that for the past several centuries of Western hegemony have been viewed as inferior people. If this can occur in the near future, it will in no small part be due to the success that Women's Studies itself has had in its own struggle to be genuinely inclusive in the study of the majority of humankind: women.

BEAUVOIR, SIMONE DE b. 1908. **The Second Sex** (1953). Classic existentialist study of women's "historical and contemporary" place in Western culture—a secondary place, the author insists, one that has shrunk their personality, limited their freedom, and twisted their relations with men. A work of remarkable sweep, learning, and intelligence. *H—Knopf; P—Random*.

————. **A Very Easy Death** (1964). Moving autobiographical contribution to the growing literature on mothers and daughters. *o.p*.

Becoming Visible: Women in European History. See "History," page 297.

BERNARD, JESSIE b. 1903. **The Female World** (1981). Encyclopedic examination of women's sphere, written by one of America's leading sociologists in the areas of women, marriage, and the family. *H & P—Free Pr*.

Black Women in White America (1972). Ed. Gerda Lerner. An extraordinary compilation of historical documents by one of the founders of the new women's history. Her more theoretical work appears in **The Majority Finds Its Past: Placing Women in History** (1979). First title: *P—Pantheon, Random*. Second title: *H & P—Oxford U Pr*.

BROWN, RITA MAE b. 1944. **Rubyfruit Jungle** (1973). An exuberant, picaresque novel about a young lesbian from Pennsylvania in the 1960s—already something of a classic. *P—Bantam*.

COLES, ROBERT b. 1929 and JANE HALLOWELL COLES. **Women of Crisis: Lives of Struggle and Hope** (1978). This choice collection of six interviews with poor women from different American traditions often reads like fiction and affirms the artistry of ordinary existence. *P—Dell*.

COWAN, RUTH SCHWARTZ b. 1941. **More Work for Moth-**

ers: **The Ironies of Household Technology from the Open Hearth to the Microwave** (1983). While industrialization liberated women from much household production, increased consumption of goods transformed the home and introduced higher expectations of domestic life that continue to fall primarily on female members of the household. *H—Basic*.

DAVIDOFF. **The Best Circles.** See "History," page 300.

DOUGLAS, ANN b. 1942. **The Feminization of American Culture** (1977). Searching critique of sentimental Victorian culture, forged, Douglas argues, by an alliance of middle-class women readers and writers, clergymen anxious about their declining influence, and publishers eager to benefit from a new consumerism. *P—Avon*.

DUBLIN, THOMAS b. 1946. **Women at Work: The Transformation of Work and Community in Lowell, Massachusetts, 1826–1860** (1979). Study of the early textile industry as it mushroomed in rural New England, initially depending on the labor of farm girls, quickly meeting labor resistance in the 1830s and 1840s, and then shifting to an immigrant labor force. *H & P—Columbia U Pr*.

EHRENREICH and ENGLISH. **For Her Own Good.** See "Sociology," page 332.

EISENSTEIN, ZILLAH. **The Radical Future of Liberal Feminism** (1981). Examination of liberal individualism—from the period of John Locke to the Carter administration—and its occasional inclusion of a radical, subversive vision of womanhood. *H & P—Longman*.

Families, Politics, and Public Policy: A Feminist Dialogue on Women and the State (1983). Ed. Irene Diamond. A challenging group of original essays reflecting the growing debate on the future of family policy in our pluralistic society. *P—Longman*.

Feminist Frameworks: Alternative Theoretical Accounts of the Relations Between Men and Women (2nd ed. 1984). Eds. Allison M. Jaggar and Paula S. Rothenberg. Beyond a continuing interest in theory, the new edition offers acute insights from radical and socialist feminists and feminists of color. *H—McGraw*.

FIORENZA, ELISABETH SCHUESSLER b. 1938. **In Memory of Her: A Feminist Theological Reconstruction of Christian Origins** (1983). In reconstructing an original, early Christian theology, this scholarly feminist history seeks to transform androcentric assumptions about Christian culture as a whole. *H & P—Crossroad NY*.

FIRESTONE. **The Dialectic of Sex.** See "Sociology," page 333.

FLEXNER. **Century of Struggle.** See "History," page 304.

FRIEDAN. **The Feminine Mystique.** See "Sociology," page 333.

GILBERT, SANDRA M. b. 1936 and SUSAN GUBAR b. 1944. **The Madwoman in the Attic** (1979). A full-scale study of the female tradition in 19th-century writing. Learned yet immensely readable, especially valuable on Austen, the Brontës, and Dickinson. *H & P—Yale U Pr.*

GILLIGAN, CAROL b. 1936. **In a Different Voice: Psychological Theory and Women's Development** (1982). This brilliant, controversial work argues that a morality of responsibility—favoring interdependence and affiliation—is more significant for women, whereas men tend to pursue a morality of rights, supporting individualism and separation. *H & P—Harvard U Pr.*

GLÜCKEL. 1646–1724. **Memoirs of Glückel of Hameln** (1977). Tr. M. Lowenthal. The life of a pious Jewish woman from northern Germany at the turn of the 17th century, as recorded during her two widowhoods. Documents her courageous struggle for personal and family survival and self-respect. *P— Schocken.*

GORDON, MARY b. 1949. **Woman's Body, Woman's Right: A Social History of Birth Control in America** (1976). One of several new studies that revise our understanding of the Victorian era as a period of controversy in which women already sought their sexual and reproductive self-determination. *H—Viking Pr; P—Penguin.*

HARRIS, ANN S. b. 1937 and LINDA NOCHLIN b. 1931. **Women Artists, 1550–1950** (1976). Beautiful catalog of a major art exhibit, with excellent biographical sketches of the artists placed in their historical context. *o.p.*

HORNEY. **Feminine Psychology.** See "Psychology," page 342.

HURSTON, ZORA NEALE 1903–1960. **I Love Myself When I Am Laughing . . . A Zora Neale Hurston Reader** (1979). Selections from the folkloristic essays, autobiographical writings, and fiction of this writer of the Harlem Renaissance. *P—Feminist Pr.*

HUSTON, PERDITA b. 1936. **Third World Women Speak Out** (1979). Interviews with mostly rural women from Tunisia, Egypt, Sudan, Kenya, Sri Lanka, and Mexico, reflecting on the promise and hardships coincident with modern economic and social development. *H & P—Praeger*.

In Her Own Image: Women Working in the Arts (1980). Eds. Elaine Hedges and Ingrid Wendt. Graphic artists, poets, musicians, photographers, and dancers writing about their work; also brief biographical sketches of forgotten women artists and essays son the arts and social change. *H & P—Feminist Pr*.

JOSEPH, GLORIA I. and JILL LEWIS. **Common Differences: Conflicts in Black and White Feminist Perspectives** (1981). Black and white women affirm their "difference, collaboration, commitment, and caring." *P—Doubleday*.

KANOWITZ. **Women and the Law.** See "Politics," page 310.

KESSLER-HARRIS, ALICE b. 1941. **Out to Work: A History of Wage-Earning Women in the United States** (1982). Detailed, authoritative survey of women's employment since the colonial period, with special emphasis on industrialization. *H & P—Oxford U Pr*.

KIRKHAM, MARGARET. **Jane Austen, Feminism and Fiction** (1983). This study explains Austen's ironic and subtle feminism—the Enlightenment surviving into the postrevolutionary romantic era. *H—B&N Imports*.

The Lesbian Issue, vol. 9, no. 4 of **Signs: Journal of Women in Culture and Society** (1985). Eds. Estelle Freedman et al. State of the scholarly art on lesbianism: articles on history, literature, friendships, lesbian communities; documents and book reviews, as well as exemplary exchanges on two earlier reviews. *H & P—U of Chicago Pr*.

Men's Studies Modified: The Impact of Feminism on the Academic Disciplines (1981). Ed. Dale Spender. Useful introduction of major issues facing teachers dedicated to a transformation of the curriculum. Arranged according to major academic disciplines, and includes a good basic bibliography for each. *H & P—Pergamon*.

Midnight Birds: Stories of Contemporary Black Women Writers (1980). Ed. Mary Helen Washington. Composed in the wake of the new feminism, these stories give a "wide-angle" view of black womanhood as sturdier, angrier, prouder, and more defiant than that suggested in a similar anthology published in the mid-1970s. *P—Doubleday*.

MILLETT, KATE b. 1934. **Sexual Politics** (1970). One of the ancestral books of the women's movement, Millett traces the patriarchal bias that operates in Western society and dissects such "culture heroes" as D. H. Lawrence, Freud, Henry

Miller, and Norman Mailer. [Mailer has responded with *The Prisoner of Sex* (1971), a work both polemical and testamental.] *o.p.*

MITCHELL, JULIET b. 1940. **Psychoanalysis and Feminism: Freud, Reich, Laing and Women** (1974). A daring defense of Freud's radical significance for feminists, based not so much on his view of femininity but on that more fundamental construct of psychoanalysis leading to a thorough examination of the patriarchal system that oppresses women. A reclamation of fantasy, desire, and the unconscious is analyzed as part of the normal human and therefore female condition. *P—Random.*

MOERS, ELLEN 1928–1979. **Literary Women: The Great Writers** (1976). An already classic study in feminist criticism that identifies various types of heroines in female fiction from the late 18th to the early 20th centuries. *o.p.*

Mothering: Essays in Feminist Theory (1983). Ed. Joyce Trebilcot. Nurturing, womb envy, maternal thinking, and the impact of Freud are among the issues finely argued, mostly by philosophers, in essays that address controversies raised by feminist scholars—a work not conceivable ten years ago. *H & P—Rowman & Allanheld.*

NODDINGS, NEL. **Caring: A Feminine Approach to Ethics and Moral Education** (1984). Examination of ethical rather than natural caring, seen as an encounter shaped by a fundamental view of the human condition: not as alone and anguished, but as related and with a capacity for joy. *H—U of Cal Pr.*

OKIN. **Women in Western Political Thought.** See "Politics," page 309.

OLSEN. **Tell Me a Riddle.** See "The Short Story," page 199.

———. **Silences** (1979). Bold, beautiful, and sensitive reflections on women writing literature, and why they often stopped, temporarily or permanently. Composed by a writer who struggled against her own silencing, the effect not only of economic hardships but more basically of the whole range of sexual politics that she helped to articulate. *H—Peter Smith; P—Dell.*

RICH, ADRIENNE b. 1929. **Of Women Born: Motherhood as Experience and Institution** (1976). Antiromantic, angry, visionary, and scholarly work by one of America's most influential contemporary feminist poets and critics. Exemplifying the second wave of feminist scholarship, its persuasive power derives from the artistry with which she weaves and interprets her own and other women's personal, often painful experience with conclusions drawn from the first decade of the new feminist scholarship. *H—Norton; P—Bantam.*

ROBERTSON. **An Experience of Women.** See "History," page 302.

SHOWALTER, ELAINE b. 1941. **A Literature of Their Own: British Women Novelists from Brontë to Lessing** (1977). In search of a distinctive female literary tradition as a subculture within a male culture, this critic examines both famous and now-forgotten English novelists and traces three successive stages of self-consciousness in the tradition: the feminine (1840–80), the feminist (1880–1920), and the female (1920–   ). *H & P—Princeton U Pr.*

TAYLOR, BARBARA b. 1950. **Eve and the New Jerusalem: Socialism and Feminism in the Nineteenth Century** (1983). Part of the feminist dialogue with the left, this careful historical study explains how the English Owenites sought to shape the future of industrial society, including familial and sexual relations. An interesting companion piece to Dublin (page 353). *H & P—Pantheon.*

TENTLER, LESLIE WOODCOCK. **Wage-Earning Women: Industrial Work and Family Life in the U.S., 1900–1930** (1979). How both employment and unemployment came to characterize working-class women's lives as the industrial economy reached its maturity. *H & P—Oxford U Pr.*

TOMALIN, CLAIRE. **The Life and Death of Mary Wollstonecraft** (1974). Biography of a daring English feminist living in an era of truly revolutionary change that inspired her major feminist treatise, *The Vindication of the Rights of Woman* (1792). See WOLLSTONECRAFT, below. *P—NAL.*

Toward an Anthropology of Women. See "Anthropology," page 328.

Victorian Women: A Documentary Account of Women's Lives in Nineteenth-Century England, France and the United States (1981). Eds. Erna Hellerstein et al. This choice selection of documents, arranged according to woman's life cycle, is a model of class-conscious historical scholarship, with excellent introductory sections. *H & P—Stanford U Pr.*

WALKER. **The Color Purple.** See "American Minority Cultures: Black," page 125.

WALKOWITZ, JUDITH R. **Prostitution and Victorian Society: Women, Class and the State** (1980). A study of the resistance to the Contagious Diseases Act of the 1860s in Great Britain, especially by the Ladies' National Association, headed by Josephine Butler, who saw the legislation as a blatant example of sex and class discrimination. *H & P— Cambridge U Pr.*

WILLIAMS. **Psychology of Women.** See "Psychology," page 342.

WOLLSTONECRAFT, MARY 1759–1797. **A Vindication of the Rights of Woman** (1792). A vehement statement of the oppression, the disabilities, and indignities women suffer. Despite its passion, it is penetrating and balanced, its general observations still valid. Not until the 20th century has her *Vindication* been accorded deserved recognition. *H & P—Biblio Dist; H—Garland Pub; P—Norton, Penguin.*

Women and Colonization: Anthropological Perspectives. See "Anthropology," page 329.

Women and Russia: Feminist Writings from the Soviet Union (1984). Ed. Tatyana Mamonova. Essays composed by women of special courage: as penalty, some of them suffered perpetual exile from the country ostensibly committed to solving the woman question. *H & P—Beacon Pr.*

Women and the American Economy. See "Economics," page 322.

Women in Medieval Society. See "History," page 299.

WOOLF, VIRGINIA 1882–1941. **A Room of One's Own** (1929) and **Three Guineas** (1938). In these still timely essays, composed during the fateful interwar years of impending fascism, the British novelist and critic ponders the subtleties of female oppression, especially as they are manifested among the growing social class that confidently raised "the daughters of educated men." In 1929, she dissected the fundamental relationship between financial and creative autonomy. In 1938, she concluded that in woman's tension between acceptance and rejection as outsider lay the promise of a more civilized world of greater liberty, equality, and peace. *H & P—HarBraceJ.*

Journals and Other Publications

Feminist Studies, % Women's Studies Program, University of Maryland, College Park, MD 20742.

Frontiers: A Journal of Women Studies, Women Studies Program, University of Colorado, Boulder, CO 80309.

New Directions for Women, New Directions for Women, Inc., 108 W. Palisade Ave., Englewood, NJ 07631.

On Campus with Women, Project on the Status and Education of Women, Association of American Colleges, 1818 R St. N.W., Washington, DC 20009.

SAGE: A Scholarly Journal on Black Women, Sage Women's Educational Press, Box 42741, Atlanta, GA 30311-0741.

Signs: Journal of Women in Culture and Society, University of Chicago Press, 5801 S. Ellis Ave., Chicago, IL 60637.

Sojourner: The Women's Forum, 143 Albany St., Cambridge, MA 02139.

The Women's Review of Books, Wellesley Center for Research on Women, Wellesley, MA 02181.

Women's Studies Quarterly (and Supplement), **Women's Studies International,** The Feminist Press, Box 334, Old Westbury, NY 11568.

(for a current list of women, projected on the status and importance of women's associations of American College. 1512 K St., N.W., Washington, DC 20005.

Avidad, Salome, *American Jewish Women. Jewish Women: a Documentary* ... Ste. Br. ... Alba, ... 1981. ($14).

Signs: Journal of Women in Culture and Society. University of Chicago Press. 5801 S. Ellis Ave. Chicago, IL 60637.

Sargent ... *The Women: a Journal* ... ... Ridley St., Cambridge, MA 02139.

The Women's Review of Books. Wellesley Center for Research on Women. Wellesley, MA 02181.

Women Scholars. Chairman (and subscription). Women's Bibl... as ... with. The Feminist Press, Box 334 Old Westbury, NY 11568.

PART V

Sciences

CHAPTER 29

Physical Sciences and Mathematics

PAUL FRIEDMAN

One distinction of the human species is its continuous curiosity about the universe it inhabits: We have always felt a need to know, understand, and explain the workings of our physical world, its nearly infinite range—from galaxies to subatomic particles. Science and mathematics were the first steps humankind took away from superstition and mystery toward rational explanation of natural phenomena.

Since the Greek philosopher-scientists and Arab mathematicians of antiquity developed the first reasoned concepts about the cosmic and the microcosmic, science has undergone many revolutions. Between the 16th and 18th centuries came the towering figures who shaped modern science: Leonardo, Bacon, Galileo, and Newton foremost among an extraordinary group. In the 19th century, Faraday and Maxwell led the way to remarkable discoveries in electricity and magnetism, thermodynamics, and the statistical theory of heat, while Gauss, Euler, and Riemann thrust mathematics beyond the boundaries set in the neoclassical age by men like Descartes.

The 20th century has produced the most explosive revolutions in all the sciences as well as in mathematics. None would have been possible had not Einstein and Planck first demolished classical physical theories concerning fixed motion and time. Others have since extended Einstein's quantum revolution (Bohr, Heisenberg, Born, and Dirac among them) and contributed a new scientific vocabulary: pulsars, quasars, quarks, and charms. Awesome developments have taken place elsewhere in the sciences too. In chemistry, Woodward's virtuoso syntheses of organic molecules ranks with Dalton's atomic theory in the 19th century. Advances in molecular biology rival those in nuclear physics, projecting both promise and peril. The computer, too, has grown from a useful tool of science and mathematics to a major specialization that poses problems vexing to science and society.

We have landed on the moon, synthesized genes, and replaced the room-sized computers of the 1950s with desktop personal devices. Faced with such accomplishments, people often respond excessively: Some mindlessly exalt scientists, esteeming them as nearly superhuman; others comprehensively damn them, regarding them as the primary source of our societal woes. A salutary corrective to each extreme would be to read objective, accurate, comprehensible studies and to share in frank, informative views expressed by scientists themselves.

We need to know more about scientific creativity, its philosophical and psychological roots, and we need to understand more fully the social, economic, and moral implications of the discoveries our scientists have made. Public television series such as "Nova," "Dimensions in Science," and "The Living Planet" serve admirably to keep us informed. The list of books below—each of them significant, informative, and entertaining—will also lead toward insight and understanding.

General Science

ARMITAGE. **The World of Copernicus.** See "Biography," page 203.

BEDINI, SILVIO, A. b. 1917. **Thinkers and Tinkers** (1975). This American bicentennial history traces the course of American science, invention, and technical ingenuity from the time of discovery to Independence. *H—Landmark Ent.*

BERNSTEIN, JEREMY b. 1929. **Science Observed** (1982). One of the best from a prolific and talented writer. Particularly good insights into the origins of artificial intelligence research. Illuminating on Einstein and Schrödinger. *H— Basic.*

BRONOWSKI, JACOB 1908–1974. **The Ascent of Man** (1974). A stunning and monumental work that runs from the beginnings to today. This clear, fresh, lucid book should be read and reread and the TV series based on it seen and reseen. *H & P—Little.*

HARRÉ, ROM b. 1927. **Great Scientific Experiments** (1981). A cut above the usual sourcebook in science. The experimenters brilliantly represent the scope, methods, and values of science from Aristotle to Konrad Lorenz. *H & P—Oxford U Pr*.

HOFSTADTER, DOUGLAS b. 1945. **Gödel, Escher, Bach** (1979). A tour de force: elements of Lewis Carroll and Galileo. Sometimes difficult, always rewarding. *H—Basic*.

HOLTON, GERALD b. 1922. **The Scientific Imagination** (1978). Important case histories centering on the process of scientific discovery—elegantly presented and rich in insight. *H & P—Cambridge U Pr*.

Physical Science

The Ingenious Dr. Franklin (1956). Ed. Nathan G. Goodman. A short and engaging collection of Franklin's scientific letters reissued for the bicentennial. *H & P—U of Pa Pr*.

JEANS, JAMES 1877–1946. **The Universe Around Us** (4th ed. 1944). Relegating mathematics to footnotes, this great astronomer relates physics, chemistry, and geology to astronomy. *H—Ridgeway Bks*.

KISCH, BRUNO 1890–1966. **Scales and Weights** (rev. ed. 1976). The history, methodology, and equipment of a subject that is often taken for granted. *o.p.*

McCULLOUGH, DAVID b. 1933. **The Great Bridge** ((1972). Recounts fascinatingly the engineering and the social impact of the world's greatest, though not longest, bridge, the Brooklyn. *P—Avon, S&S*.

MEDAWAR, P. B. b. 1915. **Advice to a Young Scientist** (1979). Useful and interesting contribution from a distinguished scientist. Invaluable for those contemplating careers in research, but good reading for all. *H & P—Har-Row*.

OPPENHEIMER, J. ROBERT 1904–1967. **Science and the Common Understanding** (1966). The significance of science today is explained by one who actively applied moral principles in his work. *o.p.*

A Random Walk in Science (1973). Eds. R. L. Weber and E. Mendoza. The ultimate anthology, saturated with wit, wisdom, history, and fun, for anyone interested in science. *H—Heyden*.

SCHRÖDINGER, ERWIN 1887–1961. **Science, Theory and Man** (1957). Nine essays on people and the changing world, introducing the reader to the philosophical outlook of one of the founders of the new science. *o.p.*

WIENER, NORBERT 1894–1964. **Cybernetics** (2nd ed. 1961). One of the most original and influential books of this century, opening the door to the computer age. *P—MIT Pr.*

————. **God and Golem, Inc.** (1964). Explores, at the amateur's level, the ethical and religious problems growing out of the human development of machines. *P—MIT Pr.*

Physics

ANDRADE DE SILVA, J. and G. LOCHAK. **Quanta** (1969). Good nonmathematical treatment of the development of quantum theory. *o.p.*

BARNETT, LINCOLN K. 1909–1979. **The Universe and Dr. Einstein** (rev. ed. 1957). One of the soundest and clearest expositions of relativity and quantum theory. *o.p.*

BORN, MAX 1882–1970. **The Restless Universe** (2nd ed. 1951). A Nobel laureate guides the intelligent reader step by step through the maze of molecules, atoms, subatomic particles, and nuclear physics. Has delightful illustrations in the form of flip-over "animated sequences." *P—Dover.*

————. **The Born-Einstein Letters** (1970). This epic correspondence of two great physicists between 1916 and 1955 has often been quoted by other greats of the "Quantum Era." The insights and philosophical implications are devastating, but some letters are incomprehensible to the lay reader. *o.p.*

CALDER, NIGEL b. 1931. **The Key to the Universe** (1977). A clear presentation of modern physics at a popular level. Lucid coverage of Feynman diagrams and quarks. *H—Viking Pr; P—Penguin.*

CLARK, DAVID H. **Superstars** (1984). Supernovae: their history and origin. A useful general introduction of modern astronomy and cosmology. *H—McGraw.*

DE BROGLIE, LOUIS b. 1892. **New Perspectives in Physics** (1962). The founder of wave mechanics challenges the Copenhagen interpretation (statistical basis of quantum physics). *o.p.*

DYSON, FREEMAN J. b. 1923. **Disturbing the Universe** (1979). Fascinating mix of autobiography, philosophy, and contemporary history from an outstanding physicist, mathematician, and humanist. Compelling reading. *H & P—Har-Row*.

Einstein—A Centenary Volume (1979). Ed. A. P. French. A treasury of material on the life, work, and worth of Einstein as a scientist and human being. Its value is enormously enhanced by perceptive contributions from illustrious contemporaries of Einstein. *H & P—Harvard U Pr*.

FEINBERG, GERALD b. 1933. **What Is the World Made Of?** (1978). Twentieth-century physics—quarks, hadrons, and the like. *P—Doubleday*.

GAMOW, GEORGE 1904–1968. **Biography of Physics** (1961). One of the best by this notable physicist. It covers classical and modern physics with a masterly blend of exposition, anecdotes, and illustrations. *o.p.*

————. **Mr. Tompkins in Paperback** (1966). Modern physics as dreamed by Mr. Tompkins. Thoroughly delightful and solidly informative. *H & P—Cambridge U Pr*.

————. **Thirty Years That Shook Physics** (1966). Quantum theory explained with a minimum of mathematics and a maximum of clarity; contains many anecdotes, photographs, and biographical sketches, *o.p.*

HEISENBERG, WERNER 1901–1976. **Physics and Beyond** (1971). Heisenberg provides further insights into the giants of modern physics: Sommerfeld, Pauli, Bohr, Einstein, and Planck. He also explains what it was for him to be a German in Germany during World War II. *P—Har-Row*.

HOFFMANN, BANESH b. 1906 and HELEN DUKAS. **Albert Einstein** (1972). A touching and poignant biography for the general reader by one of Einstein's collaborators and his secretary. *P—NAL*.

KEVLES, DANIEL b.1939. **The Physicists** (1978). A critical history of the ascent of American physics. *H—Knopf*.

NICHOLSON, IAN. **Gravity, Black Holes and the Universe** (1981). An accurate, readable, popular treatment of modern cosmology. *H—Halsted Pr*.

PAIS, ABRAHAM b. 1918. **Subtle Is the Lord** (1982). Arguably the best of a number of excellent biographies of Albert Einstein. Includes a thorough summary of his work. *H & P—Oxford U Pr*.

RUSSELL, BERTRAND 1872–1970. **The ABC of Relativity** (3rd rev. ed. 1969). A popular account of the meaning and significance of relativity by a great mathematician and equally great philosopher. *P—NAL*.

VON BAEYER, HANS C. b. 1938. **Rainbows, Snowflakes and Quarks** (1984). Basic themes of physics exemplified in everyday phenomena and extended to current concepts. Informative and interesting. *H—McGraw*.

Chemistry

ASIMOV, ISAAC b. 1920. **Asimov on Chemistry** (1974). Entertaining and instructive essays on a variety of chemical topics. *H & P—Doubleday*.

CAGLIOTI, LUCIANO and MIRELLA GIACCONI. **The Two Faces of Chemistry** (1983). The positive and negative impacts of chemistry on modern society are critically examined. *H—MIT Pr*.

CASSIDY, HAROLD G. b. 1906. **Science Restated** (1970). Superior text for nonscientists; covers physics and chemistry from first principles to present complex status. *H—Freeman C*.

Chemistry and Crime (1983). Ed. Samuel M. Gerber. Entertaining exploration of the connection between crime writers such as Arthur Conan Doyle and Dorothy Sayers and modern forensic science. Argues that the techniques of fictional detectives have influenced modern analytical techniques. *H—Am Chemical*.

Chemistry and Modern Society (1983). Eds. John Parascandola and James C. Whorton. Wide-ranging glimpse of chemistry in 20th-century America. Geochemistry, drug therapy, synthetic fuels, and chemical warfare research are among the topics covered. *H & P—Am Chemical*.

FARBER, EDUARD b. 1892. **Milestones of Modern Chemistry** (1965). Collection of original papers describing the great discoveries of scientists ranging from Mendeleev to Bohr. *o.p.*

GARARD, IRA D. b. 1888. **Invitation to Chemistry** (1969). Instructive history from ancient origins to recent developments. *o.p.*

IHDE, AARON J. b. 1909. **The Development of Modern Chemistry** (1964). A comprehensive history of chemistry—well illustrated and with extensive and informative appendixes. Some knowledge of chemistry is needed. *P—Dover*.

MARK, HERMAN F. b. 1895. **Giant Molecules** (1966). Easy to understand, comprehensive, and lavishly illustrated introduction to a field of major importance by the man who made much of it happen. *o.p.*

PANETH, F. A. 1887–1958. **Chemistry and Beyond** (1964). Selected writings on chemical and philosophical topics by a great chemist—from alchemy through meteorites to Goethe and Kant. *o.p.*

Mathematics

ASIMOV, ISAAC b. 1920. **Asimov on Numbers** (1975). Easy and interesting reading; covers a range of mathematical topics. *P—PB*.

GUILLEN, MICHAEL. **Bridges to Infinity** (1984). Essays on major themes in modern mathematics; a clear and engrossing look at the mathematical imagination. *H & P—J P Tarcher*.

KLINE, MORRIS b. 1908. **Mathematical Thought from Ancient to Modern Times** (1972). Comprehensive and highly informative—sometimes difficult. *H—Oxford U Pr*.

KRAMER, EDNA E. b. 1902. **The Nature and Growth of Modern Mathematics** (1982). Comprehensive history and overview of modern mathematics; includes a useful biographical appendix. *H & P—Princeton U Pr*.

LIEBER, HUGH S. and LILLIAN L. LIEBER. **The Education of T. C. Mits** (rev. ed. 1970). Old but good. *P— Norton*.

MENDELSSOHN, KURT A. G. 1906–1980. **The Quest for Absolute Zero** (1966). An engaging historical account of the approach to absolute zero. Nonmathematical, this book clearly treats one of the physical limits. *P—Taylor & Francis*.

Precision Measurements and Fundamental Constants (1970). Eds. D. N. Langenberg and B. N. Taylor. A collection of papers given at the 1970 International Conference of the National Bureau of Standards, summarizing the consistent, basic constants of present-day science. Requires some mathematical sophistication. *o.p.*

RUCKER, RUDY. **The Fourth Dimension** (1984). Moves from flatland to hyperspace. Full of mind-stretching concepts and paradoxes. *H—HM*.

ULAM, STANISLAW M. 1909–1984. **Adventures of a Mathematician** (1976). The autobiography of a prodigy of our day, full of entertaining anecdotes about such giants as Von Neumann, Fermi, Gamow, and others. *P—Scribner*.

The World of Mathematics (1956). Ed. James R. Newman. A four-volume anthology of mathematical literature from the Greeks to modern times, compiled for both amateur and expert. *o.p.*

Geology

CALDER, NIGEL b. 1931. **The Restless Earth: A Report on the New Geology** (1972). A lucid, well-illustrated survey for the nonspecialist of theories concerning the earth's crust (plate tectonics, continental drift, formation of mountains and ocean basins) and the origin and evolution of life. *P—Penguin.*

GAMOW, GEORGE 1904–1968. **A Planet Called Earth** (1963). A clear, illuminating account of the earth's geological and biological history. *o.p.*

PARKER, DONALD B. **Inscrutable Earth** (1984). Essays of general interest on modern geology. *H—Scribner.*

Computer Science

Note: No attempt has been made to select programming guides for Basic, Pascal, Fortran, etc. There are a huge number available at every level from a host of publishers. Choice of a programming guide depends on the background of the reader, the computer used, and the potential application.

BEAR, JOHN b. 1938. **Computer Wimp** (1983). A great combination of "on the money" advice and engaging and humorous presentation. Bear covers the range of pitfalls faced by the PC owner—from purchase to upgrade to repair—and offers eminently useful solutions. Highly recommended. *H & P—Ten Speed Pr.*

BERNSTEIN, JEREMY b. 1929. **The Analytical Engine** (rev. ed. 1981). History of the development of the computer from Leibniz, Pascal, and Babbage to Von Neumann and the present age. Easy reading. *o.p.*

CASE, JOHN. **Digital Future** (1985). An intimate history of the development of personal computers, full of fascinating anecdotes and information. *H—Morrow.*

Computers and the World of the Future (1962). Ed. Martin Greenberger. The impact of computers on human endeavor as seen by Norbert Weiner, C. P. Snow, and many others. *o.p.*

CRICHTON, MICHAEL b. 1942. **Electronic Life: How to Think about Computers** (1983). Breezy, sensible, and interesting introduction—includes programs. *H—Knopf.*

DEKEN, JOSEPH. **The Electronic Cottage** (1981). An ambitious, successful examination of the present and future roles of the home computer. Lucid explanations of the principles of computer operation and programming are an estimable feature. *H—Morrow.*

EAMES, CHARLES 1907–1978 and RAY EAMES. **A Computer Perspective** (1973). A splendid, marvelously detailed and effective photographic history of the computer. The text and pictures are a seamless match. *H—Harvard U Pr.*

FEIGENBAUM, EDWARD A. and PAMELA McCORDUCK b. 1940. **The Fifth Generation** (1983). A searching look at Japan's effort to preempt the computer field. A thorough exposition of the background of the proposed artificial intelligence computer and of Japan's game plan for producing it is coupled with a warning of the consequences of American failure to compete. *H—A-W; P—NAL.*

GOLDSTINE, HERMAN b. 1913. **The Computer from Pascal to Von Neumann** (1980). A pioneer's informed picture of the development of modern computers. A detailed personal look at the beginning of the modern era. Read this with the Eames's *A Computer Perspective. H & P—Princeton U Pr.*

KIDDER, TRACY b. 1945. **The Soul of a New Machine** (1981). The compelling story of a group of whiz kids led by a charismatic genius and their struggle to create a superminicomputer for Data General. Their trials, triumph, and tragedy are superbly chronicled by a master at his craft. *H—Little, Thorndike Pr; P—Avon.*

MICK, COLIN K. and STEFAN T. POSSONY. **Working Smart** (1984). Excellent guide to personal computer hardware and software. Chock full of information on how they work and advice on what is needed for particular applications. *H—Macmillan.*

Science Fiction

Much good reading and some good science and provocative social thought can be found in science fiction. This edition of *Good Reading* omits a selective list of science fiction titles not because we undervalue either their general worth or their academic legitimacy (many colleges have already introduced a course of science fiction into the curriculum) but because the books rated as best are hard to determine with any degree of objectivity.

Science fiction reading buffs may well be the best source for books to start with. Or you might consult *Anatomy of Wonder: Science Fiction* (2nd ed. 1981, Bowker), a critically annotated guide to some 2,000 of the best adult and juvenile science fiction titles.

Without recommending "best titles" (which are much in dispute), we do recommend that you encounter at least the following novelists (who are recognized as masters of the genre). Each has written at least one science fiction masterpiece (and a few have written two or more) that is either good literature or sound science or usually both. If you choose to read science fiction, do not miss Isaac Asimov, Ray Bradbury, John Brunner, Arthur C. Clarke, Robert A. Heinlein, Aldous Huxley, Ursula LeGuin, Walter Miller, Larry Niven and Jerry Pournelle, Kurt Vonnegut, and H. G. Wells (one of the founders of the genre).

CHAPTER 30

Biological Sciences

STANLEY WECKER

. . . if the ultimate aim of the whole of science is, as I believe, to clarify man's relationship to the universe, then biology must be accorded a central position, since of all of the disciplines it is the one that endeavors to go to the heart of the problems that must be resolved before that of "human nature" can even be framed in other than metaphysical terms. Consequently, no other science has the same significance for man. . . .

— Jacques Monod, *Chance and Necessity*

Mindful of these words by the late biologist and Nobel Laureate Jacques Monod, the reader may wish to ponder these possible "resolutions" to some biological problems:

- Multiple choices of a human insulin gene are inserted into bacterial cells which become miniature insulin-producing "factories"—meeting the future needs of millions of diabetics.
- "What is life?" takes on new meaning as NASA's automated *Viking* spacecraft lands on the surface of Mars and conducts experiments to determine whether Mars nurtures primitive living organisms.
- Computer programs that model the movement of naturally occurring chemical substances through ecological systems may also suggest the path of toxic wastes and pollutants.
- Living mammalian embryos are removed from their natural mothers and transplanted into the uteri of surrogate females of *different* species. The results—a horse gives birth to a zebra; one species of monkey delivers a normal offspring of another.

373

- The discovery of cancer-initiating "oncogenes" in most normal cells leads researchers to hope that mechanisms triggering the malignant process may soon be revealed.
- More complete fossil evidence spurs a new understanding of the pace and mode of evolutionary change—and inadvertently fuels a controversy about creation versus evolution.

What do these apparently unrelated "resolutions" have in common? They are not possibilities but realities, not science fiction but scientific events of the past decade. And they represent only a minute sampling of the multiple activities engaging the time and energy of today's biologists. Not since the downfall of classical physics at the beginning of the 20th century has a revolution of like intensity swept through a modern science.

Diversity enriches contemporary biological systems at every level. Biologists study the properties of matter in more forms than do their counterparts in the physical sciences. Molecules, cells, tissues, organs and organ systems, individual organisms, populations, communities, ecosystems, the entire biosphere, even the potential existence of life on other planets—all fall within the scope of contemporary biology. Each of these levels can be organized variously, giving rise to an impressive array of biological disciplines, among them molecular biology, cytology (the study of cells), cell physiology, cytogenetics (heredity), histology (the study of tissues), anatomy, physiology, developmental biology, genetics, ecology, taxonomy (classification), and evolution.

To compound the complexity, the more than two million species of living organisms occupy five different kingdoms: Monera (bacteria), Protista (one-celled organisms having characteristics found in both plants and animals), Fungi, Plantae, and Animalia—an additional order of diversity that permits yet another approach to biology: taxonomic fields of study. This plethora of "-ologies," moreover, is pursued by a host of special "-ists": virologists, bacteriologists, protozoologists, algologists (algae), mycologists (fungi), botanists, entomologists (insects), malacologists (mollusks), herpetologists (snakes), ornithologists, mammalogists, and the like. And since the boundaries *between* biology and the physical sciences are often indeterminate, add those biologists who follow truly interdisciplinary careers as biophysicists, biochemists, biometrists, paleoecologists (studying environmental systems of the past), and exobiologists (studying the potential for life elsewhere in the universe).

The by-products of scientific revolutions are not limited to new areas of knowledge arising from basic research, however, and the current ferment in biology is no exception to this general rule. Even as modern physics ultimately produced a catalog of useful products (television, transistors, personal computers, semiconductors, and, some may argue, nuclear power plants), the initial applications of biotechnology, as we learned at the outset, are now being realized.

But there is an important difference. Because biology is unique in its concern with *living* entities, it has always engaged our interest in a most special way. This distinctive focus upon life does not imply renewed support for those long-discarded "vitalistic" theories that hold that life is qualitatively different from the universal laws of nature necessary to order and understand the physical world. Nor (creationists to the contrary) can any science legitimately deduce its laws from any account of a supreme being. What biology urges, rather, is that we take pleasure in the color, form, and movement of nature, that we grow aware of natural diversity and beauty, and that, as living creatures ourselves, we cherish our special relationship with the nonhuman fellow travelers on our fragile planet.

Just as the daffodils, skylarks, and white whales of earlier times inspired Wordsworth, Shelley, and Melville, the new biology has shaped a different kind of literary figure—the practicing scientist dedicated to rendering his world intelligible to the educated layperson. A few of them merit special attention here: the incredibly prolific Isaac Asimov (more than 300 books); the witty, incisive authors and columnists Stephen Jay Gould (*Natural History Magazine*) and Lewis Thomas (*The New England Journal of Medicine*); and the late microbiologist and Pulitzer Prize–winning humanist, René Dubos. Others have emerged from their laboratories as television personalities. As Thoreau, Burroughs, and Muir introduced earlier generations to the wonders of the natural world, so Jacob Bronowski, Jonathan Miller, Carl Sagan, and David Attenborough have aroused public interest in science with such remarkable television series as "The Ascent of Man," "The Body in Question," "Cosmos," "Life on Earth," and "The Living Planet."

A growing number of highly esteemed science writers, often in collaboration with scientists, have focused on the more controversial areas of biology, areas in which deep-seated philosophical differences and moral dilemmas abound. The reading list that follows reflects the explosive increase in the number of books about such topics: the conflict between evolution and creationism; the bitter, often politicized debates about sociobiology; the threat of environmental degradation linked with population growth, depletion of resources, pollution, and the like; and, more recently, the debate about recombinant DNA technology, the ethical consequences of tinkering with the master molecule from which both genes and dreams are fashioned.

Few people realize that at least 80 percent of *all* the scientific papers *ever* published have appeared during the past forty years— most of them in an ever-expanding number of scientific journals. Good reading is available here too for interested nonspecialists from a broad range of popular and semipopular monthly and bimonthly magazines: *Natural History, National Geographic, Smithsonian, Audubon, Environment, The Sciences, Scientific American, American Scientist, Bioscience, Science Digest, Science '85,* and *Discover* (the science version of *Time* magazine). Good science and good reading are not mutually exclusive. Were he still alive, C. P. Snow, the scientist and novelist who warned of the growing dichotomy between the "two cultures," would have been pleased at this development.

A final cautionary word may be in order: The primary goal of this diverse bibliography is more than entertainment. To be ignorant of or indifferent to the scientific and technological revolutions that chart the future course of biological research would be tragic. We must be informed and alert to monitor the use and application of biotechnology as well as to assure the freedom of the scientific community from undue social and political pressure.

ASIMOV, ISAAC b. 1920. **Asimov's New Guide to Science** (rev. ed. 1984). One of the more recent of this prolific author's 300-plus books, this comprehensive work covers most of the major topics in science in a logical order. Almost half deals with biological subjects, and Asimov has few equals in making technical concepts understandable to laypersons. *H—Basic*.

ATTENBOROUGH, DAVID b. 1926. **Discovering Life on Earth** (1982). Like the BBC television series broadcast on PBS, the book offers a dynamic and epochal history of nature—from the origin of life to the emergence of human beings. *H—Little*.

————. **The Living Planet: A Portrait of the Earth** (1985). A virtual geography of life, this book, the inspiration for the PBS television series, ranges from tropics to tundra and from ocean depths to mountaintops while exploring the strategies different species use to survive. *H—Little*.

BASKIN, YVONNE. **The Gene Doctors: Medical Genetics at the Frontier** (1984). The wide range of biomedical applications of the recent advances in molecular genetics are described in this nontechnical introduction, with consideration also given to the ethical implications of the new procedures. *H—Morrow*.

CARR, ARCHIE b. 1909. **So Excellent a Fishe: Tales of Sea Turtles** (1984). The remarkable story of how an air-breathing creature navigates 1,400 miles of open ocean without apparent landmarks to seek its birthplace. *H—Scribner*.

CARSON, RACHEL 1907-1964. **The Sea Around Us** (1951). A sensitive, gracefully written account of the origin, history, and dynamics of the sea by the very first editor of this *Good Reading* chapter on Biological Sciences. *H—Oxford U Pr; P—NAL*.

————. **Silent Spring** (1962). The toxic effects of DDT and other pesticides have been well documented since, but this seminal volume did more to launch the environmental movement than any other single work before or after. *H—HM; P—Fawcett*.

CHERFAS, JEREMY. **Man-Made Life: An Overview of the Science, Technology and Commerce of Genetic Engineering** (1982). A useful overview of a rapidly expanding field, which will give the reader an understanding of both the relevant basic science and the specialized techniques involved. *H—Pantheon*.

CHRISPEELS, MAARTEN b. 1938 and DAVID SADAVA. **Plants, Food, and People** (1977). Given the severe famines in parts of Africa and the general challenge of sustaining a burgeoning human population, this highly readable little book tells succinctly what plants are and how they function. *H & P—WH Freeman*.

COLINVAUX, PAUL b. 1930. **Why Big Fierce Animals Are Rare: An Ecologist's Perspective** (1978). Readers will welcome this lively serving of modern ecology's central ideas. Written in a clear, attractive style, each chapter explores a different theme, beginning with a paradox and ending with a report on the current status of our knowledge. *H & P—Princeton U Pr*.

DAWKINS, RICHARD b. 1941. **The Selfish Gene** (1976). A nontechnical exposition that extends evolutionary theory into such social areas as altruistic and selfish behavior, aggression, and the natural history of sex differences. *P—Oxford U Pr*.

DETHIER, VINCENT G. b. 1915. **To Know a Fly** (1963). Makes the study of the housefly a humorous, personal, and fascinating adventure. *P—Holden-Day*.

DUBOS, RENÉ 1901–1982. **So Human an Animal** (1968). A Pulitzer Prize–winning effort by an eminent microbiologist who is philosophically concerned with a variety of dilemmas relating to the human condition. This particular work centers on problems associated with life in a technological society, but unlike others who have echoed this theme, Dubos offers an optimistic prescription for a hopeful future. *P—Scribner*.

————. **The Wooing of Earth** (1980). Here (after several volumes in the intervening years) Dubos' focus is on man's relationship to nature from a broad historical and biological perspective. o.p.

EHRLICH, PAUL b. 1932 and ANNE EHRLICH b. 1933. **Extinction: The Causes and Consequences of the Disappearing of Species** (1981). A strong argument that maintaining the diversity of life on an increasingly crowded planet is in nature's best interest and our own as well. *H—Random; P—Ballantine*.

ERRINGTON, PAUL 1902–1962. **Of Predation and Life** (1967). Based on a lifetime of research, this work dispels a number of widely held beliefs about the relationships between predators and their prey. *P—Iowa St U Pr*.

FUTUYMA, DOUGLAS J. b. 1942. **Science on Trial: The Case for Evolution** (1982). Both a well-documented survey of the evidence for evolution and a rebuttal of modern creationist views, this enjoyable book is a must for anyone interested in the full dimensions of the current controversy. *H & P— Pantheon*.

GOULD, STEPHEN JAY b. 1941. **Ever Since Darwin: Reflections in Natural History** (1977). This compendium of essays gleaned from the author's monthly columns in *Natural History Magazine* is a remarkable tour de force and aptly illustrates why Gould is considered to be one of the most creative and popular of all modern science writers. In topics ranging from race, sex, and violence to the life and times of Charles Darwin, these essays are models of clarity and wit, and the insights generated will well reward even the most casual of readers. Enjoy! *H & P—Norton*.

————. **The Panda's Thumb: More Reflections in Natural History** (1980). *H & P—Norton*.

————. **The Mismeasure of Man** (1981). A documentation of the historical and contemporary misuse of biology to justify notions of racial inferiority, this widely acclaimed book explores some of the saddest and more bizzare chapters in the history of science. *H & P—Norton.*

————. **Hen's Teeth and Horse's Toes: Further Reflections in Natural History** (1983). *H & P—Norton.*

GRANT, SUSAN. **Beauty and the Beast: The Coevolution of Plants and Animals** (1984). Plants and animals interact in a variety of ways and this fascinating little book describes the adaptive strategies involved. *H—Scribner.*

GRIBBON, JOHN and JEREMY CHERFAS. **The Monkey Puzzle: Reshaping the Evolutionary Tree** (1982). The authors argue for a new view of human evolution, basing their case on information drawn from a wide variety of scientific fields. *H—Pantheon; P—McGraw.*

HARDIN, GARRETT b. 1915. **Nature and Man's Fate** (1959). Beginning with a historical account of the development of Darwin's theory and the debate that followed its publication, this versatile interpreter of biological thought goes on to speculate about the human future in light of the knowledge of genetics and heredity developed in the first half of the 20th century. *o.p.*

HARSANYI, ZSOLT b. 1944 and RICHARD HUTTON b. 1949. **Genetic Prophecy: Beyond the Double Helix** (1981). This timely book describes both the revolutionary benefits and the ethical dilemmas of genetic forecasting, which has the capacity to predict human health and behavior. *H—Rawson Assocs.*

HEINRICH, BERND b. 1940. **Bumblebee Economics** (1979). A brilliant introduction to insect and plant relationships that uses references to Adam Smith to focus on the management of energy resources by one of nature's most adaptive creatures. *H & P—Harvard U Pr.*

JOHANSON, DONALD b. 1943 and MAITLAND EDEY b. 1910. **Lucy: The Beginnings of Humankind** (1981). The story of the dramatic discovery of our oldest fossil ancestor and the controversial change it makes in our view of human origins. (See LEAKEY, following, for a different version of our family tree.) *P—Warner Bks.*

JUDSON, HORACE FREELAND b. 1931. **The Eighth Day of Creation: Makers of the Revolution in Biology** (1979). This highly acclaimed historical account of the course of molecular biology tells the story of the discoveries and of the remarkable people who made them. *H—S&S.*

KAVALER, LUCY b. 1930. **Mushrooms, Molds, and Miracles** (1965). The mythology, natural history, and human importance of fungi, captivatingly recounted. *o.p.*

KELLER, EVELYN FOX b. 1936. **A Feeling for the Organism: The Life and Work of Barbara McClintock** (1983). The story of a life dedicated to science made even more compelling because the subject is a woman, because her work was only belatedly recognized, and because she recently became a Nobel laureate. *H & P—WH Freeman.*

KITCHER, PHILIP b. 1947. **Abusing Science: The Case Against Creationism** (1982). The arguments set forth here utilize both biological evidence and a philosopher's knowledge of the nature of science itself to refute the "scientific" claims of contemporary creationists. *H & P—MIT Pr.*

KONNER, MELVIN b. 1946. **The Tangled Wing: Biological Constraints on the Human Spirit** (1982). Remarkably free from ideology and dogmatism, this important book synthesizes the extraordinary accumulation of knowledge that has enlarged our insight into the biological basis of human behavior and emotions. *H—HR&W; P—Har-Row.*

KOREY, KENNETH. **The Essential Darwin** (1984). The first in the Masters of Modern Science series (Robert Jastrow, ed.), this volume combines stimulating, interpretive commentary and selections from Darwin's major works. *H & P—Little.*

KRUTCH, JOSEPH WOOD 1893–1970. **The Twelve Seasons** (1949). Many have written well about the country year but few with more deliberate dedication to the biological in nature than this literary critic and professor of English. *H—Ayer Co.*

LAYCOCK, GEORGE b. 1921. **The Alien Animals: The Story of Imported Wildlife** (1966). While the pitfalls in this game of wildlife roulette are many and the sources few, the efforts to introduce "foreign" animals continue. This account of the process includes some of the most remarkable tales in natural history. *o.p.*

LEAKEY, RICHARD b. 1944 and ROGER LEWIN. **Origins** (1977). Disputing the view that aggression is rooted in our genes, this handsomely illustrated volume describes the biological and cultural determinants that shaped the course of human evolution. (See Johanson above for a somewhat different view of our family tree.) *P—Dutton.*

LORENZ, KONRAD Z. b.1903. **King Solomon's Ring** (1952). A delightful, pioneering introduction to animal behavior by a

Nobel laureate who represents an ethological point of view emphasizing genetic determinance. *P—Har-Row, NAL*.

————. **On Aggression** (1966). Aggression is presented as an essential part of the social life of animals, and its purported role in the evolution and development of human behavior is forcefully argued. *P—HarBraceJ*.

MATTHIESSEN, PETER b. 1927. **The Tree Where Man Was Born** (1983). A magnificent portrait of past and present relationships of the humans and animals that have lived together on the East African plain for countless eons. This perceptive, award-winning author is one of the finest and most prolific of the contemporary nature writers. *P—Dutton*.

MEDAWAR, PETER B. b. 1915 and JEAN S. MEDAWAR. **The Life Science: Current Ideas in Biology** (1977). While some of its specific content is unavoidably dated, this slender, highly readable work by a Nobel laureate and his equally well-known wife nevertheless identifies and explores many of the major frontiers of biological knowledge. *H—Har-Row*.

MILLER, JONATHAN b. 1934. **The Body in Question** (1979). A historical account of the major discoveries pertaining to the normal functioning of the human body, this highly entertaining and informative work is a companion volume to the popular BBC television series of the same title. *H & P—Random*.

MONOD, JACQUES 1910–1976. **Chance and Necessity: An Essay on the Natural Philosophy of Modern Biology** (1971). The outstanding French biochemist and Nobel Prize winner sweeps away the "animist" conception of man that has dominated virtually all Western world views. Drawing on contemporary genetic principles to deny the concepts of destiny and evolutionary purpose, he suggests an entirely new way of looking at ourselves. *P—Random*.

MOSS, CYNTHIA b. 1940. **Portraits in the Wild: Animal Behavior in East Africa** (2nd ed. 1982). With a major focus on the recent findings of her own research on elephants and an updated account of the plight of the highly endangered black rhino, the hidden lives of 15 species of African mammals are revealed. Especially recommended for all who have visited or hope to visit this unique area. *P—U of Chicago Pr*.

RESTAK, RICHARD b. 1942. **The Brain** (1984). Complete with more than 150 full color and black-and-white illustrations, this engrossing account captures the excitement of the acclaimed PBS television series of the same name. *P—Bantam*.

SAGAN, CARL b. 1934. **The Dragons of Eden** (1977). The

award-winning author and astronomer's account of how we evolved, how our brains and those of other animals work, and why intelligent beings from other worlds will be sufficiently like us to permit interstellar communication. *H—Random; P—Ballantine*.

SAYRE, ANNE b. 1923. **Rosalind Franklin and DNA** (1975). While Rosalind Franklin's work contributed substantially to the discovery of the molecular structure of DNA, she received virtually no credit during her lifetime. This controversial book provides both an absorbing scientific drama and an intimate view of what it's like to be a gifted woman in a male-dominated profession. *H & P—Norton*.

SCHALLER, GEORGE B. b. 1933. **The Year of the Gorilla** (1964). One of the most insightful modern studies of the great apes by a devoted and accurate reporter who literally lives unarmed with his various animal subjects in their wild domain; full of pleasant writing, appealing drawings, and peaceful beasts. *H & P—U of Chicago Pr*.

————. **The Deer and the Tiger** (1967). A unique account of the relationship between this highly endangered cat and its major prey species. It is at the same time an eloquent plea for wildlife management and conservation. *P—U of Chicago Pr*.

SCIENTIFIC AMERICAN LIBRARY. An undertaking of breath-taking proportions, with magnificently illustrated texts by some of the foremost scientists of our time. Thirteen volumes on selected topics in the natural sciences have already been produced (by mid-1985) with others to follow. Of special interest biologically are Richard Lewontin's **Human Diversity** (1982), Thomas A. McMahon and John Tyler Bonner's **On Size and Life** (1983), and Christian de Duve's two-volume **A Guided Tour of the Living Cell** (1984). *H—WH Freeman*.

SHEPARD, PAUL b. 1925. **The Tender Carnivore and the Sacred Game** (1973). A free-ranging commentary on human behavior and ecology in light of our hunting past. The author advocates a blueprint for the future that integrates the desirable qualities of hunter-gatherer existence and the rapid pace of modern life. *o.p.*

SPARKS, JOHN b. 1939. **The Discovery of Animal Behavior** (1982). A biological detective story, this companion volume to the PBS television series reviews the investigations of animal nature from medieval times to the present. *H—Little*.

STANLEY, STEVEN M. b. 1941. **The New Evolutionary**

Timetable: Fossils, Genes, and the Origin of Species (1981). The heated debates taking place in evolutionary circles revolve around the tempo of evolutionary change. If the new ideas advanced in this nontechnical account are correct, we shall have to rethink our traditional views of the ascent of man and the balance of nature. *P—Basic*.

TAYLOR, GORDON RATTRAY 1911–1981. **The Great Evolution Mystery** (1983). This alternate selection of the Book-of-the-Month Club describes the major noncreationist objections to some of Darwin's basic ideas and reviews alternative explanations in the light of knowledge derived from a number of scientific fields. *H—Har-Row*.

THOMAS, LEWIS b. 1913. **The Lives of a Cell: Notes of a Biology Watcher** (1974). A delightful little book by one of America's most accomplished physicians and medical researchers, making it clear why the author is one of our most gifted science writers. The essays, gleaned from Dr. Thomas's columns in the prestigious *New England Journal of Medicine*, reflect on a wide variety of topics and open up a universe of knowledge and perception that cannot fail to provide the reader with a new vision of humankind and the world around us. *H—Viking Pr; P—Bantam, Penguin*.

————. **The Medusa and the Snail: More Notes of a Biology Watcher** (1979). *H—Viking Pr*.

TIPPO, OSWALD b. 1911 and WILLIAM LOUIS STERN b. 1926. **Humanistic Botany** (1977). For the many readers interested in botany, this nontechnical text covers all of the essential features of plant form and function and describes the ways plants interact with and are used by people. *H—Norton*.

VAN LAWICK-GOODALL, JANE b. 1934. **My Friends the Wild Chimpanzees** (1967). A charming and informative book narrates the challenges and rewards of years of painstaking field observations of man's closest primate relatives. *o.p.*

WATSON, JAMES b. 1928. **The Double Helix** (1968). An insider's revealing account of the discovery of the molecular structure of DNA and the race to win the Nobel Prize. *H—Atheneum; P—NAL, Norton*.

WILSON, EDWARD O. b. 1929. **On Human Nature** (1978). An extension of the ideas set forth in his highly controversial book *Sociobiology*, Wilson's goal is to apply biological thought to social sciences and humanities in a manner that avoids the social Darwinist legacy of the last century. Many will disagree, but the controversy is still with us and both sides deserve to be read. *H—Harvard U Pr; P—Bantam*.

ZINSSER, HANS 1878–1940. **Rats, Lice, and History** (1935). A masterful account of the role played by mammals and insects in spreading a human disease that affected the course of history. Still a classic in its field. *H—Little*.

A Note About Ecology and the Environment

Increasing knowledge about depleted natural resources (the near extinction of certain mammal, bird, and fish species) and the widespread pollution of air and water has compelled awareness of the counterproductive results of the Faustian will to dominate and exploit the environment. Most of the books cited here have identified ecological and environmental problems and suggested social and political programs as resolutions. Some, however, argue that practical approaches have failed and urge instead pursuit of philosophical and spiritual insights such as are offered by "ecosophy," a term blending the physical environment ("eco") and wisdom ("sophia").

For the materials that follow, we acknowledge the work of Professors George Sessions and Paul Shepard.

BROWN, LESTER b. 1934 et al. **The State of the World 1985** (1985). An annual publication of the Worldwatch Institute that uses many information sources to monitor changes in global resources and the factors that affect environmental quality. *H & P—Norton*.

CLAPHAM, WENTWORTH B. b. 1942. **Natural Ecosystems** (2nd ed. 1983) and **Human Ecosystems** (1981). A valuable two-volume work, the first of which reviews basic ecological principles, which the second uses to provide an understanding of the interplay of ecological factors and social forces that shape human relationships with the natural environment. *P—Macmillan*.

COLINVAUX. **Why Big Fierce Animals Are Rare.** See "Bilogical Sciences," page 377.

COMMONER, BARRY b. 1917. **The Closing Circle** (1973). Close to a definitive study of ecology and its relationship to modern industrial civilization. A primer for those interested in the options open in the struggle for a livable world. *H—Beekman Pubs*.

DEVALL, WILLIAM and GEORGE SESSIONS. **Deep Ecology** (1985). An overview of the contemporary environmental movement and a discussion of Arne Naess's principles of deep ecology and "ecosophy," together with the historical sources of ecosophy. Suggestions for direct ecological action and ways of life are forwarded. *H—Gibbs M Smith*.

GUPTE, PRANAY. **The Crowded Earth: People and the Politics of Population** (1984). A former foreign correspondent for the *New York Times* visits five continents on a UN-sponsored journey to explore the present and potential effects of continued (although slower) world population growth. *H—Norton*.

MILLER, GEORGE TYLER b. 1902. **Living in the Environment** (1983). An outstanding textbook in ecological principles and environmental problems that argues that we must move away from industrial society to deep ecological, sustainable earth futures. *H—Wadsworth Pub*.

SHEPARD, PAUL b. 1925. **Nature and Madness** (1982). Shepard argues that there is a "normal ontogeny" for childhood development. Modern industrial society fails to provide childhood rituals for bonding to wild nature. The resulting alienation from nature lies at the basis of contemporary environmental destruction. *H—Sierra*.

————. **The Tender Carnivore and the Sacred Game.** See page 382.

WORSTER, DONALD b. 1941. **Nature's Economy** (1984). A leading environmental historian traces the development of ecology since the 17th century. He discusses Gilbert White, Darwin, Thoreau, and Leopold, among others, and concludes with a chapter on ecology and ecophilosophy. *H & P—Cambridge U Pr*.

PART VI

Special Section

PART VI

Special Section

Summary

I: General Bibliographies and Indexes

II: General Encyclopedias

III: Fact Books (almanacs)

IV: Atlases and Gazetteers

V: Dictionaries
> English language: *unabridged; desk; etymology; synonyms; usage; slang*
> foreign languages

VI: General Biographical Collections
> collections: *current: U.S. and world; historical: U.S. and world*
> bibliography

VII: Literature
> encyclopedias: *general, drama and poetry; American, English, classical and European*
> quotations
> histories: U.S. and English
> bibliography

VIII: The Arts
> encyclopedias: *general, architecture, decorative arts, photography*
> bibliography

IX: The Performing Arts
> encyclopedias: *theater, film, music, jazz, opera, dance, ballet*
> bibliography

X: Philosophy, Religion, and Folklore
> encyclopedias: *philosophy, religion, bible, folklore, mythology*
> bibliography

XI: History
> World and U.S.; *encyclopedias, chronologies, surveys, atlases*
> bibliography

XII: The Social Sciences
> encyclopedias: *general, anthropology, business and economics, politics and government, psychology, sociology*
> statistics
> bibliography

XIII: The Sciences and Technology
> encyclopedias: *general, astronomy, biology, geology, computers*
> bibliography

CHAPTER 31

Reference Books

GEORGE N. THOMPSON

What Is a Reference Book?

Knowledge is of two kinds: we know a subject ourselves, or we know where we can find information on it.—Samuel Johnson, 1709–1784, English writer and scholar (see page 50)

A reference book is one we consult whenever we need to know a fact, an explanation of an idea or theory, or the history of an event or biography of a person. Some reference books are an end in themselves, like an encyclopedia, atlas, or biographical collection, whereas others are only the first step in the process of solving our problem, like a bibliography, which tells us what books or periodical articles discuss a subject we are interested in.

All reference books are designed to suit the needs of a special class of reader. Sometimes what is special about the reader is that there is nothing special about his or her interests or background, but often, however, the reader is assumed to have some special interest, training, or experience in the subject that the book covers, and the compilers will refer to basic concepts and use technical terms without explanation. To someone with such an interest, the entry in a general reference book may seem superficial; but a specialized book may be too difficult for a beginner to use. Books of both sorts are cited in the sections that follow.

To illustrate the variety of reference books, suppose we want some information on an artist—Michelangelo, for instance. If all we want is the year of his death, that fact (but little more) is in the biography section of **Webster's Ninth New Collegiate Dictionary** (*Merriam-Webster Inc.*). There is a paragraph on his life and achievements in the **Webster's New Biographical Dictionary** (*Merriman-Webster Inc.*), and a longer entry, but still one to be measured in paragraphs, in **The New Columbia Encyclopedia** (*Columbia U Pr*). **The New Encyclopaedia Britannica's** (Ency Brit Ed) article is more than five pages, whereas the **Encyclopedia of World Art** (*Jack Heraty*) has twenty-six pages, with many illustrations. If we want to know the current interpretations of some aspect of his work, and to consider the facts and arguments various scholars have offered to support their opinions, then we will probably turn to **Art Index** (*Wilson*) to be directed to articles that have been published in the major art periodicals. When we read the articles in the encyclopedias and magazines, we may want to have a basic dictionary of critical terms handy, such as **The Penguin Dictionary of Art and Artists** (*Penguin*).

Because the listings that follow can mention only a sampling of the many useful reference books found in even a public library or a small college library, it is generally useful to discuss our research problems with a librarian.

I: General Bibliographies and Indexes

A bibliography is a list of books or of books and periodical articles. An index lists the contents of certain periodicals, usually by subject. When a periodical article is cited, the name of the author and the title of the article are given, as well as the name of the journal where it was published, with the exact date and page. If a summary of the article is also given, that is called an *abstract*.

Books in Print (*Bowker;* called **BIP**) lists the books currently available from U.S. publishers by author and title. It is supplemented by **Subject Guide to Books in Print** (*Bowker*) and kept up to date by **Forthcoming Books** (*Bowker*).

The catalog of a college or public library is a kind of bibliography. The **National Union Catalog** (*Rowman & Allanheld;* called **NUC**) not only is a catalog of the books in the Library of Congress but also lists the books reported to the Library of Congress by libraries all across the United States and Canada. The **Union List of Serials** (*Wilson*) and **New Serial Titles** (*Bowker*) together do a similar job for periodicals.

The **Reader's Guide to Periodical Literature** (*Wilson*, from 1900) is an index to about 170 of the periodicals most likely to be found in public libraries. **Magazine Index** (*Information Access Co.*) covers hundreds of similar magazines for the most recent five years. **Humanities Index** (*Wilson*, from 1974) covers about 300 of the major academic and professional journals in a number of the fields of the arts and humanities. A companion index is **Social Sciences Index** (*Wilson*, from 1974). Between 1965 and 1974 both were part of **Social Sciences and Humanities Index**, which, in turn, had been called **International Index** from 1916 to 1965. Essays in selected books, particularly in the humanities, are indexed in **Essay and General Literature Index** (*Wilson*, from 1900).

Public Affairs Information Service Bulletin (the *Service*, from 1915; called **PAIS**) is a very useful index to articles, books, pamphlets, and government publications on current issues. The **New York Times Index** (*New York Times*) covers the paper from its founding in 1851. In addition, for recent years there are indexes available to the *Washington Post*, *The Christian Science Monitor*, and the *Wall Street Journal*, as well as a few major regional papers.

Book reviews in mainly popular magazines are indexed in **Book Review Digest** (*Wilson*, from 1905), which also usually quotes briefly from the review. More searching reviews from cultural, academic, and professional magazines can be found through **Index to Book Reviews in the Humanities** (*Thomson*, from 1960). In addition, for recent years, **Humanities Index** (*Wilson*) offers a supplement listing reviews in the periodicals it covers, as do **Social Sciences Index** (*Wilson*) and **Readers' Guide to Periodical Literature** (*Wilson*).

The **Guide to Reference Books** (9th ed., *ALA*, 1976), with its supplements, is extensive and well annotated. **Where to Find What** (*Scarecrow*, 1984) is much less complete but is up to date and conveniently arranged. **The New Library Key** (3rd ed., *Wilson*, 1975) is a self-teaching manual to all aspects of library use and research.

II: General Encyclopedias

The standard general encyclopedias are **The New Encyclopaedia Britannica** (15th ed., 30 vols., *Ency Brit Inc.*, 1980), **The**

Encyclopedia Americana (30 vols., *Grolier Ed Corp*, 1984), and *The World Book Encyclopedia* (22 vols., *World Bk*, 1984). Recent editions of the *Britannica* have been in three major sections: a **Propaedia,** or outline of knowledge (1 vol.): a **Macropaedia** (19 vols.), which has long articles on major subjects, including people; and a **Micropaedia** (10 vols.), which has brief entries on people, places, events, literary works, animals, plants, etc., and definitions of technical terms in many areas. All of the entries in the *Macropaedia* are summarized in the *Micropaedia*. The *Americana* is arranged in a single sequence, and although a number of the very specific topics covered in the *Britannica's Micropaedia* are not found in the *Americana*, the range of the two encyclopedias and the length of their entries are, in general, similar. The *World Book* is aimed at young adults.

The New Columbia Encyclopedia (4th ed., *Columbia V Pr*, 1975) is a one-volume encyclopedia that offers brief, clear articles on a remarkable range of topics. **The Concise Columbia Encyclopedia** (*Columbia U Pr*, 1983) is greatly abridged but also updated. The **New Century Cyclopedia of Names** (3 vols., *P. H*, 1954) is a useful handbook of people, places, events, literary works and characters, and mythological and biblical figures.

III: Fact Books

Both **The World Almanac** (*Newspaper Enterprise Assn*, from 1868) and **Information Please Almanac** (*S&S*, from 1947) give a wide range of statistics and other facts on the United States, the world, and indeed the universe, and embrace numerous diverse lists—boxing champions, train wrecks, colleges, skyscrapers, space flights, etc.

IV: Atlases and Gazetteers

The most expensive atlases have large pages, permitting very detailed maps, and usually a large section of information on geological, historical, social, and economic topics, illustrated with diagrams, charts, graphs, pictures, and, of course, maps.

Inexpensive atlases from the same publishers have smaller and fewer maps and may include less supplemental information. But if these inexpensive atlases are less informative, they are still useful and certainly easier to handle and shelve.

Among the large atlases are **The Times Atlas of the World: Comprehensive Edition** (2nd rev. ed., *Times Bks*, 1984), **The New International Atlas** (*Rand*, 1982), **Prentice-Hall Great International Atlas** (*P-H*, 1981), and **Hammond Medallion World Atlas** (*Hammond Inc*, 1984). *The Times Atlas* has more, larger, and more detailed maps than the others. *The New International* stresses regions that are population centers or are economically important. The *Great International* devotes more pages to charting the world's environment and economy than the others. Only the *Hammond Medallion* maps each state of the United States on a separate page, with population and other data on the facing page.

The Prentice-Hall New World Atlas (*P-H*, 1984), the **Hammond Citation World Atlas** (*Hammond Inc*, 1982), **The New Rand McNally College World Atlas** (*Rand*, 1985), and Rand McNally's **Goode's World Atlas** (16th ed., *Rand*, 1982) are all good home atlases. Other atlases, like the **New York Times Atlas of the World** (2nd rev. ed., *Times Bks*, 1983) and **Ambassador World Atlas** (*Hammond Inc*, 1982) are intermediate in scope and price.

All of these atlases naturally concentrate on the land areas of the earth. **The Times Atlas of the Oceans** (*Van Nos Reinhold*, 1983) covers the environmental and economic aspects of the oceans and ocean floor, with maps, graphs, illustrations, and text. Both Hammond and Rand McNally also produce globes.

Webster's New Geographical Dictionary (*Merriam-Webster Inc.*, 1984) gives short entries on countries, towns, and geographic features such as rivers and mountains. The entries in **The Columbia-Lippincott Gazetteer of the World** (*Columbia U Pr*, 1962) are longer, often including historical information and noting landmarks. **The Worldmark Encyclopedia of the Nations** (6th ed., *Wiley*, 1984) is in five volumes, by region, and gives basic social, political, economic, and environmental data.

V: Dictionaries

Webster's Third New International Dictionary of the English Language (*Merriam-Webster Inc*, 1961) is the best of the large (unabridged) one-volume dictionaries. Recent printings have had a sizable supplement of new words and meanings. An expanded version of this supplement is also published separately (**9000 Words,** *Merriam-Webster Inc,* 1983). The current printing (1983) of **Webster's New Twentieth Century Dictionary of the English Language** (*S&S,* 1966) includes a few words added since earlier printings, but unlike *Webster's Third,* it usually lists synonymous words without discriminating and some of the illustrations are murky. The **Random House Dictionary of the English Language** (unabridged ed., *Random,* 1966) is also a lesser choice.

The largest of all English dictionaries is the **Oxford English Dictionary** (13 vols., *Oxford U Pr,* 1888–1933; called *OED*). It traces the history and meaning of words in English from their earliest recorded use, showing how they have changed and developed. A *Supplement* includes 20th-century changes (3 vols., of 4 expected, *Oxford U Pr,* 1972–   ). Both the **Dictionary of American English on Historical Principles** (4 vols., *U of Chicago Pr,* 1936–44) and **A Dictionary of Americanisms on Historical Principles** (2 vols, *U of Chicago Pr,* 1951) track the history of distinctively American words and phrases.

An etymological dictionary concentrates on the history of words themselves, rather than meanings, indicating the language from which each word in English was borrowed, and may carry the history back through several previous languages. **The Oxford Dictionary of English Etymology** (*Oxford U Pr,* 1966) supplements and revises the etymologies given in the *Oxford English Dictionary.* **Origins: A Short Etymological Dictionary of Modern English** (4th ed., *Macmillan,* 1966, o.p.) is also useful.

Among smaller dictionaries ("desk" or "college" dictionaries), the **Webster's Ninth New Collegiate Dictionary** (*Merriam-Webster Inc,* 1983) is the most recently revised, and the 1984 printing even includes some minor corrections. Both it and the **Webster's New World Dictionary of the American Language** (2nd college ed., *S&S,* 1982) are well illustrated, and offer annotated lists of synonymous words, along with entries on notable people, places, and literary characters.

The entries in **Webster's New Dictionary of Synonyms** (*Merriam-Webster Inc,* 1984) are brief, useful essays clarifying the subtle differences in meaning and connotation among synonymous words. Less precise is **Roget's International Thesaurus** (4th ed., *TY Crowell,* 1977) which groups sets of synonyms logically, under broad categories.

The Little English Handbook (4th ed., *Scott*, 1984) is a basic, sensible guide to grammar and usage. **The Elements of Style** (3rd ed., *Macmillan*, 1979; called "Strunk and White") takes a more authoritarian approach, but has the goal of helping users to write well, not merely correctly.

VI: General Biographical Collections

Who's Who in America (43rd ed., *Marquis*, 1984) is a biennial biographical directory giving basic information on prominent living Americans. It is supplemented by regional and professional volumes, and by **Who's Who of American Women** (13th ed., *Marquis*, 1983). **Who's Who** (136th ed., *St Martin*, 1984) is the British equivalent, and **Who's Who in the World** (7th ed., *Marquis*, 1984) and **International Who's Who 1985–86** (49th ed., *Europa*, 1985) cover eminent people worldwide. **Current Biography** (*Wilson*, from 1940), a monthly publication, gives short character sketches of people in the news.

The **Dictionary of American Biography** (10 vols., *Scribner*, 1928–37; called *DAB*) provides accounts, sometimes long ones, of eminent or notorious dead Americans, from Abraham Lincoln to Jesse James. the entries from this and its first six supplements are condensed in the **Concise Dictionary of American Biography** (3rd ed., *Scribner, 1980)*. It may be supplemented by **Notable American Women** (3 vols. and supplement, *Harvard U Pr*, 1971–80) and the **Dictionary of American Negro Biography** (*Norton*, 1982). The corresponding British works are the **Dictionary of National Biography** (22 vols. and 8 supplements, *Oxford U Pr*. 1885–1981; called *DNB*) and **The Concise Dictionary** (2 vols., *Oxford U Pr*, 1901–70).

Webster's New Biographical Dictionary (*Merriam-Webster Inc*, 1983) has brief entries on eminent dead people of all eras worldwide. Biographical articles from certain periodicals and books are indexed in **Biography Index** (*Wilson*, from 1946).

VII: Literature

Key Sources in Comparative and World Literature (*Ungar*, 1983) is an annotated bibliography of bibliographies and other reference books that are useful for the study of literature.

Cassell's Encyclopaedia of World Literature (new rev. ed., 3 vols., *Morrow, o.p.*, 1973) has entries on authors and surveys of national literatures and of literary styles and forms. The **Encyclopedia of World Literature in the 20th Century** (rev. & enlarged ed., 4 vols., *Ungar*, 1981–84) is a similar guide to modern world literature, as is the **Columbia Dictionary of Modern European Literature** (2nd ed., *Columbia U Pr*, 1980).

The **Princeton Encyclopedia of Poetry and Poetics** (enlarged ed., *H & P—Princeton U Pr*, 1974) covers topics in poetry (but not individual authors) and literary theory. A **Handbook to Literature** (4th ed., *H & P—Bobbs*, 1980) defines critical terms, with particular reference to English and American literature.

The **Reader's Encyclopedia of World Drama** (*TY Crowell*, 1969) includes articles on playwrights, plays, and other topics, while the **McGraw-Hill Encyclopedia of World Drama** (2nd ed., 5 vols., *McGraw*, 1983) has surveys of national dramas and articles on playwrights.

Most of the volumes of the **Dictionary of Literary Biography** (40 vols. to date, *Gale*, 1978–   ) have biographical and critical articles on the writers of an era of American or British literature, with illustrations. **The Oxford Companion to American Literature** (5th ed., *Oxford U Pr*, 1983) and **The Reader's Encyclopedia of American Literature** (*TY Crowell*, 1962) cover writers, major works, literary movements, and other topics. **The Oxford Companion to English Literature** (5th ed., *Oxford U Pr*, (1985) and **The New Century Handbook of English Literature** (rev. ed., *P-H, o.p.*, 1967) emphasize authors, works, and characters. The **Reader's Encyclopedia of Shakespeare** (*TY Crowell, o.p.*, 1966) has long entries on each play, as well as entries on other writers, scholars and critics, and actors and theater people associated with his works.

The first volume of **Literary History of the United States** (4th ed., 2 vols., *Macmillan*, 1974) is the history; the second volume contains bibliographies. **The Concise Cambridge History of English Literature** (3rd ed., *H & P—Cambridge U Pr*, 1970) includes chapters on Commonwealth literatures.

Encyclopedias that deal with the authors and major works of specific foreign literatures are **The Oxford Companion to Classical Literature** (2nd ed., *Oxford U Pr, 1937); **Crowell's Handbook of Classical Literature** (*P—TY Crowell*, 1964); the **Oxford Companion to French Literature** (*Oxford U Pr*, 1959); the **Oxford Companion to German Literature** (*Oxford U Pr*, 1976); the **Dictionary of Italian Literature** (*Greenwood*, 1978); and the **Oxford Companion to Spanish Literature** (*Oxford U Pr, 1978*), which also covers Spanish-American literatures.

Granger's Index to Poetry (7th ed., *Columbia U Pr*, 1982); the **Fiction Catalog** (10th ed., *Wilson*, 1980), for novels; **Short Story Index** (*Wilson*, from 1900); and **Play Index** (*Wilson*, from 1949) all help to locate where a work of literature has been published, and all list works by theme or locale.

The Oxford Dictionary of Quotations (3rd ed., *Oxford U Pr*, 1979) is arranged by author alphabetically. **Bartlett's Familiar Quotations** (15th ed., *Little*, 1980) is arranged chronologically, by author's year of birth. Both the **Home Book of Quotations** (10th ed., *Dodd*, 1984) and **The New Dictionary of Quotations** (*Knopf*, 1942) are arranged by subject.

Humanities Index (see Section I) identifies the most widely read periodicals in literary history and criticism, but the most complete literary bibliography is the annual **MLA International Bibliography** (*Modern Lang*, from 1921).

VIII: The Arts

The **Encyclopedia of World Art** (15 vols. and supplement, *Jack Heraty*, rev. ed. 1972–83) offers substantial articles on all aspects of the visual arts, illustrated with photographs, drawings, and diagrams. The articles in the **McGraw-Hill Dictionary of Art** (5 vols., *McGraw*, 1969) are much shorter, but take into account some artists of secondary importance excluded from the *Encyclopedia*. **The Oxford Companion to Art** (*Oxford U Pr*, 1970) ranges over world art, including biographies and definitions of technical terms, in one large volume. **The Penguin Dictionary of Art and Artists** (5th ed., *P—Penguin*, 1984) is a similar book, but pocket-sized and limited to Western art since the late Middle Ages. Volume I of **The Encyclopedia of Visual Arts** (*P-H*, 1983) is a history, with chapters on the arts of Africa and the countries of Asia, while volume 2 is a biographical dictionary. Both volumes are extensively illustrated.

The Penguin Dictionary of Architecture (3rd ed., *P—Penguin*, 1980) has short entries on architects, architectural styles and schools, and building types. The entries in **A Dictionary of Architecture** (rev. ed., *Overlook Pr*, 1976) are rather longer, with many illustrations.

The Oxford Companion to the Decorative Arts (*Oxford U*

Pr, 1975) and the **Dictionary of the Decorative Arts** (*Har-Row*, 1977) include furniture, jewelry, pottery, textiles, etc., with brief entries on artists, materials, and techniques, but the *Companion* adds longer survey articles on basic topics. Both are illustrated.

The **International Center of Photography Encyclopedia of Photography** (*Crown*, 1984) covers photographers, movements and schools, and technical terms, with many illustrations. The **Photograph Collector's Guide** (*H & P—NYGS*, 1979), more widely useful than its title suggests, has an illustrated biographical section, a chronology, and a glossary of terms. The entries in the **Macmillan Biographical Encyclopedia of Photographic Artists and Innovators** (*Macmillan*, 1983) supply fuller biographies, as well as longer bibliographies of critical studies.

Art Index (*Wilson*, from 1929) surveys the major periodicals in all the visual arts.

IX: The Performing Arts

Unlike the drama encyclopedias mentioned in Section VII, **The Oxford Companion to the Theatre** (4th ed., *Oxford U Pr*, 1983), and **The Oxford Companion to the American Theatre** (*Oxford U Pr*, 1984) emphasize the stage and plays in performance, with entries on actors, theaters, theater companies, and stagecraft, as well as on playwrights.

The Film Encyclopedia (*TY Crowell*, 1979) has entries on actors, directors, screenwriters, and others active in U.S. and foreign filmmaking, and also defines technical terms. It is usefully supplemented by the critical plot summaries in **International Dictionary of Films and Filmmakers: Volume I: Films** (*St. James Pr*, 1984).

The **New Grove Dictionary of Music and Musicians** (20 vols, *Macmillan*, 1980) includes composers, performers, orchestras, instruments, and styles and forms of music, of all eras and countries. The **New Oxford Companion to Music** (2 vols, *Oxford U Pr*, 1983) is similar in range, but is aimed at the general reader and omits performers, while adding entries on operas, songs, and other named compositions. The entries in **The New College Encyclopedia of Music** (rev. ed., *Norton*, *o.p.*, 1976) are brief but informative, and often supply musical quotations or portraits. The **Harvard Dictionary of Music** (rev.

enl. ed., *Harvard U Pr*, 1969) is limited to definitions of technical terms, among them musical forms and instruments.

The Dictionary of the Opera (*S&S*, 1983) has brief entries on composers, performers, and operas. Detailed plot summaries, with descriptions of arias, etc., are furnished in **The New Kobbés Complete Opera Book** (*Putnam Pub Group*, 1976).

The Ballet Goer's Guide (*Knopf*, 1981) includes illustrated summaries of ballets and a survey of steps. **The Complete Guide to Modern Dance** (*Doubleday*, *o.p.*, 1976) covers American choreographers, with analyses of their major works. **Biographical Dictionary of Dance** (*Schirmer Biks*, 1982) gives short entries on choreographers and dancers, including tap dancers and other popular performers.

Humanities Index (see Section I) catalogs a number of periodicals in all these fields, although *Art Index* (see Section VIII) offer better coverage of film periodicals. Film reviews are listed in *Humanities Index*, the *Readers' Guide*, *Magazine Index*, and the *New York Times Index* (see Section I), as well as in *Art Index*. These same indexes, except for *Art Index*, cite reviews of stage productions, chiefly from New York City. Reviews of recordings are listed in the *Readers' Guide*, *Magazine Index*, and the *New York Times Index*.

X: Philosophy, Religion, and Folklore

The **Encyclopedia of Philosophy** (4 vols., *Macmillan*, 1973) has extensive essays on philosophers and philosophical schools, movements, and problems. The **Dictionary of the History of Ideas** (5 vols, *Scribner*, 1968–74) encompasses basic concepts from the history of culture and thought. **A Dictionary of Philosophy** (2nd ed., *P—St Martin*, 1983) provides brief entries on philosophers as well as philosophical terms and problems.

A Dictionary of Comparative Religion (*Scribner*, 1970) furnishes data on beliefs, deities, and practices of religions worldwide. **The Penguin Dictionary of Religions** (*Penguin*, 1984) has brief entries on sects and practices, with a particularly good bibliography. **The Oxford Dictionary of the Christian Church** (2nd ed., corrected, *Oxford U Pr*, 1974) is a historical handbook of people, practices, and denominations.

The **Encyclopedia Judaica** (16 vols, *Macmillan*, 1971–72) embraces people, places, events, and other topics of all eras in

Jewish history and culture. A ten-year supplement (the "Decennial Book," *Jerusalem: Ency Judaica*, 1982) takes account of developments of 1972–81. **The New Catholic Encyclopaedia** (15 vols. and 2 supplements, *McGraw*, 1967–79) is a general encyclopedia, but one that emphasizes Catholic history and doctrine. **The Encyclopedia of Islam** (new ed., *Humanities*, 1960–   ) surveys all the Islamic lands and includes their arts, literature, and history.

The Interpreter's Dictionary of the Bible (5 vols. and supplement, *Abingdon*, 1962–76) and the **New Westminster Dictionary of the Bible** (*Westminster*, 1970) have entries on people, places, objects, animals, etc., mentioned in the Bible and are illustrated with maps and photographs. **The Westminster Historical Atlas to the Bible** (rev. ed., *Westminster*, 1956) and the **Oxford Bible Atlas** (2nd ed., *Oxford U Pr*, 1974) offer maps of the major eras of biblical history and an extensive explanatory text; the Oxford atlas also includes a detailed index to its text. **The Macmillan Bible Atlas** (rev. ed., *Macmillan*, 1977) has numerous small maps of regions, cities, and events, with explanatory captions.

Funk and Wagnalls Standard Dictionary of Folklore, Mythology, and Legends (*TY Crowell*, 1972) affords information about gods, heroes, and supernatural beings; superstitions and practices; and symbols and objects. **Crowell's Handbook of Classical Mythology** (*TY Crowell*, 1970, *o.p.*) gives detailed entries on characters and places in Greek and Roman myth.

Humanities Index (see Section I) is a guide to the basic journals in all these fields.

XI: History

The **Dictionary of World History** (*Nelson*, 1973) and the smaller **Macmillan Concise Dictionary of World History** (*Macmillan*, 1983) have brief entries on people, events, and other topics. **The Oxford Classical Dictionary** (2nd ed., *Oxford U Pr*, 1970) surveys Greek and Roman history, culture, and society, including biographies. For coverage in depth of American history, see the **Dictionary of American History** (rev. ed., 8 vols, *Scribner*, 1976), which includes entries on events, documents, ideas, places, and other topics. The **Concise Dictionary of American History** (*Scribner*, 1983) is abridged and omits a few entries entirely, but also adds some entries on recent issues. The **Scribner Desk Dictionary of American History** (*Scribner*, 1984) is even further abridged, perhaps excessively so. Biographies are found in the *Dictionary of American Biography* (see Section VI). These works may be supplemented with the **Encyclopedia of Black America** (*McGraw*, 1981) and **The Negro Almanac** (4th ed., *Wiley*, 1983); both include biographies and survey articles, and the *Almanac* gives statistical data from the 1980 census.

An **Encyclopedia of World History** (5th ed., *HM*, 1972) and the **Encyclopedia of American History** (6th ed., *Har-Row*, 1982) are both chronological lists of events, with brief explanatory notes and good indexes. **Facts on File** (*Facts on File*, from 1940) is a weekly summary of major events in the United States and the world.

A series of standard multivolume histories of the Western world, all written by teams of scholars, are the **Cambridge Ancient History** (3rd ed., *Cambridge U Pr*, 1970–; original ed. 1923–39, in 12 vols.); the **Cambridge Mediaeval History** (2nd ed., *Cambridge U Pr*, 1966–; original ed. 1924–36, in 8 vols.); and the **New Cambridge Modern History** (14 vols. *H & P—Cambridge U Pr*, 1957–79). Cambridge University Press has also published a number of other important collaborative histories, among them the **Cambridge History of Africa** (5 vols. to date, 1975–) and the **Cambridge History of China** (4 vols. to date, 1978–).

The **Times Atlas of World History** (rev. ed., *Hammond Inc*, 1984) and **The Times Concise Atlas of World History** (*Hammond Inc*. 1982) illustrate cultural, political, and economic history from the earliest times to the 1970s, with full attention to Africa and Asia. Both also give extensive explanatory texts; the unabridged *Atlas* adds a brief encyclopedia of names. The **Rand McNally Historical Atlas of the World** (*Rand*, 1981) has fewer and simpler maps, but it also supported by an accompanying text. An approximately 150-page supplement of historical maps appears in the *Hammond Medallion World Atlas* (see Section IV), which emphasizes the history of the United States and Western Europe. The **Atlas of American History** (rev. ed., *Scribner*, 1978) offers excellent, detailed coverage of the United States.

Humanities Index (see Section I) surveys the major periodicals on U.S. and world history. **America: History and Life** (*ABC-Clio*, from 1964) includes a very full account of social, cultural, and intellectual history and gives abstracts of most entries. A companion series, **Historical Abstracts** (*ABC-Clio*, from 1955) covers the history of the rest of the modern world. A convenient place to begin research in American history, however, is the **Harvard Guide to American History** (rev. ed., 2 vols., *H & P—Harvard U Pr*, 1974), which lists books and some articles, by period or topic. This can be supplemented by the annotated bibliographies after each chapter of **America: A Narrative History** (2 vols., *H & P—Norton*, 1984), which emphasizes recent books.

XII: The Social Sciences

The articles in the **International Encyclopedia of the Social Sciences** (17 vols. and supplement, *Macmillan*, 1968–79) discuss in depth the theories of all the social sciences. **A Dictionary of the Social Sciences** (*Free Pr*, 1964) is a one-volume handbook of basic concepts.

The **Dictionary of Business and Economics** (2nd ed., *Free Pr*, 1984) offers clear, usually brief definitions, complemented by terms from related fields, such as accounting and sociology, and names of government agencies and programs.

The **American Political Dictionary** (6th ed., *H & P—HR & W*, 1982) has entries on political terms and federal laws, court cases, and government agencies, past and present.

The **Encyclopedia of Psychology** (4 vols., *Wiley*, 1984) includes biographical entries as well as articles on theories, experiments, and tests, with references to a 280-page bibliography. The **Longman Dictionary of Psychology and Psychiatry** (*Longman*, 1983) defines terms briefly. **The Encyclopedic Dictionary of Psychology** (*MIT Pr*, 1983) supplies fewer but longer entries, with bibliographies.

The **Penguin Dictionary of Sociology** (*P—Penguin*, 1984) has brief entries on concepts and terms, with extensive bibliographical references.

The **Europa Yearbook** (*Europa*, from 1926) reviews the United Nations and other international organizations and the nations of the world, with summaries of social and political topics, general economic statistics, and information on major cultural and other institutions, including banks and the press. **The Statesman's Yearbook** (*St Martin*, from 1864) provides statistics as well as a more extensive survey of the government, society, and economy of the nations of the world. More detailed accounts of the nations of the Third World can be found in three other Europa publications: **Middle East and North Africa** (from 1948); **Africa South of the Sahara** (from 1970); and **The Far East and Australasia** (from 1969). For a sampling of the data collected by federal agencies, see the **Statistical Abstract of the United States** (*Gov Printing Office*, from 1879).

Social Sciences Index (see section I) lists the major periodicals in these fields. For articles on business topics, see **Business Periodical Index** (*Wilson*, from 1958).

XIII: The Sciences and Technology

The **McGraw-Hill Encyclopedia of Science and Technology** (5th ed., 15 vols., *McGraw*, 1982) has entries on numerous aspects of mathematics, the biological and physical sciences, medicine, and technology and is kept up to date by a yearbook. An abridged, one-volume version is the **McGraw-Hill Concise Encyclopedia of Science and Technology,** which adds some entries taken from other McGraw-Hill reference works. The larger **Van Nostrand Scientific Encyclopedia** (6th ed., 2 vols., *Van Nos Reinhold,* 1984) offers a remarkable range of information in well-illustrated articles, some of considerable length. Although there is much overlap between the *McGraw-Hill Concise* and the *Van Nostrand,* each work includes a surprising number of topics not in the other. In addition, the *McGraw-Hill Concise* tends to give specific topics separate, brief entries, while the *Van Nostrand* tends to give references from specific headings to broader topics, discussing the specific aspect in its context.

None of the above works includes biographical entries. **The Dictionary of Scientific Biography** (16 vols. and supplement, *Scribner,* 1970–80) and the **Concise Dictionary of Scientific Biography** (*Scribner,* 1981) are sources for biographical information about dead scientists of all eras and countries. Scientists active during this century, including many living scientists, appear in **McGraw-Hill Modern Scientists and Engineers** (3 vols., *McGraw,* 1980).

The **McGraw-Hill Dictionary of Scientific and Technical Terms** (3rd ed., *McGraw,* 1983) gives short, sometimes dense, definitions, with many illustrations. An abridged version is **McGraw-Hill Dictionary of Science and Engineering** (*McGraw,* 1984). **The Penguin Dictionary of Science** (5th ed., *Penguin,*

1979) deals with mathematics, physics, and chemistry and is complemented by **The Penguin Dictionary of Biology** (7th ed., *Viking Pr*, 1978), which also supplies particularly clear definitions of current terms, and by **A Dictionary of the Natural Environment** (*Wiley*, 1978), a well-illustrated dictionary of terms from geography, geology, oceanography, and meteorology.

The Anchor Dictionary of Astronomy (*P—Doubleday*, 1980) furnishes brief entries on planets, stars, and galaxies and definitions of technical terms. The **Atlas of the Solar System** (*Rand*, 1983) has chapters on the sun, the planets, and the moon; it is illustrated with maps, drawings, and many spectacular photographs. The **New Atlas of the Universe** (*Crown*, 1984) and **The Telescope Handbook and Star Atlas** (rev. ed., *TY Crowell*, 1975) survey the solar system and those stars and galaxies most of interest to star watchers, and include star maps and lists of astronomical objects, with commentary and photographs.

The Audubon Society Encyclopedia of Animal Life (*Crown*, 1982) and **The New Larousse Encyclopedia of Animal Life** (*Larousse, o.p.*, 1980) are beautifully illustrated surveys of animal families, with emphasis on the vertebrates, and more particularly on the mammals. **The Encyclopedia of Mammals** (*Facts on File*, 1984) surveys the general biology, habits, and role in the environment of the families of mammals, with annotated lists of individual species. **Walker's Mammals of the World** (4th ed., 2 vols., *Johns Hopkins*, 1983) is a very scholarly work, illustrated to inform rather than to dazzle, yet it manages to be steadily interesting. **The Great Book of Birds** (*Dial, o.p.*, 1975) describes the appearance and behavior of the birds of the world. **The Audubon Society Encyclopedia of North American Birds** (*Knopf*, 1980) has entries only on those species of birds found in the United States and Canada, but its articles on bird anatomy, behavior, and ecology are of general use. The **Oxford Companion to Animal Behavior** (*Oxford U Pr*, 1982) has long articles on general aspects of the instincts and capacity for spontaneous actions in vertebrates and invertebrates.

The Computer Glossary (3rd ed., *P-H*, 1983) is a guide for the perplexed. Those who already are familiar with computers and want to know more may prefer the **Dictionary of Computing** (*Oxford U Pr*, 1983) or the **Encyclopedia of Computer Science and Engineering** (2nd ed., *Van Nos Reinhold*, 1982).

General Science Index (*Wilson*, from 1978) focuses on about 90 of the most widely read science periodicals, including a few specifically aimed at the nonscientist. **Biology Digest** (*Plexus*, from 1974) chooses periodicals accessible to the nonscientist, abstracts articles, and is particularly good on nature and the environment. Most of the reader-friendly computer magazines are indexed in *Magazine Index* (see Section I).

INDEX

The ABC of Relativity, 367
ACT Guide to Children's Television: How to Treat TV with TLC, 254
Abe, Kobe, 85
Abish, Walter, 185
Abnormal Psychology: Current Perspectives, 340–41
About Chinese, 82
Abraham, Henry J., 310
Abrahams, Peter, 91
Absalom, Absalom!, 181
Abu Al-Ala Al-Ma'arri, 67
Abusing Science: The Case Against Creationism, 380
Achebe, Chinua, 91
Ackerman, James S., 227
Acocella, Joan, 340
Acosta, Oscar "Zeta," 129
The Acquisitive Society, 322
Adair, John, 329
Adam Bede, 155
Adamczewski, Jan, 36
Adams, Henry, 24, 227
Addison, Joseph, 52
Adivar, Halide Edib, 69
Adolphe, 137
Advancement of Learning, 32

Adventures in the Skin Trade, 201
Adventures of a Mathematician, 369
The Adventures of Augie March, 186
The Adventures of Conan Doyle, 230
Adventures of Huckleberry Finn, 177
The Adventures of the Chicano Kid and Other Stories, 130
The Adventures of Tom Sawyer, 177
Advice to a Young Scientist, 365
Aeneid, 16
Aeschylus, 6
Aesop, 6
Aesthetics and History in the Visual Arts, 262–63
AFRICA, 88–95
Africa in History, 93–94
Africa Must Unite, 95
Africa South of the Sahara, 403
The African Image, 95
African Music: A People's Art, 93
The African Origin of Civilization, 94

African Religions and Philosophy, 290

African Systems of Thought, 290

Afro-American Anthropology, 324–25

After the New Criticism, 241

After the Tradition: Essays on Modern Jewish Writing, 71

Against Interpretation and Other Essays, 242

Against Nature, 139

Against the American Grain, 241

Against the Stream: Critical Essays in Economics, 320

Agamemnon, 6

Age of Analysis, 285

The Age of Charlemagne, 24

The Age of Enlightenment, 52

The Age of Humanism, 263

The Age of Louis XIV, 48

The Age of Reason, 55

The Age of Reason Begins, 48

The Age of Religious Wars, 1559–1689, 300

The Age of Revolution and Reaction, 1789–1850, 300

The Age of the Avant-Garde, 261

The Age of the Great Depression, 1929–1941, 305

The Age of the Reformation, 299

The Age of Voltaire, 58

Agnon, Samuel Joseph, 70

Ahlstrom, Sydney E., 291

Aidoo, Ama Ata, 91

Aiiieeeee! An Anthology of Asian American Writers, 115

Aké, 93

Alan Turing: The Enigma, 230

Alarcón, Pedro Antonio de, 137

al-Ayyam: A Passage to France, 68

al-Ayyam: An Egyptian Childhood, 68

al-Ayyam: The Stream of Days: A Student at the Azhar, 68

Alba, Victor, 104

Albee, Edward, 220

Albert Einstein, 367

Albrecht-Carrié, René, 299

The Alchemist, 34

Alcott, Louisa May, 173

Alegría, Ciro, 99

Aleichem, Sholom (Shalom Rabinowitz), 195–96

Alfred Stieglitz and the American Avant-Garde, 230

Alice in Wonderland, 154

The Alien Animals: The Story of Imported Wildlife, 380

Alienation and Economics, 322

Alinsky, Saul D., 331

All Men Are Brothers, 83

All Quiet on the Western Front, 149

All Said and Done, 227

All the King's Men, 192

Allen, Gay Wilson, 227

Allen, Harry Cranbrook, 299

Al-Mutanabbi, Abu Al-Tayyib Ahmad Ibn Al-Hussain, 67

Alter, Robert, 71

Abu Al-Tayyib Ahmad Ibn Al-Hussain, 67

Amado, Jorge, 99

Ambassador World Atlas, 393

The Ambassadors, 175–76

America: A Narrative History, 402

America: History and Life, 401

America Is in the Heart: A Personal History, 115–16

The American, 175

American Court Systems: Reading Judicial Process and Behavior, 310

AMERICAN INDIAN, see NATIVE AMERICAN

American Indian Myths and Legends, 108

American Indian Women: Telling Their Lives, 108
The American Indians, 112
American Indians of the Southwest, 109
AMERICAN MINORITY CULTURES, 106–31
AMERICAN NOVELS, 170–77, 178–92
American Photography: A Critical History 1945 to the Present, 270
AMERICAN POETRY, 207–12
American Poets from the Puritans to the Present, 206
The American Political Dictionary, 402
American Politics: Policies, Power and Change, 311
An American Portrait, 303
American Presidency Series, 303
American Revised Standard Version (of the Bible), 288
The American Scholar, 243
The American Songbag, 268
An American Tragedy, 180
Americana, 392
The Americans: The Democratic Experience, 303
America's Fascinating Indian Heritage, 108
America's Music from the Pilgrims to the Present, 267
Amis, Kingsley, 162
Anabasis, 8
The Analects, 81, 258
The Analytical Engine, 370
Anand, Mulk Raj, 83
Anarchism: A History of Libertarian Ideas and Movements, 309
Anastasi, Anne, 340
Anatomy of Criticism, 240
The Anatomy of Melancholy, 33
The Anatomy of Revolution, 300
Anaya, Rudolfo, 129

The Anchor Dictionary of Astronomy, 404
ANCIENT AND MEDIEVAL HISTORY, 298
Ancient Evenings, 189
Ancient Greek Literature, 8
The Ancient Greeks, 9
ANCIENT HISTORY, *see* ASIA; GREECE; HISTORY; MIDDLE EAST; ROME
And Quiet Flows the Don, 150
And Still the Waters Run, 109
And Then We Heard the Thunder, 124
Anderson, Jervis, 126
Anderson, Maxwell, 220
Anderson, Sherwood, 179
Anderson, W. R., 267
Andrade, Carlos Drummond de, 99
Andrade de Silva, J., 366
Andreas Capellanus, 21
Anglo-Saxon Attitudes, 169
Animal Farm, 167
Anna Karenina, 140
Annie Allen, 123
Anouilh, Jean, 220
Anshen, Frank, 249
Anthology of Chinese Literature: Vol. I—From Early Times to the Fourteenth Century; Vol. II—From the Fourteenth Century to the Present, 79
An Anthology of French Poets from Nerval to Valéry, 213
An Anthology of German Poetry from Hölderlin to Rilke in English Translation, 214
Anthology of Japanese Literature, 79
Anthology of Korean Literature: From Early Times to the Nineteenth Century, 80
An Anthology of Mexican Poetry, 99

An Anthology of Modern Arabic Poetry, 67
An Anthology of Roman Drama, 14
Anthology of Spanish Poetry: From the Beginnings to the Present Day, 214
Anthony, Katharine, 36
ANTHROPOLOGY, 323–29
Anthropology and Art, 325
Anthropology of the City, 325
Antigone, 8
Anti-Intellectualism in American Life, 305
Antonin Artaud, 229
Antonius, George, 73
The Anxiety of Influence, 239
Apollo in the Democracy, 265
Apologia pro Vita Sua, 232
Apologies to the Iroquois: With a Study of the Mohawks in High Street, 113
Apology for Poetry, 36
Appointment in Samarra, 182
Apuleius, Lucius, 14
The Arab Awakening, 73
Arabian Nights, 67
ARABIC LITERATURE, 67–68
Arabic Writing Today, 67
Arcadia, 35
ARCHAEOLOGY, see ANTHROPOLOGY; GREECE; HISTORY; MIDDLE EAST; RELIGION
ARCHITECTURE, 265–66
The Architect's Eye, 266
Arciniegas, Germán, 104
Arendt, Hannah, 308
Argonauts of the Western Pacific, 327
Ariès, Philippe, 331
Ariosto, Lodovico, 32
Aristophanes, 6
Aristotle, 6, 277–78, 308
Armah, Ayi Kwei, 91

Armelagos, George, 326
Armenian Folk-Tales and Legends, 72
Armenian Legends and Poems, 72
ARMENIAN LITERATURE, 71–72
Armitage, Angus, 227
Armstrong, David, 252
Arnason, H.H., 261
Arnold, Matthew, 207, 238
Arnott, Peter, 222
Aronson, Elliot, 340
ART, see FINE ARTS
Art and Architecture in France: 1500–1700, 37
Art and Existentialism, 263
Art and Life in America, 263–64
Art and Politics in the Weimar Period, 265
Art as Experience, 278
Art Index, 390, 398
The Art of Courtly Love, 21
The Art of Humanism, 38
The Art of Love, 15
The Art of Making Dances, 268–69
The Art of Southeast Asia, 87
Art of the Middle Ages, 24
The Art of the Novel, 240
The Art of the Print, 261
Art since 1945, 262
Artaud, Antonin, 222
Arthurian Romances, 21
Artistic Theory in Italy, 37
As I Lay Dying, 181
The Ascent of Man, 364
Ashley, Maurice Percy, 299
ASIA, 74–87
ASIAN NATIONS, SMALLER, 80–81
ASIAN-PACIFIC, 114–19
Asians in America: Filipinos, Koreans and East Indians, 117–18

Asimov, Isaac, 368, 369, 376
Asimov on Chemistry, 368
Asimov on Numbers, 369
Asimov's New Guide to Science, 376
Aspects of the Novel, 240
The Assistant, 189
Astrology in the Renaissance, 38
ASTRONOMY, *see* PHYSICAL SCIENCES
Asturias, Miguel Angel, 99
At Swim-Two-Birds, 167
The Atlantic Monthly, 243–44
Atlas of American History, 401
Atlas of the Solar System, 404
ATLASES, *see* REFERENCE BOOKS
Attack and Die: Civil War Military Tactics and the Southern Heritage, 305
Attar, Farid Addin, 68
Attenborough, David, 376
Attridge, Derek, 205
Atwood, Margaret, 162
Aubrey, John, 44
Auchincloss, Louis, 185
Auden, W. H., 210, 238
Audubon, John James, 227
The Audubon, Society Encyclopedia of Animal Life, 404
The Audubon Society Encyclopedia of North American Birds, 404
Auerbach, Erich, 238
Augustine, Saint, 14, 278
Aunt Julia and the Scriptwriter, 103
Aurora Leigh, 207
Austen, Jane, 153
Austin, J. L., 284
Austin, William W., 266
Authorized Version of the Bible, 44
Autobiographical and Political Writings, 55

AUTOBIOGRAPHY, *see* BIOGRAPHY
Autobiography, 33 (Cellini), 54 (Franklin), 228 (DuBois), 232 (Mill), 234 (Steffens), 235 (Wright), 235 (Yeats)
The Autobiography of a Brown Buffalo, 129
The Autobiography of a Turkish Girl, 70
The Autobiography of Alice B. Toklas, 234
Autobiography of an Unknown Indian, 83–84
The Autobiography of LeRoi Jones, 227
The Autobiography of Malcolm X, 231
The Autobiography of Miss Jane Pittman, 124
Autobiography: The Story of My Experiments with Truth, 84
The Autumn of the Patriarch, 101
The Awakening, 173
Awoonor, Kofi, 93
Axel's Castle, 242
Ayer, A. J., 284
The Aztecs of Mexico, 105
Azuela, Mariano, 100

Bâ, Mariama, 91
Babbitt, 182
Babel, Isaac, 196
The Bachelor of Arts, 84
Bacon, Francis, 32–33
Bad Blood: The Tuskegee Syphilis Experiment, 334
Bagdikian, Ben, 252–53
Bailey, Hugh C., 303
Bailey, Thomas Andrew, 303
Bainton, Ronald H., 299
Baker, Carlos, 227
Baker, Herschel, 37
Balanchine, George, 268

Balanchine's Complete Stories of
the Great Ballets, 239
The Balcony, 220
Baldwin, James, 122
The Ballet Goer's Guide, 399
Ball-Rokeach, Sandra J., 253
Balthazar, 164
Balzac, Honoré de, 137
Baraka, Imamu Amiri, 210, 227
Baran, Paul, 317
Barber, Richard W., 24
The Barber of Seville, 52
Barchester Towers, 158
Barnes and Noble Art Series, 262
Barnet, Richard J., 317
Barnett, Lincoln K., 366
Barnhart, Edward N., 118
Barnouw, Erik, 253
Baroque and Rococo Architec-
ture, 49
Baroque and Rococo Art, 47
Barr, Alfred H., Jr., 262
Barren Ground, 181
Barrow, R. H., 16
Barth, John, 185, 196
Barthelme, Donald, 186, 196
Barthes, Roland, 248
Bartlett's Familiar Quotations,
397
Barzun, Jacques, 266
Basham, A. L., 83
Basho, Matsuo, 85
Basic Works (Aristotle) 277
Baskin, Yvonne, 377
Bate, W. Jackson, 57
Bateson, Mary Catherine, 325
Batouala, 92
Battaille, Gretchen, 108
Batterberry, Michael, 24
Bauer, P. T., 317
Bautier, Robert-Henri, 24
Bazin, Germain, 47
Bear, John, 370
Beattie, Ann, 196
Beaumarchais, Pierre Caron de, 52

Beaumont, Francis, 44
Beauty and the Beast: The
Coevolution of Plants and
Animals, 379
The Beautyful Ones Are Not Yet
Born, 91
Beauvoir, Simone de, 227, 352
Bebey, Francis, 93
Becker, Carl Lotus, 57
Becker, Ernest, 332
Beckett, Samuel, 143
Becoming Visible: Women in
European History, 297
Bedini, Silvio A., 364
Beerbohm, Max, 162–63
Beers, Burton F., 297
Beethoven, 233
Before the Mayflower: A History
of Black America, 126
A Beggar in Jerusalem, 192
The Beggar's Opera, 54
Behaviorism, 340
Behind Mud Walls: 1930–1960,
85
Behn, Aphra, 44
Being and Nothingness, 285
Being and Time, 279
Being Indian in Hueyapan, 326
Bel-Ami, 139
Beliefs, Attitudes, and Human
Affairs, 343
Bell, Quentin, 227
Bellamy, Edward, 173
Bellow, Saul, 186
Bem, Daryl J., 343
Benedetti, Mario, 100
Bennett, Arnold, 163
Bennett, Lerone, Jr., 126
Bentley, Eric, 222
Benz, Ernst, 293
Beowulf, 21
Berenson, Bernard, 37, 262–63
Bergen, Bernard J., 336
Berger, Peter L., 332
Bergson, Henri, 284

Berkeley, George, 52, 278
The Berkshire Studies in European History, 299
Berle, Adolf A., 317
Berlin, Isaiah, 227
The Berlin Stories, 165
Berlioz, Hector, 227–28
Berlioz and His Century, 266
Berlitz, Charles, 248
Berman, Harold J., 310
Bernard, Jessie, 352
Bernard Berenson: The Making of a Connoisseur, 233
Bernstein, Jeremy, 364, 370
Bernstein, Leonard, 266
Bery, Wendell, 239
Best American Plays, 218
The Best and the Brightest, 312
The Best Circles, 300
The Best of Saki, 200
The Betrothed, 139
Beti, Mongo, 91
Betrayed by Rita Hayworth, 102
Between Man and Man, 284
Beyond the Waste Land: A Democratic Alternative to Economic Decline, 317
Bhagavad Gita, 83, 289
Bhagavad-Gita: Song of God, 289
The Bhagavadgita, 289
The Bible and Ethics in the Christian Life, 291
Bierce, Ambrose, 196
The Big Money, 180
Billiards at Half Past Nine, 143
Billy Budd, 176
Billy Phelan's Greatest Game, 188
Bingo and the Sea: Two Plays, 220
Biographical Dictionary of Dance, 399
BIOGRAPHY, 224–35
Biography Index, 395
Biography of Physics, 367

BIOLOGICAL SCIENCES, 373–85
Biology Digest, 404
Birch, Bruce, 291
The Birds, 6
The Birth of the Republic, 1763–89, 58
Bishop, Elizabeth, 210
BLACK, 120–26
Black Boy, 235
Black Elk Speaks, 111
Black English: Its History and Usage in the United States, 248
Black Fire: An Anthology of Afro-American Writing, 125
Black Poets of the United States: From Paul Laurence Dunbar to Langston Hughes, 206–07
Black Rain, 86
A Black Theology of Liberation, 292
The Black West, 126
Black Women in White America, 352
Black Women Writers (1950–1980): A Critical Evaluation, 125
The Blackfeet: Raiders on the Northwestern Plains, 109
The Blacks, 220
Blacks in Antiquity, 95
Blake, Robert, 228
Blake, William, 53
Blau, Joseph, 293
Bleak House, 155
Bless Me, Ultima, 129
The Blind Owl, 68
Bloch, Marc, 24
Bloom, Harold, 239
Blotner, Joseph Leo, 228
Blume, Friedrich, 37, 266–67
Blunt, Anthony, 37
Boas, Franz, 108, 263, 325
Boccaccio, Giovanni, 33

Bodley, John H., 325
The Body in Question, 381
Boethius, 14
Bogin, Meg, 24
Böll, Heinrich, 143
Bond, Edward, 220
Bone, Robert, 125
Bonner, John Tyler, 382
The Book of Beasts, 21
The Book of Daniel, 187
the Book of Laughter and
    Forgetting, 147
Book Review Digest, 391
Books in Print, 390
Boorstin, Daniel J., 303
Bootzin, Richard R., 340
Borges, Jorge, 100
Borinquen: An Anthology of
    Puerto Rican Literature, 129
Born, Max, 366
The Born-Einstein Letters, 366
The Bosses, 100
Boswell, James, 53
BOTANY, see BIOLOGICAL
    SCIENCES
Bousquet, Jacques, 263
Bowen, Catherine Drinker, 228
Bowen, Elenore Smith (Laura
    Bohannan), 325
Bowen, Elizabeth, 163
Bower, Faubion, 85
Bowie, Henry, 263
Bowker, Gordon H., 341
Bowles, Samuel, 317, 332
Bowra, C. M., 8
Bradbury, Ray, 196
The Brain, 381
Braine, John, 163
Braudel, Fernand, 299
Brave New World, 165
Braverman, Harry, 332
Brazil on the Move, 104
Bread and Wine, 150
The Breast of the Earth: A
    Survey of the History,

Culture and Literature of
    Africa South of the Sahara,
    93
Brecht, Bertolt, 220, 222
Brecht on Theatre, 222
Breunig, Charles, 300
The Bride Price, 91
Brideshead Revisited, 169
The Bridge of San Luis Rey, 183
Bridges to Infinity, 369
A Brief Life, 102
Brief Lives, 44
Brighton Rock, 166
Brinton, Crane, 297, 300
Britannica: Propaedia, Macro-
    paedia, Micropaedia, 391–92
BRITISH NOVELS, 151–58,
    159–69
BRITISH POETRY, 207–12
Broch, Hermann, 144
Brockett, Oscar, 222
Brogan, Terry, 205
Bronowski, Jacob, 364
Brontë, Charlotte, 154
Brontë, Emily, 154
Brook, Peter, 222
Brooks, Cleanth, 205
Brooks, Gwendolyn, 122
The Brothers Karamozov, 138
Brown, Claude, 123
Brown, Dee, 108
Brown, Lester, 317, 384
Brown, Lloyd W., 93
Brown, Rita Mae, 352
Brown, Robert McAfee, 292
Browne, Edward G., 68
Browne, Sir Thomas, 33, 44
Browning, Elizabeth Barrett, 207
Browning, Robert, 207
Bruce, C. Loring, 325
Brustein, Robert, 222
Bruun, Geoffrey, 301
Buber, Martin, 284
Buddenbrooks, 147
Buddhism, 288, 293

Building a Sustainable Society, 317

Bulgakov, Mikhail, 144

Bulletin of the Atomic Scientists, 244

Bullivant and the Lambs, 163

Bullough, Donald, 24

Bulosan, Carlos, 115–16

Bulwer-Lytton, Edward, 16

Bumblebee Economics, 379

Bunyan, John, 45

Burckhardt, Jacob, 37

Burgess, Anthony, 163

Burke, Edmund, 53

Burner, David, 303

Burnham, Walter Dean, 310–11

The Burning House, 196

The Burning Plain and Other Stories, 103

Burns, Robert, 53

Burroughs, William, 186

Burtle, James L., 321

Burton, Robert, 33

Burtt, Edwin A., 78

Bury My Heart at Wounded Knee, 108

Bush, Douglas, 37

Business Periodical Index, 403

Butler, Samuel, 154

Butterfield, Sir Herbert, 57

Byron, 231

Byron, Lord (George Gordon Noel), 207

Byzantium: Greatness and Decline, 73

Cable, George Washington, 173

Caesar, Gaius Julius, 14

Caesar and Christ, 16

Caglioti, Luciano, 368

Calder, Nigel, 366, 370

Caldwell, Erskine, 179–80, 196

Call It Sleep, 182

The Call of the Wild, 182

Calvino, Italo, 144

Cambridge Ancient History, 401

Cambridge History of Africa, 401

Cambridge History of China, 401

Cambridge History of Classical Literature: Latin Literature, 16

Cambridge Mediaeval History, 401

Camel Hsiang-tsu, 82

Campbell, Jeremy, 248

Camus, Albert, 144, 239

CANADIAN NOVELS, *see* BRITISH NOVELS

Cancer Ward, 150

Candide, 56

Cane, 124

The Canterbury Tales, 21

The Cantos, 211

Čapek, Karel, 144

Capital, 320

Capitalism, Socialism and Democracy, 321

Capote, Truman, 186, 196

Carcopino, Jerome, 16

CARIBBEAN, *see* LATIN AMERICA

Caring: A Feminine Approach to Ethics and Moral Education, 356

Carlson, Marvin, 222

Carlson, Neil R., 341

Carlyle, Thomas, 57

Carmen, 139

Carpentier, Alejo, 100

Carr, Archie, 377

Carroll, Lewis (Charles L. Dodgson), 154

Carson, Rachel, 377

Cartier-Bresson, Henri, 269

Cary, Joyce, 163

Casanova de Seingalt, Giacomo, 53

Case, John, 370

Cassell's Encyclopedia of World Literature, 396
Cassidy, Harold G., 368
Cassirer, Ernst, 57, 284
Castaneda, Carlos, 292
Castel, Françoise, 332
Castel, Robert, 332
Castellanos, Rosario, 100
Castiglione, Baldassare, 33
The Castle, 146
The Castle of Otranto, 56
Castle Rackrent, 155
Cat and Mouse, 146
Cat Country, 82
Catch-22, 188
The Catcher in the Rye, 191
Cather, Willa, 47, 180
Catlin, George, 108–09
Catullus, Gaius Valerius, 14
Caught in the Web of Words, 232
Celebrations and Attacks, 240
The Celestial Omnibus, 197
Céline, Louis-Ferdinand (Destouches), 144
Cellini, Benvenuto, 33
CENTRAL AMERICA, *see* LATIN AMERICA
Centuries of Childhood: A Social History of Family Life, 331
Century of Struggle, 304
Cervantes Saavedra, Miguel de, 33
César Vallejo: The Complete Posthumous Poetry, 103
The Challenge of Scandinavia, 302
Chambers, E. K., 37
Chance and Necessity: An Essay on the Natural Philosophy of Modern Biology, 381
Chandler, Alfred D., 317
A Change of Light and Other Stories, 100
A Change of Skin, 101
Changes in the Land, 109

Character and Conflict, 218
Charles Dickens, 230
Charles Stewart Parnell, 231
Charles Sumner and the Coming of the Civil War, 304
The Charterhouse of Parma, 140
Chase, Gilbert, 267
Chase, Marian T., 248
Chase, Stuart, 248
Chastel, André, 263
Chaucer, Geoffrey, 21
Chaudhuri, Nirad, 83–84
The Chauvinist and Other Stories, 118
Cheever, John, 186–87, 196
Chekhov, Anton, 196, 220, 239
CHEMISTRY, 368–69
Chemistry and Beyond, 368
Chemistry and Crime, 368
Chemistry and Modern Society, 368
Chen, Jack, 116
Cherfas, Jeremy, 377, 379
Chéri and the Last of Chéri, 145
Cherry, Colin, 248
Chesterfield, Lord, 53
Chesterton, Gilbert Keith, 228
Chestnutt, Charles Waddell, 123
The Cheyennes: Indians of the Great Plains, 110
CHICANO-HISPANIC, 127–31
Chief Modern Poets of Britain and America, 205
Childe, V. Gordon, 298
Childhood and Society, 343
Children and Adolescents: Interpretive Essays on Jean Piaget, 343
Children Is All, 200
The Children of Sánchez, 104
Children of Violence, 166
Children's Books on Africa and Their Authors, 95
The Child's Understanding of Number, 344

CHINA, 79, 81–83
China Men, 117
The China Reader, 82
China's Economic Revolution, 317
Chinese Americans, 117
The Chinese Mind, 286
The Chinese of America, 116
Chinese Thought from Confucius to Mao Tse–tung, 81
Chinweizu, 93
Chippewa Customs, 109
Chodorow, Nancy, 343
Choephoroe, 6
Chomsky, Noam, 248, 284, 312, 332
Chopin, Kate, 173
Chrétien de Troyes, 21
Chrispeels, Maarten, 377
Christ Stopped at Eboli, 147
Christendom Divided: The Protestant Reformation, 39
Christian Faith and Other Faiths, 290
Christian Social Teachings, 291
Christopher and His Kind, 230
Christopher Columbus, 231
Chronicle of a Death Foretold, 101
Chronicles of America, 303
Chronicles of England, France, and Spain, 22
Chu, Louis H., 116
Churchill, Sir Winston, 297, 301
Chute, Marchette, 47
Cicero, Marcus Tullius, 14, 239
Cicero's Letters to Atticus, 239
CINEMA, see FILM
The City of God, 278
City of Night, 131
Civilisation, 263
Civilization: A Personal View, 37
Civilization and Capitalism: Vol. 1 The Structure of Everyday Life; Vol. 2 The Wheels of Commerce; Vol. 3 The Perspective of the World, 299
The Civilization of Rome, 16
The Civilization of the Renaissance in Italy, 37
Clapham, Wentworth B., 384
Clark, David H., 366
Clark, Kenneth M., 37, 263
Clash of Cultures, 326
The Classic Theatre, 218
CLASSICAL LITERATURE, see GREECE; ROME
The Classical Tradition, 10
Claudine at School, 145
Claudine in Paris, 145
Clea, 164
Cleaver, Eldridge, 123
Clemens, Samuel L., see Twain, Mark
A Clockwork Orange, 163
The Cloister and the Hearth, 26
The Closing Circle, 384
The Clouds, 6
Clough, Shepard Bancroft, 300
Cloward, Richard A., 336
The Clown and His Daughter, 69
Clyde, Paul H., 297
Cobban, Alfred, 57
Cocteau, 234
Cognition and Reality: Principles and Implications of Cognitive Psychology, 341
The Cold Fire: Alienation and the Myth of Culture, 336
Cole, Arthur C., 305
Coleridge, Samuel Taylor, 207
Coles, Jane Hallowell, 352
Coles, Robert, 352
Colette, Sidonie Gabrielle, 144–45, 196–97
Colinvaux, Paul, 377
Collins, Wilkie, 154
Colón, Jesus, 129
Colonial American Poetry, 45
Color, 123

Color of Darkness, 200

The Color Purple, 125

Columbia Dictionary of Modern European Literature, 396

The Columbia-Lippincott Gazetteer of the World, 393

The Combat, 92

The Coming Crisis of Western Sociology, 334

The Coming of the Civil War, 303

The Coming of the French Revolution, 58

The Coming of the Revolution, 306

Commentaries, 14

Commentary, 244

Common Differences: Conflicts in Black and White Feminist Perspectives, 355

The Common Reader: First Series, 242

Commoner, Barry, 384

Commonweal, 244

COMMUNICATIONS, 251–55

Communications and the Future, 253

Comparative Politics, 312

Comparative Study of Political Elites, 312

Compass History of Art Series, 262

The Compleat Angler, 47

The Complete English Poems, 33

Complete Greek Tragedies, 5

The Complete Guide to Modern Dance, 399

A Complete Guide to Therapy: From Psychotherapy to Behavior Modification, 342

Compton-Burnett, Ivy, 163

The Computer from Pascal to Von Neumann, 371

The Computer Glossary, 404

A Computer Perspective, 371

COMPUTER SCIENCE, 370–71

Computer Wimp, 370

Computers and the World of the Future, 371

Concentration Camps North America: Japanese in the United States and Canada During World War II, 116

Concise Cambridge History of English Literature, 396

The Concise Columbia Encyclopedia, 392

The Concise Dictionary, 395

Concise Dictionary of American Biography, 395

Concise Dictionary of American History, 400

Concise Dictionary of Scientific Biography, 403

Conditioned Reflexes: An Investigation of the Physiological Activity of the Cerebral Cortex, 340

Cone, James H., 292

Confessions, 14 (Augustine), 56 (Rousseau)

Confessions of an English Opium-Eater, 228

Conflict and Concord, 299

Confucius, 81

Confucius and the Chinese Way, 81

Congreve, William, 45

Conjectures and Refutations, 241

A Connecticut Yankee in King Arthur's Court, 177

Conquest of Mexico, 105

Conquest of Peru, 105

Conrad, Joseph, 163, 197

The Consolation of Philosophy, 14

Constant, Benjamin, 137

Constitution of the United States, 53

Constitutional Civil Liberties, 310

CONSTITUTIONAL LAW, 310
Constitutional Law, 310
Consuming Passions: The Anthropology of Eating, 326
Contact: Human Communication and Its History, 253
Contemporaries from the Nineteenth Century to the Present, 240–41
Contemporary America: The National Scene Since 1900, 306
Contemporary American Poetry, 205
Contemporary Chicano Theatre, 129
Contemporary French Poets, 213
Contemporary German Poetry, 214
CONTEMPORARY HISTORY, 301–03
Contemporary Indonesian Poetry: Poems in Bahasa Indonesian and English, 80
Contemporary Israeli Literature: An Anthology, 71
CONTINENTAL NOVELS, 135–41
CONTINENTAL POETRY, 213–15
The Continental Renaissance, 1500–1600, 39
The Continuity of American Poetry, 206
The Convention and the Constitution: The Political Ideas of the Founding Fathers, 310
Conversations with Ogotemmeli, 326
Copper, James Fenimore, 173–74
Coover, Robert C., 187, 197
Copland, Aaron, 267
Corneille, Pierre, 45

Corporate Control, Corporate Power, 319
Cortázar, Julio, 100
Coulton, George G., 24
The Count of Monte Cristo, 138
The Counterfeiters, 145
The Country of the Pointed Firs, 176
The Courtier, 33
Cousin Bette, 137
Cowan, Ruth Schwartz, 352
Cows, Pigs, Wars, and Witches, 326–27
Coyote Was Going There, 109
A Crack in the Mirror, 325
Craig, Albert M., 78
Craig, Gordon, 302
Crane, Hart, 210, 239
Crane, Stephen, 174, 197
Cranes at Dusk, 86
Craven, Avery Odelle, 303
The Creative Process, 261
Creel, H. G., 81
Crèvecoeur, St. John de, 53
Crichton, Michael, 371
Crime and Punishment, 138
The Crime of Sylvestre Bonnard, 138
Critical Perspectives on Lusophone Literature from Africa, 93
CRITICISM, 236–42
The Critique of Judgment, 280
The Critique of Practical Reason, 280
The Critique of Pure Reason, 280
Croce, Arlene, 268
Crombie, A. C., 24, 38
Cronon, William, 109
Cross Currents in Seventeenth-Century English Literature, 48
The Crowded Earth: People and the Politics of Population, 385
Crowding and Behavior, 344

Crowell's Handbook of Classical Literature, 396

Crowell's Handbook of Classical Mythology, 400

Crowell's Handbook of Elizabethan and Stuart Literature, 40

Crusade in Europe, 302

The Crusades, 25

Cry, the Beloved Country, 92

CUBA, *see* LATIN AMERICA

Cullen, Countee, 123

Culler, Jonathan, 239

Culture and Anarchy, 238

The Culture of Cities, 265

Culture, Society and the Media, 253

Cummings, E.E., 210

Cunha, Euclides da, 100

Cunliffe, Marcus, 57

Curie, Eve, 228

Curran, Charles E., 291

Current Biography, 395

The Current Crisis in American Politics, 310

Curti, Merle, 303–04

Cybernetics, 366

Cyrano de Bergerac, 49

Da Vinci, Leonardo, 33

Dada: Art and Anti-Art, 264

Daedalus, 244

Daiches, David, 228

Daily Life in Ancient Rome, 16

D'Alembert, Jean Le Rond, 53

Daly, Mary, 332

The Damnable Question, 300

The Damnation of Theron Ware, 174

Dana, Richard Henry, 228

DANCE, 268–69

Dance in Its Time, 269

A Dance to the Music of Time, 167

Dangerfield, George, 300

Dangerous Currents: The State of Economics, 322

Daniels, Roger, 116

Danks, Joseph H., 341

Dante Alighieri, 21

Daredevils of Sassoun: The Armenian National Epic, 72

Darío, Rubén, 100

The Dark Child, 92

Darkness at Noon, 147

Darley, John M., 344

Darnton, Robert, 57–58

Darwin, Charles, 228

David Copperfield, 155

David of Sassoun, 72

Davidoff, Leonore, 300

Davidson, Basil, 93–94

Davies, Robertson, 164

Davis, Arthur P., 125

Dawkins, Richard, 377

Dawn to the West: Japanese Literature in the Modern Era, 86

Day by Day, 211

The Day of the Locust, 183

The Day of the Scorpion, 168

De Broglie, Louis, 366

de Duve, Christian, 382

De Forest, John William, 174

da la Mare, Walter, 197

De Quincey, Thomas, 228

The Dead Father, 186

The Dead Sea Scriptures, 289

Dead Souls, 138

Dean, Vera Micheles, 297

Dear Theo, 234

Death in Life: Survivors of Hiroshima, 344

Death in Midsummer and Other Stories, 86

The Death of a Nobody, 149

The Death of Artemio Cruz, 101

The Death of the Heart, 163

Death on the Installment Plan, 144

Debo, Angie, 109

A Decade of Hispanic Literature: An Anniversary Anthology, 129

The Decameron, 33

The Decapitated Chicken and Other Stories, 102

Declaration of Independence, 53

The Decline and Fall of the Roman Empire, 17

Deconstruction: Theory and Practice, 250

Deconstructive Criticism: An Advance Introduction and Survey, 249

Dederer, John Morgan, 304

Deep Ecology, 385

Deep Song: The Dance Story of Martha Graham, 269

The Deer and the Tiger, 382

Deetz, James, 112, 325

DeFleur, Melvin L., 253

Defoe, Daniel, 47, 53

Deken, Joseph, 371

Delacroix, Eugene, 228

Deloria, Vine, Jr., 109

The Democratic South, 304

Demosthenes, 6

DeNitto, Dennis, 269

Densmore, Frances, 109

The Deptford Triology, 164

Derrida, Jacques, 284

Descartes, René, 278

DESIGN, 265–66

Destiny of Fire, 25

The Destruction of Black Civilization, 95

Detained, 92

Dethier, Vincent G., 378

Deutsch, Babette, 205

Deutsch, George, 345

Devall, William, 385

The Development of Modern Chemistry, 368

Developmental Psychology: An Introduction, 341

The Devil in Massachusetts, 49

Devkota, Laxmiprasad, 87

Dewey, John, 278

The Dialect of Sex: The Case for Feminist Revolution, 333

Dialogues, 282

Dialogues of the Dead, 7

Dialogues of the Gods, 7

Diamond, Stanley, 325

The Diaries of Paul Klee, 231

Diary of a Young Girl, 229

The Diary of Samuel Sewall, 47

Díaz del Castillo, Bernal, 104

Dickens, Charles, 58, 155

Dickinson, Emily, 208

DICTIONARIES, *see* REFERENCE BOOKS

Dictionary of American Biography, 395

Dictionary of American English on Historical Principles, 394

Dictionary of American History, 400

Dictionary of American Negro Biography, 395

A Dictionary of Americanisms on Historical Principles, 394

A Dictionary of Architecture, 397

Dictionary of Business and Economics, 402

A Dictionary of Comparative Religion, 399

Dictionary of Computing, 404

Dictionary of Italian Literature, 397

Dictionary of Literary Biography, 396

Dictionary of National Biography, 395

A Dictionary of Philosophy, 399

Dictionary of Scientific Biography, 403

Dictionary of the Decorative Arts, 398

Dictionary of the History of Ideas, 399

A Dictionary of the Natural Environment, 404

The Dictionary of the Opera, 399

Dictionary of the Social Sciences, 402

The Dictionary of World History, 400

Diderot, Denis, 54

Didion, Joan, 104

Diehl, Charles, 73

Digital Future, 370

Dillard, J. L., 248

Dinesen, Isak (Baronesse Karen Blixen), 197

Ding Ling, 81

Dinner at the Homesick Restaurant, 191

Diop, Cheikh Anta, 94

A Diplomatic History of Europe Since the Congress of Vienna, 299

A Diplomatic History of the American People, 303

Discipline and Punish: The Birth of the Prison, 333

Discourse on Method, 278

Discovering Life on Earth, 376

Discovery and Conquest of Mexico, 104

The Discovery of Animal Behavior, 382

Discovery of the Mind in Early Greek Philosophy and Literature, 10

Disputation and Dialogue, 290

Disraeli, 228

Dissent, 244

A Distant Mirror: The Calamitous Fourteenth Century, 26

Disturbing the Universe, 366

The Divided Self, 342

The Divine Comedy, 21

A Division of the Spoils, 168

The Diwan of Abu Tayyib Ahmad ibn al-Hussain al-Mutanabbi, 67

Dr. George Washington Carver, 229

Dr. Jekyll and Mr. Hyde, 157

Dr. Zhivago, 148

Doctorow, E. L., 187

A Documentary History of Religion in America, 291

Dodds, E. R., 8

Dog Soldiers, 191

Dog Years, 146

Dolbeare, Kenneth M., 311

The Don Flows Home to the Sea, 150

Don Quixote, 33

Doña Barbara, 101

Doña Flor and Her Two Husbands, 99

Doña Perfecta, 140

Donald, David, 304

Donleavy, J. P., 187

Donne, John, 33

Donoso, José, 101

Dorfman, Ariel, 253

Dos Passos, John, 104, 180

Dostoevski, Fedor, 137

Dostoevsky: The Seeds of Revolt, 1821–1849, 229

Dostoevsky: the Years of Ordeal, 1850–1859, 229

The Double Helix, 383

Douglas, Ann, 353

Douglas, Norman, 164

Douglass, Frederick, 123

Down These Mean Streets, 131

Drabble, Margaret, 164

The Dragons of Eden, 381–82

DRAMA, 216–23

Drama on Stage, 218

A Dream of Red Mansions (Hung Lou Meng), 83
Dream of the Red Chamber, 83
Dreiser, Theodore, 180
Dryden, John, 45
Du, Nguyen, 87
Du Bois, William E. B., 94, 123, 228
Dublin, Thomas, 353
Dubliners, 198
Dubos, René, 378
Dudley, Donald R., 16
Due to Circumstances Beyond Our Control, 253
Duff, J. W., 16
Dukas, Helen, 367
Dumas, Alexandre, 47, 138
Dunbar, Paul Laurence, 123
Dunn, Richard S., 300
Durant, Ariel, 47–48, 58
Durant, Will, 8–9, 16, 38, 47–48, 58, 286
Durkheim, Emile, 332
Durrell, Lawrence, 164
Dürrenmatt, Friedrich, 145
Dutton, Bertha P., 109
The Dyer's Hand, 238
Dyson, Freeman J., 366–67

Eagle Against the Sun: The American War with Japan, 306
The Eagle and the Serpent, 102
Eagleton, Terry, 248
Eames, Charles, 371
Eames, Edwin, 325
Eames, Ray, 371
Early Greek Poetry and Philosophy, 9
Early History of Rome, 15
Early Poems 1935–1955, 102
Earthly Powers, 163
East Across the Pacific: Historical and Sociological Studies of Japanese Immigration and Assimilation, 116
EAST AND SOUTHEAST ASIA, 74–87
East Asia: Tradition and Transformation, 78
East to America: A History of the Japanese in the United States, 119
The Eastern Orthodox Church, 293
Eat a Bowl of Tea, 116
Eckstein, Alexander, 317
Eclogues, 16
Eco, Umberto, 145, 249
ECOLOGY, see BIOLOGICAL SCIENCES
Economic and Philosophical Manuscripts, 281
The Economic Development of Medieval Europe, 24
Economic Philosophy, 321
Economic Report of the President, 317–18
ECONOMICS, 314–22
Economics: An Introductory Analysis, 321
Economics and the Public Purpose, 318
Economist, 244
The Economists, 321
Economists at Bay: Why the Experts Will Never Solve Your Problems, 319
The Economy: Old Myths and New Realities, 319
Ecstatic Religions, 327
Edel, Leon, 229
Edelman, Murray J., 311
Edey, Maitland, 379
Edge of the Storm, 103
Edgeworth, Maria, 155
The Education of Henry Adams, 227
The Education of T. C. Mits, 369

Efuru, 92
The Egghead Republic, 149
The Egoist, 157
Ehrenreich, Barbara, 332–33
Ehrlich, Anne, 378
Ehrlich, Paul, 378
Eichenberg, Fritz, 261
Eichner, Alfred S., 318
Eight Great Comedies, 218
Eight Great Tragedies, 218
Eight Men, 202
Eighteen Twenty-Six Journal of
    John James Audubon, 227
18TH CENTURY, 50–58
The Eighth Day of Creation:
    Makers of the Revolution in
    Biology, 379
Einstein, 229
Einstein—A Centenary Volume,
    367
Eisenhower, Dwight D., 302
Eisenstein, Sergei, 269
Eisenstein, Zillah, 353
Either/Or, 284
Ekwenski, Cyprian, 91
El Bronx Remembered, 130
Eleanor of Aquitaine and the Four
    Kings, 25
The Electronic Cottage, 371
Electronic Life: How to Think
    about Computers, 371
The Elementary Forms of the
    Religious Life, 332
The Elements of Style, 395
Eliot, George (Mary Ann Evans),
    155
Eliot, T. S., 210, 220, 239
Elizabethan and Metaphysical
    Imagery, 41
Elizabethan Critical Essays, 33
Elizabethan Narrative Verse, 33–34
The Elizabethan Renaissance: The
    Cultural Achievement, 40
The Elizabethan Renaissance: The
    Life of Society, 40

The Elizabethan World Picture,
    41
Elkind, David, 343
Elliott, John Huxtable, 300
Ellison, Ralph, 123–24
Ellmann, Richard, 229
Elsie Venner, 175
Emecheta, Buchi, 91
The Emergence of Modern
    America, 1865–1878, 305
Emerson, Ralph Waldo, 208, 239
Émile, 56
Emma, 153–54
The Empty Space, 222
Enclave, 130
Encyclopedia Judaica, 399
The Encyclopaedia of Islam, 400
The Encyclopedia Americana,
    392
Encyclopedia of American
    History, 400
Encyclopedia of Black America,
    401
Encyclopedia of Computer
    Science and Engineering,
    404
The Encyclopedia of Mammals,
    404
Encyclopedia of Modern Archi-
    tecture, 265
Encyclopedia of Opera, 267
Encyclopedia of Philosophy, 399
Encyclopedia of Psychology, 402
The Encyclopedia of Visual Arts,
    397
Encyclopedia of World Art, 390,
    397
An Encyclopedia of World
    History, 401
Encyclopedia of World Literature
    in the 20th Century, 396
ENCYCLOPEDIAS, see REFER-
    ENCE BOOKS
The Encyclopedic Dictionary of
    Psychology, 402

The End of Liberalism: The Second Republic of the United States, 311

End of the Road, 185

The Endangered Planet, 312

The Enduring Art of Japan, 87

Engerman, Stanley L., 304

The Engineer of Human Souls, 150

ENGINEERING, *see* PHYSICAL SCIENCES

England's Eliza, 34

English, Deirdre, 332

ENGLISH DRAMA BEFORE SHAKESPEARE, 22

English Drama: 1580–1642, 34

English Literature in the Earlier Seventeenth Century: 1600–1660, 37

English Literature in the Sixteenth Century, 39

English Lyrics of the Medieval Period, 22

ENGLISH NOVELS, *see* BRITISH NOVELS

The English Poems of George Herbert, 34

The English Reformation, 40

English Versification, 1570–1980: A Reference Guide with Global Appendix, 205

The Enlightenment, 300

The Enlightenment: An Interpretation, 58

The Enneads, 282

Enormous Changes at the Last Minute, 200

Enquiry Concerning Human Understanding, 279

The Epic of Latin American Literature, 105

The Epic of the Kings, 68

Epitaph of a Small Winner, 102

Equality and Efficiency: The Big Tradeoff, 320

Equality, the Third World and Economic Delusion, 317

The Era of Theodore Roosevelt: 1900–1912, 306

Erasmus, Desiderius, 34

Erewhon, 154

Erikson, Erik H., 343

Erikson, Kai T., 333

Ernest Hemingway: A Life Story, 227

Eros and Civilization: A Philosophical Inquiry into Freud, 335

Errington, Paul, 378

Esau and Jacob, 102

Essay and General Literature Index, 391

An Essay Concerning Human Understanding, 46, 281

Essay on the Principles of Population, 55

ESSAYS, 236–42

Essays in Criticism, 238

Essays in Understanding Latin America, 105

Essays of Elia, 241

Essays of Three Decades, 241

The Essential Darwin, 380

The Essential Gandhi, 84

Esslin, Martin, 222, 229

Estampas del valle y otras obras, 130

Esteves, Sandra Maria, 129

Esther Waters, 157

Ethan Frome, 183

ETHICS, 291

The Ethics, 283

Ethnic and Tourist Arts, 325–26

Ethnographic Film, 327

Eugénie Grandet, 137

Eumenides, 6

Euripides, 6–7

Europa Yearbook, 402

Europe and the French Imperium, 301

Europe and the People without History, 329

Europe in the Fourteenth and Fifteenth Centuries, 298

Europe in Transition, 1300–1520, 38

Europe: The World of the Middle Ages, 298

European Economic History, 300

EUROPEAN NOVELS, *see* CONTINENTAL NOVELS

Evans-Pritchard, Edward E., 326

Eve and the New Jerusalem: Socialism and Feminism in the Nineteenth Century, 357

Evelyn, John, 45

Even the Rat Was White: A Historical View of Psychology, 344

Ever Since Darwin: Reflections in Natural History, 378

Everyday Life in Medieval Times, 26

Everything in Its Path: Destruction of Community in the Buffalo Creek Flood, 333

Everything That Rises Must Converge, 199

Ewen, David, 267

Ewers, John C., 109

Existence and Being, 279

Existentialism from Dostoevsky to Sartre, 286

Experience and Nature, 278

An Experience of Women: Pattern and Change in Nineteenth-Century Europe, 302

Experimental Psycholinguistics: An Introduction, 341

Extinction: The Causes and Consequences of the Disappearance of Species, 378

Eysenck, H. J., 343

Fables, 6 (Aesop), 467 (La Fontaine)

Fabliaux: Ribald Tales from the Old French, 22

Facing Mount Kenya, 94

The Fact of a Doorframe: Poems Selected and New, 1950–1984, 211

Facts on File, 401

Faerie Queene, 36

Fagan, Brian M., 326

Fagunwa, Daniel Orowole, 91

Fairbank, John K., 78, 297

Falk, Richard, 312

Fallico, Arturo B., 263

Families, Politics, and Public Policy: A Feminist Dialogue on Women and the State, 353

Family: Turbulent Stream; Spring; Autumn, 82

Family Installments, 131

Family of Man, 270

Famous Utopias of the Renaissance, 34

Fanon, Frantz, 94

Fanshen: A Documentary of Revolution in a Chinese Village, 81

FAR EAST, *see* EAST AND SOUTHEAST ASIA

The Far East, 297

The Far East and Australasia, 403

Far from the Madding Crowd, 156

The Far Side of Paradise, 232

Farb, Peter, 249, 326

Farber, Eduard, 368

A Farewell to Arms, 181

Farewell to Manzanar, 86

Farrell, James T., 180, 197

Farrington, Benjamin, 9

Fathers and Sons, 140

Faulkner, 228

Faulkner, William, 180–81, 197

Faust, 54

Fay, Sidney Bradshaw, 302
Federal Reserve Bank of Atlanta, 318
The Federalist Papers, 311
Feeling and Form, 205
A Feeling for the Organism: The Life and Work of Barbara McClintock, 380
Feest, Christian F., 109
Feigenbaum, Edward A., 371
Feinberg, Gerald, 367
Felita, 130
The Fellowship of the Ring, 168
The Female World, 352
The Feminine Mystique, 333
Feminine Psychology, 342
FEMINISM, *see* WOMEN'S STUDIES
Feminist Frameworks: Alternative Theoretical Accounts of the Relations Between Men and Women, 353
Feminist Studies, 358
The Feminization of American Culture, 353
Ferdowsi, Abulghasem, 68
Ferguson, Wallace K., 38
Festinger, Leon, 343
Feudal Society, 24
Ficciones, 100
FICTION, *see* NOVELS; SHORT STORY
Fiction and the Figures of Life, 240
Fiction Catalog, 397
Fielding, Henry, 54
Fifth Business, 164
The Fifth Generation, 371
Fifty Major Documents of the Twentieth Century, 302
Filler, Louis, 304
FILM, 269–71
Film and the Critical Eye, 269
The Film Encyclopedia, 398
The Film Experience, 270

Film Form, 269
The Film Sense, 270
The Financier, 180
Fin-De-Siecle Vienna: Politics and Culture, 301
Finding the Center: Narrative Poetry of the Zuñi Indians, 109–10
FINE ARTS AND PERFORM- ING ARTS, 259–71
Finley, M.I., 9
Finnegan, Ruth, 94
Fiorenza, Elisabeth Schuessler, 353
The Fire of Liberty, 54
Firestone, Shulamith, 333
The First Circle, 150
Fischer, Louis, 84
Fisher, Anthony D., 112
Fisher, Sydney, 73
Fitzgerald, F. Scott, 181, 197, 239
Fitzhugh, William W., 109–10
Five Economic Challenges, 319
Five Modern Noh Plays, 86
A Flag for Sunrise, 191
Flaubert, Gustave, 138, 239–40
Fletcher, John, 44
Flexner, Eleanor, 304
Flexner, James T., 58
The Flies, 100
The Flight from the Enchanter, 167
Flower, Elizabeth, 286
The Flowering of the Middle Ages, 263
Flowers of Fire: Twentieth Century Korean Stories, 80
Focal Encyclopedia of Photogra- phy, 270
Fogel, Robert W., 304
Fonteyn, Dame Margot, 268
For Her Own Good: 150 Years of Experts' Advice to Women, 332–33

For Whom the Bell Tolls, 182

Forbes, 244

Force and Statecraft: Diplomatic Problems of Our Time, 302

Ford, Ford Madox (Ford Madox Hueffer), 164

Foreign Affairs, 244

Forell, George W., 291

Forest of a Thousand Daemons, 91

The Forest People, 329

The Forgotten People: Cane River's Creoles of Color, 305

Form and Function, 265

The Formation of the Economic Thought of Karl Marx, 320

Forster, E. M., 163–66, 197, 240

The Forsyte Saga, 166

Forthcoming Books, 390

The Fortunes of Nigel, 49

The Forty Days of Musa Dagh, 150

The 42nd Parallel, 180

Forty Viziers, 70

Foucault, Michel, 38, 333

The Foundations of Early Modern Europe, 1460–1559, 300

Four Arguments for the Elimination of Television, 254

Four Major Plays of Chikamatsu, 79–80

Four Russian Plays, 218

Four Verse Plays (Anderson), 220

The Fourth Dimension, 369

Fowler, James W., 293

Fowles, John, 166

Fox, George, 45

Fox-Genovese, Elizabeth, 303

France, Anatole, 138, 145

France: An Interpretive History, 297

Frank, Anne, 229

Frank, Francine, 249

Frank, Gelya F., 327

Frank, Joseph, 229

Frank, Philipp, 229, 284

Frankel, Hermann F., 9

Frankenstein, 157

Frankl, Viktor, E., 342

Franklin, Benjamin, 54

Franklin, John Hope, 304

Fraser, Antonia, 48

Frederic, Harold, 174

Free to Choose, 318

Freedman, Jonathan, 344

Freeman, Douglas Southall, 229

Freire, Paulo, 333

The French Lieutenant's Woman, 166

The French Revolution, 57

French Sociology: Rupture and Renewal Since 1968, 335

Freud, Sigmund, 342

Freyre, Gilberto, 104

Friedan, Betty, 333

Friedlander, Judith, 326

Friedman, Milton, 318

Friedman, Rose, 318

Friendly, Alfred W., 253

Frisch, Max, 145

Froissart, Jean, 22

From Sand Creek, 111–12

From Slavery to Freedom: A History of Negro Americans, 304

From Surabaya to Armageddon: Indonesian Short Stories, 80

From the Country of Eight Islands: An Anthology of Japanese Poetry, 80

From the Dark Tower: Afro-American Writers, 1900–1960, 125

Frontiers: A Journal of Women Studies, 358

Frontiers of Anthropology, 326

Frost, Robert, 210

Fry, Roger E., 261

Frye, Northrop, 240
Fuentes, Carlos, 101
Fugard, Athol, 220
Fung Yu-Lan, 81
Funk and Wagnalls Standard
  Dictionary of Folklore,
  Mythology and Legends, 400
the Futile Life of Pito Perez, 103
The Future of Architecture, 266
The Future of Partnership, 292
Futuyma, Douglas J., 378
Fuzuli, Mehmet, 69–70

Gabriela, Clove, and Cinnamon,
  99
Gaddis, William, 187
Gaines, Ernest J., 124
Galbraith, John Kenneth, 318
Gall, Sally M., 206
Gallegos, Rómulo, 101
Gallistel, C. R., 344
Galsworthy, John, 166
Gamow, George, 367, 370
Gandhi, Mohandas K., 84
Garard, Ira D., 368
García Márquez, Gabriel, 101
Garcilaso de la Vega, 101
Gardner, Howard, 341
Gargantua and Pantagruel, 35
Garin, Eugenio, 38
The Garrick Year, 164
Graza, Roberto J., 129–30
Gaskell, Elizabeth, 156
Gass, William, 187, 197, 240
Gautier, Théophile, 138
Gay, John, 54
Gay, Peter, 58, 300
Geertz, Clifford, 326, 344
Gelman, Rochel, 344
Gender, 334
Gender: An Ethnomethodological
  Approach, 344
The Gene Doctors: Medical
  Genetics at the Frontier, 377

General Science Index, 404
A General Selection from the
  Works, 342
The General Theory of Employ-
  ment, Interest, and Money,
  319
A Generation of Materialism,
  1871–1900, 301
Genet, Jean, 145, 220
Genetic Prophecy: Beyond the
  Double Helix, 379
Genovese, Eugene, 303
Geoffroy de Villehardouin, 22
Geoffroy of Monmouth, 22
GEOLOGY, 370
George, Alexander L., 302
George Washington: Man and
  Monument, 57
German and Italian Lyrics of the
  Middle Ages, 22
Germinal, 141
Gestalt Psychology, 340
Ghana: The Autobiography of
  Kwame Nkrumah, 95
The Ghost Dance Religion and
  the Sioux Outbreak of 1890,
  111
Giacconi, Mirella, 368
Giant Molecules, 368–69
Gibbon, Edward, 17
Gibney, Frank, 85
Gibson, James, J., 344
Gide, André, 145
Giedion, Sigfried, 265
Gies, Frances, 25
Gies, Joseph, 25
The Gift, 327
Gigi, Julie de Carneilhan, and
  Chance Acquaintances,
  144–45
Gilbert, Sandra, M., 354
Gilligan, Carol, 354
Gilmore, Myron, P., 38, 301
The Ginger Man, 187
Ginsberg, Allen, 210

Gintis, Herbert, 332
Giordano Bruno and the Hermetic
  Tradition, 41
Gipson, Lawrence Henry, 306
Giraudoux, Jean, 220
Gissing, George, 156
Gitlin, Todd, 253–54
Glasgow, Ellen, 181
Gleitman, Henry, 341
Glick, Clarence, 116
Global Reach, 317
Glückel, 354
Glucksberg, Sam, 341
Go Tell it on the Mountain, 122
The Goalie's Anxiety at the
  Penalty Kick, 146
God and Golem, Inc., 366
Godan: The Gift of a Cow, 84
Gödel, Escher, Bach, 365
Gods and Men, 298
God's Bits of Wood, 92
God's Little Acre, 179
Goethe, Johann Wolfgang von,
  54
Goffman, Erving, 334
Gogol, Nikolai, 138–39, 197
Going After Cacciato, 190
Going Steady, 270
Going to the Dance, 268
The Golden Apples of the Sun,
  196
The Golden Ass, 14
The Golden Bowl, 176
The Golden Century, 299
The Golden Fruits, 149
Golden Latin Artistry, 17
The Golden Serpent, 99
Golding, William, 166
Goldman, Marshall I., 318
Goldoni, Carlo, 54
Goldsmith, Oliver, 54
Goldstine, Herman, 371
Goldstone, Richard Henry, 229
The Golestan, 69
Goncharov, Ivan, 139

The Good Companions, 167
Good Company, 334
A Good Man Is Hard to Find,
  199
Good Morning, Midnight, 168
The Good Soldier, 164
The Good Soldier Schweik, 146
Goodbye, Columbus, and Five
  Short Stories, 200
Goodbye, Gutenberg: The
  Newspaper Revolution of the
  1980s, 254
Goode, Judith Granich, 325
Gordimer, Nadine, 91
Gordon, David M., 317
Gordon, Mary, 354
Gosling, Nigel, 270
Gottfried von Strassburg, 22
Gould, Stephen Jay, 378
Gouldner, Alvin W., 334
GOVERNMENT, see POLITICS
The Governmental Process,
  311–12
Garham, Shirley, 229
A Grain of Wheat, 92
Grammatical Man: Information,
  Entropy, Language, and
  Life, 248
The Grandissimes, 173
Granger's Index to Poetry, 397
Grant, Michael, 9, 17
Grant, Susan, 379
Grantham, Dewey W., 304
Granville-Barker, Harley, 38
The Grapes of Wrath, 183
Grass, Günter, 146
The Grass Harp and A Tree of
  Night and Other Stories, 196
The Grass Roof, 87
Graves, Robert, 9, 17
Gravity, Black Holes and the
  Universe, 367
Gravity's Rainbow, 190
The Great Book of Birds, 404
The Great Bridge, 365

The Great Cat Massacre: And Other Episodes in French Cultural History, 57–58
The Great Evolution Mystery, 383
Great Expectations, 155
The Great Gatsby, 181
Great Jewish Thinkers of the Twentieth Century, 294
The Great Pianists, 268
The Great Plains, 306
The Great Psychologists from Aristotle to Freud, 340
Great Sanskrit Plays in Modern Translation, 84
Great Scientific Experiments, 365
Great Voices of the Reformation, 294
The Great Wheel: The World Monetary System, 321
GREECE, 3–11
The Greek Anthology, 5
The Greek Experience, 8
Greek Lyrics, 54
The Greek Myths, 9
The Greek Philosophers, 11
Greek Science, 9
Greek Sculpture, 264
The Greek Stones Speak, 10
Greek Tragedy, 10
Greek Tragic Poetry, 10
The Greek Way, 9
The Greeks, 10
The Greeks and the Irrational, 8
Green, Henry (Henry Vincent Yorke), 166
Green, Jonathan, 270
The Green Huntsman, 140
Green, Philip, 311
Greenblatt, Stephen, 38
Greene, Evarts B., 305
Greene, Graham, 166
Greenough, Horatio, 265
Greiner, William R., 310
Griaule, Marcel, 326

Gribbin, John, 379
Grierson, H. J. C., 48
Griffiths, Paul, 267
Grimm, Harold J., 300
Grimmelshausen, Hans Jacob Christoffel von, 45
Gropius, Walter, 265
Grout, Donald Jay, 267
Grove Press Modern Drama, 218
The Growth of American Thought, 303
Growth of the Soil, 146
Gubar, Susan, 354
Guerrillas, 167
A Guide to Post-Keynesian Economics, 318
Guide to Reference Books, 371
A Guided Tour of the Living Cell, 382
Guillaume, Alfred, 293
Guillaume de Lorris, 22
Guillemin, Jeanne, 110
Guillen, Michael, 369
Gulliver's Travels, 56
Guntekin, Resat Nuri, 70
Gunther, Gerald, 310
Gupte, Pranay, 385
Gurr, Andrew, 38
Guthrie, Robert V., 344
Gutman, Robert, 229
Guzmán, Martín Luis, 101
Gyn/Ecology: The Metaethics of Radical Feminism, 332

Habermas, Jurgen, 334
The Habsburg Monarchy, 1800–1918, 301
Hacker, Louis Morton, 304
Hadas, Moses, 9
Hafiz, Khaja Qavamaddin, 68–69
Hakluyt, Richard, 34
Halberstam, David, 312
Hale, J. R., 38
Halecki, Oskar, 297

Hall, Calvin, 341
Hall, Edward T., 249, 326
Hall, John W., 85
Hall of Mirrors, 191
Haller, William, 48
Halliday, Jon, 85
Hallucinogens and Shamanism, 326
Hamilton, Alexander, 311
Hamilton, Edith, 9
Hammarskjold, Dag, 229
Hammond Citation World Atlas, 393
Hammond Medallion World Atlas, 393
Hamsun, Knut, 146
A Handbook of Christian Theologians, 294
Handbook of North American Indians, 110
A Handbook of Literature, 396
A Handful of Dust, 169
Handke, Peter, 146
Hard Times, 155
Hardin, Garrett, 379
Harding, Vincent, 126
Hardy, Thomas, 156, 208
The Harlem Renaissance Remembered, 125
Harlem Shadows, 124
Harper, Douglas, 334
Harré, Rom, 365
Harrington, Michael, 334
Harris, Ann S., 354
Harris, Marvin, 326
Harrison, George B., 38–39
Harrison, Jane, 9–10
Harsanyi, Zsolt, 379
Hartt, Frederick, 39
Hartz, Louis, 308
Harvard Dictionary of Music, 398
Harvard Guide to American History, 402
Hašek, Jaroslav, 146
Haskell, Arnold, 268

Haskins, Charles Homer, 25
Hawkes, John, 187
Hawkes, Terence, 249
Hawthorne, Nathaniel, 48, 174, 198
Hay, Denys, 298
Hay Otra Vez Poems, 131
Hayakawa, S. I., 249
Hayek, Friedrich A., 318
Hayes, Carlton J. H., 301
A Hazard of New Fortunes, 175
Hazlitt, William, 240
Head, Bessie, 92
The Heart Is a Lonely Hunter, 188
Heart of Aztlan, 129
Heart of Darkness, 163
The Heart of the Matter, 166
The Heavenly City of the Eighteenth-Century Philosophers, 57
Hedayat, Sadegh, 68–69
Heer, Friedrich, 25
Hegel, Georg W. F., 278–79
Heidegger, Martin, 279
Heider, Karl, 327
Heilbroner, Robert L., 318
Heinrich, Bernd, 379
Heisenberg, Werner, 367
Hellenistic Culture, 9
Heller, Joseph, 188
Heller, Walter W., 319
Hellman, Judith Adler, 104
Hellman, Lillian, 220
Helplessness: On Depression, Development, and Death, 342–43
Hemingway, Ernest, 181, 198, 240
Henderson, Harold G., 85
Heninger, S. K., 39
Henry, O. (William Sydney Porter), 198
Henry, Robert S., 305
Henry James, 229

Hen's Teeth and Horse's Toes: Further Reflections in Natural History, 379

Herbert, George, 34

Hercules, My Shipmate, 9

Herculine Barbin: Being the Recently Discovered Memoirs of a Nineteenth-Century French Hermaphrodite, 333

Herman, Edward S., 319

Herman, William, 269

A Hero of Our Time, 139

Herodotus, 7

Herr, Richard, 300

Herrick, Robert, 46

Herring, Hubert C., 104

Herself Surprised, 163

Herzog, 186

Hesiod, 7

Hesse, Hermann, 146

Hession, Charles, 229

The Hidden Dimension, 326

A High Wind in Jamaica, 166

Higham, Charles, 230

Highet, Gilbert, 10, 17

Hildesheimer, Wolfgang, 230

Hilgard, Ernest, R., 341

Hillerbrand, Hans, J., 39

The Hills Beyond, 202

Hindu Myths, 84

Hindu Religious Tradition, 293

Hinduism, 84

Hinojosa, Rolando, 130

Hinton, William, 81

Hippolytus, 7

Hirmer, Max, 264

Historical Abstracts, 402

Histories, 8

HISTORY, 295–306

History, 7

A History of American Labor, 321

History of American Life Series, 305

History of Art, 261

History of Civilization, 297

The History of England, 48, 298

A History of Far Eastern Art, 78–79

History of Greek Literature, 9 (Hadas), 10 (Lesky)

History of Italian Renaissance Art, 39

History of Latin America, 104

A History of Literary Criticism in the Renaissance, 41

History of Modern Art, 261

A History of Modern France, 57

A History of Modern Poetry: From the 1890s to the High Modernist Mode, 206

History of Philosophy, 286

A History of Philosophy in America, 286

A History of Poland, 297

A History of Russia, 301

A History of Song, 267

The History of Surrealism, 264

History of the Arabs from the Earliest Times to the Present, 73

History of the English-Speaking Peoples, 297

A History of the Jews, 291–92

History of the Kings of Britain, 22

History of the Monroe Doctrine, 306

History of the Theatre, 222

A History of Western Music, 267

A History of Western Philosophy, 286

Hitchcock, 271

Hitti, Philip Khuri, 73

Hoban, Russell, 188

Hobbes, Thomas, 279

Hodges, Andrew, 230

Hodier, Andre, 267

The Hoe and the Horse on the Plains, 110

Hoebel, E. Adamson, 110
Hoffmann, Banesh, 367
Hofstadter, Douglas, 365
Hofstadter, Richard, 305
Holder, Preston, 110
Holmes, Oliver Wendell, 175
Holton, Gerald, 365
The Holy Koran: Text and
    Explanatory Translation, 289
Homans, George C., 334
Home Book of Quotations, 397
The Home Book of Verse:
    American and English
    1580–1920, 205
The Homecoming, 221
Homer, 7
Homer, William Innes, 230
Hookham, Hilda, 81
Hopkins, Gerard Manley, 208
Hopkins, Thomas J., 293
Hopscotch, 100
Horace (Quintus Horatius Flaccus),
    14–15
Horney, Karen, 342
The Horse's Mouth, 163
Hosokawa, Bill, 119
The House by the Medler Tree,
    141
A House for Mr. Biswas, 167
House Made of Dawn, 111
The House of Mirth, 183
The House of the Seven Gables,
    174
Houseboy, 92
Houseman, Alfred Edward, 208
Houston, James D., 86
Houston, Jeanne Wakutsuki,
    86
How Europe Underdeveloped
    Africa, 86
How German Is It, 185
How to Read a Film: The Art,
    Technology, Language,
    History, and Theory of Film
    and Media, 254

How to Read Donald Duck:
    Imperialist Ideology in the
    Disney Comic, 253
Howard, Jane, 230
Howe, Irving, 240
Howells, William Dean, 175
Hudson, Charles, 110
Hudson Review, 244
Hughes, Langston, 124, 126, 210
Hughes, Richard, 166
Hughes, Robert, 263
Hughes, Ted, 210
Huizinga, Johan, 25
Human Diversity, 382
Human Ecosystems, 384
Humanistic Botany, 383
Humanities Index, 391
Hume, David, 279
Humphrey, Doris, 268–69
Humphreys, Christmas, 293
Hungry Wolf, Beverly, 110
Hunt, John Dixon, 230
Hurston, Zora Neale, 124, 354
Huss, Roy G., 270
Husserl, Edmund, 279–80
Huston, Perdita, 354
Hutton, Richard, 379
Huxley, Aldous, 166
Huysmans, Joris Karl, 139

I, Claudius, 17
I Lost It at the Movies, 270
I Love Myself When I Am
    Laughing . . . A Zora Neale
    Hurston Reader, 354
I Stand Corrected: More on
    Language, 250
Ibn Khaldun, 67
Ibsen, Henrik, 220
Ibuse, Masuji, 86
The Iceman Cometh, 221
Ideas, 279–80
Ideas and Men, 297
The Ides of March, 17

If on a Winter's Night a Traveler, 144

Ihde, Aaron, J., 368

Iliad, 7

Illich, Ivan, 334

Illusion in Art: A History of Pictorial Illusionism, 264

The Illustrations from the Works of Andreas Vesalius, 36

The Imitation of Christ, 23

The Immoralist, 145

Imperialism: The Highest Stage of Capitalism, 319

In a Different Voice: Psychological Theory and Women's Development, 354

In Dubious Battle, 183

In Her Own Image: Women Working in the Arts, 354

In Memory of Her: A Feminist Theological Reconstruction of Christian Origins, 354

In Nueva York, 130

In Praise of Folly, 34

In Praise of Love, 26

In Search of the Primitive, 325

In the Heart of the Heart of the Country, 197

In the Heart of the Seas, 70

In the Light of History, 301

In the Middle of the Road, 99

In the Midst of Life, 196

In the People's Republic, 313

Index to Book Reviews in the Humanities, 391

INDIA, 83–85

India: A Wounded Civilization, 84

Indian Dances of North America, 110

Indians, 112

Inevitable Revolutions, 104

The Influence of Sea Power upon History, 1660–1783, 298

Information Please Almanac, 392

The Ingenious Dr. Franklin, 365

Inkeles, Alex, 334

The Innocent Voyage, 166

An Inquiry into Meaning and Truth, 282

Inscrutable Earth, 370

Inside Prime Time, 253

Intelligence Controversy: H. J. Eysenck vs. Leon Kamin, 343

The International Center of Photography Encyclopedia of Photography, 398

International Dictionary of Film and Filmmakers: Volume I: Films, 398

International Encyclopedia of the Social Sciences, 402

International Index, 391

INTERNATIONAL RELATIONS, 312–13

International Who's Who, 395

The Interpretation of Cultures, 326

The Interpreter's Bible, 289

The Interpreter's Dictionary of the Bible, 289, 400

Introducing Shakespeare, 38–39

Introduction to African Religion, 94

An Introduction to Brazil, 105

An Introduction to Chinese Literature, 82

Introduction to Classical Arabic Literature, 68

An Introduction to Haiku, 85

Introduction to Oriental Civilizations: Sources of Indian Tradition, 78

Introduction to Personality, 341

Introductory Lectures on Psychoanalysis: A General Introduction to Psychoanalysis, 342

Introductory Readings on Language, 249

Inua: Spirit World of the Bering Sea Eskimo, 109–10
Invisible Man, 123–24
Invitation to Archeology, 325
Invitation to Chemistry, 368
Ionesco, Eugène, 220–21
Irons, Peter, 116
Ironweed, 188
The Irrepressible Conflict, 1850–1865, 305
Irving, Washington, 198
Isherwood, Christopher, 156–66, 230
Ishi in Two Worlds, 110
Islam, 293
Island: Poetry and History of Chinese Immigrants on Angel Island, 1910–1940, 116
ISRAELI LITERATURE, 70–71
The Issa Valley, 148
Istanbul Boy, 70
Italian Humanism: Philosophy and Civic Life in the Renaissance, 38
Italian Painters of the Renaissance, 37
Italian Poetry: A Selection from St. Francis of Assisi to Salvatore Quasimodo, 214
Italian Poetry, 1960–1980, 214
The Italian Renaissance, 40, 299
Ivanhoe, 26

Jabra, Ibrahim Jabra, 67
Jackson, Shirley, 198
Jackson, W. T. H., 25
Jacobean Drama: An Anthology, 218
Jacobson, Norman, 308–09
Jaeger, Werner, 10
Jahn, Janheinz, 94
James Joyce, 229
James, William, 240, 280, 293, 339–40

Jamieson, Perry D., 305
Jane Austen, Feminism and Fiction, 355
Jane Eyre, 154
Janson, Horst W., 261
JAPAN, 79–80, 85–87
Japan, 85 (Hall), 86 (Sansom)
Japanese Americans: The Evolution of a Subculture, 117
Japanese Inn: A Reconstruction of the Past, 87
Japanese Theatre, 85
Jay, John, 311
Jean de Joinville, 22
Jean de Meun, 22
Jeans, James, 365
Jefferson, 58
Jefferson, Thomas, 55
Jeffrey, Ian, 270
Jensen, Merrill, 305
The Jerusalem Bible, 288
The Jewel in the Crown, 168
Jewett, Sarah Orne, 176
Jewish Society Through the Ages, 73
Jews and Arabs, 73
Joan of Arc, 26, 233
Johanson, Donald, 379
John Keats, 234
John Maynard Keynes, 229
John Milton: Complete Poems and Major Prose, 35
John XXIII, Pope, 230
Johnson, Chalmers, 319
Johnson, Edgar, 230
Johnson, Samuel, 48, 55
Jones, Ernest, 230
Jones, James, 188, 334
Jones, LeRoi, *see* Baraka, Imamu Amiri
Jones, W. T., 286
Jonson, Ben, 34
Jordan, Archibald Campbell, 94
Joseph Andrews, 54

Joseph Conrad: The Three Lives, 231
Joseph, Gloria I., 355
The Joseph Tetralogy, 148
Josephy, Alvin M., 110
Journal of a Soul, 230
A Journal of the Plague Year, 47
Journey to Ixtlan, 292
Journey to the End of the Night, 144
Journey to the West, 83
Joyce, James, 166, 198, 240
Judaism in America: Adventure in Modernity, 293
Jude the Obscure, 157
Judgment Day, 180
The Judiciary: The Supreme Court in the Government Processes, 310
Judson, Horace Freeland, 379
Jumpers, 221
Jung, Carl G., 342
The Jungle, 183
Justice at War, 116
Justine, 164
Juvenal (Demicus Junius Juvenalis), 15

Kael, Pauline, 270
Kafka, Franz, 146, 198
Kagan, Jerome B., 344
Kalidasa, 84
Kang, Younghill, 87
Kanowitz, Leo, 310
Kant, Immanuel, 280
Kao Ngo, 83
Kaplan, Justin, 230
Kaplan, Susan A., 109
Karl, Frederick, Robert, 231
Karl Marx, 227
Karnow, Stanley, 305
Katz, William Loren, 126
Kavaler, Lucy, 380

Kawabata, Yasunari, 86
Kaye, Evelyn, 254
Kazantzakis, Nikos, 147
Kazin, Alfred, 240–41
Keats, John, 241
Keene, Donald, 86
Keller, Evelyn Fox, 380
Keller, Helen, 231
Kelly, Amy, 25
Kemal, Yashar, 70
Kenilworth, 40
Kennedy, William, 188
Kenyatta, Jomo, 94
Kesey, Ken, 188
Kessler, Suzanne J., 344
Kessler-Harris, Alice, 355
Kevles, Daniel, 367
Key Sources in Comparative and World Literature, 396
The Key to the Universe, 366
Keynes, John Maynard, 319
Keywords: A Vocabulary of Culture and Society, 251
Khayyám, Omar, 69
Khonkhai, Khammaan, 87
Kidder, Tracy, 371
Kierkegaard, Soren, 284
Kikumura, Akemi, 117
Killens, John O., 124
Kim, 166
Kim, Illsoo, 117
King, Coretta Scott, 231
King James Version, 288
The King Must Die, 10
King Solomon's Ring, 380–81
Kings and Philosophers, 1689–1789, 300
The King's Peace, 301
The King's War, 301
Kingsley, Charles, 157
Kingston, Maxine Hong, 117
Kipling, Rudyard, 166, 198
Kirkham, Margaret, 355
Kisch, Bruno, 365
KissKissBangBang, 270

Kitano, Harry H. L., 117
Kitcher, Philip, 380
Kitto, H. D. F., 10
Klee, Paul, 231
Kline, Morris, 369
Knapton, Ernest John, 297
The Knight and Chivalry, 24
Kodomo No Tame Ni—For the Sake of the Children: The Japanese American Experience in Hawaii, 118
Koestler, Arthur, 147
Kohler, Wolfgang, 340
Kongi's Harvest, 93
Konner, Melvin, 380
The Koran, 289
The Koran Interpreted, 289
The Korean Diaspora: Historical and Sociological Studies of Korean Immigration and Assimilation in America, 117
Korey, Kenneth, 380
Kosinski, Jerzy, 188
Kovel, Joel, 342
Krailsheimer, A. J., 39
Kramer, Edna E., 369
Kramer, Hilton, 261
The Kreutzer Sonata, 140
Kristeller, P. O., 39
Kristin Lavransdatter, 26
Kroeber, Theodora, 110
Krutch, Joseph Wood, 380
Kuhn, Thomas S., 334–35
Kundera, Milan, 147
Küng, Hans, 293
The Kung San: Men, Women and Work in a Foraging Society, 327
Kwakiutl Ethnography, 108

La Carreta Made a U-Turn, 130
Le Feber, Walter, 104
La Fontaine, Jean de, 46

Labor and Monopoly Capital: The Degradation of Work in the Twentieth Century, 332
The Labyrinth of Solitude, 105
Labyrinths, 100
Lacey, Robert, 39
Laclos, P. A. F. Choderlos de, 55
Lady Chatterley's Lover, 166
Lafayette, Madame de, 46
Lahr, John, 222
Laing, R. D., 342
Lamb, Charles, 241
Lamont, Corliss, 289
Landmarks of the World's Art, 262
Landscape into Art, 263
Lang, Paul, Henry, 267
Langer, Susanne K., 205
Langland, William, 23
Langness, L. L., 327
Language: An Introduction to the Study of Speech, 250
LANGUAGE AND COMMUNICATIONS, 246–55
Language and the Sexes, 249
Language in Thought and Action, 249
Language, Truth, and Logic, 284
Lannoy, Richard, 84
Lao She, 82
Lao Tzu, 82
Lardner, Ring, 198
Larkin, Oliver W., 263–64
L'Assommoir, 141
The Last Days of Pompeii, 16
Last Tales, 197
The Last Tycoon, 181
Latané, Bibb, 344
The Late George Apley, 182
Later the Same Day, 200
LATIN AMERICA, 96–105
Latin America: A Cultural History, 104

Latin America Between the Eagle and the Bear, 104
Latin Poetry in Verse Translation, 14
Laubin, Gladys, 110
Laubin, Reginald, 110
Laviera, Tato, 130
Lawrence, D. H., 166, 198, 210, 241
Laycock, George, 380
Laye, Camara, 92
Lazarsfeld, Paul F., 335
La Corbusier (Charles-Edouard Jeaneret-Gris), 265
Leakey, Richard, 380
Learning Non-Aggression, 327
Learning to Look: A Handbook of the Visual Arts, 262
Leatherman, Leroy, 269
Leaves of Grass, 209
Lee, Richard B., 327
Lee, Sherman E., 79
Lefebvre, Georges, 58
Left Brain, Right Brain, 345
Legitimacy in the Modern State, 309
Legs, 188
Leibniz, Gottfried Willhelm von, 46
Leitch, Vincent, 249
Lekachman, Robert, 319
Lelia: The Life of George Sand, 231
Lély, Gilbert, 231
Lem, Stainslaw, 147
Lemert, Charles, 335
Lenin, V. I., 319
Lenin: Notes for a Biography, 234
Lentricchia, Frank, 241
Leonardo Da Vinci, 37
Lermontov, Mihail, 139
Les Liaisons Dangereuses, 55
Les Misérables, 139

The Lesbian Issue (Signs: Journal of Women in Culture and Society), 355
Lesky, Albin, 10
Lessing, Doris, 166
A Lesson from Aloes, 220
LETTERS, 236–42
Letters, 47 (Sévigné), 56 (Walpole)
Letters and Notes on the Manners, Customs, and Conditions of the North American Indians, 108
Letters from an American Farmer, 53
Letters of Anton Chekhov, 239
Letters of D. H. Lawrence, 241
The Letters of F. Scott Fitzgerald, 239
The Letters of Gustave Flaubert, 239–40
The Letters of Hart Crane, 239
Letters of James Joyce, 240
Letters of John Keats, 241
The Letters of Virginia Woolf, 242
Letters to His Son, 53
Levi, Carlo, 147
Lévi-Strauss, Claude, 327
Levitation, 200, 279
Levy, Julien, 231
Lewin, Roger, 380
Lewis, Clive S., 39, 294
Lewis, I. M., 327
Lewis, Jill, 355
Lewis, Oscar, 104
Lewis, Sinclair, 182
Lewis, Warren H., 48
Lewontin, Richard, 382
Leyla and Mejnun, 69–70
Lezama Lima, José, 101
The Liberal Imagination, 242
The Liberal Tradition in America, 308
Liberalism in the New South, 303

Liberation, Revolution, and Freedom: Theological Perspectives, 292

Lichtenstadter, Ilse, 68

Lichtheim, George, 309

Lieber, Hugh S., 369

Lieber, Lillian L., 369

Liebling, A. J., 254

The Life and Death of Mary Wollstonecraft, 357

The Life and Times of Cotton Mather, 49

The Life and Times of Rembrandt, 49

The Life and Work of Sigmund Freud, 230

Life in a Medieval Castle, 25

Life in a Medieval City, 25

The Life of Greece, 8–9

The Life of Michelangelo, 232

Life of Petrarch, 41

The Life of Reason, 285

The Life of Samuel Johnson, 53

The Life Science: Current Ideas in Biology, 381

Life Studies, 211

Lifton, Robert J., 344

Light in August, 181

The Lime Twig, 187

The Limits to Growth: A Report for the Club of Rome's Project on the Predicament of Mankind, 335

Lincoln, Eric, 126

Lincoln and the Radicals, 306

Lindblom, Charles, 312

Lindzey, Gardner, 341

LINGUISTICS, see LANGUAGE AND COMMUNICATIONS

Link, Arthur S., 306

Lin-Tung Tan, 82

Lippard, Lucy, 264

Lipscomb, George D., 229

The Literary Essays of Ezra Pound, 241–42

A Literary History of Persia, 68

A Literary History of Rome: From the Origins to the Close of the Golden Age, 16

A Literary History of Rome in the Silver Age; Tiberius to Hadrian, 16

Literary History of the United States, 396

Literary Theory: An Introduction, 248

Literary Women: The Great Writers, 356

The Literature of the Middle Ages, 25

A Literature of Their Own: British Women Novelists from Brontë to Lessing, 357

The Little Disturbances of Man, 200

The Little English Handbook, 395

Little Women, 173

Liu Wu-Xi, 82

Lives, 8

Lives: An Anthropological Approach to Biography, 327

The Lives of a Cell: Notes of a Biology Watcher, 383

Lives of Illustrious Men, 36

The Lives of the Artists, 36

The Lives of the English Poets, 48

Living in the Environment, 385

The Living Planet: A Portrait of the Earth, 376–77

Livy (Titus Livius), 15

Lo Kuan-Chung, 82

Lochak, G., 366

Locke, John, 46, 281

Logical Positivism, 286

Lolita, 189

London, Jack, 182, 199

The Lonely Crowd, 336

Long Day's Journey into Night, 221

The Long Valley, 201
The Longest Journey, 165–66
Longfellow, Henry Wadsworth, 208
Longman Dictionary of Psychology and Psychiatry, 402
Long-time Californ': A Documentary Study of an American Chinatown, 118
Look Homeward, Angel, 183–84
Looking Backward, 173
Loon Lake, 187
Lope de Vega Carpio, Félix, 34
Lorca, Federico García, 221
Lord Jim, 163
Lord of the Flies, 166
The Lord of the Rings, 168
Lorenz, Konrad Z., 380–81
Lorenzo de' Medici and the Renaissance, 39
Lost in the Funhouse, 196
The Lost Steps, 100
The Lost Universe: Pawnee Life and Culture, 113
The Lottery, 198
The Lover, 71
Loving, 166
Lowell, Robert, 210
Lowi, Theodore J., 311
Lowry, Malcolm, 166
Lu Xun (Chou Shu-Jen), 82
Lucian, 7
Lucien Leuwen, 140
Luckmann, Thomas, 332
Lucky Jim, 162
Lucretius, 281
Lucy: The Beginnings of Humankind, 379
Lukacs, Georg, 309
Lullies, Reinhard, 264
Luo Kuan-Chung, 82
Lyman, Stanford M., 117
Lyons. F. S. L., 231
Lyrics of the Troubadours and Trouveres, 22

Lysistrata, 6
Lytle, Clifford, 109

MLA International Bibliography, 397
Macaulay, Thomas B., 48
Maccoby, Eleanor E., 344
McConnell, Grant, 311
McCorduck, Pamela, 371
McCullers, Carson, 188–89
McCullough, David, 365
McCunn, Ruthanne Lum, 117
MacDonald, Dwight, 241
McDonald, Forrest, 303, 305
McFadden, Thomas M., 292
McGraw-Hill Dictionary of Art, 397
McGraw-Hill Dictionary of Science and Engineering, 403
The McGraw-Hill Dictionary of Scientific and Technical Terms, 403
The McGraw-Hill Encyclopedia of Science and Technology, 403
McGraw-Hill Encyclopedia of World Drama, 396
McGraw-Hill Modern Scientists and Engineers, 403
Machado De Assis, Joaquim Maria, 102
Machiavelli, Niccolò, 34
McKay, Claude, 124
MacKendrick, Paul L., 10
McKenna, Wendy, 344
McKinney, Howard, 267
McLuhan, Marshall, 254
McMahon, Thomas A., 382
The Macmillan Bible Atlas, 400
Macmillan Biographical Encyclopedia of Photographic Artists and Innovators, 398

Macmillan Concise Dictionary of World History, 400
MacNeice, Louis, 211
McNeill, William H., 297
McQuail, Denis, 254
McTeague, 176
McWhiney, Grady, 305
Madame Bovary, 138
Madame Curie, 228
Madariaga, Salvador de, 104, 231
Mademoiselle de Maupin, 138
Madison, James, 311
The Madwoman in the Attic, 354
Magazine Index, 371
Magaziner, Ira C., 319–20
MAGAZINES, 243–46
Maggie: A Girl of the Streets, 174
The Magic Mountain, 147–48
The Magus, 166
Mahabharata, 84
Mahan, Alfred, 298
Mahatma Gandhi and His Apostles, 232
Mailer, Norman, 189
Main Street, 182
Major Trends in Jewish Mysticism, 294
The Majority Finds Its Past: Placing Women in History, 352
Make Prayers to the Raven, 111
Makers of Contemporary Architecture, 265
Making Bricks Without Straw: Nathaniel Greene's Southern Campaigns and Mao Tse-Tung's Mobile War, 304
Making News: A Study in the Construction of Reality, 254–55
The Making of an American, 233
The Making of Economic Society, 318
The Making of the Modern Mind, 298

The Makioka Sisters, 87
Malamud, Bernard, 189, 199
Malavika and Agnimitra, 84
Malcolm, 190
Malcolm, Janet, 335
Malcolm X, 231
Malinowski, Bronislaw, 327
Malory, Sir Thomas, 23
Malraux, André, 147, 261
Malthus, Thomas Robert, 55
Man in the Holocene, 145
The Man Without Qualities, 148
Manchild in the Promised Land, 123
Mandel, Ernest, 320
Mandela, Nelson, 94
Mander, Jerry, 254
Mandeville, John, 23
Man-Made Life: An Overview of the Science, Technology and Commerce of Genetic Engineering, 377
Mann, Thomas, 147, 199, 241
Mannerism: The Painting and Style of the Late Renaissance, 263
Manon Lescaut, 55
Man's Evolution, 325
Man's Fate, 147
Man's Most Dangerous Myth: The Fallacy of Race, 328
Man's Search for Meaning, 342
Mansfield, Katherine, 199
Mansfield Park, 153
The Manticore, 164
The Manuscript Books of Emily Dickinson, 208
Many Mexicos, 301
Manyoshu, 80
Manzoni, Alessandro, 139
Mao Dun, 82
Mao Tse-Tung, 82
Maran, René, 92
The Marble Faun, 174
Marcel Proust, 232

Marchand, Leslie, 231
Marcus Aurelius Antoninus, 281
Marcuse, Herbert, 335
Margaret Mead, 230
Margins of Philosophy, 284
Margot Fonteyn: Autobiography, 268
Marías Aguilera, Julián, 286
Marie de France, 23
Marius the Epicurean, 17
Mark, Herman F., 368–69
Markings, 229
Marquand, J. P., 182
Marquis de Sade, 231
The Marriage of Figaro, 52
The Marrow of Tradition, 123
Marshall, Alfred, 320
Martha Graham, 269
Martí Joan de Galba, 23
Martínez, Max, 130
Martorell, Joannot, 23
Maru, 92
Marvell, Andrew, 46
Marx, Karl, 281, 320
Marxism: An Historical and Critical Study, 309
Marxism and Human Liberation, 309
Mary Barton, 156
The Masnavi, 69
Mass Communication Theory: An Introduction, 254
Mastai, Marie-Louise, 264
The Master and Margarita, 144
Master Harold and the Boys, 220
The Master of Ballantrae, 158
Master Photographers, 270
Masterpieces of the Orient, 79
Masters and Slaves, 104
Masters of Modern Drama, 218
Masters of World Architecture, 265
Mathematical Thought from Ancient to Modern Times, 369

MATHEMATICS, 369–70
Matlin, Margaret, 341
Matson, Floyd W., 118
Matsubara, Hisako, 86
Mattelart, Armand, 253
Matthiessen, Peter, 381
Maugham, W. Somerset, 166–67, 199
Maupassant, Guy de, 139, 199
Maurer, Armand, 25
Mauriac, François, 148
Maurois, André, 231
Mauss, Marcel, 327
The Maximus Poems, 211
Mayer, Hans E., 25
The Mayor of Casterbridge, 156
Mbiti, John S., 94, 290
Mead, George Herbert, 335
Mead, Margaret, 327
Meadows, Donnella H., 335
Meaning in the Visual Arts, 39–40
The Meaning of Meaning, 285
The Meaning of Truth, 280
The Meanings of Modern Art, 264
Means, Gardiner C., 317
Medawar, Jean S., 381
Medawar, Peter B., 365, 381
Medea, 7
MEDIA, *see* LANGUAGE AND COMMUNICATIONS
The Media Are American, 255
The Media Monopoly, 252–53
Mediaeval and Early Modern Science, 38
The Medici, 299
Medieval and Early Modern Science, 24–25
Medieval Drama, 22
Medieval Fables, 23
MEDIEVAL HISTORY, *see* HISTORY; MIDDLE AGES
MEDIEVAL LITERATURE, *see* MIDDLE AGES

Medieval Panorama, 24
Medieval People, 26
Medieval Philosophy, 26
Medieval Technology and Social
    Change, 27
Medieval Women, 26
The Medieval World, 25
Meditations, 281
The Mediterranean and the
    Mediterranean World in the
    Age of Philip Second, 299
The Medusa and the Snail: More
    Notes of a Biology Watcher,
    383
Mee, Charles L., 39
Mehta, Ved, 232
Melendy, H. Brett, 117–18
Meltzer, Milton, 126
Melville, 232
Melville, Herman, 176, 199, 208
Memed, My Hawk, 70
Memento Mori, 168
Memoir of an Art Gallery, 231
Memoirs of Bernardo Vega, 130
Memoirs of Glückel of Hameln,
    354
Memoirs of Hadrian, 17
Memoirs of Hector Berlioz,
    227–28
Memoirs (also Chronicles) of the
    Crusades, 22
Men of Good Will, 149
Mendelssohn, Kurt A. G., 369
The Meno, 282
Men's Studies Modified: The
    Impact of Feminism on the
    Academic Disciplines, 355
Mere Christianity, 294
Meredith, George, 157
Mérimée, Prosper, 139
Merkl, Peter H., 312
Merleau-Ponty, Maurice, 284–85
Merton, Robert K., 335
Merton, Thomas, 232
Metamorphoses, 15

Metaphysical Lyrics and Poems
    of the Seventeenth Century,
    46
The Mexicans: The Making of a
    Nation, 104
MEXICO, see LATIN AMERICA
Mexico in a Nutshell and Other
    Essays, 103
Mexico in Crisis, 104
Meyerhoff, Barbara G., 327–28
Mick, Colin K., 371
MIDDLE AGES, 18–27
MIDDLE EAST, 63–73
The Middle East, 73
Middle East and North Africa, 403
Middlemarch, 156
Midnight, 82
Midnight Birds: Stories of
    Contemporary Black Women
    Writers, 355
Midnight's Children, 84–85
Milestones of Modern Chemistry,
    368
Milgram, Stanley, 335
Miliband, Ralph, 311
Mill, John Stuart, 232, 285, 320
The Mill on the Floss, 155
Miller, Arthur, 221
Miller, Edwin H., 232
Miller, George Tyler, 385
Miller Henry, 182
Miller, Jonathan, 381
Miller, Perry, 58
Miller, Stuart Creighton, 118
Millett, Kate, 355–56
Millon, Henry A., 49
Mills, C. Wright, 336
Mills, Gary B., 305
Milosz, Czeslaw, 148
Milton, John, 35
Mimesis, 238
The Mind Managers, 254
Mind, Self, and Society from the
    Standpoint of a Social
    Behaviorist, 335

Minding America's Business, 319–20

Mine Boy, 91

Minimal Art, 261

Miracle, 294

Miracle by Design: The Real Reasons Behind Japan's Economic Success, 85

Mirak, Robert, 72

Mischel, Walter, 341

Mishima, Yukio, 86

The Mismeasure of Man, 378–79

Miss Lonelyhearts, 183

Miss Ravenel's Conversion from Secession to Loyalty, 174

Mistral, Gabriela, 102

Mitchell, Joseph, 113

Mitchell, Juliet, 356

MITI and the Japanese Miracle, 319

Mizener, Arthur, 232

Moby Dick, 176

Modern Art: 19th and 20th Century Selected Papers, 264

Modern Brazilian Short Stories, 102

The Modern Corporation and Private Property, 317

Modern Egyptian Drama: An Anthology, 68

Modern Germany, 298

Modern Greek Poetry, 214

Modern Hebrew Poetry, 71

MODERN HISTORY, 299–301

A Modern Instance, 175

Modern Israeli Drama: An Anthology, 71

Modern Latin America, 104

Modern Music: The Avant Garde Since 1945, 267

Modern Persian Short Stories, 69

Modern Poetic Sequence: The Genius of Modern Poetry, 206

Modern Science and Its Philosophy, 284

Modern Spanish Poems, 215

Modern Theatre, 219

The Modern Tradition: Backgrounds of Modern Literature, 205

Modern Tragedy, 223

Modern Varieties of Judaism, 293

Modes of Thought, 285

Modulor, 265

Modulor 2, 265

Moers, Ellen, 356

Mohr, Nicholasa, 130

Molière (Jean Baptiste Poquelin), 46

Moll Flanders, 53

Momaday, N. Scott, 111

Monaco, James, 254

Monkey, 83

The Monkey Puzzle: Reshaping the Evolutionary Tree, 379

Monod, Jacques, 381

Monopoly Capital, 317

Mont-Saint-Michel and Chartres, 24

Montagu, Ashley, 325, 328

Montaigne, Michel de, 35

Montesquieu, Charles de, 55

The Moon and the Bonfire, 148

Mooney, James, 111

The Moonstone, 154

Moore, G. E., 285

Moore, George, 157

Moore, Gerald, 95

Moore, Marianne, 211

Moore, Ruth E., 232

The Moral Judgment of the Child, 340

Moravia, Alberto, 148

More Work for Mothers: The Ironies of Household Technology from the Open Hearth to the Microwave, 352–53

Morgan, Charles H., 232
Morgan, Edmund S., 58
Morganthau, Hans, 312
Mori, Toshio, 118
Morris, Ivan, 86
Morris, Wright, 189
Morrison, Toni, 124
Le Morte Darthur, 23
Moses, 228
Moss, Cynthia, 381
Most of P. G. Woodehouse, 202
Mothering: Essays in Feminist
    Theory, 356
MOTION PICTURES, *see* FILM
Mountain Wolf Woman, 328
Mountolive, 164
The Moviegoer, 190
Mowry, George E., 306
Mozart, 230
Mphahlele, Ezekiel, 95
Mr. Clemens and Mark Twain,
    230
Mr. Jefferson, 58
Mr. Sammler's Planet, 186
Mr. Tompkins in Paperback, 367
Ms., 244
The Muckrakers, 304
Mueller, Claus, 249–50
Muhammad, 233
Muir, Edwin, 211
Müller, Ronald E., 317
Mumbo, Jumbo, 124
Mumford, Lewis, 265
Muntu: An Outline of the New
    African Culture, 94
The Muqaddimah: An Introduc-
    tion to History, 67
Murasaki, Lady, 86
Murdoch, Iris, 167
Murphy, 143
Murphy, Murray G., 286
Murray, K. M. Elisabeth, 232
Museums and Women, 201
Mushrooms, Molds, and Mira-
    cles, 380

MUSIC, 266–68
Music in History, 267
Music in the 20th Century, 266
Music in Western Civilization,
    267
The Music School, 201
Musical Instruments and Their
    Symbolism in Western Art,
    268
Musil, Robert, 148
Muslim Saints and Mystics, 68
My Antonia, 180
My Bondage and My Freedom,
    123
My Friends The Wild Chimpan-
    zees, 383
My Life as a Man, 191
My Life with Martin Luther
    King, Jr., 231
My Michael, 71
My Name Is Aram, 201
Myrdal, Gunnar, 320
Mysticism, 294
The Myth of Sisyphus and Other
    Essays, 239
Mythologies of the Ancient
    World, 73
Mythology and the Renaissance
    Tradition in English Poetry,
    37
Myths of the Greeks and
    Romans, 9

Nabokov, Peter, 111
Nabokov, Vladimir, 189, 232
Nadar, 270
Nadeau, Maurice B., 264
Naipaul, V. S., 84, 167
The Naked and the Dead, 189
Naked Lunch, 186
Naked Masks, 221
The Name of the Rose, 145
Nana, 141
Narayan, R. K., 84

Narrative of the Life of Frederick Douglass, an American Slave, 123

The Narrow Road to the Deep North and Other Travel Sketches, 85

The Nation, 244

The Nation Within, 109

National Review, 244

National Union Catalog, 390

NATIVE AMERICAN, 106–13

Native American Testimony, 111

Native American Women: A Contextual Bibliography, 111

Native Arts of North America, 109

Native Son, 125

Native Tongues, 248

Natural Ecosystems, 384

NATURAL HISTORY, *see* BIOLOGICAL SCIENCES

Naural History, 245

The Nature and Functions of Law, 310

The Nature and Growth of Modern Mathematics, 369

Nature and Madness, 385

Naure and Man's Fate, 379

The Nature of the Child, 344

The Nature of the Non-Western World, 297

Nature's Economy, 385

Nausea, 149

Navajo Religion: A Study of Symbolism, 112

The Navajos, 112–13

NEAR EAST, *see* MIDDLE EAST

The Necessary Angel, 242

Nee, Brett De Bary, 118

Nee, Victor G., 118

Needleman, Jacob, 292

The Negro Almanac, 401

The Negro Novel in America, 125

Neihardt, John G., 111

Neill, Stephen Charles, 290

Neisser, Ulric, 341

Nelson, Richard K., 111

Nepali Visions, Nepali Dreams, 87

Neruda, Pablo, 102

Neruda and Vallejo: Selected Poems, 102

Nerval, Gérard de, 139–40

Nesin, Aziz, 70

Neurotic Styles, 343

Nevins, Allan, 305

Nevins, Deborah, 266

New American Nation Series, 305

The New Art, 261

New Atlantis, 32

New Atlas of the Universe, 404

New Cambridge Modern History, 401

The New Catholic Encylopaedia, 400

New Century Cyclopedia of Names, 392

New Century Handbook of English Literature, 396

The New College Encyclopedia of Music, 396

New Columbia Encyclopedia, 390

A New Companion to Shakespeare Studies, 39

The New Dictionary of Quotations, 397

New Directions for Women, 358

The New Encylopaedia Britannica, 390, 391

The New England Mind, 58

The New English Bible, 288

The New Evolutionary Timetable: Fossils, Genes, and the Origin of Species, 382–53

New Grove Composer Biography Series, 267

New Grove Dictionary of Music and Musicians, 398

The New International Atlas, 393

The New Kobbe's Complete Opera Book, 399

The New Larousse Encyclopedia of Animal Life, 404

The New Library Key, 391

The New Nation, 305

The New Oxford Book of American Verse, 206

The New Oxford Book of English Verse, 1250–1950, 205

New Oxford Companion to Music, 398

New Perspectives in Physics, 366

The New Rand McNally Cosmopolitan World Atlas, 393

A New Reader's Guide to African Literature, 95

The New Religions, 292

The New Republic, 245

The New Russian Poets, 1953–1968, 215

New Serial Titles, 390

New Urban Immigrants: The Korean Community in New York, 117

New Webster's Biographical Dictionary, 390

The New Westminster Dictionary of the Bible, 400

New Writing from the Middle East, 69

New York Review of Books, 245–46

New York Times Atlas of the World, 393

The New York Times Index, 391

The New Yorker, 246

The Newberry Library Series, 111

Newman, Edwin, 250

Newman, John Henry, 232

Newnham, Richard, 82

Newsweek, 246

Newton, Eric, 264

Ngugi, James (Ngugi Wa Thiong'o), 92

Niane, Djibril Tamsir, 92

Nibelungenlied, 23

Nicholson, Ian, 367

Nicolas Copernicus and His Epoch, 36

Nicomachean Ethics, 6, 277

Niels Bohr, 232

Nietzsche, Friedrich, 281–82

The Nigger of the Narcissus, 163

Night, 192

The Nightmare of Reason: A Life of Franz Kafka, 232–33

Nilda, 130

The Nine Guardians, 100

9000 Words, 394

1984, 167

1919, 180

19TH-CENTURY AMERICAN NOVELS, 170–77

19TH-CENTURY BRITISH NOVELS, 151–58

19TH-CENTURY CONTINENTAL NOVELS, 135–41

Nineteenth Century Sculpture, 264

Nkrumah, Kwame, 95

No Easy Walk to Freedom, 94

No Man's Land, 221

No-No Boy, 118

No Sweetness Here, 91

Nochlin, Linda, 354

Nock, Albert J., 58

Nocturnes, 93

Noddings, Nel, 356

Norman Thomas: The Last Idealist, 234

Norris, Christopher, 250

Norris, Frank, 176

The North American Indians, 112

The Norton Anthology of Modern Poetry, 205

The Norton Anthology of Poetry, 205–06

The Norton History of Modern Europe, 300

Nostromo, 164

Notable American Women, 395

The Notebooks, 33

Notes from Underground, 137

Novak, Michael, 320

NOVELS, 135–92

Novus Ordo Seclorum: The Intellectual Origins of the Constitution, 305

Now That the Buffalo's Gone, 110

The Nude, 263

Nussbaum, Frank L., 301

Nuyorican Poets, 130

Nwapa, Flora, 92

Oates, Joyce Carol, 190

Obedience to Authority: An Experimental View, 335

Oblomov, 139

O'Brien, Tim, 190

The Obscene Bird of Night, 101

O'Casey, Sean, 221

O'Connor, Flannery, 190, 199

O'Connor, Frank, 199

The Octopus, 176

The Odd Women, 156

Odes (Pindar), 7

Odyssey, 7

Oe, Kenzaburo, 86

Oedipus Rex, 8

Of Grammatology, 284

Of Human Bondage, 166

Of Predation and Life, 378

Of Women Born: Motherhood as Experience and Institution, 356

O'Faolain, Sean, 199

O'Flaherty, Wendy, 84

Ogawa, Dennis, 118

Ogden, C. K., 285

Ogilvie, R. M., 17

Oglala Religion, 112

O'Hara, John, 182, 199

Okada, John, 118

Okin, Susan Moller, 309

Okun, Arthur M., 320

Old Goriot, 137

Old Mortality, 49

The Old Regime and the French Revolution, 58

Old Times, 221

The Old Wives' Tale, 163

The Old World and the New, 1492–1650, 300

Oldenbourg, Zoe, 25

Oliver Twist, 155

Olsen, Tillie, 199–200, 356

Olson, Charles, 211

Omensetter's Luck, 187

Omoo, 176

Omotso, Kole, 92

On Aggression, 381

On Becoming a Person, 342

On Being a Christian, 293

On Campus with Women, 309

On Deconstruction: Theory and Criticism after Structuralism, 239

On Human Communication: A Review, a Survey and a Criticism, 248

On Human Nature, 383

On Liberty, 285

On Photography, 270

On Revolution, 308

On Size and Life, 382

On the Laws of Japanese Painting, 263

On the Nature of Things, 281

One Day in the Life of Ivan Denisovitch, 150

One Fat Englishman, 162

One Flew over the Cuckoo's Nest, 188

One Hundred Armenian Tales and Their Folkloric Significance, 72

One Hundred Middle English Lyrics, 22

One Hundred Poems from the Japanese, 80

One Hundred Years of Solitude, 101

O'Neill, Eugene, 221

O'Neill: Son and Artist, 233

O'Neill: Son and Playwright, 233

Onetti, Juan Carlos, 102

Ong, Walter, 250

O'Nolan, Brian ("Flann O'Brien," "Myles na Gopaleen"), 167

Oppenheimer, J. Robert, 365

Oral Literature in Africa, 94

Orality and Literacy: The Technologizing of the Word, 250

Orations, 6

The Ordeal of Richard Feverel, 157

The Order of Things: An Archaeology of the Human Sciences, 38

The Oresteia, 6

ORIENT, *see* ASIA

Origin and Originality in Renaissance Literature, 40

Origins, 380

Origins: A Short Etymological Dictionary of Modern English, 394

The Origins of Modern Science, 57

Origins of World War, 302

Orlando Furioso, 32

Ornstein, Robert E., 345

Oritz, Alfonso, 111

Ortiz, Simon, 111–12

Orwell, George, 167, 241

The Other America, 334

Other People's Worlds, 169

Other Voices, Other Rooms, 186

O'Toole, James, 321

Our Lady of the Flowers, 145

Out of My Life and Thought, 233

Out to Work: A History of Wage-Earning Women in the United States, 355

Outlaws of the Marsh (Shui Hu Chuan), 82

An Outline of European Architecture, 266

The Overcoat, 139

The Overcoat and Other Tales of Good and Evil, 197

Ovid (Publius Ovidius Naso), 15

Owen, Roger C., 112

Owen, Wilfred, 211

Oxford Bible Atlas, 400

Oxford Book of American Verse, 206

Oxford Book of Seventeenth-Century Verse, 46

The Oxford Classical Dictionary, 10, 400

The Oxford Companion to American Literature, 396

Oxford Companion to Animal Behavior, 404

The Oxford Companion to Art, 397

Oxford Companion to Classical Literature, 396

The Oxford Companion to English Literature, 396

Oxford Companion to French Literature, 396

Oxford Companion to German Literature, 396

Oxford Companion to Spanish Literature, 397

The Oxford Companion to the American Theatre, 398

The Oxford Companion to the Decorative Arts, 397

The Oxford Companion to the Theatre, 398

The Oxford Dictionary of English Etymology, 394

The Oxford Dictionary of Quotations, 397

The Oxford Dictionary of the Christian Chruch, 399
Oxford English Dictionary, 394
Oyono, Ferdinand, 92
Oz, Amos, 71
Ozick, Cynthia, 200

Pa Chin (Li Fei-Kan), 82
Pagan Mysteries in the Renaissance, 41
Paideia, 10
Paine, Thomas, 55
The Painted Bird, 188
Painter, George, 232
Painter, Sidney, 26
PAINTING, 262–65
Pais, Abraham, 367
Pale Fire, 189
Paley, Grace, 200
Palladio, 227
The Palm-Wine Drinkard, 93
Palmer, Robert Roswell, 300
Pamela, 55
Pancake, John S., 306
The Panda's Thumb: More Reflections in Natural History, 378
Paneth, F. A., 369
Panofsky, Erwin, 39–40
Parade's End, 165
Paradise Lost: The Decline of the Auto-Industrial Age, 321
Paradiso, 101–02
Parker, Donald B., 370
Parkes, Henry B., 298
Parry, John Horace, 300–01
Parsons, Talcott, 336
Parzival, 24
Pascal, Blaise, 46–47
A Passage to India, 166
Pasternak, Boris, 148
Pater, Walter H., 17
Paterson, 212
Paton, Alan, 92

Patrides, C. A., 40
The Patriot Chiefs, 110
Pavese, Cesare, 148
Pavlov, Ivan P., 340
Pawel, Ernst, 233
Paz, Octavio, 102, 105
Pearce, Roy Harvey, 206
Pedagogy of the Oppressed, 333
Pei, Mario, 250
Peirce, Charles S., 285
Pelican History of Art, 262
The Pelican History of the Church, 291
The Peloponnesian Wars, 8
Penguin Book of French Verse, 214
Penguin Book of German Verse, 214
Penguin Book of Greek Verse, 214
Penguin Book of Hebrew Verse, 71
Penguin Book of Spanish Verse, 215
The Penguin Book of Turkish Verse, 70
The Penguin Dictionary of Architecture, 397
The Penguin Dictionary of Art and Artists, 390, 397
The Penguin Dictionary of Biology, 404
The Penguin Dictionary of Religions, 399
The Penguin Dictionary of Science, 403
The Penguin Dictionary of Sociology, 402
Penguin Island, 145
Penrose, Roland, 233
Pensées (Thoughts), 46
People of the City, 91
Pepys, Samuel, 47
Perception, 341
Percy, Walker, 190

Pérez Galdos, Benito, 140
PERFORMING ARTS, *see* FINE ARTS AND PERFORMING ARTS
PERIODICALS, *see* MAGAZINES
Perkins, David, 206
Perkins, Dexter, 306
Pernoud, Regine, 26, 233
PERSIAN LITERATURE, 68–69
Personae, 211
A Personal Anthology, 100
A Personal Matter, 86
Persons and Places, 233
Peter Abelard, 26–27
Peters, Edward Murray, 298
Petrarch, Francis, 35
Petrarch: Selected Sonnets, Odes and Letters, 35
Pétrement, Simone, 233
Petronius, Gaius, 15
Pevsner, Nikolaus, 266
Peyote Hunt: The Sacred Journey of the Huichol Indians, 327–28
The Phaedo, 282
Phenomenology and the Crisis of Philosophy, 279–80
The Phenomenology of Mind, 278–79
Phenomenology of Perception, 284–85
Philippine Short Stories: 1941–1955, 80–81
Philosophical Investigations, 283
Philosophical Papers, 284
Philosophical Writings 46 (Leivniz), 285 (Peirce)
PHILOSOPHY, 272–86
The Philosopy of History, 278–79
The Philosophy of Humanism, 289
The Philosophy of Symbolic Forms, 284
The Philosophy of the Enlightenment, 57

Phoenix, 241
Photograph Collector's Guide, 398
PHOTOGRAPHY, 269–71
Photography: A Concise History, 270
PHYSICAL SCIENCES AND MATHEMATICS, 363–72
The Physicists, 367
PHYSICS, 366–68
Physics and Beyond, 367
Physics and Metaphysics, 277
Physiology of Behavior, 341
Piaget, Jean, 340
Picasso: His Life and Work, 233
A Pictorial History of Black Americans, 126
The Picture of Dorian Gray, 158
Pictures from Brueghel and Other Poems, 1950–1962, 212
Piers Plowman, 23
Pietri, Pedro, 130
Pigeon Feathers and Other Stories, 201
Pigs for the Ancestors, 328
Pilgrim's Progress, 45
Pill, David H., 40
The Pillow Book of Sei Shonagon, 86
Pindar, 7
Piñero, Miguel, 130
Pinson, Koppel S., 298
Pinter, Harold, 221
The Pioneers, 173–74
Pioneers of Design, 266
Pioneers of Photography, 270
Pirandello, Luigi, 221
Piszek, Edward J., 36
Piven, Frances Fox, 336
The Plague, 144
Plagues and Peoples, 298
A Planet Called Earth, 370
Plants, Food, and People, 377
Plath, Sylvia, 211
Plato, 7, 282

Plautus, Titus Maccius, 15
The Play: A Critical Anthology, 219
Play Index, 397
PLAYS, *see* DRAMA
The Playwright as Thinker, 222
The Pleasures of Anthropology, 328
The Pledge, 145
Plotinus, 282
Plumb, John Harold, 40, 299, 301
Plutarch, 8
Pocho, 131
Poe, Edgar Allan, 200, 208
Poems from the Divan, 68
Poetics, 277
POETRY, 203–15
Poetry Handbook: A Dictionary of Terms, 205
The Poetry of Black America: Anthology of the 20th Century, 206
The Poetry of Robert Frost, 210
Poets in a Landscape, 17
Point Counter Point, 166
The Political Economy of the Black Ghetto, 322
A Political History of Japanese Capitalism, 85
Political Parties in the American System, 311
POLITICS, 307–13
Politics, 308
Politics Among Nations, 312
Politics and Markets: The World's Political-Economic Systems, 312
Politics and Vision: Continuity and Innovation in Western Political Thought, 309
The Politics of Communication: A Study in the Political Sociology of Language, Socialization, and Legitimation, 249–50

The Politics of Prejudice: The Anti-Japanese Movement in California and the Struggle for Japanese Exclusion, 116
Polo, Marco, 23
Polsby, Nelson, 311
Polybius, 8
The Poor Christ of Bomba, 91
Pop Art, 264
Pope, Alexander, 55
Popper, Karl 241
Popul Vuh: The Sacred Book of the Ancient Quiché Maya, 102
The Portable Elizabethan and Jacobean Poets, 35
The Portable Greek Historians, 6
The Portable Greek Reader, 6
The Portable Jung, 342
The Portable North American Indian Reader, 112
The Portable Renaissance Reader, 35
The Portable Roman Reader, 14
Porter, Katherine Anne, 200
Portillo de Trambley, Estela, 130–31
Portnoy's Complaint, 190–91
The Portrait of a Lady, 175
Portrait of the Artist as a Young Man, 166
Portraits in the Wild: Animal Behavior in East Africa, 381
Possony, Stefan T., 371
Pouillon, Fernand, 26
Pound, Ezra, 211, 241–42
Powell, Anthony, 167
Power, Eileen, 26
The Power Elite, 336
The Power of Words, 248
Powers, William K., 112
Praeger World of Art Paperbacks, 262
Pragmatism, 280
The Prairie, 174

Precision Measurements and Fundamental Constants, 369

Prefaces to Shakespeare, 38

PREHISTORY, *see* ANTHRO-POLOGY; GREECE; HIS-TORY; MIDDLE EAST; RELIGION

The Prehistory of European Society, 298

Prejudice, War, and the Constitution, 118

Preliminary Discourse to the Encyclopedia of Diderot, 53

The Prelude: A Parallel Text, 209

Premchand (Dhanpat Rai Strivastava), 84

Premises and Motifs in Renaissance Thought and Literature, 40

Prentice-Hall Great International Atlas, 393

The Prentice-Hall New World Atlas, 393

Prescott, William Hickling, 105

The Presentation of Self in Everyday Life, 334

Presidential Elections, 311

The Press, 254

Prévost, Antoine, 55

Pricksongs and Descants, 197

Pride and Prejudice, 153

Pride and Solace; The Functions and Limits of Political Theory, 308–09

Priestley, J. B., 167

Primitive Art, 263

PRIMITIVE ARTS, *see* AN-THROPOLOGY; FINE ARTS; GREECE

The Prince, 34–35

The Princess of Cléves, 46

The Princeton Encyclopedia of Poetry and Poetics, 206, 396

The Principal Upanishads, 289

Principles of Economics, 289

Principles of Political Economy, 320

Principles of Psychology, 339–40

Pritchett, C. Herman, 310

Pritchett, V. S., 200

Private Power and American Democracy, 311

Problems and Other Stories, 201

Proctor, Raja, 87

The Professor's House, 180

Profile of Man and Culture in Mexico, 105

Prolegomena to the Study of Greek Religion, 9–10

Prometheus: The Life of Balzac, 231

Prose Keys to Modern Poetry, 206

Prostitution and Victorian Society: Women, Class and the State, 357–58

The Protestant Ethic and the Spirit of Capitalism, 336–37

The Protestant Reformation, 35

Proust, Marcel, 148–49

The Psychiatric Interview, 343

The Psychiatric Society, 332

Psychoanalysis and Feminism: Freud, Reich, Laing and Women, 356

Psychoanalysis: The Impossible Profession, 335

Psychological Testing, 340

PSYCHOLOGY, 338–45

Psychology, 341

The Psychology of Consciousness, 345

Psychology of Women, 342

PSYCHOTHERAPY, 342–43

Public Affairs Information Service, 391

Pudd'nhead Wilson, 177

A Puerto Rican in New York and Other Sketches, 129

Puerto Rican Obituary, 130

The Puerto Rican Poets, 131

Puig, Manuel, 102
Purdy, James, 190, 200
The Pursuit of Inequality, 311
Putnam, Robert D., 312
Pym, Barbara, 167
Pynchon, Thomas, 190

Qualitative Analysis: Historical and Critical Essays, 335
Quanta, 366
Quartet, 168
Quartet in Autumn, 167–68
Queen Elizabeth, 36
Queen Victoria, 234
The Quest for Absolute Zero, 369
Quine, W. V. O., 285
Quint, David, 40
Quiroga, Horacio, 102

R. E. Lee, 229
Rabbit Is Rich, 191
Rabbit Redux, 191
Rabbit, Run, 191
Rabelais, François, 35
Rabinow, Paul, 328
Race and Economics, 322
Race, Language and Culture, 325
The Race of Time: Three Essays on Renaissance Historiography, 37
Racine, Jean, 45
The Radiance of the King, 92
The Radical Future of Liberal Feminism, 353
Radin, Paul, 112, 328
Ragtime, 187
Rain of Scropions and Other Writings, 130–31
The Rainbow, 166
Rainbows, Snowflakes and Quarks, 368
The Raj Quartet, 167
Rameau's Nephew and Other Works, 54

Ramos, Samuel, 105
Rand McNally Historical Atlas of the World, 401
Rand McNally's Goode's World Atlas, 393
Randall, John Herman, Jr., 298
Random House Book of Twentieth-Century French Poetry, 214
Random House Dictionary of the English Language, 394
A Random Walk in Science, 365
Ransom, John Crowe, 211
Rappaport, Roy A., 328
Rasmussen, Larry D., 291
Rats, Lice, and History, 384
Rauch, Basil, 302
Rawls, John, 309
Rawson, Philip, 87
Rayback, Joseph G., 321
Reade, Charles, 26
Reader-Response Criticism: From Formalism to Post-Structuralism, 250
Reader's Encyclopedia of American Literature, 396
Reader's Encyclopedia of Shakespeare, 396
Reader's Encyclopedia of World Drama, 396
Reader's Guide to Periodical Literature, 391
Readings in Eastern Religious Thought, 288
Readings in Philosophy, 286
Rebel Angels, 164
Rebellion in the Backlands, 100
Rechy, John, 131
Recognitions, 187
Recollected Essays, 1965–1980, 239
RECORDS, see DRAMA; POETRY
The Rector of Justin, 185
The Red and the Black, 140

The Red Badge of Courage, 174
Reed, Ishmael, 124
REFERENCE BOOKS, 398–405
Reflections, 222
Reflections of Fieldwork in
  Morocco, 328
Reflections on Language, 248,
  332
Reflections on the Revolution in
  France, 53
REFORMATION, 28–41
The Reformation, 38
The Reformation Era, 1500–1650,
  300
Regulating the Poor: The
  Functions of Public
  Relief, 336
Reich, Robert, 319
Reichard, Gladys A., 112
Reinventing Anthropology, 328
Reischauer, Edwin, O., 78
Religio Medici, 44–45
RELIGION, 287–94
Religion and Morality, 291
Religion and the Rise of
  Capitalism, 49
Religion for a New Generation,
  292–93
Religions of Man, 290
The Religions History of the
  American People, 291
Remarque, Erich Maria, 149
Remembrance of Things Past,
  148–49
The Renaissance, 38
Renaissance and Baroque Music,
  37, 266–67
The Renaissance and English
  Humanism, 37
RENAISSANCE AND REFOR-
  MATION, 28–41
Renaissance and Renascences in
  Western Art, 40
Renaissance Exploration, 38
The Renaissance in Italy, 41

The Renaissance of the Twelfth
  Century, 25
Renaissance Self-Fashioning from
  More to Shakespeare, 38
Renaissance Thought and the
  Arts: Collected Essays, 39
Renault, Mary (Mary Challans),
  10
Repertory in Review: 40 Years of
  the New York City Ballet,
  269
The Reproduction of Mothering:
  Psychoanalysis and the
  Sociology of Gender, 343
The Republic, 7, 282
Residencias, 102
Restak, Richard, 381
The Restless Earth: A Report on
  the New Geology, 370
The Restless Universe, 366
Return from the Stars, 147
The Return of the King, 168
The Return of the Native, 156
Return to Laughter, 325
The Revolt of the Cockroach
  People, 129
The Revolutionary Generation,
  1763–1790, 305
Reyes, Alfonso, 103
Reynolds, Nancy, 269
Rheims, Maurice, 264
Rhys, Jean, 168
The Rhythms of English Poetry,
  205
Riasanovsky, Nicholas V., 301
Rice, Eugene F., Jr., 301
Rich, Adrienne, 211, 356
Richard Wagner, 229
Richards, I. A., 285
Richardson, Samuel, 55–56
Richter, Hans, 264
Rickshaw Boy, 82
Riddley Walker, 188
Riesman, David, 336
The Rights of Man, 55

Riis, Jacob, 233
The Rise and Fall of the Third Reich, 302
The Rise of Anthropological Theory, 327
Rise of Modern Europe, 300
The Rise of Puritanism, 48
The Rise of Silas Lapham, 175
The Rise of the West: A History of the Human Community, 297–98
The Rites of Passage, 329
The Rivals, 56
Rivera, Edward, 131
Rivera, Tomás, 131
The Rivers of America, 306
Rizal Y Alonso, José, 87
The Road of Serfdom, 318
Robbe-Grillet, Alain, 149
Robert Frost, 234
Robertson, Priscilla, 302
Robinson, Edwin Arlington, 211
Robinson, Joan, 321
Robinson Crusoe, 53
Rodinson, Maxime, 233
Rodney, Walter, 95
Roethke, Theodore, 211
Rogers, Carl, 342
Roget's International Thesaurus, 394
The Role of the Reader: Explorations in the Semiotics of Texts, 249
Rolfe, Sidney E., 321
Romains, Jules, 149
Roman Civilization: Sourcebook, 17
Roman Literature and Society, 17
The Romance of the Rose, 22
Romanesque Art, 264
The Romans, 16
The Romantic Rebellion, 264
Romanticism and Realism: The Mythology of Nineteenth-Century Art, 264

ROME, 12–17
Rome in the Augustan Age, 17
Romero, José Rubén, 103
Room at the Top, 163
A Room of One's Own, 358
Roosevelt from Munich to Pearl Harbor, 302
Rosalind Franklin and DNA, 382
Rosen, Charles, 264
Rosenberg, Stanley D., 336
Rosencrantz and Guildenstern Are Dead, 221
Rosenthal, M. L., 206
Roses and Thorns: The Second Blooming of the Hundred Flowers in Chinese Fiction 1979–1980, 79
Rosman, Abraham, 328
Rossetti, Christina, 208
Rostand, Edmond, 49
Roth, Henry, 182
Roth, Philip, 190–91, 200
Rothschild, Emma, 321
Rousseau, Jean Jacques, 56
Rousseau and Romanticism, 58
Rowell, Henry T., 17
Rowling, Marjorie, 26
Rowse, A. L., 40
Royal Charles: Charles II and the Restoration, 48
Royal Commentaries of the Incas and General History of Peru, 101
The Rubáiyát, 69
Rubel, Paula G., 328
Rubyfruit Jungle, 352
Rucker, Rudy, 369
Ruether, Rosemary, 292
Rules and Representations, 284
Rules and Radicals, 331
Rulfo, Juan, 103
Rumi, Mawlana Jalal Addin, 69
Ruoff, James E., 40
Rushdie, Salman, 84–85

Russell, Bertrand, 242, 282, 286, 367
Russell, John, 264
Russell, Letty M., 292
Russian Poetry: The Modern Period, 215

Sachar, A. L., 291–92
Sachs, Curt, 269
Sacred Books of China, 290
SACRED TEXTS, 288–90
Sadava, David, 377
Sa'Di Mosleh-Addin, 69
Safire, William, 250
Sagan, Carl, 281–82
SAGE: A Scholarly Journal on Black Women, 359
Sahlins, Marshall, 328
Saint Thomas Aquinas, 228
Saki (H. H. Munro), 200
Salinger, J. D., 191, 200
Salmagundi, 246
Salvador, 104
Samuel Johnson, 55 (Johnson), 57 (Bate)
Samuels, Ernest, 233
Samuelson, Paul A., 321
Sandburg, Carl, 211–12, 268
Sands, Kathleen M., 108
Sansom, Sir George B., 86
Santayana, George, 233, 285
Sapir, Edward, 250
Saroyan, William, 201
Sarraute, Nathalie, 149
Sartre, Jean Paul, 149, 285
Satanstoe, 174
Satires (Juvenal), 15
Saturday Night and Sunday Morning, 168
The Satyricon, 15
Savior Hold My Hand, 131
Sayre, Anne, 382
Scales and Weights, 365
The Scarlet Letter, 48

Schaar, John, 309
Schaller, George, 382
Schapiro, Meyer, 264
Scharf, Aaron, 270
Schell, Orville, 82, 313
Scherer, Joanna Cohan, 112
Schevill, Ferdinand, 299
Schiller, Herbert, I., 254
Schmidt, Arno, 149–50
Schmidt, Nancy J., 95
Schoenbaum, S., 40, 233
The Scholars, 83
Scholem, Gershom, 294
Scholes, Robert E., 250–51
Schonberg, Harold C., 268
The School for Scandal, 56
Schooling in Capitalist America: Educational Reform and the Contradictions of Economic Life, 332
Schopenhauer, Arthur, 282–83
Schorske, Carl E., 301
Schrödinger, Erwin, 366
Schulz, Bruno, 201
Schumacher, E. F., 321
Schumpeter, Joseph, 321
Schurmann, Franz, 82
Schweitzer, Albert, 233
Science, 246
Science and Human Behavior, 340
Science and the Common Understanding, 365
SCIENCE FICTION, 372
Science Observed, 364
Science on Trial: The Case for Evolution, 378
Science Restated, 368
Science, Theory and Man, 366
Scientific American, 246
Scientific American Library, 382
The Scientific Imagination, 365
Scott, Paul Mark, 168
Scott, Sir Walter, 26, 40, 49, 58
Screwtape Letters, 294

Scribner Desk Dictionary of American History, 401

SCULPTURE, 262–66

The Sea Around Us, 377

The Second Sex, 352

Second Skin, 187–88

The Second World War, 301

Seize the Day, 186

Selected Letters of Oscar Wilde, 242

Selected Poems and Langston Hughes, 124

Selections from Russian Poetry and Prose, 215

The Selfish Gene, 377

Seligman, Martin E., 342–43

Sembène, Ousmane, 92

Semiotics and Interpretation, 250–51

Seneca, Lucius Annaeus, 15

Senghor, Léopold Sédar, 93

El Señor Presidente, 99

Sense and Sensibility, 153

The Senses Considered as Preceptual Systems, 344

Sent for You Yesterday, 125

A Separate Reality, 292

Sessions, George, 384

Seven Gothic Tales, 197

Seven Long Times, 131

The Seven Storey Mountain, 232

1777: The Year of the Hangman, 306

17TH CENTURY, 42–49

The Seventeenth-Century Background, 49

Sévigné, Marie, Marquise de, 47

Sewall, Samuel, 47

Sex and Temperament in Three Primitive Societies, 327

Sexism and God Talk: Toward a Feminist Theology, 292

Sexton, Anne, 212

Sexual Politics, 355–56

Seznec, Jean, 40–41

Shadows on the Rock, 47

Shaeffer, Louis, 233

Shakespeare, William, 35

Shakespeare, a Survey, 37

The Shakespearean Stage, 1574–1642, 38

Shakespeare's England, 41

Shakuntala, 84

The Shapes of Change, 269

The Shaping of Black America, 126

Shapiro, David, 343

Shapiro, Karl, 206

Shaw, George Bernard, 221

She Stoops to Conquer, 54–55

She-Wolf and Other Stories, 202

Shelley, Mary Wollstonecraft, 157

Shelley, Percy Bysshe, 208–09

Shenfan, 81

Shepard, Paul, 382, 385

Shepard, Sam, 221

Sheridan, Richard Brinsley, 56

Sheyk-Zada, 70

Shih, Nai-An, 82–83

The Ship, 67

Shirer, William, 302, 303

The Shock of Recognition, 242

The Shock of the New, 263

Sholokhov, Mikhail, 150

Short Eyes, 130

A Short History of China, 81

A Short History of Chinese Philosophy, 81

Short Letter, Long Farewell, 146

SHORT STORY, 193–202

Shorty Story Index, 397

Showalter, Elaine, 357

The Sickness unto Death, 284

Sidney, Philip, 35–36

Siegel, Marcia, 269

Signs: Journal of Women in Culture and Society, 359

Silences, 356

The Silent Don, 150

The Silent Language, 249
Silent Spring, 377
Silk, Leonard, 321–22
Silko, Leslie M., 112
Sillitoe, Alan, 168
Silone, Ignazio, 150
Silverman, Kenneth, 49
Silverstein, Norman, 270
Silvert, Kalman H., 105
Simone Weil, 233
Simplicus Simplicissimus, 45
Simpson, Lesley Byrd, 301
Sinclair, Upton, 183
Singer, Isaac Bashevis, 201
Singh, Khushwant, 85
Sir Gawain and the Green
    Knight, 23
Sir Walter Raleigh, 39
Sister Carrie, 180
Siva: The Erotic Ascetic, 84
Six Yuan Plays, 79
Sketch Book, 198
Sketches from a Hunter's Album,
    201
Skidmore, Thomas E., 105
Skinner, B. F., 340
Skira Art Books, 262
Skocpol, Theda R., 336
Škvorecký, Josef, 150
Slaughterhouse Five, 192
The Sleepwalkers, 144
Small Is Beautiful: Economics As
    If People Mattered, 321
Smith, Adam, 56
Smith, Anthony, 254
Smith, David G., 310
Smith, Huston, 290
Smith, Peter H., 105
Snell, Bruno, 10
Snow, C. P., 168
Snow Country, 86
Snow White, 186
Snowden, Frank M., Jr., 95
So Excellent a Fishe: Tales of
    Sea Turtles, 377

So Human an Animal, 378
So Long a Letter, 91
The Social Animal, 340
Social Behavior: Its Elementary
    Forms, 334
The Social Construction of
    Reality: A Treatise in the
    Sociology of Knowledge, 332
The Social Contract, 56
Social Development: Psychologi-
    cal Growth and the
    Parent-Child Relationship, 344
Social Sciences and Humanities
    Index, 391
Social Sciences Index, 391
Social Theory and Social
    Structure, 335
The Social Transformation of
    American Medicine: The
    Rise of a Sovereign Profession
    and the Making of a Vast
    Industry, 336
Sociobiology: The New Synthe-
    sis, 337
The Sociological Imagination, 336
Sociological Theory: An Introduc-
    tion, 336
SOCIOLOGY, 330–37
Socrates to Sartre, 286
Sojourner: The Women's Forum,
    359
Sojourners and Settlers: Chinese
    Migrants in Hawaii, 116
The Solitary Singer, 227
Solomon, Maynard, 233
Solzhenitsyn, Alexander, 150
Some Main Problems of
    Philosophy, 285
The Song of God, 83
The Song of Roland, 23
Song of Solomon, 124
Sonnets from the Portuguese, 207
Sons and Lovers, 166
Sontag, Susan, 242, 270
Sophie's Choice, 191

Sophocles, 8
Sorauf, Frank, 311
Sorell, Walter, 269
The Sorrows of Young Werther, 54
The Sot-Weed Factor, 186
The Soul of a New Machine, 371
Soul on Ice, 123
The Souls of Black Folk, 123
The Sound and the Fury, 180–81
Source Readings in Music History: The Renaissance, Vol. 2, 36
Sourcebook in Indian Philosophy, 286
Sources of Chinese Tradition, 78
Sources of Japanese Tradition, 78
SOUTH AMERICA, *see* LATIN AMERICA
South Wind, 164
SOUTHEAST ASIA, 74–87
The Southeastern Indians, 110
Sowell, Thomas, 322
Soyinka, Wole, 93
Space, Time and Architecture, 265
Spaeth, Harold J., 310
Spain, 300
The Spanish American Short Story: A Critical Anthology, 103
Spark, Muriel, 168
Sparks, John, 382
Speak, Memory, 232
The Speaking Tree; A Study of Indian Culture and Society, 84
The Spectator, 52
Spector, Ronald, 306
Spenser, Edmund, 36
Spicer, Edward H., 112
Spingarn, Joel E., 41
Spinoza, Baruch, 283
The Spirit of Democratic Capitalism, 320

The Spirit of the Laws, 55
The Splendid Century, 48
Sportsman's Sketches, 140
Springer, Sally P., 345
Stafford, Jean, 201
Stages of Faith, 293
Stanford, W. B., 10
Stanley, Steven M., 382–83
Starkey, Marion L., 49
Starr, Paul, 336
The State in Capitalist Society, 311
The State of the World 1985, 384
States and Social Revolution: A Comparative study of France, Russia, and China, 336
The Statesman's Yearbook, 402
Statistical Abstract of the United States, 403
Statler, Oliver, 87
Steegmuller, Francis, 234
Steele, Sir Richard, 52
Steffens, Lincoln, 234
Steichen, Edward, 270
Stein, Gertrude, 183, 234
Steinbeck, John, 183, 201
Stendhal (Henri Beyle), 140
Steppenwolf, 146
Stern, Robert A. M., 266
Stern, William Louis, 383
Sterne, Laurence, 56
Stevens, Wallace, 212, 242
Stevenson, Robert Louis, 157–58, 242
Sticks and Stones, 256–66
Stodelle, Ernestine, 269
The Stoic, 180
Stone, Robert, 191
Stone Age Economics, 328
The Stones of the Abbey, 26
Stoppard, Tom, 221
Stories by Contemporary Japanese Women Writers, 80
Stories from a Ming Collection, 79

Stories from El Barrio, 131
Stories of Three Decades, 199
The Story of Elizabethan Drama, 39
The Story of Language, 250
The Story of My Life, 231
The Story of Philosophy, 286
The Story of the Confederacy, 305
Storyteller, 112
Stowe, Harriet Beecher, 177
Strachey, Lytton, 234
Strange Things Happen Here, 103
The Stranger, 144
Strangers and Brothers, 168
The Street of Crocodiles, 201
Strictly Speaking: Will America Be the Death of English?, 250
Strindberg, August, 221
Structuralism and Semiotics, 249
Structuralism and Since: From Levi-Strauss to Derrida, 251
Structuralism in Literature, 250
The Structure of Evil: An Essay on the Unification of the Sciences of Man, 332
The Structure of Scientific Revolutions, 334–35
Structures of the Church, 293
Studies in Classic American Literature, 241
Studies in Iconology: Humanistic Themes in the Art of the Renaissance, 40
Studies in Islamic Poetry, 67
Studs Lonigan, 180
A Study of History, 298
Stumpf, Samuel, E., 286
Styron, William, 191
Subject Guide to Books in Print, 390
Subtle Is the Lord, 367
The Subversive, 87
Suicide, 332

Sula, 124
Sullivan, Harry S., 343
Summa Theologica, 283
The Sun Also Rises, 181
Sun Chief, 112
The Sun Shines Over the Sanggan River, 81
Sundiata, 92
Sunflower Splendor: Three Thousand Years of Chinese Poetry, 79
Superstars, 366
The Suppliants, 7
Supply-Side Economics in the 1980's, 318
Supreme Court Policy-Making: Explanation and Prediction, 310
Surfacing, 162
The Survival of the Pagan Gods, 40–41
Suzuki, D. T., 285
Swanberg, W. A., 234
Sweezy, Paul M., 317
Swift, Jonathan, 56
Swinburne, Algernon Charles, 209
Sylvie, 139–40
Symbolic Anthropology, 328
Symonds, John Addington, 41
The Symposium, 282
The System of Modern Societies, 336
Sze Mai-Mai, 83

Tabb, William, K., 322
Tacitus, Cornelius, 15
Tagore, Sir Rabindranath, 85
A Tagore Reader, 85
Taha Hussein, 68
The Tale of Genji, 86
Tale of Kieu, 87
A Tale of Two Cities, 58
Tales Alive in Turkey, 70

Tales from Thailand, 81

Tales of Power, 292

The Tangled Wing: Biological Constraints on the Human Spirit, 380

Tanikawa, Shuntaro, 87

Tanizaki, Junichiro, 87

Tao T Ching, 83

Taoism: The Parting of the Way, 83

The Tapestry of Culture, 328

Tawney, Richard H., 49, 322

Taylor, Alan John Percival, 301

Taylor, Barbara, 357

Taylor, Gordon Rattray, 383

Taylor, Joshua C., 262

The Teachers of Mad Dog Swamp, 87

Teachings from the American Earth: Indian Religion and Philosophy, 112

The Teachings of Don Juan, 292

The Teaching of the Compassionate Buddha, 78, 288

The Telegraph, 140

The Telescope Handbook and Star Atlas, 404

Tell Me a Riddle, 199–200

Ten Broek, Jacobus, 118

The Tender Carnivore and the Sacred Game, 382

Tender Is the Night, 181

Tennyson, Lord (Alfred), 209

Tentler, Leslie Woodcock, 357

Terence (Publius Terentius Afer), 15–16

Terra Nostra, 101

Tess of the d'Urbervilles, 156

The Tewa World, 111

Textual Strategies: Perspectives in Post-Structuralistic Criticism, 251

Thackeray, William Makepeace, 158

The Theaetetus, 282

The Theater in Its Time: An Introduction, 222

Theater of Memory: Three Plays of Kalidasa, 84

The Theatre and Its Double, 222

The Theatre of Revolt: An Approach to Modern Drama, 222

Theatre of Tennessee Williams, 221

Their Eyes Were Watching God, 124

Them, 189–90

Theogony, 7

THEOLOGY, see RELIGION

Theology in a New Key: Responding to Liberation Themes, 292

Theories of Learning, 341

Theories of Mass Communications, 253

Theories of Personality, 341

Theories of the Theater, 222

A Theory of Justice, 309

The Theory of the Leisure Class, 322

The Theory of the Modern Stage, 222–23

There Is a River: The Black Struggle for Freedom in America, 126

Thérèse, 148

The Thin Red Line, 188

Things Fall Apart, 91

Thinkers and Tinkers, 364

Third World Women Speak Out, 354–55

Thirty Years That Shook Physics, 367

This Was Harlem: A Cultural Portrait: 1900–1950, 126

Thomas à Kempis, 23

Thomas Aquinas, Saint, 24, 283

Thomas, D. M., 168

Thomas, Dylan, 201, 212

Thomas, Edward, 212
Thomas, Lewis, 383
Thomas, Piri, 131
Thompson, Lawrance, 234
Thoreau, Henry David, 234
Thornton Wilder, 229
Thousand Pieces of Gold: A
  Biographical Novel, 117
A Thousand Years of Vietnamese
  Poetry, 81
The Three-Cornered Hat, 137
Three Dialogues Between Hylas
  and Philonous, 278
Three Guineas, 358
Three Kingdoms: China's Epic
  Drama, 82
Three Lives, 183
The Three Musketeers, 47
Three Novels: Molloy; Malone
  Dies; and The Unnamable,
  143
Three Plays, 221
Three Ways of Thought in
  Ancient China, 83, 289
Three Who Made a Revolution,
  303
Through Harsh Winters: The Life
  of a Japanese Immigrant
  Woman, 117
Through Navajo Eyes, 329
Thucydides, 8
Thurber, James, 201
The Thurber Carnival, 201
Thurow, Lester, 319, 322
Tierney, Brian, 26
Tillyard, E. M. W., 41
The Timaeus, 282
Time, 246
The Time of Indifference, 148
The Time of the Hero, 103
Time on the Cross: The
  Economics of American
  Negro Slavery, 304
The Times Atlas of the Oceans,
  393

The Times Atlas of the World:
  Comprehensive Edition, 393
The Times Atlas of World
  History, 401
The Times Concise Atlas of
  World History, 401
The Times Survey of Foreign
  Ministries of the World, 302
The Tin Drum, 146
Tippo, Oswald, 383
Tirant lo Blanc, 23
The Titan, 180
To Be a Pilgrim, 163
To Know a Fly, 378
To the Lighthouse, 169
Tocqueville, Alexis de, 58
Tolkien, J. R. R., 168–69
Tolstoi, Leo, 140, 242
Tolstoy, 234
Tolstoy's Letters, 242
Tom Jones, 54
Tomalin, Claire, 357
Tono Bungay, 169
Toomer, Jean, 124
Torn Between Two Lands:
  Armenians in America, 1890
  to World War I, 72
Torres-Ríoseco, Arturo, 105
Toth, Marian Davies, 81
Touches of Sweet Harmony:
  Pythagorean Cosmology and
  Renaissance Poetics, 39
Toward a Rational Society:
  Student Protest, Science,
  and Politics, 334
Toward an African Literature, 94
Toward an Anthropology of
  Women, 328
Toward the Decolonization of
  African Literature, Vol. 1,
  93
Towards a New Cold War, 312
The Towers of Silence, 168
Toynbee, Arnold J., 298
Tractatus Logico-Philosopicus, 283

Trade and Dominion, 300–01

Train to Pakistan, 85

Transition and Tradition in Moral Theology, 291

Travels, 23

A Treasury of Asian Literature, 79

A Treasury of the Theatre, 219

A Treatise Concerning the Principles of Human Knowledge, 52–53

The Tree Where Man Was Born, 381

Trevelyan, George M., 298

Trevor, William, 169

The Trial, 146

The Trickster, 112

Trilling, Lionel, 242

Tristan, 22

Tristes Tropiques, 327

Tristram Shandy, 56

The Triumph of American Capitalism, 304

The Triumph of Science and Reason, 301

Troilus and Criseyde, 21

The Trojan Women, 7

Trollope, Anthony, 158

Tropic of Cancer, 182

Trotsky, Leon, 234

Troyat, Henri, 234

The Truce, 100

Truffaut, François, 271

Truman, David, 311–12

A Trumpet to Arms: Alternative Media in America, 252

Tsao Hsueh-Chin, 83

Tube of Plenty: The Evolution of American Television, 253

Tuchman, Barbara W., 26

Tuchman, Gaye, 254–55

Tunstall, Jeremy, 255

Turgenev, Ivan, 140–41, 201

TURKISH LITERATURE, 69–70

The Turn of the Screw, 175

Turnbull, Colin, 329

Tutuola, Amos, 93

Tuve, Rosemond, 41

Twain, Mark (Samuel Langhorne Clemens), 177

Twelve African Writers, 95

Twelve Makers of Modern Protestant Thought, 294

The Twelve Seasons, 380

Twelve Who Ruled, 300

The Twenties, 235

20TH-CENTURY AMERICAN NOVELS, 178–92

20TH-CENTURY BRITISH NOVELS, 159–69

20TH-CENTURY CONTINENTAL NOVELS, 142–50

Twentieth-Century Italian Poetry: A Bilingual Translation, 214

Twenty-three Plays: An Introductory Anthology, 219

Two Adolescents, 148

Two Cheers for Democracy, 240

The Two Faces of Chemistry, 368

Two Gentle Men: The Lives of George Herbert and Robert Herrick, 47

Two Leggings: The Making of a Crow Warrior, 111

Two Novels of Mexico, 100

The Two Sources of Morality and Religion, 284

The Two Towers, 168

Two Treatises of Civil Government, 46

Two Years Before the Mast, 228

Tyler, Anne, 191

Typee, 176

Ulam, Stanislaw M., 369

Ulysses, 166

The Ulysses Theme, 10

The Unanswered Question, 266

The Unbearable Lightness of Being, 147
Uncle Tom's Cabin, 177
Uncle Tom's Children, 202
Under the Volcano, 166
The Underdogs, 100
Underhill, Evelyn, 294
Underhill, Ruth, M., 112–13
Understanding Media: The Extensions of Man, 254
Understanding Poetry, 205
Undset, Sigrid, 26
UNESCO Art Series, 262
Union List of Serials, 390
The United States and China, 297
UNITED STATES HISTORY, 303–06
The Universal Baseball Association, Inc., J. Henry Waugh, Prop, 187
The Universe and Dr. Einstein, 366
The Universe Around Us, 365
Unpopular Essays, 242
The Unresponsive Bystander: Why Doesn't He Help?, 344
The Untouchable, 83
The Unwelcome Immigrant: The American Image of the Chinese, 1785–1882, 118
Up Against the Fourth Wall, 222
Up from Slavery, 234–35
The Upanishads, 289
The Upanishads: Breath of the Eternal, 289
Updike, John, 191, 201
Urban Renegades, 110
Urvasi, 84
U.S.A., 180
USSR in Crisis, 318
Utilitarianism, 285

Vaillant, George, 105
Valency, Maurice J., 26

Valenzuela, Luisa, 103
Vallejo, César, 103
Van Gennep, Arnold, 329
Van Gogh, Vincent, 234
Van Lawick-Goodall, Jane, 383
Van Loon, Hendrik W., 49
Van Nostrand Scientific Encyclopedia, 403
Vanity Fair, 158
Varga ve Gulsah, 70
Vargas Llosa, Mario, 103
Varieties of Religious Experience, 293
Vasari, Giorgio, 36
Veblen, Thorstein, 322
Verdi, 235
Verga, Giovanni, 141, 202
Vergil (Publius Vergilius Maro), 16
A Very Easy Death, 352
Vesalius, Andreas, 36
Vespasiano da Bisticci, Fiorentino, 36
The Vicar of Wakefield, 54
Victims of Progress, 325
Victorian England, 301
Victorian Woman: A Documentary Account of Women's Lives in Nineteenth-Century England, France and the United States, 357
Vietnam: A History, 305
Viking (Penguin) Book of Folk Ballads of the English-Speaking World, 206
The Village in 1970, 85
Villanueva, Tino, 131
Villareal, José A., 131
Villette, 154
Villon, François, 24
A Vindication of the Rights of Woman, 358
The Violent Bear It Away, 190
Virginia Woolf, 227
Virginibus Puerisque, 242

The Visible Hand: The Manage-
  rial Revolution in American
  Business, 317
Vision and Design, 261
Voices of Modern Greece:
  Cavafy, Sikelianos, Seferis,
  Elytis, and Gatsos, 214
The Voices of Silence, 261
Volpone, 34
Voltaire (Francois Marie Arouet),
  56
Von Baeyer, Hans C., 368
Vonnegut, Kurt, 192
Voss, 169
The Voyage of the Beagle, 228
Voyages and Discoveries, 34
The Voyeur, 149

Waddell, Helen, 27
Wage-Earning Women: Industrial
  Work and Family Life in the
  U.S., 1900–1930, 357
Waggoner, Hyatt, H., 206
Wagley, Charles, 105
Wagner, Jean P., 206–07
Waiting for Surabiel, 87
Walden, 234
Waldo Emerson, 234
Waley, Arthur, 83
Walker, Alice, 125
Walker's Mammals of the World,
  404
Walkowitz, Judith R., 357–58
Wallace, Walter L., 336
Walpole, Horace, 56
Walton, Izaak, 47
The Waning of the Middle Ages,
  25
The Wapshot Chronicle, 186
The Wapshot Scandal, 187
War and Peace, 140
The War of the End of the
  World, 103
War with the Newts, 144

Ward, Aileen, 234
The Warden, 158
Warner, Langdon, 87
Warner, Rex, 11
Warren, Robert Penn, 192, 205
Washington, Booker T., 234–35
Washington: The Indispensable
  Man, 58
Watching the Dance Go By, 269
Water Margin, 83
Watson, James, 383
Watson, John B., 340
Watson, Robert I., 340
Waugh, Evelyn, 169
Waverley, 58
The Way and Its Powers, 290
The Way of All Flesh, 154
The Way of Chinese Painting,
  83
The Way of Lao Tzu, 82, 290
The Way of the Ways, 82
The Ways of My Grandmothers,
  110
The Ways of Religion, 290–91
We, 150
We of the Mountains: Armenian
  Short Stories, 72
The Weaker Vessel, 48
The Wealth of Nations, 56
Webb, Walter Prescott, 306
Weber, Max, 363–37
Webster's New Biographical
  Dictionary, 395
Webster's New Dictionary of
  Synonyms, 394
Webster's New Geographical
  Dictionary, 393
Webster's New Twentieth
  Century Dictionary of the
  English Language, 394
Webster's New World Dictionary
  of the American Language,
  394
Webster's Ninth New Collegiate
  Dictionary, 390, 394

Webster's Third New International Dictionary of the English Language, 393

Wechsberg, Joseph, 235

Wecter, Dixon, 305

Wedgwood, Cicely Veronica, 301

Weglyn, Michi, 118

Weisskopf, Thomas E., 317

Weisskopf, Walter, 322

Welch, Holmes, 83

Wells, H. G., 169

Weltfish, Gene, 113

Welty, Eudora, 202

Werfel, Franz, 150

West, Nathanael, 183

Western Europe in the Middle Ages, 26

The Westminster Historical Atlas to the Bible, 400

Westward Ho!, 157

Wharton, Edith, 183

What Is Modern Painting?, 262

What Is Sociology, 334

What Is the World Made Of?, 367

What to Listen for in Music, 267

When Prophecy Fails: A Social and Psychological Study of a Modern Group that Predicted the Destruction of the World, 343–44

When the Lights Go Down, 270

Where to Find What, 391

White, Lynn, 27

White, Patrick, 169

The White Hotel, 168

Whitehead, Alfred North, 285

Whitman, Walt, 209

Whittier, John Greenleaf, 209

Who Designs America?, 266

Who's Afraid of Virginia Woolf?, 220

Who's Who, 395

Who's Who of America, 395

Who's Who in the World, 395

Who's Who of American Women, 395

Why Are We in Vietnam?, 189

Why Big Fierce Animals Are Rare: An Ecologist's Perspective, 377

Wide Sargasso Sea, 168

Wideman, John Edgar, 125

The Wider Sea: A Life of John Ruskin, 230

Wiener, Norbert, 366

Wiesel, Elie, 192

Wildavsky, Aaron, 311

Wilde, Oscar, 158, 209, 242

Wilder, Thornton, 183, 221

Wilkins, Ernest H., 41

Wilkinson, L. P., 17

The Will to Believe, 240

The Will to Power, 281–82

Willett, John, 265

Willey, Basil, 41, 49

William Shakespeare: A Compact Documentary Life, 40

William Shakespeare: A Documentary Life, 233

Williams, Chancellor, 95

Williams, Juanita H., 342

Williams, Raymond, 223, 251

Williams, T. Harry, 306

Williams Tennessee, 221

Williams, William Carlos, 212

Wilson, Angus, 169

Wilson, Edmund, 113, 235, 242

Wilson, Edward O., 337, 383

Wilson, Robert A., 119

Wind, Edgar, 41

Windelband, Wilhelm, 286

Winesburg, Ohio, 179

The Wings of the Dove, 175

Winternitz, Emanuel, 268

Winter's Tales, 197

The Wisdom of Catholicism, 294

The Wisdom of Lao Tzu, 290

Wise Blood, 190

Wiser, Charlotte Viall, 85

Wiser, William H., 85
Wish, Harvey, 306
Witchcraft, Oracles, and Magic among the Azande, 326
With a Daughter's Eye, 325
Wittgenstein, Ludwig, 283
Wodehouse, P. G., 202
Wolf, Eric, 329
Wolfe, Bertram David, 303
Wolfe, Thomas, 183–84, 202
Wolfram von Eschenbach, 24
Wolin, Sheldon, 309
Wollstonecraft, Mary, 358
The Woman in the Dunes, 85
Woman of Her Word: Hispanic Women Write, 131
The Woman Warrior, 117
Woman's Body, Woman's Right: A Social History of Birth Control in America, 354
Women and Colonization: Anthropological Perspectives, 329
Women and Russia: Feminist Writings from the Soviet Union, 358
Women and the American Economy, 322
Women and the Law, 310
Women Artists, 1550–1950, 354
Women at Work: The Transformation of Work and Community in Lowell, Massachusetts, 1826–1860, 353
Women in Love, 166
Women in Medieval Society, 299
Women in Music: An Anthology of Source Readings from the Middle Ages to the Present, 268
Women in Western Political Thought, 309
Women of Crisis: Lives of Struggle and Hope, 352
Women Poets of Japan, 80

The Women Troubadours, 24
Women Writers in Black Africa, 93
The Women's Review of Books, 359
WOMEN'S STUDIES, 346–59
Women's Studies Quarterly, 359
The Wonder That Was India, 83
The Wonderful World of Dance, 269
Woodcock, George, 309
Woodrow Wilson and the Progressive Era, 306
Woodstock, 49
The Wooing of Earth, 378
Woolf, Virginia, 169, 242, 358
Word and Object, 285
Word Play: What Happens When People Talk, 249
Words in the Blood, 113
Wordsworth, William, 209
Word in America, 321
Working Smart, 371
Works and Days, 7
The Works of Love, 189
World Almanac, 392
The World and Africa: Inquiry into the Part Which Africa Has Played in World History, 94
The World as Will and Representation, 282–83
The World Book Encyclopedia, 392
World History of the Dance, 269
The World of Cartier-Bresson, 269
The World of Copernicus, 227
The World of George Washington, 59
The World of Gwendolyn Brooks, 122–23
The World of Humanism 1453–1517, 38
The World of Mathematics, 370

The World of Odysseus, 9
The World of Rome, 17
The World of the French
    Revolution, 300
The World of the Shining Prince,
    86
World of Wonders, 164
The Worldly Philosophers,
    318–19
The Worldmark Encylopedia of
    the Nations, 393
The Worlds of Jazz, 267
Worster, Donald, 385
Worth, Sol, 329
The Wretched of the Earth, 94
Wright, Frank Lloyd, 235, 266
Wright, Richard, 125, 202, 235
Writing Degree Zero, 248
Writings and Buildings, 266
Wu Ching-Tsu, 83
Wuthering Heights, 154

Xenophon, 8

. . . Y no se lo trago la
    tierra (and earth did not part),
    131

Yale Review, 246
The Yalu Flows, 87
Yañez, Augustin, 103
Yankee from Olympus, 228
Yates, Frances, 41
The Year of the Gorilla, 382
Years of Infamy: The Untold
    Story of America's Concen-
    tration Camps, 118
Yeats, William Butler, 212, 235
Yehoshua, Abraham, 71
Yerba Buena, 129
Young, George M., 301
Young Lonigan, 180
The Young Manhood of Studs
    Lonigan, 180
Yourcenar, Marguerite, 17
Yusuf-I Meddah, 70

Zamyatin, Yevgeny, 150
Zen Buddhism, 285
Zerner, Henri, 264
Zinsser, Hans, 384
Zola, Émile, 141
ZOOLOGY, *see* BIOLOGICAL
    SCIENCES
Zorba the Greek, 147
Zuleika Dobson, 162–63